Some Early
TRAVIS COUNTY, TEXAS
Records

Abstracted & Compiled By:
Mrs. Jane Summer

Southern Historical Press, Inc.
Greenville, South Carolina

Copyright 1979
By: The Rev. Silas Emmett Lucas, Jr.

All rights reserved. No part of this publication may be reproduced, stored in a retrieval system, transmitted in any form, posted on to the web in any form or by any means without the prior written permission of the publisher.

Please direct all correspondence and orders to:

www.southernhistoricalpress.com
or
SOUTHERN HISTORICAL PRESS, Inc.
PO BOX 1267
375 West Broad Street
Greenville, SC 29601
southernhistoricalpress@gmail.com

ISBN #0-89308-129-9

Printed in the United States of America

DEDICATED TO:

MRS. ALICE DUGGAN GRACY, and
her late husband

DAVID CALDWELL GRACY.

INTRODUCTION

TEXAS LAND

173,682,674 acres. YES, 173 million, plus acres. TEXAS was land rich and in money, cash, a pauper.
It paid its debts in land, built the present CAPITOL BUILDING, at a cost of 3,025,000 acres and used 49,530,334 acres for educational and eleemosynary institutions.
Disposition of TEXAS land actually began while SPAIN held MEXICO and TEXAS as part of its colonial empire.

In the areas around Nacogdoches, San Antonio, and the Rio Grande Valley SPAIN gave away several large tracts of land. Some of the KING'S RANCH is in this area. When MEXICO obtained her independence, she granted title to large areas of TEXAS land. The means by which MEXICO disposed of these lands were three: SALE, SPECIAL GRANTS and EMPRESARIO contracts. (These were to men who contracted to settle a given number of families in a given area.) The most famous of these contracts was the contract with MOSES AUSTIN and STEPHEN F. AUSTIN, his son. Approximately 26,250,000 acres of land were granted by SPAIN and MEXICO. TEXAS recognized the legitimacy of titles to land granted by SPAIN and MEXICO.

TEXAS parted with land in three ways: SALE, GIVEN AWAY, some traded for services rendered in the TEXAS war of INDEPENDENCE and its officials.

Land was given away to encourage immigration, reward good citizens and veterans for military service, encourage settlement and improvement of land; help the growth of railroads and other internal improvements, and for educational purposes and systems.

HEADRIGHTS:

There were four classes of HEADRIGHTS:
FIRST was granted by the delegates who adopted the CONSTITUTION of the REPUBLIC of TEXAS in March 1836, at Washington-on-the Brazos. It provided that "all persons except Africans and their descendants, and Indians, living in TEXAS on the day of the Declaration of Independence, are entitled to headright grants, if they be heads of families, one league, and one labor (la-bour) and if single man, 17 years of age or older, one-third of a league."

SECOND CLASS HEADRIGHT CERTIFICATES went to heads of families and single men who arrived in TEXAS as immigrants after the Declaration of Independence and prior to October 1, 1837, provided, they remained in the REPUBLIC of TEXAS three years and performed the duties of citizenship. Heads of families were to receive certificates for 1280 acres and single men a certificate for 640 acres.

THIRD CLASS HEADRIGHT CERTIFICATES were granted to heads of families and single men who immigrated to TEXAS after October 1, 1837, and before January 1, 1842. Single men who were heads of families were entitled to 640 acres of land and single men to 320 acres of land. All colonial grants are to be found among THIRD CLASS CERTIFICATES. The REPUBLIC encouraged immigration by contractingwith men who agreed to settle a number of immigrants on public lands.

FOURTH CLASS CERTIFICATES were issued to immigrants who arrived in TEXAS after Jan. 1, 1840, and before Jan. 1, 1842. Young men who were permanent residents and 17 years of age before Jan. 1, 1840, were eligible for these certificates. Heads of families could receive 640 acres, and single men 320 acres. The recipients were required to perform the duties of a citizen for three years.

Among the famous men connected with TEXAS history who received FIRST CLASS CERTIFICATES were: JAMES BOWIE and DAVID CROCKETT, who died at the Alamo. THOMAS LAGOW, received a FIRST CLASS CERTIFICATE. He came to TEXAS in November, 1835. His property is where the present city of Dallas is located, on White Rock Creek.

THE GENERAL LAND OFFICE OF TEXAS:

One of the first permanent governmental structures erected after the original capitol building, which burned, was a GENERAL LAND OFFICE. With all the land which belonged to the STATE of TEXAS, it was necessary to provide a place to keep the records for all this land.

In December 1854, Professor Doctor C. C. STREMME, designed and drafted the first GENERAL LAND OFFICE BUILDING. It was, and is still standing, at the southeast corner of the original "CAPITOL SQUARE". Dr. STREMME held many titles, one was at the Court of Emperor NICHOLAS I, of RUSSIA.

The first COMMISSIONERS of the GENERAL LAND OFFICE Were: JOHN P. BORDEN, 1837 to 1841, and THOMAS WM. WARD, 1841 to 1848. The Commissioners of the GENERAL LAND OFFICE are elected officials, just as the Governors of the State are elected.

The dominion over which the two men served as the first COMMISSIONERS was what is now TEXAS, plus more than one-half of NEW MEXICO, parts of KANSAS and COLORADO and WYOMING. Plus out to three (3) marine leagues into the Gulf of MEXICO.

The GENERAL LAND OFFICE of the STATE of TEXAS, is now located in its fourth building. It is a storehouse of GREAT historical as well as genealogical interest. HOWEVER, these records are not accessible to the public. The Clerks, who are very accommodating and helpful, will search a given name, and advise and show the interested party what is on file in the TEXAS GENERAL LAND OFFICE ARCHIVES on such name. Copies of these documents may be obtained for a reasonable fee, and very promptly.

NOTE: In requesting information on a patent or patentee, or member of the ARMY of the REPUBLIC of TEXAS, request all material in the folder. Sometimes there may be a number of documents on file in a man's folder, pertaining to the PATENTEE, SOLDIER, his assignee, and/or their families.

There are many interesting items to be found in the files of the GENERAL LAND OFFICE:

THE SPANISH ARCHIVES. These archives contain some four thousand (4000) original titles written in Spanish and issued by the Spanish and Mexican authorities when TEXAS was under their dominion. In addition, some 4000 sets of field notes, written in ENGLISH by American Surveyors during the colonization program initiated by SPAIN and carried out by MEXICO. Some of these are dated as far back as 1745, but most are for the period of 1823 to 1835.

MAP of TEXAS, showing parts of adjoining states, compiled by STEPHEN F. AUSTIN.

MUSTER ROLL of the ARMY of the REPUBLIC OF TEXAS.

CERTIFICATE to SAMUEL G. POWELL, dated February 3, 1854, for 320 acres of land for building, within the STATE of TEXAS the STEAMBOAT "BETTY".

BEAUTIFUL MAPS by Proffessor Doctor C. C. STREMME. Tyler County map, dated May 1858, and Houston County map dated October 1868.

PAYROLL RECORD of WILLIAM S. PORTER (O. HENRY), 1887

MAP of KENT COUNTY, 1889 by WILLIAM S. PORTER (O. HENRY).

An original certificate for MILITARY SERVICE:

THE REPUBLIC OF TEXAS (:)
    COUNTY OF AUSTIN   (:)   This is to certify that ALEXANDER ISBELL, has appeared before us, the BOARD of LAND

COMMISSIONERS for the County of Austin, and proved according to law, that he arrived in TEXAS previous to the second day of May 1835, and that he is a single man and that he is entitled to one third of a league of land under the 22 sect. of the land law being under the age of seventeen years and having received a honorably discharge for a tour of duty, upon the condition of paying at the rate of 3 dollars 50 cts. for every labor of irrigable land 2 doll. 50 cts. for every labor of temporal or arable land and one doll. 20 cts for every labor of pasture land which may be contained in the survey secured to him for his certificate.

GIVEN UNDER OUR HANDS in San Felipe de Austin this second day of March eighteen hundred thirty eight.

ATTEST:
LOUIS KLEBERG c. o.B (Sgd.) ROBERT KLEBERG) associate
(SGD) J. LaFAYETTE HILL)

ENDORSED: File 169 Gonzales Co.
1st Class Headright
Ctf. ALEXANDER ISBELL

(CERTIFICATE)
GENERAL LAND OFFICE, AUSTIN, TEXAS, Oct. 5, 1978.
I, BOB ARMSTRONG, Commissioner of the General Land Office of the State of TEXAS, do hereby certify that on the reverse hereof is a true and correct copy of the original of this instrument now on file in this office together with all the endorsements thereon.
IN TESTIMONY WHEREOF, I hereunto set my hand and affix the seal of the said office the day and date first above written.

(Sgd.) BOB ARMSTRONG
COMMISSIONER of the
general land office.

OFFICIAL SEAL AFFIXED.
The seal says: GENERAL LAND
OFFICE of the STATE of Texas.

ANOTHER MILITARY CERTIFICATE:

"REPUBLIC of TEXAS"

No. (cannot read)   320 acres

KNOW ALL MEN TO WHOM THESE PRESENTS SHALL COME, THAT JOHN H. ISBELL having served faithfully and honorably for the term of four months from the twentieth day of July 1836 until the twentieth day of Nov. 1836, and being honorably discharged from the ARMY of TEXAS is entitled to Three hundred twenty acres Bounty Land, for which this is his CERTIFICATE.
And the said JNO. H. ISBELL is entitled to hold said Land, or to sell, alienate, convey and donate the same, and exercise all rights of ownership over it.
THIS CERTIFICATE will be transferable by a deed before any competent authority, with witnesses to the same.
IN TESTIMONY WHEREOF, I have hereunto set my hand at Houston the thirty first day of January 1838.

(Sgd.) BARNARD E. BEE, Sec. War.

APPROVED Nov. 11, 1854,
James S. Gillett, adjt. Genl.
ENDORSED: The signature of JOHN H. ISBELL.
ENDORSED: Milam Bounty.
Bounty Warrant 320 acres, JOHN H. ISBELL, Filed Aug. 3/54 "to be appv. by adjt. genl."

(sgd) F. W. ROBERTSON, Reg. (Sc) Mg13948
Rondian

A CERTIFICATE OF THE GENERAL LAND OFFICE IS STAMPED ON THE REVERSE OF THE ABOVE, And the offiicial seal is affixed.

(See next sheet for conveyance of the above bounty warrant)

REPUBLIC of TEXAS   (;)
COUNTY OF HARRIS   (:)   KNOW ALL MEN BY THESE PRESENTS, that I, JOHN
H. ISBELL for and in consideration of the sum
of Fifteen doll. to me paid by WM. J. HUTCHINS of the City of Houston,
have GRANTED, BARGAINED, SOLD, ALIENATED and CONVEYED and DELIVERED
possession of to WM. J.HUTCHINS, hisheirs and assigns all my right,
title and interest in and to Bounty Land Warrant issued to me on the
31st Jany. 1838 for sevices rendered in the army of TEXAS NO.....
for three hundred & twenty acres..

signed by B. E. BEE, Sec. of War.

TO HAVE AND TO HOLD said certificate for three hundred & twenty acres
of land to him the said WM. J. HUTCHINS, his heirs and assigns forever
and I, the said J. H. ISBELL for myself my heirs and assigns the title
to and peaceable possession of said certificate will WARRANT and
DEFEND against the claims or demands of all persons whatever.

GIVEN UNDER MY HAND & SEAL this 26th day of Jany. 1846.
(Sgd.)   J. H. ISBELL (SS)

WITNESS: J. P. BOWLES

THE STATE OF TEXAS   (:)
COUNTY OF MILAM   (:)   This day personally came and appeared before
me, F. A. HILL, a NOTARY PUBLIC in and for
said County, JESSE P. BOWLES, a personto me well known, who upon.
oath sayeth that he saw J. H. ISBELL sign, sell and deliver the foregoing instrument of writing bearing date 26th day of January 1846, for
all his interest therein contained and set forth, and that he signed
the same as a witness at the request of the parties.

WITNESS MY HAND AND OFFICIAL SEAL this 25th day of October, 1854.
(Sgd.) F. A. HILL
NOTARY PUBLIC, M. C._____

ENDORSED: File 1093
Milam Bounty, J. H. ISBELL, to CONVEYANCE WM. J. HUTCHINS filed Nov.
3, 1854, certified copy for J. H. ISBELL.

JOHN H. ISBELL deed WM. J. HUTCHINS Bounty Land 320 acres.

CERTIFICATE OF GENERAL LAND OFFICE STAMPED ON REVERSE SIDE, and the
seal of the GENERAL LAND OFFICE duly affixed.

(All of the foregoing are in handwriting, except the certificate by the
Commissioner of the General Land Office.)

ABBREVIATIONS:

Admr.	Administrator or administratrix;
Apr.Apprs.	Appraiser, appraisers;
A/245	Record Book "A" page 245 of a given County;
Asgne.	Assignee;
Ack.	Acknowledgment;
A/J	Abstract of a judgment, debt reduced to judgment;
Aff.	Sworn statement, regarding some matter of which there is not a legal or court record. An affidavit of heirship names the persons or heirs of a deceased person or person, who d. without leaving a will or other Probate Proceedings;
Atty.	Attorney, either representative in court or by Power of Attorney;
BCT	Bastrop County, Texas (other counties same)
b.	born, ca or location;
CJWCT	Chief Justice Williamson County Court;
CJ	Chief Justice;
CJ Sup.Ct.	Chief Justice of Texas Supreme Court;
CCC	Clerk County Court;
ch.	children;
Cert. of Title	Issue by General Land Office, prior to Patent to land;
cc	Certified copy, from another county or state or other legal authority;
ca	approximate time;
Community survivorship	This is a TEXAS legal proceedings where either husband or wife dies without leaving a will, and the estate is small and their assets were all community property. (Texas is a community property state, and all property acquired during marriage is community property, regardless of who was the breadwinner);
Counties	The counties in TEXAS are not the same as the Land Districts;
DC	District Court, or clerk;
DT	Mortgage on real estate;
Deft	Party or parties against whom legal proceedings have been filed;
Dpty.	An appointed assistant to an elected official;
d.	died, date or place;
Div.	Divorce;
et al	and others;
et ux	and wife;
et vir	and husband;
ex parte	Only one person interest in a given court proceedings;
Est.	Estate of deceased person, or minors or NCM;
Extr.	Executor, executrix, appointed under will to handle estate;
Ex O NP	Ex officio NOTARY PUBLIC:
fs	femme sole (single woman);
Gdn/Guad.	Guardian;
HD	Homestead designation; (Texas homesteads are exempt from forced sale, if properly declared and used)
Intestate	died without will;
JP	Justice of Peace
JP & EXO	Justice of Peace, with authority to take acknowledgments;
labor	TEXAS Land Measure (la-bour) 177.1 acres of land;
Lien	A mortgage against real estate;
Land Districts	Not the same as counties;
League	4428 English acres of land, a TEXAS land measure;
M/L	Marriage license;
m.	married, date or place;
Mech. Lien.	Lien by a builder or laborer against real estate;
M. O. G.	Minister of the Gospel;
Mtg.	This is a mortgage against real estate;
NP	NOTARY PUBLIC
nee	maiden name;
N. C. M.	Latin phrase for a person of unsound mind;

O. L.   Oil Lease;
PA   Power of attorney;
Pat.   Instrument patenting title to TEXAS land toa patentee;
Ptf.   Party or parties filing law suit;
QCD or QC   Quitclaim deed;
Rem.Disab.
of minority   This is a TEXAS proceedings for giving minors right to sign
               legal papers before becoming of age, where there is no
               appointed guardian;
SWD   Special Warranty Deed;
sm.   single man;
Spl.gdn.   In law suits a judge presiding can anddoes appoint a
               special guardian to represents minors before his court;
Seq. of
prop.   CSA levied and sold property of northern sympathizers
               by sequestration proceedings against their property;
Transcript
TRSPT   Transcript by another county clerk regarding papers on
               record ina given county, which should also be of record
               in the County where the TRANSCRIPT is recorded;
TCT   Travis County, Texas;
unm   un married;
vs   Law suit against other persons
Wmson. Co.   Williamson County, Texas.

THE
CITY OF AUSTIN

CAPITAL of the REPUBLIC of TEXAS and the STATE OF TEXAS.

Created and established by Act of the CONGRESS of the REPUBLIC of TEXAS April 3, 1839, and platted and drawn by WILLIAM H. SANDUSKY, and surveyed by S. C. WILCOX, under the direction of the CONGRESS of the REPUBLIC of TEXAS.

The land was selected by a committee appointed by the CONGRESS of the REPUBLIC of TEXAS, and then condemned by the same CONGRESS in proceedings held in the County of Bastrop, REPUBLIC of TEXAS. And under the direction of the same CONGRESS the CITY of AUSTIN was planned and laid out and surveyed for the capital of the REPUBLIC of TEXAS.

The origial plan, under the direction of the CONGRESS of the REPUBLIC provided ground spaces for CAPITOL SQUARE, SCHOOLS, LIBRARY, CEMETERY, HOSPITAL, COURT HOUSE, JAIL and various PARKS. The 40 acres shown on the plat as "COLLEGE HILL" became the University of TEXAS, and no private individual or company has ever owned the "original 40 acres".

Some ninety years after the condemnation proceedings held in Bastrop County, Republic of Texas, a dispute continued, which had arisen in said condemnation proceedings against THOMAS JEFFERSON CHAMBERS, one of the owners of the property so condemned in 1839. This dispute was settled by a deed which is of record in Vol. 374, pages 204 et seq. of the Travis County Deed Records. This deed was given by "the heirs of THOMAS JEFFERSON CHAMBERS to the whole of the original City of Austin, it is recited..." on July 29, 1831 the STATE of COAHUILA andTEXAS then one of the states of the REPUBLIC of MEXICO granted eight (8) leagues of land to THOMAS JEFFERSON CHAMBERS, and the same was located June 20, 1835 on the east bank of the Colorado River, then in Bastrop County, later Travis County, Republic of Texas. April 3, 1839 the GOVERNMENT of the REPUBLIC of TEXAS condemned 5004 acres of the THOMAS JEFFERSON CHAMBERS grant for the seat of government of the REPUBLIC.."

Fifty-nine(59) men signed the DECLARATION of INDEPENDENCE of the REPUBLIC of TEXAS, March 2, 1836. One was a native of England, one of Scotland, one of Ireland, one of Canada, thirteen of Virginia, ten of Tennessee, eight of North Carolina, Five of Kentucky, four of South Carolina, four of Georgia, two of New York, two of Pennsylvania, one of New Jersey and one of Mississippi, and two of Texas, native born in San Antonio de Bexar.

These, and their counter=parts, and ambassadors, empresarious, consulates of other Nations, as well as other foreign dignitaries, came to the new NATION with it's vast areas of varied soils and timber. They brought with them their families and their fortunes. And with these came the "COMMON MAN" with his family, seeking his fortune.

This is but a partial history of a few of these people as shown by the records in the Travis County Court House. The deeds from the County Clerk's Office; wills and probate from the County Court and law suits from the District Courts of Travis County, Texas. Texas was a REPUBLIC for TEN years, ONLY, but the Travis County Records continued, uninturrupted, by the change from REPUBLIC to STATE, and through the difficulties of the war between the STATES.

The vindictive and irreclaimable bad character of Geronimo leaves but little doubt that he will never cease from attempting to block the progress of civilization or become reconciled to the monotony of a peaceful existence as a government pet, unless thoroughly converted by cold lead into such a condition as would make him good aboriginal anatomical subject for some medical museum. Of the renegades who two years ago consented to return to their reservations, he was the last to put in an appearance, and that his good treatment by the authorities during his stay on the reservation was worse than thrown away, is simply demonstrated by the thirty-six victims whose lives were brutally sacrificed by his savage wantonness.

EPH - Jan. 1883:

Original words to "DIXIE" by Dan Emmett from his own manuscript:

> I wish I was in the land of cotton,
> Old times dar am not forgotten,
> In Dixieland whar I was bawn in,
> Arly on a frosty mawnin'.
>
> Ole Missus marry Will de weaber,
> Will he was a gay deceaber,
> When he put his arm around her,
> He looked as fierce as a forty-pounder.
>
> His face was sharp as a butcher's cleaber,
> But dat didn't seem a bit to greab'er,
> Will run away, missus took a decline,
> Jer face was de color ob de bacon rine.
>
> While Missus libbed, she libbed in clober,
> When she died, she died all ober,
> How could she act de foolish part
> And marry the man who broke her heart?
>
> Buckwheat cakes and cawn meal batter
> Make you far or a little fatter,
> Here's a health to the nex' ole missus,
> An' all de gals as wants to kiss us.
>
> Now if you want to dribe away sorrow,
> Come and hear dis song tomorrow,
> Den hoe it down an' scratch de grabble,
> To Dixie's land I'm bound to trabble.
>
> Chorus:
> I wish I was in Dixie hooray, hooray?
>   In Dixie land
>   We'll take our stand
> To lib an' die in Dixie
> Away, Away, Away, down souf in Dixie!
> Away, Away, Away down souf in Dixie!

PC 373, EST. MARIA L. JONES, decd. 1867, minors: KLEBAR JONES, THOS. H JONES, RUFUS R. JONES, EMMA LEE, CHAS. H. LEE & ISAAC V. JONES,heirs of MARIA L. JONES: MARIA L., OLIVIA & LINTON JONES, 8 children. THOMAS H. JONES, surviving husband

Transcript 1/234 Title Bond, June 22, 1836, ISAAC DECKER to GEO. W. SPIER. WIT: GREENLIEF FISK, JAMES W. MOORE, JAMES HAGGARD.

Transcript 1/40 Title Bond Aug. 18, 1836, GEO. W. SPEAR, WM. HEMPHILL of San Augustine Co. Texas, to MATTHEW CARTWRIGHT, WIT: JACOB GARRETT, A. HORTON, GEO. TULL, THOS. B. GARRETT, JNO. CALDWELL, L. C. CUNNINGHAM, JC Bastrop & Ex Of. NP. Says: DAVID A. CUNNINGHAM stated GEO. W. SPEAR ack. Feb. 20, 1838.

A/342 ISAAC DECKER of Montgomery Co. Texas, to MATTHEW CARTWRIGHT of San Augustine Co. Tex. WIT: R. D. RAMSEY, THOS. P. DAVEY, ack. by GEORGE MORRISON, NP, MONTGOMERY Co. Texas. Mar. 13, 1848.

37/291 WD April 1, 1877 JOHN M. SWISHER to C. WAVERLY DANIEL.

274/562 QC Dec. 28, 1910 NOEL WINSTON LeSUEUR, Smith Co. Texas, SAML. J. LeSUEUR, Jefferson Co. Tex. all right, title,etc in mother's estate LELAH N. LeSUEUR, who d. July 5, 1894 to W. N. LeSUEUR

275/105 WD April 30, 1915, W. N. LeSUEUR, LELAH LeSUEUR, feme sole, of TCT to W. A. MAYNE

54/621 Deed Feb. 26, 1883 Sept. 8, 1879, R. D. WELLS to JAMES WELLS, bond of title, shows RICHARD B. WELLS, sm May 4, 1883 and CAROLINE fs sole heirs of JAMES WELLS, decd..

PC 1298 ATHALIANN CAROLINE WEBER, d. Feb. 27, 1888, LOUIS WEBER, indp. Extr. also known as CAROLINE WEBER, formerly A. C. WELLS, wife of LOUIS WEBER to bros. and sister and decendants of sister: MRS. LUCY ANN LEWIS, et vir D. K., ELIZA JANE GOOD, MARY ANN PIERCE who m. JOSEPH TRIPLETT, Bradley Co. Tenn., bros. REUBEN BURCH, CALLOWAY BURCH et ux SARAH JANE, Hot Springs, Ark., MARTIN BURCH & HOUSTON BURCH.

C. W. DANIEL (was of BERGEN, DANIEL & GRACY Abstract Co. Austin, Texas)

98/611 Aug. 31, 1890 Aff. says CAROLINE WELLS, decd. debts and funeral expenses of R. D. WELLS, decd. son of CAROLINE WEBER, decd.

344/595 Aff. JOHN A. SHAW m. TEXANNA C. GOODRICH, d. Feb. 10, 1923;(1) A. A. SHAW, son decd. to wife BESS A.; (2) J. W. SHAW decd.(3) DAISY B. SHAW, d. Mar. 17, 1935, (4) KATE E. SHAW & (5) LAURA A.SHAWm.W.H. GOODMAN.

706/572 Aff. TEXANNA C. SHAW, d. Aug. 5, 1834, DAISY DEEN d. Mar.17, 1935.
PC 166 ESTATE GIDEON WHITE, decd. filed Apl. 27, 1843, by ELIZABETH WHITE, wife of Dallas Co. Ala.WILL dated Jan. 3, 1838,dau.CORNELIA JANE m. ENOCH JOHNSON, ELIZABETH ANN m. MARTIN MOORE, LOUISA MARIA d.2/1/54 m. EDWARD SEIDERS, d. June 16, 1892; REBECCA CAROLINE m. JAMES W. THOMP-SON & NARCISSUS LUCINDA WHITE, WIT: JAS. C. CRAIG, T. M. JACKSON, JOHN SMITH and JOHN (X) TOLMAN, Aprs. May 16, 1853, W. W. HORNSBY, A. P. BOYCE, REUBEN HORNSBY. LOUISA SEIDERS d. Feb. 1,1854, left 3 sons: EDWARD G., HENRY B. & PINCKNEY W. SEIDERS. EDWARD SEIDERS m.(2)LETITIA.

642/11Aff. heirship GEO. DITTMAR, d. Jan..1899, his wife, EMELIA J. d. July 10, 1938, she was dau. of WM. WENDE, decd. Ch: W. MARTIN DITTMAN, d. Dec. 22, 1932, his wife was WALLY d. May 2, 1917; ADOLPH DITTMAR, wife DORRACE, MATILDE, fs and GEO DITTMAR and wife AUGUSTA; ANNE von QUINTUS, JOHN A. DITTMAR, d. Nov. 19, 1937, he m. TILLIE & div. Jan. 10 1935; had EDNA KREUNCKE, who m. ALVIN; MARY m. RUSSELL FIEMSTER and JOHN A. and ALMA who m. PAUL HAMNER, GEO. B. DITTMAR et ux MARTHA, ROSA J. SPILLMAN, m. EDWARD SPILLMAN, EMILIE R. m.EMIL SCHUTZE, MARY A m. MAX EHRLICH, FRANK J. DITTMAR et ux ALMA and CLARA J. m. WILLIE FEUERBACKER.

844/240 Aff. May 20, 1947, CASPER DITTMAR, patentee, land Cert. Mar. 30 1850. He came to Texas ca 1853, he and wife d. of cholera 1855 in Gillespie Co. Texas, intestate: 4 ch: CHATERINE (CATHERINE) m.ANTON A NEBGEN, MARTIN DITTMAR, Gillespie Co. Tex. d. April 6, 1881; GEO. D. DITTMAR m. EMILY J. WENDE and ANNIE m. J. STULER d. Blanco Co. Tex Mar. 30, 1876.

PC 5403 MATHILDE DITTMAR was div. from JOHN DITTMAR, she was dau. of JOSEPH BECK et ux MATHILDE and had sister LYDIA, who m. OTTO SPILLMAN Mentions WALLY RILEY, who m. H. B. RILEY and had 3 ch. not named

B/35 Transfer of Cert of Title (this is county surveyor's record,TCT) ROBT. COMPTON to JOSIAH FISK June 6, 1941, 640 ac. No. 326, granted by Jasper Co. Texas, Bd. of Ld. Commrs. Jan. 1, 1849. WIT: S. W. RALPH, JOHN L. BAKER, ack. June 10, 1846, by ROBERT COMPTON, before JAMES DELLENEY, NP Jasper Co. Tex. surveyed Mar. 19, 1850 by JAMES R. PACE surveyor, P. MILLICAN, ...EDWARD...chainmen.

161/496 Deed June 25, 1900 JOSIAH FISK to J. G. BURNEY (Fisk of LaSalle Co. Ill.)

E/8 WD Nov. 7, 1849, GEO. W. DAVIS to DAVID F. BROWN. WIT: T. T. FITZ-SIMONS, F. E. FITZSIMONS, LEVI PENNINGTON.

D/206 WD GEO. W. DAVIS to JAMES CUNNINGHAM, Mar. 20, 1850. WIT: J. MINER, JAMES R. PACE (refers to R. E. FLANNIGAN tract)

Q/363 Constable's deed Dec. 18, 1865 GEO. W. DAVIS, et ux EMILINE P. to gd. CATHARINE DAVIS sole representative of our son R. M. DAVIS. She is under age.

Q/368 Deed Dec. 12, 1865 GEO. W. DAVIS, et ux EMELINE P. to son WM.J.

Q/365 Deed July 17, 1860 GEO. W. DAVIS et ux EMILIE to B. H. DAVIS, son and his wife, ELVIRA T..

T/558 deed July 14, 1870 G. W. DAVIS to W. F. WELLS.

173/607 WD Dec. 12, 1901 P. C. WELLS, J. M. WELLS, W. T. WELLS and AMANDA LaRUE, a feme sole.

E/343 deed July 9, 1851, GEO. W. DAVIS to ROBT. E. FLANNEGAN. WIT: B. PAYNE, I. P. DAVIS

H/313 WD June 26, 1855 ROBT. E. FLANEGAN et ux MARY D. to RADCLIFF PLATT. WIT: A. A. CARLETON, JOHN B. COSTA.

PC 3529 EST. SAM M. PLATT, decd. minor child.of SAM M. PLATT who d.Mar 6, 1903 TCT; SAM M. PLATT b. Dec. 15, 1891, JOE H. PLATT b. Feb. 18. 1894; ONA PLATT b. Jan. 2, 1899; COLON M. PLATT, b. Aug. 11, 1902,all minors and MOLLIE L. PLATT and LENORA CAMPBELL et vir GILBERT.

X/395 Deed Jan. 3, 1873 GEO. W. DAVIS (EMILINE P. decd) to dau.MARTHA ANN, 2 sons, WM. J. & GLENN OWEN DAVIS to ELVIRA T. DAVIS, wife of son B. H. DAVIS, GEO. ENGLAND, JAMES ENGLAND, Ch. of dau. SARAH (SALLIE) decd., JAMES W. ENGLAND, their guardian. MARTHA ANN m. W. H. MAYTUM and d. 9/18/1877.

91/427 QC Jan. 6, 1890 J. W. ENGLAND of Lampasas Co. Texas, to sons GEO. D. & JAMES W. ENGLAND, JR.

91/639 Deed Jan. 13, 1890 GEO. ENGLAND of Midland Co. Tex. to W.L.DAVIS

315/335 deed Mar. 3, 1900 JAS. W. ENGLAND, JR. of Harris To.W. L.DAVIS

75/270 Receipt J. M. DAVIS et ux H. A. to MRS. E. T. DAVIS,mother
338/57 Aff. Jan. 23, 1922 by W. L. DAVIS, 56 years old,son of B. H. and ELVIRA T. DAVIS, both decd. B. H. d. intestate TCT Mar.14, 1882 and she d. Sept. 12, 1918.

V/513 Deed April ...1870 JANE McFARLAND, ABLE McFARLAND, M. J. & R.J. McFARLAND, legatees of J. A. CALDWELL, decd. JANE McFARLAND, MOTHER and heir of decd. children of JOHN S. YOUNG, FRANK P. YOUNG, MARY J. PAINE, et vir W. S., EMMA J. BLACK et vir THOS. BLACK, legatees of S. C. COLVILLE, decd. to ANN PITTS.

W/693 deed July 30, 1872 C. R. JOHNS to FLORENCE GLEEN et vir JOHN W.

60/474 Deed Aprl 23, 1884 FLORENCE R. GLEEN et vir JOHN W. of New Orleans, La. to ELLEN C. McDONALD wife of JOHN.

D/27 Patd.Oct. 30, 1832 JOHN BURLESON.

A/186 deed Oct. 29, 1840 JOHN CARTWRIGHT to THOS. PUCKETT of TCT (CARTWRIGHT of San Augustine Co. Tex.) bounded by JAMES GILLELAND,lea. and JACOB BURLESON 1/2 lea. WIT: M. CARTWRIGHT, L. H. MOFFITT.

R/76 PA Oct. 25, 1860 LORENZO D. PUCKETT of Karnes Co. Tx. to CYRUS PUCKETT, property of his mother NANCY PUCKETT and father of THOMAS.

R/77 PA Mar. 11, 1867 CALEB GARRETT et ux IRENE of Douglass Co. Ill., names THOS. PUCKETT & NANCY, who d. in TCT April 6, 1859 to CHANCEY R. PUCKETT and CYRUS PUCKETT TCT

PC 74, filed Oct. 3, 1860 by WM. S. HOTSCHKISS, father of minors: DANIEL 14, MARY under 14, CORELIA under 14, said WM. S. HOTSCHKISS was husband of a child of NANCY PUCKETT. AARON BURLESON, GILES W. BURDITT R. M. JOHNSON, JOHN T. ALEXANDER & WILLIAM M. WILSON, appraisers

136/562 Aff. 1896 by MARY S. HOTSCHKISS second wife of WM. S. HOTSCH- KISS, whose first wife was HANNAH who d. 1852, leaving DANIEL, MARY E. CORELIA T., & MARTHA F., DANIEL d. 1846, no issue, MARY E. m. JOHN CHAMPION, CORELIA T. m. JAMES L. BROWN, MARTHA F. m. THOS. BOSTICK.

R/78 partition April 8, 1867 THOS. PUCKETT, CALEB GARRET et ux IRENE PUCKETT GARRETT of Douglas Co. Ill.; WM. S. HOTSCHKISS Heirs of Danl W. & gd. of CORELIA T. HOTSCHKISS, MARTHA E. HOTSCHKISS BOSTICK, JOHN CHAMPION et ux MARY E. HOTSCHKISS CHAMPION,heirs at law of HANNA B. PUCKETT HOTSCHKISS, LORENZO D. PUCKETT, Karnes Co. Tex; CYRUS PUCKETT MIRANDA PUCKETT, NATHANIEL MOORE and wife, EUCELIA PUCKETT MOORE,heirs of NANCY PUCKETT who d. April 6, 1859, Ack. before ALBERT BROWN,NP TCT

28/417 Deed Feb. 5, 1875 A. L. McRAE et ux MARANDA to CYRUS PUCKETT. WIT: W. S. HOTSCHKISS, Z. T. FULMORE.

S/69 PA Jan. 28, 1869 CALEB GARRETT et ux IRENE to CHAUNCEY P. PUCKETT THOMAS PUCKETT d. Nov. 14, 1868.

S/20 PA Feb. 13, 1869 CALEB GARRETT et ux IRENE of Douglas Co. Ill., LORENZO D. PUCKETT of Karnes Co. Tex.; CYRUS PUCKETT of Uvalde Co. Tex MIRANDA PUCKETT, NATHANIEL MOORE et ux EUCELIA, MARTHA E. BOSTICK,JOHN CHAMPION et ux MARY E., JAMES L. BROWN et ux CORELIA T., TCT.; THOS. PUCKETT d. Nov. 14, 1868 in Ill. intestate; 320 acres sold to L.B. D. LANE, R. S. JAMESON, land on VALLANORA Lea. Cherokee Co. Tex.; JOHN J. KENNEDY, Harrison Co. Tex. land out of JOHN M. DOR, league

171/446 deed Sept. 1, 1893 CYRUS PUCKETT, SR. et ux M C. TCT to sons LEON & CYRUS, JR.

205/288 Agreement Oct. 15, 1906 between M. C. PUCKETT, widow TCT, LEON PUCKETT, TCT & T. W. PUCKETT, Runnells Co. Tex. her sons.

DC 15, Fall Term 1850 filed Oct. 15, 1850 GEO. HANCOCK vs. THOS. J. McKINNEY, cites HORATIO CHRISMAN as Alcalde to SAML. L. WILLIAMS,agt. for SANGIAGO del VALLE

B/78 WD Sept. 2, 1839 BARTLETT SIMMS to ISAAC W. BURTON, Bastrop Co. Texas before L. C. CUNNINGHAM, CJ WIT: E. PORTER & J. C. SIMS

A/263 WD Feb. 23, 1841, BARTLETT SIMS to JAMES & ELIJAH CURTIS, WIT: WM. C. W. SIMS, JAMES H. GILLESPIE

B/139 WD Jan. 26, 1846 SAMUEL HIGHSMITH to JOSEPH ROWE

F/336 WD Feb. 15, 1858 ROBERT MITCHELL to 1/3 ch: and heirs of JOHN D. HENRY, decd.; 1/3 MEREDITH WALTON and 1/3 JAMES T. BENSON, ELIZ. B. HENRY widow of JOHN D. HENRY decd.; MEREDITH W., ELY T., HUGH G., DAVIS N., JOHN R., MARY I., AMANDA M., THOMAS I., JAMES M. & FRANKLIN D. HENRY

DC 187 filed April 19, 1855 MARTHA MITCHELL vs. MINUS C. & JESSE BURDITT & JOHN T. MILLER

DC 642 filed April 19, 1855, MEREDITH WALTON, JAMES B. BENSON, ELIZABETH B. HENRY widow JOHN D. HENRY decd., MEREDITH W. & HUGH G. HENRY heirs of full age, vs. ELIZ. T., DAVIS N., JOHN R., MARY ⁻., AMANDA M., THOMAS J., JAMES M., FRANKLIN D. & TEXANNA C. HENRY, minor children.

830/529 PATENT June 19, 1861 to JOHN E. LINN, bounty warrant No. 1484 issued by Adj. General Jan. 21, 1854.

110/577 July 25, 1849 PATENT to ALEX. DUNLAP by virtue of unconditional headright cert. by Brd Land Comrs. of Victoria Co. Tex. Dec. 5, 1853.

N/86 Wd Nov...1857 JOHN E. LINN of TCT to RICHARD SCHWAB. WIT: M.FARLEY, SAMUEL JONES, before ALEX W. SNEED NP, Milam Co. Tex. by wit: M.FARLEY.

27/512 deed April 21, 1873 J. T. DUNLAP to bros. RICHARD G. & WILLIAM C DUNLAP. ack. Henry Co. Tenn by J. T. DUNLAP

27/ 512 PA JOHN H. DUNLAP of Henry Co., Tenn. appoints ARTHUR R.CROZIER of TCT to sell lands in Texas belonging to estates of RICHARD G. and/or E. ALEX DUNLAP.

27/513 PA Aug. 12, 1874 RIPLEY E. DUNLAP of Gibson Co. Tenn. to ARTHUR R. CROSIER

41/491 PATENT to JAMES T. DUNLAP July 31, 1874 of Nashville, Davidson Co. Tenn. to JAMES H. WILLIAMS of Lebannon, Ky.

46/224 WD Aug. 17, 1878 JAMES H. WILLIAMS to DAVID WALKER, both of Mason Co. Ky.

57/290 Sept. 12, 1883 LEVI HERSHALL to W. C. SCRUGGS of Green Co.Tenn.

A/424 WD Jan. 15, 1840 HENRY MARTIN, Sabine Co. Tex. to LEANDER C. CUNNINGHAM by Cert. 25, Bd. Ld. Com. SABINE Co. surveyed by THOMAS H. MAYS, Bastrop Co. commissioned surveyor ack. before WM. P. WYCHE, CJSCT WIT: B. HERSHAL, WM. PALMER

H/545 Mtg. Sept. 17, 1855 LEANDER C. CUNNINGHAM of Bastrop Co. Tex.to BENJAMIN A. SHEPHERD, ANDREW J. BURKE, Harris Co. Tex. WIT: P. R.TURNER M. B. HIGHSMITH, ack. Sept. 21, 1855, before JOSEPH O'CONNER, NP Bastrop County Texas

55/263 cc Judgment May 4, 1860 B. A. SHEPHERD, ANDREW J. BURKE, vs.L.C. CUNNINGHAM & CO.(HENRY CROCKERON) from Harris Co.Tex.sold to GEO.SEALY.

88/395 SWD Oct. 19, 1885 GEO. SEALY of Galveston Co. Tex. to McDONALD TOWNSEND TCT 2 notes, payable at office of BALL HUTCHINGS & CO.

88/393 WD Oct. 10, 1889 McDONALD TOWNSENDet ux SERENA M., of Bastrop Co. Texas to OSCAR BOESEL TCT

PATENT July 7, 1847 to JAMES WEBB assignee of W. H. W. JOHNSON, O. L. 39, Div. A, Austin City Outlots TCT

D/545 Rel.Sept. 9,1851 RACHAEL E.WEBB, wife of JAMES WEBB. WIT:JAMES W. WEBB & P. W. HERBERT, ack. before WARREN KINNEY, NP Nueces Co.Tex.

31/414 WD Jan. 28, 1876 JAMES H. RAYMOND to S. G. KINGSBERY

48/157 WD Dec. 6, 1880 S. G. KINGSBURY to CH. L. FORSTER & JAMES H. RAYMOND.

119/97 WD Sept. 6, 1893 C. L. FORSTER et ux MAHALA to W. J. FORSTER

254/561 WD Jan. 22, 1918 H. A. WROE to MRS. JENNIE PURSLEY

322/297 Aff. Dec. 23, 1921 by W. MASSEY, RE: HIRAM PURSLEY et ux JENNIE decd. 7 Ch. div. 23 years ago, Ch: WM. d. sm 34 years ago no issue; MYRTLE d. single, ELIZABETH m. M. H. McGEE, d. about 1920, she d. at birth of only son ROBERT BRUCE McGEE (Now 16 years) SAM now living, J. W., now living, AUGUST d. when a child, and 332/297 says JENNEY PURSLEY d. 1918.

A/563 WD Sept. 5. 1843 JOHN WOOD to SAML. JAMES WOOD, MOSES WOOD, WIT: D. LAUGHLIN, WM. BRATTON.

B/119 WD Feb. 25, 1845 MOSES WOOD & SAML. J. WOOD to JOSEPH W. ROBERTSON. WIT: A. W. LUCKETT, THOS. FREEMAN before A. J. HARRELL ccc TCT

D/415 PATENT Feb. 20, 1850 to EDWIN NASH, ASSIGNEE

D/416 WD Jan. 20, 1851 EDWIN NASH to WM. M. WILSON

K.240 WD Feb. 18, 1856, WM. W. WILSON to BENJ. F. OWEN, WIT: J. T. DUFFAU, JUSTIN DEVIDSON

PC 1053, Community survivorship EST. PAUL DEATS, decd. filed Jan. 25, 1885 by surviving wife, ELIZABETH H. DEATS; he d. June 11, 1885, 6 ch. MARY, T. A., ROBERT A., ELIZA A., MARTHA F., and PAUL M. DEATS. Appraisers JOS. SPENCE, W. E. CARPENTER, JNO. O. JOHNSON

D/654 Tax deed Aug. 15, 1850 JOHN CARROLL, assessor and Col. to A. B. McGILL. WIT: T. B. BECK, WARREN L. THOMAS.

F/327 QC Nov. 7, 1853 ASHFORD B. McGILL to JOHN T. CLEVELAND, WIT: JOHN T. ALLAN, GEO. L. WALTON

H/359 WD Aug. 1, 1855 J. T. CLEVELAND to CHAS. DEXTER CLEVELAND, WIT: GEO. L. WALTON, JOHN H. CONNOR.

Q/54 CC sequestration of property of CHAS. D. CLEVELAND of State of Calif. Jan. 14, 1863. Then came J. T. CLEVELAND et ux LOUISIANA, who claim to be parents of CHAS. D. CLEVELAND & J. T. & LOUISIANA CLEVELAND faithful citizens of Confederate States and say land is vested in them.

Q/57 WD May 26, 1863 J. T. CLEVELAND, Blanco. Co. Tex. to JOS. WRIGHT ack. by J. T. CLEVELAND before PERL PRIESTLEY, NP TCT

V/565 PA Sept. 22, 1871 C. C. CLEVELAND, San Francisco, Calif to J.T. CLEVELAND of Burnet Co. Tex. WIT: FRANK V. SCHUDDER, DANL.McCAULEY, F. V. SCUDDER, Comr. for Tex. resident of City and Co. SanFrancisco Cl.

I/365 Wd Mar 6, 1855 A. B. McGILL to WM. C. AINSWORTH, WIT: CHAS. CONEY, CHAS. A. CROSBY

H/414 Wd Aug. 28, 1855 WM. C. AYNSWORTH to MRS. LYDIA LEE, WIT:R.A.H. CARLETON, A. B. McGILL.

P/435 WD May 29, 1860 ABNER LEE et ux LYDIA To WM. A. HAMILTON

S/128 WD April 15, 1869 WM. A. HAMILTON of Milam Co. Tex. to ELIZABETH TEABE (E. E. M. TEABAUT) & JANE H. HAMILTON, WIT: J. N. HAMILTON LOUISE T. NAGLE, THOS. J. RAY.

37/613 Wd May 9. 1877 JOS. WRIGHT et ux RACHEL, to R. P. WRIGHT

30/457 Deed July 19, 1877 JOS. WRIGHT et ux RACHEL, love and affection for dau. LOUISA J. WALLING, et ux of GEO. W. WALLING, SR.

28/495 AGMT. Oct. 29, 1874 PENINA BROWNING, surviving wife of C. C. BROWNING decd. and MRS. MARY P. GLASSCOCK & SARAH E. WHIPPLE wife of J. W., daus. of C. C. & PENINA BROWNING, Comrs. appointed: W. M. WILSON, WASHINGTON ANDERSON & ROBT. WRIGHT.

52/251 Wd April 14, 1882 HENRY HIRSCHFIELD to JAMES WOOD SMITH. WIT: DON WILSON, W. S. SMITH

377/28 Aff. April 7, 1925 GEO. W. WALLING, SR. d. TCT Feb. 29, 1916, wife LOUISA J. sur. whom he m. Dec. 24, 1855; Ch: CATHERINE WALLING m. P. C. WELLS (now decd) she d. Aug. 6, 1936, he d. May 29, 1913; CORA m. JAMES A. WALLING she d. April 25, 1912 and had 4 Ch: ANNIE SCHERMERHORN wifeof JAMES, CATHERINE SILLIMAN wife of W. B., ROBERTA BICKLEY, wife of CHAS., & AMY WILLIAMS wife of JAMES: ROBT. W. WALLING GEO. W. WALLING, JR., THOS. B. WALLING, MARY ELLA m. CHAS. C. WILKINS, RICHARD B. WALLING, LOUISE m. LUKE C. ROBERTSON d. Sept. 17, 1909, she d. Nov. 24, 1910, no ch. CLARIBEL m. A. B. CLARKSON, she d. Sept. 25, 1919 and he d. Sept. 14, 1919 in Corpus Christi, Texas storm, had one child HELEN CLARIBEL m. JAMES A. RUSSELL, JR. 1932.

C/9 WD Dec. 30, 1846 ALFRED W. LUCKETT to MORGAN C. HAMILTON, WIT: JAMES BAKER, B. F. JOHNSON before CHAS. MASON, NP TCT

D/244 QC May 16, 1850 MORGAN C. HAMILTON to NOWLAND M. LUCKETT. WIT: D. C. CADY, JNO. F. MULLOWNEY.

PC 218 NOLAND W. LUCKETT, filed Dec. 3, 1855; he d. Oct. 13...by Thos. M. DUVAL & L. HORACE LUCKETT. WILLappoints DUVAL & JNO. S. SUTON, Extr. and CODICIL APpoints L. H. LUCKETT, Extr. said L. H. LUCKETT is cousin of decd. 2 Ch. minors and wife, survive, father and mother dead. Will dated Mar. 23, 1853 names dau. MARY JANE LUCKETT, son ALFRED THOUSTON LUCKETT, WIT: W. P. deNORMANDIE, EDWARD F. PECK. CODICIL, made at Woodville, Wilkinson Co. Miss. Oct. 13, 1855. WIT: JOSHUA DORSEY, E. J. ELDER, DANL. H. PROPER, FRANCIS GILBERT, FRANK CONRAD Clerk, PC. FRANK BROWN, THOS. H. JONES, WM. O'CONNELL, JAS. P. DAVIS & JNO. T. ALLAN, Appraisers. Guardianship by LEVIN H. LUCKETT, resident TCT says ALFRED T. LUCKETT & MARY JANE LUCKETT, under 14 and 21 years DC 1204, MARY JANE CHALMERS et vir WM. HUGH CHALMERS, vs. LEVIN H. LUCKETT, THOS. H. DUVAL, executor, WM. LUCKETT decd. PC min. E/238 filed Mar. 29, 1870 ESTATE MARY JANE CHALMERS, decd.

PC 136 filed...1872 EST. THOS. G., DAVID G. & JULIA V. CHALMERS, minors by HUGH CHALMERS. 1877 says JULIA 18 y. and WM. HUGH CHALMERS now resident of D. C., D. GLENN, THOS. GREEN & JULIA HALL et vir W. K., JULIA VAUGH CHALMERS waived service to discharge.

251/25 aff. Feb. 6, 1912 by H. M. METZ and H. G. LEE; N. M. LUCKETT was hus. of ANNA C., d. Mar. 25, 1853; ANN C. d. 185...left surviving ALFRED, MARY JANE, 185..m. LEIGH CHALMERS, she d. 1870 and he d. had 3 children.

54/525 PARTITION DEED Dec. 28, 1882 D. G. CHALMERS of d. cb, JULIA CHALMERS HALL of Galveston Co. Tex. wife of E. E. HALL and D. G. CHALMERS and THOS. G. CHALMERS

D/63 Deed Feb. 20, 1840 THEO. BISSELL, m. man to SOLOMON B. CONLY, BastropCo. Tex. WIT: GEO. C. TENNILLE, C. L. LOCKHART, ack. by GEO. C. TENNIEHILL, before C. C. deWITT, CJ Gonzales Co. Tex. Apl.4, 1849

B/155 Deed Sept. 14, 1845 JOHN C. WOODALL to JAMES PARK, TCT in Milam grant, WIT: W. HARRISON, JOHN H. GILLESPIE.

DC 403 JAMES PARK & WILLIAMSON S. OLDHAM, GIDEON G. PACE, DAVID OLDHAM & J. J. JOHNSON, 1854 May 1866, WM. WALTON Esq. guardian ad litem for minor heirs of D. OLDHAM, decd. Mar. 5, 1867 death of ptf. is noted Mar. 4, 1868, CLEMENT R. JOHNS, admr.with will annexed of JAMES PARK decd. DAVID B. OLDHAM, left widow ELVIRA & minor ch: SALLIE JANE and JOHN O. OLDHAM.

PC 382 JAMES W. PARK, 1867, WILL probated in Franklin, Williamson Co. Tenn. Oct. 1866. ROBT. S. BLLLEW, Judge, DAVID CAMPBELL had will dated Aug. 25, 1866. JAMES PARK HAMMER and wife, MAY heirs had land inTCT to DAVID CAMPBELL 1280 acres in Johnson Co. Tex. and HUGH & DAVID CAMPBELL when 21; to WM. PARK and FRANCES PARK (WM.'s sister) the pro= ceeds of their father's estate to H. PARK NEELY to HENRIETTA PARK CAMPBELL & DOCTOR J. P. HAMMER's wife. JOHN W. HAMMER, JR., JAMES PARK & JOHN PARK, JR. land in Ellis Co. Texas; papers in hands of WILLIAM A. PARK's widow.

328/270 Mar. 5, 1921 MRS. CORNELIA BECKETT, widow of WM. K. BECKETT,dcd.

328/258 deed Mar. 26, 1921 W. L. BECKETT, THOS. A. BECKETT, C. H. BECK- ETT, MARY D. BECKETT & OLLA BECKETT, MINNIE BRODIE wifeof J. C., G. H. BECKETT of Tehama Co. Cal. to mother, MRs. CORNELIA BECKETT.

441/326 Aff. WM. KARR BECKETT et ux CORNELIA JONES BECKETT, he d. July 1922 and she d. March 1947

58/69 deed Oct. 9, 1883 W. K. BECKETT to school, 2 acres on Manchaca road, TCT on T. BISSELL survey, 1915 book 285/282 deeded back to BECKETTS...school known as ROBERTS SCHOOL HOUSE.

K/759 deed Oct. 13, 1855 ABNER H. COOK Mtg. to F. W. CHANDLER,trustee M. C. HAMILTON. WIT: JOHN T. ALLAN, GEO. T. BOARDMAN.

F/417 deed Jan. 21, 1854 BARTON RENICK to ABNER H. COOK (he was a home builder in Austin and built the Governors"mansion in 1853)

F/15 deed Dec. 4, 1851 DAVID G. ADAMS to BURTON L. RENICK, WIT: JOHN CARROLL, FRANCIS E. ADAMS,

M.252 deed Mar. 20, 1858, A. H. COOK to WM. C. PHILLIPS

B/64 Title Bond, July 17, 1839, DANL. BROWNING to HENRY ADAMS, Bastrop Co. Tex. WIT: JOHN J. GRUMBLES, J. PINCKNEY HILL.

No. 36 DC HENRY ADAMS, Spring Term 1848 TCT Court vs. heirs of DANIEL BROWNING, decd.

F/41 deed May 20, 1852 HENRY ADAMS of Dallas Co., Ala. to JOHN G. GRUMBLES, TCT

F/179 WD Dec. 21, 1852 JOHN J. GRUMBLES to JAMES E. BOULDIN, WIT: G. W. SCOTT, JOHN B. COSTA.

G/484 AGREEMENT April 25, 1853 JAMES G. SWISHER, JNO. M. SWISHER, JAMES H. RAYMOND & JAMDS E. BOULDIN. WIT: JOS. LEE, H. B. SLAUGHTER H. L. UPSHAW, surveyor TCT district

PC 645 Est. JAMES E. BOULDIN, SR., filed July 22, 1876; he d. July 13, 1876; JAMES E. BOULDIN, JR. petitioner. WILL dated July 13, 1876, land in St. Clair and Benton Counties, Missouri, about 6 miles from Warsaw known as White Sulphur Spgs. tract 400 acres; lot on Morgan St. St. Louis, Mo. 1/3 to ch. of son DAVID W. 1/3 to ch. of JAMES E. BOULDIN, JR. and 1/3 to ch. of dau. MARY V. FOX, LILLIE, SIDNEY, NELLIE, LACKEY & FRANCIS ST. JOSEPH FOX, and dau. CONSTANCE T. COOK decd. July 24, 1882, Ch. CONSTANCE, EARNEST COOK & LILLIE RECTOR & ELIZABETH TERRELL g.ch. and to friend J. W. LAWRENCE, WIT: J. W. LAWRENCE & J. C. SAUNDERS

91/505 QC Dec. 21, 1889, JAMES E. BOULDIN of Pettis Co. Mo. and his ch: JAMES E. BOULDIN, JR., MINTOR T. BOULDIN, ROBT. E. BOULDIN, WM.,MINNIE E. BOULDIN of Pettis Co. Mo...WIT: JOSEPH E. CARTER and H. C. SINNETT
P. C. 921 filed Sept. 4, 1883 CONSTANCE T. COOK by husband A. H. COOK, JR. she d. July 24, 1882.

PC 1167, filed Sept. 8, 1886, by ABNER H. COOK says he is father of minors (mother d. July 24, 1862) LINDA MAY, HUGH BOULDIN, ALEX TERRELL CONSTANCE 18 in 1892 and EARNEST 14 in 1892.

88/102 deed Oct. 4, 1889 ABNER H. COOK to CONSTANCE COOK love and aff. and because of her physical inf. all right, interest, etc. I have as surviving heir of CONSTANCE COOK in and to estate inherited by decd. wife from her grand father JAMES E. BOULDIN.

PC 785 J. M. FOX applicant, transcript from court in San Francisco Co. Calif. guardian (aptd. July 16, 1880) minors: SIDNEY FOX, NELLIE FOX, LACKEY F., LILLY FOX and FRANCIS ST. JOSEPH FOX. States this is anxilliary proceedings of Montana guardianship, Gordon Co. Montana.

PC 784 JOSEPH M. FOX, Sept. 2, 1880 JOSEPH M. .. FOX appointed guardian by San Francisco Co., is uncle by marriage of minors; DAVID W. BOULDIN JR, d. prior to April 15, 1890, POWHATTAN W. BOULDIN & JAMES E. BOULDIN

PC 1221 JAMES E. RECTOR decd. d. Nov. 27, 1886, at Kyle, Hays Co. Tex wife LILLA B. & 4 ch: J. BOULDIN RECTOR 13 yr., RICHARD T. RECOTOR 11 y. LIZZIE 9 yrs. and ARTHUR 7 years.

PC 1354 Sept. 5, 1888 guardianship J. BOULDIN RECTOR, RICHARD TO., LIZZIE & ARTHUR. Land in Travis, Menard, Kerr and Erath counties, Tex

DC 8930 filed March 29, 1889 JAMES E. BOULDIN d. July 13, 1876, land to grand children, ch. of W. D. BOULDIN, J. E. BOULDIN, JR., ELIZABETH TERRELL, decd. and MARY VA. FOX, decd. defts. J. E. BOULDIN, M. T., R. E. & WM. and MINNIE BOULDIN are grandchildren of JAMES E. BOULDIN and wife, MINNIE: 1/48 as heirs of JAMES B. BOULDIN one of three ch. who d. intestate, and without issue, defts. W. D. BOULDIN, JR., W. P. & J. E. BOULDIN, are children of D. W. BOULDIN & BELL B. And grandchildren of JAMES BOULDIN, their son; defts. LILLA RECTOR gd. JAMES E. BOULDIN dau. ELIZABETH TERRELL, decd. and ARTHUR J. TERRELL, defts. LINDA MAY MURPHY, TERRELL COOK, CONSTANCE COOK & EARNEST COOK ch. CONSTANCE COOK decd. formerly TERRELL, a grandchild of J. E. BOULDIN and dau. ELIZABETH TERRELL, decd., HUGH COOK d. after the death of mother CONSTANCE COOK.

589/523 PATENT, STATE of COAHUILA & TEXAS to WILKINSON SPARKS, sm. July 21, 1835, introduced by R. M. WILLIAMSON, agent for EMPRESARIO BENJ. R. MILAM. WIT: TALBOT C. CHAMBERS, J. H. SCAGGS, L, C. CUNNINGHAM

108/180 deed Dec. 21, 1892 WILKINSON SPARKS of Harris Co. Ga to W.A. FARLEY & J. R. LAWRENCE, before A. F. TRUETT, Clk.Sup. Court (Ga).

C/544 WD Aug. 8, 1858 WILKINSON SPARKS to PATRICK C. JACK, WIT: JAMES P. McKINNEY, E. M. DEAN, ack. by J. P. McKINNEY, July 21, 1849, A. B. McGILL, CCC TCT

E/56 BOND FOR TITLE, PATRICK C. JACK to WILKINSON SPARKS of Ga. WIT: JAMES F. McKINNEY, E. McLEAN, ack. by EPHRAIM McLEAN, witness, Mar. 18, 1850, A. F. JONES CJ Galveston Co. Texas

D/225 deed Mar. 29, 1850 REUBEN R. BROWN of Brazoria Co. Tex. to PETER McGREAL & JOHN L. LEWIS & SEYMOUR R. BONNER of G. THOS. G. MASTERSON, NP Brazoria Co. Texas

D/395 CC COURT of Brazoria Co. Texas, Jan. 1, 1851 PATRICK C. JACK d. 1844 intestate; THOMAS F. McKINNEY appointed administrator March 29, 1850, WIT: P. deCORDOVA, JAMES G. SWISHER

D/572 deed Mar. 20, 1852 PETER McGREAL of Brazoria Co. Texas to JOHN HORAN, WIT: WILLIAM P. MILES, WILLIAM O'CONNELL

PC 247 SEMOUR R. BONNER, decd. D. C. FREMEAN, JR., filed Sept. 3, 1858 BONNER d. more than 12 months ago out of state; FRANK BROWN, O. H. CULLEN & J. M. BLACKWELL, appointed appraisers.

P/83 deed Feb. 20, 1861 F. W. CHANDLER, E. B. TURNER to JOHN RABB, WIT: GEO. R. SCOTT, WM. O. OTIS

Q/95 deed April 22, 1861 JOHN RABB to VIRGIL S. RABB. WIT: JNO. T. ALEXANDER, L. S. FRIEND.

Q/96 deed April 22, 1861, V. S. RABB to TEXAS RABB, my youngest brother

W/787 deed Aug. 23, 1872 TEXAS RABB to ISAAC SMITH

52/248 deed Mar. 29, 1881 P.A. ISAAC SMITH et ux MARY to E. W. SHANDS

PC 1069 Community survivorship Oct. 6, 1885 LEONARD HICKLES sur. husb. ANNA C. d. June 13, 1885, 2 mns.ch. MARY MATILDA 15 yr. and JACOB LEBRECHT MAX HENKELS 4 years (HENKELS & HINCKELS, etc.)

DC 24,104 TTT filed June 23, 1906 J. T. BRACKENRIDGE vs. J. W. HAMMETT JIM McLEMORE, BOB SIMPSON, JASPER BROWN, BUDDY BROWN, CAL RAY & ED. ANDERSON

207/10 aff. by EUGENE BREMOND & JOHN H. ROBINSON, JR. Dec. 7, 1905,GEO. HANCOCK d. Jan. 2, 1879 survived by wife, LOUISA who d. Nov. 2, 1903 and son LEWIS HANCOCK.

V/600 deed Nov. 16, 1871 B. GRAHAM to A. H. WILKINS of New Orleans, Par. of Orleans, WIT: GEORGE T. GRAHAM, J. C. RAYMOND

C/354 deed April 23, 1847 THOMAS H. MAYS, Bastrop Co. Texas to SARAH LEE, TCT WIT: J. H. GILLESPIE, R. L. REDING

C.486 QC April 28, 1849 JOSEPH LEE et ux SARAH to HALL MEDLIN, TCT, WIT JAMES L. MALONE, ARCHIBALD MARTIN, before JOE MINOR, CJ

D/441 deed May 28, 1850 HALL MEDLIN to WILLIAM A. HADLEY

D/203 SWD Mar. 19, 1850 HALL MEDLINto WILLIAM BRADFORD, WIT:ENOCH MORSE

K/598 SWD Nov. 4, 1852 WILLIAM BRADFORD to A. W. ANDERSON, WIT: J. H. RUSSELL (?)

DC 920 filed April 7, 1856 FRANCIS KELLY vs. HALL MEDLIN, WILLIAM CASE, & OLIVER H. HEDGECOXE, Nov. 14, 1866, death of plaintiff, MARY A. KELLY, surviving wife prosecutes.

PC 272 EST. FRANCIS KELLY filed Feb. 1, 1860 Comm. survivorship states: FRANCIS KELLY d. Jan. 2, 1860, JOSEPH D. SHEPHERD, WILLIAM SATTLER, ED PITZAH, WILLIAM SAUER, & CHARLES ORLENDORF, appointed appraisers. CH: MARY ANN, WM. T.,JNO. W., & MARY JANE KELLY

DC 17,999 filed Mar. 26, 1902 MARY L. ARCHER fs. HAROLD H. DIESON,MINORS by next friend C. H. DIESON of Travis Co. vs. (C. H. bro. of W. G.DIESON) SETH B. REED, J. M. REED of Los Angeles Co. Calif. property bought by SETH B. REED May 5, 1840 and his wife, ELEANOR, who d. Dec. 23,1901 CH: JOHN M. REED, over 21, 1902, MARY L. REED ARCHER, widow of W. W. ARCHER, ANN ELIZA wife of W. G. DIESON, she d. Oct. 5, 1888, left HAROLD H. DIESON, says SETH B. REED, long since moved to Calif. EXH."A" (family record attached to aff.) BARTON REED b. in Mt. Pleasant, Tnws. Jefferson Co. Ohio, May 19, 1819; ELEANOR ROGERS b. Roeberry Tnsw.Washington Co. Ohio, Feb. 5, 1824; BARTON REED & ELEANOR ROGERS m. May 7, 1840, JAMES MADISON REED son B & E b. May 26,,1841; MARYMUM LAVINA REED dau. BARTON & ELEANOR, b.Aug. 28, 1844, in Arora, Dearborn Co. Ind.; ANN ELIZA REED dau. B & E, b. St. Charles, Mo. June 6, 1847. J. J. GASSER & H. M. METZ & J. R. BEARD commissioners to partition.

58/336 deed Nov. 27, 1883 to CHARLES THIELE from LIZZIE PAGE NELSON, fs New York.

171/592 Conf. deed Jan. 29, 1890 FANNIE B. NELSON MERCER et vir, now of Richmond, V. she formerly of York Co. Va.

F/46 WD May 28, 1852 HENRY ADAMS of Dallas Co. Ala. to JAMES H.RAYMOND

G/394 WD Nov. 22, 1853, JAMES H. RAYMOND, JOHN M. SWISHER to STERLING W. GOOD RICH, WIT: HENRY P. BREWSTER, P. deCORDOVA

PC 410 Community survivorship filed July 14, 1868, by MARY A. GOODRICH surviving wife of S. W. GOODRICH. He d. May 18, 1868.

57/12 WD June 26, 1883, LUCY L. DAVIS et vir I. V. to R. H. KINNEY

PC 1405 filed Mar. 19, 1889 SMITH EVANS KINNEY & FRANCIS GRACE KINNEY, over 21, MRS. FRANCES G.KINNEY, widow of ROSWELL H. KINNEY, decd. and LILLIAN B. KINNEY under 14 years.

190/192 WD Dec. 18, 1903, F. G. KINNEY sur. wife of R. H.; S. E.: F.G.: KINNEY fs. and L. B. KINNEY fs. of TCT and LUETTA KINNEY LINDSAY wife of W. G. of Detroit, Mich. to HENRY MAUTHE.

Div. 23,879 TCT filed Mar. 13, 1906 CARRIE ISABEL MAUTHE vs. HENRY MAUTHE m. Oct. 8, 1904,Harris Co. Tex. She was CARRIE ISABEL KLOTZ.

445/238 Aff. Re: E. L. WHITEHEAD, et ux MRS. HATTIE C. she d.prior to Sept. 23, 1914 left sur. hus. E. L. & R. L. son, MRS. CLAIRE J.SINCLAIR wife of L. B. dau; MRS. C. ISABELL HARGRAVES wife of C. E.; MRS. PEARL TERRELL wife of JOHN O.: MRS. BEULAH BEATRIX STALNAKER, wife of GUY C. & L. K. WHITEHEAD, son, of Miller Co. Ark.

PC 45 JAMES W. SMITH d. intestate Jan. 22, 1841, ANGELINA D.SMITH his widow and THOS. W. SMITH, his father apptd. administrators.

B/227 WD May 13, 1846 ANGELINA D. SMITH, Washington Co. Tex. to ASHFORD B. McGILL, Williamson Co. Tex. WIT: B. F. TARVER, STEPHEN R. ROBERTS, before WM. H. EDWING, CJ & EX NP Williamson Co. Texas

B/341 WD Jan. 4, 1847 ASHFORD B. McGILL to CHARLES KLEIN, both TCT WIT: T. W. ALGONER, H. LOHMAN.

U/99 deed Nov. 1, 1870 J. H. THACKARD et ux CHRISTINA, Galveston Co.Tex present and future estate of father of grantor JOHN HENRY LOHMAN, also all right in estate of ANTONETTE LOHMAN decd. to JOHN HENRY LOHMAN and his present wife, ROSINE

U/100 deed Nov. 7, 1870 same as above by ELIZABETH (X) BARINGER and husband J. C., of Limestone Co. Texas

U/101 same as above Nov. 3, 1870 by THEODORE LOHMAN et ux MARY (X) of Jackson Co. Texas

PC 1951 ESTATE P. C. TAYLOR d. Nov. 11, 1895 will dated Oct. 30, 1895 MARY ANN surviving wife, DAUS. BELL & BESSIE.

DC 31,992 TTT filed May 3, 1915 GUY A. COLLETT vs. unknown heirs of WILKINSON SPARKS, W. A. FARLEY, JOHN R. LAWRENCE, LEE SIMPELMAN, HARRY G. W. ISAACS, REUBEN HORNSBY, SR., JNO. D. HENRY, THOS. H. JONES,SAML. MORGAN, SUSAN & GEO. F. MOORE, WM. H. CUSHNEY, THOS. J. CHAMBERS, D. THOMAS, L. HORTSON, PETER McGREAL of Brazoria Co. Tex; THOS. WARREN PATRICK C. JACK, TOM ZIMPLEMAN, WALDINE ZIMPELMAN KOPPERL, wife of MONTZ, C. S. COOK, D. T. W. DIGNAN, JONAS DANCER, JOSEPH NEWSHAM.

W/388 PATENT Sept. 23, 1854 to MATTHEW CARTWRIGHT, assignee of WM. WOFFORD,Sept.1,1845, transferred to CARTWRIGHT, Aug. 31. 1849.

PC 1539 MAURICE B. MOORE, Comm. survivor. MRS. BELLE MOORE, sur wife Oct. 4, 1890 TOM HEFFINGTON, H. M. METZ, H. G. WICKES, appraisers 307/384 Aff. KARL EH, m. PAULINE SCHNEIDEWIND, Dec. 24, 1892,she d. Mar.12,1899; 3 ch: CLARA m. FRITZ WENDLAND, HERMAN F., and HERMINE m. PAUL PAKRANT d. Jan. 14, 1929, intestate 2 ch: RAY & IRENE m. F. L.

CAMFIELD, WILLIAM or WILHELM was child of PAULINE SCHNEIDEWIND (out of wedlock) not a son of KARL EH. KARL EH, m. (2) FREIDRIKA SCHNEIDEWIND, sister of PAULINE, his firstwife, April 28, 1900. Had: FRIEDA m. T. J. CUNNINGHAM and HILDA m. A. H. PRIEM.

PATENT to ULRICH WUTHRICH Jan. 5, 1842 by REPUBLIC of TEXAS.

PC 76 EST. ULRICH WUTHRICH, d. Aug. 3, 1844, intestate no kin in Republic of Texas, petition by LOUIS CAPT.

D/565 PA Jan. 27, 1852 LUCIA WUTHRICH, mother of ULRICH WUTHRICH, CHRISTIAN MICHAEL, MATES, PETER & JOHANN, bros. of ULRICH WUTHRICH, and ANNA E. & LUCIA FRANKHAUSER, wife of SAML. sisters of JOHANN ULRICH WUTHRICH: agreement ack. in German, consulate of U. S. A. inSwitzerland secy. of St. Craton Bern Switzerland, N. BUCHARD, consul

D/509 AGREEMENT Dec. 8, 1851 with above and JOSEPH W. ROBERTSON, ack. JOHANN ULRICH WUTHRICH, agent and J. W. ROBERTSON in TCT

DC 882 HENRY P. HILL of Muscogee Co. Ga., vs. JOHN J. GRUMBLES & MORGAN C. HAMILTON of TCT. JOHN J. GRUMBLES d. ca May 1, 1869, CAROLINE his widow; PETER B., JOHN D. of San Saba Co. Tex. MARTHA STANLEY, wife of WM. H. of Williamson Co. Tex. and JOSEPH W. GRUMBLES, Hays Co. Tex; JANE GRUMBLES, MARY PLUMLEY wife of J. T. of Williamson Co. Texas; SAML. G., MEDORA, ANDERSON, Minor children.   J. M. REID, jury foreman

F/346 PA HENRY P. HILL, Spalding Co. Ga..Sept. 6, 1853 to WM. P.STOKES and WM. H. STEWART, atty. of Harris Co. Tex. WIT: DAVIS WILLIAMS, A. BELLAMY, JP, and JAMES S. WOOD, Clk. Inferior Ct. JASON BURR, Justice. (evidently Spalding Co. Ga. as Texas officials not so named)

Z/459 PA Sept. 20, 1872 HENRY P. HILL of Giffin, Ga. to WM. A.STEWART Houston Co. Tex.; land in TCT, City of Austin, and Denton Co. Texas, assignee of HENRY HARMAN (bounty warrant) WIT: JOHN H. LEME, JNO. O. WALLS, FREDERICK D. DISMUKES, ordinary, J. R. McCORMICK,Denton Co.Clk.

Z/457 deed 1280 acres RUFUS McLILLAN assignee of A. SANCHES, cert. issued to JOHN MOLE or MALE 1/3 Lea. ack.Spalding Co. Ga. and WM. A. STEWART, Ellis Co. Texas

DC 8428 filed Nov. 8, 1887 H. P. HILL vs. N. G. SHELLY, O. T. & H. B. KINNEY, F. DOHME, R. J. BRACKENRIDGE, NATHAN WOODS, W. A. TIPTON, WM. TEAGUE, F. SWISHER, JACOB STERN, C. H. ALDEN, J. S. COPES, MRS. R. SLINGER (service..sheriff says she is dead) ALEX EANES, G. T. ROBB, DANIEL P. KINNEY, J. D. PARISH, MRS. HENRIETTA BEHNKE (service..sheriff says she is dead) MRS. C. HUNTER, MILTON JACKSON, JOSEPH MODEN, R. J. SWANCOAT, et ux LIZZIE, CHARLES STOKES & DOUGLAS WOODS.

123/369 CARL OSCAR STARK, JOHAN (JOHN) AUGUST, HERMAN,LOENTINA (TINA) ROSALIE FORSBERG, grandchildren SARAH LOGREN, SALLIE ALMA, dau. of decd. dau. AMANDA CHRISTINA LOGREN.

474/162 Aff. Dec...1964 ALBERT, d. 1956, & HILDA (HULDA) BERKMAN d. 1940, she was HULDA STARK m. 1907 1 time, each, son: CLAUDE T. BERKMAN b. Feb. 20, 1909 LOUISE b. Oct. 2, 1910 d. May 3, 1963 unm

74/12 Aff. of adoption Dec. 6, 1886 H. J. & NANCY A. DOUGHTY, adopt EUGENE HOLLAND, male, minor about 6 years old, son of MRS. SALLIE HOLLAND, widow, was apprenticed by order of TC court.

235/462 aff. Oct. 8, 1909 MRS. NANCY A. DOUGHTY d. April 9, 1903

PC 639 Guardianship NEWTON GIVENS LANE 19, JAMES LANE 17 and ANNIE LANE 13 years old, she m. J. R. BLOCKER, filed Feb. 28, 1876, by R. N. LANE, surviving parent 1/3 interest ELIZABETH SWISHER

K/472 WD Sept. 25, 1856, T. J. CHAMBERS to WAYMAN F. WELLS, WIT: M. I.

WELLS, THEO. P. SPENCE, JAMES M. SWISHER, CCTCT by Aug.SWARTZ, Dpty.

K/186 Cert. Feb. 1, 1838 by A. HORTON, Pres. and NATHL. HUNT, asst.Comr WIT: JOHN C. BROOKE, Clk. appeared THOS. D. HENDRICKS, Ld. Commissioner San Augustine Dist. arrived year 1825 sm Republic of Texas of San Augustine Co. Tex. June 8, 1940 ,G. W. BLOUNT ccc & THOS. C. BARRETT, dpty.

K/187 CERTIFICATE TRANSFER Nov. 12, 1839, D. (X) HENRICK to MORRIS MAY WIT: WM. G. LONG, K. L. ANDERSON, ALEX M. DAVIS, CJ & NP

K/187 CERTIFICATE TRANSFER June 8, 1840 MORRIS MAY, San Augustine Co. Tex. to HENRY MORGAN, WIT: JAMES MATTHEWS, C. B. RITCHIE.

K/188 CERTIFICATE TRANSFER May 14, 1844 J. A. CHAFFIN, admr. de bonis non of EST. HENRY MORGAN, decd. to JOHN C. BROOKS, San Augustine Co. Texas. WIT: W. C. DUFFIELD, A. M. DAVIS

D/706 WD Nov. 8, 1852 JOHN C. BROOKE of San Augustine Co. Tex to RADCLIFF PLATT, TCT. WIT: JOHN C. ROHTE, L. W. WILLIAMS, F. V. McKEE, NP San Augustine Co. Texas

G/252 CERTIFICATE TRANSFER May 4, 1853 JNO. C. BROOKE,San Augustine Col. to H. W. SUBLET, TCT. WIT: J. A. GREER, C. I. POLK.

G/493, SWD Dec. 27, 1853 JOHN C. BROOKE et ux MARGARET T., San Austin Co. Tex. sole heirs of J. A. BROOKE decd.WIT: F.V.McKEE & J.R.SHELTON

F/529 WD Mar. 4, 1854 HENRY W. SUBLET to O. H. MERONEY, TCT refers to land in name of ANTO. FORSYTHE, THOS. D. HENDRICK & JNO. A. PRICE

L/144 WD Feb. 21, 1856 H.W.SUBLETT to JOSIAH FISK. WIT: M. H. BOWERS

H/447 WD Sept. 13, 1855 H. W. SUBLETT to DAVID K. ROSS. WIT: O.FLUSSER JAMES P. NEAL

T/320 WD May 28, 1870 ALBERT A. FULKES to WAYMAN F. WELLS

P/352 WD...1862 WAYMAN F. WELLS to STEPHEN CUMMINGS, et ux NANCY G., WIT: EDWARD LaRUE, L. M. LaRUE.

31/537 SWD WAYMAN WELLS et ux MAYE E. to AMANDA LaRUE land in TCT and Lampasas Counties, Texas

158/508 partition deed April 18, 1899 among children of WAYMAN F. WELLS and MARY E. WELLS: AMANDA LaRUE, PETER C. WELLS, J. M. WELLS, d. Aug. 15, 1914, W. T. WELLS & G. H. WELLS

277/93 Aff. Aug. 28, 1915 J. M. WELLS, m. Jan. 21, 1886 MARGARET DILLINGHAM, CH: MARY EVA b. Sept. 10,1891, Lucille b. August 4, 1894

PATENT Oct. 12, 1840 to A. BALDINGER, City of Austin lot.

F/27 Partition decree cc from Probate Court Galveston Co. Texas, June 5, 1847, ANDREW BALINGER to PETER DURST, decd. and widow and heirs of JOHN W. DURST.

T/24 WILL, Aug. 28, 1848, JOHN ULRICH DURST decd. to ch. of bro.PETER DURST to sister BARBARA WILD, MATODI (MATHLODI) ANNA CATHERINE JESSNEY & JACOB & SABEL JESSNEY

P/174 deed April 2, 1861 JOHN C. TRUBE et ux VERONICA DURST, WARFORD (HARFORD) LONG, et ux CATHERINE to SOPHIE TRUBE, wife of HENRY J.

T/27 PARTITION Feb. 8, 1870 SOPHIE BOCK widow of PETER DURST, SOPHIE, CATHARINEA & VERONICA, minor ch. of PETER DURST

330/127 Aff. Oct. 25, 1920, JAMES W. SMITH d. Oct. 21, 1920 et ux MARGARET SMITH d. Sept. 1, 1899, Austin TCT, NANNIE A. CRISER, TarrantCo.

ALFRED SMITH d. Rochester, Minn., Sept. 18, 1920, wife decd.CH:JEANNETE sw, MYRA B. sw, ALFRED SMITH, JR. sm, AMELIA FULLER, FanninCo. Texas, ROBERT C. d. July 13, 1900 sm, MARY E. b. Sept. 10, 1872 d. unm,MAGGIE MILLS d. Sept. 7, 1876 and J. W. SMITH, JR. Tyler, Smith Co.,Texas

C/415 Title Bond Oct. 2, 1848 W. D. PARIS, TCT to MARTIN MOORE TCT. WIT A. B. McGILL, JOHN WAHRENBERGER.

PC 268 ESTATE MARTIN MOORE, decd. d. Dec. 18, 1859, 5 ch. all minors and wife, ELIZABETH ANN (does not name children)

PC 3715 SARAH E. MOORE, et parte filed June 14, 1873 she is over 17 y. dau. MARTIN & E. A. MOORE

PC 1604 ESTATE JOHN HANCOCK,NCM 69 years E. B. HANCOCK son and widow SUSAN E., died shortly thereafter and estate administered under same No

B/247 PATENT, REPUBLIC OF TEXAS to E. HAIRSTONE

A/449 Cert. July 6, 1840 REPUBLIC OF TEXAS to HENRY WILCOX by JAMES H. STARR, secy. of the Treas.WIT: TIMOTHY McKEAN, F. T. HERRING

B/247 deed Jan. 2, 1846 EZEKIEL HAIRSTONE to D. B. BASFORD, says same let purchased by W. P. THORPE, July 6, 1840, WIT: THOS. WARD, L. MOORE ack. ANDERSON J. HARRELL, CCC TCT

C/163 Wd Dec. 10, 1847 ASHFORD B. McGILL to H. D. BOHLS. WIT: MARTIN MOORE, JOHN BROTHERS.

M/507 Bond for Title, Oct. 11, 1858, DEITRICH BOHLS et ux ANNA (H.D)

PC 356 EST. D. BOHLS, filed May 26, 1866 by MRS. ANNA BOHLS, JOHN E. MOWINKLE (MOWINCKLE)

303/110 aff. by EMELINE BLOMEKE, was dau. D. BOHLS,decd. and wife, ANNA D. BOHLS m. twice in old country, 1 child of first m. WILLIAM (2) 7 ch. THEODOR, GUSTAV, OLENA, who m. H. SPILLMAN & EMILINE who m. A. BLOMEKE now decd. JACK ED BOHLS & HENRY B. an infant who d. young; HENRY BOHLS d. sm prior to 1876; and after D. BOHLS d. ANNA m.____WIELAND: she was widow 1882; D. BOHLS is same to whom JUAN DELGARDO sold 177 ac.pat.TCT

PC 878 EST. JOHN J. STUDOR, decd. filed Dec.15, 1881, he d. Nov. 29, 1882 sm unm only heirs sister ROSIANA BARBARA KUPFER & BRO. HENRY STUDOR and sister ELIZABETH STUDOR

56/22 WD Feb. 21, 1883 ROSENA BARBARA KUPFER et vir T. S. of San Diago, Duval Co. Tex; HENRY STUDOR & ELIZABETH STUDOR, Zurich Switzerland

PC 2640 EST. JULIA O. WHEAT, decd. nee BERTRAM d. Harrison Co. Texas, heirs: MOSES H. WHEAT & 3 sisters: AGNES MOELLER, wife of H. W. of N.Y. EMMIE HUPPERTZ, & DORIS MILLER et vir W. J. of Runnels Co. Texas

313/90 cc ESTATE GEO. W. SPIER (SPEAR, SPEER) Fayette Co. Rep. Tex.d. Dec. 29, 1838,intestate, JOHN W. SCALLORN & REBECCA J.SPIER, admrs.D.S. KARNEGAY, Clerk, N. W. EASTLAND, Judge, WILLIAM NABORS, Dept. Shf. JEROME B. ALEXANDER, Depty. Clk. Bond, JOHN W. SCALLORN, & REBECCA J. SPIER, per WILLIAM A. FARRIS & WILLIAM SCALLORN, securities; REBECCA J. SPIER, WIDOW & MARIAM SCALLORN, dau. only heirs, J. B. McFARLAND, CJ FCT, N. W. FAISON, CCC L. P. WEBB, SHF.

A/330 Feb. 6, 1844 M. H. NICHOLSON to HARRIETT E. NICHOLSON, WIT: WILLIAM COCKBURN, A. COLEMAN, before JAMES M. LONG, CJ & EX O NP TCT

D/29 PATENT Oct. 16, 1848 JAMES H. RAYMOND, GEO. W. WOOD, governor, and GEORGE W. SMYTHE, COMR. GENL. LAND OFFICE

B/   QC Jan. 11, 1849 JAMES H. RAYMOND et ux MARGARET I. to THOMAS T. FAUNTLEROY. WIT: H. E. McCULLOCH, JOHN HORAN.

L/455 WD June 26, 1857 JAMES H. RAYMOND to MATTHEW HOPKINS, WIT: H. H. HAYNIE, JAMES F. JOHNSON

O/162 WD and street, Mar. 15, 1860 MATTHEW HOPKINS, JAMES H. RAYMOND, JAMES F. JOHNSON, ALEX. GREGG, mentions GEO. GLASSCOCK. WIT: JAMES M. SWISHER, D. CORWIN, surveyor.

V/348 WD Mar.17, 1870 JAMES H. RAYMOND to JOHN G. JAMES & C. A. JAMES.

PC 1176 EST. SAML. HARRIS, decd. filed Feb. 2, 1887, RHOADS FISHER, appl. says: SAML. HARRIS d. Sept. 3, 1886, Greensbrier Co. West Va. WILL dated July 13, 1885, appoints RHOADS FISHER of TCT & SAML. PAGE, heirs of MARGARET PAGE of Albermarle Co. Va. WIT: JOHN HANCOCK, E. B. HANCOCK T. S. MAXEY

W/611 Aff. June 27, 1872 BERNARD RADKEY, filed claim against JOHN G. JAMES for work done on TEXAS MILITARY INSTITUTE (3 story rock bldg. still being used as residence, 1977)

CHRIS. A. JAMES m. MISS MARGARET E. TOOLE, Dec. 10, 1872, TCT

210/195 Aff. by MOLLIE O'CONNER, Re: J. R. CARROLL, d. June 9, 1907 TCT et ux JANE d. Aug. 1876, Effingham Co. Ill. Ch: LEWIS VINCENT, RACHEL AMANDA m. W. N. MONROE, MARY ELLEN m. CHARLEY CONES, JOHN WESLEY, KITTIE JANE m. HALLUM WOOD, baby d. in infancy

278/354 aff. Re: J. N. BOYD (DR) d. ca 1872 Austin TCT wife AMY EWING, J. E. (EARNEST) and ALICE McKELVY et vir J. J.

F/40 PATENT to B. W. DEAN, Mar. 5, 1852, assignee of JOHN S. SPENCE

F/ 40 WD May 20, 1852 B. W. DEAN to JOHN C. HYDE, WIT: A. B. McGILL, JOHN B. COSTA

N/196 Assignment S. G. HAYNIE to FRANK BROWN, O. H. CULLEN, JOHN B. COSTA trustees, says 12½ ac. cedar land, deeded JOSIAH FISK to TIMOTHY McKEAN Sept. 3, 1859 and by McKEAN to FRANK BROWN, Oct. 13, 1853, receipt of JOHN A. GREEN, admr. of LAMAR MOORE

R/518 WD Jan. 1, 1869 MARGARET F. RUTLEDGE(formerly M. F. CARTER, NEE OLIPHANT)

PC 1099, EST. A. H. ROBINSON, COMM. SURVIVORSHIP Jan. 28, 1886, by PAULINE ROBINSON, Sur. wife, he d. April 11, 1885, left 7 ch: BESSIE 16 JOHN 14½, AL 12, MARY 12, KATE 11, PAULINE 5 and JOSEPHINE 4 mos.

W/150 says ALFRED H. ROBINSON, decd. minors: ALFRED H., JR., JOSEPHINE & PAULINE...C. J. FISHER atty. ad litem Jan. 12, 1895

S/530 WD Jan. 1. 1870 JOHN H. ROBINSON to ELLEN OWENS, orphan niece of my wife, ELIZABETH

138/566 WD April 22, 1890 ELEN FULHAM, widow, nee OWENS, of San Francisco, Calif. to JOHN H. ROBINSON, SR.

PC2059 WILL: JOHN H. ROBINSON, SR. dated Feb. 20, 1896 he d. April 10, 1897 to wife, ELIZABETH 2 sons JOHN H. & ALONZO and to son of my wife's niece LEO FULHAM, and dau.in-law PAULINE BREMOND ROBINSON, dau. LIZZIE SWANCOAT

873/527 PATENT, REPUBLIC OF TEXAS to PHILIP McELROY, a married man, of USA, Oct. 16, 1832, SAMUEL M. WILLIAMS agt. SAML. P. BROWNE, surveyor Adj. Colonist REUBEN HORNSBY, W. T. LIGHTFOOT, witnesses

B/156 WD Mar. 2, 1845 HENRY McELROY of Fort Bend Co. Rep. of Tex. to WM ADKINSON of TCT line between YOUNG & McELROY down creek to ELIZABETH McELROY's pasture taken out of PHILIP McELROY sur. WIT: JAMES T. DYER, DANIEL FRENCH, bef ore C. C. DWYER CJ & EX O N^P.Fort Bend Co. Tex

B/28 WD Dec. 3, 1844 HENRY McELROY , Harris Co. Tex. to JAMES YOUNG TCT says down line to ELIZABETH HUBBARD's line, cor. WM. D. THOMAS. WIT: ZADOCK HUBBARD, JOHN BUCHANNAN, I. CASTANEA, WM. FERGUSON, all Harris Co. Tex

B/68 Deed Dec. 3, 1848 HENRY McELROY to WM. D. THOMAS, mentions FRANCELLA McELROY's corner. WIT: ZADOCK HUBBARD & JOHN GREEN, JR.

39/128 Aff. heirship Nov. 1, 1877 CHAS. S. McELROY of Fort Bend Co. Tex. son of PHILLIP McELROY, after death of PHILIP McELROY, widow m. GEO. W. POWELL, 1 child GEO. POWELL: PHILLIP McELROY will was probated in Harris Co. Texas, 1844, CH: ELIZABETH m. HUBBARD, FRANCELLA HENRY d. unm. Aug. 14, 1866, ack. before H. S. SOMERVILLE, CCFB Co. Texas

V/188 cc partition J. W. HENDERSON, I. A. SOUTHMAYD, JOHN FITZGERALD

Y/278 Partition Feb. 20, 1872 JAMES G. ADKISSON et ux ELIZA, DAVID R. FULWINDER, et ux M. A., SAMPSON C. MOORE, et ux MARY J. (was widow of WM. ADKISSON, decd.) WM. ADKISSON, sole heirs WM. ADISSSON, decd.

PATENT issued JAMES COLEMAN, July 16, 1857 surveyed June 25, 1858, L. H. LUCKETT, dept. surveyor Travis Dist. DANL. DAVIS & WM. WYATT, chain carriers.

E/187 Certificate transfer Mar. 1, 1840 JAMES COLEMAN to JOHN FISK, for 1280 acres of land Jasper Co. Texas, Jan. 10, 1840. WIT: JOHN WALKER, CHAS. BROWN, ack. by JAMES COLEMAN before MARTIN PALMER, NP Jasper Co.

PATENT to JACOB TARRANT Sept. 1, 1845, surveyed April 4, 1853, L. N. LUCKETT dept. surveyor, Travis Dist. J. BROWN, ELIJAH PATE, ch. carrs.

PC 192 EST. JOHN C. HYDE, Decd. July 14, 1854, by THOS. FREEMAN, d. July 13, 1854 no kin in Tex. R. H. PAGE, JOHN T. ALLEN & J. VANCLEAVE aprs. NANCY HYDE formerly NANCY HANCOCK now NANCY TONGATE, et vir M. TONGATE. She m. JOHN C. HIDE Oct. 28, 1845, Fort Bend Co. Tex. no ch. and deceased not survived by parents, sisters or brothers.

217/314 Aff. NANCY TONGATE, was widow Feb. 15, 1868, JASPER STEWART Dec. 20, 1869, JAMES R. PACE, Co. surveyor, A. MORRISON & A. I. (J) SANFORD, chainers.

160/168 deed June 9, 1900 A. J. SANFORD et ux ELIZA to sons, EARL PALM SANFORD, PEARL MAY SANFORD, LEWIS TELIE SANFORD, all Wmson Co. Tex

202/187 Deed Sept. 5, 1904 JAMES F. RAGLAND et ux ADELIA to ALICE L. WALDEN, wife of ...

204/402 Sept. 5, 1905 ALICE L. WALDEN et vir L. R. WALDEN

PATENT, March 29, 1835 STATE of COAHUILA & TEXAS to WM. CANNON, m. man with family Bastrop Co. Tex. WM. CANNON d. intestate Dec. 10, 1851, WM. R. CANNON his son administered estate shows: He first m. MARY d. 1831=32 came to Texas 1835 with 2 sons WM. R. & CHAS. C., CHAS d. intestate 1836. 1852 AGNES K. CANNON sued WM. R. CANNON as surviving wife of WILLIAM CANNON (she of Williamson Co. Texas)

76/623 cc EST. JOHN A. WINSTON, decd. d. Dec. 1871, from Mobile Co. Ala Jan. 15, 1872 JOEL W. JONES. WILL, JOHN ANTHONY WINSTON Dec. 30, 1868 before JOHN A. dePRAS, SMITH CULLANE, & JOHN C. BOGLE dau. MRS. AGNES W. GOLDSBY and husband and her children: WM. O. WINSTON of Sumter Co. and JOEL W. JONES of Mobile, and EDWARD W. PETTUS of Selma, Indp. Extrs CODICIL: April 9, 1869.."..it may be porbable that my gdau. may have from her paternal gf.estate more than her brothers, executors ordered to even out..."

137/185 deed June 20, 1893 to FELIX E. SMITH, W. H. THAXTON

PC 1480 EST. FELIX E. SMITH, d. Feb. 5, 1890 intestate, widow and ch: W. H. THAXTON applies, is son-in-law of decd. husband of NANNIE S. Bond W. H. THAXTON $50,000.00 R. F. ROUNDTREE, ABE WILLIAMS, JAMES W.

SMITH, WADE M. SMITH, W. S. SMITH & W. D. MILLER, sureties.

418/165 Aff. NANNIE THAXTON, dau. FELIX E. SMITH d. Mar. 11, 1890;MARY S. SMITH d. Nov. 22, 1916; WILL S. SMITH, BETTIE A. SMITH ROUNDTREE, MAMIE SMITH THAXTON, MATTHEW M. SMITH, JOHN T. SMITH, JAMES M SMITH, WADE M. SMITH, JR.. and MARY SMITH CAMPBELL, FELIX E. SMITH, RUTH HELEN & GEO. d. infants; JAMES M. SMITH d. unm Feb. 13, 1899; JOHN T. SMITH, minor d. unm Sept.23, 1900; WILL SMITH d. Oct. 29, 1915, left. Ch. but was a widower; GILBERT STOVALL SMITH d. intestate and unm Dec. 8, 1917 NOVELLA WADE SMITH legal age and lives at Marfa, Texas; WM. ROGERS SMITH of age, lives in Falls Co. Tex.; BETTIE A. SMITH, widow of R. F. ROUND-TREE (he d. July 20, 1893) she d. April 1, 1926,, left SMITH ROUNDTREE MUSIDORS ROUNTREE, wife of L. L. MONTGOMERY, HALL L. ROUNTREE, HERBERT ROUNTREE, GORAN ROUNTREE and ROBT. F. ROUNTREE, JR., all of age and living except ROBERT F., JR. who d. unm under age ca 1908; MARY SMITH CAMPBELL d. intestate April 30, 1923, surv. by hus. WM. H. CAMPBELL and ch: JAMES LAWRENCE of Gilray, Calif. FELIX MORRIS, b. 1908 of Merced, Calif. and RUTH HELEN B. May 7, 1910, MATTHEW M. d. testate, Jan. 10, 1924; ELMORE L. ANDERSON SMITH of Dallas, 2 adult sons MATHEW M. JR., and STEPHEN GIRARD, NANNIE SMITH THAXTON, widow of W.H. THAXTON who d. Sept. 5, 1925; had HENRY J., MARY T. STOVAL wife of V. A., and FELIX S. THAXTON & CLARA SCOTT wife of PAUL R. SCOTT, Dallas and 2 children who d. in infancy ca 1891.

M/363 deed July 6, 1858 E. S. JOHNSON & CORNELIA J. WHITE JOHNSON to ABNER H. COOK.

C/519 June 8, 1849 deed to WM. COCKBURN, JOHN C. LEE, LEML. BRACKEEN

178/253 Jan. 13. 1902 A. FAULKNER d. intestate and no ch. Dec. 1, 1901 widow NELLIE, whom he m. Mar 9, 1872 and 2 sisters, MARY J. of TCT and EMRETTA E. PARKER, a fs. of Harris Co. Tex. and niece MARY A. ACKERMAN WIFE OF JESSE of Red Hook, Dutches Co. NY, MARY A. A. only child of JAMES A. M. FAULKNER decd. brother of A. FAULKNER, and a nephew A. F. McCORD of Dallas Co. Texas, only child of sister JULIA C. McCORD, decd.

DC 3627 LOUIS P. COOKE, MARY L. HARDY wife of JOHN F., VIRGINIA B. TALBOT fs. and CORA K. RICE, filed Mar. 31, 1873, sole heirs of father LOUIS P. COOKE, who d. 1849 and wife MARY A. vs. ALFRED GROOMS & JOS. LEE, Nov. 2, 1876, agreed judgment, VIRGINIA & RICHARD BENNETT are minor children of CORA RICE, decd. RICHARD BENNETT by aff. proves himself entitled to share of mother's part; CORA K. BENNETT, formerly RICE, formerly COOKE.

C/419 Manclovia, State of COAHUILA & TEXAS, June 24, 1835, to THOMAS JEFFERSON CHAMBERS, superior Judge of the Judicial Circuit of Texas, done at Monclavia, July 29, 1834, citizen IRA R. LEWIS, Special Commrs VIDAURI JUAN ANTONIO PADILLO, secy. T. J. CHAMBERS, selected a tract on eastern margin of Colorado River, April 17, 1834, beginning at Cascade Creek, at village of San Felipe of Austin, MANUEL MA VALDEZ, IRA R. LEWIS, WILLIAM L. CAZNEAU, LEWOLON D. EDWARDS, CJ of Co. of Matagorda, June 16, 1838

PATENT May 4, 1859 to I. A. PASCHAL

M/262 DEED April 24, 1858, GEO. W. PASCHAL to wife, MARCIA. WIT: THOMPSON HALLETTE, IRVING ROOT, ask. before S. CROSBY NP TCT

PC 757 filed Mar. 19, 1880 BETTY PASCHAL WRIGHT dau. of MARIA PASCHAL who d. Sept. 30, or Oct. 1, 1865, MRS. E. P. WRIGHT, dau. WILL: April 17, 1862, MARIA PASCHAL to son WM. D. PRICE (?) to dau. BETTIE, says present husband is GEO. W. PASCHAL.

238/60 WD Nov. 27, 1909 AMY K. WRIGHT et ux FRANCIS W., BESSIE EMILY HORNSBY et vir JESSE, MARY E. LAMAIR fs. JOHN C. BURROWS, et ux LENORA M. to JAMES SASSMAN.

238/547 Aff. Dec. 9, 1909 knew JOHN BURROWS, et ux ELIZABETH, he d. Aug 18, 1893, and she d. May 29, 1909; 4 ch: AMY K. m. FRANCIS WRIGHT, BESSIE EMILY m. JESSE HORNSBY, MARY E. m CHARLES LAMAIR, now widow and JOHN C. BURROWS.

G/460 WD Jan. 20, 1854 WILLIAM R. CANNON of Bastrop Co. Texas to NATHANIEL TERRY of Ala.

K/208 WD Feb. 24, 1855 NATHANIEL TERRY of Tarrant Co. Texas, to JOHN ANTHONY WINSTON, of Ala.

60/601 WD May 15, 1884 WILLIAM O. WINSTON, Extr. of J. A. WINSTON Est. and JOHN A. GOLDSBY, JOEL W. GOLDSBY only and sole heirs of decd. WM. O. WINSTON, ack. before CHARLES COOKE, NP SUMPTER Co. Ala., and JOHN A. GOLDSBY & JOEL W GOLDSBY ack. before R. B. OWENS NP Mobile Co. Ala

43/421 WILL: HENRY SWIFT, August 20, 1867, CHARLES A. RAPPALIO & FRANCIS SUMNER, Ind. Extrs. wife, CAROLINE, dau. ALICE MAYHENE and son FREDERICK son HENRY SUMNER SWIFT, son FRANK S. SWIFT.

238/60 JAMES SASSMAN d. Nov. 27. 1909, JOS$_{IE}$ IDA SASSMAN d. Dec. 8,1915 PC 5758 guardianship: ANNIE 20, THOS. V. 18; ARCHIE CLIFFORD 16; ISABEL 12, WM. F., over 21, sold to JOE W. SASSMAN (LELA MAY) deed May 6,1924. JAMES SASSMAN m. MYRTLE M. CARSON

AUSTIN CO. TEXAS voting districtVoting Precincts 1867 (these were taken by U. S. ARMY personnel): HERMAN HENNINGER 1867 had been in Texas 19 y. b. Prussia was in 12th III Vol. Calv. naturalized Dec. 16, 1865,in Brazoria Co. Texas.

C/422 Admr's deed Oct. 23, 1848, cc from Bastrop Co. Tex. GEO. W. DAVIS administrator of JAMES P. DAVIS, decd. to JULIA ANN BACON (says hereby divesting all other heirs of said JAMES P. DAVIS, decd.?)WIT: JAMES R. D JONES, ROBERT M. ELGIN

D/611 WD Aug. 5, 1851 JULIA (X) ANN BACON to son THOMAS H. BACON. WIT: ISAAC M. BROWN, J. B. BACON

F/340 WD Nov. 26, 1853, THOMAS H. BACON et ux MARTHA E. to TIMOTHY B. MORRIS

D/43 WD Feb. 26, 1849 JULIA ANN BACON to JAMES W. REILY, and WILLIAM REILY. WIT: G. W. DAVIS, J. B. BACON

574/80 PATENT, Nov. 1849 to JOSEPH W. ROBERTSON

PC 445 EST. JOSEPH W. ROBERTSON, d. Aug. 8, 1875 petition by GEORGE L. ROBERTSON, will says GEORGE L. ROBERTSON is son.

38/548 Wd Aug...1877 GEORGE L. ROBERTSON to mother, L. L. ROBERTSON

59/259 WD July 24, 1883 MOSES RAYNER to AUGUST FUHRMANN

253/565 Aff. Nov. 30, 1907 by CHRIS KOFAHL & B. BLENDERMANN, RE: AUGUST & EMILIE FUHRMANN, he d. May 2, 1906, had 6 Ch: HANNAH, over 21 m. DENNIS SHEEHAN, of Dublin, Texas, Erath Co.; HELENE over 21, WALLIE, now 18 y. m. ROSS SMITH, TCT, ROBERT over 21 of Erath Co.; CHARLES over 21, Williamson Co. Tex. and AUGUST, JR. over 21 m. EFFIE, TCT

PC 9418 EMILIE FUHRMANN d. April 8, 1939 wills to HELEN FUHRMANN

204/616 PATENT Oct. 10, 1905 to T. B. BAILEY, assne. of G. W. BAILEY

159/90 QC May 30, 1899, G. W. BAILEY et ux JULIA to T. B. BAILEY, ack. before J. L. WALLACE, JP, Burnet Co. Texas

204/615 WD Oct. 31, 1905 T. B. BAILEY et ux LOU to J. J. GREGG, ack. before J. B. PANGLE, Burnet Co.,Texas

602/60 Aff. April 9, 1935 E. U. COX bought 320 ac. of BB & C. RY. Nov. 6, 1912, V. E. COX & B. M. COX, Grayson Co. Tex. div. Sept. 25, 1914 She d. April 11, 1916 no ch. He m. WILLIE A...

L/547 WD Aug. 25, 1857 L. FELLMAN to DANIEL BLUM of New Orleans, LA.

DC 16,623 filed Mar. 8, 1900 MRS. JANE P. VALENTINE fs. of Queens Co.NY vs. W. J. JOHNSON et ux AUGUSTA, JOSEPH STUMPF sur. partners of BROWER & STUMPF, JOSEPH STUMPF, Extr. EST. P. BROWER, decd. all TCT.

cc Harrison Co. Texas, July 14, 1845 GARLINGTON C. DIAL, appointed overseer of road Marshall to Wallings Ferry to ALSTON COLEMAN

A/116 April 3, 1838, surveyors notes, JOHN B. ROBINSON. Bond for Title Oct. 29, 1835 at Mina. GREENLEIF FISK, J. C. CUNNINGHAM & REUBEN HORNSBY to and with JOHN B. ROBINSON & E. D. HARMON

126/516 cc proceedings in JOHN B. ROBINSON EST. Aug. 25, 1841, NANCY (X) ROBINSON sur. wife of J. B., who d. June 15, 1839, and she signed waiver for estate Feb. 1849 as NANCY STRAWN, admrs. and W. B. STRAWN.

E/352 deed June 12, 1851 CALVIN BARKER et ux NANCY (X) of Williamson Co. Texas to SAMUEL PARKS, TCT

I/143 deed May 2o, 1854 CALVIN BARKER, Williamson Co. Tex. to ISAAC WILDBAHN, of patent of 1/3 lea. June 4, 1841.WIT:B.GOOCH & D.W.McFADIN

JESSE C. TANNEHILL survey to him not recorded, and an old affidavit not recorded, made by W. A. BLACKBURNFeb. 1, 1896, states he m. dau of NATHANIEL TOWNSEND decd. by his 2nd wife, ANGELINA L. TOWNSEND: 1st. wife of NATHANIEL TOWNSEND was MARIA who d. ca 1840 leaving 4 ch. and her husband surviving. Ch: HALSEY, MARIA, NATHL. J. & BENJ. R.; HALSEY & MARIA d. young and are buried in Austin Cemetery (Oakwood) NATHL. was killed at Gettysburg during Civil War. BENJ. R. was sole heir of his mother July 28, 1865.

Affidavit, not recorded by A. R. MORRIS, Feb. 1896, says knew MISS LUCRETIA RAY family of TCT; they were single (she and her sister Miss. E. A. RAY) August 1, 1875, and were sistersof J. R. RAY.

1/88 Transcript, deed JESSE C. TANNEHILL to NATHANIEL TOWNSEND, April 25, 1835; WIT: THOS. I. GAZLEY, Judge, Jurisdiction Mina. JESSE BART= LETT & E. M. PEASE, J. W. BUNTON, D. C. BARRETT, July 4, 1840and JOHN RICE JONES Aug. 10, 1840. SAMUEL R. MILLER, recorder.

Q/360 deed July 28, 1865 BENJ. R. TOWNSEND to ANGELINA L. all int. as heir of decd. mother, MARIA and decd. bros. and sisters. Ack. July 28, 1865 before SAML. R. BETTS, Judge U. S. DC Southern NY

X/433, deed Oct. 18, 1872 JOHN DOUGHTY to J. R. RAY

T/367 deed June 25, 1870 ANGELINA TOWNSEND to LUCRETIA RAY & E. A. RAY to N. E.corner JOSHUA PATTERSON's 100 ac.

C/16 PATENT Nov. 12, 1846 to JAMES O. RICE

C/18 WD Jan. 25, 1847 JAMES O. RICE to REUBEN HORNSBY, said he sold other half to WILLIAM CUSTARD.

C/193 WD Jan. 22, 1848, JAMES O. RICE to ISAAC HARRIS

F/120 WD Aug. 20, 1851 ISAAC HARRIS to JESSE HARRIS

G/149 WD April 18, 1853, JESSE (X) HARRIS et ux SARAH to THOS. HUDDLESTON.

F/218 Wd April 18, 1853 ISAAC HARRIS to JOHN BRACHEE (BRICHE, BRACKER, BRAKER, present day spelling)

K/795 Wd Oct. 11, 1856 JOHAN BRECHE to wife, AUGUSTA & CH.: FREDERICK, AUGUST & HENRY NEELY my step-son, TCT

251/178 WD MARY JANE NEANS, widow of WILLIAM, Oct. 22, 1909 to son CHARLEY NEANS

I/363 deed Nov. 10, 1854 A. B. McGILL to C. C. BROWNING (CHRISTOPHER C.) WIT: JOHN T. ALLAN, SAM H. RENICK

PC 11044, BEN RADKEY, filed May 2, 1885; he d. Aug. 20, 1883; MARY L. sur. wife 4 CH: STEPHEN D.13, OLIVER H.9, MARTIN A.7 & MARY A. 4years.

256/95 June 29, 1918 infant boy b. Feb. 22, 1918 JOHN WESLEY adopted by J. M. MORRIS et ux M. E. they also had natural children, W. L. MORRIS & LILLIE CLOUD, wife of R. L. CLOUD

A/34 QC April 10, 1840 JAMES S. LESTER, WM. M. EASTLAND of Fayette Co. Texas to J. C. TANNEHILL. WIT: B. MANLOVE

V/215 WD Feb. 8, 1871 WM. M. WILSON et ux MARY E. to PAUL DEATS of Llano Co. Texas. WIT: GEO. T. GOYE (GAYE)

B/498 WD Jan. 18, 1849 JOSIAH FISK to GEORGE A. FISHER

L/299 WD Jan. 2, 1850 JOSIAH FISK to MILTON PERRY

715/143 PATENT Feb. 29, 1892, to HENRY COCHERON (CROCHERON) Bastrop Co. Tex. assignee of JOHN APPLEGATE by virtue of land cert. 345 issued to JOHN APPLEGATE by Bd. Land Comrs. Shelby Co. Tex. Mar. 9, 1838, and transferred to COCHERON Mar.22, 1839.

26/161 Wd Dec. 12, 1873 JESSE A. & JOSEPH T. McCUTCHIN of Williamson Co. Tex. to J. G. KILLOUGH. WIT: O. N. HOLLINGSWORTH & JNO. A. GREEN

27/65 WD July 1, 1874 I. G. or J. G. KILLOUGH to J. W. HANNIG

36/132 SWD Oct. 3, 1874 JOSEPH W. HANNIG & O. N. HOLLINGSWORTH et ux K. G. K. HOLLINGSWORTH to M. D. MILLER of Williamson Co. Texas.

43/482 WD June 13, 1879 M. D. MILLER et ux SOPHIE W. to WILLIAM SUTTON all of Williamson Co. Texas.

54/106PA M. D. MILLER to A.P. WOOLDRIDGE. (MILLER and wife, SOPHIE W. of Summitt Co. Colorado, and WOOLDRIDGE of TCT. He was Mayor of Austin)

S/428 COMMRS. REPORT, DENNIS CORWIN, CHAS. A. CROSBY & P. W. NOWLIN, filed Nov. 3, 1869 for partitionof Est. MARY J. GOOD (nee REDING) wife of WM. GOOD, heirs of ROBERT S. REDDING: WM. M., MARY J. m. WM. GOOD, MINERVA J. m. HUGH ODUM, JOSEPHINE REDDING m. JONATHAN ROGERS, LAURA REDDING & KATE m. CATO BALLARD

DC 10,515 filed 1892 EST. PETER KLEIN, decd. transferred from PC because of disqualification of WILLIAM von ROSENBERG, JR., Co. Judge; MARY N. KLEIN petitioner, PETER KLEIN d. June 26, 1886 TCT WILL to wife MARY N. KLEIN, WIT: THOS. H. WHELESS, WM. von ROSENBERG, JR. June 7, 1886

104/18 Feb. 25, 1892 T. B. WHEELER of San Patricio Co. Texas and E. T. MOORE, TCT to heirs of PETER KLEIN, decd.

97/472 Affidavit Mar. 15, 1892 MARY J. KLEIN sur. wife, PETER J. KLEIN, JOHN P. KLEIN & ELIZABETH GUSEWELLE (GUISEWELLE) wife of FRED A., only children of PETER J. & MARY J. KLEIN to AMERICAN POWDER MILLS, Boston, Mass.

G/397 Nov. 22, 1853 STERLING W. GOODRICH to JAMES G. SWISHER, JAMES H. RAYMOND, JNO. M. SWISHER, JAMES M. SWISHER. WIT: CHAS. CONNEY and B. G. GOODRICH

EX PARTE 3837 PC removal of disabilities of minority of TEXAS E. GOODRICH fs. over 19 and under 21 years, Oct. 10, 1875, date of judgment.

PATENT September 29, 1845 to JAMES SMITH

PC 78, ALFRED SMITH & ELIZABETH B. SMITH petitioners, JAMES SMITH d. 1845, ELIZABETH B. sur. wife, JAN. 28, 1845, non cupative will dated Jan. 24...he d. Jan. 26. C. L. WING, AARON BURLESON, JAMES H. MATTHEWS, Dec. 29, 1845, ELIZABETH B. SMITH apt. gdn. ad litem for CAROLINE A., JOHN F., MARY E. & SUSAN A., minor children of JAMES SMITH decd.

28/84 deed Dec. 11, 1874 ELIZABETH B. SMITH to dau. MARY E. MATTHEWS

PC 6072 ERIC MATTHEWS, PAUL, ANNE & ROSA, minor children of FRANK and MARY E. MATTHEWS.

276/250 aff. May 14, 1909 E. K. SMILEY & A. M. SMILEY are bros. of EMMA S. WEST, wife of NORTH K. WEST of Franklin, Vanago Co. Pa.; he d.Jan... 1899, EMMA d. April 1899, m. 1 time 5 ch. 3 girls and 2 boys; girls d. young and unm, no issue; CLARENCE WEST oldest, New Castle, Laurence Co Pa. HARRY d. TCT Never married.

276/251 Aff. May 22, 1909 W. L. GILFILLAN TCT was raised in Franklin, Vanago Co. Pa. knew WEST and wife, CLARENCE & HARRY S. WEST, their sons HARRY S. WEST d. a few months ago.

276/252 Aff. CLARENCE. E. WEST b. Venango Co. Pa., July 14, 1861, HARRY S. WEST came to Austin TCT June or July 1893, d. Jan. 14, 1909

PATENT, Jan. 16, 1841 REPUBLIC of Texas to WM. H. JOHNSON & TALK & BECK

A/59 deed 1840 ANSON JONES to JOHN TALK & J. B. BECK. WIT: D. W. SNAVES & BENJ. GRAYSON

DC 9121 filed Aug. 21, 1889, CYNTHIA T. REEVES et vir WM. T., ABBIE JANE HARRIET wife of JOHN, L. M. LORENZO BARRETT, minor by his uncle THOS. TALK. ARMAND COOKER wife of DILLARD COOPER, ELIZA TAYLOR wife of JOS.C. & THOS. TALK, all heirs of JOHN TALK decd. vs. MRS. DELIA CLARK.

G/163 deed May 4, 1853 MATTHEW CARTWRIGHT of San Augustine Co. Tex. to JAMES G. SWISHER. WIT: JOHN M. SWISHER, EDWARD FONTAINE.

F/260 deed June21, 1853, JAMES G. SWISHER to HUGH TINNIN.

L/619 deed Oct. 1, 1857 JAMES G. SWISHER to FRANCIS T. DUFFAU. WIT: J. JUSTIN DAVIDSON,JAMES R.PAN(?) (DUFFAU is spelled thus, not AN)

Q/201 deed April 21, 1864 FRANCIS T. DUFFAU to MARY W. GREEN, trustee for JOHN HEMPHILL GREEN, wife and son of late GENL.THOS.GREEN, WIT: D. W. C. BAKER
PC 574 May 28, 1874 THOMAS GREEN, minor over 14 years chooses JOHN A. his uncle as guardian refers to R. N. LANE vs. ELIZA C. GREEN et al 1873 DC TCT; says THOMAS GREEN same as JOHN HEMPHILL GREEN

61/224 deed July 10, 1884, TOM GREEN TCT lease "part of estate of my f. GEN.TOM GREEN,decd." to D.A.J.HOWELL.WIT: TOM G.CHALMERS & H.SCHMIDT.

180/144 Deed July 24, 1902 G. R. FREEMAN et ux MARY F. to BAYLOR UNIV. reserves life estate in home HAMILTON, HAMILTON CO. TEXAS.

235/517 Rel.Aug 20, 1909 of $4000. note dated Nov. 10, 1895 by ED RUST ex PHEBE. She d. prior to 1909, 1 ch. CARRIE CRAWFORD, wife of .J. M. CRAWFORD, no other children named.

234/170 aff. May 26, 1909 by MRS. BETTIE GROOMS HELM, widow of THOMAS HELM decd. she is dau. of ALFRED GROOMS & BETSY GROOMS decd. m. 1 time BETSY GROOMS d. Nov...,1883. They had 2 ch: 1 d. infancy and affiant. ALFRED GROOMS d. 1887.

207/19 Aff. Dec.7; 1905 by EUGENE BREMOND et ux RE: GEO. HANCOCK d. intestate, Jan. 2, 1879 left wife, LOUISA and 1 son, LEWIS

68/228 April 27, 1886 LEWIS HANCOCK & ELIZA LOUISA, widow to JOHN HANCOCK

120/50 rel Oct. 5, 1893 LEWIS HANCOCK to SUSAN E. HANCOCK sole devisee of JOHN HANCOCK decd.

PATENT to L. C. CUNNINGHAM Sept. 27, 1845 issued by Ld. Bd. Comrs. of Bastrop Co. Tex., Mar. 29, 1838.

D/261 SWD Nov. 15, 1849 LEANDER C. CUNNINGHAM of Bastrop Co. Tex. to MATTHEW CARTWRIGHT of San Augustine Co. Texas. WIT: JAMES H. GILLESPIE, HIRAM S. MORGAN

W/380 partition May 30, 1871 heirs MATTHEW CARTWRIGHT, decd. AMANDA CARTWRIGHT sur. wife; COLUMBUS C., A. P., LEANDER, ANNA W., wife of BENJ. T. ROBERTS, MARY C., wife of JAMES H. INGRAM, MATTHEW CARTWRIGHT JR., ACK BY ALL IN San Augustine Co. Texas, before W. A. McCLANAHAN, NP & EX O.

W/386 May 30, 1871 shows persons, as above also land in Anderson,Collin, Denton, Ellis, Hill, Hopkins, Van Zandt, Victoria, Wood, Jack, Kaufman, Sabine, San Augustine, Shelby and Upshaw counties in Texas.

H/543 Mtg. Sept. 17, 1855 LEANDER C. CUNNINGHAM, Bastrop Co. to BENJ. A SHEPHERD & ANDREW G. BURKE, Harris Co. Tex. states we, LEANDER C. CUNN-INGHAM, HENRY COCHRAN composed firm of LEANDER C. CUNNINGHAM & CO. WIT: P. R. TURNER, M. B. HIGHSMITH before JOSEPH O'CONNER NP BCT

S/228 Shf. deed July 8, 1869 L. C. CUNNINGHAM et al by RADCLIFF PLATT, Shf. TCT to GEORGE SEALY.

55/375 SWD July 15, 1882, GEORGE SEALY, J. H. HUTCHINGS firm BALL HUTCH-iNGS & CO. to M. DAVIS, Galveston Co. Tex. before JOHN ANDIANSE, NP

B/425 PA Sept. 6, 1841 Arkansas Co...HEMPSTEAD MORGAN CRYER & MILDRED CRYOR, alias MILDRED DUTY, LaFayette Co. Ark. to JOSEPH F. SMITH, Refugeo Co. Tex. to settle successions of SOLOMON , RICHARD, GEORGE and MATTHEW DUTY.

A/234 Bond for Title Nov. 30,1839, L. C. CUNNINGHAM to SOLOMON DUTY.

A/234 deed Aug. 5, 1858 L. C. CUNNINGHAM to heirs SOLOMON DUTY of Burleson Co. Tex. not named. WIT: H. McLESTER & PHIL CLAIBORN. ACK.Burleson Co. by PHIL CLABURN who takes the deed as agent and atty. of heirs of S. DUTY before SANDY SHOEMAKE, cc.

53/154 cc from Burleson Co. Texas. WILL: MARGARET M. DUTY, July 19, 1859 to g. dau. LUCY MARGARET DUTY MUNSON, appoints JOHN SAYLOR esq. of Washington Co. Tex. Guardian of gd. WIT: JOHN W. HAY, ALBERT A.JORDAN.

53/156 Aug. 2, 1882 deed LUCY M. D. BURNS, formerly MUNSON only heir, EST. SOLOMON DUTY et ux ROBERT BURNS, Harris Co. Texas

DC 15,545 DC TCT, THE SCOTTISH AMERICAN MORTGAGE CO. LTD. filed Oct.29, 1898, vs. J. H. BOOTY, et ux MARY, Williamson Co. Tex. P. A. SCHAEFER, Williamson Co. Tex., JAMES R. JOHNSON, J. M. BOROUGH, ANDREW SISLER, WM. L. GRAVES, GEORGE PFLUGER, GUSTAV SCHROMANN, W. H. WAY, R. L.BROWN, JOHN R. DOOM, et ux LILIE H., KATE HAMILTON, MAY HAMILTON, minorsFRANK, CARRIE, EVERETT & TOMMIE HAMILTON all minors of FRANK HAMILTON, allTCT; JACK HAMILTON, South Bend, St. Joseph Co. Indiana, GEO. W. BRACKENRIDGE & FRED HUGG, JR., Bexar Co. Tex. D. D. ATCHISON, Galveston Co. Tex. ERIC P. SWENSON, SWEN ALBIN SWENSON, members of S. M. SWENSON & SONS, firm composed of S. M. SWENSON, ERIC P.SWENSON & SWAN ALBIN SWENSON, ERIC P. & SWEN ALBIN SWENSON of New York City, SUSAN M. SWENSON and MARY E. SWENSON beneficiaries under will of S. M. SWENSON decd. NY City
C/534 PATENT June 11, 1849 to JAMES H. RAYMOND.

68/100½ WD JAMES H. RAYMOND to JAMES R. JOHNSON, July 7, 1876.

PC 2309 EST. JAMES R. JOHNSON, decd. WILL: WM. B. WORTHAM, Extr., et ux not named, dated Sept. 4, 1900. WIT: MILES F. BYRNE, JOHN H. WHITIS

DC 13,823, TCT Mar. 29, 1900, ROBERT A. SMITH, trustee, vs. MADDOX BROS co-partnership: JNO. W. & FRANK M. MADDOX & C. E. ANDERSON, JAMES H. RAYMOND & CO., JAMES R. JOHNSON, MARGARET RAYMOND, J. S. MYRICK.

185/129 WD Dec. 6, 1902 MARY C. JOHNSON, widow, TCT ALEX C. JOHNSON, Jefferson Co. Tex., RAYMOND JOHNSON, Gillespie Co. Tex., & BEN J. JOHNSON, Bexar Co. Tex. to H. P. N. GAMMEL, TCT. Ack. MARY C. JOHNSON, before THOS. F. TAYLOR, NP TCT, RAYMOND JOHNSON, before J. F. CHANEY NP Gillespie Co. Tex., BEN F. JOHNSON before PETER JONES, NP Bexar Co. Tex. and ALEC C. JOHNSON before THOMAS F. TAYLOR, NP TCT

AJ 5/102 April 25, 1898 TCT Co. Ct. favor of FRANK CARBON (?) against R.E. WALDEN, J.R. RAYLAND, H. P.N. GAMMEL, L.M. ODOM & Z. T. FULMORE

DC 26,104 EX PARTE, MARCIA JOHNSON, minor dau. of..removal of dis. of minority (between 19 and 21 years) Dec. 9, 1909

I/442 WD April 26, 1870 (conveys land obtained in deed F/31 Sept. 8,1849 GEO. W. DAVIS to heirs of JOS. PORTER BROWN), J. FRAZIER BROWN, SALLIE F. BRACKENBROUGH, et vir M. C., of San Saba Co. Tex. sole surviving heirs J. PORTER BROWN, decd.

44/259 from Dist. Ct. San Saba Co., Tex. Sept. 1879, JAMES F. BROWN, ptf. vs. ALBERT P. BROWN, MARY A., & SARAH C. BROWN, minors under 21 ch; of ADELLA MOORE, and her husband JAMES F. BROWN

300/134 partition deed Sept. 12, 1917 W. R. E. BOOTH & J. S. BOOTH, sons MRS. A. C. BOOTH, who d. TCT Nov. 12, 1886 and R. C. BOOTH d. TCT Aug. 31, 1917; WM. RUSSELL E. BOOTH and wife, MOLLY, homestead designation 323/490 July...Swisher Addition (south Austin)

313/96 cc EST. MARION SCALLORN decd. Fayette Co. Tex. Mar. Term 1851, NEILL ROBISON, Judge, petitioner THOS. J. SCALLORN, sur. hus.; WM. G. WEBB, atty. filed Feb. 24, 1851; N. W. FAISON CCC, bondsmen: R.B.(T or P. B.) SORRELL, W. A. FAIRIE $6000.00 L. P. WEBB. Shf. apprs. Mar. 31, 1851, WASHINGTON SAWYERS, WM. SCALLORN, FRANCIS KARNES. Notes of THOS. & DAVID ADAMS. July Term 1853 Hon. J. C. CABANESS, CJ, CHANDLER & McFARLAND, atty.; a/c of STEPHEN SCALLORN, July 25, 1853, J. MOORE, shf. Nov. 5, 1853, JOHN HANCOCK bought land.

PC 399 EST. GEO. W. GLASSCOCK, Sr. petition filed Mar. 30, 1868. WILL: Feb. 28, 1868, dau. MARGARET C. BOATNER, wife of S. W., other children GEO. W. JR., ELIZABETH J. LOGAN wife of A. T. (m. TALBOT) ALBERT H. GLASSCOCK, ANDREW J. (H), SARAH J. GLASSCOCK, ANNA B. GLASSCOCK, all minors, Feb. 2, 1870. ANNA B. m. W. C. ALLEN

K/432 deed April 27, 1856 STERLING W..GOODRICH to BEVERLY G. GOODRICH

N/300 WD June 6, 1858 B. G. GOODRICH to GEO. W. GLASSCOCK & O. H. MILLICAN, WIT: WM. BYRD, before J. T. McLAURIN cc TC

B/15 August 9, 1841 PATENT to WAYMAN WELLS

F/75 Wd Feb. 10, 1851, WAYMAN F. WELLS et ux MARY E. of Bastrop Co. Tex and SAMUEL PARKS, TCT WIT: P. P. LUCKETT, DAVID EPPRIGHT.

B/157 PATENT April 14, 1841 GORDON C. JENNINGS

A/451 WD Oct. 14, 1841 WILLIE AVERY, admr. GORDON C. JENNINGS, decd. to SEABORN J. WHATLEY, Bastrop Co. Tex.

A/499 deed Nov. 27, 1841, JAMES P. WALLACE, Bastrop Co. Tex. to JAMES ROGERS. WIT: JOHN C. ANDERSON, JAMES H. GILLESPIE.

L/392 LEASE May 21, 1850, THOS. JEFFERSON CHAMBERS of Bastrop Co. Tex to DAVID THOMAS, also Bastrop Co. leases 8 leagues, property known as CHAEMEAN MILL, east bank of Colorado River, near present MT. BONNELL. WIT: PHIL CLAIBORN, DAVID HALDEMAN.

M/540 LEASE Nov. 30, 1858, T. J. Chambers to F. S. RAY, SAYS DAVID Thomas had under lease May 1850 to Dec. 1855; NORMAN MILL (?) WIT: ALEXANDER EANS, JOHN BROWN

S.548 deed Jan. 7, 1870 N. F. CAMBELL et ux JOSEPHINE H., Washington Co. Tex. to R. F. CAMPBELL, Bastrop Co. Tex. ack. before CHAS. C. WILLIAMS CCC Washington Co. Tex.

S/552 Deed Dec. 14, 1869 R. F. CAMBELL et ux PHEBE J., Bastrop Co. Tex to DANIEL R. PAYTON, Bastrop Co. ack. before W. C. LAWHON, NP BCT

26/113 Admr. deed April 8, 1872 ESTATE THOS. J. CHAMBERS decd. to DANIEL R. PEYTON.

36/83 Deed D. R. PAYTON et ux AMANDA B. to I. & G. N. RR. Sept.28,1876

79/211 PA Dec. 12, 1887 to JOHN B. JOURDON, ZECHARIST P. JORDON, W. L. GILES, ESTATE GEO. W. JOURDON, decd. Ch: JAMES JORDAN, GEO. W. JOURDON FANNIE P. JORDON or ANNE who m. JAMES FISHER, FREDERICK JOURDON D. Oct 14, 1887; MRS. H. E. WALDEMORE, GEO. W. d. Oct. 14, 1887, MARY C.JORDON m. WM. ALFORD his first wife, she d. Mar. 1881 had Ch: B. S. ALFORD, CHAS. ALFORD, JANNICE ALFORD & JULIA & MOLLIE: SALLIE JORDAN now GILES m. W. L. GILES, AMANDA B. JOURDAN m. D. R. PEYTON, JENNIE L. JOURDAN m. J. C. MAXWELL & J. C. MAXWELL gd. CHAS., JULIA & MOLLIE ALFORD, minor ch. of MARY C. ALFORD m. SPRINKLE, JOHN B. JOURDAN, ARCH P. JOURDAN, JULIA E. JOURDAN m. OSCEOLA C. CATO. (PEYTON, PAYTON, JOURDAN JORDAN are spellings used by various members of these two families)

163/624 deed Dec. 10, 1900 MRS. A. B. PAYTON, JNO. W. PAYTON, E. F. PAYTON, ANDREW J. PAYTON, EULA P. & DORA PEYTON to GEORGE JONES

392/340 PA E. F. PAYTON, EULA, DORA PALMER et vir CHAS. O., LURA P. BELL R., BEULAH HILTON et vir LEE..PALMER, PAULINE PEYTON to B. N. PAYTON SOLE AND ONLY HEIRS MRS. A. B. PEYTON decd.

PATENT May 20, 1846 to MARTHA G. MORROW, she m. EDWIN HARRY of Cherokee Co. Tex. V/781 PA May 26, 1871 MARTHA G.HARRY to SON C. E.

101/168 HD Feb. 19, 1891 J. W. WHITT et ux R. H.

DC 12,439 1896 J. W. WHITT 1/2 in. JESSE WHITT, & T. J. WHITT & THOMAS HENRY, WM. WHITT, NANCY KIRK, PATRICK WHITT, LIZZIE WEST, GEORGIA McGOWAN, BELL PRIEST, HOLLY SMITH & JOHN WHITT, evidently children and grand children of R. W. WHITT, decd.

PATENT July 3, 1961 to JAMES W. TALBOTT, assignee J. A. YBARBO I/79 TCT, surveyors Journal Oct. 1, 1853 survey made for JESSE BURDITT, assignee of JOSE ANTONIO YBARBO, cert. 224, issued by Bd. Ld. Comrs. Nacogdoches Co. Tex. Feb. 8, 1838, JAMES RAILEY, FRANK MOORE, chain carriers, L. H. LUCKETT, Dept. Co. Surveyor H. L. UPSHUR, Dist. Surveyor Travis Dist.

Q/650 Deed Dec. 31, 1866 ELIAS W. TALBOT of Williamson Co. Tex. to CHAS. P. & THOS. TALBOT, Middlesex Co. Mass. same patented to JOSEPH W. TALBOT, transferred to ELIAS W. TALBOT, Jan. 1, 1863 says CONDILANUS YBARBO.

U/187 WD Feb. 9, 1873 CHAS. P. & THOS. TALBOT of Lowell, Mass by agt. and atty. E. B. TURNER of Austin, Tex. love and affection for brother ELIAS W. TALBOT of Georgetown, because our brother has met with mis=
fortunes.
X/60 WD Sept. 6, 1872 ELIAS W. TALBOT to JOSEPH KAUFMAN

Z/216 WD Dec. 13, 1873 JOSEPH KAUFMAN et ux THERESA J. to THOMAS J. WHEELER, ack. before A. W. MORROW.

DC 4774 suit on note July 3, 1876, J. W. PAGE vs. T. J. WHEELER on JOSE ANTONIO YBARBO & CANDELARIS YBARBO surveys.

364/259 Aff. Aug. 8, 1924, G. T. LINDSEY, TCT is 76 years old knew R. W. TURNER et ux SARAH H.: R. W. TURNER d. ca 1907 leaving wife and 8 ch: 3 boys and 5 girls: BELL TURNER, R. R. TURNER, GEO. M., and wife ANNA, LENORA wife of C. E. HALL, JENNIE L. wife of W. L. HALL, BESSIE S. wife of W. P. COOK, NELLIE wife of PETER COOK, SARAH J. wife of L. L. WESTEN, SARAH J. d. 1920 in Burnet Co. Tex. L. L. WESTEN did not remarry. Her estate is in PC Burnet Co. Texas.

100/80 WD Oct. 20, 1890 HORACE SEELY sm to BURT McDONALD

102/548 WD Jan. 12, 1892, BURT McDONALD sm to D. C. McMARTIN

734/58 WD Sept. 4, 1843, ERNEST J. HEPPENHEIMER et ux RUTH NORRIS of Hudson Co. N. J.

295/349 Aff. RE: ERHARDT FRUD (FRUITT, FRUTH) et ux THERESA d. Nov. 10 1895; BETTIE (ELIZABETH) m. JOE D. MOORE, DC 18,409; L. A. m. DAVID A. CYPHER DC 18,408; Mathilda m. JOSEPH STUMPF. CHRISTINA M. m. CHAS. ING, MARY FRUTH, THERESA m. LOUIS FELTEN, g. ch: NICHOLAS LEWIS (LOUIS) FELTEN, PETER JOSEPH FELTEN, FRANK JAMES FELTEN, MARY THERESA FELTEN, LOUISA B. FELTEN, JULIA BETTIE (ELIZABETH) all of Santa Clara Co. Calif in 1902 and JOHN ISIDORE FELTEN TCT.

43/56 deed Aug. 18, 1877 O. N. HOLLINGSWORTH et ux K. G. K. to W. H. LOVE et ux LELIA

74/134, 1886 W. H. LOVE vs. LEILA LOVE DC 9522 July 21, 1890, divorce
173/48 April 1, 1901 extension signed LIELA CLAY LANE;
245/554 Feb. 1911 LENA CLAY LANE to MARGUERITE TURNER LOVE WINN;
286/222, 1916 MARGUERITE TURNER LOVE WINN to nephew HENRY HOXIE LADD
302/532 Rel MARGUERITE TURNER LOVE WINN, now wife of LOUIS N. GRAY

DC 24,415 TCT heirs HARRY (HENRY) B. KENNEY et ux MARTHA A. d. Mar.5 1890; HARRIET S. PASCHALL (child of von ROSENBERG) m. EMMETT PASKELL (PASCHALL), MARY K. DeWAR (child) m. HAMILTON deWAR, PERCY E. GALLANT GSON VON ROSENBERG, MARY ALLEN BRENNAN gdau. von ROSENBERG, FRANK GWYNN GSON VON ROSENBERG, IVAN A. GWYNN gson von ROSENBERG, HARRY B. KINNEY, ED P. KINNEY, HATTIE B. KINNEY, CHILD: HENRY HAMILTON DeWAR, minor, MARGARITE ALLEENE DeWAR & HAL P. P. DeWAR, minors. (KINNEY, KENNEY, KINNIE)

960/336 PATENT Dec. 10, 1841 REPUBLIC of TEXAS to JAMES WEBB

D/377 deed Dec. 10, 1850 JAMES WEBB to M. C. & ANDREW J. HAMILTON, Many lots in Austin patented to WEBB, assignee of W. H. JOHNSON, July 3, 1847; JOHN WOOD, July 3, 1847; H. M. BEATY same date and ROBERT H. WYNNE Oct. 23, 1848. WIT: JAMES F. JOHNSON, JOSEPH LEE

T/506 Deed April 21, 1870 ALEX H. BARNES to THOS. B. WHEELER. WIT: E. HIGBY, WM. O. OTIS. (HIGBY, HIGSBY, HIGGSBY)

V/378 deed July 8, 1871 MORGAN C. HAMILTON to ANDREW J. & MARY J. HAMILTON

29/437 confirmation deed widow MARY JANE HAMILTON, MARY HAMILTON MILLS wife of W. W., FRANK H., BETTY H., & LILLY HAMILTON, Ch. of ANDREW J. HAMILTON, all TCT LILLY is under 21 years, adk. June 4, 1875

DC 7748 Travis Co. CELESTE LOOMIS & 2 minor ch: LYDIA MAY & SIMON CHRISTIAN LOOMIS. SIMON LOOMIS & EDWARD CHRISTIAN were partners, and SIMON LOOMIS DIED.

PC 1822 filed April 5, 1894 guardianship: IRVING EGGLESTON, applicant CHRISTIAN LOOMIS about 19 y. both parents dead. LYDIA MAY LOOMIS signed as bondsman.

153/9 correction deed June 24, 1897 MARY HAMILTON MILLS et vir W. W. MRS. LILLY MALONE, widow.

293/484 aff. by CHAS. WOLF, Mar. 19, 1917: JOSEPHINE WOLF, wife of CHAS d. Dec. 13, 1901 CH: JOSEPHINE M. WOLF & CHAS. WOLF, only heirs. She is now MRS. C. A. PETERS. CHAS. WOLF d. May 12, 1913.

39/349 PA Oct. 1, 1877, to ALFRED P. LUCKETT by SUSAN E. LUCKETT, widow of ALFRED decd. and mother of L. HORACE LUCKETT, decd. BASIL H. LUCKETT EDWARD L. LUCKETT, JOHN H. LUCKETT, T. DADE LUCKETT, H. POWELLLUCKETT, HENRY H. LUCKETT, LOUISE LUCKETT MOORE, wife of W. W. MOORE, and ALFRED P. LUCKETT ch. of ALFRED & SUSAN E. LUCKETT

PC 213 of Bastrop Co. Tex: WILL, ROBERT L. REDDING, dated Feb. 26,1849, to JANE ELIZABETH, wife WILLIAM MAC TYSON. CH: MARY INDIA, MINERVA JANE wife of HUGH S, MARGARET LAURA sw 1866; NANCY JOSEPHINE sw 1866; CATHERINE ELIZABETH m. A. J. BALLARD, NANCY JOSEPHINE m. JONATHAN ROGERS, before 1873 and was not of age Nov. 17, 1866.

37/513 deed Feb. 3, 1876 N. S. RECTOR to JAMES A. WRIGHT. WIT: N. A. RECTOR, W. B. DUNN

O/441 deed Sept. 10, 1860 JOHN BRAKE et ux AUGUSTE (X) to R. A. RUTHERFORD. FREDERICK, AUGUST BRAEKE & HENRY NEELY now minors.

51/435 or 455 deed Jan. 26, 1882 recites on July 31, 1880 ROBERT A. RUTHERFORD, JR., Agreed with G. R.FREEMAN of Hamilton Co. Tex. atty. to sue for partition of community property of father and decd. mother, at time of her death and brothers C. N. (CHARLES NEELY) Never gives date of her death or her name.

252/58 deed Oct. 22, 1909 WILLIAM NEANS, JR. et ux FANNIE E. to HENRY NEANS, JR. interest inherited from decd. WILLIAM.

252/56 deed Feb. 17, 1912 MARY JANE NEANS to dau. MATTIE NEANS HAMMOND wife of CHAS. HAYES HAMMOND.

251/500 deed Oct. 10, 1912 MARY JANE NEANS to dau. MOLLIE NEANS BURMINGHAM wife of D. W., and also deed to son HENRY, JR.

DC 5767 filed Dec. 22, 1881 C. N. RUTHERFORD & R. A. RUTHERFORD, JR. recites: PARTITION com. property of R. A. RUTHERFORD, SR. and decd wife ELIZABETH. She d. 1861

688/615 deed AMANDA TATUM, widow of JAMES, decd. of McLennan Co. Tex.to J. F. HAIR of Bexar Co. Tex. 42.860 acres known as JOSEPHINE ROBINSON home place, N. of 53 acres BEN MANNING old home place being old home place of JOSEPHINE ROBINSON, decd. which she gave to her husband JAMES TATUM and he possessed for years before he d. She, JOSEPHINE ROBINSON was mother of JAMES TATUM. He held property over 20 ys. before he died.

274/24 Aff. Feb. 17, 1915. WILLIAM SHANKS, FANNIE CRAWFORD & EASTER DAVIS of TCT SAM BLACK; their father d. ca 1905 m. (2) first to MARY JANE MADISON, mother of affiant ca .18..: 9 Ch, who reached maturity: GEO. BLACK of Coyle, Okla. JACK BLACK, TCT, WILLIAM BLACK who d. ca 1896 leftwi dow and 8 Ch: NANCY DAVIDSON, widow of COYLE, Logan Co. Okla; GEORGE BLACK, AMY SHANKS, wife of WILLIAM TCT, HARRIET CLAYTON wife of JOHN TCT, EASTER DAVIS, widow TCT; MARIA RAMEY, widow, Ellis Co. Tex; SAM & MARY JANE BLACK had no real estate at death of MARY JANE ca 1866; (2) MILLIE ca 1868 4 ch: SAM BLACK, JR. TCT: HENRY BLACK,TCT MARY BUFORD, widow, TCT DAVID BLACK, Coyle Okla, MILLIE 2nd wife had 2 ch. by previous marriage; CHARLIE WILLIAMS of Mart, McClellan Co.Tex. and B. FRANK WILLIAMS, Falls, Co. Tex; WILLIAM BLACK son of SAM & MARY JANE now decd. his widow; CAROLINE BLACK, widow, TOM BLACK, Coyle Okla. ADAM K. BLACK, RICHARD BLACK, CHARLES BLACK & CLAUD BLACK, TCT, BEULAH d. ca 1910, SELISTINE BLACK & ETHEL BLACK, TCT; DEAMS or GEANIE BLACK m. P. B. OLDHAM, somewhere in east Texas. Deed March 29, 1873 to SAM BLACK.

427/576 1928: R. W. HOLLER, sm MARY HOLLAR fs. SALLIE BAYS, wife of J. S. TCT: DORSEA McCLAIN wife of J. M., Childress Co. Tex.; NANNIE LINDSAY, wife of C. M.,Wichita Co. Tex.; W. M. BRYANT, sur. hus. MITTIE HOLLAR BRYANT, decd. Parker Co. Tex.; H. R. BRYANT, King Co. Tex. Ruth BRYANT, fs. Parker Co.,Texas; PEARL BRYANT fs. Dallas Co. Tex. being all children MITTIE HOLLAR BRYANT, decd. A. P. HOLLER decd. King Co. Tex. Our parents S. W. & LUCRETIA HOLLAR, both decd.

428/357 Aff. re-dated Oct. 1928: W. W. HOLLAR et ux LUCRETTA both decd. m. 1 time only: THEODORIA (known as THEODORIO & DORSIA) wife of J. M. McCLAIN,Childress Co. Tex; NANNIE LINDSAY wife of C. H., Wichita Co.Tex SALLIE(Once SALLIE VOWTER) now wife of J. S. BAYS, TCT MARY HOLLAR fs. TCT; ARMINTA (MATTIE) wife of W. H. BRYANT, Parker Co. Tex. now decd. hus. and Ch. W. H. BRYANT, RUTH BRYANT, PEARL BRYANT fs. and M. B.BRYANT A. P. HOLLAR now decd. d. testate and sur. widow AMMIE. A. H. HOLLAR decd. (HENRY) d. intestate left widow MRS. CARRIE HOLLAR and several ch names unknown. (HOLLAR, HALLAR)

I/346 PATENT Feb. 5, 1846 to THOS. H. MAYS assignee of DANIEL J. GILBERT

Q/307 deed Sept. 17, 1875 ROBERT J. TOWNES, E. T. EGGLESTON, RICHARD A. TOWNES of Carroll Co. Miss. by will devised to ch. of said ROBERT J. TOWNES 1/2 personal estate &c and balance when R. A. TOWNES, widow,died 1855 the negroes were sent to Texas to ROBERT J. TOWNES by agent with MRS. BETTIE TOWNES, widow of RICHARD A. BLACK.

DC 2841 Jan. 26, 1869 J. J. THORP, pet. note vs. C. S. WEST, extr. EST. R. J. TOWNES, decd. E. T. EGGLESTON, MILA T. MORRIS, et vir J. B.,POLLY, ALFRED, PATTIE, ALLEN COBB & EVERARD TOWNES, minors.

236/529 PATENT to ISAAC DECKER, introduced by R. M. WILLIAMSON, agent for Impresario BENJAMIN R. MILAM, represents himself to be married man with family Mar. 16, 1835, Town of Mina (Bastrop) BARTLETT SIMS,survey onS. side Colorado River, from Austin, begins about where the south end of Bridge on Ny 35 crosses Colorado River opposite Holiday Inn, up river to mouth of spring branch which is now BARTON SPRINGS (SPA) 5 labors (177 ac) arable and 20 pasture land. L. C. CUNNINGHAM, asst. to A. GARCIA, ASST.

O/461 deed Sept. 10, 1860 T. J. CHAMBERS of Chambers Co. Tex. to JOSIAH FISK. ack. by CHAMBERS in Williamson Co. Texas.

D/116 deed Mar. 16, 1849 JOSIAH FISK to THOMAS WHITE. WIT: A. B. McGILL, W. M. THOMPSON.

N/203 deed Feb. 12, 1859 JOHN B. (X) WHITE, SAMUEL E. WHITE, ELEAZER H. WHITE, JOEL ELAM et ux MARY L., all of Bond Co. Ill., to JOHN M. WHITE before S. A. PHELPS, JP Bond Co. Ill.; cert. of J. P. E. GASKINS, ccc Bond Co. Ill.

P/380 deed JOHN M. WHITE, TCT Mar. 5, 1861 to CECELIA TOWNSEND. WIT: FRANK F. BRICHTAG, L. W. COLLINS.

P/376 Mtg. April 2, 1862 shows MARTIN W. TOWNSEND et ux CECELIA

143/15 cc from McCrockin Co. Ky. will of B. H. WISDOM to executors, as trustees for 3 ch. and ch. of decd. son: HENRY gson. his parents both dead until he is 21; GEORGE C. WALLACE, WILLIAM E. CAVE, extrs. June 2, 1896, WIT: H. C. OVERBEY, HENRY BURNETT

F/325 San Francisco Co. Calif. to GEORGE JOHN DURHAM, WIT: D. C. CODY, W. W. LYON, before WM. H. RHODES, Tex. Comr. for Calif.

F/526 deed Mar. 1, 1854, JAMES G. SWISHER to JOHN I. ROGERS. WIT:WILLIE R. JONES, JAMES E.B OULDIN.

38/102 PA Mar. 21, 1870 J. I. ROGERS of Boyle Co. Ky. appoints W. L. ROBARDS & A. M. JACKSON, before JNO. B. NICHOLS, clk. Boyle Co. Ky.

R/257 Mar. 4, 1868 JNO. I. ROGERS, of Perry Co. Ala., and JOHN S. BOYD of Harrison Co.Ky. T. WHERRITT, CHCC

V/26 deed Jan. 7, 1871, J. S. BOYD to SARAH A. BUNTON TCT

40/154 Feb. 23, 1878 DESHA BUNTON et ux SARAH

DC 7990 filed Sept. 4, 1886, SARAH A. BUNTON vs. JOHN BUNTON of Kimble Co. Tex.; that prior to 1870 she m. DESHA BUNTON; 1881 DESHA d. 1 ch. and son and only child was by a former wife who d. many years before ptf. m. DESHA BUNTON

DC 7740 Dec. 9, 1883 SARAH A. WALTON vs. E. PAYSON WALTON m. June 3, 1885, B. C. WELLS, foreman of Jury.

88/290 aff. Oct. 19, 1889 SARAH A. KELLAM formerly SARAH A. BUNTON, hus A. B. KELLAM sold BUNTON home place (austin) and went to Hot Springs,Ark

PATENT, Mar. 1, 1849 to M. FARLEY assignee of THOS. G. FOSTER

D/217 deed June 6, 1849 MOSSILON FARLEY to TIMOTHY McKEAN. WIT: J. R. JONES, D. C. CODY

F/342 Deed Oct. 7, 1853, TIMOTHY McKEAN to M. C. HAMILTON. WIT: JOHN R. McCALL, FRED W. MOORE

K/404 deed April 1, 1856 MORGAN C. HAMILTON to WM. P. deNORMANDIE

L/517 deed July 25, 1857 WM. P. deNORMANDIE et ux CATHARINE S. to THOMAS C. COLLINS. WIT: J. L. REED, H. M. DeCORDOVA

L/677 MTG. Sept. 14, 1857 THOS. C. COLLINS to W. P. deNORMANDIE. WIT: CHAS. CONEY, A. H. PARISH.

N/489 deed Oct. 13, 1859 CHAS. G. WILCOX et ux MARY K. to ROBERT M.WILCOX decd. Jan. 13, 1863. Mar. 3, 1868 DALLAS WILCOX surviving wife

DC 3044 filed Jan. 30, 1871 DALLAS JOHNSON et vir RICHARD M. vs.BOBBIE M. WILCOX, DALLAS m. ROBERT M. WILCOX Oct. 5, 1859 he d. Dec. 13,1862 leaving widow DALLAS and 2 ch. ALICE who d. June 7, 1868 and BOBBIE (da u) July 19, 1868 m. RICHARD M. JOHNSON. Feb. 6, 1871 FERGUS KYLE appointed guardian for minor deft.

86/500 deed Aug. 29, 1889 DALLAS JOHNSON et vir R. M. to BOBBIE M.WILCOX

216/530 aff. by R. M. JOHNSON et ux DALLAS, former wife of R. M.WILCOX decd. lived on land from year 1858 house burned ca 1898; 1858 to 1868 GEORGE H. GRAY lived on land; 1869 R. A. BOYCE et ux ANN BOYCE lived on land..probably as tenants, as this was farm land, an OULOT of Austin.

520/607 May 17, 1935 MARY E. JOHNSON CRADDOCK, of Commerce, Tex. dau. R. M. JOHNSON et ux DALLAS KYLE JOHNSON; R. M. JOHNSON d. Nov. 26,1914 DALLAS KYLE JOHNSON d. July 20, 1922, both intestate; MISS BOBBIE M. WILCOX d. Sept. 18, 1923 unm and no issue; R. M. JOHNSON et ux DALLAS KYLE JOHNSON had: son JOHN R. JOHNSON, 3 daus. FANNIE A. JOHNSON,MARY E. JOHNSON, JOSEPHINE G. JOHNSON d. Jan. 7, 1935; MARY E. JOHNSON m. H. F. CRADDOCK July 10, 1930.

622/36 aff. 1939 R. M. JOHNSON had been m. before he m. DALLAS but wife d. and no ch. born; DALLAS d. July 20, 1922, left FANNIE A. JOHNSON, MARY E. J. CRADDOCK & JOHN R. JOHNSON

365/352 deed Nov. 13, 1924 JNO. R. JOHNSON of Biloxi, Miss. fmrly TCT JOSEPHINE JOHNSON ack. Harrison Co. Miss.

PATENT Oct. 19, 1848 to ERHARD FRUD, Book 430/284 deed records E/71 WD Aug. 4, 1849 E. FRUIT, and wife, JANE to WILLIAM COCKBURN. WIT: LOUIS HORST, WILLIAM SCHILLER

C/259 PATENT Sept. 1, 1846 to JULIET JAYNES. ALBERT C. HORTON, governor

C/260 WD Jan. 25, 1848, JULIET JAYNES to A. H. HOPKINS. WIT: JOHN S. PATTON, JOSEPH FISK.

C/516 Wd June 8, 1849 ANDREW H. HOPKINS, et ux JANE to WILLIAM COCKBURN WIT: THEO. P. CARTMELL, P. M. W. HALL

F/324 PA filed Nov. 2, 1853 WM. COCKBURN of San Francisco to GEO. JOHN DURHAM. WIT: D. C. CADY, WM. W. LYON, ACK. before WM. H. RHODES, Comr. appointed by Gov. of Texas

PC 174 EST. MARY J. COCKBURN, decd. filed by GEO. J. DURHAM, June 11, 1853 she d. 185..hus. WILLIAM COCKBURN, resident of Calif. says to send residue of his (Wm. Cockburn's) family consisting of 4 children. Does not name them.

F/325 Admr. deed Nov. 2, 1853 GEO. J. DURHAM, administrator to JOSEPH WRIGHT. WIT: JOHN T. ALLAN, A. B. McGILL.

M/533 WD Nov. 1, 1858 JOSEPH WRIGHT to NANCY H. RAGSDALE. WIT: HENRY THOMAS, R. C. SHELLEY.

R/91 Homestead designation July 23, 1867 NANCY H. RAGSDALE says home in Galveston, Texas, Dickinson Bayou, known as ALLEN LEWIS place

R/92 July 23, 1867 NANCY H. RAGSDALE to W. M. SIMS, guardian of MARGARET N., JAMES W. & WALTER G. RAGSDALE.

U/227 WD Feb. 1, 1871 NANCY H. RAGSDALE of Brazos Co. Tex. to JAMES W. & WALTER G. RAGSDALE & MARGARET N. BEALL, nee RAGSDALE

U/479 WD April 17, 1871 JAMES W. RAGSDALE & WALTER G. RAGSDALE of Burleson Co. Texas to THOS. J. & MARGARET N. BEALL

PC 1226 EST. MRS. ELIZABETH H. MITCHELL apl. by A. W. TERRELL, filed April 26, 1887 father of HOWARD D. TERRELL, minor; MRS. E. H. MITCHELL d. April 21, 1887 TCT; MRS. NANNIE WOOD wife of CAMBELL WOOD of San Saba Co. Tex. and CULLEN DOUGLAS of Sumner Co. Tenn. (bro. of ELIZABETH H. MITCHELL) NANNIE WOOD is gdau. of late husband, DR. JAMES MITCHELL and to her g.son HOWARD D. TERRELL

B/183 PATENT, to WILLIAM HINES, Sept. 26, 1845.

A/422 Wd Mar. 8, 1840 WILLIAM HINES to LEANDER C. CUNNINGHAM, part of Cert. No. 105 issued by Bd. of Ld. Comrs. of Sabine Co. Tex. surveyed by THOS. H. MAYS, surveyor, Bastrop Co. Tex. WIT: JOHN WYCHE, H. H. LOVING ack. before WM. P. WYCHE, CJ & EX O NP Sabine Co. Texas

AUSTIN AMERICAN, Newspaper published in Austin, Texas, Sunday Oct.3, 1965:
C. W. WIMBERLY, son of RUFUS WIMBERLY, descendant of PLEASANT WIMBERLY for whom the little town of WIMBERLY, Hays Co. Texas is named.

MORMON MILLS, on Hamilton Creek, S. E. corner Burnet Co. & Travis County

OLD ANDERSON MILL, on Cyrpess Creek, western part of Travis Co.

BURLESON MILL, after Tex. Rev. GENL. ED BURLESON on San Marcos River Hays County, Texas

994/605 aff. by ED GRIFFIN resident TCT 65 years past; knew HENRY MAUTHE, (1950) decd. HENRY MAUTHE m. 1 time to CARRIE ISABEL WHITEHEAD who had previously m....KLOTZ. No. ch. divorced Mar.15, 1906.

C/52 PATENT to WALKER WILSON March 12, 1835.
B/279 ..1841 WALKER WILSON of Bastrop Co. to LEANDER C. CUNNINGHAM, Paid Mar.12,1835 by SLAUGHTER,admr. of EST. STEPHEN F. SLAUGHTER, decd.

N/423 Dec. 29, 1851 LEANDER C. CUNNINGHAM et ux ANN, and AUGUSTUS B. SLAUGHTER son of ANN, states LEANDER C. CUNNINGHAM was appointed 1838 PC Bastrop Co. Tex. as administrator of ESTATE STEPHEN F. SLAUGHTER, father of AUGUSTUS B. SLAUGHTER. JAMES H. GILLESPIE bought land Sept. 18, 1842.

L/467 Mtg. June 5, 1857 A. B. SLAUGHTER of Bastrop Co. Tex., S. H. GARRETT, trustee for MARTIN MITCHELL. WIT: S. G. NORVELL, N. J. NORVELL

O/300 same dt. June 1, 1860 to WM. H. GARRETT, MARTHA H. MITCHELL.

PC 370 Feb. Tern 1867 ANN P. SLAUGHTER of TCT sur. wife of AUGUST B. SLAUGHTER June 25, 1866; W. C. LURRY et ux ANN P. she was wife of A. B. SHAUGHTER m. W. C. LURRY, Dec. 19, 1869.

DC 3375 TCT MARTHA M. MITCHELL vs. W. C. LURRY et ux ANNE, CORA B. SLAUGHTER, FRANCES A. SLAUGHTER, ALICE V. SLAUGHTER & LUCY A. SLAUGHTER minors. W. H. GARRETT is now resident Bell Co. Tex. J. M. DENTON was appointed special guardian of minors.

DC 4339 TCT Mar. 23, 1875 ANNA P. LURRY, resident of San Marcos (Hays Co. Texas) vs. WM. C. LURRY, JOHN H. ROBINSON & ALFRED H. ROBINSON, CORA B. SLAUGHTER, now BARTON: FRANCES A. SLAUGHTER, son now 16; ALICE V. SLAUGHTER, 13 and LUCY ANN 8. She and W. C. LURRY had ROY LURRY now 2 years on May 5; note to J. C. N. NELSON, subpeona to PAUL von ROSENBERG MRS. C. EVANS, JOE PICKETT, W. C. DAVIS, R. B. EVANS, J. P. McARTHUR, MRS. A. M. BURDETT & RICHARD KING, T. W. NOLEN, A. A. HUGHES, JOHN C. WILSON & FELIX SMITH, W. R. DAVIS, A. P. BLOCKER, JAMES P. McARTHUR, WM SWANK, GEO. B. ZIMPELMAN, Shf. by JNO. P. BROOKS, P. P. PENDLEY, WM. THAXTON, F. SLAUGHTER, H. SLAUGHTER, F. E. SMITH, gd. ad litem CORA B SLAUGHTER m. ROBERT BARTON, MR. J. C. WILSON a neighbor, W. C. LURRY says had property in La and Texas, replevy bond: W. C. LURRY, principal March 31, 1875, DESHA BUNTON, PETER SCHMIDT, O. H. CULLEN & M. J. DENTON. Case was completed Nov. 1, 1876 and ROY wax awarded to his mother

PC 510 Oct. 10, 1872 J. F. RICHARDSON, Judge 27th Dist CT. TCTFELIX E. SMITH, CORA B. SLAUGHTER, FRANCES A., ALLICE V. & LUCY A. minors, all under 14 years except CORA who is in Limestone Co. in school; May 16, 1882 ANNA P. McCUISTION, gd. says ALICE CHAPPEL, F. A. SLAUGHTER, et ux MARY, July 11, 1885, Liberty, Texas, receipt for part of estate. Manchaca, Feb. 14, 1885, ALICE V. CHAPPEL et vir, WM. C., JOHN J. McCUISTION m. ANNA P. SLAUGHTER LURRY Sept. 29, 1880, Feb. 1885, all of LUCY SLAUGHTER ESTATE received, J. E. CAMPBELL, JOHN McCUISTION and J. J. DAVIS, commissioners.

H/545 Mtg. Oct.23, 1885 SAML. K. JENNINGS to PETER deNORMANDIE, TRUSTEE EDWARD TEN EYCK & ALFRED & A. TEN EYCK. WIT: ALEX. EANES & WM.K. BROWN

5 8/613 Jan.21, 1884 MRS. DOROTHY D. ALEXANDER, widow, FORMERLY DOROTHY D. THOMPSON, MRS. LAURA E. LANE, formerly LAURA E. THOMPSON, et vir JOHN LANE, all Grimes Co. Tex. MRS. LANEY L. THOMPSON PATTERSON et vir M. E., Falls Co. Tex; W. D. THOMPSON, Blanco Co. Tex.; W. R.THOMPSON, Limestone Co. all heirs of JACKSON THOMPSON, decd.

26/348 PA May 7, 1874, MARY H. (X) PRICE of Limestone Co. Tex. dau and heir of JAMES C. NEILL, who d. 1848 in Montgomery Co. Tex. to WM. E. ROGERS, Hill Co. Tex. WIT: T. M. PENTELL, JOSEPH WOOD, B. R. TYNS, NP

29/308 PA June 15, 1874 WM. E. ROGERS to J. E. RECTOR

29/130 Deed W. E. ROGERS to H. C. FORD April 3, 1875 WIT: H. F. OTTOWAY WILEY DANIEL before N. J. KING, JP NP Bosque Co. Texas

DC 4908 filed Mar. 3, 1877 W. E. ROGERS, H. C. FORD vs. JOHN C. WILSON MRS. RHODA WILSON, SCOTT WILSON, T. W. NOLEN, THOS. E. STANLEY, B. CHOTE, JNO. C. HAMILTON, ROBT. & JOS. HAMILTON, ISAAC HAMMETT, WM. R. DAVIS, JAS P. McARTHUR, J. H. TULL, THOS. TUMEY, Miss MARY HAMILTON, MRS. ELLA HAMILTON KEEN, et vir.
B/34 Jan. 15, 1845 WM. CANNON of Bastrop Co. Tex. to JAMES C. NEILL WIT: PRESTON CONLEE, W. H. GARRETT, L. C. CUNNINGHAM, NP BCT.

DC 4360 filed Mar. 25, 1875 MARY H. PRICE, widow of Limestone Co.Tex. vs. THOS. E. STANLEY, SR., et ux MARY E., BECKER F. STANLEY, GEO. T. STANLEY, ELIAS S. STANLEY, THOS. W. NOLAN, JOHN C. WILSON, et ux and DAVID M. WILSON & DAN WILSON

B/419 July 10, 1847 GEO. J. NEILL to PRESTON CONLEY, Bastrop Co. Tex. WIT: GEO. HANCOCK, ALEX WILLIAMS

46/539 April 30, 1880 THOS. W. NOLAN, SARAH J. NOLEN, mentions land of BECKER F. STANLEY. WIT: JAMES E. RECTOR

F/460 Feb. 3, 1854, WILLIAMSON S. OLDHAM to JOHN C. JOHNSON. WIT: FRANCIS T. DUFFAU, THOS. F. McKINNEY, A. W. TERRELL

C/370 deed Mar. 6, 1848 THEO. BISSELL of Victoria Co. Tex. to ROWLAND A. ROBBINS of Baltimore, Md. mentions I. OR J. C. WOODALL & MATTHEW CARTWRIGHT. WIT: EDWARD BISSELL, CHAS. A. JOHNSON. ack. by T. BISSELL before GEO. W. PALMER, NP Victoria Co. Texas

X/23 PA June14, 1869 to W. C. PHILLIPS by RUSSELL ROBBINS, ROWLAND A. ROBBINS, CHAS. W. LORD et ux LAURA G., only heirs of ROWLAND A. ROBBINS decd. our father. WIT: to C. W. LORD, et ux, P. H. HOFFMAN, WM. H. HILL WIT: RUSSELL ROBBINS, ROWLAND A. ROBBINS, NATHANIEL GILL, WM. H. CLARKSON. ACK. by LORD et ux before WM. B. HILL, Comr. for Texas in Md. by R. ROBBINS & R. A. ROBBINS before CHAS. NETTLETON, Comr. for Tezas in NY.

DC 2842, 1869 JAMES PARK vs. SARRAH HARRIS wife of J. W. HARRIS (she formerly widow of JOHN C. JOHNSON, Hays Co. Texas)

DC 20,513 filed Feb. 18, 1903 MARTHA HEISSNER, et vir GEO. D. she dau of THOS. W. NOLEN, d. Mar. 19, 1900, et ux SARAH LANE d. Feb. 16, 1895 S. F. NOLEN, B. E. NOLEN, H. C. NOLEN, W. A. NOLEN, MRS. ANNIE DAVIS MRS. MARTHA HEISSNER, THOS. NOLEN d. Jan. 17, 1899; MARY DAVIS d. Feb. 1, 1881; and MYRA HEISSNER d. June 23, 1899, no issue; THOS. NOLEN had MARY, HOMER, LIZZIE & MITCHELL, d. Aug. 10, 1893, no issue. MARY DAVIS d. Feb. 1, 1881; CORDIE DAVIS, MARY DAVIS, FINAS DAVIS & JOE DAVIS, JENNIE DAWSON, Wife of N. A. , Orange, TEXAS. AND DAISY THRASHER FINAS d. 1887 (Aff. 321/109 and 312/108)

B/130 Deed Jan. 15, 1845 WM. CANNON Bastrop Co. Tex. to LEANDER C. CUNNINGHAM, WM. M. SNODDY. WIT: PRESTON CONLEE,H.W.GARRETT, R. L. REDING CJ BCT

G/567 Aff. JUNE 21, 1852 ISAAC HAMMETT, STATES THAT WM. M. SNODDY DEC SOLD TO DONALD SMITH OF BASTROP CO. TEX. OCT. 19, 1849, land in TCT on Onion Creek and on Jan. 1, 1850, SMITH transferred said bond for title to ISAAC HAMMETT & CORNELIUS M. HEMPHILL, admr. made deed.

M/315 Mt. Mar. 2, 1858 ISAAC HAMMETT to W. B. & H. M. BURDITT, as sureties to GILES BURDETT, JESSE F. BURDETT, admr. N. W. BURDITT, decd. mentions deed to JOHN H. TULK. WIT: J. C. WEST, J. T. McLAURIN

W/66 Feb. 13, 1859 ISAAC HAMMETT et ux MARTHA G. to NATHL. TOWNSEND land adjoining B. CHOTE, JNO. H. TULK, SEBRON G. SNEED, JOSEPH SCRIVNER and MARTIN W. TOWNSEND. WIT: GEO. H. GRAY, O. H. CULLEN

R/278 deed ISAAC HAMMETT et ux MARTHA J., May 13, 1868 to JOHN C.WILSON WIT: J. H. TULK, L. HAMMETT

39/213 deed Nov. 24, 1877 MARTHA J. HAMMETT, widow of ISAAC HAMMETT, decd. JACKSON, WASHINGTON, JOSEPH B., WILLIAM B., ISAAC M., MARTHA J. PREWITT and husband JOHN T. to JOHN C. WILSON

47/535 deed Aug. 31, 1880 JNO. C. WILSON to wife, MILDRED R.

D/407 deed Feb. 15, 1850 GEO. J. NEILL to BENJ. CHOTE, Bastrop Co. Tex WIT: B. F. JOHNSON, JAMES COLE.

49/381 deed Aug. 23, 1879 BENJ. CHOTE et ux MARY (X) to son FRANCIS F. CHOTE. WIT: J. L. D. HILLYER, A. R. CLARK, JOHN C. BONNER

92/23 deed Nov.14, 1889, FRANK F. CHOTE et ux LULA H.to JOHN C. WILSON

30/159 deed Aug. 4, 1875 RHODA WILSON, ELIA. P.fs and DON & W. SCOTT WILSON, TCT to DAVID M. WILSON.

67/517 deed April 15, 1886 D. M. WILSON et ux MARY to GEO. W.GLASSCOCK Williamson Co. Texas.

202/321 partition Feb. 2, 1897 MILDRED R. WILSON, sur. wife J. C.WILSON d. intestate Mar. 27, 1893, CH: MOLLIE W. PUCKETT et vir W. W., Hays Co W. S. WILSON, TCT (JENNIE L.) ANNA McGEE et vir JOHN T., Williamson Co. Tex., J. M. WILSON T. CT, J. B. WILSON, MILDRED E. MILLER, et vir W.D., JR. TCT, SALLIE B. SLOSS et vir M. M., Hays Co.; D. M. WILSON, JR., R. L. WILSON, Galveston Co. Tex., B. H. WILSON, Tarrant Co. Tex., (SARAH) ALBERT S. WILSON, TCT, EDNA WILSON TCT m. NORMAN CROSLIN, mentions land in Henderson Co. Tex. (aff.257/511 by W. H. CULLEN confirms that JNO. C. & MILDRED R. were m. 1 time only.)(Aff. 257/454 says JNO. C. WILSON was not in Ny 1894 and did not execute a mortgage)

DC 4869 filed Jan. 26, 1877 SUSIE M. TOWNSEND, PAULINE TOWNSEND, ANNA L BLACKBURN et vir WM. A., vs. ANGELINA L.(sur.wife) BENJ. R. TOWNSEND (sold to other heirs) JAMES W. TOWNSEND, minor, PALMER G. TOWNSEND, MINOR, PAULINE S. TOWNSEND m. 1889,WM. J. CULBERTSON, W. A. BLACKBURN d. 1909; MRS. ANNIE BLACKBURN d. Mar. 7, 1911. WILL PC 3533 to ch: WM. D. BLACKBURN, NATHL. T. BLACKBURN, HENRY P. BLACKBURN (ncm), HELEN ELIZABETH and ALEX L. BLACKBURN of age 1912. J. B. ROBERTSON, gdn.H.P. BLACKBURN ncm; WILLIAM D. BLACKBURN and wife MARY B., Harris Co.Texas NATHL. T. BLACKBURN, Galveston Co. Tex. HELEN E. BLACKBURN, Harris Co. Tex., ALEX. L. BLACKBURN Yavapoi Co. Arizonia. NATHL, TOWNSEND d. June 11, 1864.

M/388 July 31, 1858 boundary line agmt. S. B. REED, W. B. MABEN & W.C. PHILLIPS

234/366 Aff. J. A. MATTHEWS of Cuyahoga Co. Ohio, Asst. Treas. THE GUARDIAN SAVINGS & TRUST CO. of Cuyahoga, knew JOSEPH M. GASSER of Cleveland Co. Ohio (d. Mar. 12, 1908) left widow KATHERINE F. GASSER and 1 child JOSEHINE G. PETEE, wife of JAMES

P/113 gift deed April 3, 1861 JAMES E. BOULDIN to grand children: CONSTANCE TERRELL, MARY LEE TERRELL, LILLA TERRELL, EARNEST BOULDIN TERREL ARTHUR TERRELL, CH. of decd. dau. ANN ELIZABETH late wife of Judge ALEX. W. TERRELL. WIT: J. T. McLAURIN, L. H. LUCKETT, FRANK BROWN

A/286 PATENT to GEORGE W. SPEER (SPIER, SPEAR) Mar. 31, 1841.

G/217 deed Feb. 17, 1852 REBECCA J. SPIER, Fayette Co. Tex. to JOHN HANCOCK. WIT: T. M. BLACKMORE, WM. SCALLORN, ack. before W. G. WEBB May 14, 1853 NP TCT

143/510 deed Aug. 16, 1897 SUSAN E. HANCOCK INDP. EXTRX JOHN HANCOCK & E. B. HANCOCK, son.

499/157 Aff. Feb. 20, 1889 PEET CARLSON m. (1) LOTTIE WESTLING, she d. Oct. 30, 1893; CARL EDWARD CARLSON, Ft. Worth; LILIE BERKMAN, wife of ROBERT, Bishop, Tex., PETER C. CARLSON m.(2) HILDA D. WESTLING Dec.17, 1896; HENRY G. CARLSON, Austin had 9 CH: ESTHER EDBORG, wife of ANTON, LAURENCE CARLSON, HERBERT, IRENE, PETE C., & ALBERT C.

I/15 deed May 20, 1854 JOHN S. SPENCE to MICHAEL SUMMERROW, both TCT WIT: D. C. SABIN, T. H. TUMEY

Q/299 Feb. 26, 1863 PA, MICHAEL SUMMERROW,Upshur Co. Tex.to JNO.SPENCE

Q/299 deed Nov. 6, 1865 MICHAEL SUMMERROW by JNO. SPENCE to M. EDWARD SUMMERROW of Lafayette Co. Texas.

Q/341 deed Jan. 1, 1866 M. EDWARD SUMMERROW to ELECTRA SUMMERROW, love and affection for mother, boht TCT

Q/572 deed Oct. 10, 1866 MICHAEL SUMMERROW et ux ELECTRA to E. B. TURNER

226/324 Aff. 1909 W. P. SUMMERROW grandson of MICHAEL who d. Onion Creek TCT May 5, 1870 and grandmother who d. Nov. 16, 1898.

371/550 deed Mar. 14, 1925 E. B. MILLICAN, Lampasas Co. Tex., O. H. MILLICAN, JAS. H. HART, W. D. HART, FRED P. HART, MARY P. HILL, widow all TCT; LOUISE Z. BROWN wife of J. A. BROWN, Harris Co. Tex., LILLIE FORBES wife of A. A., Harris Co. nieces and nephews of FRED PECK decd. TCT to MARY P. HART.

399/314 1927 Aff. FRED PECK d. Feb. 22, 1925, son R. H. PECK & MARY sisters: FANNIE PECK MILLICAN, wife of E. B., PHOEBE PECK JAMES, wife of THOMAS H., MARY E. HART, wife of JAMES P., SALLIE d. in infancy; E. B. MILLICAN, & FANNIE MILLICAN d. prior Feb. 22, 1925, 2 ch: O. H. TCT & E. B. MILLICAN, Lampasas Co. Tex., PHOEBE P. JAMES and THOMAS H. d. before 1925, 3 ch: LOUISE Z. BROWN, St. Louis, Mo. , LILLIE FORBES, Harris Co. Tex. MARY P.HILL, TCT, MARY E. HART, hus. JAMES H. HART & W. D. HART & FRED P. HART, TCT.

B/45 deed Jan. 7, 1840 J. PORTER BROWN TO DAVID F. BROWN, refers to deed from GEO. W. DAVIS. WIT: DAMON COATS

I/472 deed April 11, 1955, D. F. BROWN to A. J. HAMILTON (ANDREW) ack before SAM J. P. McDONNELL (or DOWETT) NP Caldwell Co. Tex. mentions JOHN HANCOCK & BERRY GILLESPIE, LEASAL HARRIS and others, vs. J. N. HARDEMAN

K/735 deed Sept. 20, 1856 A. J. HAMILTON to WM. P. MABEN. WIT: F. W. CHANDLER, E. B. TURNER

Q/327 deed Dec. 7, 1865 W. P. MABEN et ux MARY ANN to GEO. HANCOCK

794/39 PATENT Dec. 10, 1841 to JAMES WEBB.

PATENT July 3, 1847 to ANSON JONES.

C/555 Deed Jan. 29, 1849 ANSON JONES to JAMES B. SHAW, Washington Co. Tex. WIT: W. H. VINSON ack. by JONES before STEPHEN R. ROBERTS

D/647 Bond for Title Oct. 31, 1850 THOS. T. FAUNTLEROY, Col. U. S. ARMY & SWANTE M. SWENSON, JOHN HERNDON, 2 notes dated at Richmond, Mar. 17, 1849. Fort Bend Co. Tex. land. WIT:JAS.G.SWISHER,ED. BURLESON

D/648 PA July 15, 1852 THOS. T. FAUNTLEROY of U. S. ARMY,appoints JAS B. SHAW to convey to JAS. H.MATTHEWS, ack. by TH. T. FAUNTLEROY, St. Louis, Mo. July 15, 1852 before EDWARD W.SHANDS, Comr. for Tex. in Mo.

F/145 deed Oct. 15, 1852 HENRY SCHULZ to CHRISTIAN WILHELM, lot patented to THOS. P.CARTMELL, July 27, 1850.WIT: JOHN B.COSTA, JOHN T. ALLAN

C. W. WHITIS d. 1877 will 1/2 property to wife, FLORENCE and 1/2 to 8 ch: RUFUS, MARY, JOHN, FLORENCE, GERTRUDE, CHAS. P., THOS. P. & ELLEN P. WHITIS. QC Mar. 14, 1899 MRS. FLORENCE WHITIS, GERTRUDE, MOLLIE, MRS. FLORENCE BELL et vir THAD C., RUFUS, CHAS. W., THOS. P. & JOHN H.

158/302 deed Feb. 3, 1876 L. W. SIMPSON et ux MARY E. TCT to J. S. SIMPSON Colorado Co. Texas, our bodily heir.

37/431 deed Feb. 26, 1877 L. W. SIMPSON et ux MARY E. to JANE C. BURLESON, wife of AARON BURLESON as her separate property.

PC 2109 JANE C. BURLESON d. TCT April 18, 1898, buried by husbandAARON BURLESON in Austin to sons EDWARD, RUFUS C., dau. JANE DEATS, wife of ROBT. A., LIBBIE MATTHEWS, wife of DAN B., TENNIE HILL wife of CHAS. W. HILL, and nephew FRANK R. TANNEHILL.

DC 3715 SARAH E. MOORE, June 14, 1873 removal of disabilities of minority over 19 y. parent: f. d. mother E. A. MOORE

129/539 Aff. Aug. 16, 1894 filed May 20, 1895 MRS. SALLIE ARLITT, Dau MARTIN & (SARAH) ELIZABETH ANN MOORE, f. d. Dec. 18, 1859, mother d. New Orleans...1873, intestate. (1) KATE L. MOORE b. 1849 m. BEN.THOMPSON, Nov. 26, 1863, he d. 1884 in San Antonio, /Tex. wife and 2 ch: BENJ. J. who d. Sept. 12, 1893 intestate and unm and KATE F. THOMPSON who will be 21 Dec. 1894; KATE L. THOMPSON m. (2)...BAKER and she d.; JAMES G. MOORE d. 1851 lives in Austin (3) LOUISA MOORE b. 1853 d. Galveston 1871 unm, intestate; (4) MOLLIE MOORE b. 1855 m. HENRY D.CONNER Mar. 19, 1873 d. Calif. 1875 and she d. about 6 or 7 years ago no ch. in Austin (5) SALLIE MOORE b. 1859 m. JAMES K. FARRELL Sept. 2, 1893 he d. Silver City, New Mex. Dec. 21, 1881 and she m. (2) May 25, 1889 FRED R. ARLITT

PC 3469 OTTOMAN R. SHUBERT decd. filed Sept. 13, 1910. He was resident of U. S. A., d. Schleiz, principality of Reus, Empire of Germany July 27, 1910, left widow ANNA and a married dau. ERNA BUELLEMANNet vir PAUL R. and 2 dau. FRIEDA and HILDEBARD all residents of Germany

DC 4445 JAMES MONROE SWISHER, petition filed June 1, 1875, he and deft JOHN MILTON SWISHER are ch. of JAMES G. SWISHER and wife, ELIZABETH: he'd. Oct. 7, 1862 and she d. April 25, 1875; RICHARD N. LANE sur husband of ANNIE LANE, nee SWISHER. NEWTON GIVENS LANE, JAMES S. LANE ANNIE LANE, minor children of ANNIE d. Sept. 13, 1864; JAMES G.SWISHER was owner of Ferry at foot of Congress Av. Austin; note of JOHN H. ROBINSON and J. M. LITTEN dated April 4, 1882 deed Book 52, p. 370 ANNIE LANE BLOCKER et vir J. R., (she dau. ANNIE SWISHER who was dau. of Capt. J. G. and wife, ELIZABETH)

N/66 Mtg. Feb. 12, 1859 ISAAC HAMMETT et ux MARTHA G. to M. W. TOWNSEND, WIT: GEO. H. GRAY, CJ TCT & O. H. CULLEN

O/188 deed Marcl 1, 1860 ISAAC HAMMETT to JAMES T. McLAURIN

DC 26 (suit to settle title disputes in early Travis Co.) ISAAH FISK, GEO. SESSIONS, JOHN PHILLIPS, DAVID McKENSIE, ROWLAND McKENSIE, JOHN McKENSIE, CHAS. F. COMPTON, GEO. W. DAVIS, JAMES RILEY, JAMES CUNNINGHAM, THOS. VANN, REBECCA SPIER, MARTIN MOOR, EDWARD SEIDERS, ENOCH S. JOHNSON, THOS. ADAMS, JAMES WALL, JANE ROBINSON, THOS. H. MAYS,FRANCIS KELLY, HALL MEDLIN, JOS. W. ROBERTSON, WM. CUSTARD, JOEL MINER, JAMES BENNETT and DAVID GREGORY, fall Term.

L/393 May 19, 1857 ENOCH JOHNSON et vir, CORNELIA J. to GEO. HANCOCK

257/454 Aff. July 13, 1913 J. M. WILSON says he is son of MILDRED E. MILLER (nee WILSON) wife of W. D.MILLER, JR.; that affiant's father JNO. C. WILSON was not in STATE of New York, 1894, or any other time and did not execute Mtg. to DAVID L. HAWKINS, in Vol. 131/87 TCT records

257/511 aff. July 11, 1913 W. H. CULLEN: JOHN C. WILSON et ux MILDRED R. both decd. TCT m. 1 time only; MOLLIE WILSON wife of W. W. PUCKETT, W. S. WILSON, ANNIE MEGEE wife of JOHN T., J. M. WILSON, J. B. WILSON, MILDERED E. MILLER wife of W. D, MILLER, J., SALLIE B. SLOSS wife of M. M. SLOSS, D. M. WILSON, JR., R. L. WILSON, B. H. WILSON, A. S. WILSON and EDNA WILSON

88/203 deed Oct. 4, 1889 ABNER H. COOK to CONSTANCE COOK dau. because of Physical injury, she was lame.

DC 7984 filed Aug. 28, 1886 W. C. PHILLIPS, surviving husband of PENELOPE PHILLIPS who d. intestate Oct. 7, 1882, vs. J. HALL PHILLIPS, MARY E. PHILLIPS, FLORIDA PHILLIPS, minor, WILLIAM P. PHILLIPS, minor

WALTER D. PHILLIPS, minor, FLEECIE M. PHILLIPS HOLMES, wife of
WALTON HOLMES, ED. B. HANCOCK, Esq. guardian for minors.

699/457 PATENT to SANTIAGO del VALLE, State of Coahuila and Texas,May
29, 1832, THOS. H. BORDEN, surveyor, SAML. M. WILLIAMS, atty. for
SANTIAGO del VALLE now Secy. of the Supreme Gov. of the State of Geona
Vicario, on Onion Creek, Burro or Garrapatas 10 leagues within expired
contract of Empresario BENJ. R. MILAM, above Bexar Road. SANTIAGO del
VALE, inhabitant of Town of San Buenava, Leona Vicario, 17th...1832,
LETONA, JOSE MIGUEL FALCON, citizen, HORACIO CHREISMAN, Prin. and
constitutional Alcalde, Town of San Felipe de Austin, Horatio CHRISMAN
WIT: W. T. LIGHTFOOT (This survey and the one to JOSE ANTONIO NAVARRO
were the first surveys in Travis County (present) on south side of
Colorado River. BERGSTROM FIELD, Air Base, covers most of the two, now)

C/197 Disclaimer Jan. 25, 1848 BARTLETT SIMS. WIT: B. F. JOHNSON,
JAMES G. SWISHER.

B/51 SWD July 16, 1835, SAML. M. WILLIAMS to MICHAEL B. MENARD. WIT:
W. F. LIGHTFOOT, C. C. GIVENS, ack. by WILLIAMS Aug. 7, 1843, R. D.
JOHNSON, CJ EX O NP Galveston Co. Tex

EST. NATHANIEL H. WATROUS, decd. THOS. F. McKINNEY petition filed Mar.
7, 1846; THOS. F. McKINNEY, Admr. JAS. M. LONG, CH & EX O Probate Judge
3665 acres west side Colorado River above res. of MR. BURDITT.(southR.)

D/26 PA Oct. 22, 1849 LYDA ANN WATROUS, Shelby Co. Ala. to JOHN C.
WATROUS, Galveston. Settlement of ESTATE of her late son NATHANIEL H.
WATROUS and she is sole and universal heir.

D/344 PA Jan. 28, 1850 JOHN C. WATROUS to HENRY B. MARTIN, before
OSCAR FARISH, Clk. Galveston Co. Jan. 29, 1851.

C/ 258deed Feb. 28, 1848, THOS. F. McKINNEY, to THOS. H. JONES, WIT:
T. C. COLLINS, WM. D. STAMPER

E/216 deed LYDIA ANN WATROUS to WASHINGTON D. MILLER, Mar. 26, 1851,
she of Shelby Co. Ala., next to A. C. HORTON, MR. OLIVEA now resides
and a MRS. DAVIS, WIT: HENRY B. MARTIN, atty. JOHN M. SWISHER, JAMES
B. SHAW

P/496 deed Sept. 18, 1862 THOS. BARRETT & H. H. STINER, of Richmond
Co. Ga. by agent, and atty in fact G. (J) M. STERN to JOHN T. MILLER,
upper corner heirs ROBERT DAVIS, line between CHAPMAN. WIT: FRANCIS
T. DUFFAU, HUGH A. HARRELSON before SAM T. SCOTT, NP

M/127 WD FEB. 1, 1858 JOSEPHUS M. STEINer, TCT to THOS. BARRETT & HENRY
H. STEINER, City of Augusta, Ga. WIT: P. deCORDOVA, A. H. FARISH

R/18 deed May 20, 1867 love and affection BENJ. A. RISHER to wife
NANNIE C. RISHER

1791/119 cc. EST. T. J. CHAMBERS, order of Galveston Co. Court July 26
1869, Vol. 6, p. 707 to 724 P. C. records of sales by ABBY C. THOMPSON
and hus. CYRUS THOMPSON, HON. EDWARD T. AUSTIN, CJ: sales to: 1. B. H.
DAVIS, 1092 acres TCT; 2 and 3 no name; 4. J. T. VAN; 5. CHAS. JOHNSON
6. THOS. H. BACON, 7. ELIJAH C. J. DIESON, 8. WM. GREENWOOD, 9 and10
Geo. Hancock, 11, J. D. McGaRY. 12 ALFRED H. LONGLEY, 13. ELLEN REID,
14, 15, 16 H. N. DUBLE, 17. C. W. WHITIS & JAMES H. RAYMOHD, Falls Co.
Tex. to H. N. DUBLE, 18. NELSON RECTOR TCT. THOS. M. JOSEPH, attorney

642/362 PATENT Mar. 3, 1842 REPUBLIC of TEXAS to A. W. LUCKETT

PC 50 guardianship Jan. 29, 1856 LEVIN H. LUCKETT, TCT, ALFRED T.
LUCKETT, minor under 14 and MARY JANE LUCKETT minor over 14.

DC 1204, 1857 MARY JANE CHALMERS, WM. LEIGH CHALMERS vs.LEVIN H.LUCKET
THOS. H. DUVAL, extr. EST. N. M. LUCKETT, decd.and L. H.LUCKETT gdn.

of ALFRED T. LUCKETT, minor. Mar. 29, 1870 JAMES COLE, A. R. MORRIS, WM. M. WALTON, appraisers for MARY JANE CHALMERS, decd. land in Williamson Co. Texas, part of J. DOVER, headright survey.

54/525 PARTITION Dec. 28, 1882 D. C. CHALMERS of D. C., JULIA CHALMERS HALL, wife of W. M. HALL of Galveston, Texas, and THOS. G. CHALMERS,TCT

Q/710 PATENT to CHARLES KLEIN, Nov. 13, 1848.

28/239 deed Oct. 26, 1874, CAROLINE NEWMANN, (formerly CAROLINE KLEIN) of Weisen Canton St. Callan, Switzerland, and ALBERTINE STEUSSEY(formerly KLEIN) TCT & ARNOLD KLEIN of TCT all children of BARBARA KLEIN lateof TCT to CHARLES KLEIN, their father.

43/409 Trustees deed June 11, 1879 to MRS. CAROLINE NEWMAN (otherwise WAHRENBERGER) WIT: F. KUEHNE, J. G. PALM

27/98 Mtg. July 13, 1874, CHAS. KLEIN to J. W. MANNING, and EUGENE BREMOND, trustee

44/255 Wd Aug. 23, 1879 CAROLINE NEWMANN WAHRENBERGER, widow, TCT to SAMUEL LUCKSINGER, TCT

97/38 WD May 6, 1890 SAMUEL LUCKSINGER et ux MARY, TCT to JAMES H. ROBERTSON & J. E. WILDBAHN

113/219 WD JAMES H. ROBERTSON & J. E. WILDBAHN to F. SCHUBER, TCT

240/273 WD Feb. 13, 1910 WILDBAHN LAND CO. to W. P. COCHRAN, OTTO EBELING, JOHN C. TOWNES, Pres. and JNO. K. DONNAN, secy. of WILDBAHN LAND CO. TCT.

241/512 WD Aug. 3, 1910 T. H. BARROW to W. K. WARD, Ellis Co. Texas

Plat 2/225 deed ack. by W. K. WARD, before GEO. L. GRIFFIN, NP, Ellis Co. Texas

277/304 deed Dec. 30, 1921 WILDBAHN LAND CO. to all stockholders, MRS. LUCY H. MARTIN wife of JOHN H., of San Saba Co. Tex., EDGAR E. TOWNES Harris Co, Tex., MRS. ANNE T. FINCH wife of H. H. TCT, JNO. C. TOWNES, JR. Harris Co. Tex. and JNO. C. TOWNES, SR. TCT

367/234 Aff. June15, 1923 by JNO. C. TOWNES, JOHN H. MARTIN of San Saba Co. Texas, heirs of LUCY H. MARTIN she d. before August 1922.

PC 5814 EST. JOHN C. TOWNES (SR) d. Dec. 18, 1923 application by ANNA T. FINCH TCT, EDGAR E. & JOHN C. TOWNES, JR., of Harris Co. Tex. WILL: Aug. 15, 1922 (holographic) to 3 children: EDGAR E. & JOHN C. TOWNES, JR. Harris Co. and ANNA T. FINCH, TCT. Inv. by C. S. POTTS, GEO. C. BUTTE, IKE D. WHITE.

5/616 AJ May 1, 1900 ROBERT A. SMITH, trustee vs. MADDOX BROS. & ANDERSON co-partnership JNO. W. MADDOX, F. M. MADDOX, C. E. ANDERSON, JAMES H. RAYMOND & CO.,JAMES R. JOHNSON, MARGARET J. RAYMOND & J. S. MYRICK

180/226 Tr. note Dec. 14, 1903 MARY C. JOHNSON to JAMES BYRNE, ack. before ROBERT J. HAMMOND, NP TCT

5/102 A.J. April 25, 1898 FRANK CABRON vs. R. E. WALDEN, J. P. RAGLAND H. P. N. GAMMEL, L. M. ODOM, Z. T. FULMORE on appeal bond.

5/112 AJ Aug. 13, 1898 JOHN D. SAMUELSON vs. THE LIDEL & H. P. N.GAMMEL

216/550 WD Aug. 1, 1907 H. P. N. GAMMEL et ux JOSEPHINE M. to F. H. SMITH, ack. before J. M. PATTERSON, NP TCT

7/14 AJ 1908 in M. M. JOHNSON CT. PCT. No. 3, favor E. M. SCARBROUGH & R. H. HICKS. (Thesepeople originally came to Rockdale, MILAM Co. Texas SCARBROUGH came to Austin established a large dept. store)

186/259 Mtg. Nov. 8, 1905 MARY C. JOHNSON, widow to A. H. YARRINGTON, trustee, W. H. THAXTON, before ASHBY S. JAMES, NP TCT

252/560 Transfer Jan. 22, 1910 MARY C. JOHNSON to FANNY PFAEFFLIN

253/263 Trs. April 11, 1912 MARY P. TURNER fs to WH. W. ELLIOTT of Sierra Co. New Mex. before OTTO EBELING, NP TCT

2/242 PLAT filed Jan. 23, 1913 by F. H. SMITH et ux EMMA WALKER SMITH before C. WENDLANDT NP TCT

254/99 WD Dec. 9, 1912 F. H. SMITH et ux EMA WALKER SMITH to LOUIS CARL EGGELING.

250/436 Feb. 11, 1913 W. FRANK HOWARD et ux JULIA A. & W. H. NELSON before P. A. WILDE, NP TCT

265/563 cc EX PARTE, MARCIA JOHNSON, minor H. PFAEFLIN Esq. before R. E. WHITE, Judge Dec. 9, 1900, D. J. PICKLE, Clk.S. A. PHILQUIST, dpty

265/564 cc PA Mar. 1, 1912 MARCIA E. JOHNSON fs Harlingen, Cameron Co. Tex. to B. F. JOHNSON same place before MILLER F. PENDLETON, Np Cameron Co. Tex., A. M. J. WEBB, Clk. by E. E. MOORE, depty.Cameron Co. Tex.

353/115 Rel. Sept. 20, 1923 HELENE PFLUGER, widow, CHRISTIAN PFLUGER she before WM. PFENNIG, NP TCT he before ALFRED ALBERS, NP Williamson Co. Tex.

M/197 Trustees deed Mar. 20, 1858 WM. C. PHILLIPS et ux PENELOPE

R/125 WD Sept. 14, 1867 W. C. PHILLIPS to JOHN HANCOCK. WIT: JOHN B. COSTA, C. W. WEST, ack. before L. W. COLLINS, NP TCT

99/252 WD May 1, 1890 WM. C. PHILLIPS of Jackson Co. Missouri to WALTER H. HOLM, ack. before STEWART TAYLOR, NP JACKSON CO. MO.

138/426 WD July 28, 1897 WALTON H. HOLMES to G. L. BRINKMAN, both of Jackson Co. Mo. Ack. before WM. A. SATTERLIE, NP Jackson Co. Mo.

147/287 SWD Ack. Aug. 7, 1897 G. L. BRINKMAN, Jackson Co. Mo. to W. F. LEBOLD, Galveston Co. Tex. Ack. before CHAS.H.SPILMAN, NP Jackson Co.Mo

149/194 Mtg. Aug. 28, 1897 W. F. LEBOLD et ux LILLIAN to D. W. DOOM, trustee for FANNY GRAY, ack. before J. R. DAVIS NP Galveston Co. Tex.

234/346 Rel July 3, 1909 FANNY GRAY PLATT et vir RADCLIFF PLATT, JR. to W. F.LEBOLD

108/406 PA July 19, 1897 WM. F. LEBOLD of Galveston Co. Tex. to C. H. LEBOLD TCT before CHAS. J. STUBBS, NP Galveston Co. Texas

154/123 WD WM. F. LEBOLD to J. M. GASSER of Cleveland, Ohio

217/594 QC JOSEPHINE G. PETEE et vir JAMES C., to KATHERINE F. GASSER of Cleveland, Ohio. WIT: LAWRENCE H. FOX, ANDREW SEYMOUR, before C. R. MEGRATH, NP Cayahoga Co. Ohio, CHAS. P. SALEM cc of Common Pleas

226/624 LEASE May 1, 1903 J. M. GASSER, Cleveland, Ohio and J. B. GASSER et ux LUCY TCT, J. J. GASSER, ack. before GUSTAV A. LAUBSCHEO, Np, Cyahoga Co. Ohio, J. B. GASSER et ux LUCY, before WM.BRUEGGERHOFF, Np TCT

286/109 Wd June 6, 1916 STACY-ROBBINS CO. to NORMAN A. CHIAPPERO etux MARY CATHERINE BOUTALL CHIAPERRO

549/567 Aff. June 28, 1934 O. G. ECKHARDT et ux LILA T. & JAMES H. WIMBISH TCT, MRS. VIRGINIA F. WIMBISH, widow, TCT d. intestate June 19, 1934.Widow of J. A. H. WIMBISH m 1 time, 2CH; LILA T. ECKHARDT, JAMES H. WIMBISH

K/440 Bond for Title April 26, 1856 E. S. C. ROBERTSON to M. TONGAT, cons. gold watch and chain and seal valued at $100.00 WIT: C. S. WEST, NELSON MERRILL.

DC 1314 Fall Term 1857 filed July 9, 1857 E. S. C. ROBERTSON vs. M. TONGAT, J. G. SWISHER, foreman of Jury, C. T. GREEN, Shf. by D. N BLACKWELL July 13, 1857 not served, Nov. 20, 1857 issued Feb. 22,1855 filed June 2, 1858 served April 21, 1858 J. M. BLACKWELL, Shf. TCT T. C. CATIN, depty.

M/511 Nov. 8, 1858 J. M. BLACKWELL, Shf. to NATHANIEL TOWNSEND, Nov. 25, 1853 surveyed: HUGH COLLINS & D. ADAMS, chain carriers, L. H. LUCKETT surveyor.

PC 348 EST. NATHANIEL TOWNSEND, decd. filed Jan. 12, 1866, by F. W. CHANDLER, son BENJ. B. TOWNSEND of Mason Co. Tex.;to wife ANGELINA L. TOWNSEND, Extr. & Extrx. NATHANIEL TOWNSEND d. Oneida Co. N. YTrenton. WILL dated Oct. 5, 1863 WIT: ALBERT H. CARLISS, ALICE F. MERRIMAN

A/336 April 26, 1941 EST. GEO. W. SPIER to GIDEON WHITE; ACK. JOHM W. SCALLORN admr. & REBECCA J. SPIER, admrx. Fayette Co. Tex. N. W. EAST-LAND, CJ & EX O NP Fayette Co. Texas

105/247 cc order by JOHN P. EHLENGER, cc Fayette Co. Tex. by JOSEPH COTTON, depty. at LaGrange, July 12, 1892

C/113 SWD Oct. 15, 1846 MARTIN MOORE et ux ELIZABETH ANN, EDWARD SEIDERS et ux LOUISA M., JAMES THOMPSON et ux CAROLINE REBECCA, and NARCISSA WHITE fs to CORNELIA JOHNSON

F/386 WD Sept. 26, 1853 REBECCA J. SPIER to JOHN HANCOCK ack. before N. W. FAISON, cc Fayette Co. Tex.

C/344 SWD Oct. 15, 1846 heirs GIDEON WHITE, CORNELIA JOHNSON, wife ENOCH, LOUISA M. SEIDERS, et vir EDWARD, CAROLINE REBECCA THOMPSON and hus. JAMES, & NARCISSA WHITE to ELIZABETH ANN MOORE,

D/26 PA Oct. 22, 1849 LYDA ANN WATROUS, Shelby Co. Ala, to JOHN C. WATROUS, Galveston, Texas, settlement of EST. son NATHANIEL H. WATROUS and is sole anduniversal heir

PC 466 Guardianship, BENJ. A. RISHER, apl. and father of ALETHEA,HARRY, ADA, LAURA & KATE, minors under 14 years. Bond SAM T. SCOTT, S. B. BRUSH, sureties R. A. SMITH, T. D. MOSELEY, W. L. GLASSCOCK, apprs. May 3, 1881, apl. by ALFRED C. EVANS, filed May 3, 1881 shows: HENRY C. RISHER(m)about 18, ADA, f. 16, LAURA B. 14 and N. KATIE RISHER 11 ye orphan children of BENJ. A. RISHER & NANNIE E. RISHER, decd. NANNIE d. Jan. 22, 1870, BENJ. d. Dec. 10, 1880; the other sister is ALETHA E., wife of O. I. HALBERT, McLennan Co. Tex., ALFRED O. EVANS is uncle,bro of NANNIE E. RISHER, decd. Receipt by H. C., ADA, LAURA B., N. KATIE June 7, 1890, before M. H. PARK, Np McLennan Co. Tex

105/160 Rel May 19, 1892 HARRY C. RISHER, ADA & LAURA B. RISHER m. W. M. SLEEPER

V/93 WD April 4, 1871 J. B. SEDWICK to HENRY BROWN, WIT: E. M. PEASE, AL LOCKETT.

38/332 Trans. July 26, 1877 HENRY (X) BROWN and wife, HENRIETTA (X) note of LUCINDA BRADLEY, WIT: JOS. SPENCE, R. A. CHADWICK, FRANK BROWN

197/121 Sept. 30, 1904, NELSON BROWN et ux MARGARETTA, heirs of LURINDA BROWN, formerly LURINDA BRADLEY and MISS LILIE RUSSELL wife of DANIEL A RUSSELL, only child of NELSON BROWN & LURINDA BROWN, WIT: F. A. CRASFORD, A. RYSINGER, NELSON BROWN, and MARGARETTE, ack. before JNO. B. VINSON, NP TCT, LILLIE RUSSELL & DANIEL A. RUSSELL , before GEO. W. PARSONS, NP Los Angeles Co. Calif.

39/618 deed Oct. 6, 1874 HENRY BROWN et ux HENRIETTA to KATE WILLIAMS
WIT: GEO. HANCOCK, Z. T. FULMORE.

59/572 deed Oct. 8, 1883 KATE (X) WILLIAMS et ux DAVID to MALONEY
BROWN & LILLIE BROWN

202/260 Aff. Nov. 26, 1904 HENRIETTA BROWN sur. wife HENRY BROWN,decd.
m. to HENRY BROWN who d. Oct. 27, 1886; CH: JAMES L. BROWN, over 21
and m.; ROBERT BROWN b. Jan. 17, 1873 d. Oct. 23, 1895, 1 dau. BEATRICE
d. in infancy

199/62 WD Dec. 24, 1904 JAMES L. BROWN et ux MATTIE B. of Tarrant Co.
Tex. to mother HENRIETTA BROWN, love and affection.

104/13 PA Mar. 24, 1892 DENNIE BROWN to HENRIETTA BROWN

235/429 Aff. Oct. 9, 1909 WILLIAM THIELE d. Feb. 14, 1908 never m. but
1 time, left wife ANNA & 11 ch: (aff. 267/96 says she d. May..1902) CH:
EDWARD A|THIELE (301/223 says he is 42 years old Dec. 1, 1917), JULIA
O. wife of THOS. D. METCALFE, Dallas, Tex., OTTO F. THIELE, ROBERT E.
THIELE, CHRISTINE THIELE wife of FRANK BURNS, Houston, Tex., and ALICE
H. THIELE , all over 21 years; WM, T. THIELE, minor PC 3163 filed Mar.
26, 1908 over 14; JOSEPHINE S. THIELE, MATTIE A., RICHARD A. & JAY D.
minors.

C/521 PA Jan. 28, 1846 DAVID G. BURNETT et ux HANNAH E. to JAMES WEBB

D/45 Mar. 29, 1848 SAMUEL G. HAYNIE to WM. COCKBURN

D/75 Nov. 12, 1849 WM. COCKBURN to JOHN HEMPHILL

PC 295 Jno. HEMPHILL est. 1862, C. S. MILLETT, admr. pro tem C. S. WEST
admr. April 29, 1862, F. W. CHANDLER, admr.

V/558 deed May 21, 1871 deed JOHN HEMPHILL heirs to THE STAR STATE
SAVINGS ASSN.

387/250 Aff. April 8, 1926, by BLISS ROBISON SPILLAR TCT Knew J. E.
PAULS and wife, CORNELIA, of Bastrop Co. Tex., J. E. PAULS d. Bastrop
Co. 1926, left wife and EDWARD CONRAD PAULS, MRS. KATHRYN ALICE PAULS
HEYE wife of OTTO JOSEPH, MRS. RUBY CORNELIA PAULS SPILLAR wife of
BLISS ROBISON SPILLAR and MRS. NELLIE LENORA MARGARET PAULS MOHLE
wife of FLAVIUS DOWN MOHLE

67/365 QC Mar. 12, 186 T. J. HOUSTON et ux VICTORINE to SAM LUCKSINGER

3/597 AJ JUDGMENT July 3, 1922 Harris Co. Tex., HAMILTON BROS. CO. a
partnership, W. E. HAMILTON, JR., G. H. HAMILTON, B. J. HAMILTON & A. L
HAMILTON

OLD FISKVILLE CEMETERY across Walnut Creek, northeast part of present
CITY OF AUSTIN:

"JESSE BURDITT, and wife, MILDRED. He b. 1790 came to Travis County, Te.
1844 d. April 4, 1878. HIs sons JESSE F. BURDITT, JR., & NEWELL F.
BURDITT fought with SAM HOUSTON in battle of San Jacinto & JESSE F.
BURDITT, JR., also served with TERRY'S TEXAS RANGERS, CIVIL WARand
fought at Shiloh. He d. Ark. at age 35 a POW of Feds. NEWELL d. a
few months after his father"

325/613 Mtg. Aug. 6, 1921 JANIE DEATS et vir R. A. DEATS (my share of
my mother's estate, ELIZABETH H. DEATS decd.) bounded by TOWNSEND on
east N. by JOSEPH SPENCE & JAMES MATTHEWS & WEST by Austin Town tract.

R/366 deed Aug. 10, 1868 JOHN HANCOCK to E. L. BACON, before F. W.
SUTOR NP TCT

DC 42,594 R. A.DEATS et vir, filed 1926 vs. T A. DEATS, ELIZA A. THRASHER, P. M. DEATS, MARTHA BURLESON, MARY E. DEATS & R. A. DEATS are children of MRS. E. H. DEATS. WILL: dated Mar. 28, 1929, MARY E. DEATS, TO: sister, MARTHA BURLESON et vir R. C. BURLESON; niece NORMA BURLESON BAKER, niece MADGE BURLESON CLARK, LOIS THRASHER, niece, great niece DORIS BAKER, 2 sisters, ELIZA A. THRASHER, MARTHA BURLESON to brothers T. A. DEATS, P. M. DEATS to sister ELIZA A. THRASHER

601/593 Aff. 1939 land to PAUL DEATS by WM. M. WILSON et ux MARY M. d Feb. 8, 1871; PAUL DEATS d. June 11, 1885 left wife ELIZABETH H. and children (see Vol. U/212)

68/100 WD July 7, 1876 JAMES H. RAYMOND to JAMES R. JOHNSON, ack. before J. S. MYRICK NP

M/137 WD Feb. 28, 1857 REBECCA J.SPIER, THOMAS J. SCALLORN, sur. hus. MARION SCALLORN and gdn. of her minor heirs; deed to satisfy bond for tit le GEO. W. SPEAR to NORMAN WOODS, then NICHOLAS McARTHUR and then to...GORDON, JOSEPH MORELAND & M. B. LAMAR and which bond is now owned by JAMES B. SHAW. Ack. before CHAS. S. LONGCOPE, CJ Fayette Co. Tex.

M/339 QC June 11, 1858 JAMES B. SHAW to JOSEPH MORELAND, WIT: J. T. MORELAND, GEORGE I. DURHAM, befoe JAMES M. SWISHER, per J. H. THOMPSON depty. ccc TCT

41/109 Rel Mar. 18, 1878 JOHN HANCOCK to JOSEPH MORELAND. WIT: JOHN B. COSTA, WM. F. NORTH, before O. H. CULLEN, NP TCT

37/323 PARTITION heirs JOSEPH & M. A. MORELAND of Freestone Co. Tex.dec REBECCA L. FORREST wife of G. B., Madison Co. Tex., LORA L. CALDWELL wife of J. L., Falls Co. Tex., MARY A. THOMPSON wife of J. R. & A. T. MORELAND, J. J. MORELAND & L. L. MORELAND, all Freestone Co. Tex. Ack. before F. G. GULLETTE Np Freestone Co. Tex. E. K.FOREE, NP Madison Co. Tex. and M. H. CURRY ccc Falls Co. Tex.

W/67 QC GEO. W. SCALLORN & MISS ELIZABETH R. SCALLORN of Fayette Co. Tex. to F. W. CHANDLER, TCT

120/273 Rel Dec. 30, 1893 STATE NATIONAL BANK of Austin to WILLIAM WELLMER, LOUIS H. YOUNGER, ROBERT W. WALLING, W. W. DEAN & A. B. DEAN

DC 10,969 filed Feb. 18, 1893 JAMES H. RAYMOND, JAMES R. JOHNSON & FRANK HAMILTON dba J. H. RAYMOND & CO. (bankers) vs. JOHN W. MADDOX, FRANK M. MADDOX, CHAS. E. ANDERSON dba MADDOX BROS. & ANDERSON & E. B. HANCOCK

108/251 WD Dec. 14, 1893 WM. WELLMER to C. A. PETERSON, deed Mar. 22, 1894 Vol. 141/383 shows: LOUISA PETERSON, wife of C. A. PETERSON

PC 2412 EST. EDWARD WM. WELLMER, decd. Nov. 5, 1901 WILL: dated Nov. 16 1893 to wife, LENA. All. WIT: A. P. WOOLDRIDGE, M. C. MILLER, Z. T. FULMORE, M. C. GRANBERRY, atty. JNO. W. HORNSBY cc TCT CHAS.HUPPERTZ, depty. Nov. 11, 1902 J. M. DAVIS, Shf. & G. S. MATTHEWS, Depty., A. R. MORRIS, JAS P. HART, H. M. METZ, appraisers

178/395 WD July 26, 1902 MRS. LENA WELLMER to G. A. BERGSTROM before J. M. PATTERSON, NP TCT

V/754 ADmrs. deed, MRS. ABBY C. THOMPSON admrs. EST. THOMAS J. CHAMBERS decd. and wife of CYRUS THOMPSONto JAMES DOXEY, land in part ordered sold last Monday June 1871 by DC 18th JUDICIAL DIST. CT. Galveston Co.

52/54 deed ROW Oct. 12, 1881 SPENCER DOXEY and wife, HARRIETT to AUSTIN & N. W. RY. CO.

DC 20, 409 filed Dec. 11, 1902 MARY HOWARD et vir VS. HARRIET DOXEY, owns 5/6 undivided interst 30 acres, only child of SPENCER & HARRIETT A DOXEY. He d. Jan. 14, 1902, SPENCER DOXEY m. HARRIETT, mother of MARY HOWARD, and she d. and he married HATTIE.

246/550 QC Nov. 29, 1911 G. A. BERSTROM, et ux AMANDA to CARL A.WIDWN

261/187 WD Nov. 26, 1913, CARL A.WIDEN et ux ELIN AUGUSTA to C.H.TAYLOR

281/279 Dec. 21, 1915 C. H. TAYLOR et ux BEULAH

PC 2210 EST. JAMES DOXEY d. Sept. 6, 1899, WILL: filed Dec. 16, 1899 dated June 24, 1891 to wife MARGARET DOXEY

170/181 PA Sept. 7, 1901 ANNA SCHUWIRTH widow & DORA C. SCHUWIRTH fs. ANNA sur. wife of GEO. SCHUWIRTH, DORA only child.

232/118 WD Nov. 12, 1908 MARGARET J. DOXEY widow of JAMES D. & THOS. A. DOXEYall DEWITT Co. Tex

184/132 WD Feb. 5, 1903 GEO. W. WALLING, JR., to E. S. KIRKPATRICK of Trinity Co. Texas

180/99 Oct. 6 1903 shows: E. S. KIRKPATRICK & wife MAGGIE L.

170/73 PA Nov. 1, 1905, E. S. KIRKPATRICK et ux MATTIE L. of McCulloch Co. Texas, to W. A. BOSWELL, TCT

244/475 WD Jan. 12, 1911 MRS. ROSA FREES et ux of WM. of Lackawana Co Pa. MRS. LELIA BERNHEIM et vir MAX, Logan Co. Okla., SAM, MORRIS, LAURA & JOHN HIRSHFIELD TCT all children of HENRY HIRSHFIELD, decd to mother MRS. JENNIE HIRSHFIELD

CEMETERY 8600 Manchaca Road, South Austin, Travis County, Texas On land setled by THOS. EDWARD STANLEY and wife, HOLLAND GATLIN, 1849. HOLLAND GATLIN STANLEY'S aunt was NANCY HANKS, ABE LINCOLN'S mother. HOLLAND d. July 4, 1863; THOS. EDWARD STANLEY d. 1881, M. S. NOLEN b. March 6, 1822 d. Jan. 12, 1872.

OAKWOOD CEMETERY, Austin: THOS. J. PALMER, June 24, 1846, April 16, 1918; MARY E. PALMER, Feb. 14, 1844, Jan. 6, 1911.

27/504 deed DEC. ... 1872 EST. NATHANIEL TOWNSEND to J. C. HARPER

39/560 Mar. 20, 1877 deed J. C. HARPER, et ux S. E. to WILSON WOODY

39/561 deed Nov. 12, 1877. W. WOODY et ux SARAH A. to A. J. SANFORD

141/577 deed Sept. 5, 1899 A. J. SANFORD to JOHN TOUNGATE, ack. at Liberty Hill, H. C. FOWLER, NP WILLIAMSON COUNTY TEXAS

101/304AFF. JNO. E. CAMPBELL, DENNIS CORWIN, MAR. 28, 1891. JESSE C. TANNEHILL D. BEFORE 1868 and wife before that time; WM. J., JOHN J., MRS. JANE C. BURLESON, MRS. CYNTHIA B. MINER, MRS. SARAH T. BENNETT heirs of decd. brother FRANK F. TANNEHILL.

R/258 deed Mar. 11, 1868 to WILL TANNEHILL, GEO. H. BENNETT, SARAH F. TANNEHILL ,NATURAL REPRESENTATIVES OF FRANCIS R. TANNEHILL TCT decd. JOEL MINOR, CYNTHIA B. MINOR, ack. ELM CO. Iowa, April 7, 1868, J.J. TANNEHILL, AARON BURLESON to Bro. WM. J. TANNEHILL. WIT: AUG. F. OTTO

100/314 deed June 4, 1868 WM. P. TANNEHILL et ux MARY ANN to LEVI BURLESON

Z/293 deed Dec. 23, 1869 WM. J. TANNEHILL et ux MARY ANN to PETER BELL DEMPS, BUCK BELL, (WM.) ELIAS BELL,PLAS DAVIDSON, AARON HANCOCK

DC 7455 filed Feb. 4, 1885 AMELIA BRASS vs. G. M. BRASS, SR., & J. MATILDA, CLARA, AMELIA, JR., PAULINE & IDA all ch. minors; says father andmother of G. M. BRASS, SR. living in Germany. Emma d. Dec. 1884

H/498 Oct. 6, 1955 ANDREW J. HAMILTON, FREDERICK W. CHANDLER & JOHN F. GRUMBLES TCT purchased at shf's sale under execution of judgment of Tex Supreme Court July 19, 1853 in favor of THOMAS JEFFERSON CHAMBERS vs. HENRY P. HILL, MOSES L. PATTEN. WIT: A. H. CHALMERS, T. J. RANDOLPH

K/595 SWD June 20, 1856 JOHN J. GRUMBLES to ANDREW J. HAMILTON, land in H. P. HILL survey TCT and in Leon Co. Tex. on Buffalow Creek, issued to me Feb. 21, 1848. WIT: JOHN B. COSTA, STEPHEN DAVIS

E/440 PATENT Oct. 27, 1848 DAVID H. FARR.

E/440 deed Dec. 17, 1850 DAVID HENRY FARR to RICHARD S. MORGAN. WIT: WM. O'CONNELL, JOHN B. COSTA

E/441 deed Feb. 15, 1851 RICHARD S. MORGAN to GABRIEL M. MORGAN. WIT: SABASTAIN KRAFT, A. LEE

E/465 deed Feb. 21, 1852 GABRIEL M. MORGAN to JOSEPH LIMRICK. WIT: R. S. MORGAN, JOHN B. COSTA

30/116 deed July 24, 1865 JOSEPH (X) LIMERICKet ux ELIZABETH to NELSON S. RECTOR. WIT: WM. M. WILSON, MOSES RAYNOR, ACK. JAMES W. SMITH NP TCT

32/499 PA Aug. 2, 1876 JOSEPH LIMERICK et ux ELIZABETH to WM. M. WILSON before JAMES NEILL, NP and Ex o. NP TCT

72/426 deed in trust Feb. 24, 1887 JOSEPH LIMERICKet ux ELIZABETH L. to EUGENE BREMOND, has been advisor and friend for years and they need assistance in old age.

85/610 deed Feb. 11, 1889 EUGENE BREMOND to ST. MARY'S CHURCH (shows they were both dead)

DC 9523 filed July 23, 1890 PATRICK McHUGH, CATHERINE McLAUGHLIN Mc BRIDE, widow of PATRICK DOLAN, ISABELLA McLAUGHLIN McHUGH et ux of JOHN MARY McLAUGHLIN BROWN et ux DANIEL, ELLEN ANN McLAUGHLIN sw, ELLEN,MARY ANN & ROSE ANN McLAUGHLIN, all single women all of these of Tyrone Co. Ireland; CHARLES McLAUGHLIN of Coatbridge near Glasgow, Scotland; MARY ANN McELLENNY et ux BERNARD of Tyrone Co. Ireland; JOHN McGILL of Dongal Co. Ireland, BRIDGET McGILL, PATRICK McGILL, also Dongal Co. Ireland; ANDREW BOYLE & CATHERINE BOYLE, both of Londonderry, ISABELLA McGILL of Tyrone Ireland, vs. MICHOLAS A. GALLEGHER of Galveston, Texas,Bishop of CATHOLIC CHURCH of TEXAS; that they are lawful heirs of JOSEPH LIM- ERICK, who d. ca. 1888 (ELIZABETH d. before JOSEPH).

DC 23,347 filed Nov. 18, 1905 FREDERICKA PETRI vs. HENRY PETRI m. in Ger. Nov. 26, 1881; to Austin, 1884, 3 ch. minor son and dau. awarded to plaintiff; HENRY PETRI, stock furniture and business of salon known as "PHOENIX SALOON".

DC 40 PETITION filed Feb. 13, 1850 SAMUEL CRAFT, administrator EST. WM. BARTON, vs. HENRY P. HILL, MARY JANE BARTON, widow and admr. WAYNE BAR- TON, decd. WAYNE was son of WILLIAM; venue changed to Washington Co.Tex April 22, 1847; JAMES WEBB, atty for HENRY P. HILL says HILL is non res- ident; citation by publication in "SOUTHWESTERN AMERICAN" Feb. 18,1850.

F/139 Tax deed Aug. 15, 1850 JOHN CARROLL. assessor to R. D. McANNELLY WIT: W. P. deNORMANDIE, G. M. MORGAN

K/151 deed Jan. 11, 1856 R. D. McANNELLY to A. J. HAMILTON, F. W. CHANDLER, J. J. GRUMBLES. WIT: GEO. W. GRAY, T. S. ANDERSON, before F. T. DUFFAU

G/367 Shf. deed Nov. 1, 1853 H. P. HILL, MOSES L. PATTON, ptf. in error THOMAS JEFFERSON CHAMBERS deft. in error, THOS. GREEN, clk. Supreme Court, July 19, 1853 to MORGAN C. HAMILTON, JOHN J. GRUMBLES, GEO. W. SCOTT, sheriff nearest corner about 1 1/4 miles west of new capital, Austin, WIT: GEO. H. GRAY, T. S. ANDERSON. Mar. 1861 published "SOUTH- ERN INTELLIGENCE" Austin, Texas.

B/178 Mar. 3, 1846 THOS. H. MAYS to PETER MacGREAL. WIT: PRESTON CONLEE JOE MAGGINSON, ACK. before ANDERSON J. HARRELL, CCC TCT

C/120 July 29, 1847 PETER MacGREAL of Brazoria Co. Tex. to RICHARD PAYNE JONES. WIT: CHAS. LEONARD, ALEX HORN

I/347 Mar. 6, 1855 CHAS. C. FRANKLAND, CLINTON TERRY of Brazoria Co. Tex. assignees of R. P. JONES, decd. & FRANCIS KELLY, TCT: AMBROSE LANFEAR of New Orleans, La. and JOHN BARNES of London, England.

PC 1900 LEILA KAVANAUGH, no will. She d. April 1918 Withita Falls, Tex oldest dau. EVA K. m. had 1 child MOSSIE (now) BROWN; LENA K. m.BENTON div. both decd. d. in Phoenix, Ariz. 4 living sons in 1918...KAVANAUGH m. ROBERT ALLEN STERN, Ft. Worth; GEO. MATTHEW d. Pheonix, CLEM KAVANAUGH, in Detroit to MOSSIE M. BROWN, EVA KAVANAUGH, minor QC to MOSSIE BROWN; MATTHEW KAVANAUGH QC to HATTIE MAE K. STEIN, LENA QC to EVA, ROBERT QC to MOSSIE, their father was JACOB (JAKE) KAVANAUGH

PC 5, filed Feb. 28, 1848, AARON BURLESON, application shows: JAMES BURLESON, father and gdn. of his 2 minor ch: ICABUD EARPE BURLESON & LAFAYETTE BURLESON, JAMES d. Jan. 13, 1848; 1864 AARON BURLESON gdn. shows guardianship dismissed.

1/38 TRANSCRIPT Feb. 6, 1838, deed EDWARD BURLESONto JAMES ROGERS, trustee for BURLESON WARREN & MARGARET WARREN, minors. WIT: BARTLETT SIMS, SAMUEL R. MILLER.

D/552 WD Mar. 20, 1852, JAMES ROGERS et ux RACHAEL to JOSHIA PATTERSON

ALFRED SMITH and decd. wife ANN: 4 gch: ANNA CASTLEMAN, MAGGIE CASTLEMAN,ALFRED CASTLEMAN & RICHARD WALTON CASTLEMAN

ELLEN J. FRAZER decd. 1913 to FRANK deLASHMUT, son-in-law, dau. E. B. deLASHMUT, son JOHN H., son JOHN H. McWILLIAMS surviving children of decd. dau. AGNES C. McWILLIAMS WEBER

573/567 Aff. by P. deCORDOVA Sept. 10, 1890 knew PAYTON W. NOWLIN d. 1884 left: LUCY A. DANCY, widow, Sept. 4, 1884; SUSAN B. RANDOLPH wife of C. H., ANNA E. LeSUER and hus. C. M.; MARY O. DINKINS, 1890 fs. Vol. 93/71 and ADDIE ROBINSON, fs. Vol. 62/60 Ch. of PAYTON W. NOWLIN and MARTHA W. NOWLIN

183/181 WD Feb. 4, 1903, P. W. JOBE sm of TCT love and affection for nephew C. P. RANDOLPH.

Y/191 cc ESTATE R. L. REDDING decd. June 25, 1849, JAS. SMITH CJ, MARK M. ROGERS, SHF. JAMES H. GILLESPIE CCC, WM. M. PERRY proved will of R. L. REDDING, decd. M. M. ROGERS, E. H. CASTLEMAN &...appraisers. Oct. 10, 1870 J. M. FENNEY depty. for R. F. CAMPBELL clk. will dated Feb. 26, 1849 ROBERT L. REDDING to wife, JANE ELIZABETH, CH: WILLIAM MAC, MARY INDIANA, MINERVIA JANE m. HUGH ODOM, MARGARET LAURA, NANCY JOSEPHINE m. JONATHAN ROGERS, CATHERINE ELIZABETH m. A. J. BALLARD

Q/527 July 21, 1866 WM. J. GOOD et ux MARY R. GOOD (REDDING) of Hays Co. Tex. to SAMUEL M. WRIGHT

236/607 Aff. Jan. 26, 1909 R. M. CASTLEMAN, knew W. S. TYSON who was killed in Battle of Val Verde, Feb. 21, 1862, and his wife E. JANE TYSON, who was widow of ROBERT L. REDDING.

F/321 WD July 12, 1853 ARCHILOUS SILLSBEE of Clinton Co. Mich. to J. C. McGONIGAL of Matagorda Co. Tex. all right, title and interest as heir and legatee of brother ALBERT SILLSBEE, land patented in TCT to ALBERT SILSBEE, assignee of H. T. DAVIS, Feb. 5, 1841; assignee FRANCISCO GARCIA to ALBERT SILSBEE for military service; land on Lampasas River, Bell Co., also for military service,land in Live OakBayou Matagorda Co.patented PENTECOST LEA sold by GEO. ELLIOTT to ALBERT SILLSBEE; MATAGORDA CO. land granted WILLIAMSTONE decd. , and sold to

ALBERT SILSBEE, Matagorda Co. Tex. by CHAS. EDWARDS, land in Jackson Co Tex. WIT: W. J. JEMSON, JAS. W. GRANGER.

PC 199 JAMES M. McGONIGAL petitioner filed Dec. 12, 1854, on JOSEPH C. McGONIGAL who d. recently, SAMUEL HARRIS replaces JAMES McGONIGAL who renounded his executorship.

1/62 WD Aug. 1, 1854 HENRY CROCKERON of Bastrop Co. to HENRY W. SUBLET WIT: D. W. C. BAKER, GEO. P. BOARDMAN.

N/270 WD April 13, 1858 H. CROCHERON to heirs of JESSE BURDITT. WIT: BENJAMIN DECHERD, JOHN HANCOCK.

275/410 QC Jan. 9, 1915 ERIN RUTHERFORD, surviving wife of R. A. RUTHERFORD, LIZZIE fs. and ELMER RUTHERFORD surviving children and heirs of R. A. RUTHTHERFORD, decd.

498/531 Aff. C. E. ROBERTS, Feb. 20, 1934, RE: R. L. WHELESS, LILLIE M WHELESS, m. June4, 1901; R. L. WHELESS d. April 22, 1918; R. L.WHELESS had 3 Ch. by prior m. to CARRIE BROWN from whom he was div. CH. ROBERT NORMAN & MAUD WHELESS ASTOLL wife of F. G.; ELIZABETH wife of C. W. STURDIVANT, NELL GUSTAFSON wife of F. W., JAMES WHELESSand wife, RUTH, SADIE WASHBURN wife of HOWARD, MILDRED WHELESS fs. and GLADYS WHELESS fs. and LENA WHELESS 19 years old.

A/315 PATENT to JOSE ANTONIO JAVARRO 7 leagues July 10, 1833, 2/3 in Travis County and 1/3 in Bastrop County. This is one of the signors of the TEXAS DECLARATION of INDEPENDENCE.

A/321 WD April 2, 1833 JOSE ANTONIO NAVARRO to JOHN CALDWELL.

A/558 deed June 22, 1842 JOHN CALDWELL to JAMES BAKER, WIT: ROBERT LOVE, H. H. H. HAYNIE

D/284 WD Jan...1846, JOHN CALDWELL to WM. L. & L. S. HANCOCK. WIT: LEMUEL FENTRESS, A. H. COOKE

50/335 cc ESTATE W. L. & LEWIS S. HANCOCK decd. JOHN HANCOCK extr. ESTATE LEWIS S. HANCOCK decd.

K/205 WD, Nov.24, 1854, JOHN HANCOCK to ALBERT C.& ROBERT JONES. WIT: GEO. HANCOCK, T. C. JACKSON

PC 189 JAMES BAKER decd TCT Mar 23, 1854, WM. R. BAKER, JOHN R. W. BAKER. WIT: JAMES BAKER, their father d. Feb. 13, 1854, MRS. FRANCES BAKER sur wife

T/171 WD April 9, 1870 E. C. JONES, admr. his father A. C. JONES to R. A. JONES (ELIZABETH C. surv. wife of A. C. JONES) WIT: JNO. E. CAMPBELL, WASH...BONNER

29/215 WD Oct. 4, 1871 D. J. husband of C. W. CRISER to W. C. JONES, division line between ROBERT JONES & CRAWFORD JONES

W/603 WD Oct. 5, 1871 W. C. JONES, R. A. JONES, ELIZABETH C. JONES & DELIA J. CRISER (nee JONES) et vir C. W. all heirs of A. C.JONES to ROBERT JONES

31/344 QC Aug. 23, 1875 WM. C. JONES and mother ELIZABETH C. JONES

V/238 & 340 Nov. 10, 1909 ROBT. JONES d. July 16, 1909 TCT left son R. F. JONES & dau. MATTIE A. PEARCE wife of THOS. P., & LOUISA J. FOSTER, widow.

E/432 WD Jan. 9, 1852, JOHN CALDWELL, Bastrop Co. Tex. to THOS. P. WASHINGTON. WIT: JOHN S. CRAFT, S. S. FRIEND, JOHN B. COSTA

A/264 PATENT Feb. 26, 1841 to JAMES ROGERS
A/565 deed Sept. 22, 1843 JAMES ROGERS To SAMUEL G. POWELL, both Bastrop Co. WIT: JAS. H. GILLESPIE, S. HIGHSMITH

B/154 WD SAML. G. POWELL of Matagorda to THOS. B.POWER

Y/36 PA Sept. 18, 1870 PREMELIA A. R. THOMPSON, widow W. D. THOMPSON decd. ALEXANDER C. THOMPSON, DANIEL D. THOMPSON, LOUISA R. GORDON, wife JOHN GORDON, JASPER M. THOMPSON, BETTIE J. JOHNSON, wife JOHN O., LEONORA L. & KNOX THOMPSON children of W. D. THOMPSON.

F/478 SARAH J. NOLEN, wife of THOS. W. NOLEN was dau. of THOMAS E. & HOLLAND W. STANLEY

PC 6785 WILL: EMELINE WILLIAMS "It being my desire that what I have in this world shall go to those in whose veins trickles a lifeblood in common with that of mine" July 3, 1922

31/22 Oct. 9, 1875 J. W. , T. M. & A. E. JONES

98/120 SARAH ANN GLENNON wife STEPHEN, he d. Nov. 16, 1923, she never had any children and d. June 10, 1935; JOHN ROONEY d. Nov. 17, 1882 willed to KATIE ROONEY, who m......

PC 15,051 THOS. LYNCH came to Austin 1875; 2 ch. SARAH ANN, m. STEPHEN GLENNON, she d. June 3, 1887; CATHERNE m. (1) JOHN ROONEY, d. Nov. 17, 1882, had: TOM MORTON ROONEY d. Dec. 31, 1903, JOHN FRANCES d. May 12, 1950; KATHERINE (KATE) who d. Jan. 22, 1952; EDDIE d. young and unm; (2) JOHN H. HANSEN 1884, 1 son, HENRY FRED. HANSEN, JOHN H. HANSEN d. Mar. 16, 1914, WILLIAM S. HOTCHKISS d. TCT 1889 m. HANNA B. PUCKETT In 1841 she d. TCT 1852 b. Mo. (2) MARY E. had MARTHA E. who m. BOSTICK WHITTEN, DANIEL W. d. 1864 young unm; MARY E. m. JOHN CHAMPION, CORELIA T. d. 1879 m. JAMES L. BROWN who d. and she m. ROBERT J. WILLENBURG Had MABEL W. d. 1900 m. WILL F. DIETERICH, MARY E. HOTCHKISS had: WM. H.d. 1886 left widow KATE WESTFALL and 1 ch. RALPH HOTCHKISS who d.when about 8 years of age; OSCAR T., MILTON S. & DeWITT H.

GEORGE HANCOCK b. Tenn. April 11, 1809, reared in Ala. came to Texas 1835, m. LOUISE LEWIS dau. of IRA R. LEWIS in Matagorda Co. Tex. 1855 oneson LEWIS

M/179 WD Aug 20, 1854 TIMOTHY B. MORRIS et ux MARY to JOHN HANCOCK. WIT: JOHN E. BYBEE, JAMES W. HANCOCK.

H/199 deed Dec. 21, 1854 WM. M. RILEY etux CLEMENTINE B. to JAMES W. RILEY

I/465 WD May 1, 1855 JAMES W. RILEY et ux SARAH RILEY to JOHN HANCOCK. WIT: JOHN B. COSTA, WM. C. REAGEN

J. C. TALLEY b. Mar. 11, 1826, Ordained Minister Dec. 1858 (BAPTIST) Settled in Texas, 1853, wife E. D., b. Aug. 11, 1852 d. Oct. 10, 1905 buried in small cemetery in edge BURNET CO. near Travis Co. line.

CEMETERY TRAVIS CO. off Bastrop Highway, near Bergstrom Field: SARAH S. S. McCALL June 6, 1833, Feb. 7, 1907; LOUISE S. MEEK wife of JOHN W. b. May 5, 1841, d. Mar. 10, 1882

FIELDING G. SMITH d. Dec. 22, 1944 TCT WILL dated Nov. 30, 1936 to be buried in family cemetery at Rome, Ga.; nephew H. EDWING DEAN, extr. and trustee; sisters AGNES S. DEAN & LEE ELLEN SPARKS, 6 nieces, JULIA DEAN ANDERSON of Athens, Ga. NELLIE STEWART DEAN of Atlanta, Ga. MARION DEAN NIXON, BOGGIE MAY DEAN, JANE DEAN MILLER & LEE DEAN TEMPLE all of Rome, Ga.

"NEW ERA" published in Austin, Texas, April 1846.

B/258 Aug. 26, 1847 ALFRED SMITH, WILL. d. May 15, 1883, filed Dec..1 1883, R. M. CASTLEMAN son-in-law, extr. 4 g.ch: ANNA M. CASTLEMAN MITCHELL, MAGGIE CASTLEMAN m. BELL, RICHARD WALTON d. Mar. 4, 1906 m. LENA, WILL of AMELIA E. CASTLEMAN wife of R. M., July 4, 1879 dau. of ANN & ALFORD SMITH says uncle JAMES W. SMITH

R/30 ABNER MATTHEWS d. TCT 1863 and wife, ASCENATH d. 1851; NANCY H. THOMPSON of Tipton Co. Tenn (she also known as AGNES H.) heirs JOHN DeKALB THOMPSON she d. left 1 ch: E. S. MATTHEWS, Limestone Co. Tex. 1886; MARY D. FRANKLIN wife ROBERT E., TCT, JAMES H., JOHN G., ESTHER H., EZEKEL S. & ELIZABETH PAYNE wife BANYAN, MARTHA M. MONROE, ROBERT E. MATTHEWS.

Y/626 WYMAN F. WELLS and wife, MARY EMILY: AMANDA LaRUE, wife GEO. F., PETER K. WELLS, GEO. HENRY, JONES MORGAN & WAYMAN THOMAS WELLS

97/103 TCT ADA EICKBAUM wife LOUIS & CAMBY CAHILL wife of J. D., at McNEIL, Aug. 30, 1890, 640 ac. H. P. HILL survey, home of WILL C.SMITH "THE HERMIT"

PATENT Feb. 28, 1842 REPUBLIC OF TEXAS to ALEXANDER T. GAYLE

C/223 deed Feb. 1, 1848, ALEXANDER T. GAYLE of Jackson Co. Tex. to JAMES H. MATTHEWS, TCT. WIT: THOS. H. DUVAL, H. M. METZ

ST. DAVID'S EXPICOPAL CHURCH, 300 East 7th Street, Austin, Texas,ALTAR PIECE in memory of FANNY CHALMERS ROBERTS (1847-1883) at dedication Jan 1, 1933 were HENRY ROBERTS of london, JOHN GORDON ROBERTS, Austin and ALBERT SAML. ROBERTS of Va. and these three sons were young when their mother d. Feb. 5, 1883. DR. JOHN CHALMERS, father of FANNY b. 1801, Halifax Co. Va. m. MARY HENDERSON in 1827 in Miss. 1838-39, 1840 to La=Grange, Texas. He was secy. of Treas. of REPUBLIC of TEXAS, 1841,published "THE NEW ERA" & "THE TEXAS DEMOCRAT" Jan. 1, 1847; DR. CHALMERS was stabbed, FANNY b. 4 mos. later. The other 5 ch: SARAH & MARY, wife of TOM GREENE, MRS. CHALMERS d. 1851; TOM GREEN, reared her orphan ch. TOM GREEN and wife had 3 ch. of their own. He b. Va. and educated in Tenn. and came to Texas 1835. TOM GREEN was a Brig. Genl. Civil War. d. April 11, 1864 and ALEXANDER CHALMERS also killed Civil War; ELIZA (LIZZIE) CHALMERS m. COL. JAMES P. MAJOR. Col. GREEN buried beside four of his children. 6 others survived him: FANNY CHALMERS m. ALBERT SAMUEL ROBERTS of Va. Nov. 21, 1868.

M/49 Mtg. Dec. 26, 1857 JAS. H. MATTHEW S to WM. F. HENDERSON, admrs. EST. E. H. HENDERSON, decd. Murry Co. Tenn. & RICHARD M. JOHNSON, tr.TC

R/469 Wd Nov. 14, 1868 JAMES H. MATTHEWS et ux LOUISA D. TCT to N. M. A. LACKEY, TCT

T/4, WD Jan. 24, 1870 J. H. MATT HEWS, et ux LOUISE D. TCT: ELIZABETH A. & LUCRETIA RAY, L. W. COLLINS, NP TCT

39/285 Wd July 24, 1877 N. M. A. LACKEY TCT to wife, U. G. LACKEY (formerly U. G. MANOR) O. H. CULLEN NP TCT

47/365 Wd July 12, 1880 MRS. U. G. LACKEY et vir N. M. A. to E. E. BONNER, Bastrop Co. Tex. H. B. BARNHART, NP TCT

48/440 WD Jan. 27, 1880 E. E. BONNER etux BETTIE J. TCT to E. T. MOORE WIT: H. C. RANDOLPH, ROBERT H. HANNA

61/281 Wd July 12, 1884 A. M. DAVIDSON to MARY E. DAVIDSON, both TCT no relationship shown.

91/312 WD JAN. 4, 1890 ELIZABETH A. & LUCRETIA RAY both fs TCT to J. E. BONDS and wife, R. E.

122/194 Rel. Mar. 15, 1895 J. R. RAY to BONDS, C. W. DANIEL NP TCT

196/18 WD May 20, 1905 J. E. BONDS et ux R. E. TCT to JOHN R. ROBINSON et ux LULA, TCT

204/309 Trf. Aug. 8, 1905 J. E. BONDS etux R. E. to HARRIETT R. BOAK widow TCT
206/312 Wd Nov. 2, 1905 MRS. MARY E. BEVERLY (formerly MRS. MARY E. DAVIDSON, wife A. M., decd.TCT WIT: MYRTLE B. SMITH, JNO. H. MULLINS NP

244/143 Aff. Jan. 9, 1911 by WALLACE & ELDRIDGE ANDERSON, SR.,ELDRIDGE ANDERSON m. MISS JULIA KINCHEON Sept. 11, 1909, son affiant ELDRIDGE SR., and bro. WALLACE ANDERSON, ELDRIDGE ANDERSON, SR was m. to EVA MARTIN Dec. 4, 1907 and was div. from her May 24, 1910, TCT, is not the same as the man who m. JULIA KINCHEON, but his father, affiant E. A. SR has not remarried. WIT: LUCK THOMPSON, MONROE WHITE,W. P. MABSON, SR.

212/475 Wd Dec. 17, 1906 MARY E. BEVERLY, widow of W. D. BEVERLY decd. formerly MARY E. DAVIDSON widow of A. M. DAVIDSON, decd.

232/182 WD Sept. 39, 1908 HARRIET R. BOAK, widow TCT to T. H. ELDER et ux LENNIE L.

241/163 Wd May 23, 1910 T. P. ROBINSON et ux MARY A. TCT to PHILIP BOSCHE, F. H. JONES, NP TCT

240/364 Wd May 28, 1910 PHILLIP BOSCHE to A. J. GATLIN of Mills Co.Tex before C. A. SATTERWAITE, NP TCT

243/59 WD V. V. WARWICK et ux MINNIE E. TCT to THEODORE OLLE TCT

293/68 WD Feb. 1, 1917 OTTO TIEMAN et ux KATTIE to THEODORE OLLE

413/312 WD Jan. 23, 1928 THEODORE OLLE et ux EMMA to N. R. JACKSON (MD) HERMAN BECKER (LUMBER CO.) A. W. SPECKELS, D. DAUGHERTY fs

272/520 PA Aug. 11, 1924 MRS. D. DAUGHERTY of NY City to VAN M. SMITH (Note PA does not so state, but she was mother-in-law of her agent)

AFF. IN RE: JAMES ROGERS (headright) he d. TCT: JAMES ROGERS et ux RACHEL had 5 ch; ED. H. ROGERS,JOSEPH B. ROGERS, MARY E. wife of WM. H. SARAH B., wife of MINAS C., NANCY wife of BEN T. GAULT, SR. got deed to 535 ac. ROGERS HEADRIGHT Jan. 23, 1867 TCT; BEN T. GAULT, SR. d. April 5, 1895 intestate NANCY D. d. o/b Jan. 22, 1935; CH. JOHN M. d. Feb. 26 1936; SARAH ELLEN m. McELROY, she d. Mar. 13, 1914; JAMES (JIM) R. SR. d. April 3, 1897; JOSEPH F. d. April 28, 1933; BEN T. JR. d. Mar. 1, 1914; RACHEL R. d. unm Nov. 27, 1949; EDWARD H. d. Dec. 2, 1943; MARY B. CEARLEY d. Oct. 23, 1950; JAMES (JIM) SR. m. JULIA VADA BARNES and got 100 ac. part 535 ac; had RENA G. SMITH, widow of EARL, MURIEL GAULT (CLAY) PHILLIPS wife of DON, VEDA fs; JOE H., JAMES R., JR. RUTH d. 1954 unm; aff. made by JAY W. BARNES, SR. who is a brother of VADA GAULTet ux JIM G., bought 100 ac. Feb. 1, 1906 (212/81)

A/82 May 20, 1839 April 17, 1840, JAMES P. WALLACE of Bastrop Co. Tex. to R. L. REDING, Bastrop Co. Tex. WIT: H. CROCHERON, WILLIS TATUM, JAMES M. LONG

C/373 deed Sept. 28, 1847 ROBERT L. REDING to JOSIAH FISK

W/171 Wd Feb. 14, 1872 DAVID RILEY et ux MARY J. of TCT to THOMAS E. CATER TCT

W/356 Mt. Mar. 22, 1872 THOMAS E. CATER to MARGARITTA

26/462 Wd April 28, 1874 CHARLES G. JONES TCT to R. W. RILEY

26/441 Mtg. April 28, 1874 R. W. RILEY et ux S. M. to JOSEPH HARRELL

29/521 Wd July 1, 1875 R. W. RILEY et ux SARAH M. (W) to STEPHEN D. HILL

28/521 WD Jan. 3, 1875 R. W. RILEY et ux SARAH W. to JAMES A. ALVIS

PC 1647, 1892 EST. STEPHEN D. HILL decd. WILL: dated Mar. 8, 1892, wit: T. CASWELL, W. W. DEEN, A. B. DEEN to wife, ELVIRIA A. HILL, to son IRA B. HILL when 21, dau. HATTIE M. when 21, to four daughters living in the northern states, only blessings and best wishes.

173/202 Aff. ELVIRA A. HILL, widow says IRA B., was 21 Nov. 19, 1904

196/398 deed S. D. HILL ESTATE Oct. 12, 1905 to HATTIE M., she m. ALLEN E. HANCOCK.

PC 10,143 ESTATE MRS. ELVIRA A. HILL decd. d. Sept. 7, 1941, to IRA B. HILL and dau. HATTIE MAY

Q/438 WD April 10, 1866 ELIZABETH A. MOORE sur. wife, MARTIN MOORE decd. to JOHN HANCOCK, both TCT, WIT: JOSIAH FISK, JAMES F. BROWN. Ack. by J. FISK before PETER B. LOWE

B/59. 1/2, WD July 16, 1845 JAMES P. WALLACE to ROBERT L. REDDING "My donation cert. for 1 league of land granted and donated by Congress of the REPUBLIC of TEXAS for and in consideration of wounds received in the service of said REPUBLIC, dated Bastrop Co. Dist. Ct. Fall Term 1841" ATTEST: H. COCHERON, N. BOYCE

D/14 Feb.111 1849 WD WM. R. REDING et ux ISABELLA M. to PEYTON W. NOWLIN, Bastrop Co. Texas

D/15 QC Feb. 19, 1849 JANE E. REDING et ux of ROBERT S. Bastrop Co. to PEYTON W. NOWLIN

62/60 SWD Sept. 4. 1884 ANNIE E. LESUER of Williamson Co. Tex; SUSAN B. RANDOLPH et vir C. B., LUCY A. DANCY, widow TCT heirs at law of PEYTON W. & MARTHA M. NOWLIN decd. to ADDIE ROBINSON & MARY O.DINKINS TCT: NOTE: D. N. ROBINSON d. Aug. 21, 1888 PC TCT and willed all property to wife, ADDIE

93/71 deed Mar. 19, 1890 MARY O. DINKINS fs. to ADDIE ROBINSON fs. TCT to E. T. MOORE, W. J. MONTGOMERY, JOHN B. RECTOR, THAD. A THOMPSON R. M. THOMSON & JAMES H. ROBERTSON, TCT

185/182 aff. Jan. 21, 1903 by ADDIE ROBINSON, widow, dau. of PAYTON W. NOWLIN et ux MARTHA M., both decd. m. 1 time only, CH: ANNIE E. LeSUEUR, SARAH B. RANDOLPH, LUCY A. DANCY, MARY O. DINKINS & ADDIE ROBINSON, 2 sons and a dau. MATTIE J. & PEYTON D. & DRURY who died before parents died, all single and not married

266/17 AGREEMENT Mar. 16, 1914 shows W. P. COCHRAN of Oklahoma City Ok. and OTTO EBELING, TCT.

338/304 Deed and disolution of WILDBAHN LAND CO. Dec. 30, 1921; MRS. LUCY H. MARTIN, et vir, JOHN H., of San Saba Co. Tex; EDGAR E.TOWNS, Harris Co. Tex., MRS. ANNE T. FINCH et vir H. H. FINCH, TCT, JOHN C. TOWNES, JR. Harris Co. Tex and JNO. C. TOWNES, SR., TCT

364/267 WD MRS. LUCY H. MARTIN, widow, San Saba Co. Tex. JNQ. C.TOWNES atty. for ANNA T. FINCH and hus. HERBERT H. FINCH, EDGAR E. TOWNES and JNO. C. TOWNES, JR., Harris Co. to C. M. KELLA, TCT

A/166 Aug. 23, 1840 Mtg. JOHN R. SLOCUMB & HORACE PRESTON SAVERY $300. notes for money or its equivalent in Texas money and Negro Girl: CAROLINE. WIT: J. MINER, GEORGE R. TULON, before J. W. SMITH, CJ & EX O. Endorsed: "SAM WHITING to pay for recording Clerk's fee $1.31 and Notary fee $1.00"

26/535 WD May 13, 1874 P. W. HALL et ux SARAH J. of Robertson Co. Tex F. M. HALL, et ux ANNIE, also Robertson Co. to GEO. W. GLASSCOCK, ELIZABETH J. LOGAN, TCT, ALBERT H. GLASSCOCK, Williamson Co. Tex. and ANDREW J. GLASSCOCK, Williamson Co. Tex.

DC 3484 Filed June 6, 1873, ELIZABETH J. LOGAN, div. A. T. LOGAN and Sept. 11, 1876 she m. S. G. TALBOT

126/605 DEED to CARL FUHRMANN, City of Austin

414/179 AFF. Feb. 7, 1938, GEORGE PETER HACKENBERG d. City of Austin, Jan. 8, 1904 m. CAROLINE von SCHAACK d. April 30, 1908, at Caxachie NY married Jan. 8, 1854, 3 CH: MAE DANNIE b. 1858 m. 1877 J. M. THORNTON, JAMES b. 1857 d. Springfield, Ohio, 1862; NEWTON b. 1860 d. Springfield Ohio 1862, CH. of MAE DANNIE THORNTON, GEORGE H. THORNTON and JAMES J. THORNTON, killed in railway accident Hidalgo Co. Texas, unm

906/240 PATENT Feb. 22, 1842 REPUBLIC OF TEXAS to THOMAS W. SMITH

PC 54, ESTATE THOS. W. SMITH d. Aug. 6, 1841, REBECCA SMITH, refused to act and HARVEY SMITH appointed administrator.

D/79 WD Nov. 30, 1849 LORENZO VANCLEVE, heir THOS. W. SMITH

D/94 WD Dec. 7, 1849 FENWICK SMITH heir THOMAS W. SMITH

F/197 deed Jan. 17, 1853 WM. SMITH of Starr Co. Tex., heir THOMAS W. SMITH

D/426 deed Sept. 30, 1850 HARVEY SMITH to WM. H. CUSHNEY

PC 165 EST. WM. H. CUSHNEY d. Nov. 24, 1852 at Independence, Washington Co. Texas. wife was LYDIA JANE, 2 minor ch: MARY JANE 6 years, and WILLIAM H., JR. 7 years. Jan. 29, 1855, MARY JANE CUSNEY m...BURLESON

170/377 PA May 10, 1911 MAMIE E. von KRAMER et vir F. C. of Frankfort on Main, Prussia German Empire, she was dau. WALTER TIPS to A. C. GOETH & EUGENE TIPS.

F/324 PA ack. Mar 29, 1853 WM. COCKBURN ack. San Francisco Co. Calif. to GEORGE JOHN DURHAM, TCT. WIT: D. C. CADY, W. W. LYON before WM. H. RHODES, commissioner of Texas for California

H/337 WD July 21, 1855 JOSEPH WRIGHT to K. L. HARRALSON, G. M. FLOURNOY A. L. ROBARDS.

K/261 WD Feb. 23, 1856 MARCIA P. CHALMERS et vir ALEXANDER H. CHALMERS to DAVID HEFFINGTON, WM. LONG

DC 3049 TCT PHILIP JOBE & JNO. H. ROBINSON vs. H. LACY et ux M. A (formerly wife of WM. E. LONG, decd.) JOSEPHINE LONG, wife of JOHN LONG, decd. son of WM. LONG, decd. LUCINDA LONG & VIRGINIA LONG, minor children of WM. E. LONG decd. all of Houston Co. Texas

26/600 deed June 3, 1874, MARTHA . LACY, relict of WM. E. LONG, decd. Lake Waco, Tex., LUCINDA E. & EMILY J. LONG only sur. ch. of WM. E. LONG, decd. Houston Co. Texas.

BAPTIST CHURCH: Freindship Baptist Church in Hays Co. Barton Creek on Long Branch between Cedar Valley & Fitzhugh (TCT) split as of Dec.1860 to SHILOH SCHOOL near Oak Hill (TCT) and became FRIENDSHIP BAPTIST CHURCH 1870; other group remained BARTON CREEK BAPTIST CHURCH, MACADONIA BAPTIST CHURCH in Webberville (TCT) 1851; ONION CREEK BAPTIST CHURCH 1857 and CREEDMOORE BAPTIST CHURCH 1890.

39/583 Jan. 22, 1878 J. H. WOFFORD to EMILY WEEMS (formerly FORD) DC 4180 EMILY VANGRANDT m. DR. WOFFARD Ch: HENRY, ROBERT DAVIS: then m. DR. JOSEPH ROWE ch: HORACE ROWE, EMILY ROWE m. FORD, (2) WEEMS & (3) CH. ARTHUR ROWE d. unm and JOSEPHINE

398/220 PATENT March 11, 1841 to WILLIAM LEWIS, SR.

PETER MANSBENDEL, was a Swiss woodcarver, and made fine furniture for years and years in Austin.

G/283 Transfer of certificate Mar. 6, 1838 WILLIAM LEWIS, SR. and wife
ELIZABETH of Zavala, Jasper Co. Tex. to THOS. B. HULING, same co. ack.
before A. G. PARKER, CCC Jasper Co. Tex. WIT: PALMON SHERWOOD, HARDY
PACE

G/282 deed July 26, 1843 JAMES LEWIS of Polk Co Tex. to son WM. LEWIS
G/284 deed Aug. 9, 1852 JOHN P. LEWIS of Jasper Co. Tex. to son WM. LEWIS

31/285 deed Oct. 6, 1855 SINGLETON F. THOMPSON (S. G.) to ISAAC HAMMETT
WIT: JACKSON HAMMETT, JOHN T. PRUITT Oct. 1, 1872. ISAAC HAMMETT et ux
MARTHA (X)

42/169 deed Feb. 25, 1878 heirs of THOS. B. HULING decd. Lampasas Co.
Tx. to ELIZABETH, JOHN A. HULING, ALAMANTA BARTLETT et ux of J. C.
WM. N. HULING et ux SAIDIE R., HENRY HILL et ux R. D., M. B. HULING
THOMAS HULING by W. W. BLAKE, atty. TILFORD BEAN, I.V.DEAN (BEAN)

Aff. Dec. 9, 1910 HENRY B. MILLARD son of COL. HENRY MILLARD, d.about
1843, member of firm THOS. B. HULING & CO. dissolved Jan. 20, 1839.
2 Ch. affiant and FREDERICK S. MILLARD d. years ago.

208/202 aff. by MARTHA E. HOTCHKISS, her father was WM. S. HOTCHKISS d.
about 1889, Austin m. (1) HANNAH B. PUCKETT, 1841 she d. 1852 left 4
Ch: MARY E. HOTCHKISS m. JOHN CHAMPION, CORELIA T. m. (1) JAMES L.BROWN
d. 4 years later (2) m. ROBERT H. WILLENBURG, left 1 ch. MABLE who m.
WILLIAM F. DIETRICH, CORELIA T. H. d. Sept. 1879; WM. HOTCHKISS m. (2)
MARY E. had: WM. HENRY d. 1886, leaving widow MRS. KATE WESTFALL
HOTCHKISS and 1 ch. RALPH d. at 18 y; OSCAR T. HOTCHKISS, now living;
MILTON S. HOTCHKISS, now living and DeWITT H. HOTCHKISS, now living.

PC 362 ESTATE HUGH TINNIN, Decd. 1866, MARY H. TINNIN, surviving wife

T/104 PATENT Mar. 8, 1849 WM. S. HOTCHKISS, assignee of SAML. G.HAYNIE

611/517 PATENT to ISIAH KIRBY, June 14, 1863.

Q/41 April 20, 1839 ISIAH KIRBY, JR., Montgomery Co. Tex. to CYRUS
DICKERMAN & N. D. WESTCOTT same Co. WIT: WM. N. BOWEN, SIGNEY BARRETT
MICAJAH BARRETT, ack. Grimes Co. Tex. G. M. MOONING clk. Dec. 31,
1862, by SIDNEY BARRETT, witness

Q/42 April 27, 1838 R. D. WESTCOTT & CYRUS DICKERMAN, WIT: WM. McRAE,
SIDNEY BARRETT

P/541 deed May 1, 1844 MICAJAH BARRETT to FRANCIS BRICHTA. WIT: L.ROSE
C. MYER of La. Parish & City of New Orleans by L. ROSE before J. M.
HOLLAND, Commissioner of Tex. Mar. 14, 1846, ENDORSEMENT: MICAJAH
BARRETT to BRICHTA June 14, 1839 WIT: M. H. BEATY, THOS. W. CAMPFULL

PC 198 Dec. 26, 1854 FRANCIS BRICHTA, SR. d. Dec. 14, 1854, New Orleans
La. by wife, AMELIA, he d. intestate and FRANCIS BRICHTA, JR., was
bondsman; JAMES M. LITTLE, NATHANIEL TOWNSEND, sureties, and S. M.
SWENSON

602/546 PATENT to heirs of J. A. MILLER, dec. April 29, 1871

48/539 deed April 5, 1862 CHAS. W. MILLER, extr. andlegatee JOSEPH A.
MILLER to THOMAS ANDERSON, Bastrop Co. Texas

293/332 cc Transfer of cert. of PATENT April 29, 1863, heirs of MICHAEL
PEVETO, decd. MICHAEL PEVETO, SR. to WM. ARMSTRONG says: PATENT TO JR.
son of Sr. who died in army of Tx. near Harrisburg (Houston) WIT:
H. B. & A. E. FORCE, Orange Co. Tex.; JANE ARMSTRONG d. prior to
death of husband, WILLIAM who d. April 9, 1871; JAMES ARMSTRONG sole
devisee 1885 was of age

Q/182 Feb. 20, 1864 JOHN HARRELL to NICHOLS HAYS, JNO. M. KING &
W. H. D. CARRINGTON, ack. Williamson Co. Tex.
605/347 PATENT to WM. A.KING, April 8, 1863.

PC 1353 ESTATE WM. A. KING, d. April 22, 1888 TCT.

P/540 June 20, 1861 PATENT to FRANKLIN JOHNSTON

605/348 PATENT Jan. 2, 1890 to THOMAS ANDERSON, assignee of O. W. NICHOLS, confederate Script Oct. 10, 1881 and trsf. ANDERSON Jan. 10, 1889

MILTON A. THORP, b. Mar. 3, 1847, wife MARY TENNESEE JOLLY b. May 13, 1854 in TCT. CHILDREN:
JOHN WM. THORPE b. 1873 d. Big Springs, Tex. 1948; NANCY ELIZABETH b. July 25, 1875, Austin m. G. H. MAYS, Sr. he d. San Marcos, Tex, 1946; MARY JANE b. April 26, 1879, m. JEFFERSON BARNES; DORA b. 1881 m. CARL B. WITHROS, Mexia, Tex.; CHARLES JEFFERSON THORP b. 1883 d. TCT 1938. MELVIN M. b. 1885 TCT; CHRISTI ANN b. 1887 d. 1940 m. LAWRENCE FERGUSON d. 1930; CARRIE b. 1889 d. 1930 m. MARSHALL FERRELL, he lives in Round Rock, Tex. ERA PEARL b. May 18, 1890 m. B. N. PAYTON, he d. Aug. 12 1937; MABEL JULIA b. 1892 d. 1953 m. WALTER NEAL he d. before 1953; and an infant b & d July 25, 1896, Jollyville TCT. B. N. PAYTON & ERA PEARL THORP had NORMAN PAYTON b. Sept. 6, 1914; JOY THRUMAN, b. Nov.20, 1916, Harris Co. Tex. MABEL JULIA b. Jan. 20, 1918 m. FRANK KUNZE, Corpus Christi, Tex. JOEL BRADFORD a twin son and his twin GERALD LEE b. Sept. 26, 1919 d. Dec. 1, 1919; HOMER LEON b. Mar. 24, 1921, St. Louis Mo. dau. b & d 1923; DANIEL RUFUS PAYTON and wife AMANDA JOURDAN m.1865 in Caldwell Co. Tex; JOHN WESLEY b. June 11, 1866 TCT d. Sept. 30,1929 m. LaRUE LENTZ, EPHRAM b. 1869 d. June 27, 1940, Lubbock, Tex. m.... MAGGY FULKS, ANDREW b. 1873 d. Feb. 5, 1938 in northwest Tex. m. KATE FULKS, JANE b. 1875 d. 1896, sw; EULA LEE b. Oct. 2, 1877, DORA b. 1881 m. CHARLEY O. PALMER, DARRELL RUFUS b. and d 1879; BRADFORD N. b. June 2, 1885 d. 1931

D/728 Aug. 15, 1850 Tax deed JOHN CARROLL, Tax assessor and collector to J. M. W. HALL, WIT: WARREN L. THOMAS, GEO. H. GRAY

39/130 WD Mar. 11, 1875 JOSEPH HARRELL to J. D. HUNT, of Fayette Co. Tex. WIT: DENNIS CORWIN, J. B. GILDART, J. M. DENTON

41/27 deed April 29, 1878 JOHN D. HUNT to MARRIE E. HUNT (wife?) both of Fayette Co. Tex. ack. THOMAS O. MULLEN, Clk. FCT

50/280 WD Oct. 25, 1881 J. D. HUNT et ux M. E. late of Fayette Co. now of Bell Co. Tex. to W. T. & M. A. BUSH of Bell Co. Tex.

64/15 cc ESTATE W. T. BUSH decd. Inv. property in Waco and TCT; M. C. BUSH, H. WRIGHT, W. H. HARKEY notes, also T. HILL, CHAS. MORROW, L. H. DAVIS notes, charged MRS. E. M. KING and notes and interest etc. as per statements etc. of div. & c. M. T. BUSH & E. M. KING, W. K. HAMBLIN, M.W. DOURON, chosen by heirs of W. T. BUSH, deed to partition their father's estate only 4 lawful heirs, viz: E. M. KING (MRS.W.M.). CATHERINE BUSH, ANNIE BUSH & McT. BUSH. ACK. CATHERINE & ANNIE & McT. BUSH Nov. 23, 1883 before W. H. BURGESS, JP & EX. O NP

64/18 cc W. T. & MARY A. BUSH, inv. she is family of MRS. MARY A. PAINE, homestead in Salado, Bell Co. Tex.

64/23 PA Feb. 1, 1884 CATHERINE BUSH of Hamilton Co. Tex. to McT. BUSH Bell Co. before SIMPSON LOYD, JP NP Feb. 25, 1884

64/24 Wd June 19, 1884 ANN BUSH HEBITS et vir J. C. of Hamilton Co. Tex. McT. BUSH, Bell Co. Texas

93/387 PA May 14, 1890 THOS. MORRALL to SON BENJAMIN MORRALL
97/125 WD Oct. 9, 1890 E. M. KING et vir of Tarrant Co. Tex. to J. H. HENDERSON, M. A. KOPPERL, THEODORE B. COMSTOCK, CHAS. L. CONDIT, JAMES C. NAGLE, F. M. COVERT & E. F. McCARTY

459/550 cc Los Angeles, Calif. THEO. BRYANT COMSTOCK decd. he d.July 26, 1915, res. Los Angeles, Calif. WILL dated Mar. 11, 1897; BLANCHE HUGGINS COMSTOCK, 55 y. of Los Angeles, sur. wife; Bros. and sisters:

ARTHUR, decd. GEO., EDWARD & ARTHUR, all over 21 of Cleveland, Ohio; ELLA COMSTOCK RODGERS 60 years, sister of Atlanta, Ga., RAYMOND COMSTOCK, bro. 54, Kansas City, Mo., ANNA M. COMSTOCK 52, Kansas City Mo. JESSIE R. COMSTOCK 50 of Kansas City, Mo. WILL: THEODOR BRYANT COM= STOCK of Prescott Co. Yavapi, Territory of Arizona to wife, BLANCHE HUGGINS COMSTOCK, WIT: R. E. SLOAN, HENRY J. STEIL.

A/180 Mtg. Nov. 23, 1840 H. W. HAMMER to LAMAR MOORE, trustee, L. S. HANCOCK. WIT: J. R. MILLER, GOLDEN DENMAN

A/243 trustee's deed Dec. 26, 1840 LAMAR MOORE, trustee to D. W. C. VARY,. WIT: JOHN M. SHREVE, IRA MUNSON

A/244 deed Feb. 6, 1941 D. W. C. VARY to WM. S. ORR, before M. H. BEATY CCC TCT, WIT: CHAS. deMERSE, WM. C. BEVINS

136/599CONFIRMATION July 5, 1882 JOHN deKALB THOMPSON, of Tipton Co. Tenn. only child of NANCY H. THOMPSON settlement of his g.father,ABNER MATTHEWS, est. d. TCT 1867, J.DeK. THOMPSON, mother NANCY H. THOMPSON was represented by E. S. M. MATTHEWS, PA Sept. 29, 1866, rec. R/30 before D. BROWN, NP Tipton Co. Tenn

66/356 WD Jan. 13, 1886 E. S. MATTHEWS et ux E. J. of Limestone Co.Tex.

142/60 aff. April 28, 1896 by E. S. MATTHEWS, son ABNER MATTHEWS d. 1863 et ux ASCENATH MATTHEWS d. 1851 TCT only marriage 11 ch:(2nd. m. before his death): MARY D. m. ROBERT E. FLANIKEN, JAMES H. MATTHEWS, JOHN C. MATTHEWS, ESTER H. MATTHEWS, E. S. MATTHEWS, ELIZABETH J. wife of BANYAN PAYNE, MARTHA MATTHEWS m. P. A. MONROE, he d. 1864-5; NANCY H. also called AGNES H. MATTHEWS d. prior to 1880 wife of ROBERT A. THOMPSON and d. prior 1880; ROBERT F. MATTHEWS, all over 21,Jan.1,1867

36/3 WD Sept. 23, 1876 EDWARD SEIDERS (surviving heirs LOUISA) to sons HENRY B. SEIDERS & PINKNEY W. SEIDERS

36/6 partition deed Sept. 13, 1876 LOUISA W. SEIDERS d. TCT Feb. 1,1854 leaving hus. EDWARD SEIDERS, 3 sons EDWARD G., HENRY B., & PINKNEY W.

B/18 PATENT REPUBLIC OF TEXAS Nov. 24, 1841 to MONROE BLESSING

C/381 Sept. 29, 1846 WD HENRY BLESSING toMARTIN MOORE, WIT. P. ENGELBACK, WM. LEFTWICH, ZILLER MACHAEL. Blessing of Comal Co. Tex.

PC 1942 filed Nov. 6, 1895 ALBERT F. BUDINGTON D. Oct. 15, 1895 no will left wife, REBECCA V. and minor daus. FANNIE LANE, wifeof H. S., MAUD JOHNSON wife of T. J. D. JOHNSON & IDA MASSEY wife of ANDREW MASSEY, CARRIE BOOKER fs. and RALPH W. BUDDINGTON, son.

247/186 Aff. 1911 by T. B. COCKRAN an atty. JOHN SPARKS, governor of Nevada 1908, d. 1908

326/400 aff. Nov. 15, 1920 by MRS. MARY JANE GILL, widow; BEN THOMPSON was her bro. he m. KATE L. MOORE, BEN T. D. 1884, San Antonio, leaving wife and BEN, JR. who d. 1893 intestate and unm & KATE F., who is now m. to JOE B. PRICE and lives in Bastrop Co. Tex., KATE m.....BAKER (?) and lived in Paris, Texas, MRS. BAKER did not have a child orchildren.

340/406 Aff. 1922 MRS. CARRIE SIMMONS 60 years of age, wife of DAVID P. was dau. of A. G. BUDDINGTON

I/462 Mtg. May 3, 1855 NATHANIEL TOWNSEND to RANDOLPH W. TOWNSEND of NY City. WIT: JOHN B. COSTA, A. B. McGILL

51/268 WD Dec. 31, 1881, JAS. H. RAYMOND to PETER HANNIFORD et ux MILLIE

50/574 Wd Nov. 1, 1881 PETER HANIFORD, et ux MILLIE to CHAS. WOLF.

115/213 Mtg. PETER HANIFORD, JAMES HANIFORD, JOSEPH HANIFORD & SUSAN NICHOLS et vir W. M.

255/326 aff. Mar. 1, 1913 JOSEPH HARRIFORD (HEREFORD, HARRIFORD, HAIRIFORD) son of PETER. These were ex-slaves

256/327 AFF. Feb. 24, 1913 by MRS. SUSIE M. ROBERTSON fs. dau.NATHANIEL & ANGELINA L. TOWNSEND; father m. (1) MARIA & (2) ANGELINA L. d. prior to July 28, 1865; MARIA had 3 ch. d. as infants and BENJ. R. TOWNSEND.

227/482 APPOINTMENT Oct. 14, 1908 JAMES BYRNE of MAMIE BRYNE, WILL, P.C. 4241 TCT appoints TIMOTHY & ROGER BYRNE, bros. and sister MRS. MARY C. LEONARD, and Nephew JOHN BYRNE extrs. CH. MARY C. LEONARD, MRS. E. D. BOND, MARGUERITE, MILES, JR. and JAMES LEONARD, Dau. MRS. ROGER BYRNE, Ft. Worth, Tarrant Co. Tex. bro. PATRICK BYRNE of Rolaugh, Parish of Kilcar, Co. Donegal, Ireland; cousin JOHN HEGARTY of Shalvey, Parish of Kilcar, County of Donegal, Ireland; cousin MISS MARY McBREARTY of same; niece MISS MARGARET McGUIRE, Coraghbeg, Parish of Kilcar..; nephews JOHN BYRNE and niece MISS BRIDGET BYRNE, CH. of decd. bro. JOHN & ROGER, his wife, MRS. R. H. BURNE her maiden name being MAMIE BYRNE, my dau. DC TCT 39,012 MAGGIE McBREARTY LOUGHRAN, ANNIE McBREARTY FORD in addition to the above in will.

400/250 Aff. Re: MRS. MARY C. LEONARD, MILES LEONARD, JR., and wife, LANIER b. Feb. 9, 1900; MISS MARY McBREARTY d. prior to Jan. 28, 1922; left JOHN McB., ANNIE McB. FORD and MAGGIE McB. LOUGHRAN, bros. and sisters of MARY MARGARET LEONARD m. LOFTON C. WELLS.

A/4 deed GEORGE W. SPEAR, Fayette Co. Tex. July 10, 1838 to NORMAN WOODS WIT: JAMES ROBERTSON, WM. M. ROBINSON, mar. 9, 1839.

A/5 deed Mar. 9, 1839 NORMAN WOODS, Fayette Co. Tex. to NICHOLAS McARTHUR of Bastrop Co. Tex.

A/5 deed Feb. 10, 1840 NICHOLAS McARTHUR to THOS. G. GORDON, JOSEPH MORELAND & MIRABEAU B. LAMAR, before JAMES S. SMITH CJ TCT

A/108 Rel. Sept. 1, 1840 A. C. MacFARLANE to THOS. G. GORDON note to DICKINSON (DICKERSON) & McFARLAN. WIT: P.W. HUMPHREYS, WAYNE BARTON

A/145 deed Sept. 2, 1840 THOS. G. GORDON to JAMES A. COLWELL, WIT: SAML. R. MILLER, JAMES F. EDRINGTON

E/101 partition Nov...1840 mentions D. K. WEBB,SR.sgd.MIRABEAU B. LAMAR, THOS G. GORDON, HARVEY KENDRICH, ROB POTTER. WIT: S. R. MILLER & J.D.PARKS

F/391 deed Nov. 27, 1853 JOSEPH MORELAND, Macon Co. Ala. to JAMES B.SHAW TCT. WIT: ROBERT DAUGHERTY, Judge Circuit Ct. Ala.

E/108 PA April 27, 1850 JOSEPH McFARLAND, Tuskogee, Macon Co. Ala. to. WM. F. Moreland, same co. before LOUIS ALEXANDER cc Macon Co. Ala.

F/330 PA filed 1853 MIRABEAU B. LAMAR of Galveston Co. Tex. to WASHINGTON L. HILL, TCT, before A. F. JONES NP TCT

H/140 deed Nov. 24, 1854 T. J. CHAMBERS of liberty Co. Tex. to JOHN W. HARRIS, Matagorda Co., Tex. WIT: JOHN B. COSTA, A. B. McGILL, cc TCT

DC 11,093 filed May 15, 1893 D. W. THOMPSON vs. D. W. & BELLE BOULDIN, parents of D. W. BOULDIN, JR. and on Sept. 4, 1888 residing Sadalia, Pettis Co. Mo.

PC 1739 May 15, 1893 D. W. THOMPSON of Sedalia Mo. representing D. W. BOULDIN, JR. d. Ariz. Sept...1889 unm

DC 124730 TTT, MONTANDON vs. SAML. G. POWELL et al filed June 12, 1962: TCT JAMES ROGERS (RODGERS) et ux RACHAEL, EDWARD H. ROGERS et ux (1) L. A. (2) SALLY; JOSEPH B. ROGERS, THOMAS H. JONES, MARY E. HARDEMAN, (she acknowledged as ELIZABETH) wife of WM. M., SARAH B. BURDITT, et ux of MINAS G., BENJ. T. GAULT, and wife, NANCY L, JAMES C. MAXWELL, THOS BIRD, et ux POLLY ANN, TRIMBLE BIRD, JOE BIRD, OLIVER BIRD, TOM BIRD, WILLIE BIRD, I. B. BIRD, J. W. BIRD, JOHN W. BIRD et ux S. E.,WILEY AYERS, SALLY AYERS, WM. R. BIRD, AARON BURLESON, J. W. BURLESON, GILES H. BURDITT, JESSIE H. BIRDITT, admr. EST. NEWELL W. BURDITT, A. W. DAV- IDSON, J. T. McLAURIN, GEO. SANDERS, OSWALD PALMER, ALEX. HALL, JOHN A. HALL, et ux NELIA, SALLIE HOLMAN, widow, MRS. O. H. HOLMAN, WIDOW MARY E. BIRD, widow, MARY LEE, RHODA LEE, LIZZIE ELLIOTT, MRS. D. E. GRIFFIN, nee MAGGIE BIRD, et vir D. E., J. G. DRAPER (he acknowledged asJOSEPH G.) et ux DESSIE, EDWARD ALLEN PALMER son of OSWALD PALMER.

102/10 WD Jan. 8, 1902 and aff. heirship (Vol.363/581 & 359/61) W. E. ROGERS, and former wife, S. A. EGGER to CH: DORA GRUMBLES, et vir W.E. McCALL GRUMBLES, ELLEN m. AUSTIN D. DORRENBERGER, LULA m. HENRY WALKER and she d. Brown Co. Tex. Mar. 22, 1932 and he d. Stonewall Co. Tex. O Oct. 2, 1942; NORMAN m. OLIVE, WM. m. DORA, FRANK m. ETHEL, EVELYN m. N. S. MILLER, JESSIE m. ..McCUTCHEON, ROBT., LAURA DORRENBERGER (DC 4333 condemnation Nov. 23, 1940, vs. above and H. N. EGGER, R. L. EGGER, W. C. EGGER, W. C. DAFFLEMEYER, B. F. EGGER, MRS. A. L. DORREN= BERGER, SHELLY WALKER & H. S. WALKER, MRS. W. O. CAPE, for LULA who m. HENRY WALKER, Ch: WALNEITTE who m. W. O. CAPE & H. S. WALKER, SHELLY WALKER, EDWARD HUDSON, ARCHIE MORRISON, assignee Feb. 26, 1876; EPHRAIM TOUNGATE et ux C. A. to J. (JOSEPH) WILLIAMS et ux EMELINE (PC 5469) & PC 6785) MILLIE ANN RUTH HARRIS et vir to JOSEPH MUNSON 1869 & ARCHIE MORRISONto JOSEPH WILLIAMS 1876, EMMELIE WILLIAMS (Vol. 612/242) 1/5 MARY CRUMLEY, 1/5 W. T. WILLIAMS et ux DORA T. 1/5 J. HENRY WILLIAMS, 1/5 LOU MYERS, Hays Co. 1/5 ch. of MARTHA HARDIN, LONCESCIA WILKES, wife of JOE, MARTIN HARDIN, Burnet Co. ALAN HARDIN, J. M. STREET,OSCAR COLLINS, et ux BERTIE C. (Vol. 468/380) DORA T. WILLIAMS to JOE, BEN, ALBERT, EUELL CRUMLEY, LAURA BURT, et vir ERVIE, AUSTIN COLLINS, OLETA CRUMLEY PHILLIPS et vir CLEVE & HENRY WILLIAMS, ELMER CRUMLEY & LOU MYERS.

143/109 Oct. 28, 1887 THOMAS BIRD & J. B. (I. B.) BIRD, Williamson Co. Tex., SALLIE HOLMAN, widow, MRS. O. H. HOLMAN, widow, MARY E. BIRD, widow, WILIE BIRD, TOM BIRD, MARY. LEE, TCT, OLIVER BIRD, Nueces Co. Tex. to ESTATE POLLY ANN BIRD, decd. TRIMBLE BIRD (ALSO TRUMBLE)

G/703 Feb. 6, 1867 THOMAS BIRD et ux PÓLLY ANN, WILY & SALLY AYERS

Z/550 Feb. 4, 1874, WM., J. W. & J. B. BIRD

41/403 June 12, 1877 JOHN W. BIRD et ux S. E. to WM. R. BIRD

58/196 Nov. 26, 1883 JNO. W. BIRD et ux to THOMAS BIRD

PATENT May 13, 1880 to THOMAS WARD

64/625 WD Sept. 2, 1885 THOS. WOOD WARD et ux ADDA of San Saba,Co. Tex to LITTLEBERRY A. ELLIS, Fort Bend Co. Tex. before J. W. THOMAS, NP San Saba Co. Tex

80/45 WD Mar. 24, 1888 LITTLEBERRY A. ELLIS et ux AMANDA M. of TCT to JOHN CROSSLEY & SONS, LTD. (Corp. of Kingdom of Great Britton,Halifax, Yorkshire, England.
PA 86/152 Aug. 22, 1888 JOHN CROSLEY etc. to HENRY LAWRENCE GILL of NY agreement, EDWARD CROSSLY, G. MARCHITTI, directors of JOHN CROSSLEY,LTD JNO. LEACH, secy. WM. THOS. deWHIRST, DEAN CLOUGH MILLS, HALIFAC and W. M. SUDERLAND, HANSON LANE, HALIFAX, ack. BODEREY RHODES, NP Halifax W. F. GRINNEL, US consulate

84/526 WD April 1, 1889,JOHN CROSSLEY, LTD. to HERMAN WRONKOW of NY WIT: GEO. B.LAUCK & SYLENAS T.CANNON.Cert. by EDW. F. REIELY, CLK.C.NY

86/335 WD June 2, 1889 HERMAN WRONKOW et ux SERENA of New York to LITTLEBERRY A. ELLIS, TCT. WIT: M. CALHOUN KELLY, GRIFFEN THOMKINS, New York, ack.

118/606 WD Nov. 10, 1898, L. A. ELLIS et ux AMANDA to M. H. McLAURIN, J. B. SMITH, TCT. WIT: W. J. JOHNSON ack. by M. H. McLAURIN before E. M. BACON, NP TCT ack. JAMES B. SMITH before WM. J. STORMS, acting US Consular agent Jan. 22, 1894, State of Tamaupeas, City of Victoria,Mex.

115/308 Mtg. Jan. 11, 1896 JAMES B. SMITH TCT to DILLWYN PARRISH, JAMES BROWN POTTER

108/91 PA Jan. 8, 1891 DILLWYN PARRISH, JAMES BROWN POTTER to R. L. BROWN & J. GORDON BROWN, DILLWYN PARRISH before H. H. NEWMAN, consulate genral USA London and JAMES BROWN POTTER before JNO. C. NEW, Consul Genl. GEORGE C. HITT, Vice Consul Gen. London

136/132 SWD July 6, 1895 M. H. McLAURIN, JAMES B. SMITH to L. A. ELLIS

110/64 CONSTABLE'S DEED Sept. 3, 1895 J. M. DAVIS, CONST. P. C. 3 TCT (GEORGE S. CRISER & MASSIE vs. M. H. McLAURIN) to GEORGE S. CRISER

PC 2052 EST. L. A. ELLIS decd. & EST. minor LEIGH ELLIS apl. by AMANDA MITCHELL ELLIS, Mar. 16, 1897; LITTLEBERRY AMBROSE ELLIS d. Dec. 11, 1896; had land TCT, Sarbartea, Ft. Bend Co. Tex. Mount Homas, Southwood & Riverside Plantations, Ascension Parish, La. AMANDA MITCHELL ELLIS Extrx. and guardian of minor children INDIA MYRTLE (called DOROTHY) & LEIGH ELLIS, other CH. CASWELL G. ELLIS, EMMETTA A. ELLIS, PINK OWEN dau. wife of DAVID A. TURNER of Wilbarger Co. Tex.

DC 13,423 Ex Parte DOROTHY ELLIS April 12, 1897 removal of disabilities of minority, EUGENE WILLIAMS of McLENNAN Co. Tex. special guardian

108/397 PA April 12, 1897 AMANDA MITCHELL ELLIS sur. wife of L. A. ELLIS decd. INDIA MYRTLE (DOROTHY) ELLIS, EMET A. ELLIS of Fort Bend Co. Tex. and C. C. ELLIS of Ascension Parish, La. & PINK OWEN TURNER et vir D. A. TURNER, Fort Bend Co. Texas to C. G. ELLIS

174/168 CONTRACT Sept. 15, 1898 between MRS. AMANDA N. ELLIS et al and INDIA MYRTLE ELLIS Now wife of DAVID HARRELL and they ack. before T. B. COCHRAN

Mtg. 189/624 Mtg. April 24, 1904 by AMANDA M. ELLIS widow AND C. G. ELIS et ux OLIVE GRAVES ELLIS

227/261 cc WILL, C. G. ELLIS decd. from Fort Bend Co. Tex. 1906 to wife OLIVE GRAVES ELLIS says she is trusted with "our child" not named.

217/610 WD Feb. 23, 1908 AMANDA M. ELLIS, widow, LEIGH ELLIS et ux FRANCES T. TCT,OLIVE GRAVES ELLIS, Bexar Co. Tex. to H. E. FORD

226/570QC INDIA M. E. HARRELL et ux DAVID, TCT, DAVID A. TURNER, admr. EST PINK OWEN TURNER, CASSIE & RITA LEORA TURNER, SUE TURNER BREWSTER et vir E. JEFFERSON BREWSTER, Harris Co. Tex. and ELLIS AMBROSE TURNER of Dallas Co. Tex.

I/32 WD July 7, 1854 H. CORCKERON to L. B. MOORE (LARKEN B.) WIT: JOSIAH FISK, CHARLES BARNES

92/197 Deed April 16, 1880 to A. E. MOORE et ux C. A., WM. T. WILLIAMSON PAROLIC E. MOORE, et vir JOHN MAYES and R. A. MOORE of Hays Co. Tex, DOROTHULA K. MOORE et vir R. B. KYLE, MARY K. MOORE et vir, W. A., CLOPTON & ELIZABETH O. MOORE et vir, J. M. RANSOM, all of Bastrop Co Tex. all children and heirs of L. B. MOORE decd. (A. T. McKEAN & E. T.BENNETT in margin of record says sons MRS. A. C. McKEAN, decd.)

197/380 deed A. E. MOORE et ux SINIE LOU to C. G. JONES

NOTE: DC p. 54 hereof shows names of most of heirs of ED. H. GAULT to JIM GAULT 100 acres part of 535 acres patented to JAMES ROGERS (RODGERS) Heirs of JIM (JAMES R.) GAULT d. Jan. 22, 1955 wife VADA JULIA, CH: RENA G. wife of EARL SMITH, MURIEL GAULT (CLAY) now wife of DON PHILLIPS VADA GAULT, fs. JOE H. GAULT, JAMES R. GAULT, JR.

Heirs of BEN T. GAULT and NANCY ROGERS GAULT: ED H. GAULT d. Dec. 2, 1943, JOE E. d. April 28, 1933; JIM, BEN T. GAULT, JR. d. Mar. 1, 1914; JOHN M. d. Feb. 26, 1936, SARAH ELEN m. GAULT McELROY d. Mar. 13, 1914 RACHEL d. Nov. 29, 1949, never married; MARY B. CEARLEY d. Oct. 23,1950 (No will or probate proceedings on any of these persons)

JAMES ROGERS (RODGERS) and wife RACHEL: ED H. ROGERS, JOSEPH P., MARY E. HARDEMAN, wife of WM. N., SARAH B. BURDETT, wife of MINAS C. and NANCY GAULT wife of BEN T. GAULT, SR.

G/89 PATENT to A. C. CALDWELL Oct. 7, 1848.

C/428 Mtg. Sept. 23, 1848 ASABEL C. CALDWELL of Angelina Co. Tex. to GEORGE BONDIES of Nacogdoches Co. Tex. on land cert. issued by Bd. of Ld. Comrs. in the Co. of Sabine, Texas. WIT: R. A. IRIAN, CHAS. P. TAYLOR, ack. before A. NELSON, NP Nacogdoches Co. Texas.

D/67 Rel. Oct. 10, 1849 GEORGE BONDIES. WIT: NATHL. AMORY, JOHANNES FREDDERSON

C/513 WD May 26, 1848 ASABEL C. CALDWELL et ux LUCY M. of Angelina Co. Tex. to CHARLES CHEVAILLIER of Nacogdoches Co. Tex. WIT: NATHL. AMORY, WM. W. BARRETT

L/287 SWD Jan. 20, 1854 NATHL. AMORY of Nacogdoches Co. Tex. to EGGLES= TON D. TOWNES of Tuscombia,Franklin Co. Ala. WIT: JAMES STACY, RICHARD WALKER, ack. JAMES H. STARR before S. HOLMES ccc NC

E/320 deed May 15, 1847 WM. CLARK, Sabine Co. Tex. to LEANDER C. CUNN- INGHAM, Bastrop Co. Tex. WIT: JOHN M. JACKSON, CURTIS M. JACKSON, WM. B. FRAZER, CCC Sabine Co. Tex.

G/155 deed Oct. 25, 1851 L. C. CUNNINGHAM to MARCUS HULING. WIT: H. COCHERON, JAMES KNIGHT, W. H. FORREST. ack. before WARREN LARKINS,NPBCT

67/1 cc filed TCT Dec. 6, 1885, from Williamson Co. Court Mar. Term 1857 LEVY C. CUNNINGHAM, MARCUS C.HULING, WM. J. J. SCOGGINS, WM. H. HARRIS JAMES BYRON HARRIS,AUGUSTAS V. SMITH & JOHN R. SMITH, her husband; JOHN R. SMITH gd. ad litem; EMMA JANE KYLE, MARTHA T. KYLE by Gd. adl.GEO. W. PASCHAL vs. EGGLESTON B. TOWNES deft. and intervenor infant heirs of WM. H. HARRIS & MARGARET W. HARRIS KYLE. JURY: BENJAMIN ALLEN, JOSIAH DYCHES, JAMES BURRIS, JOHN SHEEL, ISAAC GARNER, PHILLIP MINER, TAYLOR SMITH, JR., JAMES PATTERSON, HENRY F. BAKER, JOSEPH T. MITHVARN, WM.F. VANPELT & WILLIAM ADE (ABE);....EDWARDS, administrator CHARLES CHEVILLIER and his widow. Commissioners appointed: ELIJAH HANSBOROUGH, EDWARD HARRINGTON, ISAAC WILDBAHN, WM. ATTWOOD & THOS. E. ROWE, Judgment June 29, 1857

C/204 cc Williamson Co. Tex. filed TCT Nov. 7, 1860 HAYDEN H. EDWARDS, administrator CHARLES CHEVAILLIER & SARAH C. CHEVAILLIER. Judgment June 29, 1857

A/214 Title Bond Mar. 27, 1840 SEABOURNE JONES WHATLEY, ABNER B. SPEAR to ROBERT M. FORBES. WIT: R. T. SMITH, ALLAN J. DAVIS

A/500 WD Dec.20, 1841 S. J. WHATLEY to ROBERT M. FORBES. WIT: CHAS. F. KING , JOSEPH WAPLES.

F/45 deed April 17, 1852 ROBERT M. FORBES of Calhoun Co. Tex. to LEVI M. BARNARD, WIT: W. M. VARNELL, WM. NICHOLS ack. before JAMES T. LYTLE Np Calhoun Co. Tex.

F/394 Wd Sept. 1, 1853 LEVI BARNARD to GEORGE A. GAMBLE TCT WIT: W. C. MONTGOMERY, JAMES RAGSDALE

F/369 Wd Nov. 16, 1853 WM. P. GAMBLE, GEORGE A. GAMBLE,Bastrop Co. Tex. to EGGLESTON D. TOWNS, WIT: SAML. PORTER

G/409 WD Nov. 18, 1852 LEVI M. BARNARD et ux MARY to EGGLESTON D.TOWNS

285/30 Aff. Mar. 3, 1916 Re: ANDERS J. ANDERSON d. 1892 in Almesaskra Socken in Jonkapings lan Kingdom of..wife CHARLOTTA G. ANDERSON d.same place 1912 CH: CARL J., E. A., OSCAR W., & JOHN ALFRED ANDERSON who emigrated to USA about 8 years ago and d. TCT Jan. 3, 1915

143/341 PATENT Sept. 23, 1880 to FRED FREYTAG, HENRY OSTEN, asgns.I & GN

138/175 Wd June 27, 1894 F. FREITAG to HENRY OTTONS

49/214 deed April 5, 1881 FREDERICK FREITAG TCT to wife CATHARINE ELSA CONVEYS: My gun, mill and all the furniture and stock of cattle branded IF

202/364 WD Feb. 22, 1905 F. FREITAG, a widow, to HENRY F. FREITAG, son WIT: JNO. O. JOHNSON, HERMAN BOHN.

40/576 WD May 13, 1878 F. FREITAG et ux CATHERINE E. (X) to CARL BECK before GEO. G. RUCKER

46/606 WD Sept. 30, 1880 to school, JAMES W. SMITH, Co. Judge, from FREDERICK FREITAG et ux ILSA. WIT: THEO. O.BOHLS, BERNHARDT PECHT

DC 25,978 TCT filed Aug. 21, 1909 WILHELMINA ALTERS, et vir HENRY, HENRIETTA ROBERTS et vir JOSEPH, J. FREDERICK FREITAG & ANNIE HAAS fs ptf. TCT vs...HENRY FREITAG, TCT

235/482 WD Oct. 9, 1909 F. FREITAG et ux ELISE had only: J. F., WILHELMINE F. et vir HENRY ALTERS, ANNA F. HAAS, widow, HENRIETTA F. et vir JOSEPH ROBERTS, HENRY FREITAG, all TCT (Henry's wife was CLARA) ELSIE FREITAG d. Feb. 4, 1903 and F. F. FREITAG d. Mar. 9, 1909

388/193 PATENT to ADAM MAAG June 27, 1846

K/455 WD April 9, 1856 ADAM MAAG of Philadelphia to HENRY THOMAS. WIT: JOHN BINNZ, commissioner of Texas and GEO. W. ASH.

41/105 deed June 28, 1878 HENRY THOMAS of Oakland, Alemeda Co. Calif. to GEORGE LINN of Rapier Co. Calif. WIT: REV. STEEN, R. M. SWANN, before W. M. BOGGS, NP Wapa Co. Calif.

49/323 WD Sept. 14, 1880 GEO. LINN to BEN RADKY

53/117 WD Aug. 10, 1882 GEO. LINN by TOM MURRAH of TCT to A. FAULKNER, Robertson Co. Tex. WIT: J. H. COLLETT, W. C. DENNY

52/277 PA April 7, 1882 GEO. LINN of TCT temporarily of Roswell, Lincoln Co. New Mex. to TOM MURRAH. WIT: A. H. WHETSTONE, JOSEPH C. LEA, before A. H. WHETSTONE, NP Lincoln Territory of New Mexico

WILL: OGLESBY S. PROPHETT, TCT dated Feb. 21, 1891, he d. Mar. 1,1894 filed April 9, 1895, was of Garland Co. Ark.: son WOODSON Z.PROPHETT, MARTHA A. DAVIS, first cousin; HENRY J. BOGGAS of Newton Co. Ga.CODICIL to grandson CHARLES WOODSON PROPHITT son of WOODSON Z. PROPHETT and EMMA C., Floyd Co. Ga.

DC 1563 filed May 7, 1858 TCT ELIAS MOSSON, HERMAN MOSSON, HART SAMUELS vs. JOSEPH WARREN, bondsmen R. M. JACKSON, J. HARRELL, J. W. ROBERTSON & JOSEPH LEE

Transfer of cert. D. J. GILBERT survey (GILBERT was singleman, who came to Texas 1835) dated 1838 S. D. PATTON, JOSIAH WILBARGER, MOSES PAGE, R. B. CRAFT, THOS. H. MAYS, SURveyor of Bastrop Co. Tex. WM.HORNSBY, JAMES ROGERS, chainmen, 1848 JAMES R. PACE, Dist. Surveyor, Travis Dist.L. H. LUCKETT, aptd. to survey, he reports July 15, 1858, GEO. W. DAVIS, JAMES R. PACE, L. H. LUCKETT, W. W. HORNSBY, JAMES ROGERS,ENOCH JOHNSON were summonsed as witnesses, subpeona to THOS. WARD, JAMES F. JOHNSON, JAMES ROGERS, W. W. HORNSBY 1859 refers to bond for title

Mar. 3, 1847 in favor of PETER MacGREAL Feb. 4, 1858 statement of facts; THOS. H. MAYS, he in Feb. 1838 as surveyor with GEO. HANCOCK, CECIL BURLESON and about 20 or 30 others (not named) mostly land owners between TANNEHILL survey and upper corner of SPEAR, thence to river, JAMES ROGERS, WM. HORNSBY tosurvey for NEOL M. BAIN (MAJOR) says in 1831 he measured to COLORADO RIVER to falls; BAIN got into a spree in Bastrop and lost his money and sold cert. JAMES HARALSON was among party as was GIDEON WHITE, WM. HORNSBY. Appeal Bond May 1, 1859,J. W. ROBERTSON, W. P. MABRIO (?) J. T. McLAURIN, on bond.

DC 11,268 TCT filed Oct. 11, 1893 EVERARD (EDWARD) T. TOWNES, left TCT Jan. 1, 1883 was 19 years old son ROBERT J. TOWNES who d. Oct. 4, 1865; PATTIE TOWNS RECTOR, NELLA T. MORRIS, POLLIE S. CARLTON, ALLEN R. TOWNS and N. COBB TOWNES.

G/78 May 17, 1852 ALBERT SILSBY assignee of F. GARCIA, HOWARD SILSBEE family of Wayne, Steuben Co. NY now of Catherine, Chomanig Co. NY to HENRY CRONKRITE of Bradford, Chomanig Co. NY; HOWARD & BPO. ARCHELAS heir of ALBERT SILSBEE of Wayne, Steuben Co. NY came to Austin's Colony, Texas, 1830-31-32 and died.

H/431 May 14, 1855 HENRY CRONKRITE to LYMAN CRONKRITE of Fayette Co.Tex

K/767 Aug. 24, 1855 LAZARUS ELLIS formerly of Wyne, Steuben Co. NY son of MARY SILSBEE decd. and bro. on my mother's side of ARCHELIUS,HOWARD & ALBERT SILLSBIE, ALBERT SILSBEE d. 1834

K/768 Dec. 18, 1854 SALLY MEREDITH wife of FRANCIS, family of SALLY HENKLEY and maiden name was SALLY ELLIS dau. MARY ELLIS now decd. who afterwards m. JOSEPH SILSBEE of Wayne, Steubens Co. Ny and she was mother of HOWARD, ARCHELIUS & ALBERT SILISBY. (different spellings)

O/278 Dec. 22, 1859 HOWARD SILSBEE to LYMAN CRONKRITE (bro. of ALBERT) who grew to manhood in Wayne, Steubens Co. Ny went to Tex. 1830-31, settled in Matagorda Co. and was killed by Indians on the San Gabriel River in company with WEBSTER STILLWELL, et al 1839.

DC 3871 CRONKRITE vs . C. A. DENNEY et al recites LYMAN CRONKRITE

PC 1685 LAVENIA H. ROGERS m. (1) B. H. THOMPSON

DC 5348 Sept. 30, 1879 EMILY WEEMS wife of JOHN B. was EMILY ROWE

DC 339 TCT THOMAS H. JONES Feb. 28, 1848, heirs DOCTOR ROBERT DAVIS who d. July 1847 his wife was EMILY and she later m. JOSEPH ROWE, May term 1854. CH. ANN ELIZA, minor, THOMAS HEARNE, minor, ISABELLA,minor, ISAAC, minor, ROBERT, minor, FRION (FRIAN), minor.

Q/691 Feb. 4, 1867 THOMAS H. JONES to wife, LOUISA

36/460 deed DAVID & MARY ANN EPPRIGHT to daus. ALICE L. & ANNA RIGGLE

252/220 Aff. ALICE L. EPPRIGHT m. (1) IRA JOHNSON he d. 1898 (2) J. M. TURNER by (1) IRA B. JOHNSON, FRANK C. JOHNSON, CHAS. P. JOHNSON,HELEN ELIZA MORSE JOHNSON fs, ALICE RUTH fs. ZUELLA m. W. J. DOUGHERTY, D. A. & MARY JANE LANE, MRS. FRANCIS LYONS, DAVID A., MARY ECKHARDT,GERTRUDE LANE SMITH, JOHN W. LANE, WALLS E. LANE

I/283 Feb. 6, 1855 SAML. G. HAYNIE to WM. A. VAN ALSTYNE

O/318 June 8, 1860 F. W. CHANDLER, E. B. TURNER to AGNES H. OLDHAM

P/556 Dec. 29, 1862 WM. S. OLDHAM et ux AGNES H. to JOSEPHUS M.STEINER

53/450 Nov. 2, 1882 CHAS. HAENELetux ELIESE & son and only child PAUL to GUSTAV WILKE
80/569 June 6, 1888 GUSTAV WILKE et ux MARY to A. B. LANGERMANN

94/35 .. 1890 A. B. LANGERMANN et ux ALTHALIE

158/551 May 6, 1899 AUGUSTUS B. LANGERMANN et ux MARIE ATHALIE to FRANZISKA von BOECKMANN

PC 2048 ESTATE EUGENE VON BOECKMANN filed Feb. 2, 1897 by FRANZESKA von BOECKMANN sur. wife, CH. ANTONIE & LAURA

198/427 Feb. 14, 1905 to MRS. ANTONIO MYER (von BOECKMANN)

199/367 May 17, 1906 THO. P. MYER et ux ANTONIO to LAURA von BOECKMANN and she m. RUDOLPH G. MUELLER (sept. 28, 1906)

T/190 PATENT Mar. 1, 1870 to MARY COOK

V/590 by JOSEPH LEE Oct. 14, 1871 MARY A. COOK wife of LOUIS P. & 4 ch: CORA K. now RICE, VIRGINIA B. now TALBOT, MARY A. COOK now HARDY & LOUIS P. COOK, JR.

307/488 Feb. 23, 1910 by MRS. EMERETTA McCALL EVANS says: MAREY ANN was dau. and that LOUIS P. COOK was a cousin of MRS. EMERETTA EVANS.

T/417 PA June 9, 1870 MARY A. HARDY of Robertson Co. Tex. to J. F.HARDY

V/596 PA Mar. 4, 1871 MARY E. RICE of White Pigeon, St. Joseph Co.Mich to HORATIO H. RICE to get property of her parents LOUIS P. & MARY A. COOK, late of Brownsville, Texas

79/12 PA Dec. 3, 1887 RICHARD P. BENNETT of Davies Co. Ky to WM. W. WOOD, Austin TCT son CORA COOK RICE BENNETT

DC 8581 filed Feb. 1, 1888 RICHARD P. BENNETT was minor Jan 1, 1879, vs. EDWARD CHRISTIAN, AUSTIN FORE, DIANA FORE, MIKE FORE, ALBERT FOSTER, JOSEPH JACOBS, LUCINDA PENN, R. S. TODD, A. S. HOUSTON, NANCY GREEN, MRS. E. WEIR & C. W. DANIEL all TCT; supplemental petition filed Mar. 3, 1888 says NANCY GREEN decd. in her stead GEO. E. GREEN, MADALINE RICHARDS, SUSAN GRUNDY & SAMUEL RICHARDS.

DC 10,010 JOHN RICHARDS TCT vs. JOHN W. BROWN, BEN H. SHROPSHIRE and W. T. CLOUD of TCT, M. ASHLAND, admr. ESTATE W. W. JEFFERSON, Galveston Co. Tex. SILAS W., FLORENCE, LILLIE & MAY JEFFERSON minor ch. of W. W. JEFFERSON, and decd. wife, they of Memphis, Tenn.

DC 28,232 filed Oct. 24, 1911 BONETA GUARDO et vir FULIASO, gd. of MARY ANN & JOHN RICHARDS, JR., ADA & ROBT. DAVIDSON RICHARDS, minors, ch. of herself and JOHN RICHARDS, decd. d. Mar. 1897; and SALLIE LOUISE DODD, et vir C. M. & BONITA PAXTON, minors.

PATENT to WILLIAM P. CORBIN Sept. 15, 1846

B/456 Tax deed WM. P. CORBIN by WM. H. CUSHNEY, assessor and collector of taxes to JAMES A. MASON

L/587 Mar. 22, 1838 Transfer of cert. WM. P. CORBIN, Brazoria Co. Tex to WILLIAM T. AUSTIN says his 1/2 interest as a married man. WIT: R. J TOWNES, WM. H. HUNT, D. HUMPHREYS

A/575 WD April 14, 1840, WM. T. AUSTIN by SAMUEL W. AUSTIN, both of Brazoria Co. Tex. to GEO. J. BYRD, of NY ack. by atty. in Galveston Co. Tex. WIT: JAMES BUTLER, M. H. KOEGH

37/516 QC April 18, 1877 HANNAH BYRD, widow and EMMA BURTNELL, IDA L. BYRD & GEO. J. BYRD, JR. only children of GEO J. BYRD, decd. late NY city allfull age to JAMES A. CHANDLER, WIT: GEO. B. JAQUES, HENRY B. BURTNELL, GEO. B. JAQUES, Com for Texas in NY City.

D/174 SWD Feb. 5, 1850 WM. T. AUSTIN, Washington Co. Tex. to EDMUND JONES, Ny, WIT: JAMES F. EDRINGTON, JAMES A. MASON

38/220 QC April 18, 1877 JAY JARVIS JONES,Fairfield Conn son EDMUND JONES lateNY to JAMES A. CHANDLER, 1 of 4 ch. and only heirs of E.JONES

38/221 QC April 18, 1877 CHARLOTTE A. HORTON of NY dau. EDMUND JONES to JAMES A. CHANDLER

38/224 QC April 18, 1877 MARY WHITEMAN dau. EDMUND JONES of NY to JAMES A. CHANDLER

38/255 EXECUTORS DEED Arpil 18, 1877, WM. B. WHITEMAN & ELIZABETH JONES extrs. EDWARD JONES decd. NY to JAMES A.CHANDLER

105/465 Aff. Dec. 14, 1892 by JOSEPH FRANKLIN of Galveston Co. Tex.knew HENRY H. WILLIAMS did business in Galveston 1845-51 came from Baltimore Md. where he died many years since.

V/743 deed June 9, 1870 HENRY H. WILLIAMS et ux REBECCA ANN, JOHN H. WILLIAMS and only surviving child. Ack. before W. W. LATIMER, commr. for Texas, resident Baltimore, Md.

490/117 April 27, 1906 JOSEPH STUMPF to JOHN H. & E. K. HAMPTON

Trf. of Cert. Land Office June 6, 1841, ROBERT COMPTON to JOSHIA FISK. WIT: S. W. RALPH, JOHN L. BAKER, ack. June 10, 1846 before JAMES DELLENEY NP Jasper Co. Tex. P. MILLICAN...EDWARD S...chainers, JAMES R. PACE survey March 1850.

36/121 Oct. 16, 1876 JAMES F. BROWN of San Saba Co. Tex. to IGN RRY

F.31 Sept. 8, 1849 GEO. W. DAVIS to JOSEPH PORTER BROWN, heirs

T/442 April 26, 1870 J. FRAZIER BROWN, SALLIE F. BRACKENBROUGH et vir M. C. of San Saba Co. Tex. (MARCUS C.)

Y/639 Oct. 18, 1873 love and affection deed C. NEELEY RUTHERFORD to father ROBERT A. RUTHERFORD, SR.

30/412 love and affection deed Oct. 30, 1874 ROBERT A. RUTHERFORD, JR. to father. WIT: ERIN RUTHERFORD & T. W. BACON

V/582 Oct. 17, 1871 R. A. RUTHERFORD to CYNTHIA A. MAXWELL for life balance to present children

30/368 July 13, 1875 THOS. Q. MAXWELL et vir VIRGINIA F. to W. W. MAXWELL

DC 2956 HON. A. H. WILLIE, CJ. STATE SUP. COURT. CHAS. S. MORSE,Clk.1883

378/79 Aff. T. O. MAXWELL, F. A. MAXWELL, VIRGINIA F. LOVING d. TCT June 25, 1925; was sister m. twice (1) 1872 to THOS. Q. MAXWELL he d. 1875 no ch. (2) m. R. J. LOVING 1877 ch; JAMES M., R. J. LOVINGd. many years ago

PC 8616 1/2 to Bro. F. P., JAMES H., JESSE W. MAXWELL, sister ELLA J. WASHINGTON, 1/6 WM. W., J. A. CARSON MAXWELL & R. HENRY MAXWELL, three yougest sons of decd. bro. WM. W. MAXWELL & 1/6 to ch. of sister (decd) LOU H. HILL, will of T. O. MAXWELL June 27, 1933

Aff. May 30, 1946 filed May 31. CYNTHIA A. MAXWELL d. TCT Aug. 24,1924 wife of ALEXANDER CARSON MAXWELL d. Mar. 26, 1871 TCT; T. .O. MAXWELL d Feb. 18, 1937 et ux MAGGIE L., W. W. MAXWELL d. May 14, 1937; B. P. MAXWELL or F. P. d. Nov. 24, 1938; F. A. MAXWELL d. Oct. 23, 1939; JAMES H. MAXWELL,JESSE W. MAXWELL, MATTHEW d. 1860 infant; MRS. VIRGINIA F. LOVING d. 1925; MRS. LOU H. HILL d. 1929; MRS. ELLA J. WASHINGTON and MRS. MILTON MORRIS: F. P. d. Nov. 24, 1938 and his wife, MAGGIE L. d Feb. 29, 1884 CH. AGNES wife of J. M. KILGORE, ANNIE L. fs. FORREST O., HARRIETT V. fs. LOUISE wife of WILBUR L. JOHNSON & FRANK H. MAXWELL, LOU H. HILL d. Mar. 16, 1929 m. A. C. HILL d. Oct. 12, 1897; OWEN HICKMAN d infancy; ELLA HILL ELKINS (CLYDE) widow, ANNIE G. HILL fs. JESSIE MAY HILL fs. ADDIE HILL wife of ROBERT L. RAMSDELL, W. W. MAXWELL m. 1 time 3 ch. W. W. JR., HENRY J. & A. CARSON d. 1940 his wife SADIE, T. O. MAXWELL m. FLORENCE PORTER d. Feb. 18, 1937 no ch. she d. Aug. 19, 1943; WM. W. MAXWELL m. LILLIE GARRETT, Aug. 10, 1894 d. Feb. 18, 1912; WM.W.

MAXWELL, JR., and R. HENRY MAXWELL

C/597 PATENT Feb. 23, 1842 to FOUNTAIN LESTER

C/599 Feb. 23, 1842 deed FOUNTAIN LESTER of Harris Co. Tex. to THOS. WM. WARD (commissioner of General Land Office) by JAMES WEBB, atty-in-fact THOS. WM. WARD is assignee of JOHN CRAYTON assignee of F. LESTER

B/271 PA Dec. 28, 1845 FOUNTAIN LESTER of Harrison Co. Tex. mentions EDWARD SMITHERSON, CHARLES C. CUSHMAN, house. WIT: D. F. WALLERS (X) JAMES CLAYTON. ACK. before R. C. DOOM ccc TCT Sept. 2, 1846

B/270 Deed Sept. 2, 1846 JOHN (X) CRAYTON to DAVID OVERTON & ELIJAH H. HARPER. WIT: LEWIS M. H. WASHINGTON, A. W. POUNCY

E/48 Trf. Nov. 1, 1849 JOHN (X) CRAYTON to THOS. W. WARD. WIT: J. de CORDOVA, S. W. BAKER

Q/232 Shf. deed Nov. 8, 1864 THOS. C. COLLINS, shf. to N. G. SHELLEY cites June 15, 1864 DC 1948 SUSAN L. WARD vs. THOS. WM. WARD, div. arrears in alimony to be sold at old "SWISHER HOTEL" S, E. corner Block 70 Austin. (NOTE: This is the northwest corner of 6th and Congress Ave) Mentions GEO. W. PASCHAL. WIT: FRANK W. BROWN, G. W. PASCHAL, ACK. before AARON F. BOYCE, CCC J. MINER, Deputy

Q/785 July 5, 1866 deed THOS. WM. WARD to SUSAN L. WARD. WIT: M. H. BOWERS, C. S. WEST, FRED CARLETON

R/156 PA Dec. 12, 1867 SUSAN L. WARD of City of NY to J. L. SLEIGHT of Galveston,Texas, before SYLVESTER LAY, Texas Commissioner for NY

544/339 PATENT Mar. 1, 1849 to MASSILLAN FARLEY

C/491 deed April 10, 1849 MASSELLAN FARLEY to JAMES G. SWISHER. WIT: WM. COCKBURN, A. V. HOPKINS

D/196 deed Mr. 14, 1850 JAMES G. SWISHER to FRANCIS DIETERICH

PC 279 EST. FRANCIS DIETERICH decd. d. TCT ...31, 1860, SARAH (C.E.) DIETERICH & C. C. BROWNING filed June 5, 1860; GEO. HANCOCK, ANDREW O. HORNE, JR., JOHN H. ROBINSON, JOHN BREMOND, JOHN B. BANKS, appraisers JAMES DIETERICH filed petition for div. July 2, 1861 vs. SARAH, widow and minor ch. THOS. ALBERT, ANNA DOROTHEA, MELCHORIA, JOHN H. ROBINSON, GEO. HANCOCK, JOSEPH LEE, JOHN BREMOND, A. C. HORNE, JR. commissioners to partition

Jan. 1, 1863 MRS. SARAH E. DIETERICH m. REV. J. W. WHIPPLE TCT, by Rev. L. B. WHIPPLE.
DC 24,086 div. filed July 2, 1906 SIDON HARRIS vs. JEANNETTA MARTELLA HARRIS, m. Dec. 15, 1902

DC 25,976 J. R. BAILY, E. B. HANCOCK, J. H. RAYMOND, JR., TCT vs. LEONIDAS SIDON HARRIS of Chooise Co. Ariz. KATHERINE LOUISE HARRIS ADAMS et virWILLIAM J. ADAMS, Jefferson Co. Tex. KENT CLAY HARRIS, Minor of San Francisco Co. Calif.; AUGUSTUS STOREY HARRIS, GLAYDS HARRIS, PATRICK SIDNEY HARRIS, JEFFERSON STOREY HARRIS, minors TCT of MARY STOREY who m. SIDON HARRIS d. May 26, 1902; IRELAND GRAVES, gd. ad litem for minors KENT CLAY, AUGUSTUS STOREY, GLADYS H., PATRICK SIDNEY and JEFFERSON STOREY HARRIS

236/47 deed Dec. 18, 1909 J. R. BAILY et ux ROSINE, E. B. HANCOCK et ux MARIE, J. H. RAYMOND, JR., et ux ALICE

O/379 agreement July 6, 1860 JAMES ROGERS, EDWARD H. ROGERS, JOSEPH B. ROGERS & THOS. H. JONES, M. C. BURDITT, commissioners, J. P. WALLACE ne. corner. WIT: C. S. WEST, JOHN HANCOCK ack. J. T. McLAURIN ccc TCT

R/473 deed Sept. 1, 1868 JOSEPH B. ROGERS et ux MARY A. to THOS. BIRD & WILEY AYERS.

R/160 partition deed Jan. 23, 1867 ED. H. ROGERS, JOSEPH B. ROGERS, MARY E. HARDEMAN, et vir WILLIAM N., SARAH E. BURDITT et vir MINUS D. ch: of JAMES ROGERS decd. et ux RACHEL to BENJ. T. GAULT & NANCY L. GAULT (she dau. JAMES ROGERS) JAMES R. PACE, surveyor

S/94 Jan. 23, 1867 MARY E. HARDEMAN, ET VIR WM. N., NANCY L. GAULT, et vir, BEN T., SARAH J. BURDITT et vir MINUS C., ch. of JAMES ROGERS decd. et ux RACHEL

S/93 Jan. 23, 1867 E. H. ROGERS et ux L. A., MARY E. HARDEMAN, et al

Q/717 Feb. 19, 1867 RACHEL ROGERS surviving wife of JAMES ROGERS decd ED. H. ROGERS & JOSEPH B. ROGERS

DC 2883 ED & JOSEPH ROGERS vs. GILES H. & J. F. BURDITT, admrs. and M. C. BURDITT, filed Oct. 3, 1870; H. N. BURDITT, H. McBRIDE, bondsmen; W. M. WALTON, JAS. A. GREEN, atty. for plaintiffs HANCOCK & WEST, atty for GILES H. BURDITT, DAVID SHEEKS, Judge; A. M. DAVIDSON, THOS. BIRD bondsmen on appeal; Hon. L. D. EVANS, Judge, Supreme Court; W. P. de NORMANDY, Clk. Sup. Ct. (EST. NEWELL W. BURDITT decd.) RADCLIFF PLATT sheriff.

290/224 QC Nov. 5, 1913 J. B. & I. B. BIRD, Williamson Co. son THOS. & POLLY BIRD, SALLIE HOLMAN, widow, TCT dau. THOS. & POLLY BIRD, MRS.O.H HOLMAN, widow, TCT dau. THOS. & POLLY BIRD, MARY E. BIRD, surviving wife WM. B., son THOS. & POLLY BIRD, WILLIE BIRD son WM. BIRD, TOM BIRD son WM. BIRD, all TCT; MARY LEE dau RHODA BIRD LEE dau. THOS. & POLLY BIRD, OLIVER BIRD, Nueces Co. Tex. and Extr. ESTATE POLLY ANN BIRD dcd LIZZIE ELLIOTT surviving wife JNO. BIRD son of THOS. & POLLY BIRD, JOE BIRD, San Patricio Co. Tex; and TRUMBLE (TRIMBLE) BIRD, MRS. S. E.BIRD GRIFFIN et vir D. E., all the heirs of THOS. BIRD and wife POLLY ANN decd. and surviving wife of JNO. BIRD, Ch. of JNO. BIRD, JOE BIRD, OLIVER BIRD, MRS. D. E. (MAGGIE) BIRD GRIFFIN & TRUMBLE BIRD.

K/684 Deed Oct. 21, 1854 J. W. BIRD et ux S. E. BIRD to A. A. FULKS 7 ac. adj. 300 ac. THOS. D. BUNDICK, JOHN C. BROOKS survey to A.A.FULKS

267/20 A. A. FULKS d. prior to 1900, ELIZABETH d. 1913; WILL & W. D. & JOHN FULKS get $1.00 each; RHODIE REYMOLDS et vir LAFAYETTE, COllins Co. Tex, MECCA PALMER et vir OSWALD, TCT, LUCRETIA ABBOTT GOSET,widow Sabastain Co. Ark. MAGGIE MARGARET PAYTON et vir E. F. PAYTON, KATE PAYTON et vir A. J. PAYTON, ANNIE DEDRICK, MARTHA CROOKS et vir HENRY Burnet Co. Tex. CHAS. FULKS, et ux BESSIE. WIlliamson Co. Tex. to E.A. PALMER, he d. Aug. 23, 1952 EDWARD ALLEN PALMER m. MYRTLE FREDA PAYTON 1922 she d. April 4, 1962.

P/103 P. A. WALTON of Bosque Co. Tex. to J. GORDON BROWN Oct. 10, 1890

G/619 PATENT May 29, 1854 to F. BRICHTA, JR. & SR.

Pc 198 FRANCIS BRICHTA, SR. decd. Dec. 25, 1854, partition AMELIA BRICHTA widow and AUGUSTUS, FRANK V., ROBERT H. BRICHTA & CECELIA B. TOWNSEND wife of M. W. TOWNSEND

136/175 deed July 29, 1895 AUGUSTUS BRICHTA of Pena Co. Ariz. to WM. R. HAMBY (original deed to HAMBY 136/104 Mar. 23, 1887)

136/362 REL says WM. R. HAMBY et ux MARY F., GARDNER RUGGLES et ux DIXIE L.

83/17 Feb. 13, 1889 MRS. MARY DUFFAU

215/302 Aff. 1907 RE: BRICHTA, CECELIA BRICHTA TOWNSEND, widow, dau. F BRICHTA et ux AMELIA, 4 ch. FRANK V., ROBERT H. d. years ago without issue; AUGUSTUS lived 1895 in Arizona & CECELIA (I/92 cites that F. BRICHTA, JR., in deed Aug. 25, 1854 was not an heir and did not inherit)

DC 41,GEO. HANCOCK vs. ALBERT C. HORTON filed Feb. 13,1850 Ptf.owner of JAMES DALY cert.1/3 Lea. JURY: LEANDER BROWN, R. F. PARKER, LEWIS HORST, AUGUST FORE, T. W. NOLEN, THOMAS J. CAMPBELL, LYMAN TARBOX

BOX, NELSON MERRELL, THOS. W. WARD, WM. M. WILSON, HIRAM BENNETT & WADE HENRY.

Aff. by G. W. MURRAY, June 2, 1928 filed same day: BELL RAMSEY, wife F. T. d. Feb. 19, 1937, J. M. & wife, MERCY P., JESSIE RAMSEY m. R. V. MURRAY, EUPHIE RAMSEY m. C. C. TAYLOR, WINNIE RAMSEY m. H. F. NITSCHKE, Raleigh, N. C.

A/376 partition May 25, 1841, Bastrop Co. THOS. F. McKINEY of Galveston Co. Tex. agent BARTLETT SIMS, Bastrop Co. NATHANIEL H. WATROUS, TCT ALBERT C. HORTON, Matagorda Co. Tex by H. S. MORGAN, atty. of Bastrop Co. Tex. WIT: JAS. H. GILLESPIE, E. T. MERRIMAN

PC 428 EST. JOHN R. McCALL decd. filed Sept. 2, 1869 by AMERICA P. sur wife,he d. 1867 had community property and small children: T. E. SNEED W. H. D. CARRINGTON, JAMES DENNIS, appraisers

30/255 deed Sept. 6, 1875 MRS. AMERICA P. McCALL to son JOHN D. McCALL

DC 4574 filed Oct. 5, 1875 THOS. E. CATER et al vs. JOHN D. McCALL: CH: EMMA McCALL BERRYMAN, WM. C. McCALL, J. S. W. C. MCCALL, heirs M. Mc DOUGAL McCALL CATER, THOS. E. CATER is gdn. ELIZA MARIA, MAGGIE, LULA V, EMMA & THOS. and AMERICA P. McCALL gdn. of her minor children: WM. C. & J. S. W. C. McCALL

407/250 PATENT Oct. 29, 1832 to JESSE C. TANNEHILLmarried man with fam.

DC 1851 filed Dec. 18, 1860, NATHANIEL TOWNSEND vs. J. C. TANNEHILL, J. J. TANNEHILL & F. R. TANEHILL, L. H. LUCKETT, dist. SurveyorTCT

86/591 deed Nov. 27, 1889 SUSIE M. TOWNSEND ROBERTSON et vir JAMES H.

173/302 aff. 1901 ELVIRA A. HILL, widow of STEPHEN D. HILL says her son IRA B. HILL became 21, Nov. 19, 1901.

DC 12,301 Div. filed Sept. 24, 1895 ELIZA M. CATER vs. THOS. B. CATER m. TCT Nov. 6, 1878; heleft June 1890; 5 ch. HAMBY M. 16 y. MARGARET 14 MARIE 9, SUSIE 7 and WALLACE 5 years.

D/118 deed Jan. 8, 1850 JAMES B. SHAW, TCT to T. T. FAUNTLEROY. WIT: JAMES M. SWISHER ack. by JAMES B. SHAW Jan. 8, 1850 before JOHN HEMPHIL CJ SUPREME COURT, TEXAS

W/456 Trustees deed May 8, 1872 to C. W. WHITIS: WILL, C. W. WHITIS d. 1877, 1/2 to wife FLORENCE bal. RUFUS, MARY, JOHN, FLORENCE, GERTRUDE, CHAS. P., THOS. P. & ELLEN P.

Transcript 1/77 deed Nov. 18, 1835 JAMES (X) BURLESON to JOSIAH WILBARGER before T. J. GAZLEY, Judge Bastrop Co. Tex. WIT: THOS. H. MAYS, E. M. PEASE, JAMES ROGERS.

Transcript 1/79 June 9, 1838 JOSIAH WILBARGER to JOHN L. LYNCH. WIT: SAML. R. MILLER, B. SIMS

A/42 JOHN L. LYNCH to JAMES SMITH Jan. 8, 1839. WIT: J. C. TANNEHILL, JAMES MANOR, bef ore JAMES W. SMITH CJ NP O TCT

G/220 June 22, 1853 JAMES W. SMITH to J. H. MATTHEWS, WIT: JOHN T. ALLEN JOHN D. FOLKS

K/25 Bond Nov. 8, 1855 SIDNEY P. BROWN et ux CAROLINE A. to JOHN D. FULKS, MARION A. HOUSTON

C/349 PATENT June 4, 1841 to HEIRS JAMES P. DAVIS

S/279 deed July 28, 1869 T. J. CHAMBERS ESTATE to THOS. H. BACON

PATENT July 1, 1841 to heirs of HENRY WARNELL, decd.

L/43 Aug. 11, 1838, WILLIAM GREESON, curator ad hoc for heirs WILLIAM
GREESON, WIT: L. B. JOHNSON, JOSIAH MAGEE, Bastrop Co. Tex. WIT:
PRESTON CONLEE, THOS H. MAYS

C/551 deed Oct. 3, 1848 EDWARD BURLESON to A. B. SPIER, admr. SEABORN
J. WHATLEY, decd. WIT: THOS. W. WARD, LAMAR MOORE

C/467 deed Feb. 10, 1849 CHAS. WALKER to GEO. BRATTON. WIT: WILLIAM
WILKS, J. MINOR.

PC 113 EST. GEO. BRATTON May 26, 1851 apts. WM. BRATTON, admr. names
wife, AMANDA & MANY CHILDREN.

H/117 AMANDA BRATTON BARGSLEY, WM. WILKS, admr. de bonis non says: WM.
C. RAIGER, admr. EST. WM. BRATTON, WIT: NELSON MERRILL, H. C. RAYMOND
A. B. McGILL. Nov. 4, 1854

PC 138 EST. WM. BAKER decd. Aug. 25, 1853, SAML. TOWNES, admr.

B/96 partition, JOHN BAKER, Guadalupe Co. Tex; ANN BAKER REAGER. TCT
WM. BAKER, Bell Co. Tex., E. S. C. ROBERTSON, gdn. RICHARD R. BAKER,
MATILDA BAKER, JANE BAKER, sons and dau. of WM. BAKER, decd. RICHARD R.
BAKER & JANE are minors, MATHILDA minor, WM. C. REAGER, gdn.

28/577 deed Mar. 9, 1874 GEO. W. WATERS, & MARY J. NEWTON to A. R.
MORRIS, JOHN M. YOUNG & E. S. MATTHEWS, trustees, PECAN SPRINGS SCHOOL
HOUSE, B. G. R. WHIPPLE, NP Jefferson Co. New York.

813/457 PATENT, HENRY P. HILL, July 14, 1835 says single man, but has
come with family)patents were issued on certain conditions of marital
status) BARTLETT SIMS, surveyor. wit; Jas. Haggard, Nathl. Mitchell,
WM. CANNON.

66/586 cc JUDGMENT, Williamson Co. Tex. HENRY P. HILL vs. A. J.
HAMILTON & F. W. CHANDLER

DC 7565 HELENA KRAUSE vs. RUDOLPH KRAUSE filed Aug. 6, 1885 m. May 27,
1868. Answer of RUDOLPH KRAUSE admits marriage and says he got divorce
in La. 1879.

PA 2446 BERTRAM KRAUSE, minor Mar. 13, 1902 by HENRY RIBBECK (friend &
extr. of RUDOLPH K. KRAUSE, will) says BERTRAM was nephew and adopted
son of RUDOLPH KRAUSE & decd. wife, ELEANOR KRAUSE. Dec. 21, 1906,final
a/c filed, says min. 21 years old.

36/458 Nov. 20, 1876 DAVID EPPRIGHT et ux MARY ANN of TCT to dau. MARY
JANE LANE, WIT: R. H. SMITH, N. P. STRAYHORN.

273/536 & 274/136 Feb. 10, 1915 MARY JANE LANE fs TCT & WALLS E. LANE
of Burleson Co. Extr. EST. A. E. LANE, decd. to FRANCES R. LYONS, TCT.
W. H. & D. A. LANE, TCT et ux MATTIE, MARY ANN ECKHARDT, et ux G. F.
BURLESON Co. Tex., JENNIE GERTRUDE SMITH, TCT, H. C. SMITH, H. CLAY
SMITH, WALLS E. LANE, BURLESON LANE, et ux MARY, JOHN W. LANE TCT etux
FRANCES E. (BETTY) LANE.

C/277 PA Jan. 28, 1848 to JAMES WEBB by MIRABEAU B. LAMAR, both TCT
"expecting shortly to connect myself with the Volunteer Army of Texas
in the service of the U. S."

C/279 Mtg. Mar. 18, 1848 MIRABEAU B. LAMAR by JAMES WEBB (now residing
in Laredo) to HUGH McLEOD, Galveston, Texas; property known as cottage
now occupied by HORATIO GROOMS, my tenant; GAZAWAY B. LAMAR of Brooklyn
NY. WIT: JOSEPH LEE, ALFRED GROOMS.

C/280 Mar. 18, 1848 HUGH McLEOD to JAMES WEBB. WIT: ROBERT S. NEIGHBORS
THOS. FREEMAN of Galveston Co. Tex.

D/59 Rel Apl. 30, 1849 MIRABEAU B. LAMAR by JAS. WEBB, atty.(LAMAR is
selling to GENL.WM.S. HARVEY, USA) WIT: JAS.B.SHAW,THOS.H. DUVAL

D/60 deed April 13, 1849 MIRABEAU B. LAMAR to WM. S. HARNEY, U. S. ARMY now stationed in Austin, Texas.

Q/29 Receivers deed April 4, 1863 (under condemnation proceedings of U. S. Judgment, Western Dist. of Tex. June Term 1862) confedrate States vs. MATILDA STANGIER, GEO. HANCOCK, sequestrated property of WM. S. HARNEY. WIT: A. W. TERREL, W. J. MECKLING, D.W.C. BAKER

Q/66 PA Feb. 25, 1863 to J. M. STEINER, TCT by SIMEON HART of El Paso Co. Tex. InRe: "ARNEY PLACE" also 1/2 interest in "STATE GAZETTE" NEWSPAPER bought of late JNO. MARSHALL.

T/279 deed May 7, 1870 WM. G. HARNEY of St. Louis Mo. to JAMES H. RAYMOND & C. W. WHITIS.

104/225 aff. RE: WHITIS, (CHAS. W) d. Sept. 1877 m. 1 time

PC 2047 ESTATE ANNA G. McKINNEY, decd. cites P. DeCORDOVA or his son

SUBP. Issued June 11, 1858 for GEO. DAVIS, WM. HORNSBY & R.HORNSBY,SR.
  do   do   July 11, 1858 for GEO. W. DAVIS, JAS. R. PACE, L. H. LUCKETT & ENOCH M JOHNSON
SUBP. Issued Feb. 20, 1858 for W. W. HORNSBY, JAMES ROGERS, HART SAMUELS HERMAN MOSSON, ELIAS MOSSON
SUBP. issued Jan. 20, 1859 THOS. WARD, JAN. 17, 1859, JAMES F. JOHNSON & July 21, 1858 JAMES ROGERS, W. W. HORNSBY, JOSEPH W. ROBERTSON

Land grants on which the Cityof Austin was located, voided all but T.J. CHAMBERS: SAMUEL GOOCHER, surveyed Feb. 20, 1838 by THOMAS H. MAYS, G. D. HANCOCK surveyed, Feb. 25, 1838; THOMAS HAWKINS Feb. 25, 1838, AARON BURLESON Feb. 25, 1838, LOGAN VANDEVER Feb. 10, 1838.

D/264 PATENT to JACOB SNIVELY Jan..1842 PA July 3,1849 JAMES SNIVELY to DAVID SNIVELY demand of JAMES RIELY, agt. Washington Co. Tex.May 1,1844

K/686 Aug. 5, 1856 STATES: I, JOSHUA BENNETT OF TCT bond to MARTHA W. HOLMAN wife of JAMES S. HOLMAN but signed JOSHUA BENNETT, JAMES BENNETT BENJ. C. BENNETT, HIRAM BENNETT, JAMES LENSING & ELIZABETH LENSING. WIT CHARLES HAMILTON, WM. STELFOX, JASPER S. HOLMAN

O/72 Jan. 17, 1860 same as signed K/686 says ELIZABETH LENSING wife of JAMES LENSING all ack. in TCT

S/5 June 3, 1868 MARTHA W. HOLMAN, I. W. HOLMAN, I. P. HOLMAN, W. F. HOLMAN & POLLY ANN B. GILLUM wife of JOHN D. residents Bastrop Co. Tex

PC 932 ESTATE CHAUNCY T. DRISCOL, minor filed Oct. 16, 1883; he is a resident of Providence R. I. under 21 parents dead.

176/88 aff. ch. of F. M. BUCHANAN & N. A. BUCHANAN, m. 1 time, lived in Williamson Co. Tex. 4 CH. 2 boys and 2 girls, J. R. & W. T. who died prior to parents death and 2 girls MARGARET B. fs. and MARY E. who m. J. T. RUTLEDGE who d. prior to Nov. 30, 1915

Transcript 1/117 J. C. TANNEHILL to JAMES I. LESTER, WM. M. EASTLAND. WIT: J. S. HOUSTON, JOHN BREEDING.

N/403 June 27, 1858 J. C. TANNEHILL to JANE C. BURLESON, his dau. wife of AARON BURLESON.

313/59 SUSAN A. SMITH dau. JAMES W. SMITH m. J. M. HARTSON prior to Feb 20, 1869; WILSON GREER had 1 ch. only dau. ELLIS GREER wife of WM. L. THOMSON of Washington Co. Ky.

Y/602 deed WILDS K. COOKE, 1850 to JOSEPH LEE for minor heirs of LOUIS P. COOKE, decd. MARY, VIRGINIA B., CORA K. & LOUIS P. COOKE

DC 3074 THEODORA HEMPHILL born out of wedlock her deed W/61 TCT

U/559 MARGARET MOFFATT, sister of whole blood, JAMES HEMPHILL & ROBERT N. HEMPHILL bros. of half blood; MARGARET HEMPHILL GASTON, Chester Co. S. C. JOHN N. HEMPHILL and ROBERT HAMPHILL only children of DAVID HEMPHILL decd. bro. of decd. HON. JOHN HEMPHILL and MARGARET & JOHN N. or JOHN W. being surviving bros. and sisters of JANE W. HEMPHILL the mother of ROBERT HEMPHILL who d. intestate and unm 1870, Fairfield Co. S.C.

U/552 WM. R. HEMPHILL May 23, 1890 of S. C., Abbeville Co.

U/551, 1870 WM. S. MOFFATT et ux MARTHA J. of Belmont Co. O. MARTHA J. being only ch. of MRS. ELIZA WILSON, sister of whole blood of JOHN HEMPHILL, decd.

U/557 PA JOHN McCALLA, Mason Co. Ind. son of MRS. JANNET McCALLA, whole blood sister of HON. JOHN HEMPHILL, decd. June 6, 1871.

U/556 Sept. 27, 1870 JANE W. HEMPHILL of Fairfield Co. S. C. mother of ROBERT HEMPHILL decd. who was son of DAVID HEMPHILL 1/2 bro. of HON. JOHN HEMPHILL, decd.

218/544 Aff.CHAS. GILLETT formerly of Austin TCT d. Baltimore, Md. Mar. 6, 1869, left wife MARY who d. Baltimore, Md. Feb. 27, 1878 Ch: MARY ELLEN m. HENRY C. HARDY, WM. WHARTON, EMILY MARGARETTA m. HENRY C. HARDY, JR., and ALICE KATE m. GEO. E. HYATT

144/357 MRS. EMILY H. JOHNS states her mother MELISSA W. HAINES, widow of JAMES HAINES (d. Mar. 7, 1877) In 1879 MELISSA bought lots in Austin with proceeds of sale of farm; MELISSA A. HAINES d. 1890, only child of EMILY H. JOHNS of Bexar Co. Tex. and her sister MRS. D. M. THORNTON Williamson Co. Tex

1/143 Transcript TITLE BOND June 18, 1838, I. DECKER to DAVID BROWNING WIT: THOS. H. BREED, GREEN I. TAYLOR, ack. by WM. FAIRFAX GRAY of Harrisburg Co. Texas. Republic of Texas. (now Houston)

1/171 Transcript WD July 11, 1839 ISAAC DECKER, Harrisberg Co. To DANL BROWNING, Fayette Co. Tex. WIT: WM. N. MOCK, J. L. POTTER, ack. by J. L. POTTER, JAMES M. LONG, depty. CCC Bastrop Co. Tex.

1/173 Transcript TITLE BOND July 17, 1839 DANL. BROWNING, Bastrop Co. to HENRY ADAMS, WIT: JOHN J. GRUMBLES, WM. PINCKNEY HILL

F/157 Field notes 131 ac. JAMES COLEMAN survey, surveyed June 25,1853 DANL. DAVIS & WM. WHEAT, chain carriers; L. H. LUCKETT, Dept. surveyor Travis Dist, H. L. UPSHURE, Dist. Surveyor Travis District.

L/172 WD Dec. 31, 1853 JOSIAH FISK to JOHN C. HYDE, WIT: JAMES COLE

F/72 field notes April 4, 1853 JACOB TARRANT 120 ac. issued to him Sept 1, 1845, surveyed April 5,1853 J. BROWN, ELIJAH PATE, chain carriers

R/25 WD Feb. 15, 1868 NANCY TONGATE to A. J. SANFORD

K/278 field notes 160 ac. JASPER N. STEWART SUR. surveyed Dec. 20,1869 JAMES R. PACE, Co. surveyor TCT A. MORRISON, A. J. SANFORD, chainers executed and corrected Nov. 15, 1873, JOHN E. CAMPBELL, surveyor TCT

V/57 SWD July 8, 1870 JASPER N. STEWART et ux ANNA to ANDREW J. SANFORD

173/371 Rel. Nov. 29, 1901 MRS. ELIZA SANFORD, S. L. SANFORD, LILLIE BESSIE SANFORD SPENCER became owners of note under will of A. J. SANFORD, PC Williamson Co. Tex. it says heir EARL MAY STANFORD (173/377 says: EARL PALM STANFORD)

464/..cc Bexar Co. Tex. PC EST. LENA DUNCKER, Mar.3, 1926 of Wilson Co. Tex. to son WM. WALTER, dau. CLARA D. son CLARK D. dau. ADDIE PLATTNER dau. ANNA WHITTIKER, LENA d. Bexar Co. Tex. Dec. 15, 1930; WALTER d. June 19, 1940 Bexar Co. Will, May 7,1940 to wife NORINE D.

694/72 Dec. 23, 1941 aff. by C. H. DUNCKER of Williamson Co. Tex. son of LENA DUNKER et vir WM. C. d. Feb..1924 m. one time only, 6 ch: WM. wife MARIE of Wilson Co. Tex. ANNIE (ADELINE) D. PLATTNER et vir IRVIN Ford Co. Kan., ANNIE D. WHITEKER et vir L. G., Ford Co. Kan., CLARA D. WARNER Et vir OSCAR, Bexar Co. Tex., CARL H. et ux THELMA, Williamson Co. Tex., WALTER H. DUNCKER, LENA d. Dec. 15, 1930, Bexar Co. WALTER H. d. 1939 wife NORINE, 1 child PATRICIA ANN.

K/470 PATENT July 24, 1855 to EDWARD M. HURST, ASGNEE JASPER GILBERT

Q/173 WD Jan. 23, 1863 EDWARD M. HURST et ux CHARLOTTE of TCT

PC 611 EST. BENJ. K. STEWART decd. d. Dec. 22, 1872 to wife SARAH: 2 sons, JESSE G. & SAMUEL N. dau. SARAH FRANCES andSonsBUD STEWART, and JAMES P. STEWART
65/512 Wd Nov. 2, 1885 J. M. WATSON to FRANK P. HEFFINGTON et ux L. J.

178/67 WILL: JULY 3, 1897 W. O. HUTCHINSON to W. O. HUTCHISON, Jr. gson and sons BEVERLY, OSCAR C. HUTCHISON & LOUIS and gdau. MARY LOUISE & ANNIE CUTHBERT dau. BEVERLY HUTCHISON and wife LEONORE S. HUTCHISON

C/598 PA 1848 FOUNTAIN LESTER of Harrison Co. Tex. to HON. JAMES WEBB

C/617 SWD Dec. 8, 1849 THOS. W. WARD to GEO. McCLINTOCK

D/300 deed July 22, 1850 GEO. McCLINTOCK et ux PHEBE to PAYTON W. NOW-LIN. WIT: B. F. JOHNSON, JOSEPH J. BOTT, before JOEL MINOR, CJ. TCT
DC 7161 P. W. NOWLIN vs. ISAAC ALFORD & POLLY

PC 341 EST. ROBERT J. TOWNES decd. d. Oct. 4, 1865CHAS S. WEST petner. appoints EVERETT T. EGGLESTON gdn. of children

PC 658 EST. N. COBB & E. T. TOWNES orphan children of R. J. TOWNES

PC 549 EST. ROBERT ADAMS decd. d. Aug...1873; petitioner WM. ADAMS,son says widow of decd. lives in Missouri; heirs HANNAH, his widow, ROBERT, JOHN, GEORGE, CORNELIUS & WM. ADAMS, all but WM. residents of Missouri

Transcript 1/8 TITLE Mar. 29, 1835 STATE COAHUILA & TEXAS to WM. CANNON in BENJ. R. MILAM colony

B/364 Wd Oct. 19, 1846 WM. CANNON, Bastrop Co. to GEO. J. NEILL. WIT: JAMES H. GILLESPIE, R. L. REDING

M/315 Mtg. Mar. 2, 1858 ISAAC HAMMETT to W. B. BURDITT, H. N. BURDITT & GILES H. BURDITT, JESSE F. BURDITT admr. of EST. N. W.BURDITT decd. WIT: J. C. WEST, ack. before JAMES M. SWISHER ccc TCT

O/118 Mtg. Mar 1, 1860 ISAAC HAMMETT et ux MARTHA G., to JAMES T. McLAURIN, trustee for JOHN C. WILSON, endorsed by Aug. F. OTTO, clk.

38/213 WD Nov. 24, 1877 MARTHA J. HAMMETT widow, ISAAC, decd; JACKSON, WASHINGTON, JOSEPH B., WM. B., ISAAC M. HAMMETT, MARTHA J. PRUITT, wife JOHN T. PRUETT, ack. before ED SUMMERROW, NP TCT

44/469 partition Dec. 20, 1879 between JACKSON, WASHINGTON, W. B., J. B., J. M., & MARTHA HAMMETT PRUETT, et vir J. T. Heirs at law of ISAAC HAMMETT & MARTHA G. HAMMETT, both decd.

51/149 WD Dec. 5, 1881 JOHN T. PRUITT et ux MARTHA J. to MRS. MILDRED R. WILSON, et ux JOHN C. WILSON

84/114 ADMRS. DEED Oct. 27, 1888 to JOHN C. WILSON by order of sale Hays Co. Ct. Dec. 3, 1884 to EST. W. B. HAMMETT decd. before JAS. G. BURLESON cc Hays Co. Tex

ALLIE C. BELCHER vs. W. C. BELCHER, div. TCT filed Sept. 16 1901 m. in Dallas, Tex. Oct. 22, 1891, CH. EUGENE HORACE 9 yr. AND JERALD GAY BELCHER 6 years.

PATENT Oct. 24, 1848 to THOMAS G. ABELL

W/16 deed Dec. 27, 1871 EUNICE E. ABELL, HARRETT M. ABELL of Buffalo, Erie Co. NY; CATHERINE J. FORBIS of Village of Fredonia, Chautauqua NY sellers to WM. A.ABELL of Buffalo, Erie Co. same land patented to THOMAS G. ABELL late of Fredonia, dec. father of buyer and sellers. WIT: to CATHERINE J. FORBUS, EUNICE E. & HARRIETT M. ABELL, W. B. CUSHING, LT. COM. U. S. Navy and A. Z. MADISON, WIT: TO CATHERINE J.FORBIS J. H. CHAMPBERLAIN & LYMAN M. BAKER. Aff. at end: THOMAS G. ABELL,late Fredonia NY d. at Buffalo, NY about May 18, 1857 leaving ch: WM.H., HARRIETT M., LOUISA R. ABELL of Buffalo, NY and CATHERINE J. FORBIS of Fredonai, NY; that about Oct. 11, 1870 LOUISA R. ABELL d. at Buffalo, that the above named mother is also dead.

119/326 cc will WM. H. ABELL, Buffalo, NY will dated Jan. 10, 1887 to 5 ch: CHARLES LEE ABELL, HARIETTE E. TOWERS, HELEN M. ABELL, ALICE LOUISE ABEL, MARY EDNA ABELL and to sister HARRIETTE M. ABELL apts. wife MARGARET gdn. of 2 infant ch. (not named) and to pay cash to WM. E. HAWKE of North Bennington VT and his wife ELIZA 200 annually during lifetime; WM. H. ABELL d. Nov. 15, 1887, MARGARET ABELL widow,HARRIETE E. TOWERS dau. CHARLES L. ABELL son and HELEN M. ABELL dau. and ALICE L. ABELL dau. 7 years and MARY EDNA ABELL 3 yr. old all NY all heirs and next of kin.

DC 31, 229 JURORS: LEONARD ECK vs. HERMAN SCHUFFER, filed Aug. 24, 1914: J. R. SEXTON, CHARLES SCHMIDT, J. G. MILLER, LOUIS J. ARMSTRONG, E. F. McCARTY, H. H. CRISWELL, J. W. BROWN, CARL SELLSTROM, E. T. HOUSTON, B. M. OSBORN, O. H. MILLICAN, foreman (one juror was dismissed byAGmt.)

945/205 PATENT to JAMES MANOR Sept. 27, 1841

111/566 deed April 8, 1912, A. E. LANE et ux MARY J. to J. E. CLAYTON et ux BRITTIE. Ack. before JAMES M. HARRIS, NP TCT

255/15 deed Nov. 23, 1912 J. E.CLAYTON et ux BRETTA to TOM PARKS et ux CERMILLER (?)

350/341 WD Dec. 9, 1921 J. E. CLAYTON to wife, BRITTIE C. ack. before HENRY FAULK, NP TCT

693/127 cc orderoffice of COMPTROLLER of CURRENCY, Wash. D. C. Nov. 26, 1926 by CHARLES W. COLLINS, acting comptroller of Currency apts. A. S. WALKER, receiver of THE FARMERS NATIONAL BANK, Manor, Tex. also C. B. UPHAM, Jan. 5, 1942 acting Compt. of Currency

A/60 deed June 6, 1840 ANSON JONES to JOHN FALK & T. B. BECK, WIT: LEVI BIGELOW, D. C. GILMORE.

A/225 Deed Dec. 24, 1840 T. B. BECK to JOHN FALK, WIT: N. M. LUCKETT, JOHN BRASHERS

A/401 deed   July 12, 1841 NEVI CHAMBERLAIN to ANGELINE D. SMITH & THOS. A. SMITH admr. JAMES W. SMITH decd. WIT: J. E. HARRELSON, before JOSEPH LEE, CJ TC ReP Texas

C/275 Constables deed Mar. 6, 1848 WM. H. CUSHING Esq. J. P., THOMAS WARD, constable; property of NEVI CHAMBERLAIN, Judgement in favor of ANGELINE D. SMITH & R. C. DOOM, Esq. a JP (Mar. 7, 1848 sold at his court room, there being no court house in Austin) to JAMES WEBB, WIT: JAMES F. JOHNSON, WM. A. REINER.

V/363 Wd July 8, 1871 ANDREW J. HAMILTON et ux MARY J.(N.J.?) TCT to MORGAN C. HAMILTON before L. W. COLLINS, NP TCT

136/78 WD July 1, 1895 MARY J. HAMILTON sur. wife of ANDREW J. HAMILTON to MRS. JULIA H. SMITH

W/147 PA Aug. 16, 1871 MORGAN C. HAMILTON to ROBT. A. SMITH before OSCEOLA ARCHER, NP TCT

32/637 WD Sept. 26, 1876 M. C. HAMILTON by R. A. SMITH agt. to JOHN B. HEADSPETH

52/605 Wd June 27, 1882 JOHN B. HEADSPETH et ux CARRIE V. to S. P. HEADSPETH

59/408 WD Mar. 16, 1883, SAML. P. HEADSPETH to IRENE E. McLAUGHLIN and W. W. McLAUGHLIN

DC 7626 filed April 30, 1885 J. F. DIGNAN vs. W. W. McLAUGHLIN et ux IRENE D., S. F. HEADSPETH, T. TRIGG, trustee, MRS. HARRIETT F. DIGNAN C. F. MILLETT.

72/406 QC Jan. 26, 1887 T. J. HOUSTON et vir VICTORINE to J. B. HEADSPETH

86/185 Title Bond Feb. 21, 1889 JNO. B. HEADSPETH et ux CARRIE V., V. A. FENNER to DELIA CLARK, ack. before A. T. PATRICK, NP TCT

PC 2170 ESTATE ROBERT JEROME HILL, d. Mar. 30, 1899, KATE E. HILL, EXTR

304/429 Aff. heirship Sept. 19, 1918 by ESTELLE LEWRIGHT dau. MARY V. LEWRIGHT, who d. TCT Aug. 13, 1915, left: J. B. LEWRIGHT of San Antonio Bexar Co. Tex. and MAUD L. WILLIE et vir ASA H. of Corsicana, Navarro Co. Tex. and J. C. LEWRIGHT who d. without issue and was 36 years old March 10, 1903 in St. Louis, Mo.

223/352 Rel. Feb. 27, 1912 FANNIE PFAEFFLIN fs. to F. H. SMITH

252/564 Rel. June 8, 1912 CITY of AUSTIN by A. P. WOOLDRIDGE, Mayor and FRED STERZING, Tax Collector.

C/264 PATENT June 8, 1841 REPUBLIC of TEXAS to GEO. W. DAVIS, beg. at N. W. corner JAS. P. DAVIS sur. and JAS. P. WALLACE survey

G/33 QC Aug. 15, 1850 JOHN CARROLL, assessor City of Austin to GEO. W. DAVIS

F/234 WD April 28, 1853 ROBERT D. FLANIKIN to LASA McKINZIE, WIT: A. B. McGILL, JOHN B. COSTA

E/145 deed July 23, 1850 JAMES CUNNINGHAM et ux SUSANNAH to LASA McKINZIE. WIT: J. HANCOCK, PHIL CLAIBORNE

PC 180 ESTATE LACY McKINZIE decd. filed Oct. 1, 1853 by ANN McKINZIE & GEO. W. DAVIS, Oct. 15, 1853. Aprs. CAPT. JAMES ROGERS, ENOCH S. JOHN-SON & NELSON MERRELL, JR., Mar. 26, 1855. JAMES McKINZIE & heirs of LASA McKINZIE, FRANCIS M. HOPKINS, SARAH E. HOPKINS, RACHAEL A. HOPKINS GEO. W. McKINZIE, MARY ANN McKINZIE, MARTHA M. McKINZIE, LASA McKINZIE FRANCIS McKINZIE, AMANDA McKINZIE & HARRIETT E.McKINZIE, all under 21 years, no guardian. BENJ. F. CARTER aptd. guardian ad litem; that ASA McKINZIE one heir and WM. ROBERTSON heirs of SARAH E. McKINZIE ROBERT-SON not residents of Texas, Mar. 26, 1855, JAMES McKINZIE, son of LACY McKINZIE decd. and ANN McKINZIE widow of decd. ASA McKINZIE & WM. ROB-ERTSON not residents of Texas; 1 share to SARAH E. ROBERTSON, nee McKIN-ZIE, DAU. 1 share to FRANCIS M. HOPKINS, SARAH E. HOPKINS & RACHAEL A. HOPKINS, minor heirs of RICHARD HOPKINS, decd. nee RICHARD McKINZIE, DAU.; 1 share JAMES McKINZIE, son; 1 share ASA McKINZIE, son; 1 share GEO. W. McKINZIE, MARY ANN McKINZIE, MARTHA McKINZIE, LACY McKINZIE, FRANCIS McKINZIE, AMANDA J. McKINZIE & HARRIETT E. McKINZIE, minors.

PC 42 guardianship LACY, FRANCIS, AMANDA, MARTHA & HARRIETT McKINZIE under 14 years and MARY ANN McKINZIE, minor, over 14 and under 21, petition by mother, ANN, they children of LACY McKINZIE

46/26 WD Dec. 22, 1879 W. F. RIBINSON et ux S. E., to T. A. FIELD, ack. before H. B. BARNHART, NP TCT

103/15 WD Aug. 19, 1891 T. A. FIELD et ux MARY ANN

52/33 RIGHT OF WAY DEED Oct. 20, 1881 W. F. ROBINSOM, et ux SARAH E. to AUSTIN & N. W. RY CO. before ALEX M. JACKSON, JR., NP TCT

PC 2172 EST. W. F. ROBINSON, decd. filed June 20, 1899; he d. April 30 1899 TCT petition by W. R. CASWELL, J. B. ROBINSON & D. A. McFALL, atty WILL: dated April 20, 1899 to ch. MOLLIE ROBINSON wife of FIELDS, J. B. S. H., HATTIE, now CASWELL and FANNIE Now DORBANDT. WIT: H.SCHIEFFER, D. A. McFALL, G. W. ALLEN, CHALRES STEPHENS, appraisers

159/398 Aff. dated Dec. 9, 1899 RE; MRS. SARAH E. ROBINSON wife of WM. F. ROBINSON d. 1897, left surviving husband and JOSEPH B., SAM., MOLLIE FIELDS, HATTIE CASWELL and FANNIE DORBANDT

825/539 Aff. April 10, 1947 H. R. HAMILTON now 58 years old knew MOLLIE FIELDS dau. of WM. F. ROBINSON, sister of HATTIE CASWELL, FANNIE DORBANDT &JOSEPH C. ROBINSON, she was also known as MARY FIELDS.

141/609 WD Jan. 17, 1900, HATTIE CASWELL et vir W. R. to JOSEPH B. ROBINSON

160/21 WD Feb. 16, 1900 FANNIE DORBANDT et vir THOS. of Lampasas Co. Tex: to JOSEPH B. ROBINSON

168/29 WD July 7, 1900 MARY A. FIELDS et vir T. A. to JOSEPH B. ROBINSON

165/75 WD July 14, 1900 SAM H. ROBINSON to JOSEPH B. ROBINSON

H/209 WD Dec. 29, 1854, GEO. W. DAVIS et ux EMELINE P. to JANE MORTON WIT: JOHN T. ALLAN, ROBERT A. A. CARLETON

U/246 PA Feb. 6, 1871 JANE MORTON to GEO. W. MORTON. ack. W. S. ERWIN Clk. CC Davidson Co. Tenn.

U/247 WD Feb. 21, 1871 JANE MORTON by atty. G. W. MORTON & B. H. DAVIS to J. P. RICHARDSON

28/361 WD Dec. 31, 1874 J. P. RICHARDSON TCT to SALEM HANCOCK. WIT: J. B. MORRIS, FRANK BROWN

W/707 WD Sept. 6, 1871 HARRIETT E. McKENZIE to SALEM HANCOCK. WIT: LACY McKENZIE

49/115 WD Mar. 1, 1881 SALEM HANCOCK et ux MOLLIE TCT to COLUMBUS BOATMAN, ack. before JAMES.A. WRIGHT, JP & EX NO TCT

49/113 WD Mar. 11, 1881 COLUMBUS BOATMAN et ux MARY to ANNIE McCARTY. WIT: JOHN DOWELL, FRITZ TEGNER, ack. FRITZ TEGNER, JP & EX NP TCT

X/580 WD Dec. 31, 1872 HARRIET E. McKENZIE TCT to WM. YATES CLARK. consideration paid by FRANCIS A. CLARK

Z/28 WD Oct. 25, 1873 HARRIET E. McKENZIE to CHAS. KIZINE

137/631 WD Oct. 29, 1896 CHAS. KAZINE et ux ANN to J. L. WILLIAMS. WIT R. W. RILEY, JOSEPH JOYNER

55/360 Wd Mar. 29, 1883 MRS. ANNIE McCARTY, ERIC F. McCARTY, A. J. McCARTY & A. B. McCARTY to B. BUSSEY, W. W. McBRIDE

62/421 WD Nov. 22, 1844 B. BUSSEY et ux MRS. F. J. to W. W. McBRIDE, rel on margin Sept. 9, 1886 B. J. KOPPERL

69/546 WD Sept 9, 1886 W. W. McBRIDE et ux MATTIE to SCOTT WEAR, et ux FANNIE

75/324 WD Sept. 9, 1887 SCOTT WEAR et ux FANNIE to MRS. PENSUELLE H. BACOT, separate property.

97/201 WD Jan. 2, 1891 P. H. BACOT et vir T. W. to L. J. WILLIAMS before RUDOLPH KRAUSE, NP TCT

152/135 WD Nov. 17, 1898 L. J. WILLIAMS et ux CARRIE C. to GEO. W. WALLING

173/30 WD Feb. 2, 1901 CHAS. (CHARLIE) KIZINE, JOE J. JOYNER, LEE PICKETT, LIZZIE PICKETT, GLEN KIZEN, TCT, GEORGE SAULS et ux FRANCES, of Williamson Co. Tex., WILL EDWARDS et ux SALLIE, FANNIE & CAROLINE KIZINE and DELPHIA KIZINE all Bexar Co. Tex. to JOSEPH B. ROBINSON

228/13 WD Aug. 24, 1907 CHARLIE KIZINE, JR., TCT to JOSEPH B. ROBINSON "my 1/15 und. int. inh. by me from grandparents CHARLIE And ANN KIZINE"

198/97 WD May 11, 1904 GEO. W. WALLING, JR. to J. D. CAHILL

196/464 Dec. 2, 1905 J. D. CAHILL et ux CAMBY

301/63 WD Nov. 19, 1917 hmstd. desig. J. B. ROBINSON et ux OTTILIE
Marriage 7/338 Jan. 21, 1891 JOSEPH ROBINSON & EDNA NITCHKE
Marriage 15/192 Dec. 5, 1908 J. B. ROBINSON & MISS OTILLIE CHARLOTTE LOESCHMANN, both Travis County, Texas

574/544 Wd Sept. 24, 1937 J. B. ROBINSON et ux OTTILIA, J. B. (JACK) ROBINSON et ux OLIVE, SAM ROBINSON et ux LARETTE, W. F. ROBINSON et ux FLORENCE & JOHN ROBINSON et ux KELSIE to JOSEPH C. ROBINSON sm

40/333 Marriage Lic. June 5, 1942 W. P. CRISMAN, JR. & MISS FARRIOR McLAURIN

873/503 aff. Nov. 20, 1947 by SAM ROBINSON son J. B. ROBINSON and first wife EDA, decd. d. 1906 no will CH: J. B. (JACK) et ux OLIVE, SAM et ux LARELLE, JOHN et ux KELSIE, W. F., et ux FLORENCE & JOSEPH C. (2) wife OTTILLIE survives J. B.

PATENT April 20, 1840, REPUBLIC OF TEXAS to THOS. GRAY

A/559 WD Sept. 4, 1843 THOS. GRAY, bastrop Co. to SAMUEL HIGHSMITH.WIT J. H. GILLESPIE & L. P. SULLIVAN by GILLESPIE before GREENLIEF FISK, CJ

F/127 deed Jam. 29, 1850 EDWARD BURLESON to JOSEPH LEE, WIT: E. B. WADE J. R. E. GOODLET

A/341 deed Dec. 6, 1839 S. HIGHSMITH to LOUIS P. COOKE, WIT: JAMES WEBB WM. A. LANE, ACK. before M. H. BEATY, CC TC Tex.

F/350 Sept. 10, 1850 SWD JOSEPH LEE to HORATIO GROOMS. WIT: RICHARD T. PARKER, TIMOTHY McKEAN

M/116 adoption Feb. 12, 1858 HORATIO GROOMSadopts HORATIO GROOMS LEE, son of my dau. SARAH LEE decd. Apts. son ALFRED GROOMS trustee if Sr. does not live until child's majority.

R/545 WD Jan. 30, 1869 ALFRED GROOMS, H. GROOMS LEE to WAYMAN F. WELLS

V/129 WD May 25, 1871 JOSEPH LEE et ux SARAH J. to WAYMAN F. WELLS

X/307 Wd Dec. 20, 1872 THERESA HIGHSMITH sur. wife and admrs. SAM HIGHSMITH decd. WIT: H. A. SMITH, B. H. DAVIS

93/156 WD Mar. 26, 1890 MARY, EMILY, AMANDA LaRUE et vir GEORGE F.LaRUE PETER C., JAMES MORGAN, THOS. W. & GEO. H. WELLS to JNO. B. RECTOR

396/576 cc EST. AGNES WACHSMAN decd. Mar. 15, 1922 admr. Lee Co. Tex and sur. husband of AGNES who d. July 24, 1921, Lee County, Tex. left ch:

HERBERT 21, ROSE BIRNBAUM 19, EMET W. 17, GEORGE 13, CLARA 5 and
ADOLPH W. 7 mos. $24,000 bond: C. L. SEELKE, J. G. KAPPLER, L. FARRIS,
JOHN SCHNEIDER, M. E. SUCHS, R. A. FALKS sureties April 11, 1923 Arps.
JOHN PROSKE, WM. GROPP & OTTO SCHULZ

PC 5800 guardianship Hays Co. Tex. CH: of MILTON KASCH son of ED
KASCH and wife who d. Nov. 22, 1937 Hays Co. Tex: MILTON EDWARD KASCH,
BETTY ANN & JAMES WARREN KASCH. MILTON KASCH was 40 years old on Nov.
22, 1947. Feb. 4, 1946 AMANDA KASCH div. MILTON KASCH in Hays Co. Tex

1005/29 Oct. 21, 1940 aff. RE: EVA HOPE ROBINSON she was EVA HOPE ANDER-
SON m. (1) JERA PAYNE THAYER 1 ch. ELIZABETH d. inf. JERA PAYNE THAYER
d. many yers. ago and EVA HOPE m. (2) E. B. ROBINSON no. ch. she d. in
Austin May 26, 1945, parents of E. B. ROBINSON d. many years ago MABEL
& FRANK ANDERSON & EDITH ANDERSON sisters and bro. and ETHEL TURNER
sister of E. B. ROBINSON only heirs of E. B. ROBINSON and EVA HOPE
ANDERSON ROBINSON.

34571107 Aff. IN RE: MORRIS, BLACKBURN & MORRIS & RAY, WILLIAM A. BLACK-
BURN Feb. 1, 1896 m. a dau. of NATHANIEL TOWNSEND, decd.by his second
wife, ANGELINA L.: 1st wife of NATHANIEL TOWNSEND was MARIA d. intestate
ca 1840 4 CH. HALSY, MARIA, NATHANIEL JR. & BENJ. R. all except BENJ.R.
d. without issue prior to death of their father; HALSEY & MARIA buried
in cemetery Austin and NATHANIEL TOWNSEND, JR. killed at Gettysburg
during Civil War on July 28, 1865. BENJ. R. was only heir of his decd.
mother MARIA. A. R. MOORIS Feb..1896 in re; Lucretia Ray & Mrs.E. A.
RAY family of TCT and were sisters of J. R. RAY, LUCRETIA & ED RAY were
minors April 1, 1875 and J. M. MORRIS et ux M. M. MORRIS sold to JOHN
W. MORRIS and wife, VALLIE S. Nov. 12, 1912 (Vol.256/95) and Dec. 12,
1899 ED. H. CARRINGTON et ux to J. M. MORRIS.

OAKWOOD CEMETERY City of Austin, Travis Co. Texas (This was the cemetery
laid out on the original plan of the City of Austin 1840) These graves
are in the southwest corner.
The following are some relatives of BENJAMIN E. EARNEST, who m. MARY
FELLS SARGENT, who was a half sister of W. E. SUMNER, father of compiler.
Most of these older persons came to Rockdale, Texas, ca 1855 from Tenn.
about 1870 moved to Austin, or some of them ca 1855.
BENJAMIN E. EARNEST 4/11/1846 (Tenn) 8/18/1924
BENNIE WOOTEN EARNEST 12/6/1882 5/18/1902
MARY FELLS EARNEST 10/24/1850 (Miss) d. May 4, 1932
JOSEPH S. EARNEST 6/13/1851 d. 4/15/1933 (bro. B. E.)
MRS. A. M. McFARLAND 7/7/1842 d. 10/3/1904 (sister B. E.)
EUCLID M. EARNEST 1/16/1818 7/5/1872 (father B. E.)
FRANCES M. EARNEST 10/25/1825 11/29/1898 (mother B. E.)
W. H. McFARLAND 11/5/1875 d. 10/12/1904, son DAVID D.10/22/1888 2 yrs.
BENNIE E. McFARLAND 9/1/1870 d 3/9/1881
JAMES E. WRIGHT 11/2/1843 d. 11/1/1904
S. E. WRIGHT son S. M. & E. A. WRIGHT 11/17/1855 d 6/7/1883
SAMUEL M. WRIGHT 12/27/1809 d 11/15/1893 wife ELIZABETH A.8/19/1819 d.
1/17/1888
MARGARET HAMILTON 3/21/1781 d. 2/ 27/1867
RACHEL WRIGHT wife of JOSEPH WRIGHT 6/21/1812 11/8/1893
JOSEPH WRIGHT 12/10/1798 d. 12/4/1898
MRS. MARY DITTRICH 83 d. 9/4/1932 at home of dau. MRS. F. W. GOLLMAN.
MRS. M. D. DITTRICH b. 1849 Arman, Austria, came to America 1892 2
stepsons survived: WM. D. DITTRICH of Edna, Texas and RICHARD DITTRICH
of Jollyville (Williamson Co. Texas)

MRS. MAGGIE DILLINGHAM BARNES 56 d. 4/4/1931. She was granddaughter of
Gov. O. M. ROBERTS, an orphan raised by him at Gov. Mansion. 3 ch: SUR:
ELLEN DILLINGHAM, S. R. & G. N. of Briggs, Texas and bro. O. M. ROBERTS
Austin; 2 half sisters, MRS. LOTTIE COOK of Lamesa, Tex. and MRS. MARY
CALVERT, Houston and 2 half bros. A. P. & O. B. ROBERTS of Austin and
uncle, ORAN ROBERTS, Austin and aunt MRS. MAGGIE SPAN, Austin

FITZHUGH CEMETERY, near Hays andTravis County lines:
J. E. CLICK 6/4/1885 d. 2/ 3/1918; E. S. CLICK 7/11/1829 d. 8/15/1912

JESSE E. LANGSTON 10/23/1837 2/10/1902 ROXNEA F. 1/16/1840 10/9/1923
MRS. ELIZABETH PRATHER 1812 - 1903
F. H. PRATHER 12/31/1845 10/13/1931 Co. "C" B. M. TEXAS CALV. CSA

FISKVILLE CEMETERY, Travis Co. Texas (north of Austin. Only the oldest birth dates were copied)
J. A. ALVIS 8/10/1829 1/21/1907
TIMOTHY CASWELL 5/1/1831 8/22/1897; JULIA CASWELL 2/16/1838 7/14/1914
ELIZABETH SMITH 10/5/1845 10/25/1886 infant of J. M. & E. SMITH died 10/18/1886
MAUD E. SMITH b 3/../1800 d. 1891
"GRANDMOTHER" CAROLINE PETERS 5/..18/10 d. Jan..1908 next to MINNIE E. WARREN 4/29/1855 d. 6/19/1919 and LYMAN WARREN 5/16/1840, 4/5/1920
WILEND ROBERTS BINJACH (MRS. L. D.) Tenn. unable to read further.
A. B. TOWNSEND 3/23/1818 2/9/1879 Masonic Emblems.
SALLIE M. TOWNSEND wife of A. B. 2/27/1862 and inf. son of A. B. & S. M. TOWNSEND 2/7/1862 d. 3/ 15/1862
WILLIAM, son of A. B. & CAROLINE TOWNSEND 1/18/1887 (?) 6/2/1870?
LOU ELLA dau. of A. B. & CAROLINE TOWNSEND 10/3/1871 8/5/1878
LULA dau. of WM. & CAROLINE CARROLL 8/15/1885 1/5/1886
WILLIAM CARROLL 10/26/1839 12/26/1903 CAROLINE CARROLL wife of W. C. CARROLL 1849, 9/13/1904
N. J. BRUNSON 2/ 5/1840 8/16/1925 MARTHA S. BRUNSON 3/13/1838, 11/10/20
BENJAMIN T. GAULT 6/26/1831 d 4/ 5/1895
GILES H. BURDITT b. Tenn 3/2/ 1818 d. 5/ 20/1903
MARY J. BURDITT d. 11/5/1905 83 y. 11 mos. 2 days
JESSE BURDITT (VAULT) b. (broken 1789(2) d. 1855 MILDRED (VAULT) BURDITT, wife of JESSIE b. 1790 d. 4/4/1870
EDWARD S. GILES 8/6/1798 7/7/1888 ?
S O U (WODMAN) THEO. M. CLARKE, Cedar Camp No. 537, Austin b. 10/24/1847 d. 1/2/1920
VIRGINIA CLARKE 11/23/1848 11/3/1928
AMANDA E. SHERMAN 1/13/1837 4/21/1912
MORGAN D. SHERMAN 11/3/1826 6/24/1882
MRS. SARAH TWEEKLE wife of FIELDER b. 1830 d. 1867
MRS. RUTH MUSE 1807 d. 1864
FIELDER TWEEDLE b. 1822 d. 1867 son of SARAH & F. b. & d 1868
W. H. WEST 3/15/1837 6/15/1905
CAROLINE FAULKNER wife of W. H. WEST 12/9/1838 6/25/1902
MARY E. SAUNDERS wife of DONALD McKINSEY d 1/27/1879
GEORGE SAUNDERS b. N. J. 2/ 3/1800 d. 10/ 20/1878
SARAH E. wife of EDWIN L. SAUDERS b. Knox Co. Ill 12/7/1840 d.11/4/27
EDWIN L. SAUNDERS 8/14/1835 d. 4/4/1902
DANIEL R. PAYTON b. 1829 d. 1889 AMANDA B.(JORDON) PAYTON 1845-1932
JAMES W. PAYTON 1875-1892

JOSIAH F. HANCOCK m. MISS MARY ANN ELIZABETH O'QUINN, dau. JAMES, Dec. 19, 1848 in Yazoo Co. Miss.

PATENT, MAY 3, 1838 to JAMES MANOR, bounty warrant No. 3164 issued by Secy. of War of Republic of Texas

PC 270 EST. PHEBE S. MANOR d. 3/12/1859 EDWARD HARRINGTON, ISAAC WILDBAHN, WM. H. HILL, NELSON S. RECTOR & THOMPSON M. RECTOR

V/648 Nov. 30, 1871; JAMES MANOR & A. GROESBECK, WM. J. HOTCHKISS, WM. R. BAKER, F. A. RICE. WIT: T. B. WHEELER, ROBERT M. ELGIN, H. HALL, ROBERT M. ELGIN before E. SIMMLER, NP Harris Co. Texas

PC 803 EST. JAMES MANOR, decd. d. at home 5/17/1881; JOHN T. HAYNES & THOS. E. ROWE, petitioners, filed June 2, 1881; CH. MRS. MATILDA J. GLASSCOCK, MRS. ELVIRA T. DAVIS, MRS. LAVINIA H. THOMPSON, MRS.CATHARINE G. WHEELER and CH. of decd. dau. MRS. ANN E. BOYCE, viz: MRS. ALICE STRICKLIN, MISS EMMA BOYCE, LEE BOYCE & GENY BOYCE and wife, ELIZABETH ANN & dau. LUCY MANOR and CH. (esse) WIT: F. M. WILDBAUM, J. W. BITTING WILL, dated May 20, 1879, CODICIL dated May 14, 1881 MISS EMME BOYCE dead. Guardianship filed Sept. 8, 1885 by M. C. ABRAMS on LUCY MANOR 9, in May 1885 and LIZZIE N. 6 in Oct. 1885; live with M. C. ABRAMS and their mother ELIZABETH A. MANOR ABRAMS.

234/258 Aff. June 25, 1909 WM. LUDECKE, & A. B. HOWELL, RE: ROBERT J.
NIXON,, d. 7/23/1906 et ux MARY E. D. d. Aug. 16, 1889, Ch: JIMMIE d.
1885, ROBERT. W. ED J., ELIZABETH, GREG. J., ETHEL, ELIZABETH m. HOTCH-
KISS, ETHEL L. m. W. H. BENNETT DC 21, 179 Sept. 6, 1904 removal of
disabilities of minority, ETHEL NIXON, above 19 years of age.

1/97 Transfeript J. C. TANNEHILL to JAMES SMITH, Sept. 25, 1838, WIT:
F. P. WHITING, ALFRED SMITH, SILAS DINSMORE.

A/41 deed JAMES SMITH to J. L. LYNCH. WIT: JAMES MANOR, J. C. TANNEHILL
Bastrop Co. Tex. but ack. before J. W. SMITH CJ TCT

1/238 Transcript PARTITION July 2, 1839 Bastrop Co. J. C. TANNEHILL,
J. S. LESTER, WM. M. EASTLAND, JAMES SMITH, JOHN L. LYNCH, SILAS DINS-
MORE, WIT: THOS. J. RABB, N. W. FAISON

1/244 Transcript SILAS DINSMORE, JAMES SMITH, J. C. TANNEHILL, J. S.
LESTER, J. L. LYNCH, WM. M. EASTLAND to ALFRED SMITH July 3, 1839. WIT:
J. W. HADEN, WM. T. HADEN, N. W. FAISON, THOS. G. RABB

A/30 Mar. 18, 1840 CHAS. DeMERSE to JAMES TRAMMELL.."about 200 yards
from road across it, made by the troups under the command of Genl.
BURLESON in the march up the country about the last of Jan. 1839".
WIT: JAMES H. BARNWELL, JOSEPH MORELAND

A/80 July 11, 1840 deed, JAMES MANOR, admr. of JOHN L. LYNCH, decd. to
JAMES SMITH

DC 253 filed Feb. 28, 1853 JAMES W. SMITH vs. ELIZABETH B. SMITH,ALFRED
SMITH, SIDNEY P. BROWN et ux CAROLINE A., JOHN F. SMITH, MARY E. SMITH
& SUSAN A. SMITH, JAMES SMITH d. of a mortal wound (by bull) on Jan.24
1845; ALFRED SMITH & JAMES W. SMITH sons by 1st. wife, AMELIA OWENS
SMITH, CAROLINE, A. S., JOHN F., MAY E. & SUSAN A. by second wife,
ELIZABETH B. HAYDEN SMITH says, then 1845 all except ALFRED were infants
(under 21) since then CAROLINE A. m. SIDNEY P. BROWN, undivided interest
in 460 acres near Austin, with JESSE C. TANNEHILL & THOMAS SMITH; many
slaves, naming them, bought in N. C. & Tenn; that JAMES SMITH moved
from Tenn, to Texas; that he sold a plantation in Tenn; the homestead
of JAMES SMITH included Outlots 30, 40, 41 in Division "A" Austin;
testimony by AARON BURLESON, BENJ. M. CLOPTON, JAMES H. MATTHEWS,
JUSTINA A. CLOPTON is sister of ELIZABETH B. SMITH, married JAMES SMITH
1832 Rowan Co. N. C., ALFRED & JAMES SMITH sons ofFirst marriage;JOHN
A. GREEN, atty. and W. L. or W. S. OLDHAM, & MARSHALL, atty.ALEXANDER
W. TERRELL, gdn. ad litem for JOHN F., SUSAN A., & MARY E.; other
attys. S. G. SNEED & THOS. H. DUVALL. COMMISSIONERS: AARON BURLESON,
ASHFORD B. McGILL, THOS. F. McKINNEY.

B/307 deed Nov. 23, 1846 EST. JAMES SMITH to THOMAS SMITH, Matagorda
Co. Texas

B/486 Jan. 6, 1849 THOMAS S. SMITH resident of Matagorda Co .. Texas

P/237 deed April 18, 1861 THOMAS SMITH of Jackson Co. Oregon, but
signed and ack. in TCT April 23, 1861 to WM. J. TANNEHILL (son of J.C.)

DC TCT July 16, 1864 SUSAN A. (SMITH) HARTSON & JOHN M. HARTSON abandoned a boy WILLIAM 11 y. and ..BARTIE girl...years. Mar. license 5/396
TCT M. B. DAVIS m. SUSAN A. HARTSON June 20, 1881

PATENT: TITLED Mar. 19, 1835 to THEO. BISSELL, a married man with
family. WIT: J. W. BUNTON, M. DUTY, A. GARCIA

D/583 deed April 24, 1852 SOLOMON B. CONLEY to WILLIAMSON S. OLDHAM.
Gonzales Co. Tex. WIT: HORATIO S. PARKER, G. F. W. RICHTER, ack. be=
fore F. CHENAULT cc Gonzales Co. Texas

1/246 Transcript July 3, 1839 same grantors to NEILAND SAWLES (SAULS)

D/252 WILL, CLEMENT R. JOHNS, will was probated In Franklintown,Williamsom Co. Tenn. O. H. CULLEN, GEO. E. ZIMPLEMAN & JOHN A. GREEN, apprs. Oct. 1, 1868 Franklin, Williamson Co. Tenn. HON. ROBERT S. BALLEW, Judge, DAVID CAMPBELL kept said will Aug. 23, 1866, JOHN S. PARK,JOSEPH L. PARK, sureties for JAMES P. HANNER, extr. WILL to JAMES PARK HANNER et ux MARY TO DAVID CAMPBELL in trust land in Johnson Co. Tex. for HUGH & DAVID CAMPBELL until 21 years of age; if JAMES PARK should die to WILLIAM PARK & FRANCES PARK, bro and sister; all property I have in their father's estate, mtg. to W. H. GILL, Clarksville, Texas; to H. PARK NEELY to HENRIETTA PARK CAMPBELL her father to receive as trustee to wife and DOCTOR J. F. HANNER'S Wife to JOHN W. HANNER, JR., JAMES PARK & JOHN PARK, JR. Ellis Co. Tex. land; papers with J. A. N. MURRAY & WM. H. GILL, Clarksville, Tex; WM. A.PARK's widow; Aug 26, 1866. WIT: JOHN B. McEWEN, THOS. K. HAYAN, JAMES PARK & WM. JOHNSON, Aug. 25, 1866 CODICIL WIT: WM. JOHNSON, JNO. B. McEWEN, THOS. K. HAMBY

R/431 Oct. 16, 1868 JAMES PARK HANNER of Williamson Co. Tenn. to WM. K. BECKETTE, WIT: L. B. & L. W. COLLINS

285/282 Aug. 28, 1915 Tr avis County Texas to ESTATE W. K. BECKETT of 2 acres, known as "ROBERTS SCHOOL HOUSE AND LAND" ..abandoned.

713/553 PATENT, REPUBLIC of Texas to THOMAS GRAY April 20, 1841, issued Jan. 19, 1838 by Bd. Ld. Comrs. Bastrop Co. field notes by THOS.H.MAYS

A/45 Nov. 13, 1839 S. HIGHSMITH to EDWARD BURLESON, land of JACOB HARRELL & WATERLOO tract and CROCHERON league and JAMES ROGERS survey. WIT: AUGUSTUS SEEGAR, JAMES WEBB, before JAMES W. SMITH cj TCT (The WATERLOO tract was the original name of the CITY OF AUSTIN)

C.540 July 1, 1848 WM. H. CUSHNEY ASSR. & COL. taxes TCT to JOSEPH LEE WIT: JOSIAH FISK, F. M. HARRIS.

A/441 Dec. 6, 1839 S. HIGHSMITH to LOUIS P. COOKE, WIT: JAMES WEBB, WM. A. LANE, ack. M. H. BEATY CCC TCT

Y/171 Deed July 10, 1852 JOSEPH LEE to ALFRED GROOMS, wit: WM. H. KIMBALL, H. W. RAGLIN

234/170 1909 MRS. BETTI GROOMS HELM widow THOMAS HELM, dau. of ALFRED GROOMS et ux BETSY GROOMS d. Nov. 1883; ALFRED GROOMS m. 1 time only; 2 ch. AFFIANT and one child who d. infancy.

573/567 Sept. 10, 1890 P. deCORDOVA says PEYTON W. NOWLIN d. 1884

183/191 deed Feb. 4, 1903 P. W. JOBE to C. P. RANDOLPH love and affection for nephew

169/548 Mtg. F. T. RAMSEY, May 23, 1902 to JASPER WOOLDRIDGE, trustee-

S/427 deed Dec. 8, 1866 SAMUEL M. WRIGHT and wife ELIZABETH to J. H. COLEMAN, Beg. S. E. cor. WM. P. WALLACE lea. near gates of J. STEELE MATTHEWS, N. E. COR. of...AINSWORTH tract sold to JOSEPH WRIGHT, part of land set apart to MARY J. GOOD formerly MARY J. REDDING cites heirs of ROB ERT REDDING: WM. M., MARY J. et ux WM. GOOD, MINERVA J. wife of HUGH ADAMS, JOSEPH REDDING, LAURA REDDING, KATE BALLARD wife of...

Q/773 Dec. 17, 1866 W. M. REDING, LAURA JOSEPHINE, H. S. ODOM et ux M. J., A. J. BALLARD and wife, KATIE. ack. Caldwell Co. Tex.

X/555 Feb. 21, 1873 JOSEPHINE ROGERS et vir JONATHAN ROGERS, JOSEPHINE REDDING on Dec. 17, 1866 was under 21 years of age now 1873 of age.

X/531 E. JANE TYSON Feb. 12, 1873 QC "by last will of my late husband, ROBERT L. REDDING, made 1849" WIT: WM. M. PERRY, N. A. RECTOR

Y/450 July...1873 N. S. RECTOR et ux HARRIETT C. RECTOR

606/174 PATENT Oct. 29, 1856 (2 lots west of present capitol bldg.) to M. C. HAMILTON assignee of A. J. HAMILTON "transfer by MORGAN C. HAMILTON to A. J. HAMILTON Sept. 15, 1856."

Z/276 May 5, 1857 M. C. HAMILTON to R. T. BROWNRIGG before A. W. TERRELL NP TCT

O/135 O. H. MILLICAN of TCT cons. paid by GEORGE W. GLASSCOCK, SR. growing out of our partnership for building of LUNATIC ASYLUM near City of Austin. (This was at West 38th and Guadalupe, now in City)

49/263 LOUIS R. HILLEBRAND (HILDEBRAND) and wife EMMA L. to THOMAS MONOGUE, April 12, 1881

295/481 July 25, 1917 MARY MONOGUE dau. of THOMAS M. & BRIDGET who m. Sept..1855, 1 time,THOMAS MONOGUE d. May 26, 1885 4 ch: MARGARET McCULLOUGH wife of JAMES H. & affiant, and THOMAS M. & WILLIAM

152/52 May 9, 1894 THOMAS MONOGUE and wife,ALBERTA of Barton Co. Mo.

163/280 April 18, 1900 BRIDGET MONOGUE & wife to ARTIE B., MELETA & EMILY L. NUMBERS

D/299 PATENT to P. W. NOWLIN June 12, 1849

DC 2995 filed Sept. 8, 1870 W. E. GOODRICH, B. G. GOODRICH, FANNIE E. BOARDMAN et ux of T., S. E. GOODRICH, MRS. M. S. THORNTON, LUCY L. DAVIS, et ux I. V., J. A. ADAMS et ux F. E. ptfs. vs. MRS. M. A. GOOD-RICH (BETTIE, TEXELEN, minors) says COL. S. W. GOODRICH died 10/1/1870 T. D. MOSELEY gdn. ad litem minors; MRS. ALBERTA ADAMS calls for CAPT. J. E. BOULDIN's west line.

27/371 partition 1874 Lists above and M. COATNEY THORNTON, BETTIE A. BRADLEY wife of LEONARD, M. B., W. E. GOODRICH of Guadalupe Co. Tex. J. ALBERTA ADAMS wife of F. E. & B. G. GOODRICH of Los Angeles Co. Calif says MARY A. GOODRICH now decd. signed S. ED GOODRICH, FRANK E. ADAMS S. E. GOODRICH, JR.

165/616 Dec. 27, 1900 LUCY L. surviving widow of I. V. DAVIS, SR. to my children: ROBERT I., MAY W., same as above

168/144 Feb. 4, 1901 grantees Vol. 165/616 and wife, F. L. MONTGOMERY to M. C. GRANBERRY

76/346 Sept. 9, 1887 F. McNICHOLAS, Galveston Co. Tex. to SIMONS & SHAW (T. F. SIMONS & FRANK D. SHAW)

286/83 cc EST. VA. HUTCHINSON KENDALL decd. Cuyahoga Co. Ohio. NATHAN KENDALL, son, Tuson, Ariz. HAYWARD H. KENDALL, son, SUSAN E. ROOT dau. of FLORENCE KELLY, decd.

PATENT to ABNER MATTHEWS Dec. 14, 1850

Y/38 Sept. 20, 1872 JOSEPH LEE et ux SARAH J., HORATIO G. LEE to JOHN HANCOCK, GEO. B. ZIMPELMAN, GEORGE HANCOCK, CHARLES S. WEST, CHARLES W. WHITIS, MINUS M. LONG, JOHN T. MILLER, EDWARD CHRISTIAN & JOHN IRELAND

37/187 JOHN HANCOCK, et al of TCT & JOHN IRELAND, Guadalupe Co. Tex. to CAPITAL STATE FAIR ASSN. .

107/52 WD Oct. 14, 1892 M. K. & T. LAND & TOWN CO. to A. C.MARCONNIER

108/248 PA Mar. 9, 1893 A. C. MARCONNIER et ux GERTRUDE L. to M. M. SHIPE, ack. WM. B. SMITH, NP Kings Co. Washington.

P. C. 1337 MATHILDA CHRISTIAN July 19, 1888 sur. wife of ED. CHRISTIAN d. April 14, 1887, 3 ch. NANNIE P. 14 y MAGGIE H. 10 yr and ED LOOMIS

722/38 1st. class Headright Cert. No. 72 1/3 Lea. issued Jan. 19, 1838 by Bd. Ld. Comr. of Bastrop Co. Texas to THOMAS GRAY

H/504 Sept. 26, 1855, SAML. STONE to MARY ANN STONE says land bought with wife's separate funds 100 ac. does not mention where it is located. WIT: THOS. H. DUVAL, FRANK GILDART

PC 238 SAMUEL STONE, Est. filed Nov. 20, 1857 MARY ANN STONE surv.wife FRANK GILDART, FRANK BROWN, O. H. CULLEN, JOHN T. PRICE. J. M. BLACK-WELL, appraisers

R/468 Nov. 7, 1868 MARY ANN STONE to SAMUEL T. STONE (Vol. 68/76 Feb.20 1886 S. T. STONE et ux to MARY A.) (18 sq. feet part of this property and father of SAMUEL STONE buried there; affd. Vol. 687/43 aff. SAML. T. STONE et ux SARAH N. STONE, lived at 401 E. 17th. Austin, Texas)

PATENT to LOUIS HORST, Oct. 7, 1848

PC 693 Feb. 9, 1878 LOUIS HORST decd. d. Jan...1878 by MARGARETHA HORST surviving wife, WILL: Dated May 10, 1870.

PC 723 MARGARET HORST filed May 10, 1879 she d. M..1879.."being old and infirm in body.." to 7 children of self and LOUIS HORST: LOUISA ROBIN-SON, EMMA FELLMAN, AUGUST HORST, MATHILDA CHRISTIAN, MARGARET KAVANAUGH CHAS. HORST, JAMES HORST, will dated July 29, 1878.

DC 3533 LOUISA ROBINSON vs. GEO. E. ROBINSON Jan. 22, 1873 for div. m. July 24, 1856 in TCT 2 Ch: MAGGIE who d. and LOUIS under age, NEILL McCASHIN, Jury foreman.

DC 3937 Feb. 2, 1874 says LOUIS ROBINSON under 14 years and request change of names to LOUISA H. & LOUIS HORST (aff. Oct. 24, 1913, Vol. 261/55 says that she still used LOUISE ROBINSON & never remarried)

F/358 Dec. 17, 1853 W. R. CANNON to BENJ. F. JOHNSON

29/280 MARY H. PRICE (X) of Limestone Co. Tex. May 14, 1875 to WM. R. DAVIS

K/471 deed May 12, 1856 WM. R. CANNON of Hays Co. Tex. to C. K. HALL WIT: JNO. A. GREEN, R. D. CARR

DC 1752 filed April 15, 1858 THOS. EBORN vs. WM. R. CANNON, Est. C. R. PERRY, MARIAH CANNON admrs. Hays Co. recites: C. R. PERRY, MARIA CANNON. Now MARIA ALLEN, W. T. ALLEN, admrs.

PC 450 EST. THOS. EBORN decd. April 1, 1871 PA JOHN A. ADAMS to JOS. NALLE admrs. THOS. EBORN d. intestate 1870 no wife or child, or parent in State of Texas; MARY L. ADAMS sister and bro. WM. EBORN & SOPHIA PAUL, M. G. BARROW

302/621 Transfer of parental authority Mar. 20, 1918 JAMES H. MACKEY an unm man of TCT agrees to adoption of JAMES WILLIS 6 mos. old son of J. H. MACKEY to MRS. S. ETHEL PERRY

302/622 adoption by MRS. S. ETHEL PERRY a fs. of TCT (also known as SALLY, SADIE (MRS. BEN) PERRY)

779/494 cc WILL, RICHARD PAYNE JONES of Medley Forest, Brazoria Co. Tex. Sept. 14, 1853..having heard of the death of my sister, MRS.ELEANOR P. FRANKLAND, revoke will made out by PETER McGREAL whilst I was in state of mental imbeculity..make solemn declaration that PETER Mc GREAL, and J. H. BARNES are of all men the worst in my opinion..appoints CHARLES COLVILLE FRANKLAND sole extr. refers to MR. JOHN BARNES of London, his partner. WIT: E. R. WISE, A. B. KRAUSS

108/44 PA Sept. 25, 1890 P.. C. SISSON (of Chambers Co. Tex) to Z. T. FULMORE

PC 272 filed Feb. 1, 1860 MARY ANN KELLY sur. wife FRANCIS KELLY, Separate property; MARY ANN, WM. T., JNO. W., MARY JANE KELLY, CHILDREN(?)

629/352 PATENT to ALBERT SILLSBEE May 24, 1839

755/42 PATENT Ja. 9, 1845 to CHRISTOPHER J. STROTHER, sold by C. J. STROTHER July 12, 1845 to STEPHEN DAVIS.

PATENT June 11, 1849 to JAMES H. RAYMOND (banker)

26/222 Mar. 24, 1876 JAMES H. RAYMOND et ux MARGARET J. to WM. NELSON

PC 687 EST. WM. NELSON decd. filed Sept. 18, 1877 by FRANK HAMILTON & ROBERT A. SMITH, WILLIAM NELSON d. Sept. 10, 1877. WILL dated Dec. 1, 1875 mentions property in SMITH and ANDERSON COUNTIES, TEXAS

241/49 Aff. by HERMAN PRESSLER, D. B. GRACY in RE: JOHN MADDOX et ux MARY D. she was formerly wife of WM. NELSON she was known as MOLLIE D. MADDOX. (aff.302/168) by F. M. MADDOX says he is bro. of JOHN W. MADDOX who m. widow of WILLIAM NELSON: MRS. HERMAN PRESSLER was a MADDOX (see Art. AUSTIN AMERICAN Dec. 14, 16, 1965)

A/362 REPUBLIC OF TEXAS April 30, 1841 to JAMES A. HAYNIE assignee of MARGUITO CASTRO

A/363 deed May 3, 1841 JAMES A. HAYNIE to AARON F. BOYCE, WIT: WAYNE BARTON, A. A. ANDERSON

A/527 Sept. 25, 1842 AARON F. BOYCE to NICHOLAS BOYCE of Bastrop Co. WIT: JAMES M. LONG, JAMES BOYCE

PC 121 EST. NICHOLAS BOYCE, decd. WILL: Oct. 16, 1849 to dau. AMANDA MULVENA NICHOLS sons: RICHARD & STEPHEN A. & BOEUERGARD, he not of age; dau. MARCELLA ELIZABETH m. TRIPLET, land near Hamilton Valley, 640 ac. Bastrop Co. used to pay debt to JOSHUA TEAGLE of Missouri; appoints bro. JAMES and SON, STEPHEN extrs. JOHN WILBARGER, THOS, ROWE, ISAAC BOYCE, appraisers

A/526 1842 NICHOLAS BOYCE of Bastrop Co. to JAMES BOYCE, WIT: AARON F. BOYCE, JAMES H. WEATHERSBEE

F/415 Jan..1854 STEPHEN A. BOYCE of Williamson Co. Tex. B. R. BOYCE of State of Calif. to THOS. J. PITT.

236/609 aff. by S. B. JESTER, nephew of MRS. SUSAN EDWARDS (now Mar.16 1910 decd) knew of SUGAR M. CAIN first husband of MRS. SUSAN EDWARDS during Mexican War 1846 he d. intestate Lampasas Co. Tex. 1869, no ch. S. D. EDWARDS, Manor, Texas, d. intestate about 1902, no ch; SUSAN CAIN EDWARDS d. 1909 WILL PC 3371 says SUSANNA EDWARDS wants to be buried by late husband S. M. CAIN in Manor, Texas, cemetery.

241/412 Mar. 2, 1910 MARY M. BOYCE et vir A. F. dau of J. Y. CAIN decd. contract dated June 5, 1870 by SUSANNAH CAIN, MARY M. BOYCE's father, J. Y. CAIN, RE: S. M. CAIN decd. 1869, ack. by BOYCE, Imperial Co.Calif

241/413 1910 EMMA TWEEDLE CARRUTH et vir T. P. dau. SARAH TWEEDLE of Lampasas Co. Tex.

241/415 S. M. CAIN TCT son J. Y. CAIN decd.

241/416 MOLLIE EDRINGTON et vir V. S. EDRINGTON TCT

241/417 M. J. EARNEST et vir J. W. EARNEST dau. of J. V. CAIN, MEDINA CO. Tex.

241/419 NETTI TWEEDLE AVERY dau. SARAH TWEEDLE et vir L. C., LlanoCo.Te

DC 26,259 filed 1910 EDRINGTON et al heirs of S. M. CAIN, C. CAIN,J.Y. CAIN, EMMA, NELLIE, MOLLIE TWEEDLE and HYMENA MUSE. ORDER appoints: A. J. EDRINGTON, CLYDE D. EARNEST, EDWARD B. EARNEST, MRS. RUTH I. WHIPPLE, J. W. WHIPPLE, MARY E. CAMPBELL, T. G. CAMPBELL, ANNA B.JARMON, R. F. JARMON, S. M. CAIN, NETTIE AVERY, L. C. AVERY, W. L. CARRUTH T. P. CARRUTH, IDA & R. M. WOMACK, R. C. BLACK, IMOGENE ATEN, IRA ATEN JOHN E. BOYCE, ELIZABETH & J. H. AVERY, ANNIE I. HUDGINS, T. E.HUGIS, BENJ. C. BOYCE, DAVID A. BOYCE, JOHN P. BOYCE.

252/280 M. J. EARNEST et vir J. W., CLYDE D. EARNEST, EDWIN B.EARNEST, MRS. RUTH I. WHIPPLE, et vir, J. W., MRS. MARY E. CAMPBELL et virT.G. Medina Co. Tex. MRS. ANNIE B. JARMON et vir R. E., TCT

H/62 Sept..1851 JAMES ALFORD, Makes application for division of ESTATE WM. H. SANDERS, decd; RICHARD HOOPER, JAMES MALONE, C. L. MANN, JOSEPH ROWE, JESSE BURDITT, commissioners. Heirs: ELIZABETH M. ALFORD,RICHARD H. SANDERS, MARTHA KNIGHT et vir THOMAS J. KING (X) WM. J. SANDERS, MARY ELIZABETH SANDERS, cc from Shelby Co. Texas

H/64 RICHARD H. SANDERS of Shelby Co. Tex. to JAMES ALFORD et ux ELIZA

H/65 1850 T. J. KNIGHT et ux MARTHA ANN, Shelby Co. Tex to JAMES & ELIZABETH ALFORD

H/63 1851 D. M. SANDERS, Shelby Co. Tex. to JAMES ALFORD

H/62 May 5, 1853 JAMES ALFORD et ux ELIZABETH M. (former wife of WM.H. SANDERS, decd. Shelby Co.)

1041/430 PATENT 1841 to JOSIAH WILBARGER, 1 labor (177 ac)

B/60 JOSIAH WILBARGER 1844 Bastrop Co. Tex. to MATHIAS WILBARGER, Bastrop Co. WIT: JOSIAH CLIFTON, LEMAN BARKER, ROBERT STEWART, DANIEL FRENCH (STEWART..STUART..STEWERT)

F/184 Sept. 1, 1852 JOHN W. WILBARGER et ux LUCY to CATHERINE C. ROWE wife of THOMAS E. ROWE

PC 210 MILLENIUM K. ALEXANDER decd. filed Sept. 5, 1855 by JOHN T. ALEXANDER, husband; she d. Aug. 3, 1855; CH. JOHN THOMAS 16, NEWTON J. 12; VIRGINIA E. 10; WM. A. 7; and EDWARD H. 5 years old

L/184 PATENT to NATHANIEL TOWNSEND 1851

Q/174 July 1862 CONDEMNING and SEQUESTERING of property of NATHANIEL TOWNSEND, . JNO. A. GREEN, receiver to ABNER H. COOK to JOSEPH M. STEINER. (This was the CSA GOV. sequestering)

Q/369 1865 to ANGELINA L. TOWNSEND, from BENJ. R. TOWNSEND, Col. of USA, Holland Patent, Queida Co. NY son of NATHANIEL, and MRS. MARIA TOWNSEND, decd.

70/192 1878 ANGELINA L. TOWNSEND, RANDOLPH W. TOWNSEND

255/327 aff. 1913 MRS. SUSIE M. ROBERTSON, fs. dau. of NATHANIEL TOWNSEND AND ANGELINA L. TOWNSEND: NATHANIEL TOWNSEND m. twice (1) MARIA d. prior to July 28, 1865 and left HALSEY, boy d. young unm; (2) ANGELINA L.; the children of first m. died young except BENJ. R. TOWNSEND

88/462 1889 deed PAULINE T. CULBERTSON, nee TOWNSEND et vir WM. J. of Edgar Co. Ill. to ANNA L. BLACKBURN

DC 863 Aug. 2, 1856 FRANCIS KELLY vs. JOSEPH WARREN

L/226 Feb. 19, 1857 P. A. FRANCIS KELLY et ux MARY ANN (being in feeble health and unable to attend to my affairs) to MICHAEL ZILLER WIT: AUGUST SCHWARTZ.

M/207 Mar. 31, 1858 JAMES TAYLOR et ux PAULINE to MOSSON et al

M/133 Feb. 17, 1858 FRANCIS KELLY et ux MARY ANN to ELIAS MOSSON, HERMAN MOSSON & HART SAMUELS land on D. J. GILBERT sur. all except participation in litigation with HAL MEDLIN. WIT: JOHN STELFOX, FRIED SUTOR

V/286 PA feb. 23, 1859 ELIAS MOSSON, Parish of New Orleans La. to H. M. & HART SAMUELS

V/287 Aug. 11, 1860 deed E. MOSSON to ROBERT J. TOWNES

pC 658 Dec. 30, 1876 petition of FRED CARLETON: 2 minors over 14; N. COBB TOWNES & E. T. TOWNES Children of R. J. TOWNES

M/58 Dec. 1, 1857 SHF. DEED to W. H. D. CARRINGTON (FRANCIS KELLY,prin. JOHN HORAN, WM. O'CONNELL, sureties,)motion C. W. DYSON,C.. KENRICK A. G. WEIR, sheriff

49/543 deed May 31, 1881 ALLEN TOWNES, Blanco, Tex. to E. M. PEASE

OAKWOOD CEMETERY, Austin, Texas, (southwest corner of oldest part)
"JULIA" WRIGHT wifeof JOSIAH WRIGHT d. 1854
R. P. WRIGHT b. Oct. 21, 1835 d. 9/1/1910
TENNIE wife of R. P. WRIGHT 1/20/1857 12/ 30/1931
LEMUEL EVANT SHELBY 1876-1938
MABEL C. WRIGHT SHELBY, 1880-1959
FANNY E. WRIGHT 1/12/1848, 10/8/1872
LAURA WRIGHT THORNE 1862, 1949
ADA WRIGHT 1868, 1950
WM. GIBSON 8/4/1874, his wife FANNIE12/22/1838 d. 1/18/1908
ANDREW GIBSON 1861, 1924
ELISSA R. GIBSON 10/5/1873, 9/3/1951
LILLIE GIBSON 12/12/1866, 1/26/1955
Dr.(?) WM. GIBSON 12/10/1863, 11/28/1930
ANNIE TIBAUT WALLING 1869-1957
LOUISA J. WALLING 12/22/1838, 9/24/1936
GEO. W. WALLING 8/6/1828, 12/29/1916
JAMES M. EARNEST 5/19/1849, 11/20/1911
FANNIE EARNEST d. 4/ 12/1937

"GENERAL GEO. W. TERRELL b. Ky. 1803 came to Texas 1840, from Miss. was associate Justice Supreme Court, Republic of Texas; 1840 Secretary of State, Republic of Tex. 1841, Atty. General 1841-2, Charge d'Affaires of theREPUBLIC of Texas to England, France and Spain, 1844-1845 d. Austin, May 17, 1846."

NEW HOPE CEMETERY, west ofHy. 29 S. of Leander, Tex. (Travis Co.):
SARAH wife of LINDSEY DAVIS b. Randolph Co. N. C. 7/10/1804, 4/7/1884
LINDSEY DAVIS b. Randolph Co. N. C..1805 d..1887?
MATHILDA MAY..4/27/1836 9/27,1903

510/193 Aff. ARTHUR von ROSENBERG et ux MARY HOLLAND m. Walker Co.Tex. Nov. 1881, she d. April 1927 he d. Aug. 30, 1934 both intestate, CH: DEVEREAUX, ROSA, AUTHUR W., NANNIE, EDNA, J. LESLIE, EDGAR

F/212 July 7, 1851 PATENT to HUDSON S. AKEN, assignee of S. G. SNEED

F/212 WD Feb. 21, 1853 HUDSON S. AKEN to JOSEPH WRIGHT, WIT: CHARLES HUGELY, THOS. FREEMAN

PC 208 EST. JOSEPH W. HAMPTON, July 30, 1855 proof by W. C. PHILLIPS, J. M. LITTON, J. M. W. HALL; owes cash; ELI C. HIGGINS owes cash; WM. SCURRY, owes cash. Decd. owned part STATE GAZETTE paper, mentions wife CYNTHIA R. HAMPTON. WIT: W. C. PHILLIPS, L. H. LUCKETT, JOSEPH BLEDSOE, R.. N. ALLEN & J. M. LITTEN, JAMES H. HUTCHINS, qualifies.

D/229 Sept. 30, 1855 widow CYNTHIA R. HAMPTON & MARY, LAURA, MARGARET, CHARLES & ROBERT HAMPTON, minor children

R/292 WD April 7, 1856 JOSEPH WRIGHT to MARY ANNETTE (dau. J. W.HAMPTON) HAWKINS.

X/118 WD Oct. 23, 1872 FREDERICK WILDE to HERMAN WILDE

252/388 cc Depositions May 8, 1912 Walker Co. Texas; MARY A. SMITH wife of S. R. SMITH m. Jan. 13, 1859 was MARY A. HAWKINS, and dau. of J. W. HAMPTON

PC 2827 EST. MRS. JESSIE FELTER, decd. dau. of CHAS. DURAND, she d. Mar. 4, 1905 in Toronto, Cana. hus: ROSCOE H. FELTER and JULIA I. ALBRIGHT (OLDRIGHT) executrix WILL, to sisters land in Canada; MARY, NELLIE, ANNIE JULIA, EMILIA, then to husband ROSCOE H. FELTER & CH. EDWARD W., GEORGE, CLARENCE DURAND.

DC 448 CHAS. L. McGEHEE & O. J. NICHOLS, partners in building TEXAS STATE CAPITOL BUILDING

E/95 JOHN POWELL, P. A. administrator MARK POWELL, decd. of Kent Co. Del. my brother JOSEPH POWELL of Kent Co. and E/96 JAMES POWELL of Kent Co. Del. my friend (?) JOSEPH POWELL all right and interest as one of the sons of JOHN POWELL.

MARY V. ARMSTRONG m. JAMES MORROW of Fayette Co. Tex. 1853

"NORTHERN STANDARD" of Clarksville, published 1849.

WM. MORROW d. Fayette Co. Tex. 1841, WM. H. BLAIR was executor

"TRUE ISSUE" published Oct. 15, 1864 in LaGrange, Fayette Co. Texas

SUSAN RICHARDSON gdau. of ASA BRIGHAM (who came to Texas 1830) m. JUDGE JOHN HANCOCK, of Austin, TCT

PRUDENCE WALKER, (mother of ELIZABETH WALKER who m. MICHAEL BUSTER) lost her husband, WM. WALKER, in Knox Co. Tenn. 1796 and 3 years later m. RICHARD MORROW & had ARMSTRONG MORROW b. 1801

JESSE GRIMES of Grimes Co. Texas, b. Duplin Co. N. C. Feb. 6, 1788; to Alabama 1817 was in Green Co. Ga. 1822. He was son SAMPSON GRIMES b. Va. and BARSHEBA WINDER of Md. JESSE GRIMES m. MARTHA SMITH, 1813. m. ROSANNA WARD, then came to Texas 1826. He d. Mar. 15, 1866 (is buried in State Cemetery, Austin, Texas)

RANDALL JONES b. Columbus, Ga., to Sabine River 1814; then to Texas with ASA HILL family. 1810 JONES left Ga. and settled in Wilkinson Co. Miss. was in War 1812 and had a store in Nacogdoches, Texas.

P/331 Dec. 31, 1853 deed to D. F. WADDELL

THOMAS F. McKINNEY is buried in OAKWOOD CEMETERY, Austin, northwest section.

PC 142 ESTATE NICHOLAS McARTHUR d. Nov. 3, 1851 (he had contract to build new Land Office Bldg..this is the building of O. HENRY fame) NICHOLAS McARTHUR'S home was at upper ferry cut near where the present Montopolis Bridge is located.

31/56 JOHN HANCOCK was to have expenses in T. J. CHAMBERS litigation. In 1852 JOHN HANCOCK got property and d. July 19, 1893, leaving wife SUSAN E. and 1 son, E. B.

Z/169 Dec. 10, 1873 JAMES W. HANCOCK & JAMES DOUGHERTY, WIT: JOHN HANCOCK.

162/156 Nov. 5, 1901 LEWIS HANCOCK et ux ELIZA H. sur. wife and children of GEORGE HANCOCK.

J. W. WAFFORD was son of EMILY DAVIS who m. JAMES ROWE

DC 25,956 suit of family of GEO. B. ZIMPLEMAN (ZIMPELMAN)

PC 387 EST. DR. ROBERT DAVIS and wife, EMILY, Later she m....ROWE, their home was above JONES FERRY, on the south side of Colorado River below the City of Austin, and in the area of the present BERGSTROM AF BASE. THOMAS H. DAVIS, his son, I. V. DAVIS m....GOODRICH, dau. of W. A. & MARY

Aff. IN RE: WILLIAM KARR BECKETT family; MRS. CORNELIA JAMES b. Feb. 6, 1853 in Tenn. d. TCT Mar. 6, 1847, TCT m. WM. KARR BECKETT 1872 he d. July 12, 1912. CH: DAVID H. d. 1944; MINNIE D. 1951 m. M. C. BRODIE d. 1956; OLLA fs; G. K. BECKETT b. 1878, d. 1950; WM. L. BECKETT b. 1884; MARY D. fs; THOMAS A. b. 1887 d 1961. SCHOOL 2 acres north corner of BECKETT FARM was named for GEO. ROBERTS.

M/394 SWISHER'S TAVERN was located on Block No. 70, Austin, northwest croner 6th and Congress Avenue.

R/180 deed SWISHER to WHITIS shows was U. S. GOV. HOSPITAL (1862-4?) on West 26th Street, Austin TCT

V/543 JAMES BURLESON to JOHN W. TAYLOR et ux NAURIN (dau. of AARON BURLESON)

DC 12,241 filed Aug. 17, 1895 SUSAN E. HANCOCK vs. EMMA J. ELDER,widow J. A., MINNIE ALTON, JAMES WM; CHAS AUGUSTUS & ARTHUR CLYDE ELDER

PC 8181 EST. W. W. CHILDRESS, decd. Sept. 17, 1934 (he was son of JOHN C.) sur. by wife, MRS. M. A. CHILDRESS, CH: MOLLIE BEARD 59 y.; THORNTON Tex.; MABEL BOATRIGHT 48 del Valle, Tex. ELLA BOATRIGHT 44 del Valle, J. T. CHILDRESS 46 San Antonio, Tex. C. A. CHILDRESS 38, Austin,BEULAH MARTIN 29 Waco, OLA BROWN del Valle; EUNICE PHILECK 35 del Valle, BEATRICE CHILDRESS 33 del Valle, MAYE CHILDRESS 31 del Valle, C. W. CHILDRESS, 23 del Valle and 3 ch. of GRAHAM CHILDRESS, ELMA 26, MICHEL 21 and LELON 19 all Del Valle, Texas. W. W. CHILDRESS m. MARY DAVIS June 27, 1885, TCT 6/283 Marriage Records.

DALLAS MORNING NEWS: Feb. 15, 1964: MRS. EDDIE HODGE, Bonham, Texas; BAILEY ENGLISH CEMETERY: JAMES TARLETON, a Golaid hero, RICHARD LOCKE, a Texas Rev. soldier & DANL. ROWLETT, graves 115 years old.

B/424 April 24, 1847 JAMES W. THOMPSON et ux REBECCA CAROLINE to THOS. OSBURN. WIT: N. M. BAIN, THOS. W. WARD

D/31 deed Mar. 17, 1849 THOS. OSBURNE to E. SEIDERS: WIT: C. C. CADY, A. B. McGILL

84/246 HOMTESTEAD DESIGNATION Dec. 26, 1888 H. B. SEIDERS et ux ALICE Lot 1 Block 13 Dickson Addn., Taylor, Williamson Co. Texas.

DC 22,463 filed April 22, 1905 RICHARD L. HANCOCK, GEO. F., REUBEN K., WAYNE, MATTIE ENNIS & SARAH E. BREWLON & MARY E. THURMAN, Baylor Co.Tex vs. T. P. WASHINGTON and ADA WHITE TCT and MELISSA HANCOCK now wife of B. C. THORPE, heirs of JOSEPH HANCOCK who d. 1902 and MARY E. HANCOCK who d. Sept. 1904

A/88 Aug. 11, 1840 THOS. G. GORDON, Mtg. to DICKERSON MacFARLANE. WIT: JAMES M. LONG, D. H. GATTIS

F/331 Oct. 28, 1853 deed MIRABEAU B. LAMAR of Ft. Bend Co. Tex. to JAMES B. SHAW

DC 317 JAMES B. SHAW vs. heirs JAMES A. CALDWELL, 1854: ROBT. CREUZBEAUR JOHN C. DUVAL, P. deCORDOVA, apptd. commissioners Nov. 4, 1854

S/299 PA June 18, 1869 JOHN S. YOUNG of Abbeville Co. S. C., WM. L.PAIN et ux MARY J., Nashville, Tenn; THOS. BLACK et ux EMMA J., Nashville, Tenn, FRANK P. YOUNG, Nashville, Tenn. but temporarily residing in Richmond, Ind. JANE L. J. YOUNG of Nashville, Tenn.; JOHN S., MARY J., EMMA J., FRANK P. YOUNG being only surviving children of JOHN S. YOUNG now decd.and JANE L. J. YOUNG as heirs of SILAS C. COLVILLE.

S/447 COMPROMISE Sept. 2, 1869 H. N. DUBLE, of GalvestonCo. Tex. and A. McFARLAND, R. J. McFARLAND, & M. J. McFARLAND of Bowie Co. Tex. and the YOUNGS named in S/299 , page 83 hereof.

T/287 PA Jan. 19, 1870 JANE McFARLAND of Bowie Co. Tex. to C. R. JOHNS CO. TCT all interest as heir of my decd. children WM. McFARLAND, SAML. N. McFARLAND & SARAH JAQUES McFARLAND, said land having been willed to my said decd. children and their bros. and sisters by JAMES A. CALD- WELL, decd.

X/579 deed June 22, 1870, JANE McFARLAND, ABEL McFARLAND, M. J. McFAR- LAND, R. J. McFARLAND, legatees of J. A. CALDWELL, decd. to CLARA MAAS

31/16 Mtg. Nov. 22, 1875 CLARA MAAS Et vir M. MAAS

R/360 Oct. 24, 1864 deed HENRY COCKERON (CROCKERON) Bastrop Co. Tex. to MILTON PERRY, WIT: J. R. GILLESPY, JOHN L.JOHNSON

R/361 Nov. 12, 1867 MILTON PERRY et ux ISABELLA of Milam Co. Tex. to R. W. RILEY, TCT. WIT: A. G. PERRY, ack. before J. T. PERRY, CCC Brazos Co. Texas

143/164 Aff. Jan. 24, 1874 by ALBERT G. RANDALL, knew THOMAS W. WHITE formerly of Bond Co. Ill., and citizen of Texas; was unm, family lived in Bond Co. Ill. near Greenville; father, ELEAZER H. WHITE and 2 bros. SAMUEL E. WHITE & JOHN G. WHITE, later living in Texas and sister MARY L. wife of JOEL ELAM

232/101 SILAS CHEEK COLVILLE to lawful children of sister JANE L. J. YOUNG et ux of DOCTOR JOHN S. YOUNG of Tenn; Georgetown tract to WM. COLVILLE RANDOLPH son of my old and much esteemed friend JAMES M. RAN- DOLPH, Crawford Co. Ark. and negro girl, LOUISA to nephew WALTER SCOTT YOUNG son of DR. JOHN S. & JANE L. J. YOUNG, CHARLES JACKSON of Fannin Co. Rep. of Tex. etrs. Dec. 13, 1842. WIT: THOS. F. SMITH, GIBSON MAY.

232/103 WILL: JAMES A. CALDWELL, land &c. in Sherman and Austin, Texas all to children of JANE McFARLAND wife of JACOB only blood relation now in Texas, cc from P.C Fannin Co. Texas

DC 5301 filed June 27, 1871 EDMUND D. PATTERSON, MAGGIE A. NICHOLS et v B. F., SAMUEL K. COWAN, minor, spl. gdn. J. K. McFALL & MARY McFALL his wife, says: JOHN S. SPENCE D. Aug. 1878, intestate no ch. MARTA M. SPENCE sur. wife; JOHN B. SPENCE left no mother or father, plaintiffs ED W. PATTERSON, MAGGIE A. NICHOLS, MARY McFALL, only dau. of ISABELL SPENCE PATTERSON now decd. who was sister of JOHN S. SPENCE decd.;SAML K. COWAN only child of JENNIE PATTERSON decd. son of SAML. COWAN, JOSEPH C. KERBY m. MRS. MARIE M. SPENCE Dec.2, 1879

909/294 PATENT to JAMES TRAMMEL Feb. 25, 1841.

C/80 Administrator's deed, WAYNE BARTON, admr. J. TRAMMEL decd. June 15 1847 "vacant succession of JAMES TRAMMEL"

DC 335, JAMES C. STEPHENSON et ux MARY JANE, ANN B. BARTON, WM. E. BAR= TON by JANE C. STEPHENSON gdn. vs. DENNIS TRAMMEL, MARGARET MODGLING, JOHN ZIVELY, deft. JURY: JOHN BRANDON, JAMES MANOR, DeWITT LOVELACE, JOSEPH L. LANE, GILES H. JOSEPHUS COWAN, JOHN A. P. CARR & WM. BARBER BOSTICK, foreman.

H/268 aff. by ELSBERRY SPARKS says he is almost 60 years old, April 20 1852, Sebastain Co. Ark., knew DENNIS TRAMMEL & MARGARET O.MODGLING since they were smallOnly ch. of DAVID TRAMMEL and wife; JAMES TRAMMEL & BURKE TRAMMEL were sons and only ch. of SAMPSON TRAMMEL, lived with their uncle, DAVID TRAMMEL, all dead except DENNIS TRAMMEL & MARGARET MODGLING, P. A. MARGARET (X) MODGLING to DENNIS TRAMMEL May 23, 1855. WIT: E. E. & NANCY HANCOCK (HAMOCK) ack. before E. E. HAMMOCK.
DC Sept. 15, 1846 HENRY ADAMS vs. NANCY BROWNING et vir DANIEL,CHRISTOP HER C. & JOHN BROWNING, MARY POTTER et vir L. J., MARTHA PATTERSON, et vir J. B., PAMELIA BOSTWICK et vir JOHN, FRANCES COX et vir WM. COX.

H/61 deed T. J. CHAMBERS of Liberty, Texas, May 15, 1854 to J. B. SHAW

V/274 deed to GEO. HANCOCK Mar. 3, 1871

266/561 cc from Chambers Co. Tex. WILL: PHILIP C. SISSON of Wallisville Chambers Co. Texas, gives to "beloved and only son PHILIP G.SISSON,"all" and appoints him executor..."I will here state that a dau. was b. to me whom I have not seen since she was in the 7th year of her age, if I have I did not know her, she is now in her 21st year, living under an assumed name and not a legal one. Thereby of her own act or at the instigation of others without consent and no disposition that I have made... to retaliate evil for evil..my said son P. G. SISSON who has stood by me in all my difficulties, personal and domestic.." Oct. 22, 1892 filed Aug. 16, 1899. P. C. SISSON d. July 25, 1899. WIT: F. R. LaFOUR, W. B. JONES

K/217 Nov. 11, 1854 deed T. J. CHAMBERS to P. C. SISSON, both of Liberty County, Texas (court house burned in this county)

N/509 deed Nov. 15, 1859 HUGH TINNIN et ux HILLEN MARY to EZEKIEL NANCE of Hays Co. Tex. WIT: THOS. C. JACKSON, J. C. KIRBY, ack. P.DeCORDOVA NP

W/526 deed April 29, 1872 EZEKIEL NANCE of Hays Co. to EDMUND J. DAVIS of TCT WIT: F. E. CUSHMAN, L. W. COLLINS, NP TCT

PC 902 EST. EDMUND J. DAVIS, d TCT Feb. 7, 1883 left only heirs ANNE E. DAVIS sur. wife and 2 sons: WALTER & BRITTON S. DAVIS, of other counties. WILL Aug. 16, 1866 at Corpus Christi, Texas to wife ANN ELIZABETH.

60/509 deed May 12, 1883 ANN E. DAVIS to WM. ROBBINS of Cook Co. Ill.

226/335 Aff. of heirship June 30, 1900 by E. P. HINDS & WM. DUNCAN of DuPage Co., Ill before LIMUS C. RUTH, NP DuPage Co. Ill. WILLIAM ROBBINS et ux MARIE S. ROBBINS m. 1 time only he d. June 20, 1889 she d. 1882. CH. JOHN S. ROBBINS, GEORGE B. ROBBINS & ISABEL M. m. WM. H. KNIGHT. Instrument shows of record in Wilbarger Co. Texas, also deed filed Feb. 13, 1914, GEORGE B. ROBBINS et ux LILLIAN E.

314/90 July 4, 1839 cc from General Land Office archives. REPUBLIC of TEXAS, FANNIN CO. That JOSHU SHARPLESS Is entitled to 640 acres of land trf. JOSHUA SHARPLESS of Fannin Co. Rep. of Texas to SILAS C. COLVILLE of same Co. dated Aug. 2, 1839. WIT: J. A. CALDWELL, RICHARD McINTIRE.

81/607 Mtf. Oct. 19, 1889, A. R. KELLUM et ux SARAH A. on 221.2 ac. BUNTON HOMESTEAD says homestead is in Hot Springs, Ark.

93/350 May 6, 1890 SARAH A. KELLUM formerly BUNTON, sells BUNTON homestead. Her ack. before D. B. GRACY, NOTARY PUB. Travis Co. May 6,1890. KELLUMS ack. before JNO. D. WARE, Notary Public, Garland Co. Ark.

95/635 deed Sept. 1, 1894 JAMES H. BELL to DAVID W. McCONOUGHY of Westmoreland Co. Pa.

43/509 deed ALEXANDER CALDER et ux AFFA Dec. 6, 1876 of Wayne Co. Pa.to A. OPPENHEIMER of Dallas Co. Texas. Ack. Delaware Co. NY

48/17 Jan. 28, 1880 AUGUST OPPENHEIMER & MRS. IDA OPPENHEIMER, nee NEWTON, of New Orleans & MESSRS. JOHN B. COTTON & CAMILLE E. GIRARDY of New Orleans, La.

DC 8145 filed Feb. 9, 1887 MARY COTTON, New Orleans, La. & NOAH R. COTTON, same, & H. N. FARLEY, residence unknown, C. E. GIRARDY (man) and J. C. McCOY of Dallas Co. Texas, are only heirs of JOHN B. COTTON decd. d. New Orleans, August ...1881. PUBLISHED "DISPATCH"Austin paper Jan. 12, 1887, ANSWER of JNO. M. McCOY states: JNO. C. McCOY d. April 30, 1887 Dallas Co. Texas
136/420 Mar. 28, 1894 deed EVA GIRARDY & HELENA GIRARDY fs of New Orleans, La. to JOSEPH N. WOLFSON, same place.

DC 12,391 filed Nov. 18, 1895 JOSEPH N. WOLFSON of New Orleans, La. vs. NOAH. R. COTTON, of Catahoula Parish, La., MRS. MARY COTTON HINCKLEY et vir, JAMES: MRS. JANE HABER, widow of FRANK: ROSINE, JEANIE & FRANK L. HABER, minors

196/49 cc Orleans Parish, La. succession of MARIE LEOPALDINE EMMA LeSUER, widow of CAMILLE E. GIRARDEY, No. 34,707; she d. July 7, 1891; Pass Christian, Miss. EVA G. 24 years, HELENA GIRARDEY 21 years

B/160 ANN McKINZIE, widow of LASA by atty. ASA McKINZIE & WM.ROBERTSON, not residents of Texas; SARAH E. ROBERTSON, formerly SARAH E.McKINZIE, dau. of decd. FRANCES M. HOPKINS, SARAH E. HOPKINS & RACHAEL E.HOPKINS minor heirs of RICHARD HOPKINS, decd. dau. of decd.

G/34 Jan. 22, 1853, G. W. DAVIS to heirs of J. PORTER BROWN

I/304 Feb. 16, 1855 ANDREW O. HORNE, SR., love and affection for wife, ELIZABETH. WIT: W. L. HILL, A. O. HORNE, JR. & JOSEPH LEE NP TCT

DC 4796 W. T. HORN, SARAH O. BROWN, et vir LEANDER, ANDREW O. HORNE,JR. of TCT., M. G. HORNE, Hill C-o. Tex. plaintiffs vs. A. A. HORNE, JOHN C. HORNE defendants of Bastrop Co. Tex. filed Feb. 25, 1865. MRS.ELIZA-BETH HORNE d. TCT. Ch: WM. HORN, M. G. HORNE, ANDREW O. HORN, JR. & SARAH O. BROWN, and A. ARCHIBALD HORN & JNO. C. HORNE, grandchildren of A. ARCHIBALD G. HORNE, decd. petitioners: WM. T. HORNE, JR, SAML. D. HORNE, SARAH M. JAQUA, JAMES M. HORNE, MATTIE L. HORNE & NELLIE G. HORN, children of WM. T. HORN, decd., MARY E. KEEL & ROBERT M. KEEL minor grandchildren of WM. T. HORNE, decd; ROBERT M. KEEL & MARY E.KEEL are children of MARIAN KEEL decd. dau of WM. HORNE, decd. WM. T. HORNE d. TCT Nov. 2, 1862. A. O. HORNE, admr. qualified Mar. 22, 1877

71/114, Nov. 4, 1886 A. G. HORNE et ux MARY C.

41/529 July 1, 1878 M. G. HORNE to wife, SUSAN C.

58/205 Nov. 16, 1883 MALCOLM G. HORNE et ux SUSAN C. of Hill Co. Tex. to AMANDA A. HORNE, a feme sole

44/571 July 7, 1879 SAMUEL D. HORNE to AMANDA A. HORNE "same land inherited from grandmother ELIZABETH HORNE, decd.."

34/26 July 30, 1877 SARAH J. JAQUA et ux A. E. to DON WILSON, trustee

PC 662 filed Feb. 12, 1877, W. T. HORNE, decd. J. W. SMITH, Jan. 1883 aptd. gdn. ad litem of minors: ROBERT & MARY KEEL, MATTIE LOU HORNE, AMANDA A. HORNE, widow of W. T. HORNE has 3/7 interest; NELLIE HORNE 1/7 interest; J. M. HORNE 1/7 interest ROBERT & MARY KEEL 1/14 each

51/148 Dec. 5, 1881 I. M. HAMMETT et ux AMERICA T.

82/350 Aff. Aug. 21, 1888 by MRS. M. J. BROWN, and MRS. R. E. CLIFTON, knew ED M. HURST et uxCHARLOTTE, that on Jan. 23, 1863 and long prior thereto HURST and wife had homestead in William Co. Tex. on N. San Gabriel 1/2 miles above Gabriel Mills 20 miles from Georgetown, Wmson Co.Tex.

26/524 May 25, 1874 JESSE G. STEWART to A. W. TERRELL, A. S. WALKER, atty. all interest from his father B. K. STEWART and atty. for O. E. STEWART, nephew of JESSIE G. STEWART, who has certain indictments by TCT grand jury.

A/365 Nov. 17, 1840 J. C. HARRELSON of San Augustine Co. Tex. toJOSEPH MORELAND. WIT: NATHAN MITCHELL, M. H. BEATY before J. W. SMITH CJ

32/159 Nov. 13, 1875 G. B. FORREST et ux REBECCA L. of Madison Co. Tex. JOSEPH R. THOMPSON et ux M. AURELIA & LEE L. MORELAND, Freestone Co.Tex J. L. CALDWELL et ux LORETTA L., A. TURNER MORELAND & J. J. MORELAND of Falls Co. Tex. heirs of JOSEPH MORELAND and wife MARY ANN

828/166 Jan. 26, 1847 PATENT to J. A. G. BROOKE.

37/297 Deed Oct. 26, 1874 JOSEPH MORELAND to M. AMELIA THOMPSON, etvir J. R. dau. of JOSEPH MORELAND. WIT: H. B. STEWART, A. T. MORELAND be= fore A. G. ANDERSON, CDC Freestone Co. Texas, by F. W. SIMS, deputy

37/320 Feb. 1, 1877 REBECCA L. FORREST et vir G. B. M., Madison Co. Tex., LORA L. CALDWELL et vir, J. L., Falls Co. Tex; MARY A. THOMPSON et vir J. R.: A. T. MORELAND, J. J. MORELAND & L. L. MORELAND of Freestone Co. only heirs of JOSEPH & M. A. MORELAND, late of Freestone Co. Texas.

37/299 JAMES L. CALDWELL et ux LORETTA L., Falls Co. Texas

26/271 April 2, 1873 States: Deed W.573 was bought by LUCIAN G.BRITTON Mtg. Oct. 6, 1875 L. HARTSON et ux ELIZA J., to E. J. DAVIS, as trustee for MRS. REBECCA BRITTON

842/152 cc ESTATE JAMES P. DAVIS, decd. from Bastrop Co. Tex. May Term 1848, GEO. W. DAVIS, administrator, No. 130 Bastrop County Court

D/612 deed of gift Aug. 5, 1851, JULIA ANN BACON to dau. ADALAIDE VANN (LAZARUS T. VAN) WIT: ISAAC M. BROWN, JOHN B. BACON

R/316 Mar. 15, 1864 DAVID ADAMS of Falls Co. Tex. to father THOMAS ADAMS of Williamson Co. WIT: F. W. CAPPS, CJ Falls Co. FRANK E. ADAMS

W/243 Dec. 15, 1871 to THOMAS ADAMS, of TCT

PA Nov. 10, 1894 ANNIE P. HARRIS, widow of JNO. W. HARRIS & CH: REBECCA P. HARRIS, LILLIE B. FISHER, et vir WALTER P., CORA L. DAVEN- PORT et vir WHARTON, all of Galveston Co. Tex. JNO. W. HARRIS of Gal- veston Co. Texas, ESTATE JOHN W. HARRIS, decd.

247/409 cc WILL, JOHN W. HARRIS of Galveston Co. (handwritten byHARRIS) (This man built the PEASE MANSION.."WOODLAWN" in Austin, 1853. When he returned to Virginia he found his intended had married another.) He sold "WOODLAWN" to E. M. PEASE, who had held a number of government- al positions in the REPUBLIC of TEXAS, and was also Governor of the State. He had only 2 children.. 2 daus. one married GRAHAM and he and his wife d. at same time, when their children were very young. The "PEASE" family raised these grandchildren...one R. NILES GRAHAM re- mained in the home of his grandparents until about 1960, when he sold it to GOVERNOR SHIVERS (former). MR. GRAHAM, moved the memorabilia of over a hundred years of family and TEXAs history into a local ware- house and donated the same to the City of Austin Public Library. The "TRAVIS ROOM" was established for the purpose of displaying and making available this vast historical donation.
    JOHN W. HARRIS willed his wife, ANNIE P. 1/5 of his estate and balance: dau. REBECCA P. HARRIS, son JOHN W. HARRIS, dau. LILLIE B.dau. CORA L. & to BRANCH T. MASTERSON for ch. of himself and ANNIE W. MASTERSON, formerly, ANNIE W. DALLMAN; BRANCH T. MASTERSON, T. W. MASTERSON, WILMAN D. MASTERSON, REBECCA B. MASTERSON, MRS. MAY M. FISHER, LEWIS FISHER & EVELYN MASTERSON.

313/453 May 31, 1919 CORA L. DAVENPORT, widow, parents were JOHN W. HARRIS & ANNIE P., he d. April 1, 1887, left wife, ANNIE P. and ch: JOHN W. HARRIS, REBECCA P. HARRIS, LILLIE H. FISHER, wife of WALTER (both d. in Galveston storm Sept. 8, 1900) and CORA L. DAVENPORT wife of WHARTON, LILLIE H. FISCHER, left 1 ch. FREDERICK KENNER FISHER,sm MRS. ANNIE P. HARRIS d. Oct. 29, 1906, was widow of JAMES WILMER DALLAM (DALLMAN) when she m. JOHN W. HARRIS, 1 ch. ANNIE DALLAM m. BURCH T. MASTERSON, she d. Sept. 9, 1900, 5 Ch. MAY M. wife of LEWIS FISHER, THOS. W. MASTERSON, JR., J. HARRIS MASTERSON, d. June 27, 1905 left wife, EVELYN P. no children and she m. DR. X. SANDOX, and WILMER D. & REBA MASTERSON, FREDERICK KENNER FISHER d. June 27, 1910 left 3 uncles, DR. WM. C. FISHER, SAM R. FISHER, & DR. F. K. FISHER and 1 aunt, MRS. ANNETTE P. ARMSTRONG.

JAMES H. MATTHEWS d. June 7, 1871, FRANK MATTHEWS, admr. LOUISA D. surviving wife and gdn. of WM. S. 17, DANIEL B. 15, MARY E. 13, JAMES

JAMES S. 12; ROBERT H. 12 and RUFUS P. MATTHEWS 5.

E/224 PATENT to CHARLES L. MANER (MANOR)

93/559 May 1, 1890 MARY E. R. HARDY et vir HENRY C., & WM. WHARTON
GILLETT of Petersburg, Va. HENRY C. HARDY, JR. et ux EMILY M., GEORGE
E.HYATT et ux KATE GILLETTE of Brooklyn, NY heirs of REV.CHAS.GILLETTE

V/682 Nov.. 1871, THOS. J. BEALL et ux MARGARET N. (she was RAGSDALE)
bros. JAMES R. RAGSDALE & WALTER G. RAGSDALE of Burleson Co. Texas

V/716 Nov. 1871 A. W. TERRELL of Robertson Co. Tex. to HEBERDEN BEALL
trustee, T. J. BEALL, Robertson Co. Texas

X/374 A. W. TERRELL, Dec. 21, 1872 to MRS. E. H. MITCHELL

PC 1226 A. W. TERRELL April 26, 1887, father of HOWARD D. TERRELL, minor
MRS. E. H. MITCHELL d. April 21, 1887, HOWARD D. TERRELL is grandson
of MRS. E. H. MITCHELL and sole descendant. WILL: MRS. NANNIE WOOD
San Saba Co. Texas, et vir CAMPBELL & CULLEN DOUGLAS of Sumner Co.Tenn
ELIZABETH H. MITCHELL to bro. CULLEN DOUGLAS, NANNIE WOOD, gdau. of
my late husband, DR. JAMES MITCHELL dated April 8, 1887. Vol. 105/4
April 9, 1892 HOWARD D. TERRELL, Boonville, Cooper Co. Mo. to A. W.
TERRELL.

P/196 June 24, 1861 DAVID G. ADAMS by agent THOMAS ADAMS to CHARLES
JOHNSON, land east of land sold to E. P. KILLINGSWORTH, Mar. 8, 1860

101/188 Feb. 10, 1891 CHARLES (X) JOHNSON et ux EMILY (X) WIT: MARY
OLIVIA JOHNSON, JOHN McDONALD

DC 18, 890 filed Sept. 20, 1902 GEO. W. BRACKENRIDGE, Bexar Co. Texas
vs. CHAS. JOHNSON, Nov. 3, 1904 supplemental answer filed by EMILIA
JOHNSON sur. wife of CHAS. J. JOHNSON, AUGUSTA LINDHOLM et vir S. L.:
HENRY JOHNSON, GUS JOHNSON, CHAS. A. JOHNSON, JULIUS JOHNSON, FRED
JOHNSON, WALTER JOHNSON, MARY JOHNSON, MATILDA BERGREN Et vir, CHAS. B.
ANNIE GUSTAVSON et vir J., & SCHARLOTTE TWINNING et vir, W. C., C. J.
JOHNSON d. Oct. 4, 1904.

S/345 deed Sept. 21, 1869 JAMES G. MOORE to A. H. BARNES undivided
1/5 interest in property of decd. father MARTIN MOORE.
Mar. lic. 2/145 TCT Nov. 24, 1863 BENJ. THOMPSON & MISS KATE L. MOORE

V/374 Aug. 18, 1871 LOUISA MOORE, Galveston Co. Tex.
DC 4790 Oct. 20, 1876, JAMES K. FARRELL et ux SARAH, nee MOORE

64/49 CC from New York: CHAS. C. NEWNING, TCT to SIMEON J. DRAKE, NY

31/100 note July 7, 1876 ALFRED E. TOWNES, Albemarle Co. Va. to DUVAL
BEALL
DC filed Feb. 16, 1865, M. C. HAMILTON vs. J. N. BAKER, No. 2284

842/335 cc MRS. ELLEN P. FRANKLAND, filed in Brazoria Co. Tex...to
nephew and sole heir CHARLES COLVILLE FRANKLAND, RICHARD PAYNE JONES
of "MEDLEY FOREST" mentions JOHN BARNES of London and his partner.

142/247 CC EST. GEO. ROCKWELL, decd. BERTRAND & GEO. A. ROCKWELL, extr
WILL of Junction City, Geary Co. Kan. dau. SUSAN R. ALBERS, gd.
CATHERINE ALBERS, ch. BERTRAND, ANNIE R. CHAFEE, KATE R. CLARKE and
THOMAS HAWLEY ROCKWELL, BERTRND & GEO. A. ROCKWELL, appointed executors
and WM. R. CLARKE of Kansas City, Mo. heirs of KATE ROCKWELL

208/398 Sept. 9, deed to ELIZABET NEY (sculptress, Austin, Texas. She
spelled her name ELIZABET)

218/389 Aff. by EDMUND D. MONTGOMERY says m. ELIZABET NEY, Sept. 10
1865 in Island of Medeira, 2 ch. dau. d. 1872, LORNE N. MONTGOMERY
b. Oct. 2, 1872, Waller Co. Texas. EDMUND MONTGOMERY d. June 29,1907.

F/144 June 3, 1852 JAMES H. RAYMOND to JOHN M. SWISHER, WIT: A. B. McGILL, N. C. RAYMOND.

DC 410 COMMUNITY SURVIVORSHIP July 14, 1868 by MARY A. GOODRICH, surv. wife of G. W. GOODRICH who d. Austin May 18, 1868.

PC 068 EST. S. W. BAKER, d. Austin, Mar. 2, 1884 dau. OCTAVIA B.ROESSLER: JENNIE WALDO BAKER and gch: MARY & JANE, daus of decd. son ANDREW BAKER; and MARY & JANE Daus. of decd. son DeWITT CLINTON BAKER, and ch. decd. son D. W. BAKER: MARY, ALICE, D. W. C., GRAHAM BAKER, NELLIE,, ELIZABETH, JULIA & ETHEL BAKER. WIT: WILL, N. T. STRAYHORN, D. C.WALKER' JACOB LESER.

DC 7167 OLIVE T. CLEVELAND KINNEY vs. DAVID P. KINNEY, filed May 17, 1884, six living children JOHN D., CHAS. D., GEO. P., OLIVEA S., OPHELIA L. & FRANCIS J. Last three are minors.(m.Jan. 16, 1859)

PC 2212 D. P. KINNEY Est. filed Dec. 21, 1899 he d. Dec. 16, 1899; BEULAH E. KINNEY, sur. wife and three sons by this m. MYRON D. 11, ROLAND D. 9, and HARVEY LEE 7, and GLADYS A. KING 1 year.

PC 2213 filed Dec. 21, 1899 guardianship on above minors.

M. S. DUNN, County Clerk Travis County for many years, b. Jan. 10, 1840, Charleston, S. C. His father came from Ireland; gf. and gm. d. on board ship, and father was adopted by MIDDLETON, and came to Texas 1848 to Seguine, Texas.

S/225 May 29, 1869 says CYNTHIA C. GLASSCOCK, decd. wife of G. W. SR.

PC 455 guardianship of ANNA E. GLASSCOCK says now, Dec. 30, 1873 wife of F. M. HALL

539/454 April 24, 1899 MRS. E. J. TALBOT, fs, Williamson Co. Tex.

PC 3105 SIMON BUTLER, decd. 1907 left property on Tennehill survey near Fort Prairie.

46/636 G. M. BRASS, SR., et ux, AMELIA, agreement, May 9, 1890 CH: GUSTAV MORITZ, JR., MATHILD PAULINE BRASS, CLARA BRASS & EUNA

PC 2205 EST, JAS. M. BUROUGHS, d. Nov.]], 1899, intestate, wife did not survive, 3 Ch: MARY ELLEN, JAMES HERILL & MARGARET. MARY was wife.

204/374 Deed Sept. 8, 1905 to SIMON FRITHIOF et ux, BRUNHILDE F. (This woman operated a beauty salon under the name of MRS. SCHNEIDER in downtown Austin, for many years. She had one child, a daughter)

DC 38,785 filed Sept. 26, 1921, ANNIE P. PANNEL vs. FULLER M. PANNEL m. May 3, 1889. No children.

A/126 cc from Bastrop Co. Tex. ESTATE, R. L. REDDING, decd. June 25, 1849, JAMES SMITH CJ., MARK M. ROGERS, Shf. & JAMES H. GILLESPIE, CC WM. M. PERRY, atty. representing estate. M. M. ROGERS, E. H. CASTLEMAN & ...GRAY appraisers. JOHN M. FINNIE, Depty. Clerk Bastrop Co. Oct. 7, 1870. WILL: to wife, JANE ELIZABETH, home in Bastrop, then Ch: WM. MAC, when he is 21 years old, MARY INDIANA, MINERVA JANE, MARGARET LAURA, NANCY JOSEPHINE & CATHERINE ELIZABETH, Will dated Feb. 26, 1849 WIT: E. A. CASTLEMAN, P. A. RUTHERFORD.

D/346 Oct. 15, 1850 T. J. CHAMBERS to BLOUNT & WM. CLEMENTS 150 acres N. Austin, now farmed by MR. AANSWORTH. WIT: S. G. SNEED, JAS. O'RICE

H/435 Aug. 21, 1855 BLOUNT & WM. CLEMENTS of Burnett Co. Texas, and SAMUEL M. RIGHT (WRIGHT) WIT: THOMAS E. SNEED, JOSEPH WRIGHT.

DC 29,416 filed Nov. 13, 1912, JAMES H. WRIGHT, CARRIE MOORMAN et vir WICKLEY, BESSIE McCONNELL et vir A. J., & HENRY WRIGHT, JR.,minor by next friend JAMES CUNNINGHAM, all of Garland Co..Ark. vs. JESSIE MADISON fs; HENRY WRIGHT, LELA BLANTON et vir JOSEPH, NOVELLA ROBINSON et vir SALEM TCT: SINA MAYS et vir, J. E., Bell Co. Tex.; EUGENE WRIGHT Tarrant Co. Tex.; MILTON & ETTA WRIGHT, minors, El Paso Co- Tex.MILTON WRIGHT d. May 1911 wife, CAROLINE d. April 1912, their son WM. M. WRIGHT d. Oct. 14, 1904, ch: JAMES, H. W., CARRIE MOOREMAN, BESSIE McCONNELL & HENRY WRIGHT, JR., children of M. & C. WRIGHT; JENNIE MADI=SON, HENRY WRIGHT, LELA BLANTON & LINNIE MAYS, EUGENE WRIGHT & NOVELLA ROBINSON & TOM WRIGHT, son M. & C. WRIGHT d. 1906, his ch: MILTON WRIGHT & ETTA MAY WRIGHT, minors.

32/549 Feb. 22, 1876 J. W. YOUNG et ux to NATHANIEL EARNEST of Shelby Co. Ill.

51/552 Feb. 16, 1882 NATHANIEL EARNEST et ux SARAH ANN, TCT

PC 1426 EST. NATHANIEL EARNEST d. May..1889. WILL, dated May 13, 1889 to only dau. JANE WEAKLEY and to wife, and other children not named. J. J. WHELESS, W. J. WHELESS, WM. BUTTERY.

589/52 PATENT to WILKERSON SPARKS July 21, 1835 says he is single man

DC 225 Sept. 21, 1852 SWANTE M. SWENSON vs. COLLIN FORBES, FORBES cut SWENSON's cedar.

N/399 July 30, 1859 S. M. SWENSON & FRANCIS DIETERICH to HUGH TINNIN

R/200 agreement Dec. 27, 1868 GEO. P. WARREN, PEYTON W. NOWLIN

I/137 Sept. 18, 1854 deed S. M. SWENSON, FRANCIS DIETERICH to PEYTON W. NOWLIN

58/598 Nov. 24, 1883 CHAS. M. LeSURER et ux ANN E. before E. A. STRICKLAND, NP Williamson Co. Tex. CYRUS H. RANDOLPH, et ux SUSAN M., MATTIE J. NOWLIN, MARY O. DINKINS, widow, ADELINE ROBINSON et ux DAVID N.

2/52 Abstract of Judgemnt against ED FLUKINGER vs. P. C. TAYLOR, R. KRAUSE, atty for plaintiff, Feb. 7, 1888.

333/190 aff. T. H. GLASS d. 1901 his wife, LENA GLASS then m. J. M. SHARP and she d. April 11, 1921; on July 22, 1892 T. H. GLASS et ux LENA adopted JOHN TAYLOR (Vol. 104/332) JOHN TAYLOR sometimes called JOHN TRAYLOR, JOHN GLASS or ROY GLASS, same place; now 1912 lives at Cape Charles, Va.

F/62 MATTHEW CARTWRIGHT to SAML. K. JENNING, JR., June 16, 1852 TCT WIT: WM. PELHAM, J. G. SWISHER

O/179 Mar. 27, 1860 ELIZA A. MOORE to ALBERT G. BUDDINGTON. WIT: EDWARD SEIDERS, PETER B. LOW.

Q/282 ANTON NEBGEN et ux CATHARINE M. Oct. 9, 1865 and GEO. DITMAR

768/327 June 17, 1867 PATENT to MARCUS THOMAS

PC 460 MARK THOMAS d. June..1871, H. McCLURE, applied letters of admin. proceeds paid over to ....HEISNER, agent for heirs.

29/151 filed April 29, 1875 GEORGE HEISNER to S. G.SNEED, County Superintendent of Schools, 2 acres for school.

471/374 April 14, 1874 PATENT to HEIRS of CASPER DITTMAR

50/280 ANTON & C. M. NEBGEN & M. DITTMAR co=heirs CASPER DITTMAR. ack. Gillespie Co. Texas, Oct. 25, 1880, GEORGE DITTMAR
Q/154 Nov. 17, 1863 A. NEBGEN et ux CATHARINE (X) M. NEBGEN & SAML. MATHER et ux ANNA.

50/282 Mar. 20, 1876, J. STULER et ux ANN, of Blanco Co. Tex...ANN STULER heir of CASPER DITTMAR

PC 2003 ESTATE GEO. DITTMAR, petition for guardianship filed May 15, 1896. GEO. B. DITTMAR, about 21 y.; ROSA J. about 18, EMILIE R. about 13 y. MARY A. DITTMAR about 10, FRANZ J. DITTMAR about 8 yr. and CLARA L. DITTMAR about 6 years, children of GEO. DITTMAR and wife EMILI J. had in the ESTATE, JOHN B. WENDE, decd. GEORGE B. DITTMAR became 21 Feb. 11, 1897 and GEORGE DITTMAR d. Jan. 18, 1899.

PC 2159 ESTATE GEO. DITTMAR, filed April 8, 1899 by EMILE J. DITTMAR surv. wife, 1. WILLIAM son 29 years TCT; A. E. dau 25 years; J. A. son 24 y., C. B. son 23, R. J. SPILLMAN wife of EDWARD SPILLMAN 21, EMILIE R. 16, M. A. DITTMAR girl 14, F. J. DITTMAR son 11 and C. A. DITTMAR girl 9.

NOTE: Nov. 7, 1845 (German Immigration ships of the ADELSVEREIN in 1845) ANTON NEBGEN on Ship "RIGS" Capt. Nesen.

I/40 Aug. 18, 1836 TITLE BOND, GEO. W. SPEIR & WM. HEMPHILL of municipality of San Augustine, Rep. of Texas to MATTHEW CARTWRIGHT. WIT: JACOB GARRETT, A. HORTON, GEO. TULL, THOMAS B. GARRETT & JOHN CALDWELL. Ack. by DAVID A. CUNNINGHAM CJ CB EX NP

394/226 Aff. MRS. BLOOMING DAVIS, sur. wife of J. J. DAVIS, SR. d.June 11, 1924 they m. Nov. 4, 1885 no children; J. J. DAVIS, SR. m. (1)MARY ELIZABETH NOLEN who d. 1882 ch: JENNIE DAVIS wife of N. A. DAWSON, of Jefferson Co. Texas; CORDELIA CORDIA DAVIS wife of R. H. ANDERSON, San Angelo, Tom Green Co. Tex.; FINIS EWING DAVIS d. Nov. 13, 1886, JOSEPH J. DAVIS, Jr., DAISY DAVIS, wife of CHESTER THRASHER, MARY DAVIS, wife of M. L. RIVERS, Elgin, Bastrop Co. Texas.

K/318 survey July 17, 1872 for BARTLEY B. MILAM, BRICE MILAM & A. THUR=MAN, chainmen, JNO. E. CAMPBELL, surveyor TCT

40/563 Mar. 30, 1878 BURRIS MILUM to JNO. H. MILUM land patented to grantor as assignee of B. M. MILAM

PATENT 1856 to ELHANAH BRUSH filed Dec. 26, 1851 issued by Augmentation Cert. 1319 Com. Harrisburg Co. Tex. Jan. 13, 1840 refers to survey made for W. D. HARRISON

X/253 Nov. 28, 1872 E. A. CABEEN et ux CATHERINE C. CABEEN to J. A. H. THURMAN, ack. before F. W. BALDWIN, JP Grimes Co. Texas

X/254 Nov. 29, 1872 W. T. LOFLIN et ux SARAH, Grimes Co. Tex. agent and atty. for MRS. LIZZIE BRUSH, Fort Bend Co. Tex. to J. A. H. THURMAN

155/428 Dec. 12, 1881 J. A. H. THURMAN et ux SARAH ANN to J. H. MILUM before F. P. HEFFINGTON, JP

54/618 J. H. MILUM et ux TENNESSEE to J. A. BRENTON (BREWTON) 1882

256/593 aff. DENNIS CORWIN before JOHN DOWELL, NP TCT: RE: SARAH LOFTON wife of WM. F. LOFTON, formerly SARAH BRUSH, CATHERINE C. CABEEN etux of E. A. CABEEN, formerly BRUSH, sole heirs of ELKANAH BRUSK

36/309 S. N. STEWART to JNO. F. OTTENS, Nov. 28, 1876

50/304 May 24, 1878, JOHN F. OTTENS to S. M. STEWART , Kimble Co. Tex

GEO. B. ZIMPELMAN and wife SARAH C.: CH. THOS 31 y. 1888; JAMES LEE 22, 1888; GEO. W. 18, 1888, and WALDINE 13, 1888.

J. C. TANNEHILL was buried in old cemetery, north end of Omega on Ladesma St..however a descendant says remains have been removed.

PATENT June10, 1847 to LUCAS MUNOS, JAMES B. SHAW, assignee, transferred to SHAW 1848.

D/636 Aug. 10, 1852 JAMES B. SHAW to JESSE BURDITT. WIT: H. H. HAYNIE
WM. I. MORTON

PC 207 ESTATE, JESSE BURDITT d. April 21, 1855 intestate. WM. B. & GILES
H. BURDITT file for administration. WM. WILKE, GEO. W. DAVIS, JAMES
ROGERS, L. B. MOORE, CHAS. WALKER, appraisers. MRS. M. BURDITT,widow
(MILDRED): Ch. WM. B., JOEL A., GILES H., HENRY H., MARTHA wife of .
A. M., MUNOS C., JESSE F., NEWELL W. decd. et ux MISSOURI C., Ch: WM.
B., THOS. MUNOS, MILDRED, NEWELL, CATHARINE, all minors. Other ch.
of JESSE BURDITT: JOSEPHINE ROWE wife of R. A. BINFORD, LAVINA ROWE,
decd. her minor son JESSE above as of May 29, 1860.

N/81 deed Feb. 19, 1859 to FREDERICK JOURDAN

241/591 by V. S. EDRINGTON 1906 HARRIETT E. JOURDAN et vir FREDERICH,
she d. prior to Mar. 23, 1885; CH. HARRIETT EMILY m. B. S. ALFORD, 3
ch: HARRIETT, J. L. BELL m. WM. WALDEMORE, no. ch. she died Williamson
Co., 1885; HARRIET ALFORD m. V. S. EDRINGTON and she d. no issue;BELL
m. OSCAR SWARTZ, AMANDA B. m. DANIEL R. PAYTON he d. intestate, Aug.
22, 1889, CH. JOHN W. EPHRAIM F., ANDREW J., BRADFORD N. (BUCK), P.
DORA, LOUISA JANE m. JAMES C. MAXWELL, JULIA E. m. O. C. CATO, SALLIE
A. m. W. L. GILES, JOHN G. JORDAN, ZACK P., GEO. W. d. Mar. 23, 1885;
GEO. W. JAMES, FANNIE P. WIFE OF JAMES V. FISHER, MARY C. (1) WM. T.
ALFORD d. Feb. 1872 had THOS. F., B. S.,JENNIE C. m. McCALL, JULIA H.
m. R. T. DAVIS, CHAS. F., MOLLIE D. m. ROBT. B. CLARK. MARY C. (2)
E. F. SPRINKLE, no ch. and she d. Mar 29, 1881

36/230 Feb. 8, 1839 (filed for record 1876) MICHAEL B. MENARD, OF
Galveston Co. Tex. and THOS. F. McKINNEY same place says SAMUEL M.
WILLIAMS executed deed in Vol. B/51 at town of San Felipe de Austin,
presence of W. H. F. LIGHTFOOT & CHAS. C. GIVENS. WIT: WM. F. MANEY,
OSCAR FARISH, ack. of Michael B. MENARD Feb. 11, 1839 before OSCAR
FARISH ccc Galveston, Republic of Texas.

A/370 PA Feb. 8, 1841 THLS. P. McKINNEY of Galveston Co. Tex. to
BARTLETT SIMMS, Bastrop Co. Tex. WIT: THOS. GREEN, E.LAWRENCE STICKNEY

B/233 deed June 29, 1846, THOS. F. McKINNEY, administrator NATHL. H.
WATROUS decd. TCT to JAMES P. McKINNEY, ack. June 29, 1846, before
JOHN S. JONES, CJ EX O NP, Galveston Co. Tex.

P/358 deed April 3, 1862 THOS. H. JONES to GEO. W. SAMPSON, ABRAM
HENRICKS, WIT: A. B. CHALMERS, FRANK L. ESTRANGE

T/166 QC Feb. 17, 1867 ISAAC V. JONES, R. R. JONES. WIT:to them
S. M. BERRYMAN, R. E. CARRINGTON, EMMA LEE wife of CHAS. H. LEE, N. L.
RECTOR and ack. by LEE before H. M. TRUEHART, NP Galveston Co. Tex.

Z/367 deed Jan. 1, 1874 W. T. DAVIS to JOHN B. WEEMS

DC 4180 filed Sept. 29, 1874 I. V. DAVIS & FRYON DAVIS, TCT, ROBT.
DAVIS, Limestone Co. Tex. vs. HORACE ROWE, EMILY WEEMS, BELLE & ANN
DAVIS, JOHN W. DOWELL, W. H. MILLER, lawyers, MILLER & DOWELL, O. B.
CALDWELL, HENRY WOFFARD, R. A. BINFORD, defendants.
1. Plaintiffs and defts. ANNA & BELL DAVIS are full bros. and sisters.
2. Plaintiffs and ANN & BELL DAVIS are 1/2 bros. and sisters of HORACE,
HENRY W. & EMILY, all are children of EMILY VAN ZANDT first wife of
DR. WOFFORD, the father of HENRY and ...DAVIS father of plaintiffs,
ANN & BELL DAVIS, and DR. JOSEPH ROWE father of HORACE & EMILY and....
BINFORD by him by a different wife (JOSEPHINE BINFORD); ARTHUR ROWE
d. ca 1873, MILLER & DOWELL & O. B. CALDWELL have interest in property
WILL of JOSEPH ROWE To dau. JOSEPHINE BINFORD, land Real and Kaufman
Cos. Tex. Will dated Aug. 8, 1864. EMILY ROWE FORD wife of MARCUS FORD

31/225 Oct. 9, 1875 J. H. WOFFORD, I. M. DAVIS, J. W. JONES et ux
E. A. all TCT
PC guardianship GEO. W. THOMPSON, minor 14 years Dec. 23, 1882, L. H.
ROGERS, wife of J. P. ROGERS says minor is her son by former marriage
BEN J. THOMPSON, decd.

91/328 deed Oct. 20, 1885 cites Aug. 12, 1882 by LUCINDA M.THOMPSON
by decd. husband JAS. A. THOMPSON in consideration of $833.33 paid
by MRS. H. ROGERS, gd. of GEO. W. THOMPSON, minor, I, LUCINDA M.
THOMPSON surviving wife of said JAMES A. THOMPSON decd. and sole heirs

39/587 deed Jan. 13, 1878 JOHN B. WEEMS et ux EMILY (formerly ROWE)TCT
in consideration of 200 AMERICAN GOLD DOUBLE EAGLES, of standard weight
and fineness now fixed by law to GEORGE NEWTON of St. Louis, Mo.

PC 1679 EST. HENRIETTA WHITLEY, decd. filed Aug. 15, 1892 says he m.
her 1883 and she d. 1890, 3 ch: JANIE or JENNIE girl 8 y. ADDIE girl
4 y. RAINIE boy 3 years.

32/536 deed Aug. 24, 1876 J. B. WEEMS et ux EMILY to JAMES W. JONES
et ux ANNIE E.

48/192 partition Jan. 1, 1877 ANNIE E. JONES, late DAVIS, ISABELLA M.
GARDNER late DAVIS as heirs of mother EMILY ROWE, decd.

185/357 Marriage contract No. 28, 1901 N. L. NORTON of Austin and
FANNIE C. PORTER of Millersberg, Ky. ack. by FANNIE C. PORTER,
Shelby Co. Ten. at Memphis, Tenn. GEO. B. COLEMAN, NP

29/414 Wd June 14, 1875 GEO. HEISSNER to CARL BERNDT. WIT: JAMES E.
RECTOR, WM. P. GAINS, NP TCT

33/49 Mtg. Feb. 7, 1877 RICHARD S. YOUNG to HENRY HIRSHFELD, trustee
ADOLPH TRAUTWEIN

53/473 WD Nov. 6, 1882 KARL BERNDT (CHARLES) et ux BABETTE of Blanco
Co. Tex. to J. C. MOELLER TCT before L. KOENEGEE cc BC texas

516/214 WD Jan. 16, 1877 (filed for record Feb. 9, 1935) SAMUEL P.
HEADSPETH to JACOB HENNIGER

517/97 Aff. Mar. 4, 1935 by MRS. ELIZABETH HENNINGER, widow of JACOB

K/453 deed Mar. 24, 1856 W. D. MILLER to W. W. CORCORAN of C. C. bor-
ders land of MRS. JOSEPH ROWE & DAVIS heirs occupied by THOMAS F. CHAP-
MAN, MRS. E. W. CROSTWAIT. WIT: FRANCIS T. DUFFAU, W. G. LOWERY

M/128 deed Feb. 1, 1858 J. M. STEINER to THOS. BARRETT & HENRY H.
STEINER, both of Augusta, Ga.

PC 837 filed Feb. 28, 1882 JOHN T. MILLER By JOHN B. RECTOR, MILLER d.
Feb. 22, 1882. Bond, JOHN B. RECTOR, Prin. and GEO. WALKER & ROBT. F.
CAMPBELL WARREN by MRS. E. A. MILLER sur. wife, GEO. WARREN, W. S.
HOTCHKISS, IRVING EGGLESTON & JNO. O. JOHNSON, appraisers.

DC 78 filed Oct. 2, 1850 cites April 15, 1846 H. B. HILL and wife
EMELINE were in possession of certain lands: CATHERINE MILLER, nee
SCHNEIDER and husband, JNO. G. MILLER vs. H. B. HILL et ux defts.
Defts. have moved beyond limits of Texas.

Q/544 Deed April 20, 1866 JOSIAH FISK to JOSIAH FISK, M. C. SHERMAN,
J. G. JOLLY, STEPHEN CUMMINGS & N. S. PARRIS, trustees, METHODIST
EPISCOPAL CHURCH

Q/766 deed June 26, 1866 JOSIAH FISK to MARTHA . JOHNSON, WIT: WM.
CLEMENTS, JOHN H. MULKEY

38/113SWD June 21, 1877 WM. GARDNER et ux ISABELLA M. to 1/2 interest
all joint real estate.
Y/539 deed Sept. 3. 1873 PETER R. BROWN et ux MARTHA A. (formerly MRS.
MARTHA A. JOHNSON) to E. W. HOLLER, begins at SE cor. JOHN MULKEYS tr.

28/27 deed Mar. 2, 1874 G. L. GANS to JOHN MULKEY, beg. at SE corner
JOHN MULKEY tract.

Q/768 June 12, 1866 deed JOSIAH FISK to JOHN MULKEY beg. at stone mound east side road AUSTIN to the Falls of the Brazos and Georgetown. WIT: WM. CLEMENTS, GEORGE SAUNDERS

R/171 deed Dec. 25, 1867 JOHN H. MULKEY et ux SUSAN E., to GEORGE SANDERS & EDWARD TIMMERMAN, WM. CLEMENTS, school trustees for Fiskville & Little Walnut Creek vicinity. WIT: AUG. F. OTTO, ccc

573/253 Aff. Aug. 25, 1931, I. J. DEEN, A. M. SHERMAN knew J. H. MULKEY d. 1898 and wife, S. E. d. 1903; CH: S. C. MEDLIN, widow, LEMASA, Texas B. J. MULKEY, Happy, Tex.;CALLIE NICHOLS, widow, Houston, Tex. J. A.MULKEY, Oklahoma City O., M. M. MULKEY d. 1909 and left: MARY MAY ROGERS, Dallas, Tex. wife of GEO., LAURA HOUSTON, New Orleans, wife of L. S., ALLEN MULKEY TCT; EUGENIA RAATZ, wife of HERBERT, TCT; J. H. MULKEY, Galveston, Tex. MARK M. MULKEY, New Orleans, Caddo Parish(?) La. O. A. SIMMONS, widow, RUTH HINGES, INEZ WILEY, L. J. JACOBS d. 1914; EUEL JACOBS, El Paso, Tex. R. P. JACOBS, Houston, VERA LAWSON, ZOE JACOBS TCT m. R. TODD FORD

73/434 April 27, 1887 C. W. BERRYMAN et ux MARY to BENJAMIN H. WISDOM Paducah, Ky.
C/261 Jan. 19, 1847, JOSIAH FISK to A. N. HOPKINS, WIT: CHAS. WRIGHT & F. DIETRICH.

C/518 June 8, 1849 A. N. HOPKINS et ux JANE to WM. COCKBURN. WIT: THEO CARTMEL, J. M. W. HALL.

H/43 June 7, 1854 EST. MAY J. COCKBURN to DAVID L. CROSS

57/66 May 2, 1883 MORGAN C. HAMILTON of Kings Co. NY love and affection for nephew WILSON F. LEWIS, Mitchell Co. Tex. and niece M. H. LANE,wife S. G. LANE (formerly M. HENRIETTA LEWIS) of Lampasas Co. Tex.

M/530 JOHN W. HARRIS to JAMES B. SHAW Nov. 22, 1858 WIT: P. deCORDOVA, J. R. RECTOR, O. FLUSSER

117/598 April 22, 1893 L. C. PEASE to JAMES WATERSTON et ux SARAH

117/155 June 1893 MRS. L. C. PEASE to JAMES A. BURDETT et ux LAURA K.

N/98 Feb. 24, 1859 JAMES D. McGARY to W. C. PHILIPS, cabin now occupied by W. C. PHILLIPS & S. B. REID, and their lime kiln

K/777 Oct. 16, 1856 LYMAN CRONKRITE, formerly Fayette Co. Tex. and as agent and atty. for bro. HENRY CRONKRITE, Bradford, Steuben Co. NY

DC 10,863 A. B. LANGERMAN vs. JOHN E. WALLACE aff. that CHAMBERS grant is a forgery.

41/79 July 3, 1878, TRUSTEES DEED to FRANK HAMILTON, ROBERT A. SMITH & JNO. S. WHITNEY, extrs. of WILLIAM NELSON decd.

58/334 Nov. 27, 1883 FANNIE B. NELSON of York Co. Va. to CHAS. THIELE.

34/80 Aug. 13, 1879 Mtg. Aug. 13, 1879 LOUIS R. HILDEBRAND 100 ac.out S. A. PUGH lea. and JESUS GOMEZ survey patent to JOHN G. HALLMAN, in Fayette Co. Tex. and sold to HILLEBRAND June 5, 1876 by W. T. BURNAM et ux SALLIE

L/219 deed Feb. 7, 1857 R. H. PECK TCT to O. J. PECK, Columbia Co.Ny

188/13 WD Mar. 1, 1899 THOS. CAVETT et ux FANNIE (widow of CHAS. ROBINSON, decd. LILLIE PEACE wife of WALTERP., ANNIE HENSON wife of WALTON, children of CHAS. ROBINSOM decd. and widow.

DC Min. C/150 JOHN ALGONER, NEWELL W. BURDITT, WM. WILKES, GEO. W.BLAIR ANDREW S. HOPKINS, PETE WILSON, JOHN McGUIRE, GEO. SASSMAN, WM. McBRIDE WM. PRIEST, LEMUEL LENSING, LEMUEL BRACKEEN, WM. D. PARRIS, REUBEN T.BOX DANL. CRAWFORD, DAVIS GREGORY, JAMES K.FARR, ENOCH MOORE, WM.BRADFORD, LACY McKENZIE, RICHARD PARRIS, PETER MILLIGAN & CALLIN FORBES.

L/170 May 13, 1853 JACOB TARRANT vy JOHN C. HYDE assignee, issued by Travis Bd. of Land Commissioners.

172/418 July...1901 LEWIS THIELE SANFORD to EARL PALM STEWART, MAY A. STEWART (deed 173/373) shows PEARL MAY to be a single man, of Williamson Co. Texas)

c/539 PATENT Dec. 21, 1846 to R. C. DOOM assignee M. C. HAMILTON, assignee of ANDELINA D. SMITH

C/538 Deed May 17, 1849 RANDOLPH C. DOOM to JAMES H. RAYMOND. WIT: JOHN FRAZER, L. R. CAMERON

57/519 Dec. 7, 1863 MATTHEW HOPKINS et ux MARY to N. G. SHELLEY

48/620 deed July 3, 1877 N. G. SHELLEY to J. G. WAIT

180/63 Dec. 24, 1895 N. G. SHELLY to sons, WM. D., JAMES J. and ROBERT M. SHELLY.

226/212 Dec. 24, 1895 N. G. SHELLEY to Ch: MOLLIE G., PERCY L. and LULA A. SHELLEY.

Z/344 Dec. 16, 1873 RUTH ADAMS sur. wife THOMAS to dau. MARGARET J. DOXEY love and aff. she to pay (on my death) $1000.00 to PERCY E. CARROLL (woman) and $500.00 to FRANK E. ADAMS. Mentions son DAVID ADAMS. (Will THOMAS ADAMS says my dau. PERCENEY CARROLL & son F. E. ADAMS)

104/23 Jan. 7, 1892 MRS. P. E. CARROLL of Washington D. C. dau of THOMAS ADAMS, TCT

36/201 Oct. 27, 1876 J. D. DOXEY et ux M. J. to A. E. REID, her heirs

165/265 Nov. 9, 1900 F. E. ADAMS of Los Angeles Co. Calif, son of THOS. ADAMS to MARGARET J. DOXEY

PATENT Mar. 3, 1842 to A. W. LUCKETT

R/431 Deed Oct. 6, 1868 deed to WM. K. BECKETT

198/40 Mar. 17, 1894 MRS. BELL MOORE to DR. R. H. EANES

B/...deed Jan. 11, 1849 JAMES H. RAY et ux to T. F. FAUNTLEROY

26/22 deed Mar. 5, 1874 S. E. GOODRICH to DR. G. T. BOARDMAN all interest in estate of MARY A. GOODRICH, and sells to W. E. GLASSCOCK, of Seguine, Texas

713/553 PATENT April 20, 184...to THOMAS GRAY

A/334 PATENT Feb. 26, 1841 to JAMES P. WALLACE 1/3 league

DC 10,080 Sept. 21, 1891 SOPHIE MEYER vs. AUGUST MEYER m. May 11, 1881 Ch. LILLIE, ALMA & ELSIE.

V/781 PA May 26, 1871 MARTHA G. HARRY to son C. E. HARRY

97/104 WD Aug. 30, 1890 ED SEIDERS et ux LETTITIA SEIDERS to ERNEST J. HEPPENHEIMER of Hudson Co. N. J

430/284 PATENT Oct. 19, 1848 to ERHARDT FRUD

F/15 TITLE BOND Dec. 4, 1851 DAVID G. ADAMS to BURTON L. RENICK. WIT: JOHN CARROLL, FRANCIS E. ADAMS

54/477 PA Sept. 7, 1881 D. G. CHALMERS of D. C. to P. deCORDOVA

Y/95 DISSOLUTION April 15, 1873 STAR STATE SAVINGS ASSN. to LEANDER BROWN, C. SPAULDING & E. C. BARTHOLOMEW

238/340 Deed Nov. 10, 1909 shows ROBERT JONES d. July 16, 1906, TCT left son R. F. JONES & dau. MATTIE A. PEARCE , wife of THOS. J., and surviving widow, LOUISA J. (FOSTER?) JONES.

203/29 Rel. May 20, 1904 S. K. MORLEY & D. B. GRACY to J. E. BONDS et ux R. E. BONDS

A/126 BOND FOR TITLE June 18, 1839 JAMES P. WALLACE to WILLIAM R. REDING of Matagorda Co. Tex. WIT: CALVIN JONES, RUSSEL B. CRAFT

B/423 QC Sept. 23, 1847 ROBERT L. REDDING to WM. R. REDDING, Bastrop Co. WIT: R. M. CLOPTON, DAVID REYMONDS.

133/263 Wd Sept. 21, 1895 SUSAN E. HANCOCK by atty. E. B. HANCOCK to T. F.PINCKNEY

255/333 WD Jan. 23, 1913 F. H. SMITH to W. FRANK HOWARD

Q/364 deed Dec. 18, 1865 GEO. W. DAVIS et ux EMELINE P. to dau. SALLIE H. ENGLAND, wife of J. W. ENGLAND

43/318 April 26, 1879 J. W. ENGLAND, gdn. GEO. D. & JAMES E. ENGLAND, JR. his minor children

212/21 deed Dec. 20, 1905 C. A. PETERSON et ux LOUISA to J. T. RAMSEY

52/370 deed April 4, 1882 ANNIE LANE BLOCKER et vir J. R. (she dau. of ANNIE SWISHER, who was dau. of CAPT. J. G. SWISHER et ux ELIZABETH) D/264 PATENT Dec. 17, 1849 to FRANCIS DEITRICH.

A/83 May 20, 1839 JAMES P. WALLACE & ROBERT L. REDING & CALVIN JONES, Bastrop Co. Tx. WIT: E. T. MERRIMAN, W. PINCKNEY HILL, and GREENLEIF FISK, CJ BCT

1/86 Transcript Sept. 17, 1838 J. C. TANNEHILL to SILAS DINSMORE, CALVIN JONES, D. C. GILMORE, SALM. R. MILLER, JOHN HARVEY, L. C. CUNNINGHAM, CJ CB NP

108/506 PA May 4, 1900 MRS. LULA C. TEMPLETON of Colorado to J. B. POPE, ack. W. A. GORDON, NP TCT

N/400 PATENT May 23, 1856 to EDWARD M. HORST, assignee of JOHN McDONALD, Bd. Land Commissioners, Matagorda Co. Tex. May 3, 1849, transferred to D. E. E. BRANNON, July 16, 1851

Q/154 WIT: W. von ROSENBERG, FRED WILHELM & W. H. KING

U/57 July 8, 1870 JASPER N. STEWART et ux ANN to ANDREW J. STANFORD

5/233 TCT M/L JOSEPH C. KERBEY m. MRS. MARIE M. SPENCE Dec. 2, 1879

W.573 April 19, 1872 T. J. CHAMBERS EST. to LEONARD HARTSON

2/145 TCT M/L BENJ. THOMPSON & MISS KATE L. MOORE, Nov. 24, 1863

PATENT Sept. 27, 1854 to STERLING C. ROBERTSON

W. 455 PATENT TO JOHN HEMPHILL June 2, 1852

153/221 Aff. ALFRED GROOMS & H. G. LEE only children of HORATTO GROOMS, decd.

C/261 deed Jan. 19, 1848 JOSIAH FISK to A. N. HOPKINS. WIT: CHAS. WRIGHT, F. DEITRICH

31/56 deed Nov. 27, 1875 JAMES H. RAYMOND & C. W. WHITIS to JOHN HANCOCK

PATENT May 19, 1852 to ANDREW O. HORNE, SR.

PATENT Mar. 7, 1841 to J. M. ODIN

DC 5247 Dec. 24, 1878 RUTHA ANN STEWART et vir H. STEWART, of Kimble Co Texas

70/256 QC Sept. 22, 1886 V. A. FENNER to SAM. LUCKSINGER, ack. C. F. HILL NP TCT

154/99 WD Oct. 13, 1892 AUSTIN REAL ESTATE & INVESTMENT CO., JAMES R. JOHNSON, Pres. J. S. MYRICK, secy. to M. M. SHIPE

W/639 Feb. 12, 1872 ADMRS. DEED ABBY C. THOMPSON, admrs. EST. T. J. CHAMBERS decd. et ux CYRUS THOMPSON. Ack. April 13, 1872 before WM. R. JOHNSON, Np Galveston Co. Tex.

96/42 SWD April 22, 1890 JNO. B. RECTOR to AUSTIN, RUNNELLS CO. LAND & LIVE STOCK CO.

B/75 BOND FOR TITLE June 26, 1841, JOHN LESSER (signed JOLOAM or JONOTHAN) to DAVID K. WEBB part of land warrant No. 1106 for 960 acres issued by BERNARD E. BEE, secy of War to me for services in the Army of the REPUBLIC of TEXAS, land on Wilbarger Creek and to convey "as soon as the REPUBLIC of TEXAS may issue me a patent to said land.." WIT: HENRY MAIGEE, JOHN BRATTON. Ack. by WIT. JOHN BRATTON, before ANDERSON J. HARRELL, CCC TC, Oct. 7, 1845, filed for record Dec.9, 1858, J. T. McLAURIN, CCC TCT

P/171 MORTGAGE, B. G. GOODRICH May 22, 1861 to S. W. GOODRICH, TCT, SLAVES: HENRY, MANDY & 3 ch. TENNESSEE, WALTON & ALEX., all now in TCT sale in trust securing notes $1750. drawn 1853 to 1856, a lien in favor of THOMAS ADAMS, Austin TCT and BAUGHN & WALKER of LaVaca (this is as it was written for many years) Texas. WIT: JAMES H. FRY, W. O. HILL, filed for record May 25, 1861, J. T. McLAURIN, CCC TCT. Ack. by B. G. GOODRICH before P. L. BUQUOR, NP Bexar Co. Texas(name is printed on seal)

53/199 deed from JAMES H. RAYMOND to W. E. BROOKS, president TILLETSON COLLEGIATE & NORMAL INSTITUTE, TCT, property on both sides of East 7th Street, at time of sale; ack. before P. deCORDOVA, NP TCT, Aug. 30,1882 F. BROWN, Clerk by ...NEILL, deputy. This deed is on a very attractive deed form by J. A. NAGLE, stationery, Austin, Texas, printers.

D/562 BILL OF SALE IN TRUST, filed April 8, 1852, JAMES A. WOODS, to JAMES L. DEMOSS, a negro girl DOCHA about 15 years old, says "a decree was recorded in the Chancery Court of Nashvilleat the Nov. Term 1850 in the case of NANCEY FOREHAND by her next friend, vs. RICHARD FOREHAND et al in which amongst other things that the Clerk Master of said Court vest the interest of the said NANCY FOREHAND in the Estate of her father JAMES DEMOSS, decd. in a negro man or a negro woman in name of JAMES L. DEMOSS in trust for sole and separate use of said NANCY FOREHAND free from the debts and control of her husband, RICHARD FOREHAND for life with remainder at her death to her children, those now in life as well as those hereafter born to said NANCY..." Signed: SAMUEL A. WOODS, WIT: A. A. McLEAN, ALANSON CROOKER, and attached to above a cert from CITY OF NASHVILLE, Davidson Co. State of Tenn. Feb. 16, 1852, be= fore EGBERT A. RAWORTH, Commissioner for State of Texas.

M/342 TIMBER DEED, T. C. COLLINS to ... JOHNSON timber off 25 acres part of SW cor. HENRY P. HILL survey on west side of Colorado River, sold at Sheriff's sale and bought in by R. M. ELGIN by ELGIN deeded toCHARLES HUGHES and J. H. COONER, by them sold to JOHN S. SPENCE, by him to THOS FREEMAN and by him to T. C. COLLINS, April 9, 1858. Ack. by THOMAS

COLLINS before JAMES M. SWISHER, CCC, J. H. THOMPSON, depty. (Austin is located on the edge of a low mountain range, and spreads east across miles of prairie land. Wood was a necessity, then, and the owners of the prairie land had 5, 10, 25 acre tracts in the"hills" for their wood)

P/17 SHERIFF'S DEED, Dec. 4, 1860 JOHN T. PRICE, Sheriff, TCT to AMOS MORRILL, sold by order DC Falls Co. Texas, in favor of C. C. OWENS,Extr vs. SAM A. BLAIN, judgment April 2, 1860, a land certificate granted to JOSEPH MATTHEWS 2/3 of league, Mar. 25, 1839, trfd. to JOHN CHAMBLER (CHAMBLEE) to be soldat the S. E. corner of Block 70, City of Austin, (this was "SWISHER'S TAVERN") before J. T. McLAURIN CCC TCT

H/222 deed July 31, 1854 NATHAN DAVIS of Panola Co. Texas to JOHN MILLER, also of Panola Co. 26 labors of land 27 miles above Austin on Colorado River, Cert. 973 Bd. Land Commrs. San Augustine, July 7, 1838, N. B. PHILLIPS, J. L. GIBBS mentioned as owner of adjoining property. WIT: J. L. GIBBS, C. S. SAVERY, ack. Panola Co. Texs. before J. HADLEY ANDERSON, Clerk.

Deed, love and affection, Sept. 6, 1858, MARY C. (X) COLLINGSWORTH TCT to dau. LUCINDA OPHELIA. TCT, a negro girl ELLEN, 6 years old. WIT: W. T. NORTON, JULIA B. BURDITT.

M/264 BILL of SALE May 5, 1858 A. B. McGILL, TCT to WM. L. T. PRINCE, 60 yearlings and oxen, subject to mortgage to GEORGE HANCOCK, & NELSON MERRILL. JOHN A. GREEN, agent for PRINCE.

A/236 BILL OF SALE Jan. 21, 1841 LAVENDER S. WILKINS, TCT to A. A. ANDERSON, TCT of negro boy "CLADE" (SHADE) 16 years old, SUBJECT to suit pending DC TCT LAVENDER S. WILKINS vs. ALEXANDER C. McFARLAND & DR. MOSES JOHNSON, WIT: LORENZO WALKER, W. KATZEBUE (?) COOK, before M. H. BEATY, CCC TCT.

G/586 Certified copy from DC TCT Spring Term 1848, HENRY ADAMS, vs. NANCY BROWNING, (widow, DANIEL BROWNING) CHRISTOPHER COLUMBUS BROWNING, JOHN BROWNING, L. J. POTTER, and wife, MARY, nee BROWNING, J. B. PATTERSON et ux MARTHA nee BROWNING, JOHN BOSTWICK et ux PAMELIA nee BROWNING WM. COX et ux FRANCES nee BROWNING, viz: DANIEL BROWNING, decd. on July 17, 1839 gave his bond for title to 2000 acres in Bastrop Co. (now Travis) on west side of Colorado River, opposite City of Austin,, part of a league granted by TALBERT CHAMBERS, commissioner, Mar. 17,1835 to ISAAC DECKER as a headright; was to have been conveyed by said DECKER to said BROWNING, July 11, 1838; was sold by BROWNING July 17, 1839 to HENRY ADAMS. BROWNING d. without having given deed; no executor oradministrator of said BROWNING estate, and a part of said defendants reside beyond the limits of the STATE OF TEXAS. ORDERED B. D. BASSFORD, Esq. Clerk of Court give deed, etc.

LEASE, Sept. 13, 1854, HORACE L. UPSHAW to THOMAS WARD, TCT Lots 9 and 10 Block 81 Original City; this is 300 block of present West 7th Street, for ten cents per annum. WIT: A. A. ALLMON, G. F. LUMPKIN, ack. says THOMAS WOOD WARD before JOHN B. COSTA, CJ TCT Sept. 14, 1854.

FIELD NOTES: 26 labors of ISAAC CAMPBELL, by virtue Cert. No. 401, issued to CHARLES Q. HALEY, assignee of JOHN W. GREEN by Bd. Land Commr. Shelby Co. and by him transferred to ISAAC CAMPBELL west side Colorado river beg. cor. S. H. REED sur. No. 50, containing 10 labors of temporal land and 16 of pasture land, Aug. 2, 1838, sgd. WILLIAM S. WALLACE, JOHN L. LYNCH, Department surveyors and CHAINERS: DAVID HUTSON, JOSEPH MANER Cert. by BARTLETT SIMMS, C. S. C. Bastrop Co. Mar. 2, 1839. TREASURY DEPT HOUSTON, June 13, 1838 Recd. of ISAAC CAMPBELL through the hands of J.P BORDEN, Commrs. Genl. Land Office $44.00 in promissory notes of the Government, JAMES H. STARR secy. of Treasurery. GENERAL LAND OFFICE Austin Nov. 23, 1839. JOHN P. BORDEN certifies true copy of field notes on file. ENDORSED: "NOT RECORDED FOR WANT OF PROOF.." This was apparently by the County Clerk, Travis County., (NOTE: There was very little currency in the country, and land certificates were used as an exchange, and many times they were forged, or altered in some manner. The clerk was being cautious.)

AFFIDAVIT. IN RE" CLARK M. STONE, land grant Jan. 4. 1839. by board
of Land Commissioners, Harrisburg, Republic of Texas, conditional cert
320 ac. CLARK M. STONE d. intestate, unm and without issue 1848 in Mon-
terry, Mexico; was emigrant to REPUBLIC OF TEXAS, Fall 1838 from Montgomery, Ala. over 17 years of age, Harris Co. his fixed place of residence; then Jackson Co. and Calhoun Co. Texas. CLARK M. STONE had no
parents or brothers or sisters now living, following are sole and only
heirs; THOMAS M. McGOWEN, uncle, of Harris Co. Texas; GEORGE R. McGOWEN
uncle; ALEXANDER McGOWEN, uncle; FANNY FERGUSON, cousin; JOSEPH FITZ-
PATRICK, cousin; JAMES McGOWEN, cousin, GEORGE McGOWEN, cousin. Thomas
M. McGOWEN & GEORGE R. McGOWEN & ALEXANDER R. McGOWEN are collateral
lines in 1st deg; FANNY FERGUSON & JOSEPH FITZPATRICK are brother and
sister and heirs of 2nd degree in line of CATHARINE FITZPATRICK, who
was an aunt of decd. and heir 1st deg; JAMES McGOWEN and GEORGE McGOWEN
are bros. and heirs 2nd. deg. in line of EDWARD McGOWEN, uncle of decd
and heir 1st degree; THOMAS M. McGOWEN ack. before S. STAFFORD, CJ
Aug. 2, 1841; J. N. MORELAND, CJ, HARRISBURG Co. EX OF. PRESIDENT BD.
LAND COMMR. associate Commr. JAMES M. McGEE by DAVIS (X) D. CULP. DEPTY
WM. R. BAKER, Clerk. Cert by J. BRASHEAR cc HARRIS CO. as correct copy
of original application of THOMAS M. McGOWEN, Nov. 9, 1860;
(NOTE: IT IS not advisable to depend upon such as the above
for heirs or other relationships of deceased persons owning land in
early TEXAS. There were many absentee land barons, and speculators,
and forgery was a common thing. SOMETIMES, 10 or 20 years later, suits
are found which prove such as the above false. Like the preceeding
paper, it is not recorded, suggesting the County Clerk did not have
sufficient proof of its truthfullness.)

REPORT OF GRAND JURY, June 11, 1872, to HON. J. W. OLIVER, presiding
Judge 27th Judicial Dist. INDICTMENTS: GEORGE W. HONEY & J. H. BURNS,
his clerk; HONEY, late TREASURER of the State of TEXAS; they have in
their possession and knowledge of the combinations to locks and safes
and vaults in said TREASURERY: A. B. BURLESON, foreman, P. R. JOHNS,
J. H. RAYMOND, J. M. SWISHER, WILLIS ROBARDS, DR. B. GRAHAM, J. M.
SWISHER, F. W. MOORE, JAMES P. McKINNEY, LEANDER BROWN & GENL. JAMES
DAVIDSON, signed by C. L. FREEMAN, ROBERT BARR, A. P. MUSGROVE (H)
BEIMER (WEIMER) JOHN W. NICHOLSON, JOHN M. HOLLAND, CEZAR (X) GIVENS.
ISAM (X) McARTHUR, NAT (X) GRUMBLES, NAT MOORE, JOHN JOHNSON, J. W.
BIRD, H. CLAY EANES, S. LOCKWOOD, WM. M. SAUNDERS, BRYCE H. BOYD and
B. TRIGG, Dist. atty. joins request for favorable consideration by
the COURT.

APPLICATION FOR CITIZENSHIP: WILLIEM BOLES, June 19, 1856. He was b.
1828 in Kingdom of Hanover; came to U. S. and Texas 1845; that he has
never borne any hereditary title or been member of any of the orders
of nobility and if any such should devolve upon him he doeth hereby
entirely renounce same; 1 year in Texas; he was not 18 when he arrived
in U. S.; renounces all allegiance to fidelity to every foreign Prince
Potentate, State or Sovereignty, whatsoever, and particularly to the
King of HANOVER of whom he was subject. :Papers say WILLIAM, he signs
WILLIEM. Application by MICHAEL ZILLER & WILLIAM SAUER, who knew him
for 1 year in Texas. MICHAEL ZILLER signs here as ZILLER MICHAEL as
elsewhere. Some places it is ZELLER.

NEW LAWYERS for TRAVIS COUNTY, TEXAS:

THOMAS J. STONE: JUNE TERM 1848, MAURY COUNTY COURT, TENNESSEE, Town
of Columbia, FIRST MONDAY IN JUNE 1848, being the 5th before WORSHIPFUL
ELIAS C. FRIERSON, ROBERT A. GLENN, JAMES M. WHITE, PARKE STREET,FRANK-
LIN A. BURKE, JONATHAN L. (S) HUNT, WM. SHARP, EDWARD R. PUCKETT, JOHN
W. WESTMORELAND and other justices (not named). MOTION of A. M. ROS-
BOROUGH, Esq.: THOMAS J. STONE, resident citizen of Maury Co. Tenn. for
more than 12 months previous, he is 21 years old, a gentleman of hon
esty, probity and good moral character, these facts be and are hereby
so certified as a preparatory step to enable said THOMAS J. STONE to
obtain a license to proctice as an attorney at law in the STATE of
TENNESSEE. WM. E. ERWIN, Clk. Maury Co. Tenn. Jan. 23, 1851 and JAMES
O. POTTER, Clerk of Circuit Court of Maury Co. Tenn. Jan. 23, 1851,
MUMFORD SMITH, sheriff; THOMAS J. STONE has taken OATH of office was

permitted to plead in said court. Another CERTIFICATE by EDWARD DILLAHUNTY, Judge Circuit Court, Jan. 24, 1851. Evidently this certificate, and copies, were brought by THOMAS J. STONE to Travis County, Texas, as evidence of his license to practice law in the State of Tennessee.

JOHN T. GRAVES: Application to be licensed, Austin, Sept. 15, 1853, JOHN T. GRAVES, applicant. BAR MEMBERS: F. W. CHANDLER, WM. WALTON, EDWARD R. PECK, W. L. OLDHAM & JOSEPH LEE. Mr. Graves presented the Committee with a license to practice in Missouri from the SUPREME COURT of that state. The committee: "We further certify that MR. GRAVES is a gentleman of good moral character and high standing in the community in which he lives..."

WILLIAM A. H. MILLER. WILLIAM A. H. MILLER, late of Gonzales County, Texas, now a resident of Travis County, Texas, requests a permanent license to practice as attorney and counselor at law in the Courts of this State. CERTIFICATE by W. V. COLLINS, Presiding Justice, Gonzales Co. Texas: CERTIFIES that WM. A. H. MILLER has been a resident of Texas for more than six months and is more than 21 years of age, and of good character. ENDORSEES: JAMES M. BURTS (BURNS), R. A. SMITH, JOHN A. GREEN, committee to examine, Saturday morning Oct. 7, 1876 and same day, before J. P. RICHARDSON he is granted license for district and all courts of Texas. Filed Oct. 9, 1876, FRANK BROWN, CCC TCT.

H. R. RUNNELS, Governor of STATE of TEXAS, on September 7, 1858, appoints T. S. ANDERSON, secretary of State.

CORONER'S BOND AND OATH, Feb. 27, 1840, MARTIN RUMPFF, principal, and N. M. LUCKETT, W. M. TIGNER, sureties. BOND to MIRA BEAU B. LAMAR, President of REPUBLIC of TEXAS, approved Feb. 27, 1840, J. W. SMITH, CJ TCT.

CORONER'S BOND AND OATH, Sept. 30, 1843, THOMAS WARD, principal and J. M. HARRELL, REUBEN HORNSBY, sureties, bound to SAM HOUSTON, President of REPUBLIC of TEXAS, $1500.00. THOMAS WARD was elected coroner by TCT on Sept. 28, 1843, approved J. M. LONG, CHF. JUS. TCT. OATH before same J. M. LONG.

CORNONER'S BOND and OATH, Aug. 26, 1848, OZWIN WILLCOX, principal and W. H. CUSHNEY, C. KYLE, sureties, and another bond Dec. 21, 1846, OZWIN WILLCOX, principal WILLIAM H. CUSHNEY, J. W. ROBERTSON, with WM. W. ATWOOD, JESS BURDITT & D. M. HARWELL, commissioners court, signing. RESIGNATION of O. WILLCOX as coroner Sept. 15, 1851, accepted Sept. 13 1851, J. MINER, CJ. (he may have moved into another precinct)

CORONER'S BOND AND OATH, Aug. 18, 1854, SAMUEL C. TAYLOR, principal and H. G. BLAKY, A. B. BURLESON, R. N. ALLEN, sureties to E. M. PEASE, as Governor.

CORONER'S BOND AND OATH Aug. 4, 1856, ALLEN E. BROWN, principal, and GEORGE HANCOCK, QUELLA I. NICHOLS to E. M. PEASE, as Governor.

CORNERS's BOND $10,000.00 (?) ROBERT H. CLEMENTS principal, J. H. BURDITT, JOHN HORAN, W. R. BAKER, W. P. deNORMADIE, WM. O'CONNELL, H. W. SUBLETT, W. B. NICHOLAS, R. H. PECK, THOS. GREEN, G. E. ROBINSON, JOHN A. GREEN, H. C. HOLMAN, MICHAEL ZILLER. Approved Aug. 23, 1858, GEO. H. GRAY, CJ. (NOTE: One wonders why a bond so large.)

CORONER'S BOND AND OATH, Aug. 20, 1860, A. N. HOPKINS, principal and FRANK BROWN, JAMES McLAURIN, approved GEO. H. GRAY, CJ

CORONER'S BOND AND OATH, Sept. 29, 1867, A. N. HOPKINS, principal, ELIAH McLAUGHLIN, F. HORNBURGER, JOHN H. ROBINSON, F. W. CHANDLER. Approved Sept. 4, 1862 by WM. H. ROBERTS, CJ.

CORONER'S BOND AND OATH, Aug. 13, 1864. JOHN M. MASSIE, principal, and L. H. LUCKETT, A. R. MORRIS, W.P. MABEN, sureties $2000.00. MASSIE was elected by the qualified electors TCT Aug. 1, 1864. He takes oath..."Constitution and Laws of the State of Texas and also the constitution and laws of the CONFEDERATE STATES OF AMERICA, so long as the STATE OF TEXAS shall remain a member of that confederacy, and swears since March 2, 1861 he has been a citizen of this state and not fought a duel..etc.." OATH before J. MINER, CCC endorsed Aug. 11, A. F. BOYCE, CCC TC

CONSTABLE'S BOND AND OATH, ROBERT H.CLEMENT S, Aug. 18, 1859 R. H. CLEMENTS, PRINCIPAL, JOSEPH LEE, W. P. deNORMANDIE, sureties, elected August 1, 1859.

MAYOR'S BOND AND OATH, May 31, 1852 GEORGE J. DURHAM as Mayor of City of Austin, with the power of JUSTICE OF PEACE. GEORGE J. DURHAM, prin. THOMAS WARD, EDWIN NASH, sureties. He was elected Mayor May 25, 1852.

RECORDER OF CITY OF AUSTIN, bond, May 5, 1847, Charles MASON, Principal STEPHEN CUMMINGS, Esq. CJ TCT. OWEN O'BRIEN, JOHN HORAN, sureties.

RECORDER of CITY of AUSTIN & EX OFFICIO JUSTICE of the PEACE: BOND and OATH, FRANCIS T. DUFFAU, principal, EDWARD (EDMUND) TEN EYCK, H. W. DAVIS, JOHN T. ALLAN (signatures are always ALLAN) sureties. Jan. 27, 1853. DUFFAU was elected Dec. 27, 1852. $6000.00 bond with THOMAS P. CARTMELL, JR., F. DIETERICH to CHIEF JUSTICE of TRAVIS COUNTY, before THOMAS WM. WARD, Mayor, Jan. 8, 1853. TEN EYCK settled about 20 miles northwest from Austin on south side of Colorado River, and a community known as "TECK" remains today.

MAYOR'S BOND Aug. 13, 1853 THOMAS WILLIAM WARD, principal, GEO. W. SAMPSON, GEORGE HANCOCK, F. DIETERICH as sureties. OATH by THOS. WM. WARD (a very legible, but unusual back handed signature, with many flourishes..reminds one of the signature of JOHN HANCOCK, only it leans the other way)

FERRYMEN and a WOMAN:

BOND AND OATH, SAMUEL STONE, to operate a ferry across the Colorado River, SAML. STONE, principal, WM. B. BURDITT, ANDERES (ANDREW ?) M. DAVIDSON, sureties. Approved; JOHN B. COSTA, CJ TCT paid $25.00annual fee Mar. 20, 1853, JAS. M. SWISHER, County Treasurer TCT Receipt No. 82 (original receipts are with these papers) filed Mar. 11, 1853, A.B. McGILL CCC TCT

RECEIPT No. 113, $25.00 to SAM STONE, Jan. 1, 1854, JAMES M. SWISHER, County Treasurer. SAMUEL STONE principal, THOMAS H. JONES, JAMES DOYLE, sureties, approved by COUNTY COURT May 16, 1854, JOHN B. COSTA CJ TCT

SAMUEL STONE, a ferry on Colorado River below and near the Cityof Austin..."and I do further swear that since the adoption of the Constitution of the State of Texas by the UNITED STATES & by the people of the State of TEXAS, that I have not fought a duel..." Oath before STEPHEN CUMMINGS, CH. JUSTICE TCT. Bond $1000.00 with SAMUEL STONE, PRINCIPAL JOSEPH ROWE, R. C. DOOM, sureties, and will faithfully perform all duties of FERRYMAN at "the lower ferry" near the City of Austin and keep the boat and ferry in good repairs and the banks of such grade as the law requires.."

MARY A. STONE, principal, J. T. McLAURIN, M. A. TAYLOR, W. A. MORRIS, H. LITTLEPAGE, Feb. 17, 1858, $2000.00 bond, Treasurer's receipt No.139 $25.00 from MARY A. STONE for 1 year Feb. 17, 1858 to Feb. 17, 1859. ED TINNIN County Treasurer.

1854 JAMES G. SWISHER, makes application (as lawful owner of land on south side of Colorado River, opposite Congress Avenue in the City of Austin) to establish publicferry; has made a contract with the Mayor

And Aldermen of saidCorporate Cityof Austin, and has acquired the use of the land on the north side of the river..filed Feb. 24, 1854.
A. B. McGILL, CCC, JOHN L. ALLAN, Dpty. JAMES G. SWISHER, principal JNO. M. SWISHER, JAS. H. RAYMOND, sureties, Receipt No. 112, $25.00 to JAMES G. SWISHER, Feb. 24, 1854, JAMES M. SWISHER, County Treasurer.

Feb. 24, 1854, JOHN G. GRUMBLES, Principal S. G. SNEED, WM. O'CONNELL, Receipts Nos. 110 and 111 (one has error) $25.00 to JOHN G. GRUMBLES, JAMES M. SWISHER, County Treasurer TCT

Sept. 18, 1854, JOHN M. RANSOM, Principal EDWARD ROBERTS, TIMOTHY Mc KEAN. Ferry at Town of Webberville on north side Colorado River. Approved Sept. 18, 1854, JOHN B. COSTS, CJ. ENDORSED "WEBBERS PRAIRIE" Receipt No. 2, $5.00 Sept. 18, 1854, with application of JOHN M. RANSOM to establish ferry opposite town of Webberville, TCT that he owns land on the north side of River, and a public road has been established. crossing the river at this place.
Feb. 20, 1855 HUGH TINNIN for ferry about one mile below City of Austin H. owns land on both sides of river, not dated, but filed Feb.20,1855 BOND & OATH, HUGH TINNIN Principal, THOS. H. JONES, A. N. HOPKINS, surities. Feb. 21, 1855, approved same day by JOHN B. COSTA, CJ TCT. Receipt No. 17, Feb. 21, 1855 E. TINNIN County Treasurer TCT

BOND and OATH FEB. 21, 1855, JAMES G. SWISHER, principal, JOHN M. SWISHER, JAMES H. RAYMOND, sureties, Feb. 21, 1855. $25.00 receipt No. 16 ED TINNIN, County Treasurer, JAMES G. SWISHER, Feb. 17, 1856, withJOHN M. SWISHER & JAMES H. RAYMOND, sureties, filed Mar. 16, 1856, A. B. Mc GILL CCC TC by JAMES P. DAVIS, deputy.

RECEIPT No. 137 Feb. 15, 1858 ED TINNIN, County Treasurer TCT $25.00 JAMES G. SWISHER, JOHN M. SWISHER & THOS. C. COLLINS, sureties, filed Feb. 16, 1858, JAMES M. SWISHER, CCC TCT by J.H. THOMPSON, deputy

# # # # # # # # # # #
FIRST FIFTY (50) pages of the FIRST PROBATE MINUTE BOOK in the new COUNTY OF TRAVIS, REPUBLIC of TEXAS:

PAGE 1: No. 1: March 31, 1840, JOHN H. GERLY appointed administrator of ESTATE WM. R. GRIMES, decd. THOS. G. FOSTER, WM. H. NICHOLSON & T. W. HUMPHREY, appointed appraisers. NOTE: Papers in Packet No. 1 say WM.R.

No. 2: Feb. 26, 1840 J. G. BURNEY appointed administrator ROBERT R. RAMEY, decd. May 4, 1840 J. B. ROBERTSON, R. H. WYNN & ...FRANCIS are appointed appraisers.

No. 3: Feb. 5, 1840 JAMES FISHER is appointed administrator of the EST BENJ. D. NOBLE, decd. JOHN P. BORDEN and D. JOHNSON appointed appraisers

No. 4: April 8, 1841 G. L. HAASS, appointed administrator EST. WM. J. WARD. April 8, 1940 D. LAUGHLIN, F. FENTRESS, FRANCIS DIETERICH, are appointed appraisers.

May 29th 1840 IRA MUNSON, of the ESTATE of JAMES ROWDEN decd. published 60 days. J. M. SMITH, Judge.

Page 3: Feb. 24, 1840 LYMAN CRANDISH by atty. JESSE TANNEHILL, administrator of ESTATE SAML. COLVIN, decd.

Page 4: CHARLES LARABIE (LARALEE) in ESTATE G. W. SAMPSON, decd.

JAMES O. CLARK, applies for appointment in ESTATE J. A. CREAREY, decd. Appraisers: MAYS GARIETY & M. JOHNSON.

JAMES O. CLARK, application in ESTATE MILTON BENNETT, decd.

HUGH McLEOD, applies for administration ESTATE BENJ. H. JOHNSON. Apprisers: A. W. LUCKETT, P. H. BELL & WM. G. COOK

PAGE 5: May 7, 1840, Wayne Barton, heir of WILLIAM BARTON, decd. WILL: (DANL. BROWNING, WITNESS) RICHARD LLOYD & ABNER S. LIPSCOMB are appointed appraisers. $20,000.00 executors bond.

JAMES McGOWAN, applies for administrtion of his brother, JOHN McGOWAN, decd. a volunteer soldier of U. S. & killed at Goliad, at the time of the murder of COL. FANNIN. July 31, published notice in "AUSTIN CITY GAZETTE".

B. H. H. BUTTS applies for administration on ESTATE JOHN HAFTER (HAFNER)

PAGE 6: THOS. G. GORDON, applies for administration on ESTATE CULLEN SPIVEY, published in "SENTINAL"

THOMAS G. GORDON, applies for administration on ESTATE WM. A. O. WADSWORTH, decd.

WM. GIBSON, applies for administration on ESTATE JAMES COOPER, decd.

CHARLES SHEPPARD, applies for administration on ESTATE CUTHBERT EDWARDS decd. Appraisers: JOHN R. SLOCUMB, N. McARTHUR, H. WARD

PAGE 7: August 8, 1840 WM. BARTON, ESTATE: Apprisers: LOGAN VANDEVER, J. M. HARVEL & DAVID BROWNING. (THIS MIGHT BE J. M. HARRELL)

Aug. 11, 1840 ESTATE JAMES COOPER: APPRAISERS: JNO. CHENAULT, JOHN M. SHREVE & JOHN C. SANDUSKY.

No. 17: THOMAS G. GORDON, applies for administration, August 12, 1840 on ESTATE J. W. COWAN (CORWIN) late volunteer soldier of U. S. & killed at Goliad, at the time of the murder of COL. FANNIN.

THOMAS G. GORDON, applies for administration on ESTATE HARRISON YOUNG, decd. a late volunteer soldier of U. S. & killed at Goliad, at the time of the murder of COL. FANNIN. July

THOMAS G. GORDON, applies for administration on ESTATE GREEN LEE, decd. a late volunteer soldier of U. S. & killed at Goliad, at the time of the murder of COL. FANNIN.

THOMAS G. GORDON, applies for administration on ESTATE JNO. M. POWER, decd. late a volunteer soldier of U. S. & killed at Goliad, at the time of the murder of COL. FANNIN.

THOMAS G. GORDON, applies for administration on ESTATE JOHN L. THORN, decd. a late volunteer soldier of U. S. & killed at Goliad, at the time of the murder of COL. FANNIN.

THOMAS G. GORDON, applies for administration on ESTATE KENNETH McKENSIE decd. a late volunteer soldier of U. S. & killed at Goliad, at the time of the murder of COL. FANNIN.

On all of the above notices to mature December 26, 1840.

August 22, 1840 ESTATE WM. BARTON, decd. WM. TRAMMEL to take the place of LOGAN VANDEVER. DAVID BROWNING and WASHINGTON SHUFF, appraisers.

August 24, 1840 CHARLES SHEPPARD, administrator ESTATE CUTHBERT EDWARDS decd. return of an inventory and appraisement.

Page 7½: August 27, 1840: JOHN H. HARVEY, applies for administration on ESTATE WM. R. GASTON, decd.

JOHN H. HARVEY, applies for administration on ESTATE JOHN N. ZINCK, decd

ROBERT BRATTON applies for administration of ESTATE WM. KIRCHER, decd.

PAGE 8: Sept. 5, 1840, SAML. FLINT, applies for administration on

ESTATE EDWARD FLINT, decd.

New bond required in ESTATE JOHN HAFTER, decd.

JOHN WOOD, CHAS. WALKER & N. SAULS, are appointed appraisers in ESTATE WM. KEPLER. Sept. 14, 1840 E. FULSOM is appointed administrator ESTATE WM. KEPLER, decd., and

PAGE 9: D. LAUGHLIN, B. F. JOHNSON & M. FARLEY are appointed appraisers ESTATE WM. KEPLER, decd.

ESTATE EDWARD FLINT, decd. APPRAISERS: JOHN WOOD, WM. WILKES & ROBERT BRATTON.

Sept. 18, 1840 E. FOLSOM administrator ESTATE WM. KEPLER, decd. interest of infant heirs, applies for moving estate to MONTGOMERY COUNTY, TEXAS, where KEPLER lived, and where heirs live. E. FOLSOM is brother-in-law of decd. COURT ORDERS estate moved to Montgomery County, Texas

PAGE 10: Oct. 3, 1840 L. R. MILLER, L. G. HAYNIE & WM. S. BEATTY are appointed appraisers ESTATE OF JOHN McGOWN, decd.

THOMAS G. GORDON, applies for administration on ESTATE JOSIAS BEALL.dcd

THOMAS G. GORDON, applies for administration on ESTATE ANTHONY BALES, decd. late a volunteer soldier of U. S. & killed at Goliad, at the time of the murder of COL. FANNIN.

Oct. 27, 1840 THOMAS G. GORDON, applies for administration on ESTATE SAMUEL B. BROOKS, decd. late a volunteer soldier of U. S . & killed at Goliad, at the time of the murder of COL. FANNIN.

THOMAS G. GORDON applies for administration on ESTATE URIAH BULLOCK decd. late a volunteer soldier of U. S. & killed at Goliad, at the time of the murder of COL. FANNIN.

THOMAS G. GORDON applies for administration on the ESTATE JAMES H. COSBY, decd. late a volunteer soldier of U. S. & kiled at Goliad, at the time of the murder of COL. FANNIN.

THOMAS G. GORDON applies for administration on the ESTATE OF GEORGE EUBANKS, decd. late a volunteer soldier of U. S. & killed at Goliad, at the time of the murder of COL. FANNIN.

THOMAS G. GORDON applies for administration on the ESTATE OF HEZEKIAH FROST, decd. late a volunteer soldier of U. S. & killed at Goliad, at the time of the murder of COL. FANNIN.

THOMAS G. GORDON applies for administration on ESTATE OF WILSON HELMS decd. late a volunteer soldier of U. S. & killed at Goliad, at the time of the murder of COL. FANNIN.

THOMAS G. GORDON applies for administration on the ESTATE OF SAMUEL A. MILLS, decd. late a volunteer soldier of U. S. & killed at Goliad, at the time of the murder of COL. FANNIN.

THOMAS G. GORDON applies for administration on ESTATE of WATKINS NOBLES decd. late a volunteer soldier of U. S. & killed at Goliad, at the time of the murder of COL. FANNIN

THOMAS G. GORDON applies for administration on the ESTATE of ROBERT A. PACE, decd. late a volunteer soldier of U. S. & killed at Goliad, at the time of the murder of COL. FANNIN.

PAGE 13: THOMAS G. GORDON applies for administration on the ESTATE of S. C. PITTMAN, decd. late a volunteer soldier of U. S. & killed at Goliad, at the time of the murder of COL. FANNIN.

Page 14: THOMAS G. GORDON applies for administration on the ESTATE of

TERRY REESE, decd. late a volunteer soldier of U. S. & killed at Goliad, at the time of the murder of COL. FANNIN.

THOMAS G. GORDON applies for administration on the ESTATE of WM. A. SMITH, decd. late a volunteer soldier of U. S. & killed at Goliad, at time time of the murder of COL. FANNIN.

THOMAS G. GORDON applies for administration on the ESTATE of JAMES WINN, decd. late a volunteer soldier of U. S. & killed at Goliad, at the time of the murder of COL. FANNIN.

All to be heard December 26, 1840.

PAGE 14: Oct. 31, 1840 A. C. MacFADAN, applies for administration on ESTATE CHARLES SCHOOLFIELD decd.

PAGE 15 Oct. 15. THOMAS G. GORDON makes $1000.00 bond on: ESTATES: J.W. COWAN, GREEN LEE, HARRISON YOUNG, JNO. M. POWER, JOHN S. THORN & KENETH McKENZIE.

No. 42, Nov. 7, 1840 ELIZABETH M. SWEENEY by atty. JOHN D. NEWALT (?) makes application on ESTATE W. B. SWEENEY decd.

JNO. W. HAYDEN, SAML. R. MILLER, & W. B. BILLINGSLEY are appointed appraisers ESTATE CHAS. SCHOOLFIELD, decd.

PAGE 16: Nov. 11, 1840, No. 44: JOSEPH A. CLARK applies for administration on estate JANE CLARK decd.

Nov. 12, 1840 D. K. WEBB, JNO. H. WILKINS & LAVENDER S. WILKINS are appointed appraisers in ESTATES OF: W. A. O. WADSWORTH, JNO. S. THORN, J. W. COWAN, KENNETH McKENZIE, HARRISON YOUNG & GREEN LEE, decd.

PAGE 17: PETER MULL decd. Nov. 16, 1840, WM. R. GASTON makes application for administration.

ELIZABETH BURLESON, applies for guardianship of JACOB BURLESON'S minor children: SARAH ANN, AARON, EDWARD & JACOB BURLESON. REUBEN HORNSBY HENRY JONES & THOMAS MOORE, are appointed appraisers.

PAGE 18: Nov. 27, 1840: GEO. B. McCLUSKY, LAVENDER S. WILKINS & JOHN H. WILKINS are appointed appraisers ESTATES THOS. D. CLARKE, decd. and HARRISON YOUNG, decd.

PGE. 19: H. K. Muse makes application for appointment in ESTATE D. B. NOBLES, decd.

PAGE 20: Dec. 26, 1840 THOS. G. GORDON is appointed administrator of ESTATES of: JOSIAH B. BEALL, decd; TIMOTHY BATES, decd. JOHN CHENAULT decd. JOHN A. F. GRAVIS & W. S. BEATY are appointed appraisers for SAM B. BROOKS.

page 21: THOMAS G. GORDON is appointed administrator of ESTATES OF: JAMES H. CROSBY, GEORGE EUGANKS, HEIZEKIAH FROST, WILSON HELMS, SAMUEL A. MILLS, WATKINS NOBLES, ROBERT A. PACE, S. G. PITTMAN, WM. A. SMITH, JAMES WYNN & PERRY REESE.

Dec. 28, 1840 G. W. BROWNING & P. V. LUMPKINS only legal heirs of KENNETH McKENZIE, are appointed administrators to replace THOMAS G. GORDON addminstrator.

PAGE 25: Dec. 29, A. W. LUCKETT, GEO. W. BONNELL & JOSEPH A. CLARK are appointed appraisers of ESTATE B. H. JOHNSON, decd. and HUGH McLEOD is administrator of ESTATE B. H. JOHNSON, decd.

PAGE 26: Jan.1 6, 1841: ROBERT POTTER, agent for JAMES WADSWORTH, father of W. A. O. WADSWORTH, who was murdered with COL. FANNIN.

New bond is ordered for J. W. COWAN, decd.

PAGE 27: Jan. 18, 1841: B. :H. H. BUTTS administrator ESTATE JOHN HAFFLER, decd. is ordered to deliver all papers into court, as he has not performed duties of administrator.

PAGE 28: Feb. 23, 1841, ANGELINE D. SMITH & THOS. W. SMITH, are making application for administraton on ESTATE JAMES W. SMITH, decd.

Feb. 24, HENRY MILLARD & CALVIN JONES, are appointed appraisers in ESTATE EDWARD FLINT, decd.

PAGE 29: J. A. CALDWELL, on March 7, 1941, makes application to be appointed administrator on ESTATE of THOMAS G. GORDON, decd.

PAGE 30: Feb. 28: JOSEPH LEE is appointed Chief Justice of Court TCT

ANGELINE D. SMITH, is widow of JAMES W. SMITH, decd.

Mar. 22, 1841 G. A. WERNLANDER applies for administration on ESTATE CONRAD HENTZE decd.

EDWARD FLINT sold land certificate to MOSES JOHNSON, Bastrop Co. Tex.

PAGE 31: Feb. 24, M. H. NICHELSON, STEPHEN HOYLE & WM. McKINZIE are appointed appraisers and GEO. L. HAASS is appointed administrator J. W. WARD, decd.

PAGE 33: May 15: JOHN HOFFLE ?

VOLNEY L. KELLOGG is appointed administrator of JOHN A. CROSBY, ESTATE and SOLOMON L. JOHNSON, F. LOYD & W. W. THOMPSON are appointed appraisers of ESTATE JNO. A. CROSBY decd. June 21, 1841.

June 25, GILMORE WEAVER is appointed administrator ESTATE ALMAN WEAVER decd.

PAGE 35: JACOB HARRELL, JOSEPH ROBERTSON, W. L. CEZNEAU, J. A. F. GRAVIS, THOS. W. SMITH & ASA BRIGHAM are appointed to appraise ESTATE THOS GORDON, decd.

PAGE 36: ESTATE CONRAD HANTZ, decd. Z. A. VANLANDER appointed administrator; GEO. LEWIS HAYS, JOHN CERELL (CARROLL?) & LEWIS HORST, apprs.

May 31, WILL...WILLIAM WALL decd. non cupative willWIT: JAS. HENDERSON & HORACE HOUGHTON...WM. MILLER, Legatee refused to act; DAVID LAUGHLIN appointed administrator with will annexed; NICHOLAS McARTHUR, WM. SIMPSON & GREENBERY H. HARRISON appraisers.

Mar. 31 DAVID LAUGHLIN, guardian MARY NORVELLA FOOT, minor $11,000.00 bond.

June 16, ALEXANDER McDONALD appointed administrator ESTATE WM. B. MELVILLE, decd; J. W. HAYDEN, DAVIS ROSS, appointed appraisers.

PAGE 38: EST. JOHN A. F. GRAVIS, decd. WM. SPENDER, appointed administrator; DANL. MURCHISON HARRISON & BERRY L. VANCLEAVE appointed aprs.

July 29, MASSELLON FARLEY is administrator of WM. A. FORCE. decd; D.K. WEBB, JOSEPH FESSENDEN & A. G. JOHNSON are appointed appraisers

PAGE 40: August 24, HARVY SMITH is appointed administrator of ESTATE THOS. W. SMITH, decd. wife REBECCA refuses to act.

August 24, 1841 NOAH SMITHWICK is appointed administrator de bonis non ESTATE RICHARD DUTY, decd.

PAGE 41: Aug 24, HARVEY SMITH is appointed administrator ESTATE THOS. W. SMITH, decd.
NANCY ROBERTSON is appointed administratrix EST.hus.JOHN B.ROBERTSON,dcd

PAGE 42: May 5, JOHN O. CLARK administator of ESTATE J. A. CREARY,decd to sell property "the promissory notes of the GOVERNMENT of TEXAS".. Sept. 27, sold land cert. for $40.00 to DAMON H. GATTIS.

PAGE 43: REPUBLIC of TEXAS, COUNTY OF TRAVIS: Messrs. E. S. PERKINS, J M. ROBERTSON & JOHN CARLOS of City of Houston, Harris County, Texas, appointed appraisers of property of JOSEPH W. GARRITY decd. of Travis Co. Texas, May 30, 1842; also land in Fort Bend Co. Texas, May 30,1842. Sgd. D. LAUGHLIN asst. Judge in absence of B. F. JOHNS, CJ TCT

PAGE 44: REPUBLIC of TEXAS, COUNTY of TRAVIS: Messrs. HENRY JONES, M. McGREAL & WILEY POWELL, Fort Bend Co. Tex. appointed appraisers of JOSEPH W. GARRITY decd.

MESSRS. SAML. WHITNEY, WM. W. THOMPSON and FRANCIS DIETRICH appointed appraisers of property of JOSEPH W. GARRITY, decd. in Fayette Co. Tex August 3, 1842.
Sheriff of Bastrop County is to appoint appraisers in Bastrop County in ESTATE A. A. ANDERSON, decd. signed June 13, 1842. D. LAUGHLIN & JAMES BAKER, associate Justices.

PAGE 45: JOHN GRUMBLES is appointed administrator ESTATE A. A. ANDERSON, decd. and OLIVER BUCKMAN & WM. CEZNEAU, are appointed appraisers of same estate. A. D. CAMBY, CJ TCT

Nov. 11, 1841: WM. W. THOMPSON & H. KLOPPENBERG are appointed administrators of ESTATE WM. KIRCHBURG, decd.; A. C. HYDE, WM. SIMPSON & FRANCIS PRENTISS are appointed apprisers.

PAGE 46: Dec. 2, WM. T. BEATY, is appointed administrator of ESTATE of DAVID K. WEBB, decd.

Oct. 24, 1842: CHARLES F. KING Appointed administrator of ESTATE GEO M. DOLSON (DOTSON) decd.

Nov. 20, 1840: HENRY JONES, BENJ. C. ROBERTSON & HENRY TERRELL, are appointed appraisers of ESTATE WM. B. SWEENEY, decd.

PAGE 47: May 11, 1843 (signed) A. COLEMAN, deputy County Clerk. (NOTE: The dates are not in order, and am presuming the book did not come until a lot of papers had accumulated and this deputy was very tired)
PAGE 49: ESTATE ALMAN WEAVER, decd. TILMAN WEAVER, administrator, Sept. 9, 1843, inventoried 640 acre certificate.

August 23, 1843, LOUIS HORST, administrator CONRAD DRISYINGER, estate by attorney JOSEPH LEE.

PAGE 50: May 29, 1843, WILLIAM BRATTON is appointed administrator of ESTATE JAMES LAMB, decd.

May 25, MAY (MARY) BELL is appointed administratrix EST. WM. BELL, decd.

PAGE 51: D. LAUGHLIN, MOSES WOOD & JOHN BRATTON are appointed as appraisers of ESTATES of WM. BELL & JAMES LAMB, decd.

May 29, GEO. K. TULON is appointed administrator EST. JAMES M.OGDEN,dec.
PACKETT NO. 1, STATE WM. H. GRIMES decd. (indexed WM. R. GRIMES) JOHN H. YERBY, petitioned the COUNTY court of Travis County to be appointed administrator of the ESTATE OF WM. H. GRIMES, decd. which is the first estate on the books in the CLERK'S OFFICE. JOHN H. YERBY stated that he was a partner of WM. H. GRIMES, decd. and he, JOHN H. YERBY had "advanced large sums of money out of his own purse on debts etc. of the said WM. H. GRIMES, decd.." None of the heirs of decd. are named or referred to in any of the papers. JOHN H. YERBY was appointed administrator, March 31, 1840, but on Dec. 31, 1841 THOMAS L. JONES was appointed administrator. The final account says: "1 gold watch appraised at $50.00 not accounted for" The ESTATE inventory listed a couple of DOWN TOWN AUSTIN CITY LOTS, and three notes, and many bills.

FIRST BOOK of MARKS and BRANDS in the Travis County Clerk's OFFICE:
(Each person appeared personally before the clerk)
JOSEPHUS SCOTT, recorded August 26, 1846, A. B. McGILL, recorder;
ALLEN ELIOT BROWN, recorded Sept. 14, 1846, R. C. DOOM, depty. recorder;
FRANCIS KELLY, recorded Oct. 2, 1846, A. B. McGILL, recorder;
HORATIO GROOMS, recorded Oct. 4, 1846;
WILLIAM SOUR, recorded Nov. 1, 1846;
SAMUEL HIGHSMITH, recorded Dec. 7, 1846;
N. M. LICKETT, recorded Jan. 11, 1847;
JOEL MINER, recorded Feb. 20, 1847;
CLAIBORNE OSBORNE, recorded Feb. 23, 1847;
THOMAS H. JONES, recorded Mar. 8, 1847;
MEUSADOR ROUNDTREE recorded Mar. 18, 1847;
JAMES YOUNG, recorded April 20, 1847;
WILLIAM D. THOMAS, recorded April 29, 1847;
GEORGE J. DURHAM, recorded May 28, 1847;"changed Oct. 22,1849" Clk.
GEORGE GOLDEN, recorded...5,1847;
LOUIS CAPT. recorded June 1, 1847;
WILLIAM S. WALLACE, recorded Sept. 13, 1847;
NELSON MERRILL, recorded Aug. 20, 1847;
ANDREW O. HORNE, recorded Aug. 29, 1847;
JAMES P. McKINNEY, recorded Sept. 26, 1847;
JOHN WAHRENBERGER, recorded Nov. 8, 1847;
CHARLES KLIEN, recorded Nov. 8, 1847;
JOHN TALK, recorded Dec. 2, 1847;
ROBERT E. FLANIKEN, recorded Mar. 30, 1848;
FERDINAND GENTRY, recorded April 15, 1848;
JAMES BOYCE, recorded April 24, 1848;
JOHN DUNCAN, recorded May 2, 1848;
A. N. HOPKINS, recorded May 5, 1848;
MARTIN MOORE, recorded May 16, 1848;
NEWELL BURDITT, recorded May 25, 1848;
JAMES P. McARTHUR, recorded May 27, 1848;
JOHN J. McCUISTIAN, recorded June 5, 1848;
HORACE BAKER, recorded June 6, 1848;
ISIAH (JHAH) BAKER, recorded June 6, 1848;
COLLIN FORBES, recorded June 13, 1848;
LEANDER BROWN, recorded June 27, 1848;
WILLIAM B. BURDITT, recorded June 29, 1848;
MARTHA BURDITT, recorded June 29, 1848;
RACHEAL B. SCOTT, recorded July 24, 1848;
ALBERT G. KIMBLE recorded July 27, 1848;
ROBERT W. MONTGUMERY, recorded July 27, 1848;
ISAAC HARRIS, recorded Aug. 1, 1848;
WILLIAM JOHNSON, recorded Aug. 19, 1848;
THOMAS OSBORNE, recorded Sept. 22, 1848;
WILLIAM CRUZE , recorded Oct. 30, 1848;
D. WALSH, recorded Nov. 24, 1848;
JOSEPH LEE, recorded Nov. 27, 1848;
JOSEPH J. MANOR, recorded Dec. 16, 1848;
JAMES H. RAYMOND, recorded Feb. 24, 1849;
MARIA BUTTS, recorded Feb. 27, 1849;
FINAS E. WARE (WEAR) recorded Mar. 25, 1849;
JAMES G. SWISHER, recorded Mar. 20, 1849;
EMMA VIRGINIA JOHNSON & SAM HOUSTON JOHNSON, recorded Mar. 27, 1849;
GEORGE BRATTON, recorded April 4, 1849;
JONATHAN TANNER recorded April 10, 1849; S. S. MULLOWNY, deputy.
THOMAS WOODS WARD, recorded April 10, 1849; A. B. McGILL, Clk.

BENJAMIN GRUMBLES, recorded May 24, 1849;
THOMAS J. MOORE, recorded May 30, 1849;
DAVID G. EDMINSTON, recorded June 4, 1849;
JOHN W. DARLINGTON, recorded June 11, 1849;
DAVID EPPRIGHT, recorded July 16, 1849;
JOSHUA BENNETT, recorded July 16, 1849;
E. R. OLIVER, recorded Aug. 3, 1849;
MARY ANN CUSTARD, recorded Oct. 2, 1849;
CHRISTOPHER M. ROESSELL , recorded Oct. 1, 1849; JOHN P. WARREN, recorded Oct. 23, 1849; VICTOR L. LABENSKI, recorded Dec. 21, 1849;

A. D. HOUSTON, recorded Dec. 25, 1849;
HALL MEDLIN, Recorded Jan. 5, 1850;
JOHN D. HENRY, recorded Jan. 11, 1850;
LEONARD S. FRIEND, recorded Jan. 30, 1850;
BENJAMIN CHOTE, recorded Mar. 8, 1850;
MARTIN CASNER, recorded Mar. 15, 1850;
THOMAS E. STANDLY, recorded Mar. 25, 1859;
SHERMAN CASE, recorded Mar. 25, 1850;
FRANCIS A. ROBEY, recorded Mar. 30, 1850;
JAMES CUNNINGHAM, recorded April 2, 1850;
JOHN G. MATTHEWS, recorded April 8, 1850;
S. D. MULLOWNY, recorded April 8, 1850;
BANYAN PAYNE, recorded April 9, 1850;
JAMES M. W. HALL, recorded April 13, 1850;
WILLIAM L. GLASSCOCK, recorded April 21, 1850;
HENRY LOHMANN, recorded April 29, 1850;
STEPHEN CUMMINGS, recorded April 29, 1850;
OZWIN WILCOX, recorded May 6, 1850;
CHARLES G. SUTTLE, recorded May 2, 1850;
QUINCY CASE, recorded May 24, 1850;
T. T. FAUNTLEROY, recorded May 30, 1850;
GILES H. BURDITT, recorded May 30, 1850;
SAMUEL SMITH, recorded June 3, 1850;
W. ·B. NICHOLUS, recorded June 3, 1850;
JOHN NEEDHAM, recorded June 3, 1850;
THOMAS W. FOSTER, recorded June 3, 1850;
MARY A. STONE, recorded June 4, 1850;
JAMES GEORGE, recorded June 4, 1850;
MARY DUTY (HENRY was written then crossed out) recorded June 8, 1850;
C. SEATON, recorded June 13, 1850;
PETER PARKER, recorded June 14, 1850;
ISAAC EPPRIGHT, recorded July 6, 1850;
JAMES H. HUTCHINS, recorded July 20, 1850;
ANGUS McLAREN, recorded July 20, 1850;
PEYTON W. NOWLIN, recorded Aug. 5, 1850;
JOHN EDWARDS, recorded Aug. 5, 1850;
JOSIAH FISK, recorded Aug. 13, 1850;
ANN E. BOYCE, recorded Aug. 15, 1850;
WILLIAM T. HORNE, recorded Sept. 9, 1850;
WILLIAM GRUMBLES, recorded Sept. 10, 1850;
BENJAMIN M. CLOPTON, recorded Sept. 14, 1850
MARCUS HULING, recorded Oct. 14, 1850;
ELLENOR RINARD, recorded Oct. 18, 1850;
HENRY THURMAN, recorded Oct. 28, 1850;
S. P. BROWN, recorded Oct. 28, 1850 (note: THIS could be "X")
ROBERT L. FERGUSON, redorded Nov. 16, 1850;
J. J. McLAURIN, recorded Nov. 21, 1850;
SAMUEL G. EDWARDS, recorded, Nov. 26, 1850;
JOHN BREMOND, recorded Nov. 29, 1850;
WILLIAM BONNER, recorded Nov. 29, 1850;
JAMES W. STANDIFER, recorded Dec. 9, 1850;
JOHNATHAN SCOTT, recorded Dec. 9, 1850;
JULINA AYRES, recorded Dec. 28, 1850;
SAMUEL K. JENNINGS, JR., recorded Jan. 1, 1851;
JOHN MEEKS, recorded Jan. 14, 1851;
CHARLOTTE HURST, recorded Feb. 12, 1851;
JOHN D. HENRY, recorded Feb. 15, 1851;
J. J. GWIN, recorded Mar. 15, 1851;
JOHN C. ROBY, recorded Mar. 22, 1851;
PALSER FLESHER, recorded April 2, 1850;
SAMUEL E. HOLLAND, recorded April 28, 1851;
JOHN F. RAPP, recorded May 1, 1851;
HARVEY H. NEWTON, recorded May 5, 1851;
MATTHEW BROWN, recorded May 5, 1851;
ADDISON LANE, recorded May 7, 1851;
JOSEPH BETZ, recorded May 24, 1851;
WILLIAM H. CUSHNEY, recorded May 26, 1851;
PHILIP HOFFMANN, recorded June 25, 1851;

THOMAS H. BACON, recorded Jun3, 30, 1851;
L. T. VANN, recorded June 30, 1851;
WILLIAM SWOUTS (SNOUTS) (brand is S H S) recorded July 5, 1851;
DAVID H. FARR, recorded July 7, 1851;
JAMES M. LANE, recorded July 8, 1851;
JOHN HARVEY, recorded July 8, 1851;
JAMES WALL, recorded July 17, 1851;
WASHINGTON D. MILLER, recorded July 30, 1851;
ERHARDT FRUT, recorded Aug. 11, 1851;
THOMAS L. CAMPBELL, recorded Aug. 15, 1851;
CHARLES T. PELHAM, recorded Sept. 15, 1851;
EDWARD ZIMMERMANN, recorded Oct. 1, 1851;
ANDREW M. COX, recorded Oct. 2, 1851;
WILLIAM P. THORPE, recorded Oct. 4, 1851;
JOHN BRAKER, recorded Oct. 18, 1851;
NATHANIEL H. ROBERTSON, recorded Oct. 21, 1851;
THOMAS A. MATTHEWS, recorded Oct. 21, 1851, A. B. McGILL by JOHN B.COSTA
ALFRED GROOMS, recorded Oct. 24, 1851;
CALVIN BELL, recorded Dec. 13, 1851;
JAMES B. BENSON, recorded Dec. 6, 1851
ANDREW JAGER, recorded Dec. 6, 1851;(YAGER)
PETER KLEIN, recorded Dec. 20, 1851;
JOHN ERNST MOWINCKEL, recorded Jan. 6, 1852;
CHRISTIAN KIRCHNER, recorded Jan. 9, 1852;
R. I. RAMBO, recorded Jan. 20, 1852;
JESSE HARRIS, recorded Jan. 31, 1852;
JOHN PHILIPS, recorded Feb. 6, 1852;
JOHN SHELTON, recorded Feb. 6, 1852;
SOLOMON STARR, recorded Feb. 23, 1852;
T. F. W. WEILCKIND, recorded Mar. 16, 1852
CALVIN H. NAYLOR, recorded April 2, 1852;
W. K. BROWN, recorded April 8, 1852;
SIMUEL ROBERT (brand is S I M) recorded April 12, 1852
N. C. RAYMOND, recorded April 12, 1852 (brand is NR)
JAMES M. TURLEY, recorded April 12, 1852;
ENOCH S. JOHNSON, recorded April 13, 1852;
HENRY D. EDWARDS recorded April 14, 1852;
LEWIS BEARDSLEY, recorded April 20, 1852;
CHRISTIAN KERCHNER, recorded April 30, 1852;
JOHN LIESSE, recorded May 8, 1852 (brand is L S)
THOMAS P. ROUNTREE, recorded May 15, 1852;
GEORGE W. RICKS, recorded May 15, 1852;
SARAH H. COCKS, recorded May 17, 1852;
H. D. COCKS, recorded May 17, 1852
NICHOLAS DAWSON, recorded May 17, 1852;
WILLIAM R. BAUCHMAN, recorded June 5, 1852;
CHARLES F. COMPTON, recorded June 9, 1852;
HUGH M. LAWHON, recorded June 22, 1852;
JOHN HEMPHILL, recorded June 30, 1852;
WILLIAM CASE, recorded MJuly 2, 1852;
JOHN CALVIN, recorded July 9, 1852
JOHN L. ARRINGTON, recorded July 9, 1852
LEWIS BARKSDALE, recorded July 15, 1852;
MARY BARKSDALE, recorded July 15, 1852;
JOHN BRACHA, recorded July 17, 1852; (this is another spelling of BRAKER)
JOHN F. SMITH, recorded Sept. 6, 1852;
MARY E. SMITH, recorded Sept. 6, 1852;
SUSAN A. SMITH, recorded Sept. 6, 1852;
FERDINAND WILHELM, recorded Sept. 17, 1852
PATRICK GUINEATY, recorded Oct. 6, 1852
ELI C. HUGGINS, recorded Oct. 25, 1852;
C. C. BROWN, recorded Oct. 25, 1852;
WILLIAM NEANS or NEENS, recorded Nov. 13, 1852; McGILL by JOHN T.ALLAN
(note: the clerk is spelling NEANS both ways)
DAVID THOMAS, recorded Nov. 22, 1852;
NORMAN AUSTIN, recorded Dec. 7, 1852;
JOHN TANEY, recorded Dec. 21, 1852;
AUGUSTUS FORE, recorded Dec. 23, 1852;
L. B. MOORE, recorded Dec. 29, 1852;

EUGENE BENNETT, recorded Dec. 29, 1852;
CHAS. SETTLE, recorded Jan. 10, 1853;
WILLIAM O. MARTIN, recorded Feb. 21, 1852;
HENRY PAPE, recorded Feb. 24, 1853;
GEORGE SUSMAN, recorded Mar. 14, 1853;
ALEXANDER JOHNSTON, recorded April 12, 1853;
A. B. SLAUGHTER, recorded April 25, 1853;
WILLIAM H. HILL, SR., recorded May 7, 1853;
GUSTAVUS KIRCHBERG , recorded May 7, 1853;
WILLIAM H. GRIMES, recorded May 16, 1853; (brand is E)
EDMUND CREUZBAUR & ROBERT CREUZBAUR, recorded May 16, 1853;
MARTHA A. R. HAGUE, recorded May 23, 1853;
RUFUS R. JONES, recorded June 3m =1853;
ISAAC V. JONES, recorded June 3, 1853;
EMILY E. JONES, recorded June 3, 1853;
ANTON NEBGEN, recorded June 3, 1853;
CAROLINE M. RAWLES, recorded Sept. 3, 1853;
MARCELLUS DuVAL, recorded Nov. 16, 1853
SAMUEL C. HOYT, recorded Nov. 26, 1853;
GEORGE B. REED, for NANNIE D. REED, recorded Nov. 26, 1853;
JOHN W. DARLINGTON, changes his brand, recorded Dec. 31, 1853;
THOS. P. CARTMELL, recorded Aug 22, 1853;
HUGH M. LAWHON has bought all the cattle branded Z belonging to
MICHAEL ZILLER by transfer from ZILLER dated June 19, 1852, change
recorded Feb. 2, 1854;
MILLENUM K. ALEXANDER, recorded Mar 8, 1854;
SAMUEL M. WRIGHT, recorded April 3, 1854;
JOSEPH LIMERICK, recorded April 10, 1854;
JAMES FAIRLEY, recorded April 17, 1854;
MADISON RIGGLE, recorded April 22, 1854;
WILHELM WENDE, recorded May 8, 1854;
THOMAS F. CHAPMAN & JOHN MARSHALL, recorded May 18, 1854;
BENJAMIN CHOATE & JAMES E. HARBER, recorded May 19, 1854
W. P. WITHERS of Caldwell Co. recorded June 3, 1854;
JOHN M. TIBAUT, recorded June 5, 1854;
CATHERINE M. NEBGEN, recorded July 1, 1854;
BRYANT O. STAVELY, recorded Aug. 30, 1854;
HENRY RATHKE, recorded Sept. 29, 1854;
RICHARD H.PECK, recorded Oct. 12, 1854;
F. DOHME, recorded Oct. 12, 1854;
WILLIAM BOLES, recorded Oct. 28, 1854;
DOVOIL T. GWIN, recorded Oct. 30, 1854;
DIETERICH BOLES, recorded Nov. 7, 1854;
AUGUST KEES, recorded Dec. 12, 1854 (brand is A K)
JAMES M. BUNTON, recorded Jan. 1, 1855;
E. S. GILES, recorded Feb. 19, 1855 (brand is 15)
ABNER P. BLOCKER, recorded Feb. 19, 1855;
JOHN W. NANCE, recorded Mar. 6, 1855;
F. G. WIERSIOH , recorded Mar 38, 1855;
PETER & JOHN WUTCHRICH, recorded Feb.April 3, 1855;
JOHN T. HAYNES, recorded April 7, 1855;
JAMES B. LITTLEPAGE, recorded April 17, 1855;
JANE & MATILDA BAKER, recorded May 1, 1855;
WILLIAM & RICHARD BAKER, recorded May 1, 1855;
JOHN BRAGA, recorded May 2, 1855;
THEODORE PECHT, recorded May 5, 1855;
J. W. BONNER, recorded May 17, 1855;
CONRAD ZUSCHLAG, recorded May. 17, 1855;
RAPHAEL MARTINUS, recorded June 5, 1855;
W. F. WELLS, recorded June 28, 1855;
HENRY PFEGER (probably PFLUGER) recorded July 27, 1855;
MARY A. E. SMITH, recorded Sept, 18k 1855;
M. TONGAT, recorded Sept. 25, 1855;
DORCASNA BRISCO, Sept. 1,25, 1855;
DAVID L. CROSS, recorded Oct. 24, 1855;
AMANDA L. GOODENOUGH, recorded Nov. 3, 1855;
WILLIAM A. PEEL, recorded Nov. 5, 1855;
THOMAS PEEL, recorded Nov. 5, 1855;

THOMAS J. STONE, recorded Feb. 16, 1857; JAMES P. DAVIS, deputy.
MRS. E. M. CROSTHWAIT, recorded Mar. 8, 1857;
HARTENSTEIN & SON, recorded Mar. 15, 1856;
WILLIAM G. WALLACE, recorded Mar. 26, 1856;
GOTTFRIED MAROHN, recorded April 4, 1856;
NANCY C. BISHOP, recorded April 12, 1856, PETER B. LOWE, deputy
BENJAMIN GAULT, recorded May 12, 1856;
DeNORMANDIE & TEN EYCK recorded May 29, 1856;
CHARLOTTE HAMPTON, recorded July 28, 1856;
JACOB SHRAVEN, recorded Oct. 9, 1856; AUGUST SCHWARTZ, deputy
GOTTLIEB SCHWARZKOFF, recorded Nov. 26, 1856; JAMES M. SWISHER, CCC
                                              AUGUSTUS SCHWARTZ,dpty.
MRS. J. A. TEN EYCK recorded June 19, 1858; J. H. THOMPSON, deputy
JOHN H. ROBINSON, recorded June 21, 1858;
MARY A.LEGETT, recorded April 18, 1857;
W. M. SIMS, recorded Sept. 18, 1857;
MICHAELS ZILLER, recorded Jan. 1, 1858;
JOHN BURLAGE, recorded Mar. 15, 1858;
J. M. TIBAUT, recorded April 3, 1858;
CHARLES JOHNSON, recorded April 13, 1858;
J. D. FAULKES, recorded June 5, 1858;
S. B. BRUSH, recorded June, 17, 1858;
COL. A. G. WEIR, recorded June 11, 1858;
MILLISSA BROWN, recorded June 11, 1858;
JOHN HENNINGER, recorded July 24, 1858;
SUSAN SETTLE, recorded Aug. 7, 1858;
WRIGHT D. JOSEPH, recorded Sept. 13, 1858; J. T. McLAURIN, Clerk
SYLVESTER T. SMITH, recorded Oct. 23, 1858;
H. H. HAYNIE, recorded Oct. 27, 1858;
JOHN H. TULK, recorded Oct. 28, 1858;
E. FELLMAN, recorded Oct. 29, 1858;
E. R. GENTRY, Nov. 8, 1858;
GEO. W. ROSE, recorded Nov. 13, 1858;
THOMAS J. HOUSTON, recorded Nov. 22, 1858;
KINCHIN BALDWIN, recorded Nov. 26, 1858;
FREIDERICK REISHOW, recorded Ded. 1, 1858;
SAMUELS & MASSON, recorded Dec. 13, 1858;
CHARLES MULLINS, Lampasas Springs &c, recorded Dec. 18, 1858;
JOEL Y. CAIN, recorded Dec. 20, 1858;
MRS. DOLLY C. PEAL, recorded Jan. 1, 1859;
CHARLES L. McGEHEE, recorded Jan. 28, 1859;
JOHN FRUIT, recorded Feb. 2, 1859; (this name several spellings)
A. G. WEIR, recorded Dec. 22, 1858;
JOHN NIXON, recorded Jan. 1, 1859;
JURIAN M. HOPKINS, transferred to E. CHRISTIAN, Jan. 11, 1859.

RECORDED IN THE BACK of the above book of MARKS & BRANDS:

RECEIVED of ASHFORD B. McGILL, clerk County Court in and for Travis Co.
one copy of the laws of Texas passed by the Legislature of the State of
Texas at 2nd session in 1847 and 1848.
                        WM. W. ATWOOD, cty. Comr. May 29, 1848

RECEIVED....by JESSE BURDITT, county commissioner May 29, 1848, but adds:
.."which copy I promise to deliver to my successor in office when
elected.."

One signed by W. H. CUSHNEY, assessor & Col. T. C. not dated.

RECEIVED by J. H. MATTHEWS,sheriff TC and adds: "..I having never re=
ceived a similar copy from any other source and which I promise to deliver to my successor in office when elected."

RECEIVED... by O. WILLCOX, Cor. notdated.

RECEIVED..A. N. HOPKINS, JP not dated.

B. D. BASSFORD, Clk. D. C. T. C. by A. N. HOPKINS, deputy. not dated

RECEIVED, .. JAMES R. PACE, Dist. surveyor, Travis District, June 5, 1848.

RECEIVED...JOSEPH LEE, Notary Public, June 9, 1848.
STEPHEN CUMMINGS, Chief Justice, Travis Co. June 10, 1848.

RECEIVED,.... G. W. DAVIS, County Comr. not dated.

RECEIVED...S. G. HAYNIE, M. L. (?)(Member of Legislature?)

RECEIVED..CHARLES MASON, Notary Public, not dated.

RECEIVED:... G. M. SCOTT, J. P. T. CO. not dated.

RECEIVED..JOHN J. MATT HEWS, County Commissioner, August 21, 1848

RECEIVED...ALBERT BROWN, Justice of Peace, Travis Co. Nov. 4, 1848.

Also in the back of the MARKS & BRANDS BOOK:

RECORDERS DOCKET: City of Austin Sept. 1, 1846

CORPORATION of the CITY OF AUSTIN
vs.
...STAMPER,"for an asalt..fine by Jury."

CORPORATION   CITY OF AUSTIN Sept. 1, 1846
vs.
WILLIAM COCKBURN "for an asolt dismissed by Jury at cost of corp."

CORPORATION   CITY OF AUSTIN Sept. 23, 1846
vs
THOS. GLASCOCK "for braking the peace fine by Jury"

CORPORATION
vs.
B. H. H. BUTTS, JURY: B. GRUMBLES, WILLIAM COCKBURN, BENJ. PIPER, C. C. CUSHMAN, LEWIS HORST & JAMES MURRY. "We the jury fine the defendant $10.00 and cost of suit" (Totalled $23.80)

CORPORATION
vs.
DAVID THOMAS "for an afray the jury return a verdict of not guilty."
                             R. C. DOOM, recorder, Nov. 23, 1846

CORPORATION
vs/
THOMAS C. COLLINS. "For an afray."...not guilty. Dec. 14, 1846

CORPORATION
VS
O. WILLCOX "for an afray" JURY: S. STONE, C. C. CUSHMAN, J. HIGHSMITH, P. GOLDEN, A. W. POWNCEY, J. C. CLEMENTS. Guilty. Fine $5.00 Dec. 14, 1846.

CORPORATION
VS.
JOHN S. FORD "for an afray. He pled guilty Dec. 14, 1846. R. C. DOOM
                                                                             recorder
CORPORATION
VS.
A. W. PUCKETT "for an afray..no evidence. corporation pays.

CITY RECORDERS COURT Dec. 14, 1846 "ORDERED by the court thatAUGUSTUS FISCHER, Esq. atty. at law be fined for contempt for profain swearing and for using obsean language $5.00 and to remain in custody of the Marshall until the fine and cost is paid. No date: "ORDERED by the court that so far as the custody of A. FISCHER Esq. atty. at law the remited.
                                     R. C. DOOM recorder

AUSTIN COUNTY, TEXAS

ELIJAH D. HOLLAND m. ELIZABETH MARSON July 20, 1840
JNO. T. HARRISON m. LESIA STANFIELD July 26, 1876
JAMES G. HEFFINGTON m. ELIZABETH JACKSON, Mar...1839 Vol. A p. 20

BASTROP COUNTY, TEXAS

78/174 Mar. 5, 1841, PATENT, STATE OF COAHUILA & TEXAS to ELISHA W. BARTON, with family. 1 League. THOMAS H. BORDEN, surveyor. MIGUEL ARCINIEGA, Comm. ROBERT TAYLOR, JR. asst. Comm. & C. C. GIVENS, asst.

PC 545 succession of J. K. MILLER, administrator of ESTATE OWEN MILLER, decd. Order discharging administrator Aug. 7, 1900; CAM TRIGG, et al heirs of OWEN MILLER vs. ELVIRA PAYNE, et al DC 2135, CAM TRIGG, FRANCES THOMPSON, LIZZIE CLEMENTS et vir GEORGE, FRANCES THORNE et vir FRANK, W. R. THORN, LIZZIE YANCY et ux of A. B., MARIAH POWELL et vir JAMES & A. L. HANLEY, BCT, MATTIE ROLLY et vir HENDERSON, Hays Co. Tx. WILEY JONES, MADISON, Co. Ala. vs. T. K. MOORE, ILSE RIDGE, et vir SOL: ELVIRA PAYNE et vir HANDY, all of Bastrop Co. Tex; OWEN MILLER d. BCT Jan. 28, 1897 a single man, parents also dead; brothers and sister are: CAM TRIGG, FRANCES THOMPSON, & LIZZIE CLEMENTS & WILEY JONES, MATILDA HANDLY, she d. before O. MILLER; FRANCES THORN, LIZZIE YANCY, MATTIE ROLLEY, MARIAH POWELL & A. B. HANDLEY, ISLEY RIDGE & Hus. and ELVIRA PAYNE, et vir, are adverse claimants, not kin. Says Jan. 1860 Monroe Co. Miss. Owen Miller and Elsie DAW, were slaves.

JAMES GEORGE (d. Alamo) J. J. BROWN, of McMahan, farmer and great g.son of JAMES GEORGE and wife, ELIZABETH, they JAMES GEORGE and wife with 3 ch. arrived in Gonzales, Feb. 20, 1830 and 2 other ch. born there: RACHEL m. JIM BROWN, MARGARET, MATHILDA m. JOSEPH ALEXANDER, MARY JANE, HENRY, JAMES GEORGE were granted land June 28. 1836 near present Lockhart, Texas. ELIZABETH (widow) m....ROWE, he d. and she m. THOMAS HASKINS: ELIZABETH ROWE, who m. JOEL CARTER, JOHN HASKINS & SARAH HASKINS m. JOSEPH HEMPHILL.

D/149 PATENT Feb. 7, 1841 REPUBLIC of TEXAS to JOHN LYTTON

D/450 deed July 15, 1842 JOHN LITTON to WM. H. JACKS (no residence for either given) WIT: JOHN G. ANDERSON & G. W. GLASSCOCK TCT

H/216 EST. WM. H. JACK decd. Nov. 9, 1848, THOS. F. McKINNEY, LAURA H. JACK, ind. extr. EST. WM. H. JACK, decd. to THOMAS J. RICE, ack. by THOS. F. McKINNEY in Galveston Co. Tex. WIT: JAMES BURKE, NANCY McKINNEY

G/164 TITLE BOND June 4, 1850 THOMAS J. RICE of Bastrop Co. to JOHN H. POPE. July Term 1851 Bastrop County Court, MARGARET RICE aptd. admrs. of THOMAS J. RICE, decd. appraisers E. MALERRY, PARKS BUNTON, C. J. STROUTHER; MARGARET RICE gdn.of minor children of THOMAS J. RICE (not named)

G/460 deed Aug. 6, 1849 JOHN LITTON et ux SARAH to FRANCIS YOAST. WIT: L. C. CALHOUN, JOHN CALDWELL

H/285 deed Jan. 16, 1852 FRANCIS YOAST et ux ELIZABETH to DAVID A. WORD WIT: SAMUEL WOLFENBARGER

23/593 Oct. 6, 1895 deed, JOHN H. POPE, home City of Austin to JOHN B. POPE.

CEMETERY on top of hill near Utley, (near Austin) Bastrop Co. Tex:
JAMES D. BRYANT, 1884-1959 et ux LULA M.
MARTIN WALKER 3/25/1814, 3/5/1889
MRS. J. S. WALKER 10/26/1831, 2/10/1909
MRS. E. A WATSON, 7/25/1855, 5/3/1931
E. A. WATSON 2/5/1847 10/10/1890
HIRAM WATSON 8/10/1878, 9/11/1900
WILLIE SANDIFER 1875=1902

ANNA M. McGINNIS wife of O. H. P. d. 11/13/1869 36 y. 1 mo. 12 d.
J. R. son of W. & S. E. ROW 10/16/186...5/ 25/1865
MARTHA J. WILSON wife of J. M., old stone could not read dates
J. G. GRESHAM 8/22/1816 d....15/1862 wife was M. L.
J. W. & A. E. BLAIR d. 1876 ?
JOURDAN SMITH 3/4/1811, 3/ 30/1873

McDADECFMENTERY, MARTHA ELIZABETH PALMER 12/6/1834, 7/22/1925
J. A. PURSER, 9/18/1873 11/12/1890

BLUE CEMETERY (rural)Lee County.
W. T. KILPATRICK 12/10/1891, a very crude stone and crude inscription,
PHYLLIS (wife of) A. A. KILPATRICK 9/9/1867
ANNA wife of T. L. BARNETT 10/25/1856 (36) 9/2/1898
ANDREW J. BARNETT, son T. L. & ANN

131/466 partition deed Oct. 9, 1857 EST. JOHN W. PORTER, met at home
of ROBERT V. PORTER in Burleson Co. Texas; land in CHAS. FERRENASH sur.
Burleson Co. & McLennan Co. Tex. H. R. & SAM CHEIRS sur. Milam Co. and
387 ac. on Niels Creek in Bosque and Bastrop Counties to ROBERT V.
PORTER, home in Burleson Co.; JOHN M. PORTER, MILTON H. PORTER, SUSAN
CATHERINE PORTER minor dau. J. B. PORTER by LINEE M. MARTIN, mother
and guardian; THOS. A. PORTER & NEWELL F.PORTER (NOTE: JOHN THORNTON
PORTER left England when he was 13 years old?)

43/473 AARON CULLING, JAMES HOLLINGSWORTH, gdn. minor heirs of AARON
CULLING, RACHAEL HOLLINGSWORTH, MARMADUKE BEATON and wife, JANE, AARON
CULLING and wife, RACHEL, JOHN (son),JANE BEATON dau. and husband M.,
ELIZA (dau) HUGHES and husband HENRY W., NANCY (dau) HUGHES and hus. S.

ERHARD DRUG STORE, Bastrop, Texas.
ADOLPH ANTON ERHARD came to Bastrop via. New Jersey from Munich. Ger.
1835. Had 2 sons: A. A. & CAYTON (youngest) The parents d. and two boys
lived with WM. NICHOLSON of Bastrop, Texas; CAYTON was in battle of
Mier & Sante Fe Expedition. He lived in San Marcos, Hays Co. Tex, and
was P. M. there and Co. Clk. and established a durg store. MRS. MARY
BRIEGER gdau. of A. A. ERHARD lived in Bastrop house. ADOLPH also
served in conf. army d. 1899 at 68 years.

H. N. BELL home Bastrop 1859 to 1866 was home of MAJOR R. D. ALLEN,
commandant of Bastrop Military Institute; the Civil War caused closing
of school. On its walls are names of CADETS: B. F. TERRY, Fort Bend Co.
May 1864; W. CATES, HORACE FRENCH, San Antonio; N. BURLESON, C. F.SHEA,
San Antonio, TExas May 19, 1864, and C. R. ADAMS May 21, 1864.
BELL BROS., W. N., H. N., SAM & D. H. bought property for their mother
Jan. 2, 1886.

JOHN ALDRIDGE house built ca 1853 sold to CAPT. JAMES W. FITZWILLIAMS
1872. J. W. FITZWILLIAM b. Wexford Co. Ireland, to Texas from Ark. after
Civil War. gdau. MISS NELL FITZWILLIAMS

JAMES HARVEY WILBARGER, son of JOSIAH, bought the home late 1850. It was
also COL. J. C. HIGGINS home. MARGARET CHAMBERS BOUGHT it, she was
formerly MRS. JOSIAH WILBARGER.

CAMPBELL TAYLOR house built 1836 as a stage stop on Old San Antonio Road.
It was owned successively by two veterans of the Battle of San Jacinto,
JESSE HALDEMAN & CAMPBELL TAYLOR.

OLD JENKINS home built ca 1836. Seven generationsof the JENKINS family
have lived there...JENKINS was County Clerk Bastrop Co. for many years.

DAVID SAYERS home built 1835 by DR. DAVID SAYERS, father of Texas Gov.
JOS. D. SAYERS.

STATE MARKER for COL. ROBERT MORRIS COLEMAN, near one of the COLEMAN
homes on SOLOMON DUTY survey 12 miles NW Bastrop, near Utley. COLEMAN
was a native of Trigg Co. Ky. b. 1799, arrived Texas 1839 (1829) Minutes
of the Ayntamiento of Mina (Bastrop) 1834 are signed by COLEMAN as

President and Alcalde; 1 of 4 Judges of Municipality of Mina;(Bastrop) was member of CONSTITUTIONAL CONVENTION Mar. 2, 1836; signed DECLARATION of TEXAS INDEPENDENCE. He was accidently drowned near Velasco at age 39, Feb. 18, 1839; his widow and one son killed by INDIANS; 2 little girls escaped and one son taken captive and home burned.

May 16, 1840 JOSEPH JONES, L. B. HARRIS and ROBERT B. CRAFT were appointed to establish a cemetery in Bastrop, Bastrop Co. Texas.

BASTROP CITY CEMETERY: (some graves of older persons)
J. C. BALSER 3/7/1810, 1/27/1875
W. C. POWELL 4/21/1830, 9/30/1899. SARAH M. POWELL 10/22/1839 10/5/1911
MAGGIE BURLESON 2/25/1897 and CHILDREN: MARTHA, MARY JANE and JOHNNY
WASHINGTON WILSON 3/2/1902, 85 years old
CHARLES JONES 1902, 75 years old
SARAH OIENS 4/21/1920, 92 years old
J. H. GILLESPIE 1839, 1885
RUFUS H. GRIMES 1814, 1863
JESSE R. GRIMES 1847, 1858
W. G. POWELL 1860, 1922
ROBERT J. WARREN 1857 1940
FRANCES WARREN 1830, 1875
NANCY WARREN 1833, 1915

McDADE CEMETERY, Bastrop Co. Texas:
WM. HAMILTON b. Jackson Co. Tenn. 2/5/1831, 3/11/1907
SUSAN R. HAMILTON 8/2/1842, 2/14/1918

NEW RED ROCK CEMETERY, Bastrop Co. Texas
ROBERT A. HARRIS 1886, 1950
BESSIE B. HARRIS 1890, 1950
MAGGIE CATCHINGS, 1886, ROBERT THEO RICKARD 1882 1940
GEORGIA E. VOIGHT 1885, 1951; GEO. F. VOIGHT 1885..
HANFORD PETTY 2/19/1875..
INEZ M. PETTY 1/4/1879, 9/15/1939
COY KING 9/1/1895, 11/20/1918
MRS. O. J. WALKER, 1/9/1850, 10/26/1927
JIM TOM WALKER 1888, 1943
TOMMIE ANDERSON, 3/9/1881, 11/30/1916
LEON C. ROSE 1883, 1961
VERLIN CALLAHAN 6/1/1895, 12/30/1917
HUGO HANKE 1881, 1939
ADOLPH JUNG 10/21/1898, 11/15/1917
REX ANDERSON 1829, 1950
SARAH J. HEMPHILL 1/31/1844, 2/6/1916
W. L. HEMPHILL 10/31/1841, 3/25/1929
J. T. HASKINS 8/3/1845, 8/27/1915
MARY HASKINS 4/30/1849, 10/4/1924
MARGARET C. GILLASPY 1854, 1950
REV. J. H. GILLASPY 1833, 1933
MINNIE S. HEMSTOCK wife of J. D. 6/1/1884, 12/27/1921
JOHN P. MURCHISON 4/3/1857, 7/20/1915
CAMERON MURCHISON 6/2/1889, 5/28/1915
WALDENA F. MOBLEY 1914, 1915
THOMAS R. MOBLEY 1874, 1928
S. B. HARRIS 12/26/1889, 1/21/1913
LOUIS GEORGE ELLIS 6/8/1832, 5/4/1915
ERASMUS W. NITE 9/24/1893, 8/14/1940
BERTHA NITE 2/13/1894..
JAKE M. AWALT 1865, 1934, ELIZA S. 1876, 1936
LILIE E. DURAN 1914, 1918
CORA A. MOBLEY 12/23/1879, 5/7/1948
THOMAS C. NITE 9/14/1866, 9/23/1931
RHODA A. NITE 9/24/1872, 8/27/1953
JOHN G. RIDDLES 1862, 1949
JULIA RIDDLES 1/26/1891, 3/5/1937
EMMA RIDDLES 8/14/1868, 3/10/1937
JIM ABNER RIDDLES 9/6/1857, 4/29/1947
T. EARL PETTY 1891, 1950
ELSIE A. PETTY 1894...

```
JOE Z. BLACK, 1873, 1927. M. ORA BLACK 1874 1940
DR. N. B. HARRIS 1857, 1927. KATHERINE HARRIS 1853, 1927
WILL E. SMITH 4/20/1885 2/20/1937.  EMMA A. SMITH 8/5/1886   11/5/1942
ROY ALBERT SMITH 5/14/1904, 11/22/1953
ANNIE SMITH 1876, 1934. JOHN WILLARD SMITH 1872, 1945
DAISY LOIS CORBELL 3/21/1826, 1934
ALTON W. CORBEEL 2/26/1908  1/6/1927
KATTIE CORBEEL 1881, 1959

At RED ROCK, back in a field off HY. No. 20 (State)
GABE LENTZ 10/22/1863, 6/30/1921, MARTHA, wife, 1/21/1866, 10/17/1918
(These are the only markers in a very small cemetery)

BEAUKISS CEMETERY, Bastrop Co. (could be in Lee Co.)
N. E. PRICE 9/9/1844, 2/17/1899
MRS. E. H. TUTTLE 2/5/1844, 6/14/1911
JOHN WARD 10/23/1847   1890
LUCY WARD 2/15/1850, 8/30/1912
DR. J. J. FINCH, 1820, 1914, grandfather
J. T. PRICE 2/13/1822  9/15/1898
DANIEL KIMBRO 2/18/1809  2/13/1883
JAMES R. PRICE 2/28/1824, 3/22/1872

RED ROCK CEMETERY (OLD) Bastrop County;
JOHN H. RHOADES 1/30/1848, 10/18/1945
DORA M. RHOADES 2/10/1844, 5/9/1928;
RONNIE L. DURAN (father) 3/19/1886 1/2/1958
OLA PEARL DURAN (mother) 11/15/1888  8/5/1948;
WM. BERRY DEMENT 8/31/1873 11/12/1935
FANNIE FRANCES DEMENT 4/10/1878 6/7/1939
WM. J. SMITH 11/14/1862, 7/4/1935
ADA C. SMITH 4/24/1876  2/23/1959
LEMMA AGNES BOOTH 9/20/1898 2/1/1924
G. DEWEY CARTER 1898 1959
GARLAND TURNER 1926
ROG ER C. TURNER 1813, 1959
W. A. PETTY 7/25/1882 1/26/1938
L. A. TURNER 7/10/1837, 2/1/1938
ADDIE E. TURNER 3/27/1847, 3/7/1944
BONNIE TURNER 1878, 1858, ELLA b. 1884...
BILL BUCKNER 9/14/1898  8/31/1960
ARRENA C. TURNER 2/10/1881, 12/23/1940
WALLACE A. TURNER 9/20/1877  1/22/1941
AUSTIN C. INGRAM 12/1/1810  3/31/1940
C. R. INGRAM (father) 12/25/1868 10/3/1928
C. L. son of C. & F. J. HENDRIX b. Bastrop Co. 12/17/1855 d. 10/2/1872
"throw frm hors 7 kild"
ELIZA LENTZ 3/24/1838  11/1/1921 "OUR MOTHER"
J. W. BUCKER 1843, 1927, MRS. BUCKNER 1848, 1933
A. D. HARRIS, 1854, ANNETTE HARRIS 1855..
ANN CASTNEE MIERS 8/9/1851  1/1/1936
H. T. MIERS 7/22/1849, 7/10/1906
DELIAH MATTINGLY 1822, 1901
JAMES PEARSON 6/1830  d. 10/28/1903
ROBERT PEARSON 3/15/1829 d. 2/29/1920
AMANDA SOIRELLS DURAN 10/5/1858  2/22/1937

ROCKNE CEMETERY, Bastrop Co.
CLARA BELL dau. J. & L. P. PROBST 9/8/1883 d. 1905
MRS. ELIZABETH MEURER 9/13/1850 8/21/1928
MRS. JOHN MEURER b. 10/13/1838...
AUGUST WENDLAND Mar. 1844 Jan. 1932
MARY WENDLAND 1/27/1854  8/13/1926

HENDRIX CEMETERY to left of No. 20, Bastrop Co. Texas:
JOHN D. HENDRIX 12/2/1863  11/18/1939
JOSEPHINE SORRELS HENDRIX 3/7/1866  6/17/1954
JAMES H. HENDRIX 1857, 1937
CORDELIA HENDRIX 1861, 1951
```

BELL COUNTY, TEXAS

198/303 April 26, 1847 PATENT to WILLIAM L. NORVILLE

N/187, deed Dec. 9, 1848, WM. L. NORVILLE to WILLIAM A. BOOTH. ack. by NORVILLE before C. A. KENABLOCK, NP LaFouche Parish, La.

EST. WILLIAM A. BOOTH, decd. Sept. Term 1866, A. J. HARRIS appointed administrator

ESTATE JOHN H. ISBELL decd. 1859 WILL B/129; AMANDA, wife, minor children ANNA, KATE & JAMES, had land in Coryell, Medina, Burnet, Haskell, Cook, Houston, McLennan, Bell, Gonzales and he inherited 1/4 of 8½ leagues of land in Gonzales Co., Texas as heir of ALEXANDER ISBELL.

E/170, 1873 JAMES R. ISBELL m. REBECCA J. JEFFRIES

L/ 39 W. H. ISBELL m. LOLA NEESCE

G/507 J. M. ISBELL m. VISTA I. MARSHALL

PC B/104, July Term 1837 GOLDSBY CHILDRESS, petitions court to be admin-istrtor of sons; JAMES FRANKLIN & THOMAS, citations to: R. CHILDRESS, CAROLINE, GOLDSBY, CATHERINE, now AMANDA CRADDOCK & JOHN CRADDOCK, ROBERT CHILDRESS, PRIOR, C. M. STICKNEY, formerly CATHERINE M. CHILDRESS wife of E. L., and AMANDA CHILDRESS CRADDOCK & CAROLINE CHILDRESS.

BLANCO COUNTY, TEXAS

CEMETERY:
E. C. HINDS, 1819, 1879 CATHERINE HINDS 1826, 1907
ISAAC DILLARD 1827, 1856
REV. WM. A. HUDSON 1816, 1892, L. M. HUDSON 1818, 1882
ALLIE A. DAVIS wf. of C. L. DAVIS 11/26/1855 d. 3/-/1867
R. N. PUGH 1849, 1877
J. W. HERMANN 1816, 1876; ALMA E. HERMANN 1826, 1905
THOMAS WILEY Mar. 1803; 12/12/1882. ELIZABETH WILEY 5/15/1803, 5/6/1900
JOSEPH CARSON 1830, 1865
THOS. S. SPEER (Mason cant read dates, very old vault)
REBECCA V. BUCHANAN 4/3/1826, 6/14/1867
SARAH B. GREEN 1819, Nov. 1881; JESSE B. GREEN 2/14/1815, 8/13/1894
JESSE A. GREEN 1848, 1871
GRANBERRY MASSEY b. Coffeville, Tenn. 6/27/1852, d. 12/31/1907
KATIE VALLMERING 6/17/1889, J...1919
JOHN M. SMITH 1844, 1895

BROWN COUNTY, TEXAS.

The court house burned here about 1875, and all the records were lost.
48/574 PATENT to MRS. MARY ANN FISK, late, she was MARY ANN LINDSEY, first wife of GREENLEIF FISK, SR. CH: ANN ELIZABETH, JAMES B., WILLIAM A., MARY E. WOOD, and JOSIAH.

BURLESON COUNTY, TEXAS

Old Fort PROVIDENCE cemetery, near Brazos River Bottom, in east part of County:
JOHN COCKRELL, SR. (F) (L) (T) at top of stone, b. Fairfield Dist.
S. C. Jan. 7, 1795, d. 8/18/1855
JOHN EDDIE COCKRELL son of JOHN & ANNIE J. COCKRELL d.4/23/1860 5 years
JOHN COCKRELL, JR. 8/2/1858 34 years
GILBERT LONGSTREET, Augusta, Ga. d. 8/2/1851, aged 68 years
DR. WM. B. NEWCOMB b. 5/24/1824 d. 3/ 26/1876
M. CROSS b. 10/27/1837 ,"Gone home, our mother", 1/8/1897.
ISAAC J. KNOX 10/4/1835 12/27/1856

A. S. JONES b. King William Co. Va. 8/26/1809 d. 3/9/1853
WM. CONNELY d.11/2/1867, 79 y. 11 mos. 25 days
W. H. CALVIN 1816, d. 11/27/1885
L. L. LEWIS 6/14/1814   9/14/1887
SARAH JANE, wife of JOHN PERSON b. 2/3/1836 d. 12/ 5/1851 & USULA ANN
b. 11/18 d. 12/ 5/1851
MARGARET E. EWING 12/10/1831, 7/13/1852
NANCY LEE 9/15/1807   4/11/1866
LACY BURNETT Dec. 1813, d. Feb. 1878
Masonic emblem, broken stone: WM. RYAN b. 2/ 27/1812 d...
NANCY A. wife of WM. broken stone, andCan only determine that one of
them died 1850
MRS. S. A. DUNN 4/8/1832 d 7/21/1900
Infant sons of W. C. & M. J. DUNN b. & d. 8/12/1889
Masonic emblem: J. J. IVEY 2/ 3/1885 80 or 30 years
HARRISON HEAD, b......d. after June 1873. Cant read the broken stones
only a part of ALBERT is still legible. According to members of the
PHELPS family still living in the area, a son and dau. of ALBERT A.
HARRISON HEAD m. a son and dau. of ....PHELPS in 1867 and 1868, in
Washington Co. Texas. According to these people the HARRISON HEAD
family died of "milk fever".

BURNET COUNTY, TEXAS

A/550 PATENT March 14, 1856 to BENJAMIN F. OWEN, assignee of CABASOS
LUCIANO.

F/491 WD Oct. 25, 1867, BENJ. F. OWEN to DAVID WEEKS

DC 564 Burnet Co. Texas, DAVIS WEEKS vs. W. W. QUEEN & L. A. QUEEN of
San Saba Co. Texas; J. A. WALK, Lampasas Co. Texas, foreclosure. Judg=
ment transferred to T. D. VAUGHAN, Burnet Co. WIT: J. G. COOK, N. J.
MILLER, sheriff.

L/13 May 28, 1879 Tax deed, N. J. MILLER, sheriff to ROBERT YOE, Burnet
Co. WIT: J. G. COOK, E. CHASE

N/547 WD July 18, 1882 A. N. W. R. R. CO. to THOS. McDONALD

W/404 Wd Oct. 25, 1891 THOS. McDONALD et ux to J. D. RILEY

F/164 BEN M. GILLESPIE m. MISS LOUISA A. GILLESPIE Sept. 1, 1884.

9/129 CHARLES R. PECK m. MISS ETHEL MAY OTTINGER, Nov. 25, 1910

2/ 2 DEATH RECORD: MRS. SUSAN M. (MARY SUE) KING d. April 1, 1918, dau
BENJ. MILES & DELILA BUNDIC, buried at Mt. Zion. Born La. 1850.

43/51 deed Jan. 1, 1906 to CHARLES PECK 23 acres SHULTZ et al surveys.

PC 125 Box 6 filed Dec. 16, 1880 LELIA MILES m. ..McCLENDON of Jones Co
Texas, JAMES C. KING, guardian. She became of age Sept. 1884, father
and mother dead; says his wife, SUSAN M. KING nearest of kin in Texas
(sister):LILIA received from F. B. MILES estate 11/11/1881, C. S. MILES
admr. These proceedings had been in La. but Parish is not given. SUSAN
M. KING was SUSAN MILES, dau. BENJ. MILES & DELILA BUNDIC, she first m.
a DR...WARD in La. he lived one week and d. of yellow fever; later she
m. JAMES C. KING.

MT. ZION CEMETERY 6 miles S. W. Bertram, Burnet Co. Texas
JAMES C. KING b. June 15, 1842, d. Dec. 4, 1920
SUE MILES KING b. July 16, 1850 d. April...1918
CLARABEL KING b. July 4, 1888 d. Oct. 26, 1952
BEN L. KING, b. March 20, 1881, d. Jan. 8, 1949

FROM FAMILY BIBLE of MRS. LOLA BAKER, granddaughter of SUE MILES KING
children of JAMES C. KING & SUE MILES KING, were:
EVA LEE b. July 6, 1876 d. Nov. 6, 1952 m. GOTCHER:

WATKINS KING (no middle name)
TECUMSEH (NICK) b. Dec. 13, 1879 d. Aug. 1945
BENJAMIN LEWIS b. Mar. 20, 1880 d. Jan. 8, 1948. Never married, was an attorney and practiced in Burnet County, Texas.
DELILA ELIZABETH b. July 25, 1883, d...m...JENNINGS
LILLIE ROSE, b. Jan. 4, 1886 d. June 11, 1958
CLARABEL b. July 4, 1888 d. Oct. 26, 1925
GRACE ANN b. Nov. 6, 1890, m. moved to Choctaw, Okla

CEMETERY between Liberty Hill and Bertram, Burnet Co. Texas:
CHARLES E. ROBERTS 1857, 1942, ELIZABETH A. ROBERTS 1869, 1957
MARTHA CLARE (CLORE) b. 1783 d. 10/11/1856
SARAH BATES b. 6/3/1808 d. 12/28/1875
CHARLES C. HICKMAN 11/7/1873 d. 12/28/1936 EFFIE M. 6/6/1880 2/24/1940
NARUNA CEMETERY, west side of Burnet Co.
BENJAMIN FRANKLIN SUMNER d. 1892, SARAH JANE POWELL SARGENT SUMNER d. 1896
W. B. ANDERSON 5/15/1812 Bedford Co. Tenn. d/ 3/10/1894
ROSETTA his wife b. 6/15/1818 Wilson Co. Ten. d. 11/27/1893
C. TALIAFERRO 9/23/1824 2/9/1891 MRS. R. H. 1840, 1913
MARTHA JANE LANE 7/2/1829   4/27/1912
JAMES I. EAVER 1/28/1818 Knox Co. Ky. 9/15/1888 his wife
RHODA S. EAVER d. 6/20/1915 88 y. 5 mos. 20 days
EMILEY wife of W. P. MARTIN 1/16/1829 d. 1/22/1897 (first m. ODIS PECK)
R. M. MORRIS 12/16/1830 12/18/1914 LUCY M. MORRIS 8/1/1840 11/21/1880
THOS. ARNOLD SEALE 4/1/1828 3/8/1883 M. A. SEALE 1/14/1812 1/2/1929
Just north of M. A. SEAL grave: S. E. BERRY 5/17/1835 5/2/1917
THOS. J. SEALE 1853 1943; EXE A.SEALE 1859 1943
HARDEN NEVILL 2/2/1805   7/16/1890
JOSEPH M. WILSON 1856   1894   MATTIE J. WILSON 1862   1948
JOHN LANDERS 7/4/1819   1/28/1909   MARY ELIZABETH 1/15/1830   2/4/1900
ELIZABETH SEAL 3/18/1803   3/24/1883
THOS. NETTLESHIP 1841   1902

WOLF CROSSING CEMETERY road between Marble Falls and Kingsland:
ISAAC N. FLUITT   1855   1918
SARAH F. FLUITT 1864 1928
F. L. GUNN 8/10/1825 8/3/1894
E. S. GUNN 3/8/1844 12/30/1919
D. FRANK FLUITT 1859 1927; S. JULIA FLUITT 1866   1951
M. E. GADDY 6/30/1858   6/17/1911
MATTIE MAUD dau. J. J. & M. M. GADY 1889 1899
E. M. HALLFORD 6/21/1851   3/21/1885
J. N. HALLFORD 11/24/1846   2/4/1890
LOLA M. TALLEY dau. W. P. & G. I. TALLEY 11/18/1880   4/8/1883
Inside iron fence, broken stone JOHN ..HALLFORD ..memroy of husband 5/5/1816 9/20/1881
LUTIE dau. T. B. & A. B. WILEY 8/7/1902   4/30/1913
'wiley' Thomas Boyed   1864, 1946 ADDIE BAILEY 1869   1931
"LEONA BAKER" old stone hand lettered no other information
One STONE: ISAAC WILEY 3/24/1842   9/24/1924 NANCY ANN 9/24/1843, 4/20/23

PECAN CEMETERY MEMORY of EARLY SETTLERS killed by INDIANS. On HY. 71:
MRS. MARGARET M. TATE 1/19/1863   7/16/1894

E. Y. WALKER, June 1816, d. 1886
JOHN BRUCE DUNCAN 4/22/1822 d. 4/6/1901 (NOTE: A man at the cemetery said a number of people were killed by INDIANS, and they were taken to this man "DUNCAN'S" place and buried. There was no record of the number nor their names, so far as this man knew)
PENELOPE DUNCAN 9/20/1788   7/1/1862
SALLIE G. BACKUS 1836   10/16/1868
JOHN K. BACKUS 2/ 3/1838   2/27/1874
PENELOPE LONG   6/24/1859   4/15/1901
B. M. GIBSON 12/25/1844 10/29/1904
SARAH JANE GIBSON   1859   1937
ELIZABETH CHILDERS   10/30/1824   6/12/1888
FRANK son of F. & M. YOAST 1/21/1859   12/7/1885

M. M. LATHAN (mother) 4/12/1849 9/19/1916
W. J. LATHAM (father) 2/18/1833 2/10/1918
ALCEMEDA BACKUS 3/8/1847 7/14/1891 on same stone SANFORD BACKUS
2/4/1840 2/13/1875
GEORGE W. GIBSON 5/16/1849 11/9/1883
CHARLES HAYNES 9/12/1814 12/28/1868

CALDWELL COUNTY, TEXAS

LOCKHART POST REGISTER; speical addition 5/6/1948

CALDWELL REGISTER, May 1879
C/248 ELIZA DANIEL m. E. M. FULLER, 10/23/1869
B/49 MRS. MARY DANIEL m. MONROE MULKEY 10/5/1867
B/77 ELLEN DANIEL m. ALICK JONES 2/ 2/1870
E/297 GEO. A. (S) DANIEL m. HARVEY HAMBY 9/8/1877 (GEORGIA A.?)
I/226 MARY L. DANIEL m. S. H. PERKLE
J/239 MISS ADDIE DANIEL m. JOHN H. BELLS 11/24/1900
E/182 OLIVER B. DANIEL m. JULIA ANN SMITH 6/1/1876
J/93 WALTER DANIEL m. MISS SARAH SPEAR 5/13/1899
K/163 B. F. DANIEL m. ROSE Z. SHUBEY
K/354 J. T. DANIEL m. DOCIA WEST

ESTATE JOHN W. MERRIWETHER b. 1832 d. 1860, probate Court Caldwell Co.

CITY OF LOCKHART CEMETERY, CALDWELL Co. (only some of the older birth dates)
ROBERT E. PALLEY 11/3/1856 1/11/1925
MELINDA E. PALLEY 11/22/1868 1/28/1948
J. H. JOLLEY (CSA) 4/30/1837 (could not read death date, father)
MRS. M..E. JOLLEY (mother) 11/8/1838 1/24/1924 C. W. RICHARDS (Capt. Co I, 31 Miss. Inf. CSA) 1829 1909
SARAH B. RICHARDS 1848 1910
JOHN LaFAYETTE LANE 1/3/1830 12/15/1917
MANERVIA ANNIE LANE 9/9/1840 1/15/1920
WILLIAM SMITH 7/17/1834 10/25/1904
J. G. LESTER 5/17/1834 4/25/1906
MRS. J. G. LESTER 8/21/1840 2/7/1918
J. N. LANCASTER 5/ 5/1827 3/31/1919
MARY A. LANCASTER 1/17/1829 12/20/1906
J. M. CARDWELL 6/18/1836 12/22/1917
MATTIE CARDWELL 4/16/1849...
H. H. FIELD 4/6/1803 1/10/1858
MARY R. FIELD 2/18/1818 1/24/1885
JAMES DALLAMITE 10/8/1799 12/30/1880; Gilley Dallamite 3/21/1803,11/10/74
WM. McGURDY 2/4/1809 9/8/1885
LUCINDA H. McGURDY 1/30/1816 3/20/1886
GEORGE W. ELLIS 9/8/1821 9/19/1857
MARTHA MILDRED ELLIS 3/12/1826 7/11/ 1880
WILLIAM ELLISON 6/29/1800 12/9/1885
REBECCA ELLISON 1803 9/3/1858
JESSIE E. son T. A. & J. ROBERTS b. 7/22/1888 d. 10/20/1899
SAMUEL SCHUPBACK 9/7/1811 10/19/1878
JOHN R. HART b. Chestertown, Md. 2/11/1800 d 12/9/1870
W. S. CARPENTER 8/1/1805 12/19/1875
MARY CARPENTER 9/1/1800 9/24/1874
NATHAN HUDSPETH 1/2/1803 2/26/1870
NARCISSA R. HUDSPETH 1811 8/28/1879
.....YATES (broken stone) b. 1789 d. 8/12/1870 JAMES YATES, dedicated to the YATES FAMILY: ANNA LIZA, FANNIE, GROVER, CLEVELAND & BRUCE)
ALEXANDER WILLIAMS 1/5/1818 9/4/1891 CSA
AMANDA M. WILLIAMS 9/23/1818 6/10/1897
W. F. KING 3/20/1826 10/11/1886
JULINA D. KING 5/7/1832 9/11/1910
J. H. WILLIAMSON 9/19/1833 9/13/1914,MARY FRANCES WILLIAMSON 1/4/1833, 6/22/1879
....CARR (broken stone) 12/28/1801 5/22/1872 GARR ?)
H. A. R. HODGES 12/31/1824 3/18/1912

JOHN T. DAVIS 12/18/1830, 3/25/1893
D. T. CAHILL 3/12/53, 5/31, 1887
LEONIDAS ROGAN, Co. "B" 26 Tex. Calv. CSA 4/8//837, 5/24/1917 on other side of stone, MARY SMITH ROGAN 3/10/1803 11/23/1862, mother of LEO ROGAN
JOHN MONTGOMERY 2/25/1804 11/26/1871
DR. JOHN G. BLANKS 2/20/1830 5/2/1897
MORGAN WHITE b. Maysville, Ky. 9/4/1845 8/2/1890
CROCKETT HARBERT d. 11/5/1885 80 years of age

LUTHERIN CHURCH CEMETERY, Maxwell, Caldwell Co. Texas:
CHRISTIAN SCHULLE 1/8/1834 5/26/1899
DOROTHEA SCHULLE 12/29/1836 7/1/1899
J. ULRICH STEINER 9/20/1833 8/20/1896 (German inscriptions)
SOPHIE STEINER 6/23/1848 12/15/1928
KAROLINA BEST 3/25/1855 10/21/1934
JACOB BEST 5/19/1841 11/23/1915
LOUISE BARTLING 11/8/1849 4/15/1940
WILHELM...9/10/1847 11/19/1914
ERNEST GUSTAF HOFFMANN 6/4/1830 in Gorlitz, Schlesien d. Maxwell Texas, 3/20/1911
CAROLINE HOFFMAN b. 12/31/1831 in Forest Bramdenerver (?)

7 graves on DOYLE farm on east side of Hy. 21, North of Reedville, before Uhland:
A. K. O. KELLY (only stone standing) 7/25/1823 7/26/1892
SAMUEL Z. DIAF 1/18/1876 10/12/1899 "He faltered by the wayside and the angels took him home"
AXIS, wife of M. D. McQUEEN, b. 12/3/1825 d. 2/27/1896, and broken stone dau. J. A. M. J. McQUEEN b. 5/5/1888 d. 1/2/1891
G. D. C. REED 2/12/1830 10/13/1898

"ROBERTS" CEMETERY, HIGH GROVE, CALDWELL COUNTY, TEXAS:
DR. JOSEPH PECAR 1814 1894
JNO. W. KELLY 8/23/1874 1931 LENNIE KELLY 1877 1960
JAMES S. SORRELLS 1827 1873
W. L. SORRELS 1835 1908
LIZZIE wife of B. M. ROBERTS 1851 1878
MRS. MARY A. SORREL 7/21/1839 1868

COLEMAN COUNTY, TEXAS

April 23, 1841 PATENT to MRS. MARY ANN FISK, late, she was MARY ANN LINDSEY, first wife of GREENLIEF FISK, SR. by Bastrop Co. District. (NOTE: FISK, was a land promotor, and had land in many counties in Texas, either in his name or the name of some of his family)

122/217 aff. Sept. 10, 1920 GREENLIEF FISK, JR. b. 2/14/1858, son of GREENLIEF FISK who d. Jan. 29, 1888, and second wife, MARY who d. 1905. SR. went to Brown County, Texas, 1860.

48/574 aff. by JOSIAH FISK, Bastrop Co. Texas; MARY ANN FISK d. ca 1850 was first wife of GREENLEAF FISK, SR.. d. ca 1880; ANN ELIZABETH CASHION JAMES B. FISK, WM. A. FISK, & MARY E. WOOD and affiant, JOSIAH FISK.

122/217 GREENLEAF FISK, JR. of Brown Co. Tex. b. Feb. 14, 1858, came to Brown Co. Tex. 1860; father GREENLEAF FISK, SR. d. in Brownwood, Jan 29, 1888; mother was MARY who d. 1905

P/403 Aff. Sept. 23, 1886 knew MRS. E. H. REED sur. wife DAVID C. REED. Sons: A. S.,T. S.;THEODORE & J. W. REED

X/382 Aff. Jan. 24, 1890 A. S. REED Runnels Co. Tex. says name of mother E. A. not E. H.

P/404 MRS. E. H. REED, T. S. REED OfBurnet Co.; A. S. REED of Runnels Co., J. W. REED of LLANO CO. TEXAS

66/191 Aff. 1908 by A. R. BROWN son OWEN BROWN d. 1892; left: A. R., R. D., A. J., IRENE BELL wife L. E., & H. H. & W. D. BROWN and JOHN BROWN who d. 1883, left surviving wife and 1 son O. J.: M. I. BROWN is surviving wife of OWEN BROWN.

COLORADO COUNTY, TEXAS

A very very old index, 1839, and no one in the County Clerk's office could determine to what it was an index: (I wished that I had copied it in its entirety, but did not)

N. C. HARRISON   THOMAS S. HEAD   JAMES G. HEFFINGTON

FAYETTE COUNTY, TEXAS

"THE JOURNAL" LaGrange, Texas, Dec. 15, 1880 (U. T. NEWSPAPER COLL) COL. JOHN H. MOORE b. 8/18/1800 d. 12/3/1880 Sumner Co. Tenn. at his sons home. JOHN H. MOORE, JR. came to Texas Spring of 1820 on Red River, 1823-4 to Colorado Co. 1827 m. MISS ELIZA CUMMINGS. They lived where LaGrange now stands. One of AUSTIN'S original 300 families.

FAYETTEVILLE CEMETERY, FAYETTE CO. TEXAS (not Catholic part)
UMBLETON GREGORY b. 9/21/1798 d 10/13/1864
MARY, wife of D. GREGORY 11/9/1809 1/30/1871
MISS..TEXANIA dau. of D. G. & MARY GREGORY b. Platte Co. Mo. 11/1/1845 d. Fayetteville, Texas 4/5/1866
H. F. DUNLAVY 9/3/1845 12/22/1874
DAVID WADE, Pvt. Anderson's Co. 74 Va. Mil. War 1812 d. 3/ 25/1861
lARGE TALL STONE: 1 side: THOMAS D. FISHER, b. Va. 1804 d. 1853 and MARTHA E. B. FISHER b. Va. 1812 d. 1853;
SECOND SIDE: THOMAS B. FISHER b. Tenn. 1835 d. 1879; ISABELLA F. BUDD b. Tenn. 1833 d. 1871;
THIRD SIDE: HARPER D. FISHER b. and d 1848, CASS M. FISHER b. 1850 d. 1851. FOURTH SIDE Blank.
SARAH E., wife of W. E. MUNGER 7/17/1832 d. 3/5/1854, LIGILIOUS S., infant of W. E. & SARAH E., b & d 1/4/1854
WILHELM DIETRICH 5/1/1826 d. 1/28/1891 (lettering in German on these 3)
CAROLINE DIETRICH 6/24/1838 5/19/1925
WILHELMINE DIETRICH 3/13/1790 12/29/1871 (part of the DIETRICH family came early to Travis County)
DOUBLE STONE: W. P. SMITH b. 1/15/1795 d. 3/18/1870. On same stone: J. C. SCATTS 11/5/1819 2/1/1874. At foot of this large stone is large flat marker placed in 1936 (TEXAS CENTL) DR. WM. P. SMITH a veteran of the TEXAS WAR for INDEPENDENCE & REGIMENTAL SURGEON atSAN Jacinto..
JAMES WALTER son of J. R. & M. J. SCATES 3/17/1878 6/8/1880
"OUR MOTHER" E. J. wife of W. H. DONATHAN 4/20/1826 2/7/1878
LARGE STONE: ISAAC RICH 1797 d. 1846; L. A. MARSHALL "My father".Nothing else on this stone.
REV. H. G. CARDEN b. Ky. 12/1/1824 8/16/1872
LOUISE BRAND 5/26/1831 11/7/1918
L. D. BRAND 5/31/1818 6/21/1878
J. E. MURRAY 12/24/1833 7/13/1879

FORT BEND COUNTY, TEXAS

THOMAS HANCOCK m. POLLY BIRD 3/11/1838
THOMAS NATHANIEL MUDD m. DELPHANA METCALF Aug. 20, 1839
1841 (license not returned): DANL. G. HARBERT & NANCY W. KIRK
Jan. 21, 1845: PERRY F. McMAHAN m. NANCY KIRK
Mar. 2, 1843: SAML. M. FROST m. MRS. HARRIET H. HEAD
Sept. 22, 1845 J. E. BUNDICK m. MISS R. ABBOTT

FREESTONE COUNTY, TEXAS

9/109 STATE of COAHUILA & TEXAS, land grant Oct. 14, 1834 to ROBERT B. LONGBOTHAN, special commissioner of (colony) Enterprise of the Citizen DAVID G. BURNETT & Empressario, longbothan, came fromU. S. A. with a wife and 7 children; JORGE ANTO NIXON, Comr. Nacogoches Oct. 15, 1834

A. HOTCHKISS, atty. in fact for JOSEPH VEHLEIN. Oct. 17, 1834 ARTHUR
HENRIE, surveyor; NATHAN AMORY, translator; GEO. ANT. NIXON, Comr. JOS.
CARRIESE, asst. BEG. N. W. cor. RIDIN GAINER sur.; N. E. cor. HUGH
SHEPPARD; N. W. cor SARAH McANULTY; MARTIN M. KINNEY (KENNEY) Spanish
translator, Austin, Texas Dec. 4, 1895

K/732 WD July 5, 1871, R. B. LONGBOTHAM et ux LUCY to A. GROESBECK, W.J
HUTCHINS, F. A. RICE & W. R. BAKER, trustees. WIT: F. HARRIS, W. G.
VEAL ack. R. B. LONGBOTHAM and wife, LUCY before C. J. TERRELL NP
Llano Co. Texas

k/776 DEDICATION of WORTHAM, TEXAS: July 28, 1871 by ABRAM GROESBECK,
W. J. HUTCHINS, F. A. RICE, W. R. BAKER, all of Harris Co. Texas,
trustees. ack. before S. SIMMLER, NP Harris Co. Tex.

K/749 Right of Way deed June 21, 1871 H. & T. C. RY by R. B. LONGBOTHAM
proved by W. G. VEAL. WIT: before H. V. HURLOCK, CDC Navarro Co. Texas

No. 520 EST. ROBERT B. LONGBOTHAM, Jan. 8,1884 THOMAS LONGBOTHAM, admr
ROBERT LONGBOTHAM decd; A. J. BERRY, J. J. STUBBS, W. M. SEELY apprs.
Bond Jan. 15, 1884, THOS. LONGBOTHAM prin. D. F. STRICKLE, J. O. LONG-
BOTHAM sureties; O. C. KIRVEN, Co. Judge Freestone Co. OATH. THOS.
LONGBOTHAM before J. R. KNIGHT, JP & EX. O. NP Freestone Co. Texas.
Jan. 15, 1884;756 acres and $200.00 cash to widow LOUISA LONGBOTHAM.

12/139 REL. April 21, 1898 THOMAS LONGBOTHAM, SR. admr. R. B. LONGBOTH-
AM and A. GROESBECK et al before C. J. TURNER NP Freestone Co. Tex.

11/382 WILL: WM. R. BAKER dated Jan. 18, 1889 of Harris Co. Texas, to
mother HANNA BAKER $400.00 annually for life; to 3 trustees E. P. HILL
PRESSLEY K. EWING, HORRACE D. TAYLOR all of Harris Co. Tex. for support
and education of gson. WM. BAKER TURNER only child of dau. LUCY BAKER
TURNER, decd. if gson dies then to four sisters of testator: MARY ANN
BAGBY, widow, EMILY TAYLOR et vir of HORRACE D. TAYLOR, JULIA W. CLARK
widow, and HARRIETT M. SZANO et vir A. A.

11/389 deed Nov. 17, 1897 E. P. HILL, PRESLEY K. EWING. H. BREASHEAR,
trustees of WM. R. BAKER who d. April 30, 1890; (BREASHEAR took place
of HORACE D. TAYLOR who d.). WM. BAKER TURNER has married and a child
was b. Aug. 1, 1897

25/347 QC July 30, 1906 H. C. PAIGE, DAVID S. PAIGE to EST. WM. B.RICE
decd. recites; D. H. PAIGE d. left wife, ANNIE E. PAIGE & 3 sons: WM.A.
HENRY C., & DAVID S. PAIGE: ANNIE PAIGE d. leaving 3 sons; then WM. A.
PAIGE d. unm and intestate left 2 bros. H. C. & DAVID S. PAIGE

11/439 PC Freestone Co. WILL: MARGARET ELIZABETH HOOD, of Cade,Navarro
Co. Teas, d. Jan. 24, 1908. WILL dated July 28, 1894 to husband W. F.
HOOD, apts. him executor,

31/389 PARTITION Oct. 7, 1909 heirs of W. F. HOOD, SR., decd. MRS.
FANNIE HOOD, widow, IDA BURLESON et vir D. D., LULA HOWARD Et vir M.;
BETTIE BURLESONet vir G. W., ELLA ROBERTS et vir K. P.; E. J. HOOD,
T. H. HOOD, W. F. HOOD, JR., JOE & H. I. HOOD.

V/593 Nov. 19, 1884 deed ABRAHAM GROESBECK, Harris Co. Tex. agmt. Mar.
22, 1868 beteen W. J. HUTCHINGS, F. A. RICE, A. GROESBECK & W. R. BAKER
trustees; ABRAHAM GROESBECK had 10 shares sold 1/8 to MRS. VAN ALSTYNE,
purchased 8, 3/4 shares of ESTATE D. H. PAIGE (this deed to BENJ. A.
BATTS) ack. ABRAHAM GROESBECK before R. A. GIRAUD NP Harris Co. Tex.

64/392 aff. Nov. 28, 1910 in RE: BENJ. A. BOTTS (BATTS) after 1861.Aff.
by B. F. WEEMS, 70 years of age, resided Houston, Harris Co. for past
40 years; BOTTS was Pres. CITY BANK of HOUSTON in 1884 until he d. 1885
that BOTTS wife and children all decd. WEEMS also knew A. GROESBECK Nov
19, 1884; WEEMS also was cashier of CITY BANK of HOUSTON, bank failed
1885; BOTTS nor his dau. no interest in property; this dau. m. bro.in-
law of WEEMS, W. A. CARRINGTON, was accidently killed several years
later; affiant was co-executor W. A. CARRINGTON'S ESTATE, with widow,

and she later died; all estate turned over to HOUSTON BANK & TRUST CO. trustee of ESTATE KATHERINE L. CARRINGTON his dau.; B. F. WEEMS, ack. Nov. 28, 1910 before H. C. HAMMERS, NP Haris Co. Cert: by HENRY SPARKS CCC Kaufman Co. Tex. by J. E. YATES, Depty. Jan. 21, 1910, cert. by TOM CRIDDLE ccc Ellis Co. Nov. 4, 1921, SUSIE JACKSON, deputy

69/83 cc PC ABRAM GROESBEK, decd. d. Feb. 6, 1886 Harris Co. W. C. ANDERS, Judge; MRS. ANNA E. GROESBECK sur. wife; BOND: ANNIE E. GROESBECK, principal and E. P. HILL, J. C. HUTCHINSON, W. A. CARRINGTON WM. D. CLEVELAND & J. H. B. HOUSE sureties, $200,000.00 Mar 8. 1886 B. A. BATTS, names MRS. MARIE A. VAN ALSTYNE

25/559 WD Aug. 4, 1882 CORNELIUS ENNIS to BRANCH T. MASTERSON, ack. be fore WM. R. JACKSON NP Galveston Co. Tex

28/22 deed Mar. 3, 1906 BRANCH T. MASTERSON to ESTATE WM. M. RICE, decd. WM. M. RICE, JR., AND JAMES A. BAKER, JR. extrs.

V/604 deed April 25, 1885 PAUL BREMOND to T. W. HOUSE

F/348, 1850 PATENT to JAMES HEAD

K/273 JAMES HEAD 1870 and wife, ELIZABETH A.

GONZALES COUNTY, TEXAS

No. 233, PATENT to JAMES H. ISBELL et ux AMANDA I., 640 acres patented to ISBELL, as he was in Battle of SAN JACINTO.

1887 MRS. L. A. ISBELL m. JOHN R. WRIGHT

Bill of sale, Nov. 5, 1859 HARRISON HEAD, Gonzales Co. Texas, cattle and hogs to son JAMES MADISON HEAD

AARON C. DANIEL m. BARBOUR JANE HEAD (dau. HARRISON HEAD and ELIZABETH) Sept. 24, 1857, by F. CHENAULT, & GEO. DANIEL, M.O.G. Gonzales Co. Tex

HAMILTON COUNTY, TEXAS

J/298 PATENT to WILLIAM A. FERGUSON, assignee of ANTHONY J. GILCHRIST Sept. 18, 1854, Milam District, Coryell Co. waters of Cowhouse Creek C. F. MATHEY'S S. E. cor. to W. S. TUBERVILLE's SW cor; THOMAS F. FREE-MAN's Corner, issued by Jasper Co. land Commrs.

J/300 June 23, 1856 W. A. FERGUSON to HENRY W. BENDY, ack. before E. J. PARSONS, Co. Clk.

J/302 deed Nov. 17, 1860 H. W. BENDY to LEWIS T. FOSTER, ack. H. GOODE ccc Jasper Co. Tex.

D/504 Oct. 18, 1873 L. T. FOSTER to ELIZABETH H. FERGUSON ack. before J. W. BALLARD, NP Shelby Co. Tex.

G/336 deed CCC Dist. Court 1270 Nov. Term 1876 from Tyler Co. Tex. JAMES H. BENDY, NAPOLEON G. BENDY, CLARA BENDY PRICEet vir W. C., & WM. NEWLAND assignee of W. H. BENDY, JR., vs. HENRY W. BENDY, SR. MARGARET M. CARLSON (BENDY) et vir, S. E., JOHN McBRIDE, J. M. BURKE commissioners and GEO. W. KIRKLAND, J. M. BUCK, Comrs. report appointed Feb. Term 1876 part of EST. MARGARET BENDY, decd. and surviving heirs H. W. BENDY, J. W. McDANIEL, recorded Vol. E, p. 434 Tyler Co. Texas District Court Minutes

I/479 Feb. 4, 1878 CLARA S. PRICE et vir W. C., before W. H. FORD NP Jasper Co. Tex.; H. W. BENDY, SR was served in Jasper Co. Texas JOHN McBRIDE, M. L. McALISTER, Comr. and W. E. DENHAM

J/334 Tax deed June 14, 1878 G. W. WADE, tax collector Hamilton Co. Tex to A. & J. C. K. Hogg. ack. before N. C. HOWARD, DCC, HAMILTON CO. Tex.

J/16 Sheriffs deed Nov. 4 , 1879 N. B. BENDY by G. N. GENTRY, sheriff Hamilton Co. Texas. to J. S. LIVINGSTON before M. S. BRUNK NP HCT sold under execution out of Tyler County, Texas

J/155 Jan. 5, 1880, ELIZABETH A. FERGUSON to PLEASANT L. FERGUSON, GEO. R., LEWIS T. FERGUSON, AUSTIN H. FERGUSON & ELIZABETH J. & CLARA E. FERGUSON ack. before A. J. RIGSBY CC Jasper Co. Texas, love and affection for children

J/314 PA 1880 ELIZABETH A. FERGUSON sur. wife of WM. A. FERGUSON, decd E. A. FERGUSON, PLEASANT L. FERGUSON, GEORGE R. FERGUSON, LEWIS T. FERGUSON, AUSTIN H. FERGUSON sons of the said ELIZABETH A. & WM. A. FERGUSON decd. CLARA E. FERGUSON, ELIZABETH J. FERGUSON, ack. before A. J. RIGSBY, cc Jasper Co. Texas April 6, 1881

J/316 May 3, 1880 deed same parties E. A. FERGUSON et ux ELIZABETH J. WM. F. FERGUSON et ux CLARA E.

J/338 QC May22, 1880 ARC'D HOGG, JAMES C, K. HOGG to FOLTS & DONNANbefore ISAAC H. STEEN, CC HCT

K/36 deed Mar. 12, 1881 W. F. FERGUSON et ux CLARA E. to T. W. FOLTS & JOHN K. DONNAN, before A. J. RIGSBY, CCH CO. TEX.

K/84 deed July...1881 WM. NEYLAND, W. C. PRICE et ux CLARA E.,EUGENE GAUCHAN et ux MADORA (formerly CARLSON) & H. W. BENDY,JR. to THOMAS W. FOLTS, JOHN K. DONNAN (Travis County Residents)

K/86 deed July 18, 1881 N. B. BENDY of Galveston Co. Texas to FOLTS & DONNAN, HENRY BROSIG, NP Galveston Co. Tex.

K/85 deed July 25, 1881 J. S. LIVINGSTON to FOLTS & DONNAN before C. W. COTTON, NP HCT

K/99 deed Sept...1881 J. H. BUNDY to FOLTS & DONNAN before J. F. HEARD cc Tyler Co. Tex

K/612 deed July 22, 1882 FOLTS & DONNANof TCT to LEWIS PAULIN

Div. LEWIS PAULIN vs. MAMIE G. PAULIN filed Dec. 4, 1885 (DC Min. D/337 Hamilton Co. Texas) 2 minor children, EDITH G. & ALBERT T. PAULIN

V/445 HD July 12, 1887 by LEWIS PAULIN before J. A. EIDSON, NP HCT

5/145 HD July 1, 1892 LEWIS PAULIN et ux LEILA I.

W/362 Rel Aug. 1, 1889 H. G. DAMON, before JAMES H. WOODS, Np Navarro Co

L/636 Rel. Oct. 4, 1897 NORMAN F. THOMPSON before A. W. CHAMBERLAIN, NP NY CO. NY

33/458 deed Jan. 9, 1907, LEWIS PAULIN to J. E. FLATT before HINER GLENN Np Central Dist. Indian Territory

30/435 Rel. LEWIS PAULIN, Dec. 19, 1909 before J. Q. A. HARROD, NP Bryan Co. Oklahoma

2/84 Jan. 7, 1894 MISS SOPHRONIA E. PHELPS m. T. A. YEAGER

MOLLIE PHELPS m. PERRY B. COX Dec. 24, 1896, 2/ 242
May 14, 1905 W. P. PHELPS to BIRDIE EARY
6/   MRS. N. V. PHELPS m. H. F. LEBERMANN, Feb. 6, 1904

BIRTH RECORD 10/341, Dec. 19, 1889 BENJAMIN FRANKLIN SUMNER b. Lanham Pct. son of JAMES HENRY SUMNER (3rd child at time of birth to mother) MARY FRANCES YOUREE, 35 at time of birth, and JAMES HENRY B. Rusk Co. Texas and MARY FRANCIS YOUREE b. Ellis Co. This is No. 6 for this mother

HARDIN COUNTY, TEXAS

130/623 aff. HARRIS MASTERSON, d. prior to 1921, m. (1) SALLIE TURNER who d. 1893, CH. HARRIS MASTERSON, JR.; RANE MASTERSON m. ...CAGE, of Harris Co. Texas; N. T., LEIGH, and RALPH who d. infancey; (2) LOUISE JANE SHARPE 1895 CH. BIRDSALL MASTERSON. CC of probate proceedings is recorded in Vol. 127, p. 314 Hardin Co.

3/136-7 (2 affds) T. R. EDMONDSON, Hardin Co. Tex, 1848. dated 1901

HARRIS COUNTY, TEXAS   (HOUSTON)

B/1 PATENT, August 5, 1818 to LUKE MOORE, (in Spanish) to STEPHEN F. AUSTIN, March 10, 1829, EST. STEPHEN F. AUSTIN, in Brazoria Co. Tex.

44/478 deed April 19, 1838 EST. S. F. AUSTIN to T. H. MYLRYNE, JAMES F. PERRY, extr. WIT: G. WILLIAM ADAMS, JNO. F. HUNTINGTON before JOHN SHEA, CJ Dec. 28, 1888 aff. by W. R. BAKER before R. S. LOVETT, NP Harris Co. Texas that G. WILLIAM ADAMS is dead; aff. by GUY M. BRYAN that JAMES F. PERRY is dead. Sept. 6, 1888.

PATENT Aug. 3, 1824 TOWN of SAN FELIPE de AUSTIN (this is not the present AUSTIN, TRAVIS COUNTY, TEXAS, but the original capital for the 300 families, and is now known as SAN FELIPE.) July 24, 1824 SYLVENUS CASTLEMAN to LUKE MOORE, with his family. BARON de BASTROP, LT. COL.DON LUCIANO GARCIA, DON JOSE ANTONIO SANCEDO, Brig. DON FELIPE de la GARZA, JOHN AUSTIN, SAML. M. WILLIAMS, ROBERT VINCE, JOHN ELAM, JOHN VINCE, JOHN COOKE, surveyor, land on Bray's and Buffalo Bayous.

F/86 Deed Feb. 20, 1840 JOHN LEVI to AUGUSTUS SENECHAL, test; RICHARD R. WILKINS, DEE DIRMLAN

191/282 deed Mar. 10, 1829 LUKE MOORE to S. F. AUSTIN, WIT: OLIVER JONES, R. M. WILLIAMSON, S. O. PETTUS, JOSEPH WHITE, CONST. ALCALDE OF AUSTIN CO. TEXAS. Asst. WIT: SAML. M. WILLIAMS and SAML. R.MILLLER

ESTATE M. H. BUNDICK, T. W. BUNDICK, administrators Feb. 28, 1837

ESTATE A. H. MILES, J. W. SCOTT, administrator
ESTATE A. GATALIN, decd. April 29, 1839, ELISHA GATLIN

EST. CORNWALL, July 1, 1839, Oct. 19, 1840 PINCKNEY HILL, admr. Bastrop Co. Texas

July Term 1839 H. J. JEWETT counsel for absent heirs of: GEO. W.CHILDRESS, GEO. M. GILLELAND & JACOB JAYS. (Childress committed suicide in Galveston, because of being without funds...only Land Script) GEO. M. GILLELAND & JACOB JAYS Were probably killed in one of the battles for TEXAS INDEPENDENCE. JOHN A. NEWLAND & W. F. GRAY were appointed to represent GEO. W. CHILDRESS heirs. He drafted the TEXAS DECLARATION of INDEPENDENCE.

ESTATE ROBERT F. ROBERTS Aug. 13, 1839, advertisement "MORNING STARR"

HAYS COUNTY, TEXAS

106/56 PATENT, state of COAHUILA & TEXAS, Feb. 21, 1833 to STEVEN V.R. EGGLESTON, a married man. ASST. STEPHEN F. SLAUGHTER.

Z/474 cc EST. S. R. R. EGGLESTON, decd. from Bastrop Co. Tex. Jan.Term 1852 JULIA, surviving wife: JULIA WALKER, MINA TURNER, ZELPHY JONES, JNO. M., ZENA P., MARIA STANDIFER, MARY DAVIS and SARAH R. partition Feb. 19, 1852, Commrs. JOHN EDWARDS, W. B. NICHOLS, WALKER WILSON JOHN TANNY.
B/51 WD...1853, JULIA ANN (X) EGGLESTON to RICHARD WELLS before WM. DUNBAR, ccc Bastrop Co. Tex. May 25, 1853.

O/216, April 1, 1881 plat of Town of DePre, later named BUDA.

64/415 cc A. N. HOPKINS, decd. C. A. TRIMBLE, D. TRIMBLE, admrs.
72/227 aff. by C. M. CARPENTER, Nov. 29, 1916 re: MRS. C. A. TRIMBLE, her husband D. A. abandoned her and left country..DePre..Buda on her ld.

E/533,Mtg. April 9, 1887 MRS. E. H. CHANDLER, widow of JAMES A. of Hays Co. she m. J. H. PARKER, June 3, 1891 M/L F/100 Hays Co. Texas

PC Oct. Term 1891 MRS. E. H. PARKER d. June 21, 1891, says R. E. CARRINGTON is brother of MRS. E. H. PARKER, petition filed Aprl 25 1892, by L. D. CARRINGTON, LOUISA CARRINGTON & W. D. CARRINGTON

53/263 WD May 14, 1907 MRS. S. A. J. CARRINGTON, widow, L. D.CARRINGTON MRS. M. E. CARRINGTON, widow, R. E. CARRINGTON, MARY CARRINGTON & W.L. CARRINGTON of TCT FANNIE E. GRAVES widow, Harris Co. and L. D. CARRINGTON, Hays Co. says: L. D. CARRINGTON, SR. left 4 Ch. R. E. d. left widow, MRS. M. E., Ch. R. E..; MARY C., and W. L., and EDITH who d.; L. D., W. D., FANNIE E. GRAVES, MRS. ELIZABETH H. PARKER, MRS. S. A.J. CARRINGTON is surviving wife of L. D. CARRINGTON, SR.

104/283 Aff. L. D. CARRINGTON SR. d. Hays Co. Feb. 12, 1897, m. (2) to MRS. S. A. J., no children

D/498 WILL: JESSE McLENDON, shows wife, JANE SEAL, her husband had one son, CHARLES, and he had one son, ISAAC D. to his son he gave land in Littleriver Co. Ark. and Red River and silver spoons. He came to Hays Co. Texas, ca 1866 through Arkansas

4/73 PATENT to WILLIAM R. BAKER, assignee of AMASA TURNER 1280 acres in Travis Land District on Rio Blanco, a branch of San Marcos River

A/74 deed Nov. 17, 1849 WM. R. BAKER of Harris Co. Texas to JACOB de CORDOVA, Harris Co. ack. before JOHN LEVI, NP Harris Co. Texas

C/4 Bond for Title, April 13, 1955 JACOB de CORDOVA, Guadalupe Co. to JAMES MONTGOMERY, Hays Co. $1000 paid in sheep. WIT: REBECCA de CORDOVA & JNO. D. PITTS, ack. before C. ERHARD, CCC Hays Co.

C/265 WD Aug. 16, 1856 JAMES MONTGOMERY to WM. C. WINTERS, both of Hays Co. Tex. WIT: A. M. LINDSEY, JAMES E. McCORD

C/261 WD Aug. 16, 1856 JAMES MONTGOMERY to MICHAEL PIERSON

C/263 WD June 4, 1856 to JOHN WILSON

C/319 WD Nov. 5, 1856 JAMES MONTGOMERY to CHARLES SHEPERD

C/488 WD June 29, 1857 ALMIRA MONTGOMERY, L. W. CHARLES to CYRUS RILEY, & DANIEL MAYES

Setp. 17, 1855 JOHN M. CUDE m. NANCY N. WINTERS, by J.B.J.OLIVER, JP

PA Jan. 7, 1861 WM. C. WINTERS to JOHN W. DAVIS, both Hays Co. "My mill tract? on JACOB WELL CREEK and part Blackwell tract of 100 acres Blanco, Texas. Ack. HENRY T. DAVIS CCC Hays Co.

56/219 WD May 16, 1866 WILLIS WINTERS & EMELINE STARR (heirs WM.WINTERS decd) They of Atascosa Co. Texas to JOHN W. CUDE, Hays Co. ack. PEYTON SMYTHE, CCC Bexar Co. Texas

PC W. C. WINTERS, decd. d. Aug...1864. No Will, petition to JAMES G. STOREY, Co. Judge Hays Co. by JOHN M. CUDE By JAMES A. WHITE, his atty W. A. YOUNG, JAMES FORA, bondsmen. New Bond Nov. 13, 1871 C. S. COOK & P. C. WOODS approved ED J. L. GREEN, Clk. District Court Hays Co. Report by J. M. CUDE, admr. before J. P. RICHARDSON, Judge 21st. Dist Ct. Hays Co., homestead 317 acres A. TURNER survey, deed 1/3 interest SOLOMON SIMMONS, Atascosa Co. WIT: by ROBERT F. NIXON, JOHN MACKEY, Exhibit of condition May 2, 1857 JAMES MONTGOMERY to WM. C. WINTERS 300 ac. to pay debts of JAMES MONTGOMERY: JOHN WILSON, C. K. JOHNS, JAMES E. BOULDIN, SWISHER, RAYMOND & CO. A. J. THOMAS, C. ERHARD TYNECK & CO. GEO. PRATER, W. DRISKILL GEO. GLASSCOCK, L.D.CARRINGTON TOTAL: $1500. J. W. DAVID, J. W. HERNDON, JAMES L. MALONE, apprs. all Hays Co. Tex. Nov. 14, 1871 G. P. BUGG, Shf. Hays Co. Ret.Jan. 29,1874

I/122 WD Mar. 5, 1874 JOHN M. CUDE et ux NANCY N. to PLEASANT WIMBERLY both of Hays Co. Ack. before I. M. BREEDLOVE, JP & NP Hays Co. Tex.

P/55 deed Nov. 30, 1881 EST. JACOB de CORDOVA, Bosque Co. Texas to T.A. COLLIER Sept. Term 1881, L. B. DAVIS, admrs. ack. by L. B. DAVIS before F. E. ADAMS, cc Johnson Co. Texas

37/337 WD April 12, 1898 PLEASANT WIMBERLY et ux AMANDA, Hays Co. to ZACK T. & ANDREW J. WIMBERLY. ACK. before T. W. THORN, NP Hays Co. Tex.

44/143 WD April 24, 1900 ANDREW J. WIMBERLY et ux FANNIE B. to CALVIN H WIMBERLY ack. before JOHN H. SAUNDERS, NP Hays Co.

52/427 WD filed Feb. 13, 1907 no date P. WIMBERLY, SR. et ux AMANDA, Z. T. WIMBERLY et ux RACHEL, Hays Co. & C. H. WIMBERLY, et ux ROSA MABLE of Hays Co. now residing in Mexico to ELI HILL: Z. T. WIMBERLY is surviving husband of his former wife MARY W. who d. intestate. Ack. P. WIMBERLY before A. W. DIBRELL Jan. 16, 1901. cc Guadalupe Co. Tex. by R. F. WILSON, Dept. ack. AMANDA WIMBERLY et vir P. WIMBERLY before S.J. PYLAND, JP PCT. 3 Hays Co. Jan. 8, 1907 same for Z. T. & RACHEL, & C. H & MABEL Feb. 11, 1907..

M/171 GRANT (PATENT) April 28, 1832 COAHUILA & TEXAS to JUAN VICENTI CAMPOS..he states on Mar. 8, 1830 he made application signed by VICTORIANA ZEPADA & VINCENTI CORTARI, ack. by ARCEMEGA June 11, 1839 be fore JOHN W. SMITH cc Bexar Co. Texas

I/251 PA Oct. 7, 1870 GUADALUPE CAMPOS ORTEGA and husband P. P. ORTIGA, SALTILLO, Mexico to W. O. HUTCHISON of San Marcos, Hays Co. Tex. ack. PABLO P. ORTEGA and wife GUADALUPE CAMPOS de ORTEGA before H. KLOCKE NP Bexar Co. by H. MacCORMACK,

L/71 PA Sept. 6, 1875 DONA GUADALUPE CAMPOS de ORTEGA only child and sole heiress of JUAN VICENTI CAMPOS decd. and husband PABLO P. ORTEGA, OF Saltello, St. of Coahuila, Rep. Mex. to DR. A. E. CARUTHERS, WIT: FRANC CUELLAR, JESUS VALDEZ CAPEDA. Ack. by FRANCISCO CUELLIR before JOHN ROSENHERMER, Np Bexar Co. JOHN D. CARUTHERS, Consul U. S. for Saltillo.

O/154 PA Sept. 30,1880 same parties to L. B. LaCOSTE of Bexar Co. Tex.

37/161 GRANT HAYS CO. TEX. Nov. 20, 1831 STATE COAHUILA & TEXAS to JUAN MARTIN de VERAMENDI. Mr. Williams commissioner in GREEN DeWITT colony Town of Gonzales, RAMON MUSQUIS, Hon. Chief Police JOSE ANTONIO NAVARRO Com. of Assistance JOSE RAMON REDFORD (BEDFORD) of Assistance THOMAS R. MILLER

B/20 cc P. C. Bexar Co. Republic of Texas, ESTATE JUAN MARTIN deVERAMINDI decd. petition filed July 12, 1839, RAFAEL GARZA & JOSEFA VERAMENDI surviving wife, C. VAN JEFS atty. JUAN G. SMITT, solicita & ERASMO SEGUIN, C. J. May term,1839, community appointment to setapart to MARIA JOSEFA VERAMENDI dau. GEO. M. DOLSON, asst. Justice M. A. VERAMENDI, gd MIGL. ARCIMEGA, A. J. RAFAEL GARZA par mi ESPOSA MA JOSEFA VERMANDI (in Spanish) mentions Mission de San Jose de Jose Ma Escalera, & Mission delREFUGIO, LasAPACHES, MANUEL NUNES, commissioner JUAN O. SMITH, MARCOS A. VERAMENDI me Tutor, JOSEFA VERAMENDI GARZA and husband RAFAEL GARZA. WIT: MANUEL PEREZ, SAM S. SMITH cc Bexar Co. Mar. 26, 1853

B/41 cc EST. VERMANDI, minors July Term 1838, SUCIAN (LUCIAN) NAVARRO gd. heirs BERRYMENDI, decd. MARCOS A. BERRYMENDI son JUAN MARTIN de VERAMENDI, WIT: VINCENTI GARZA, I. L. HOWARD admitted and appraisers ERASMOS SIGUIN, INEZ PRAL ;== cc by JAMES S. TRUEHART Bexar Co. April 29, 1849 by E. I. CROCKETT, Dist. Clk. C. ERHARD, CCC Hays Co. and note says: MARCOS A. VERAMENDI one of the sons of late JUAN M. de VERAMENDI

150/12 deed same as Vol. B p. 5 TCT) Jan. 3, 1844 MARCUS A. VERAMENDI of Bexar Co. Tex. to EDWARD BURLESON. WIT: JNO. CALDWELL, WM. LINDSAY, JOSE ANTONIO NAVARRO ack. Washington Co. Tex. Jan. 22, 1844 by JOHN CALDWELL before DAN I. TOLER, NP

A/225 April 4, 1851 WD WM. H. MERIWETHER of Comal Co. Texas to CLEMENT P. McKINNIE of Albermarle Co. Va.

A/282 PA June 20, 1851 CLEMENT P. McKINNIE of Albermarle Co. Va. to MARCELLUS McKINNIE of Hays Co. Tex. WIT: JOHN C. PATTERSON, HENRY K. COCHRIN, ack. before JNO. R. JONES JP IRA GARRETT CCC Albermarle Co.

B/100 WD May 20, 1852 CLEMENT P. McKINNIE of Albermarle Co. Va. to SHADRACK DIXON of Bossier Parish, La.

87/391 Aff. May 30, 1924 IN RE: CHARLES MEINERS, et ux MRS. AUGUSTA, 1877 CHARLES MEINERS purchased from J. W. HERNDON & J. V. HUTCHINS 40 acres and was married to first wife, EMILIE: they had 1 ch. d before 1 year; 1885 MRS. E. MEINERS d. childbirth no child living (2) m. MRS AUGUSTA BUTZ, a widow, had 1 child WILLIAM O. MEINERS

54/241 WD Dec. 27, 1907 HERMAN H. BUTZ of Pecos Co. Texas, CHARLES MEINERS et ux MRS. AUGUSTA M., CARL L. BUTZ, EMILY BUTZ, fs. Hays Co. Texas to WILLIE O. MEINERS.

99/296 Cites: MRS. AUGUSTA BUTZ had 3 ch. HERMAN H. BUTZ, CARL L. BUTZ & EMILY BUTZ.

CEMETERY on Farm Road 12, 2 miles south Dripping Springs, Hays Co.Tex.
R. (?) G. SORREL 8/29/1848   3/13/1881
W. J. NORWOOD 5/21/1847   9/15/1937
MRS. M. E. NORWOOD 2/28/1857   12/7/1934
infant son of H. (?) & B. B. ROBERTS d. 10/20/1881
B. B. ROBERTS (mother) 11/11/1835   4/13/1921
J. F. ROBERTS (father) 11/23/1835 9/23/1923
ISAAC D. ROBERTS 1/2/1872   5/7/1961
ELLA L. ROBERTS 9/5/1881 1/29/1964
H. M. SURBER 2/8/1837   8/13/1914
THOMAS H. JENKINS 12/16/1846   11/3/1925
VIRGINIA E. JENKINS 10/6/1852   11/7/1928
G. (C) A. McALISTER 11/27/1841   4/8/1911
SUSAN GLOSSON 2/3/1841   3/28/1928
JAMES GLOSSON 6/17/1837   9/15/1902
GEO. W. HOUCHINS 1828   1910
BETTIE W. HOUCHINS 1833 1905
J. M. MADDING, Co. H 8 La. Co. CSA no dates
mother MARY ELIZABETH MADDING 12/1/1853   5/31/1926
SALLIE DAVIS (mother) 12/18/1839..d...
W. W. DAVIS (father)   4/3/1838 1/4/1907
JOSEPH T. SENOUR 4/21/1836 7/20/1894
SWEN M. BERGMAN (father) b. Eks Jo Sweden 7/6/1836 5/15/1898
DANIEL P. FAIRLY 5/15/1846   2/5/1901
A. W. MATTICE 8/14/1838 4/17/1888 Co. A Michigan Co. A 8th Aug.8,1861 Discharged 7/3/1865
F. P. SORRELL 6/17/1852 4/7/1893 (?)
SALLIE SORRELL 3/12/1857   4/7/1893 (?)
MRS. A. M. SORRELL (mother) 6/15/1829 2/28/1917
T. L. SANSOM (father) 2/6/1844   4/29/1916
P. M. SANSOM (mother) 7/16/1848   1/23/1918
CHARLEY son of W. H. & N. R. BANKS 12/8/1883   12/28/1888

CEMETERY about 1 mile east of Dripping Springs Hays Co. atop high hill:
JAMES O. ROWLAND   8/15/1842   3/27/1928
MATTIE E. ROWLAND 2/3/1860   7/27/1926
L. (S) C. BROWN 12/13...age 69 years. (a very old stone)
MARY & FRANK W. wife and son of PROF. W. M. JORDAN, wife d. 6/24/1891 age 53 years. Son d. 3/28/1883 age 19 years
FANNIE ROWLAND 1844..6/8/1907
HATTIE H. wife of W. J. EDWARDS 1/21/1843   1/16/1895
WM. HOBBY 9/18/1803   12/31/1881
B. J. HINDS   1818   1884
W. T. CHAPMAN 3/8/1835   3/6/1917
M. A. CHAPMAN 3/20/1835   1/23/1924

```
B. J. MARSH 9/9/1820 (6) 2/28/1872
Infant of T. H. & W. P. EGERTON 5/31/1905 6/2/1907 another b/d 1907
JESSE McCLENDON (Mason) 1/20/1883 80 years
JANE McCLENDON 1831  1911
HERNDON infant son WM. S. & E. H. McCLENDON 7/25/1901 and died
CHARLES SEAL 1862  1937
DELLA MAE SEAL 1870  1944
Infant dau. of S. D. & E. J. GILPIN 9/28/1882
A. L. DAVIS, SR. (father) 1824  1888
Mother N. I. DAVIS 1842  1927
MARY FRANCES wife of P. (LEINNE WEBER) d. 2/28/1899
R. W. CAVETT d. 1867
VIRGINIA CAVETT wife of R. S. 1898
A. LANTERMAN 12/22/1812  5/14/1896
CATHERINE M. wife of A. LANTERMAN 5/22/1819  1/16/1900
B. M. GIBSON (father) 1838 1888 MARTHA 1843  1938
JAMES C. HALL 8/6/1855  3/13/1896
DELIND A. HALL b. Marshall Co. Tenn. 7/26/1856(?)  6/7/1892
D. JOSEPH M. POUND, Mason 1826, 1914 SARAH D. POUND 1832 1915 LOUISANA 12/14/1868  3/6/1887
HARRY WALTON infant son of H. P. & T. B. KIDD 12/18/1894  1/6/1895
J. E. LIVINGSTON 8/2/1834  7/4/1890
WM. H. ROBBINS 6/2/1845  4/(1) 2/1894
MARY J. COCKRILL wife of W. H. ROBBINS 1/1/1853  1/4/1919 mother
B. T. STEPHENSON son B. T. & NANNIE  1884  1886

CEMETERY just out of Dripping Springs, Hays Co. Tex:
B. B. ROBERTS 11/11/1835 mother 4/13/1931
J. F. ROBERTS 11/23/1835  9/23/1923
ISAAC D. ROBERTS  1/2/1872  5/6/1961

REV. F. M. WALKER 3/19/1839  9/22/1913
M. H. WALKER 1/24/1841  8/4/1913
ROBERT E. LEE, Co. B 4 Tex. Inv. CSA no dates
ELLA LEE SMITH 1867  1944
HENRY W. ROBERTS Co. I, 3 Tex. Inf. CSA 3/20/1840  7/29/1917
ELEANOR A. ROBERTS 11/20/1845  1/18/1925

MIDDLEBROOK CEMETERY, D. ROBLE farm on Henly-Drippings Springs road:
H. E. SMITH 2/10/1833  4...1880
JOSEPH J. BYARS 6/17/1842  2/20/1907 GEORGIA M. 2/14/1846  2/8/1930
MARY ANN QUICK 9/9/1836 11/1/1926
J. E. QUICK 3/15/1833  12/15/1912

OLD CEMETERY on high hill on BROOKS GOREE farm in Western Hays Co.:
A. T. DYE 5/26/1828  2/1/1916 and 3 unmarked graves.  A neighbor says
wife and wife's sister and unknown; another neighbor says wife and 2
daughters who d. with diaptheria.

PURSLEY CEMETERY on PURSLEY farm in Western Hays Co.:
BATHSEBA PURSLEY 9/20/1829  5/18/1899, WM. PURSLEY 9/10/1820 3/24/1892
ROBERT ROSS 1/3/1837  1/16/1882
GEORGE SIMON 1/28/1841  t/24/1908 SOPHIE SIMON 12/1/1851 1/28/1834
MILLS WHITLEY LAWRENCE 1/231/1837  7/13/1905
TABITHA T. HORMAN, late wife of L. KINNARD 10/13/1822 9/29/1910
P. PURSLEY very old stone 1876 only date able to read
M. A. MIDDLEBROOK 11/22/18...d. Oct. 1903
S. S. MIDDLEBROOK J...12, 1809  2/11/1893 (?)
MRS. N. (?) L. MIDDLEBROOK 3/20/1827  5/8/1910
MRS. G. A. H. STEPHENSON (built up vault) 11/14/182..9..18...
JAMES P. HALLFORD (vault of field stone) d. O...186..
MARY JANE WADE (hooded vault) 2/20/1793  3/7/1875
MRS. M. SIRMON (?) wife of G...W? 2/26/1861 d. 1881
F. L. SEWARD 8/31/1878  10/23/1880
B. V. SEWARD Jan. 1875 d...V. V. BOYD 3/5/1844 d...
```

FALL CREEK CEMETERY Hy 71, near Dripping Springs, Hays Co. Tex:
JOHN STEPHEN CAWFIELD 1878 1880; WALTER CAWFIELD 1862 1882, JAMES CAWFIELD no dates
W. C. FRANKLIN 9/11/1838 10/26/1918
MARY FRANKLIN 3/1/1837 10/9/1897
MIRANDA REID 11/28/1823 7/18/1900
"MOTHER" JANE HAYS 1/29/1847 8/21/1907
M. KENNEDY 3/4/1828 2/16/1907
E. J. KENNEDY 7/4/1829 2/15/1907
M. J. KENNEDY 1852 1845 J. B. KENNEDY 1856 1935
MAHALA D. DILLARD 2/26/1811 9/19/1890
MARY J. WITT 11/30/1835 6/25/1900
MOTHER. MRS. J. W. HOLLINGSWORTH b. Monroe Co. Ga. 7/11/1853 3/24/1924
J. S. HOLLINGSWORTH 6/3/1842 12/15/1914
MRS. G. A. HOBBS 4/17/1843 8/16/1903
J. D. HOBBS 1/9/1828 11/25/1914
JOHN HENRY SHAFFER 1824 1892 CSA Pvt. 6 Co. 17 Reg. Tex. Militia

CALHOUN CEMETERY, Hays Co. on private ranch. Some graves which would have been under CANYON LAKE were moved to this cemetery:
"W. WARWICK d. 1907" Old built-up cut stone vault. Square marker on inside of stone wall or vault: "E& E" Another inscription: "MARY WARRICK" b. 1832 Sept. 19, d. 4/1/1911
FRANK CASE 1847 1875 This grave moved from Canyon dam site.
W. W. JONES 4/26/1853 12/12/1898
THOMAS J. STAPLES d. 2/22/1919
LOUISA STAPLES 7/4/1845 2/9/1900
W. M. PLATT WOW 7/21/1900 49 years
FATHER, THOMAS DODSWORTH 11/5/1819 12/19/1896 Born Willoughby, England
MOTHER, ELIZABETH DODSWORTH 12/29/1816 d. 12/8/1896 born Tarnham, Eng.
L. S. JENNINGS 7/14/1815 in Norwich, Conn. d. 1/21/1887
AARENE E. JENNINGS 5/24/1840 1/17/1896
R. P. HARRISON 12/29/1800 d. 10/27/1880
ELIZA P. CALHOUN 5/26/1820 12/2/1919
JAMES H. CALHOUN 1811 1866
LENORA J. FIELD ISBELL 8/22/1841 12/28/1931
MARTHA A. MASSEY b. Montgomery Co. Ala. 11/13/1835 d. Hays Co.11/16/82
GEORGIA BURNS (moved from Canyon Dam Site 1849 1925
JAMES J. JENNINGS 1849 1840

MILLER CREEK CEMETERY on US 290 about 5 miles W. Henly, Hays Co. Tex.
DAVID FELPS 5/2/1804 9/16/1880
SAMUEL OLIVER infant son JOSEPH & RODY WALLER 11/12/1881 1884
WARREN HERWIG 6/21/1824 2/11/1901 ELIZABETH, wife, 3/19/1829 4/26/1896
ROSCOE H. HERWIG 2/27/1817 5/9/1924
HENRY GRUPE 12/28/1828 1/18/1906 HANNAH F. GRUPE 1/16/1832 7/13/1913
MATTIE J. MORGAN 11/4/1838 12/24/1926
THOMAS MORGAN 4/16/1826 9/30/1904
DANIEL H. MADDOX 11/18/1820 10/16/1881
SELETY wife of C. H. M. 3/15/1818 4/4/1897
ROBERT BOWLAN MADDOX Sgt. Co. F, Waul's Legion CSA 4/24/1841 4/27/1918
ANDREW MADDOX 10/4/1844 6/5/1923 Co. K Tex Calv
ELIZABETH C. MADDOX wife of L. A. 10/19/1845 12/28/1883
E. L. GREENHAW 11/18/1843 9/22/1917
A. J. BEAUCHAMP 12/9/1834 9/1/1894 SARAH J. 10/21/1841 1/20/1917
JAMES B. HUNNICUTT 10/20/1820 4/29/1896 SHANNY M. 3/28/1831 1/5/1905
JACOB FELPS 3/2/1806 4/15/1885 wife CATHERINE R. 1/9/1803 2/8/1885
BRITTON FELPS 1/22/1826 6/21/1904
BENJAMIN F. FELPS 3/19/1839 3/29/1909 IDA C. 4/10/1849 7/9/1924
Father, R. W. FELPS 12/25/1834 1/11/1890 MOTHER JULIA A. 11/18/1846, 6/10/1911
DR. JAMES ODIORNE, b. Molden, Mass. 12/26/1817 7/5/1887
SARAH. E. wife of JAMES d. 2/25/1865 ? 39 ? years
J. Y. WANSLEY 4/3/1831 2/5/1864
JOHN GRAHAM 11/5/1814 5/22/1900 M. GRAHAM 8/20/1819 10/6/1891

PATENT July 19, 1849 to heirs of WASHINGTON MITCHELL decd. killed at Golaid Mar. 27, 1836.
M/321 Aug. 17, 1859 ROBT. G. MITCHELL, MARTHA D. MITCHELL, sur. wife of RANDOLPH MITCHELL of Muscogee Co. Ga.,SARAH G.MITCHELL sur. wife

B. J. J. MITCHELL decd. same Co. and State; E. F. FLANAGAN dau. of
SARAH TAYLOR decd. sister of WASHINGTON MITCHELL decd. of Russell Co.
Ala. JULIUS H. HALSEY, Macon Co. Ga.

D/95 ROBERT G. MITCHELL, Muscogee Co. Ga. atty. for SARAH G. MITCHELL,
GERALDINE MITCHELL, JULIUS HALSEY, MARTHA MITCHELL & ELIZABETH FLANA-
GAN

CEMETERY Near JACOB'S WELL...west part of County, west of Wimberly, Tex
This well is the cornor of at least four league grants in Hays County.
It is as near an everlasting water supply as is possible. In surveying
out old Texas land grants, water was an important factor and sometimes
in order to insure the PATENTEE of water rights, a long narrow strip
of land would run down between two or three other leagues to a river
or stream.
ELLIS B. EGGER 5/19/1832 5/19/1910 LIDDIE HARRIS EGGER 5/1?/1813?
3/4/1898
MOSES BOND EGGER 11/11/1798 2/9/1883
ENCLOSED WITHIN A FENCE:
ERIC S. EDWARDS 8/2/1820 9/24/1904
"mother" ACQUILLA GILMORE 1853 1917
JOSEPH R. EDWARDS 6/4/1808 11/12/1886
JAMES L. EGGER. Co. D 24 Miss. Inf. CSA no dates.
Beside above is "MOTHER" CYNTHIA EGGER 3/17/1851 2/26/1919
LYDIA A., wife of J. J. BLACKWELL 1/4/1879 12/20/1920
"MOTHER" SARAH ANN ENGLISH 11/19/1833 6/20//1912
"FATHER" AARON ENGLISH. Pvt. Co. A 17 Reg. Tex Inf. CSA 10/29/1828,
4/ 5/1890
"OUR MOTHER" MARY F. BLACKWELL 9/20/1848 12/10/1919
DOUBLE ARCH STONE: MOTHER, ELLENOR SAULS (SOULS) b. in Ind. 2/8/1828
m. ELISHA McCUISTION 10/31/1851 d. 11/7/1902
ELISHA McCUISTION b. in Mo. 4/12/1918 m. ELLENOR RAINARD (?) 10/31/1851
12/9/1902.
ANN JENNINGS b. 8/29/1852 m. J. T. JENNINGS 11/25/1878 d. 8/22/1908 "A
FAITHFUL WIFE, A SISTER DEAR, A LOVING DAU. BURIED HERE.."

E/543 WD July 11, 1868 ALFRED SMITH to JOSEPH F. ROWLEY

F/337 WD Nov. 22, 1869 DAVID TRIMBLE to CORNELIA A. TRIMBLE, his wife
41 ac. except 50 x 150 feet N. E. corner, conveyed by TRIMBLE to MISS
MARY H. ADAMS for school purposes

PC 188 Hays Co. EST. J. A. CHANDLER, Sept. Term 1884 he d. Hays Co.July
12, 1884 intestate; petition by H. E. SHELLY; MRS. ELIZABETH H. CHANDLER
sur. wife, waives to HENRY E. SHELLY, L. D. & H. E. CARRINGTON

D/621 Mtg. Jan. 31, 1885 JACOB T. CHANDLER 1/2 interest he was co=part-
ner JAMES A. CHANDLER , DuPRE: NAMES J. T. ch. dissolved death JAMES A.

64/336 Appl. filed Mar. 6, 1885 from T. C. T. WILL: JACOB T. CHANDLER,
he d. Feb. 24, 1885 in Wallingford, Conn. resided in Hays Co. to GEO.
W. son, dau. MRS. ANNIE BARTHOLOMEW, gson CHAS. H. CHANDLER is son of
CHAS. H. CHANDLER who d. Huntsville, Walker Co. Tex. dau. CARRIE W.
CHANDLER

PC 651 guardianship THOS. E. 18 and HOWARD C. McELROY 14 minors, filed
2/6/1906

92/102 aff. Sept. 6, 1926 W. D. CARRINGTON says he is now 70 years of
age and resides Buda, Tex. for about 40 years, knew T. E. McELROY and
wife ADA m. 1 time no will; 3 ch. WM. A. son and THOS. E. son and
HOWARD D. son

92/104 aff. Sept. 6, 1926 by W. W. PUCKETT now 84 years, lived 50 years
in Hays Co. IN RE: McELROY

92/105 Sept. 6, 1926 aff. MRS. ADA McELROY now 68; T. E. McELROY d.
May 9, 1898; WM. A. was 21 on Aug. 13, 1906.

LAMB COUNTY, TEXAS

EDWARD KENSINGTON, CAPITOL FREEHOLD LAND & INVESTMENT CO. LTD.3,000,000 acres known as "CAPITOL RESERVATION" June 25, 1885, London, England.

12/1 Lamb Co. Texas records ABNER TAYLOR of Chicago, Ill., JOHN VILLEIRS FARWELL & CHARLES BENJ. FARWELL, WM. CHASE PRESCOTT, CHARLES ALBERT La TROBE, GEORGE SIMOND, ELEX BRONDON, THOMAS WM. MARTIN, CHARLES E.FEARN

1/22 Feb. 4, 1886 COVENANTS of TRUST between the CAPITAL FREEHOLD LAND & INV. CO. LTD. & THE EARL OF ABERDEEN, QUINTON HOGG, & WM. McARTHUR of Middlesex Co. England. The Right Hon. JOHN CAMPBELL HAMILTON GORDON, Earl of Aberdeen, Esq. and ALDERMAN Sir WM. McARTHUR, K. C. M. G of Holland Park Co. of Middlesex England. Land in DALHAM, OLDHAM, DEAF SMITH, PARMER, CASTRO, BAILEY, LAMB and HARTLEY Counties, Texas.

The above land was consideration for the erection of the present capitol building (ca 1880) in Austin, Texas, after the original building burned.

ABNER TAYLOR now building State Capitol Building. CHARLES FITZWILLIAMS DYBALL, London.

9/307 Sept. 29, 1913 GEO. FINDLAY of Lake, Forest, Ill., over 50 years; JOHN VILLERS FARWELL d. 1908; CHAS. B. FARWELL d. 1903; ABNER TAYLOR d. April 13, 1903; ABNER TAYLOR et ux CLARA LOUISE, both of Cook Co. Ill. He was a member of the House of Representatives 1st. Cong. Dist. Ill

3/220 WM. McARTHUR d. Nov. 16, 1887 London 78 years Knight, ALDERMAN & MERCHANT.

3/1 June 29, 1892 SIR WM. QUARTUS EWART of Belfort in Ireland, Baronet, County Autrun, Ireland Baronet

3/69 HON. AMYAS STAFFORD NORTHROPE & JOHN VILLIERS FARWELL the younger of Chicago, Ill.

LAMPASAS COUNTY, TEXAS

11/108 PATENT Oct. 8, 1852 to NELSON MOREY 640 acres in MILAM DISTRICT, Bell Co. Texas

A/164 Oct. 11, 1854 and 12/621 WD NELSON MOREY to ANDREW J. LEWIS 1/2 interest before STROUD MELTON ccc Milam Co. Texas

A/166 WD Oct. 23, 1856 ANDREW J. LEWIS to SQUIRE W.SHORT. WIT: W. E. WILLIS, R. G. WILLIS, before W. B. COVINGTON, cc Lampasas Co. Tex.

14/286 QC Jan. 15, 1857 S. W. SHORT to ROBERT LASTLEY, before G. W. SCOTT, NP LAMPSAAS CO. TEXAS

12/623 QC June 15, 1857 S. W. SHORT to IRENY SHORT

12/624 WD Aug. 8, 1872 IRENY SHORT to W. J. MEEKS, before A. P. ANDERSON CDC Lampasas Co. Tex.

W/119 Tax deed WILLIAM H. HAMMAN Tax Collector to ALBERT G. RICE, before A. G. WALKER NP Lampsasa Co. Texas

V/233 WD July 2, 1892 W. J. MEEKS and wife, S. ANN to J. M. & A. A.GRAY before A. J. McGUYER, JP & EX O. NP Lampasas Co. Tex

2/596 SWD April 18, 1898 J. M. GRAY and wife, A. A. to S H. & A. J. STRALEY before J. W. TRUSSELL, JP & EX. O NP LampasasCo. Tex.

13/295 QC A. J. STRALEY and wife, MARY E. to J. L. STRALEY, SR., before F. D. RICHARDSON, JP & EX O Lampasas Co. Texas

12/623 SWD J. L. STRALEY, S. H. STRALEY and wife FANNIE E. to C. E. MAYBEN, L. E. MAYBEN

22/223 WD Sept. 25, 1911 L. E. MAYBEN and wife M. O. to C. E. MAYBEN

8/18 Mtg. Sept. 26, 1911 C. E. MAYBEN et ux MARY E. to R. B. SENTERFITT trustee for KATE SENTERFITT

39/543 Rel. 1/5/1920 KATE TOWNSEND (evidently SENTERFITT in 1911) before A. F. MENGER, NP Otero Co. New Mex.

29/342 WD Sept. 29, 1916 C. E. MAYBEN and wife M. E. to MRS. SUSAN BURNS

39/267 deed Dec. 17, 1919 SUSAN BURNS to J. W. BURNS

128/232 Aff. MANDA ROSS, MATTIE AYERS, RE: MRS. SUSAN BURNS, d. intestate May 8, 1938 no husband; J. W. BURNS and wife, CALLIE; M. L. BURNS et ux MYRTLE; MANDA ROSS et vir O. R.; MATTIE AYERS et vir J. H.; ALICE SHED et vir G. H.; ALICE d. 1940, Lampasas Co. heirs and G. H. sur. hus. and J. T., A. E., G. H., Jr., and MYRTLE MAE MORRIS et vir S. W.; NANCY et vir A. T. SHED, JOHN W., A. T. SHED, JR., R. E., JAMES, MOLLIE PAULINE WILLIAMS et vir O. A., VIRDIE PRICE et vir EARL & S. DOYLE BLACKLOCK and wife, PAT.

CEMETERY near Lampasas:

T. H. WOLF, b. Oct. 24, 1818 Davis Co. reared in Warren Co. Tenn. came to Texas Oct. 7, 1837 d. May 13, 1892

SILAR son of WITT SHELBURN b. 1850 killed by Indians, Horse Prairie 1870.

LAVACA COUNTY, TEXAS

HACKBERRY CEMETERY, north of Halletsville, about 3 miles:
A. J. MORROW b. 1/29/1828 3/11/1899
I. D. or J. D. MORROW 1848 1929
NANCY ANN MORROW b. White Co. Va. April 22, 1815 d 6/2/1874
ELIZABETH MORROW, wife of J. D. MORROW and dau. of COL. CHAS. HARRISON b. May 17, 1849
J. F. MORROW 4/17/1841   3/ 20/1921
LOUISE MORROW 8/1/1844 10/17/1919
H. F. CHILDRESS, no markings

DC 1808 filed Oct. 23, 1873: FRANCES JANE GRIMES HEAD, et vir ALBERT, EMANUEL GRIMES, JOHN W. GRIMES et ux M. A., SARAH ELIZABETH GRIMES GODWIN, et vir JOHN vs. MARY CAMPBELL GRIMES, widow and JAMES F. GRIMES a minor, child of second m. of JOHN B. GRIMES decd. d. Feb. 18, 1873; plaintiffs are children of first marriage of JOHN B. GRIMES with MARY G. CHILDRESS in 1840 in Hart Co. Ky., she d. Feb. 8, 1862, in Lavaca Co. Texas

LEE COUNTY, TEXAS

LAWHORN SPRINGS or SMITH SPRINGS on FM 619 Lee Co.

JOHN L. SMITH b. England June 16, 1796 d. Nov. 24, 1851 was first person buried in SMITH SPRINGS cemetery.

BLUE CEMETERY,
GEORGE LEE PILLOW 4/ 22/1887 10/21/1903

COPELAND, Texas: WM. M. SMITH 4/2/1827 6/24/1893

CENETERY at CENTER POINT, near A. W. SHERRILL farm 2 mi. N. Blue:
ELEANOR AMANDA CAMERON b. 1837 Jan. 19, d. 12/25/1918
D. M. CAMERON 7/24/1827 d. 3/7/1900

LLANO COUNTY, TEXAS

O/162 WD Feb. 8, 1889 J. P. JOHNS, pres. RAMSEY MINING CO. to S. H. BUCHANAN, mentions THOS. R. DEDRICK line and surface owners of 360 ac. J. L. RENICK, N. B. FREEMAN, J. E. MADDEN, MRS. T. M. JOHNSON

39/166 WD Nov. 13, 1893 W. R. RAMSEY, Pres. RAMSEY MINING CO. to J. N. & S. M. MADDEN, part WM. von ROSENBERG patent.

I/30 WD Sept. 8, 1884 C. R. JOHNS, pres. RAMSEY MINING Co. to N. B. FREEMAN, Beg. at SE cor. THOS. TALEY 320 acre survey;

G.62 WD May 27, 1885 RAMSEY MINING Co. TO G. J. GRAY, part patent to heirs of JOSEPH MEYERHEFER Jan. 29, 1875 Beg. 730 ac. survey name of MICHAEL SCHULTZ

F/380 WD Aug. 21, 1884 RAMSEY MINING Co. to H. H. JOINER, part GERMAN EMIGRATION CO. survey Feb. 1, 1875
F/380 WD Aug. 21, 1884 RAMSEY MINING Co. to H. H. JOINER, part HENRY H. WHEELER SURVEY

N/509 WD Nov. 2. 1888 RAMSEY MINING Co. to J. T. SIMPSON Beg. 320 ac. survey GEO. HEBGER

28/306 WD Nov. 5, 1895 RAMSEY MINING CO., W. R. RAMSEY, Pres. to A. J. SIMPSON. Beg. N. E. cor. JOSEPH MENCKE survey

43/529 WD Mar. 9, 1907 MRS. SARAH A. MOORE et vir E. L., MIS.STELLA COURSEY, P. L. ROBERTS, C. C. ROBERTS, JR., JOHN ROBERTS, JAMES BACKUS et ux MATTIE, out JAMES E. BITTNER sur. R. D. McANNELLY assignee of MATHIAS HINDS Nov. 28, 1849, JOHN BUTTERY sur. from S. S. SLAUGHTER BY deed Jan. 30, 1899 and deed from F. C. STEWART to JAMES CHAPMAN et ux CELEND A to C. C. ROBERTS, SR. Mar. 24, 1899 and part JONAS DANCER sur. and THEODORE LOPEZ sur.

E/521 WD Feb. 10, 1885 RAMSEY MINING CO. to J. T. BARDIN, D. C. & A. J. BARDIN, Beg. H. BROECKER sur. and N. DAUGHERTY sur.

F/123 WD Dec. 27, 1883 RAMSEY MINING CO. to C. D. BOURLAND, SE cor. CHRISTIAN HEISE Survey

32/440 WD RAMSEY MINING CO. to JOHN F. BEASLEY, Beg. N. E. cor. sur. to heirs of FR. RICHLER

47/22 Nov. 25, 1910 F. M. RAMSEY of Lampasas Co. Tex. before W. D. ABNEY, Lampsass Co. Texs. part MARTHA J. PERRY sur. patent to O. F. GOLSON, April 20, 1885 JOSEPH CONE sur. ptd. to R. T. CALDWELL, July 5, 1859, J. BEDFORD sur. patented Oct. 25, 1873, pt. W. C. SHARP patented W. A. H. MILLER Nov. 13, 1888, part THEODORE LOPEZ sur. patented to R. S. NEIGHBORS, Feb. 28, 1849

MILAM COUNTY, TEXAS

NOTE: The court house here burned in 1874 and all records destroyed.

May 23, 1946 issue (special) CAMERON DAILY HEROLD. This gives a lot of history of local people.

SOMERVILLE COUNTY, TEXAS.

An old unmarked or labelled BOOK p. 73: ADOPTION: THOMAS HEROD, of Somerville Co. Texas, adoptedALGY (minor) male b. Jan. 7, 1877. His mother was ....HOLMS died in month of April 1877. No legitimate father

P/92 AGREEMENT, Mrs. E. E. ADAMS, decd. heirs: DELILA STEPHENS et vir M. C. A. STEPHENS, CHARLES PEAR

OCCUPATION TAX BOOK: (This is the only county in which I saw one of these)

COMMERCIAL TRAVELERS, DRUMMERS or SOLICITORS of trade: STATE COMPTROLL-ER, W. M. BRONWN:
PINUS LYONS, LIcense dated 4/25/1881;
CINCINNATUS KIDD, license dated April 20, 1881;
EUGENE WARREN, license dated May 6, 1881;
W. S. TERRY license dated April 23, 1881;

R. J. SMITH license dated May 3, 1881;
J. W. SHAKER, license dated April 25, 1881;
D. LAMPKINS, license dated April 26, 1881;
J. B. HOLLINGSWORTH license dated May 12, 1881. $50.00.
G. W. HOLLINGSWORTH license dated April 29, 1881;
J. A. LINK, license dated May 7, 1881;
D. S. ROSS, license dated April 30, 1881;
S. A. ELKINS, Galveston, Texas, license dated April 21, 1882;
P. J. WILLIS BROS. for GEO. MULLUSK, license dated April 22, 1881;
W. DAVIS, Galveston license dated April 25, 1881;
R. N. GRAHAM, license dated June 10, 1881;
M. MOSES license dated April 27, 1882;
H. H. SIMPSON license dated May 20, 1881;
P. R. BEALL license dated May 20, 1882;
B. V. COULSON, Dallas, license dated April 23, 1881;
S. B. MAYER license dated April 29, 1881;
SIMON LITTLE license dated June 30, 1881;
WARD T., SMITH license dated May 4, 1881;
EUGENE HUTCHINSON license dated May 10, 1881;
T. M. COLLINS, license dated June 15, 1881;
THOMAS P. LISMAN, license dated June 27, 1881;
EDWARD SHEEHAN license dated May 13, 1881;
W. J. FINKS licnese dated July 1, 1881;
J. R. HOBIN or HABIN, license dated June 1, 1881;
R. M. STEVENS license dated July 18, 1881;
A. J. COOPER license dated May 25, 1881;
HENRY M. FRIEND license dated May 7, 1881;
W. D. BELT license dated June 23, 1881;
JOHN H. MORTON, Louisveille, Ky. lieense dated April 23, 1881;
HOWARD W. PEAK, license dted June 21, 1881;
J. P. WILSON license dated July 1, 1881;
M. A. CHAMBERS license dated May 3, 1881;
FELIX E. MISTRAT, license dated July 27, 1881;
W. C. or T. C. HARVEY license dated May 9, 1881;
W. H. STOOKE (STOCKE) license dated July 6, 1881;
NICK D. BARRY license dated May 30, 1881;
W. W. TRIPPETT license dated April 12, 1881;
W. G. TURNER license dated June 7, 1881, and
E. ATCHISON license dated August 8, 1881.

WILLIAMSON COUNTY, TEXAS

203/54 PATENT to JNO. F. WEBER, Jan. 15, 1849.

2/ 210 1851 deed JNO. F. WEBER to THOMAS J. MOORE. WIT: J. W. CASNER, JOHN B. BUCKS

4/100 deed Oct. 13, 1852 J. T. MOORE to MICHAEL YOUNG, ack. TCT

203/57 aff. dated Sept. 13, 1897, filed Nov. 14, 1921, by JAMES WILLIAMSON. WILLIAM WILLIAMSON, m. twice: 1st. wife d. 18...had: JAMES WILLIAMSON, ELIZABETH, who m. JOHN T. SIMMONS, SUSAN, who m. J. N. BROWN LEWIS WILLIAMSON, JOHN (m.) and had 2 ch: JOHN W. & ELIZABETH now the wife of HARRISON (?) JOHN WILLIAMSON died during the civil war. There were no children by the second wife of WILLIAM WILLIAMSON.

PC 1340, WILL: P. H. DIMMITT d. Dec. 5, 1903, WIT: J. E. COOPER & R. T. COOPER, wife, MRS. MAMIE HENLEY DIMMITT, to dau. LILLIE A. DIMMITT, to 25th birthday as heir of her decd. mother, MRS. AMANDA DIMMITT. Appoints F. W. CAROTHERS, EXTR. and guardian of LILLIE C. DIMMITT, dated Aug. 27 1902; will filed Feb. 13, 1904; $105,000.00 bond; S. W. BROWN, J. D. ELLIOTT & W. F. CASEY, appraisers. Mar. 15, 1913, LILLIE A. ATKINSON, et vir CHAS. B. ATKINSON & F. W. CAROTHERS state LILIE is 23 years old and pray that she and her husband have charge of estate.

DC 5983 ESTATE P. H. DIMMITT, decd. by EXTRS. vs. J. J. DIMMITT, MRS. ROSA HUGHES et vir J. D. says P. H. DIMMITT never received his share of ESTATE J. J. DIMMITT, SR.

DC 6066 MRS. M. L. DIMMITT v. ROSA L. HUGHES et vir JOHN D. HUGHES, JNO. J. DIMMITT, F. W. CAROTHERS, LILLIE A. DIMMITT, MRS. BEULAH H. DIMMITT, LILBURN DIMMITT & JAMES H. DIMMITT, defts. filed June 21,1906 Petition says she and JOHN J. DIMMITT were married many years prior to May 9, 1864, when he died intestate leaving: W. W., C. A., P. H. J.J., LILBURN, ROSA L., now HUGHES & JOSIA, called BIRDIE DIMMITT: says she inherits dead children/s shares: BIRDIE, LILBURN & C. A. DIMMITT, decd

DC 5664 filed July Term 1904 MRS. MAMIE H. DIMMITT vs. F. W. CAROTHERS extrs. and LILLIA A. DIMMITT and MRS. M. L. DIMMITT, gdn. says MRS. AMANDA SHELL DIMMITT decd. was mother of LILLIE A. ATKINSON, LILBURN ANZETINE EUBANK was wife of CHAS. B. ATKINSON who d. 1920.

4/211 WD Feb. 8, 1853, B. MANLOVE et ux ABRELLA (X) to FRANCIS K.HUNT
3/521 DEED G. G. ANDERSON who bought from Tax Collector 3000 acres to JULIA G. HUNT, MARIA B. DUDLEY & B. W. DUDLEY

pC 349 Guardianship WALTER & ORA MILES, Minor ch. of J. T. MILES, who d. Nov. 1884 near Liberty Hill, Williamson Co. Texas.

2/366 PATENT august 19, 1844, to CLEMENT STUBBLEFIELD

18/209 WD Feb. 17, 1877, THOS. P. HUGHES to B. E. CHRIETZBERG. WIT: DUNCAN SMITH, WM. KEY

PC 389 filed April 14, 1886 by MRS. BELLE P. CHRIETZBERG, comm. sur. with B. E. CHREITZBERG who d. May 27, 1885 left wife and Ch: CHAS. P., 15 years old; EDGAR M. 13 years old; ANA MARIE 11 years old; C. PERKINS 9 years old; ROBERT HENRY 7 years old, HILLIARD TIMBROKE 4 years old d. y. unm.; EDGAR M. m. GRACE BRYSON, who d. Mar. 17....2 ch. BOND B. and EDWINIA McLUGH; ANNA MARIE m. JAKE MATTHEWS, d. 1904, had OUIDA BELLE; C. PERKINS d. 1936 m. FANNIE FOSTER d. no ch.; ROBERT HENRY m. LILIE CARTER d. leaving 1 son ROBERT HENRY, Jr. TCT

PC 5332, MRS. BELL F. CHRIETZBERG d. Austin at age of 105 years, Jan. 2, 1957. Application by EDGAR CHRIETZBERG, only surviving child; says dau and grand dau. OUIDA BELL are buried in IKE MATTHEWS cemetery

1/228 WD Sept. 14, 1847 THOMAS M. HORNSBY of Milam Co. to JULY ANN RICE, dau. THOS. HORNSBY. WIT: WM. C. REAGER, REUBEN H.HORNSBY, JR.

1/51 WD Sept. 1, 1848 THOS. M. HORNSBY to HARMON SMELSER. WIT: GREEN- LIEF FISK, ABNER GREGG, WM. MYRICK.

6/224 Deed April 12, 1853 JOHN WATES (WATTS) of Walker Co. Tex. to HADEN WATTS of Polk Co. undivided interest.

5/414 PATENT. Sept. 16, 1845 REPUBLIC OF TEXAS to heirs of PRIOR A. HOLDER, decd.

6/616 TITLE BOND, Dec. 12, 1835, PRIOR A. HOLDER to T. KENNEY, WIT: E. D. HOLDER, MARY KENNEY

2/158 cc MILAM COUNTY, TEXAS, Sept. 6, 1842 JOHN ADRIANCE vs. THOS. KINNEY, recorded judgment, sheriff's deed by JACOB B. HARRELL, depty sheriff. WIT: B. GOOCH, J. C. LEE

7/417 cc from MILAM CO. TEXAS, WM. D. THOMPSONand O. B. SMITH on Apl. 24, 1837 had assignment of Title Cert. from PRIOR A. HOLDER, he left: WM. HOLDER, MARTHA JANE, minors with THOMAS H. MAYS, admr.

7/419 cc JUDGMENT MILAM CO. DC 438: April 10, 1847, JACOB M. HARRELL, NELSON MERRILL, GEO. ERATH, apprs. and commrs. PRESTON CONLEE,Shf.BC

1/308 deed MAY 18, 1849 W. D. THOMPSON, O. B. SMITH to FREEMAN SMALLEY: WIT: WASHINGTON ANDERSON, PHILLIP HOLLAND

2/161 Deed March 25, 1851, FREEMAN SMALLEY to JAMES G. HARRELL.

5/97 Dec. 26, 1853 JAMES G. HARRELL to THOS. BACON. WIT: ED VENTREES, B. GOOCH.

6/456 1850 THOMAS H. BACON, 100 ac. home place

6/456 SWD June 5, 1850 JAMES NICHOLSON et ux CLEMENTINE: ROBERT S.SMITH et ux AMERICA N., CHAS. T. SMITH, all of Williamson Co. Tex; THOMAS J. SMITH Cass Co. Tex. by CHAS. T. SMITH, heirs of OBADIAH B. SMITH OF Giles Co. Tenn. to WM. D. THOMSON.

13/552 WD Feb. 22, 1862 JOHANNES PALM to S. M. SWENSON: WIT: SWANTE PALM, WM. BLACK

PC 1496 ESTATE HENDRICK THEOFIL STARK d. Feb. 13, 1907 Williamson Co. Tex. WILL dated Sept. 14, 1894, 1/5 each sons: CARL OSCAR STARK, JOHAN AUGUST, HERMAN STARK, dau. LONTINA ROSALIE FORSBERG and gd. SARAH LOGREN, dau. of decd. dau. AMANDA CHRISTINA LOGREN. WIT: A. J. NELSON, J. A. NELSON & C. J. H. FORSBERG (she signs MRS. TINA FORSBERG) and MRS. SALLIE ALMQUIST et vir EMIL, nee LOFGREN.

PATENT, REPUBLIC OF TEXAS To THOMAS P. DAVY, in Milam Co. Oct. 7, 1841

Deed April 14, 1842 THOS. P. DAVY et ux NANCY A. DAVY of Montgomery Co Tex. to GEO. R. MERCER: WIT: RICHARD D. HIGHTOWER, JAMES POWELL

1/125 PARTITION succession of GEO. R. MERCER, decd. Dec. 26, 1848, ELIZABETH OLIPHANT, the widow, & GEO. H. & MATTHEW MERCER, only CH. Commissioners: JOHN McCREARY, SANFORD OLIPHANT, J. K. CAMPBELL

1861 GEO. H. MERCER, MATTHEW MERCER of Walker Co. Tex. to STEPHEN CUMMINGS

12/597 QC Oct. 1, 1870 LUCRETIA HASMER et vir CHAS. B. HASMER of Cook Co. Ill., she heir of ELIJAH D. HARMON, decd.

12/598 Deed Nov. 2, 1870 EDWIN C. HARMON, LILLIAN HARMON, ELLA G. HARMON, H. LOUISA HARMON to ISAAC D. HARMON, heirs of ELIJAH D. HARMON of Cook Co. Ill. LILLIAN & H. LOUISA HARMON ack. Dec. 14, 1870 in Suffolk Co. Mass. and EDWIN C. HARMON et ux ELLA ack. Cook Co. Ill.

12/602 PA Aug. 20, 1870 ISAAC D. HARMON of TCT to W. M. WALTON

2/1 PATENT to THOS. ANDERSON, assignee of JAMES BURLESON assignee of WILEY HARRIS, March 22, 1841.

2/2 deed April 10, 1847 THOS. ANDERSON to WASHINGTON ANDERSON.

PC 819 ESTATE WASHINGTON ANDERSON, decd. W. A. TALLAFERRO, Indp. Extr. Hed. April 29, 1894, WILL: dated Mar. 2, 1893 to 4 gch: MRS. ANNIE L. MANN, MRS. FANNIE M. TAYLOR, W. A. TALIAFERRO, and CHLOE TALEAFERRO, wife: MARY ANN ANDERSON. WIT: L. M. MAYS, J. M. BLACK. apprs. J. M. BLACK, S. V. DOOLEY (DOLLEY) and R. R.HYLAND.

PC 254 guardianship filed July 27, 1882, BETTIE V. 19, FANNIE M. 15 and CHLOE H. TALEAFERRO 12. (The spellig is not consistent. The name is pronounced as TOLIVER, here)

359/78 Aff. Dec. 19, 1949 ROBERT EGGER, son of W. E. EGGER and S. A. EGGER, she d. Jan. 12, 1949.

359/61 Aff. by WALNEITTA COPE & SHELBY WALKER, son and dau. LULA WALKER nee EGGER dau. W. T. & S. A. EGGER, late of Williamson Co. and husband HENRY WALKER: WALNEITTE, wife of W. O. COPE, H. S. WALKER and SHELLY WALKER, Los Angeles, Calif. They were reared in Brown Co. Texas. LULA WALKER d. Brown Co. Mar. 22, 1932, HENRY WALKER d. Stonewall Co. Tex. Oct. 2, 1942. He never re-married

1/20 TRANSFER OF LAND CERTIFICATE, by CLEMENT STUBBLEFIELD, Feb.20,1836 to THOS. B. HULING; says land granted to him as Colonist and settler 1836 in February, from Sumner Co. Tenn. and a young man without family.

1/53 WD June 8, 1848 THOS. B. HULING to WILLIAM KNIGHT. WIT: DAVID COWAN, W. J. ANDERSON

ESTATE, DR. WM. KNIGHT, decd. filed May 13, 1851; appl. by MARY A. KNIGHT, says she is widow, joined by DR. WM. I. ANDERSON, SAML, ALEXANDER, NEAL McGAFFEY & G. W. LEMMON, appointed appraisers. B. GOOCH, NEAL McGAFFEY & W. C. DALRYMPLE are bondsmen, May 26, 1851

43/507 aff. Dec. 17, 1887 before E. A. STRICKLAND by W. K. MAKEMSON & EMZY TAYLOR. They knew WILLIAM KNIGHT: he d. Williamson Co. prior to Aug. 14, 1869, left as sole heirs: MARY A. surviving wife, JAMES, MARTHA, J. B., ELIZA, NANNIE, now FOSTER and CAROLINE now EUBANK.

329/141 Aff. Aug. 21, 1945 by R. G. EUBANK gson of WM. & MARY A.KNIGHT who d. about 50 years ago leaving: MARTHA BULLOCK, wife of B. W., J.B. KNIGHT, ELIZA MONTGOMERY, wife of JAMES, NANNIE wife of (1) WILLIAM FOSTER and (2) J. M. PAGE, JAMES KNIGHT and CAROLINE m. CYRUS EUBANK, and is affiant's mother.

2/71 Nov. 8, 1860 E. J. HEAD m. E. A. OWENS

5/505 Nov. 5, 1884 J. R. ISABELL m. M. A. MOTE

14/256 EARNEST W. PECK m. ELSIE THORNTON Dec. 24, 1911

PC 2182 J. W. PHELPS d. Feb. 4, 1918, bro. 1/5 int. R. R. PHELPS, Columbia, Tenn.; bro. NEIL S. PHELPS, Wales, Tenn, niece MRS. EUGENE SHANDS (?)

211/616 PATENT REPUBLIC of TEXAS to B. MANLOVE Aug. 19, 1845.

27/228 cc WILL from Fayette Co. Ky. dated Aug. 24, 1876, doesnnt state date of death of F. K. HUNT, will to wife, son-in-law DR. B. W. DUDLEY wife and son=in-law Extrs. and extrx. not naming any person. CODICIL: says DR. ELISHA WARFIELD father of his wife, not naming her, dated March 31, 1879

27/227 PA Sept. 14, 1881 JULIA G. HUNT, widow, F. K. HUNT and MARIE B. DUDLEY & B. W. DUDLEY of Fayette Co. ,Ky. to W. M. KEY, of Williamson Co. Ark. in Williamson Co. Sept. 14, 1881

142/559 PATENT, REPUBLIC of TEXAS, July 31, 1845 to HENRY FIELDS

4/238 Tax Deed July 15, 1850 W. C. DALRYMPLE, assr. Col. taxes for Williamson Co. to TAYLOR SMITH

DC 6890 filed 1910 Williamson Co. Texas, recites no deed from HENRY FIELDS, all plaintiffs claim under TAX DEED: J. P. BAKER, DAVID MITCHELL, C. L. SIMMONS, MRS. M. A. SMITH fs. H. C. & W. D. FOWLER, WARREN BRYDSON, E. T. CHAPMAN, C. A. MILLER, C. M. MEARS, A. B. MATTHEWS, W. O. STUBBLEFIELD, J. W. ATWOOD.

8/48 WD Nov. 20, 1859 TAYLOR SMITH to BENJAMIN SMITH

10/250 deed Sept. 27, 1866 WILEY SMITH et ux SPEEDY To A. F. AYNSWORTH

10/244 deed May 29, 1866 N. J. CRUMP to W. R. & F. C. BRATTON
PC 212 petition JOHN H. WILLIAMS resides Williamson Co., Tex. over 21 yrs. GEO. W. WILLIAMS, Wmson. Co. d. intestate Feb. 13,1881 left wife and several children; ptf. is son of surviving wife, NANCY E. First wife, SUSANA d. ca 1849 m. NANCY ca 1850; Ch: Dec. 20, 1881 parties ESTATE SUSAN WILLIAMS and SARAH ADAMS ET VIR HENRY, of Burnet Co.Tex; JOHN H. WILLIAMS, Williamson Co., FERDINAN, THOS. WILLIAM & MARTHA FRANKLIN, children of (1) NANCY WILLIAMS, now decd. all of Titus Co. Tex; WLIZABETH WILLIAMS widow of decd. Williamson Co.; & SEREPTS HUNT wife of A. J.; MARY WHITELEY, wife of SAM. & FREDONIA McCLURE et vir GEORGE and COPHRONIE WILLIAMS 14 years old,ANNIE WILLIAMS ncm. no

guardian; GEORGE WILLIAMS 14 years old.

12/600 Oct. 1, 1870 to ISAAC D. HARMON from WETHYAN L. BURLEY and husbank ARTHUR G. Of Cook Co. Ill.

12/597 Oct. 1, 1870 LUCRETIA HASMER and husband CHAS. G., Cook Co. Ill heir of ELIJAH D. HARMON, decd.

9/11 Jan. 22, 1863 JOHN M. WHIPPLE, Williamson Co. Tex. to C. C. MASON also of Williamson Co. Texas

29/217 July 14, 1883 QC NANCY BABCOCK et vir CHAS. sister of JAMES E. WHIPPLE to THOS. P. EVANS.
1/26 cc from Galveston Co. Texas; Refers to note Feb. 8, 1878,plaintiffs RICHARD S., WM. H., PETER J. WILLIS, JOSEPH G. GOLDTHWAIT and wife ELLA MAGNOLIA SEALEY and husband GEO., CAROLINE LADD and husband WM. F., composing firm of P. J. WILLIS & BRO. Galveston Co. Texas

5/173 deed to B. H. MUDD of Jasper Co. Texas, Oct 10, 1847

7/18/1849 JAMES H. GILLESPIE ccc Bastrop Co. Texas; JAMES W. SMITH 1867, Judgement from Travis County, Texas

ANDREW J. HAMILTON was provisional governor of Texas Oct. 20, 1865. (He and his brother MORGAN C., were land holders in many counties)

PATENT to ORBILLE PERRY, 1852.

7/543 QC deed Jan. 22, 1859, JOHN FISHER et ux MELANIA of Robertson Co Tex. 1/2 interest as lawful heirs of ORVILLE PERRY to HELENA JOHNSTON WIT: EDWARD W. HERNDON, ROBERT JOHNSTON

8/83 SWD Dec. 12/ 1859 ORVILLE PERRY and wife MARY ANN (X) to JAMES JOHNSON & O'BANION, states league granted to said ORVILLE PERRY, a Colonist Aug. 10, 1835. WIT: M. O. ROAKE, JOHN E. MORRIS, ack. La. Parish of Washington by MRS. MARY ANN PERRY, he did not ack. JULIUS E. WILSON, presiding Judge of 8th Judg. Dist. of La. (Washington, St. Helena, St. Tammey and Langston Parishes)

8/131 SWD Nov. 24, 1858 ORVILLE PERRY to NATHANIEL PERRY & DeWITT C. SMITH, all of the league. WIT: S. H. SMITH, D. T. STEWART, ack. Newton Co. Texas, by D. T. STEWART, WITNESS, R. C. BALLANGER, Newton Co. Tex

7/590 Deed June 25, 1859 NATHANIEL PERRY of Newton Co. Tex. atty. for BURRELL P. PERRY, heir of RICHARDSON PERRY, decd. late of Texas and JERIMIAH HENDLEY, JAMES McGEE (MAGEE) STEPHEN JARRALL & JOHN SPEERS also heirs, RICHARDSON PERRY in the right of their wives. (P.A. to JOHN SPIERS Oct. 13, 1857) to JAMES JOHNSTON, 1 league to ORVILLE PERRY, Williamson Co. Tex. and 1 leag. on Yawall (Egua) Burleson Co.Tex

22/448 cc decree 4720 TCT claims in ANTONIO FLOREZ, & NICHOLAS PORTER surveys and PULSIFER 1/3 lea. HELEN BERNHARDT et vir JOSEPH,ELIZABETH HOFFATT et vir JOSEPH, WILLIE & LOUIS HOFFATT, minors by R. J. HILL, Spl. guardian; MARTHA M. GOWAN, et vir SIDNEY M., MARY ANN JOHNSTON and JOHN C. & ELLA JOHNSTON, minors by R. J. HILL spl. guardian and HAMILTON O'BANION to ANDREW J. & ALBERT H. GLASSCOCK

4/474 PATENT July 26, 1850 to G. W. GLASSCOCK as guardian of WM.ADDISON

1/75 WD Mar. 13, 1849 GEO. W. GLASSCOCK to MATHIAS WILBARGER,ANTONIO FLORES survey. WIT: GREENLEAF FISK, J. E. CLARK, before G. T.WILLIAMS ccc Williamson Co. Texas.

1/298 deed Jan. 13, 1850 MATHIAS WILBARGER to NOAH McCUISTIAN,administration MATHIAS WILBARGER, May Term 1853 by SARAH M. WILBARGER & W. C. DALRYMPLE, EVAN WILLIAMS, JOHN J. AKE & JOHN SHELL, appraisers; bondsmen: JOHN W. WILBARGER,WEBB OWEN,$20,260. final closing August 29th

1859, PC 3/36 Williamson Co. Rec. delivery to SARAH M. WILBARGER, surv. wife and legal guardian of minor heirs, not named.

13/747 QC July 9, 1872 A. S. WALKER says ANN J. WALKER, d. intestate Dec. 14, 1865 left heirs: SARAH MARGARET & ALEXANDER S. WALKER, JR. and SARAH MARGARET d. Oct. 14, 1867 to ALEX. S. WALKER, JR. all estate of his sister and mother ANNA J. WALKER (late WILBARGER). WIT: H. C. WILBARGER, JOHN E. WALKER, W. T. DALYRMPLE, clk.

DC 1083 filed July 10, 1872 ALEX S. WALKER, JR., by next friend A. S. WALKER, SR. vs. MRS. SARAH M. WILBARGER, MRS. LOUISA WALKER and husband JOHN E., & H. CLAY WILBARGER, all parties of Williamson Co. Texas; represents that MATHIAS WILBARGER d. Feb. 1852 leavig SARAH M. his widow and ANNA JANE, LOUISA, HENRY CLAY, VIRGINIA, JAMES & MATHIAS W.children. Subsequent to 1852 JAMES, MATHIAS & VIRGINIA d. as infants; ANNA JANE WILBARGER m. May 6, 1861 A. S. WALKER, SR. d. Dec. 24, 1865 leaving two children ptf. and SARAH MARGARET who d. Oct. 14, 1867; 1/2 estate to widow, SARAH M. WILBARGER & 1/2 to LOUISA WALKER, H. CLAY WILBARGER & ptf. COMMISSIONERS: WM. C. DALRYMPLE, JOHN J. STUBBLEFIELD, RICHARD SANSOM.

ESTATE MRS. LOUISA WALKER decd. filed Oct. 21, 1903 R. T. COOPER, pet. says she d. Oct. 2, 1903 a widow, COOPER SANSOM, atty. for R. T. COOPER appl. WILL dated Sept. 26, 1903 to PRESBYTERIAN THEOLOGICAL SCHOOL at Austin & Presbyterian College for Girls at Milford, Texas, balance to nephew ALEX S. WALKER & nieces and nephew SARAH WILBARGER, ANNE M. WILBARGER, & GEORGE C. WILBARGER, apts. friend R. T. COOPER, Extr. WIT: J. E. COOPER, COOPER SANSOM, W. T. CASEY, J. M. PAGE & F. W. CAROTHERS Appraisers

6/299 PATENT Dec. 31, 1845 to THOMAS. B. HULING assignee WOODRUFF STUBBLEFIELD.

11/15 deed June 12, 1846 THOMAS. B. HULING of Jasper Co. Tex. to ELIZABETH HULING, division of community property. WIT: C. H. DELANCY, JOHN HAMILTON HULING ack. before JAMES DILLENAY, NP Jasper Co. Texas

1/407 SWD June 7, 1850 THOS. B. HULING to JOHN J. STUBBLEFIELD, the WOODRUFF STUBBLEFIELD league and labor. WIT: G. W. GLASSCOCK, JOH$_N$(X) McGINNIS

89/405 cc ESTATE THOS. B. HULING decd. by ELIZABETH HULING Suvg. wife PC Lampasas Co. Tex. 1866, April Term. LORENZO D. NICHOLS,, JACOB DOUGLASS, D. V. GRANT, apprs. WM. H. STORM, CJ Lampasas Co. Tex A. P. ANDERSON CDC Lampasas Co. Texas.

69/280 QC Dec. 7, 1894 ELIZABETH HULING, Lampasas Co. ratifies deed to THOS. B. HULING made June 18, 1850 WIT: W. D. ABNEY

35/436 WD May 18, 1885 JOHN E. WALKER to ANNE WILBARGER, widow, SARAH, GEORGE, ANNE M. & VIRGINIA WILBARGER heirs late H. C. WILBARGER.

109/262 deed Aug. 8, 1904 GEO. C. WILBARGER to sisters SARAH & ANN M. WILBARGER, estate of our deceased father H. C. WILBARGER & decd. mother MRS. ANNIE WILBARGER and decd. aunt MRS. LOUISA WALKER

161/464 WD Jan. 2, 1914 MRS. SARAH WILBARGER COOPER et vir J. E. & ANN WILBARGER fs.

176/106 Transfer note July 6, 1916 SARA WILBARGER COOPER et vir J. E. of Williamson Co. Tex. and MRS. ANNIE M. WILBARGER HARDAWAY et vir GEO. W. of El Paso Co. Texas

PATENT Nov. 20, 1847, to SAMUEL DAMON, SEN.

7/476 deed Jan. 22, 1848 SAMUEL DAMON to THOMAS DILLARD. WIT: WILLIAM L. BURK, JAMES H. BELL, ack. before J. H. BELL, Brazoria Co. Tex.

88/592 ESTATE THOS. DILLARD, decd. Burleson Co. Tex. Oct. 31, 1853,
J. W. THOMAS, C. J., M. M. HITCHCOCK, Shf. WM. H. MURRY, Clk. partition
of THOS. DILLAR ESTATE:
1. POLEMAN DILLARD & ABSOLON DILLARD,heirs of GABRIEL DILLARD, decd.
2. JOHN & SUSAH DILLARD, heirs of JOHN H. DILLARD, decd.
3. NANCY DILLARD, and 4. WILLIAM DILLARD

298/140 cc confirmation of report of Commissioners, Oct. Term 1853:
1. MARY W. CAGE.
2. MARTHA W. MARTIN and husband GEORGE W. MARTIN;
3. WILLIAM DILLARD;
4. PALEMAN DILLARD & ABSOLAN DILLARD heirs of GABRIEL DILLARD, decd.
5. JOHN & SARAH DILLARD heirs of JOHN H. DILLARD, decd.
6. NANCY DILLARD, & heirs of ELIZABETH SMITH dec.

6/413 NOV. 28, 1854,Administrators deed, WILLIAM DILLARD admr. ESTATE
NANCY DILLARD, decd.

14/451 WD Dec. 3, 1873 J. W. HOLT et ux, LUCETIA to G. W. CLUCK

24/36 deed Aug. 6, 1879 G. W. CLUCK et ux H. L., to trustees of THE
BRUSHY SCHOOL, J. STEWART, G. W. CLUCK & G. P. McCREA

71/302 WD Aug. 6, 1894 GEORGE W. CLUCK et ux H. L. to son EMMETT CLUCK

148/300 WD Jan. 5, 1911 G. W. CLUCK et ux H. L. to son C. A. CLUCK

151/623 deed Feb. 28, 1913 G. W. CLUCK et ux H. L. to son ALVINCLUCK

PC 2534 Williamson Co. G. W. CLUCK d. 8/23/1920 will of G. W. & H. L.
CLUCK husband and wife, Cedar Park, Williamson Co. Texas, dated July 3
1919 filed July 30, 1924 to heirs; MRS. ALLIE A. CLUCK ANDERSON, GEO.E,
EWELL S., CLARENCE A., JOHN O., JULIA M. CLUCK FRIEDSAM, DAVID A.,
ALVIN G., THOMAS E. CLUCK; grandchildren, Ch. dau. HARRIET M.CLUCK
MASON, decd. LONNIE (MASON) DORROH, LOUISA MASON SHERMAN & JULIE
MASON, appoints sons and dau. ALLIE A. CLUCK ANDERSON, Austin, GEO. E.
CLUCK, DAVID A. CLUCK, CLARENCE A. CLUCK & THOMAS E. CLUCK of Cedar
Park, EWELL S. CLUCK of Waco; ALVIN B. CLUCK Austin, JOHN O. CLUCK of
San Bernadino, Calif. JULIA CLUCK FRIEDSOM of Waco. and JOHN MASON
of Taylor, Texas.

317/281 aff. July 21, 1943 CLARENCE A. CLUCK, Williamson Co. m. MRS.
MYRTLE H. he d. April 13, 1933, 1 child MRS. MILDRED L. CAMPBELL wife
of FOREST G.

16/169 ROBERT C. THAXTON to GEO. F. ALFORD, C. W. HURLEY, T. W.FOLTS,
W. B. NORRIS McLEMORE, L. C. ROUNDTREE, B. R. DAVIS, G. S.MINGER,
W. J. CLARK, M. H. BONNER, J. R. HENRY, W. G. VEAL, F. A. MOODY,
Trustees Texas University Sept. 1, 1873.CHARTERED as   SOUTHWESTERN
UNIVERSITY 1875.

67/554 deed Nov. 21, 1892 LOBAN STEWART heirs by T. M. HOUGHTON agent,
(1) P. L. STEWART, SUSAN C. McCLURE & J. N. STEWART of Williamson Co.
Tex. (2) JESSE DOUGLAS & NANCY DOUGLAS Of Erath Co. Texas (3) A. J. &
T. J. STEWART, Burnet Co. Tex. (4) MAY JANE NELSON of Gonzales Co.Tex
(5) E. M. NIERHOFF, Sanonro Co.? Calif. (6) J. W. & LAURA L. GARRISON
of McCLENNAN CO. Tex (7) JOHN W. & MARY A. ANDERSON of Gillespie Co.
(8) W. F. STEWART, MARY A. & J. S. TABER, Barry C., Mo.

3/248 WILLIAM BRATTON to Texas, Mar. 25, 1851 d. prior to 1856 survived
by: 1 child WILLIAMETTA BRATTONand wife AMANDA; WILLIAMETTA m. in Travis
Co. Tex. Jan. 12, 1871, FRANKLIN (B. F.) McNEESE, and had: MOLLIE F. m
G. W. ASHER, T. R. McNEESE, EDD McNEESE, ELLEN m. W. R. SMITH, L. M.,
AMANDA m. J. M. ARCHER, LINA B. m. J. H. SMITH, BEN, W. E. & C. W..
(The house of this family is just across the Travis Co.Williamson Co.
line, and their cemetery is just inside the Williamson Co. line, on old
Merrilltown Road)

304/415 PATENT Dec. 11, 1841 REPUBLIC of TEXAS to ELISHA ALLEN (A/149)
Surveyors record shows T.A.GRAVES, depty. surveyor of Nashville Colony

4/42 Wd June 5, 1851 ELISHA ALLEN to JOHN B. CAMP, J. B. HARNS, G. B. REED. Ack. before G. B. REED cc Grimes Co. Texas

10/507 deed J. B. CAMP to H. M. RUTLEDGE

10/416 deed Sept. 24, 1867 J. B. CAMP of Grimes Co. to heirs of SUSAN RUTLEDGE my dau. and decd. wife of W. P. RUTLEDGE, Williamson Co. Tex. SAM A. RUTLEDGE, ANNIE E. HOUGHTON, JOHN T. RUTLEDGE & FRANKLIN RUT-LEDGEto be equally divided whenyoungest reaches 21 years of age

55/155 Wd Nov. 1, 1890 FRANK RUTLEDGE et ux MARTHA A.

49/315 Wd Aug. 17, 1889 FRANK RUTLEDGE et ux ALICE to T. M. HOUGHTON, WM. CHAPMAN & J. P. GLENN, trustees of School Dist. No. 5.

1/400 Jan. 20, 1839 dissolution of partnership made 1835 THOS. B.HULING HENRY MILLARD & GEO. W. GLASSCOCK: MORGAN C. HAMILTON of King Co. Ny agent for GEO. W. GLASSCOCK June 2, 1854

1/20 TRANSFER TITLE CERT. CLEMENT STUBBLEFIELD to THOS. B. HULING Feb. 20, 1836; says STUBBLEFIELD came to Texas 1836 Feb., from Tenn. single man. WIT: L. B. WALTERS, WM. DOBBS, Jasper Co. Ack. JOSEPH MOTT cj

May 13, 1851 WM. I. or L. ANDERSON & MARY A. KNIGHT file for letters of administration of DR. WM. KNIGHT decd. apprs. SAML. ALEXANDER, NEAL McGAFFEY, G. W. LEMONS, B. GOOCH, W. C. DALRYMPLE, MARY A. KNIGHT, apl. on minors: JAMES, MARTHA, CAROLINE, JOSEPH B., ELIZA & NANCY.

47/407 1887 WM. KNIGHT left 0Nly heirs: MARY A. KNIGHT, JAMES, MARTHA, J. B., ELIZA, NANNIE K. FOSTER & CAROLINE D. EUBANK (CYRUS EUBANK m. CAROLINE Feb. 12, 1863) JACOB B. HARRELL & W. H. MARTIN, appraisers

176/590 1916 and 119/167, 1906 JOSEPH ROBERTSON d. Feb. 28, 1900, in Williamson Co. Tex.; m. 3 times: (1)...d. Ark. had CHARLOTTE m. E. S. HARRIS, EUGENE ROBERTSON left Williamson Co. prior to 1906; (2) m. H. A. F. (X) arkansas, before coming to Texas she d. Feb.26, 1898: GREEN F. (L) ROBERTSON et ux MARY, M. V. ROBERTSON et ux M. E., P. N. (PERRY N.) et ux M. E., JNO. W. et ux JESSIE, C. J. (CYNTHIA) m. J.D. HALL, had dau. ANN ETHEL HALL; C. C. ROBERTSON m. JOHN Y. YARBROUGH, SALLIE E. ROBERTSON m. W. T. PAYNE no. ch. d. May 1903; (3) m. N. J... still living 1916 no children

March 10, 1836, certificate 1476 acres..WM. GRAY to GEO. W. GLASSCOCK, trustee SAMUEL PHARRASS, WM. DABBS, THOS. DUGEN & C. H. DELANCY

81/44 Feb. 9, 1897 to W. C. KING et ux AMANDA

108/313 TRANSFER OF LAND CERT. Sept. 4, 1838, BOARD OF LAND COMMRS. JASPER CO. to NATHANIEL H. COCKRAN, ASSIGNEE of CHARLES COCHRAN & GEO. W. GLASSCOCK says CHAS. COCHRAN arrived in this country in Oct. - 1835. WIT: R. W. PENNAL, clk. JAMES ARMSTRONG PRIST, THOS. B. HULING & H. W. SUDDUTH, associate commr. cc before WM. MYERS NP Jasper Co. Republic of Tex. H. I. SHELBY depty surveyor signed at Zavala Sept. 4, 1838.

1/365 deed July 31, 1849 G. W. GLASSCOCK to GREENLEAF FISK. WIT: CALVIN BARKER , G.T. WILLIAMS

7/120 deed Feb. 16, 1857 GREENEAF FISK to JOHN FAUBION. WIT: JAMES W. WILLIAMSON & JAS. McSWEENY.

ESTATE MARY A. FISK, decd. wife of GRENELEAF FISK apl. dated April 26 1858. TAYLOR SMITH, SR., ANTHONY SMITH & WM. R. WARE, APPRAISERS

8/7 JAMES B. FISK to GREENLEAF FISK Aug. 19, 1859

8/8 Sept. 1, 1859 deed ANN ELIZABETH CASHION et virTHOMAS J. to GREEN-LEAF FISK.

151/86 Aff. April 12, 1913 ANN ELIZABETH FAUBION was dau. of...CASHION wife of THOMAS J. and dau. of GREENLEAF FISK & MARY ANN who d.1853;Ch: this affiant and JAMES B. FISK, WILLIAM A. FISK, JOSIAH FISK,MARY and MARGARET J. who d. when 12 years old; affiant now wife of J. M. FAUBION

293/525 PATENT to JACOB M. HARRELL, Mar. 16, 1841. (This is what is known as OLD ROUND ROCK, TEXAS)

PC Williamson Co. filed Sept. 10, 1853 to HON. W. I. ANDERSON, CJ,JAMES G. HARRELL & MARY HARRELL (surviving wife) that JACOB M. HARRELL d. Aug.23, 1853, VENTRESS & HUGHES, attys. WILL: (Vol.2/138 PC Min) dated August 22, 1853; to wife and bro. JAMES HARRELL until son JOHN returns from Calif. JOHN to be executor with wife and guardian of dau. EUER (EMMA?); son ANDERSON HARRELL and wife, devisees. WIT: R. B. PUMPHREY, THOS. C. ELGIN, THOS. OATS, JAMES BOYCE, RICHARD SANSOM, appraisers. Application to partition Jan. 31, 1854; JOHN,ANDERSON J. & EMA (minor) only heirs. MARY sur. wife. Report of Comms. JOHN W. WILBARGER, R. D. McANELLY, STEPHEN A. BOYCE, D. C. COWAN, surveyor.

6/614 Aug. 30, 1856 A. J. HARRELL et ux to FRANKLIN JOHNSTON

8/140 May 17, 1860 FRANKLIN JOHNSTON to T. B. ASHER

7/354 Mar. 27, 1858 A. J. HARRELL et ux to L. S. ROBERTSON

8/211 Mar. 30, 1858 ANDERSON J. HARRELL et ux DORTHULA, to AMMA B. NAPIER

10/54 April 17, 1863 J. B. NAPIER et ux EMMA B. to J. W. LEDBETTER, joins T. B. ASHER, MRS. PETER BOWMAN, Round Rock SEMINARY JOINT STOCK CO., MRS. DEMASSEE, DR. BLACK.

64/473 May 6, 1893 MARTHA BLAIR to ROBERT J. YANCEY, sells old GEO. D. BLAIR homestead, next to J. W. SILLURE, G. N. CRIM

139/521 aff. by GEO. W. GLASSCOCK, JR. 64 years 1910, ANNIE E. GLASS- COCK was his sister m. (1) F. M. HALL who d. and (2) W. C. ALLEN

Feb. 8, 1858 WILL: GEO. W. GLASSCOCK, Williamson Co. dau. MARGARET C. BOATNER, GEO. W. GLASSCOCK, JR., ELIZA J. LOGAN, ALBERT H. GLASSCOCK, ANDREW J. GLASSCOCK, SARAH J. and dau. ANNIE E.

151/229 PATENT to GREENLEAF FISK land in Colonization of State of Coahuila & Texas by ROBERT LEFTWICK, April 15, 1825 and conceded to NASHVILLE CO. Oct. 15, 1827; 1 league in now Williamson Co. by GUILLERMO H. STEELE (Rubric)by MILES F. SMITH, asst. Rubric and ELIJAH S. C. ROBERTSON.

151/231 PATENT to GREENLEAF FISK, assignee of W. H. MONROE Sept. 16, 1845

151/232 PATENT to GREENLEAF FISK assignee HENRY GARMES Sept. 19, 1845. (This might be GRIMES or GOVER)

210/493 PATENT July 28, 1849 (Cert. May 3, 1841) to GREENLEAF FISK, assignee of L. B. JOHNSON(Milam Dist.) by Bd. of Land Commrs. Bastrop Co. surveyors June 1840 LUCIUS B. JOHNSON by ALLEN S. HALDERMAN, sur= veyor G. FISK, & D. FRILEY, chainmen, PATENTED July 28, 1849.

8/6 Deed Aug. 16, 1859 WM. A. FISK, son to GREENLEAF FISK, all his interest in community property MARY ANN (his mother) and MARGARET JANE (his sister) WIT: THOS. J. CASHION, OTTO KREMPKOW (?)

8/7 deed Aug. 19, 1859 JAMES B. FISK to GREENLEAF FISK

8/8 deed Sept. 1, 1859 ANN ELIZABETH CASHION et vir THOMAS J. to GREENLEAF FISK

DC 444 BENJ. JOHNSON, SAMUEL CAROTHERS, WM. JOHNSON & E. A.WALKER vs GREENLEAF FISK,WM. F., JAMES FISK,THOS. CASHION,LIDIA CASHION, JOSIAH

FISK & MARY FISK recites: GREENLEAF FISK m. MARY ANN MANLOVE 1835-6-7 and had five children; that MARY ANN MANLOVE FISK d. 1853; plea of intervension filed by MARTIN J. WELL, HENDERSON UPCHURCH, ALEXANDER WATSON & JAMES COCKRAN, cites about as original petition but adds: WATSON & COCKRAN bought May 13, 1854 of GREENLEAF FISK 720 acres part of labor patent to FISK assignee of BARTHOLOMEW MANLOVE, says GREENLEAF FISK'S first wife. Amended petition says: MRS. ANN ELIZABETH CASHION is commonly known as LIDIA; JOE A. HOUGHTON & F. W. CHANDLER atty. at law, appointed guardian ad litem minors: JOSIAH & MARY FISK, above filed prior to Sept. Term 1859; Amended petition filed Sept. 16 1859 by JAMES & NICHOLAS BRANCH & JOHN F. HEINATZ of Williamson Co. and E. C. MAULDIN of Lavaca Co. Judgment says ELISHU C. MAULDIN, intervenors: MARTIN J. WELLS, HENDERSON UPCHURCH, ALEXANDER WATSON & JAMES COCHRAN.

122/588 deed April 25, 1907 MARY UPCHURCH to MRS. CORA MAGILL

122/587 deed April 25, 1907 CORA MAGILL et vir J. D. to W. G. UPCHURCH 1/7 interest in homestead of HENDERSON UPCHURCH decd. (MARY & HENDERSON UPCHURCH, their parents.)

PC MARY ELIZABETH UPCHURCH decd. April Term 1919 WILL: MARY ELIZABETH UPCHURCH to children; MARTHA, JOHN, MOLLIE, GREEN, CORA and heirs of PHEBE. $1.00 to dau. SARAH GEORGE UPCHURCH.

193/277 Aff. RE. H. UPCHURCH d. 1892 left MATTIE L. WAGONER, widow; A. P. WAGONER, JOHN, W. G. WAGONER, MOLLIE HYLAND, widow, WILL HYLAND PHOEBE HALL, widow, A. W. HALL, SARAH G. UPCHURCH & CORA MAGREILL wife of J. D.; MARY E., widow H. UPCHURCH d. Feb. 6, 1919; JOHN, above d. Nov. 26, 1919, left his widow, LIZZIE & RUBY UPCHURCH fs, about 30 yrs of age; BERTHA UPCHURCH fs. about 28 years of age; ZORA UPCHURCH about 25 years fs.and OLA CHAPMAN wife of MASON CHAPMAN; PHEBE HALL d. 1899 left A. W. HALL sur. husband and R. B. HALL & FRANK HALL over 21 years

305/90 Aff. by J. E. BULLOCK, Dec. 17, 1940 says son of B. W. BULLOCK & MARTHA KNIGHT both decd. WM. KNIGHT d. prior to Aug. 14, 1869, survived by MARY A. KNIGHT, widow and six children. Does not name children.

21/306 WILLIAMSON COUNTY, TEXAS, to JOHN SPARKS Feb. 8, 1879.

133/148 1908 NANCY ELNORA SPARKS, 50 years old 1908, widow of JOHN SPARKS of Reno, Washu Co. Nevada and BENTON H. SPARKS, son 26 years old 1908; JOHN SPARKS d. May 22, 1908, Washoe Co. Nev. cc from Washoe Co. Nev. CHAS. M. SPARKS son 23 years, LELAND SPARKS 20 years.

116/194 QC MRS. MAUDE SPARKS MACKENZIE 30 years 1908, she was born in Lampasas Co. Texas, and husband J. A. MacKENZIE to father JOHN, all right. title and interest in estate of mother RACHEL SPARKS d. Feb. 14, 1879 of Williamson Co. and sister MAUD RACHAEL KNIGHT SPARKS d. Dec. 6, 1881.

PATENT to DAVID CURRY July 21, 1851 issued Feb. 5, 1838.

5/175 Jan. 3, 1852 DAVID CURRY to CASPAIN C. SEAY. wit: of RICHARD SANSOM, L. HAWKINS before G. GOOCH, ccc Williamson Co. Tex.

5/176 Jan. 6, 1854 CASPIAN SEAY et ux NANCY to PETER ROBERTSON, WIT: SHAD. R. EGGAN, JOSEPH R. ARNOLD.

PC PETER ROBERTSON decd. filed Sept. 27, 1859, LYDIA A. wife: He d. Sept. 22, 1857; WILL to wife, LYDIA A. ROBERTSON for life 1/2 to his sister and brother and 1/2 to her sister and brother. WIT: ED. H. VENTREES, W. A. DAVIS, PETER (X) ROBERTSON Nov. 18, 1856. JAMES H. HARRELL, JAMES PADDOCK, A. C. TAYLOR, appraisers.

12/432 April 1, 1870 LYDIA A. ROBERTSON to JOHN W. SNYDER before JOHN T. RICKS, NP Williamson Co. Tex

5/420 Sept. 29, 1851 DAVID CURRY to FRANKLIN SMALLEY. WIT: A. L. MURRY, JAMES DAWSON

10/159 May 26, 1883, JAMES K. SMALLEY et ux SINTHA A. (X) to ERZA S. SCOTT, ack. Burbon Co. Kan. by JAMES K. SMALLEY and wife, before K. K. CALDWELL, DAVID R. COBB ccc Burbon Co. Kan.

10/188 April 27, 1866 E. S. SCOTT et ux ELIZABETH J. to WM. A. M. SMALLEY before J. C. BLACK NP Williamson Co. Tex.

7/71 April 16, 1856 DAVID A. CURRY to ROBERT ELLER wit: M. FARLEY before FRANKLIN JOHNCON CJ Williamson Co.

7/109 ROBERT W. ELLER et ux MARGARET E.

4/188 Jan. 1, 1853 MARY ANN BUTLER to ZACHARIAN K. HERNDON

6/524 JUly 2, 1856 R. W. ELLER et ux MARGARET to Z. K. HERNDON

PA Feb. 8, 1871 JOHN W. TAYLOR, ISAAC M. TAYLOR sons and heirs of A. C. TAYLOR, SR., decd. and MATHILDA TAYLOR former wife of A. C. TAYLOR, SR. to A. C. TAYLOR, ack. S. M. JONES, Limestone County, Tex

DC 132 A. C. TAYLOR admr. EST. A. C. TAYLOR, decd. filed Jan. 23, 1874 vs. J. J. BRUCE, MRS. DORCUS S. TAYLOR, temporarily residing in Colorado Co. Texas, but residence is in Williamson Co. Texas

32/258 Jan. 12, 1882 J. W. SNYDER to J. D. WULFGIN, J. W. SNYDER. ack. before JNO. K. JEFFREY ccc District Wyo. Territory

33/115 Jan. 12, 1882 J. W. SNYDER et ux C. J. before JOHN K. JEFFREY Clerk DC 1st Dist. Wyo. Territory (Laramie Co.)

7/159 May 19, 1857 R. H. TOBIN to A. C. TAYLOR, 252 ac. Colorado Co. on west bank of Colorado River, part of PRESTON GIEBER survey being former residence of A. C. TAYLOR sold to R. H. TOBIN

PA 8/440 June 10, 1861 A. C. TAYLOR to JNO. W. TAYLOR.."A. C. TAYLOR is indebted to his son JOHN W. TAYLOR and his heirs for estate through decd. mother MILITA TAYLOR."

13/11 Jan. 5, 1871 A. C. TAYLOR to DUDLEY H. SNYDER all interest A. C. TAYLOR & J. B. TAYLOR & B. G. TAYLOR

13/397 Oct. 12, 1871, SARAH C. TAYLOR WARD et vir SYLVESTER (dau. A. C. TAYLOR, SR.)

PATENT Nov. 7, 1835 to ELISHA (ELIJA) D. HARMON, C. C. GIVENS, Commrs. & WM. H. STEELE, Com. NASHVILLE COLONY contracted ROBERT SEFTWICK, April 15, 1825 granted Nashville Col. Oct. 15, 1827; begins at corner of SAMUEL HAZLETT sur. and TUMLINSON sur. at town of Viesco, Nov. 7, 1835, Guillerno H. STEEL, asst. WIT: ELIJAH S. C. ROBERTSON, asst.WIT: NILES F. SMITH, General LAND Office, Houston, Mar. 20, 1838, THOMAS G. WESTON, translator, JOHN P. BORDEN, Comr. G. Ld. Office: JAMES HOWLETT, district surveyor.

2/376 PA Feb. 3, 1849 ELIJAH D. HARMON to JOSIAH FISK, WIT: S. M. SKINNER, S. G. SNEED before JOSEPH LEE, NP by SKINNER, wit.

11/250 Mar. 22, 1853 GREENLEAF FISK to CHAS. BABCOCK, adj. CHAS.BABCOCK survey. WIT: THOMAS P. HUGHES, ED. H. VENTRESS, NP Williamson Co.Tex

5/607 Jan 10, 1855 CHARLES BABCOCK to JAS. W. WHIPPLE, Williamson Co.

PATENT to MILTON HICKS, sm 8 leagues; arrived in Texas prior to Mar. 2 1835 "for wounds received at the battle of Velasco 1832 and which is a permanent disability" EDWIN WALLER, pres. A. C. HYDE, assn. commr. State of Texas, Dist. of Milam April 15, 1849. Cert. by Bd. of Land Commrs. for Brazoria Co. in Williamson Co. Beg. at SE corner TALBOT CHAMBERS lea. E. line of MOSES S. HORNSBY 1/3 league, DOVER WALTER CAMPBELL 1/4 league.

DC 129 MARY HICKS et al vs. R. E. J. & NICHOLAS GOODLETT, PHIL CLAIBORN
& GEO. W. PASCHELL, atty. ptf. MARY HICKS, heir at law (mother) of
MILTON HICKS, decd; JOSEPH H. PRESLEY, H. & AMANDA H. WILEY, CATHERINE
H. SUBLETT et vir; SAML., SARAH H. NEIGHBORS et vir, WM. NEIGHBORS &
JAMES W. HICKS, vs. BURKETT B. BOWMAN, PETER BOWMAN, JOHN DAVIS,
SHEPPARD BAKER, JOSIAH B. DAVIS, WM. A. CLOUD, JOSIAH FISK, ELISHA D.
HARMON, JOHN NICHOLAS, JAMES R. E. GOODLET, JOSEPH, MARY, PRESLEY &
AMANDA HICKS, residents of Indiana; CATHERINE, SAMUEL, SARAH & WILLIAM
of Ky. JAMES W. HICKS, of Mo.; BURKETT B. & PETER BOWMAN, JOHN DAVIS,
SHEPPARD BAKER, JOSIAH B. DAVIS, WM. A. CLOUD, residents of Williamson
Co. Tex; JOSIAH FISK, TCT ELISHA D. HARMON, JOHN GOODLETT, NICHOLAS
GOODLETT & R. E. GOODLET, are non residents; says MILTON HICKS d.
young 1839;1852 JAMES HICKS, father of MILTON HICKS d. intestate; Nov.
11, 1839, administration Bastrop Co. CHARLES K. REESE Admr. located
land cert. No. 718; ELISHA D. HARMON, family never came to Texas,
resided in Chicago, Ill.; JOHN & NICHOLAS GOODLET, sons of JAMES R. E.
GOODLETT of Indiana; JAMES FISK, chair carrier, was under 14 years;
field notes dated April 51, 1849; BARTLETT HICKMAN, cert. No. 192,
Vol. 1, page 546 Williamson Co. DC Min. Sept. 11, 1857, JURY: JAMES
O. RICE, KING FISHER, TAYLOR SMITH, SR., PHILIP MINER, J. T. MILAM,
J. W. ATKINSON, C. A. D. CLAMP, WM. AKE, JOHN CORNELISON, JOSEPH
AKE & TAYLOR SMITH, JR.

12/598 Nov. 2, 1870 QC to ISAAC D. HARMON (heirs of ELIJAH D. HARMON
decd.) Suffold Co. Mass. H. LOUISA HARMON & LILLIAN HARMON, Cook
Co. Ill. EDWIN C. HARMON et ux ELLA C.

12/600 Oct. 1, 1870 WITHYAN L. BURLEY heir of ELIJAH D. HARMON &
heir ARTHUR G. BURLEY of Cook Co. Ill.

PATENT Oct. 5, 1847 to ISAAC BUNKER

12/208 June 2, 1859 HANNA MILLER (CHAS. F. MILLER) heir of ISAAC BUNKER
ISAAC BUNKER, JR., & JOSEPH BUNKER who d. in Republic of Texas, to JOHN
E. KING, on Salado, Branch of Little River; S. CAROTHERS, N. W. Cor,
Y. DAVIS, E. line and N. MOORE, south cor. ROBUCKS survey, WIT: O.
KELLER, NICHOLAS NOEL, ack. before T. H. BAGBY, Judge PC Seneca Co.Ohio
ATTACHED IS EXHIBIT "A", aff. by R. H. MONTGOMERY "practical" surveyor
July 1884, surveyed south line of JAMES WALLA LEA. from N. E. COR.
ALEXANDER EWELL survey as patented out by AARON ROBBINS, an old
citizen and A. ROBINSON Said the 6 live oak corner were pointed out to
him by MATHIAS WILBARGER, surveyor 30 years ago, and JAMES A. RUMSEY
an old surveyor living near.

37/421 Aff. filed June 25, 1885 by JOHN E. KING says SYLVIA KING, for-
merly S. BUNKER, PILEG BUNKER, JUSTIN H. BUNKER, MATHIHALBELL B.
KINNEAR, FRANCIS KINNEAR, LIZZIE BUNKER, SLOCUM H. BUNKER, HENRY BUNKER
THOMAS S. BUNKER & HANNAH B. MILLER are all the heirs of ISAAC BUNKER
decd. and that HENRY G. & FRANK A.KING, NANNIE M. HARGROVE & C. A.
MURRAY are all the heirs of H. C. A. & E. A. KING the former being decd.

6/13 PA July 2, 1853 PILEG BUNER et al ack. in Morrow Co. Ohio, states
the ESTATE in TEX AS which has descended to us from our father ISAAC
BUNKER decd. and his two sons, our brothers ISAAC & JOSEPH both decd.
to JOHN E. KING

6/16 July 8, 1853 SLOCUM H. BUNKER & MATILDA B. (husband wife) Calhoun
Co. Mich.

12/224 Mar. 17, 1857 deed PILEG BUNKER et al to JOHN E. KING says
ISAAC BUNKER father and ISAAC BUNKER, JR. and JOSEPH, all d. in
Republic of Texas; MIHITABEL B. KINNEAR et vir FRANCIS

10/552 Mar. 31, 1860 JOHN E. KING et ux SYLVIA KING, Williamson Co.ack
11/64 HIRAM WOOD to W. J. DONNELL Sept. 9, 1868

16/347 April 27, 1875 W. J. DONNELL et ux MANERVA ANN DONNELL

DC 2553 filed Dec. 26, 1889 by MRS. EUNICE DONNELL sur. wife of W. J.
DONNELL who d. 1885 intestate vs. C. E. DONELL & ED WILEMAN says she m.
W. J. DONNEL Dec. 14, 1879

PC 522 1889 JAMES B. SHAVER of Williamson Co. asks to be appointed
gdn. of FANNIE DONNELL 18 y. who resides with petitioner in Williamson
Co. and CORA DONNELL 15 y. who resides with B. H. BUCHANAN in Fisher
Co. Texas. DONNELL place south of Corn Hill, Williamson Co.

68/521 deed Mar. 14, 1893 to W. A. QUATTLEBAUM, EUNICE DONNELL sur.
wife W. J. DONNELL decd.,, ALICE DONNELL WILEMAN et vir ED. (sgd.J.E.)
WM. DONNELL, ED DONNELL, FANNIE D. BRIDGES et vir GILFORD (sgd.W.G.)
BELL D. SHAVER et vir JAMES, & JOHN McDOUGLE, ANA & DORA DONNELL, CORA
COX et vir W. H. COX,(Fisher Co. Texas) EMMA WALKER, F. I. WALKER,
M. A. (Zura) BURNHAM & B. H. BURNHAM, Sept. 1893, ETTA MAY McDOUGLE dau
JOHN &___13 years.

149/93 aff. W. J. DONNELL, decd. survived by wife, EUNICE, dau. ALICE
WILEMAN, FANNIE BRIDGES, BELL SHAVER, CORA(X) COX, EMMA WALKER, ZURA
(M. A. or MISSOURI) BURNHAM sons W. H. DONNELL, C. E. DONNELL and his
gd. ETTA MAY McDOUGLE

PATENT Aug. 4, 1853 granted Feb. 6, 1838 to EDMUND PARSONS

38/568 Oct. 4, 1853 EDMUND PARSONS to E. J. PARSONS WIT: W. B. GOODE
& HENRY CLIBURN, Jasper Co. Texas

38/569 Oct. 4, 1853 EDMUND PARSONS to CRAGG PARSONS WIT: W. R. GOODE,
HENRY CLIBURN

38/257 cc from Tyler Co. Texas of gdn. ZENUS PARSONS for JACIN PARSONS
says minor resided with petitioner from 1876 signed. E. J. PARSONS

17/644 deed July 19, 1876 to B. L. OWEN son and only heir of F. C. OWEN
decd. of Lawrence Co. Ala., by CRAGG PARSONS of Dallas Co...ZENUS PAR-
SONS Ind. extr. and gd. E. J. PARSONS, SR., W. A. PARSONS, MARGARET PAR-
SON GOODE only sur. heirs of EDMUND PARSONS decd. our father late of
Tyler Co. Texas, to make good a title bond dated April 23, 1852
EDMUNDS PARSONS to F. C. OWEN: WIT: E. S. PARSONS

30/164 Jan. 29, 1878 B. L. OWEN of Lawrence Co. Ala. to J. T. HUGGINS

5/170 JAMES O. IRVINE et ux SARAH J. Liberty Co. Tex. Jan. 1, 1840 to
THOS. H.ESPY of Jasper Co. Texas (JAMES C. IRVINE sur. Pat. Dec. 31,
1845)

5/172 Jan. 2, 1847 THOS. H. ESPY et ux ELIZABETH M.

88/633 Sept. 4, 1876 THOMAS HODGSON to PATRICK BOURKE, bothof New
Orleans, La. conveys interest in decd. mother's estate, MARY HODGSON
P C. 2nd Dist. Parish of Orleans.

BAGDAD CEMETERY, Williamson Co. Texas:
JOHN SAUL Mar. 29, 1794 d. 70 y. 5 mos. 11 d.
DICY SAUL, 3/5/ 1798 1/9/1861
SARAH HAMILTON 9/21/1787 10/5/1871
JOHANNA E., wife of ANDY HAMILTON 11/2/1833 10/9/1912
ANDY HAMILTON 2/2/1827 9/25/1908
THOS. HAILE b. 3/6/1824 in union Dist. S. C. 10/24188...
JOHN HAILE b. S. C. 1/14/1842 2/24/1864
JOHN FAUBION b. Cock Co. E. Tenn. 2/8/1812 d. 1906
ELIZ ABETH STEPHENS wife of JOHN FABION, b. CockeCo. Tenn.
W. N. CAROTHERS b. S. C. 12/4/1825 9/25/1864?
MARGARET CAROTHERS 5/5/1790 2/5/1859
MARY J. MASON b. 3/ 31/1822 in Mecklenberg Co. N. C. 1/23/1897
C. C. MASON 5/5/1818 5/2/1865
BENJ. LEVITT 1/5/1812 8/12/1868
LUCINDA LEVITT 10/18/1830 8/7/90
GEORGE CRAVEN 10/18/08 7/1/1894_ JANE CRAVEN 8/13/1813 2/19/1888

ELIZABETH G. CLOUD 9/23/1818 5/9/1881
WM. A. CLOUD 10/26/1810 5/27/1870
ROBERT CARROLL THAXTON b. Warren Co. Tenn. 3/1/1815 5/28/1897
JOHN N. QUEEN b. Ga. 12/12/1857...

2/376 PA Feb. 3, 1849 ELIJAH D. HARMON to JOSIAH FISK. WIT: S. M. SKINNER, G. L. SNEED

5/568 Jan. 1, 1850 JOSIAH FISK to GREENLEAF FISK. WIT: B. MENEFEE, WM. A. FISK

4/250 Mar. 22, 1853 GREENLEAF FISK to CHAS. BABCOCK. WIT: THOMAS P. HUGHES, ED H. VENTRESS

NOTE in Williamson Co. abstract: LAND CERT. 713 issued to MILTON HICKS, that he arrived in this country prior to May 2, 1835 a single man, entitled to survey because of permanent disability wounds received in battle of Velasco 1832.

4/15/1849 STATE OF TEXAS, DIST. of Milam, survey for MILTON HICKS of Ld. Com. for Brazoria Co. corner TALBOT CHAMBERS & MOSES S. HORNSBY 1/3 lea. DOVER lea. and WALTER CAMPBELL lea. JAMES & GREENLEAF FISK, chain carriers; MATHIS WILBARGER, dep. sur. Milam Dist. JAMES HOWLETT dist. surveyor

1/300 PA Oct. 17, 1843 JAMES & MARY HICKS parents of MILTON HICKS of Floyd Co. Ind. who d. 1830 in Republic of Texas, intestate unm to JAMES R. E. GOODLETT, WIT: HARVEY A. & WM. A. SCRIBNER, NP Floyd Co. Ind.

301/1 PATENT to heirs of MOSES S. HORNSBY May 20, 1846 in Milam Co. to heirs 1/3 lea.

E/12 surveyors records Williamson Co. field notes Aug. 30, 1845land cert. issued to REUBEN HORNSBY admr. MOSES HORNSBY by Bd. Ld. Com. Bastrop Co. Feb. 2, 1838 Republic of Texas, Milam Co. MATTHIAS WILBARGER surveyor, Milam Co. G. FISK & DORSEY BIGGS, chain carriers, JAMES ROWLETT county surveyor

5/356 Sept. 8, 1847 REUBEN HORNSBY et ux SARAH TCT to THOMAS HORNSBY late of Burleson Co. Tex. WIT: ANGUS McLAURIN, R. HORNSBY

4/5 May 18, 1852 JOHN W. HORNSBY, FELIX HORNSBY of State of Miss. 2 of 5 heirs of MOSES S. HORNSBY to THOS. S. BACON of New Orleans, La. SUSANNA HORNSBY wife of JOHN & SARAH A. wife of FELIX. WIT: J. L. HARGRAVES, CHRISTOPHER (X) CAIN. ACK. for JOHN & SUSANNA, Covington Co. Miss. ack. J. L. HARGRASS, a WIT: to FELIX HORNSBY and wife, SARAH, Hinds Co. Miss.

5/499 Sept. 17, 1853 HADEN WATTS to ISAAC TONSEY 1/5 conveyed to JOHN WATTS by M. D. HORNSBY Dec. 10, 1852

DC 155, filed Mar. 26, 1854 DC Williamson Co. Tex. THOS. S. BACON of New Orleans, La. vs. heirs of MOSES HORNSBY, petition cites MOSES HORNSBY d. without children or surviving parents and had 5 bros. REUBEN, THOMAS, DUKE, JOHN & FELIX HORNSBY, THOS. HORNSBY deeded to ALUHEOUS P. RICE his son-in=law, of Burnet Co. Tex. who sold to HARMON SMELSER, resides on Colorado River and CHARLES BABCOCK of Williamson Co. FIELDING DAWSON & CHARLES SUTTLE residence unknown; JAMES W. S. WILLIAMSON, JOHN FAUBION of Williamson Co., DUKE HORNSBY sold his interest to JOHN WATTS resident on Trinity River; DUKE HORNSBY is a resident of Williamson Co.

DC WM. AKE & 11 others jury: SHF. of WILLIAMSON Co. and NICHOLAS BRANCH, GREENLIEF FISK & DAVID G. COWAN, Com. report of commissioners before JUDGE JOSIAH FISK, LEVI ASHER, shf. GREENLIEF FISK & D. C. COWAN

DC 371 filed Feb. 10, 1858 F. W. CHANDLER & A. H. CHALMERS, are atty. vs. THOS. M. HORNSBY refuses to make deed

7/361 May 5, 1858 SHF. DEED to CHARLES C. MASON

ESTATE C. C. MASON filed May 29, 1865 petition of MARY JANE MASON sur. wife, C. C. MASON d. May 2, 1865, Williamson Co. 8 minor ch: Application for inventory Aug. 26, 1865 by A. H. GRAHAM who m. MARY L. MASON. Apl. to give three heirs their shares; MRS.. MARY L. GRAHAM, A. S. MASON & JOHN D. MASON; reportof commissioners to partition Jan. 29, 1866,set off to ADLPHOUS MASON, LOUISA GRAHAM et vir DR. A. H. GRAHAM, JOHN MASON & CHAS. MASON, adult heirs; minor heirs are JAMES N., MAGGIE ADDIE, NANCY, BET &....

DC 146 Sept. 18, 1877 MARGARET C. FAUBION wife of J. H., ADELAIDE E. HANNA, wife of A. J. vs. J. N. MASON, ELIZABETH BELLE MASON, AUGUSTA A. MASON, MARY J. MASON, widow of C. C. MASON, Sr. vs. A. S. MASON, J. D. MASON, C. C. MASON, JR., MARY L. GRAHAM wife of A. H. GRAHAM, J. N. MASON, ELIZABETH BELL MASON & AUGUSTA A. MASON heirs C. C. MASON, SR. all residents of Williamson Co. NANCY MASON d. prior to July 1878 intestate and unm.

DC 3446 removal of disabilities of minority, filed June 21, 1897 on M. LILLIE HANNA by father A. J. HANNA

76/265 June 22, 1897 COOPER SANSOM sur. husband GUSSIE MASON SANSOM to MRS. MARGARET C. FAUGION, MRS. E. B. LAUCK, J. M. MASON & M. LILLY HANNA recites MRS. MARY J. MASON, decd.

DC 3447 filed June 22, 1897 petition Williamson Co. J. N. MASON, MRS. MARGARET C. FAUBION et vir J. H., MRS. E. B. LAUCK et vir T. H. vs. M. L. HANNA, recites MRS. M. J. MASON d. intestate Williamson Co. 1897 plaintiffs and defendants are all heirs; M. L. HANNA gd. and child of. ..HANNA nee MASON are all heirs.

26/10 Mar. 28, 1881 STEPHEN CUMMINGS et ux NANCY G. of TCT to DR. JOSEPHUS CUMMINGS et ux, TEXAS.

88/235 June 23, 1898, GUSTAV FRICK to FRITZ GANZERT

96/25 FRITZ GANZERT to KARL EHRHARDT Mar. 30, 1900

197/56 OIL LEASE, KARL EHRHARDT et ux FREDERIKA, 1920

9/11 deed Jan. 22, 1863 JNO. M. WHIPPLE to C. C. MASON, both Williamson County, Texas

13/693 deed June 15, 1872 K. W. YATES et ux A. P. (X) YATES to R. BUCHANAN.

P. C. 1520 filed 1907 JAMES RICHMOND BUCHANAN d. July 18, 1907, by J.T. RUTLEDGE, says his wife, MARY E. RUTLEDGE & MAGGIE BUCHANAN are sole heirs.

Aff. Dec. 9, 1910 HENRY B. MILLARD son of COL. HENRY MILLARD d. about 1843, members of firem of THOMAS B. HULING & CO. dissolved Jan. 20, 1839, two children, affiant and FREDERICK S. MILLARD d. yearsand years ago.

WILL, ANDREW J. NELSON dated May 1, 1895: five oldest children: SON: THOMAS EDWARD NELSON, dau. MARY BELL NELSON, son OSCAR ANDREW NELSON, dau. ADLA CHRISTINE NELSON, son CARL AUGUST NELSON, youngest son GEORGE WALTNER NELSON to wife, HEDWIG NELSON.
HOPEWELL CEMETERY, southwest part Williamson Co. near Burnet Co. line: CHARLES PECK, 1859, 1930, EMMA PECK 1865 1942
WILLIAM EARNEST PECK 1886 1965
BENNET J. JONES May 31, 1835, 8/7/1919
MARTHA JONES 7/25/1845 Nov. 18, 1930
G. W. THORNTON (GEO. WASHINGTON) (grandfather of THORNTON PECK, Lt.Col. USAF) 1853, 1937. SUSAN HEAD 1855, 1886 and JANE WILKES 1858, 1930.
D. M. THORNTON 7/23/1832 12/27/1922, MARGARET, wife of D. M. 5/13/1840 10/29/1888
MARY JONES 5/10/1830 6/18/1890
(NOTE: SUSAN HEAD (1) and JANE WILKES (2) were wives of G. W. THORNTON)

YOAKUM COUNTY, TEXAS.

12/27 PATENT, Jan. 13, 1907 to J. P. GILLIAM.

4/108, cc STATE of TEXAS vs. 12.293 THE LEON & H. BLUM LAND CO., THE ISLAND CITY SAVINGS BANK, LEOPOLD FELLMAN, of N. Y. and EDWARD RANDALL Galveston County, Texas. In year 1879, land in now Yoakum and Terry Counties surveyed by JOHN H. GIBSON: P. C., EDWARD RANDALL, decd.

7/355 EDWARD RANDALL, JR., filed Dec. 17, 1889, Will, Oct. 25, 1889 names nephew EDWARD MANSON and niece MRS. MARY RANDALL MANSON, and husband, W. F. MANSON, of Chicago, Ill. Estate probated in Galveston County, Texas.

7/519 Aff. Aug. 14, 1913 by EDWARD RANDALL his uncle, DR. EDWARD RANDALL, d. 1889, his wife, predeceased him, and there were no children

7/357 cc P. C. Galveston Co. Texas, MARY RANDALL MANSON d. Galveston Co. Texas, left husband, WM. F., niece HARRIET BALLINGER RANDALL, and nephew EDWARD RANDALL, JR.

13/76 Aff. EDWARD RANDALL, MILTON H. POTTER & CHAS. H. DORSEY, Galveston Co. Texas, MARY RANDALL MANSON d. Nov. 12, 1897, her husband, W. F. d. 1911; 2 children: MAY GRANT (GANTT) MANSON, wife of NOLAN V. ELLIS and EDWARD RANDALL MANSON, Cook Co. Ill..

12/28 WD Dec. 13, 1906 filed Jan. 1, 1917 J. P. GILLIAM and wife, BELL, of Hamilton Co., Texas.

12/86 WD Dec. 29, 1906, filed 1917 OTTO STOLLEY, et ux GERTRUDE E. T.CT to JAMES FUCHS, TCT

12/113 WD Feb. 6, 1917 CLYDE E. THOMAS to J. E. CLARK, Tarrant Co. Texas, aff. Yoakum Co. Texas, April 16, 1956, EDGAR FUCHS d. 1935 TCT never married, JAMES FUCHS, d. Jan. 12, 1939 m. MARIA, d. 1933; ALFRED E. W. FUCHS, EMMITT L. W. FUCHS, OLGA L. S. BOHLS, ADLAI A. BOHLS, LAURA E. A. BOHLS & WALTER O. W. FUCHS.

The original City of Austin, is what is now "DOWNTOWN AUSTIN, and is the area between West Avenue and East Avenue, from the Colorado River, north to 15th Street. The lots in the blocks on either side of CONGRESS AVENUE are 46 x 160 feet, with a 20 foot alley running north and south. Most of the other blocks have lots 69 x 129 feet with an alley running east and west. The offices of the various GOVERNMENTAL DEPARTMENTS of the REPUBLIC of TEXAS, were located on either side of CONGRESS AVENUE, which sweeps majestically from the Colorado River to the foot of the capital grounds.

The outlying area was plotted into OUTLOTS, with areas of from five (5) to forty (40) acres. These were used as garden plots, as well as farm and pasture plots for the residents of the DOWNTOWN area. Saparate patents were issued for each of the small DOWNTOWN lots as well as the OUTLOTS.

Some of the patentees of a few of the "OUTLOTS' of the original City of Austin, in addition to the "ROBERTSONS, SWISHERS and RAYMONDS", were:

THOMAS ABEL, MOSES AUSTIN (b. 1761 in Conn. d. Mo. 1820)

N. E. BERRY, MOORE BLESSING, STEPHEN W. BLOUNT, (b. Ga. 28 y. 1836, and youngest of the signers of the TEXAS DECLARATION of INDEPENDENCE, d. 1890); JOHN BRATTON, ROBERT BRATTON, MARY E. BULLOCK M. E. BURNETT, JAMES W. BYRON:

SAM. L. CARSON (b. N. C.) W. L. CEZNEAU, WM. CARROLL CRAWFORD, C. C. CUSHMAN:

CHAS. DeMERSE, RICHARD ELLIS (member of the first constitutional convention of ALABAMA. He was chosen President of the March 1836 TEXAS CONVENTION);

MASSON FARLEY, COLLIN FORBES:

ALEX T. GATE, WILLIAM FAIRFAX GRAY, BENJAMIN S. GRAYSON, BENJAMIN GRUMBLES:

ROBERT HAMILTON (from Scotland) JOHN HEMPHILL, A. HERRON, ANDREW N. HOPKINS, SAM HOUSTON:

J. JAYNE, CLAIRBORNE KYLE, WILLIAM LEVY:

T. McKEAN, COLLIN McKINNEY (B. N. J. 1766, the oldest of the signers), ROXINE MAAG, JAMES L. MALONE, ADAM MEGG, JOEL MINER, WILLIAM MOTLEY (b. Va. April 8, 1812, and first casualty of the new REPUBLIC, April 21, 1836, at San Jacinto, Harrisburg);

JOSE ANTONIO NAVARRO (b. San Antonio, educated in Spain) ANDREW NEAL:

MARTIN PARMER (b. Va. June 4, 1798, member of 1st Legislature of Missouri) JAMES POWER, (b. Ireland, 1788), JESSE PIERSON, ROBERT POTTER, (b. N. C. and a two term congressman of N. C.) STERLING C. ROBERTSON, ANDREW ROBINSON, ALEXANDER RUSSELL, FRANCISCO RUIZ, (B. San Antonio, educated in Spain), THOMAS J. RUSK;

JOHN R. SLOCUM, ANGELINA D. SMITH, JACOB SNIVELY, J. S. TAFT, HUGH TINNIN;

SARAH D. WALSH, ANDREW WECHSTER, U. WESTRICH, JOSEPH WIEHL, W. C. WING, ROBERT H. WYNNE, LORENZO de ZAVALA (b. Oct. 3, 1788 in Spain) and MICHAEL ZILLER.

Many beautiful mansions were erected in present "DOWNTOWN AUSTIN". One was by SWISHER. It was a large stately Greek revival in the block between West 4th Street and West 5th Street, on San Antonio Street. The SWISHERS lived there, but owned many hundreds of acres in the area, including two or three thousand acres in the ISAAC DECKER survey on both sides of South Congress Avenue across the Colorado River from "DOWNTOWN AUSTIN". When South Austin (now a part of Austin) was platted and laid out, the streets running east and west across South Congress Avenue were named for the SWISHER children.

The "ROBERTSONS" owned the land around the "FRENCH EMBASSY" This was built by France, during the years of the REPUBLIC of TEXAS.

The "RAYMOND" colonial house was located on north side of West 6th Street, west of Shoal Creek. The tall white columns of this house were later used to frontthe "GRACY BUILDING" 203-5 West 7th Street. (This is now UNIVERSITY of TEXAS property) These columns are now a part of the SCOTTISH RITE TEMPLE, 207 West 18th Street, Austin.

Many patents were issued for lots and/or outlots in the original City of Austin, as, or in payment for services to members of the Government of the REPUBLIC, and many others to members of the armed forces in the TEXAS war of INDEPENDENCE.

Many people came to TEXAS prior to March 1836 and at the time of the signing of the DECLARATION of INDEPENDENCE, there were some thirty (30) to forty (40) thousand non-Spanish speaking people within the present bounds of the State of TEXAS.

In 1822 ANDREW ROBINSON was a first settler and opened a ferry across the Brazos, in the present Washington County. His son-in-law, JOHN W. HALL, and his associates laid out a townsite in 1833, and it was named WASHINGTON, in honor of the birth place of DR. ASA HOXEY, who was born in Washington Co. Ga.

JOHN M. GOULD, and DR. RICHARD RODGERS PEEBLES, a pioneer TEXAS physician, were at Washington on the Brazos in 1835. Dr. PEEBLES received a grant of land for his service in the REVOLUTION and in 1841 moved to Austin County, locating where the present town of Hempstead, Waller Co. Texas, is now located. In 1843 he married MRS. MARY ANN ELIZABETH CALVIT GROCE, widow of JARED E. GROCE.(GROCE of Nueces Co.)

ROBERT POTTER, Native of N. C., THOS. J. RUSK, of S. C. and MARTIN PARMER, STEPHEN W. BLOUNT of Ga. JAMES POWER, of Ireland and DR. WM. MOTLEY were early patentees of TEXAS land.

JOHN A. VEATCH, arrived in East TEXAS when it was a province of MEXICO. He was authorized as an immigrant to select a league of land, and he chose his property in two parts, one three miles south of the present City of BEAUMONT, and the other near SOUR LAKE in present HARDIN COUNTY. When oil was discovered in TEXAS in late 1890-1900, the greatest oil discoveries were made on these two tracts of land.

The men who colonized TEXAS received their pay in land. STEPHEN F. AUSTIN was the first. PETERS and MERCER, located their colonies in and around present DALLAS, running all the way to the Red River. The CASTRO Colony was southwest of San Antonio and was settled by GERMANS and ALSATIANS, and some GERMANS settled in FISHER and MILLER colonies. Many persons of the GERMAN NOBILITY settled in and around present Fredericksburg, and New Braunfels.

The early TEXAS CENSUSES: show many persons in Travis County, Texas who were born in Tenn. and Kentucky. ROBERT BRATTON, b. Ind. wife B. in Ohio; WM. C. REAGER, b. Va. wife Ann b. N. Y.; W. P. THORP b. Pa.

wife in KY.; JOHN BUTTRY b. Yorkshire, England, wife in Ky.; F. WAHRENBERGER, b. Thusgna Switzerland, wife CATHERINE b. France du Nord; CHALRES KLEIN b. Switzerland, as was his wife, and NELSON MERRILL, b. Conn. and wife b. in Va.

The MEXICAN GOVERNMENT, wanted to either MEXICANIZE those non-SPANISH speaking people who had entered TEXAS or drive them out. It passed an ACT April 6, 1830 which forbade the entrance of settlers from the UNITED STATES. The early settlers called and held a CONVENTION at San Felipe de Austin (not the present City of Austin) to petition for the repeal of this April 6, 1830 law. This convention was held October 1, 1832.

WILLIAM H. WHARTON, STEPHEN F. AUSTIN, DR. JAMES B. MILLER and ERASMO SEGUIN and SAM HOUSTON were present as residents of TEXAS as was BEN MILAM and FRANK JOHNSON.

PASSPORTS were necessary to enter TEXAS at the Sabine River. These passports areon film at the BARKER LIBRARY, University of Texas. They show the names and ages of parents and children, and the names and ages of slaves, most of the time.

ADDENDA: (Not indexed)

The following is information which came to me through the family of BENJAMIN EUCLID EARNEST, who was a son of EUCLID MADISON EARNEST and FRANCES MATHILDA HAMILTON. An aunt of mine married BENJAMIN EUCLID EARNEST, and there were no descendants of his family.

I have furnished this information to several persons in Tennessee and California, who were related to these families. Because there were no descendants of this branch of this EARNEST, HAMILTON, WRIGHT family and because these people came originally to Milam County, Texas, and the court house there burned in 1874, I feel this information should be made available to as many persons as possible, and also because I have no descendants, and the information would be lost.

NOTE: Please, there were at least four different HAMILTON families in early Travis County, Texas, and there is no releationship between any two of them, so far as our Travis County Records show.

WILLIAM HAMILTON b. Va. Mar, 4, 1777, d. Tenn. Sept. 29, 1840, son of ALEXANDER HAMILTON, who d. ca1843 in Tenn;
m. MARGARET HUGLEY or HUWGBY 1795 in Tenn. she was b. Mar. 21, 1781 d Feb. 28, 1867 and is buried in OAKWOOD CEMETERY in Austin, Texas, they had 8 children:
1. ALEXANDER b. Sept. 10, 1807, d. Feb. 5, 1811;
2. PEGGY, b. Nov. 16, 1809, d. Oct. 16, 1813;
3. WILLIAM A. b. April 10, 1810, d. April 27, 1894, buried in OAKWOOD CEMETERY, Austin, Texas. (This is the CEMETERY provided for in the original plan of the CITY OF AUSTIN, 1839)
This man married JANE HUGLEY and had four children:
1. ELIZABETH ANN, b. Dec. 12, 1835, d. Nov. 4, 1913, buried in OAKWOOD CEMETERY, Austin, Texas; m. (1) JOHN M. TIBEAUT b. Mar. 27, 1820, d. Sept. 28, 1880, buried in OAKWOOD CEMETERY, Austin Texas; (2) ED CHAMBERS. No information on him)
TIBEAUT CHILDREN:
FANNIE S. m. JAMES M. EARNEST;
MARY J. or MOLLIE m. T. H. BOWMAN, 1881;
LUELLA, m. F. S. BOWMAN, 1881;
ANNIE S. m. T. B. WALLING, 1894;
JOHN M. TIBEAUT, JR. b. July 5, 1866, d. Dec. 11, 1905 in Carribean Sea

4. RACHEL HAMILTON m. JOSEPH WRIGHT, had:
ROBERT P. WRIGHT m. FANNIE (FRANCES) ELIZABETH EARNESTb. Jan. 12, 1848 d. Oct. 8, 1872, 2 children: LAURA m. FRED THORNE and ADA m. T. M. EARNEST, B. Jan. 20, 1857, d. Dec. 22, 1931.

FANNIE M. WRIGHT b...d. Jan. 18, 1908 m. WILLIAM GIBSON, had: A. J., EUGENE, JAMES W., LILLIE D. never married, ELLISA R. never m., WILLIAM B. and MINNIE who d. in infancey.
LOUISA WRIGHT m. GEO. W. WALLING.

5. JAMES HAMILTON, b. Aug. 30, 1814, M.
6. SAMUEL HAMILTON b. April 18, 1817, m.
7. ELIZABETH A. HAMILTON b. Aug. 19, 1819, d. Jan. 17, 1888 m. SAMUEL M. WRIGHT, b. Dec. 27, 1809 d. Nov. 15, 1893.

8. FRANCES MATHILDA, b. Oct. 24, 1825, d. Nov. 29, 1898, m. EUCLID MADISON EARNEST, b. Jan. 16, 1818, d. July 5, 1872; had:
AMANDA M. EARNEST b. July 7, 1842, d. Oct. 1, 1904, m. M. D. L. McFARLAND:
JAMES M. EARNEST b. May 18, 1849, d. Nov. 20, 1911, m. FANNIE TIBAUT:
BENJAMIN EUCLID EARNEST b. April 10, 1846, in Tenn. D. Aug. 18, 1924 m. MARY JANE FELLS SARGENT, b. Oct. 24, 1850, Miss. d. May 5, 1832, had 2 children, andneither had any children. (NOTE: It is from this family I received the inforamation herewith:)
FRANCES MATHILDA HAMILTON EARNEST and husband, EUCLID MADISON EARNEST had: AMANDA M. m....McFARLAND, JAMES WILLIAM EARNEST m. JENNIE CAIN (MARTHA on death certificate) This couple had 8 children, EARNEST couple.

MATTIE EARNEST m. TOM DIETERICH, had 6 children;
ANNA EARNEST m. JAMES MURDOCK, had 4 children;
JOSEPH SAMUEL EARNEST, never married;
ROBERT EARNEST m. LEE IVEY, had three children;
AMANDA m. McFARLAND, had threechildren;
ADDIE m. BURNETT, had 4 children;
FANNIE M.
JAMES WILLIAM EARNEST m. JENNIE CAIN, had 8 children
BENJAMIN E. EARNEST m. MARY JANE FELLS SARGENT.

* * * * *

JOHN W. HAMILTON m. SUZANNA HESSEY in Tenn. (No information on these)
JAMES R. HAMILTON, m. KATHERINE. He was a district judge in Travis
County, Texas, for many years. They had one son, who died when he
was about 19 years old, unm, no issue.

EVERETT HAMILTON, m. PRUDENCE TAYLOR. He was an M. D. in Travis County.
They had no chidren, and when he died ca, 1900, PRUDENCE, his widow
m. S. E. ROSENGREEN, and when he d. . she m. U. S. SEN. BAILEY. They
lived in Dallas, Texas. No children by any of these marriages.

F. Ella Hamilton, dau. of WM. A. HAMILTON, m._____STAMPER, in Tenn.
They had one sone and three (3) daughters. When STAMPER d. his widow
m. ....BISHOP, they had: NAOMI, SUZANNE and LENA, none had children.

JAMES N. HAMILTON m. LAVENIA BURDITT , 1863, in Travis County, Texas;
b. July 31, 1837, d. June 21, 1908. Both buried in OAKWOOD CEMETERY.
This JAMES N. HAMILTON willed hisproperty to his wife for life
with the remainder to the children of his sister ELIZABETH ANNE TIBEAUT
AND HIS DECEASED BROTHERS,   JOHN W. HAMILTON and CHARLES W. HAMILTON

CHARLES W. HAMILTON m. MARTHA LAVENIA ENGLISH, dau. Rev. EDMOND FLYNN
ENGLISH, and wife, MARY ANN (HARVE (?), according to an affidavit by
T. B. WALLING they had one child.

Graves on HAMILTON block in OAKWOOD CEMETERY, Austin, Texas:
JANE H. HAMILTON, b. 2/1/1815, d. 5/14/1898;
WILLIAM A. HAMILTON b. 4/10/1810, d. 4/27/1894;
JAMES N. HAMILTON b. 7/31/1837, d. 6/21/1908;
LAVENIA HAMILTON HESSEY b. 3/19/1844 d. 11/3/1922;
JAMES H. TIBEAUT b. 6/22/1856 d. 12/1/1857. (According to tradition
this man came from New Orleans, La.)
WILLIAM H. TIBEAUT 1/14/1855 d. 6/12/1855;
JOHN M. TIBEAUT, JR. b. 7/5/1866 (lost in Carribean Sea, Dec. 11,1905"
ELIZABETH A. CHAMBERS b. 1/12/1835 d. 11/4/1913;
JOHN M. TIBAUT, b. 3/27/1820 d. 9/28/1880. On the northeast corner
of the JOSEPH & RACHEL WRIGHT block is the grave marker for MARGARET
HAMILTON, b. 3/21/1781, d. 2/28/1867)

The earliest record of JOSEPH WRIGHT in Travis County, Texas, which I
have found from the records was 1855. SAMUEL WRIGHT registered his
cattle brand 1854.

Marriage records in Travis County, Texas:
1856, Vol. 1, p. 247 CHARLES HAMILTON to MARTHA MASTERSON;
1863 Vol. 2, p. 148, JNO. N. HAMILTON to L. BURDITT;
1854, Vol. 1, page 171, ELIZABETH HAMILTON to JOHN M. TIBAUT:
1883 MRS. ELIZABETH A. TIBAUT to ED CHAMBERS.

Affidavit dated Feb. 16, 1924, made by T. B. WALLING, recorded Vol. 359
p. 320, TCT:
As of June 2nd, 1894 (date of J. N. HAMILTON WILL) the children of
ELIZABETH ANN CHAMBERS, were: MRS. FANNIE S. EARNEST, MRS. MARY B. BOW-
MAN, MRS. LUCILE BOWMAN and MRS. ANNIE L. WALLING (wife of T. B.)

The children of JOHN W. HAMILTON, were: JAMES R. HAMILTON and MRS. F.
ELLA BISHOP, and the child of CHAS. W. HAMILTON was CHAS. W. HAMILTON
and that they remained alive after the death of LAVENIA HAMILTON:

DEED: dated Feb. 1, 1924 of 202.66 acres,(now in City of Austin) recorded Vol. 359, page 321 et seq. Travis County Deed Records: (NOTE: This was the home of JOSEPH WRIGHT, and was occupied by various descendants until $_{1}$924, when it was sold, it is signed by:

D. H. DOOM, surviving independent executor of the will of LAVENIA HAMILTON HESSEY, decd; JAMES R. HAMILTON, and wife, katherine; Mrs. F. ELLA BISHOP, widow, MRS. MARY J. BOWMAN, widow, MRS. LUELLA BOWMAN widow, MRS. ANNIE L. WALLING, and husband T. B. WALLING, all TCT, MRS. FANNIE S. EARNEST, widow, Dallas Co. Texas, and CHAS. W. HAMILTON and wife, HATTIE, Maury Co. Tenn.

Vol. S, page 128 TCT. This deed is W. A. HAMILTON, and wife, JANE H. to E. A. M. TEABAUT (ELIZABETH..she was sister of W. A. HAMILTON. This deed recites that WM. A. HAMILTON was a resident of Milam Co. Texas, and is dated April 15, 1869 to JOSEPH WRIGHT, brother-in-law to W. A. HAMILTON.

WILL, JAMES N. HAMILTON, who d. TCT June 21, 1908 and probated in Cause No. 3199, TCT rec. Vol.25, p. 364 Probate Records: To his wife LAVENIA HAMILTON, for life, then to my nephews and nieces, the children of my sister ELIZABETH ANN CHAMBERS, and the children of my brother JOHN W. HAMILTON, decd, and the son of my bro. CHAS. W. HAMILTON,decd to be divided on death of my wife, LAVENIA.

LAVENIA HAMILTON'S will dated 1909, she d. 1922, and the will is probated in Cause No. 5567 TCT recorded Vol. 47, page415, TCT: $500.00 to FISKVILLE CEMETERY, TCT where my father and mother are buried... to sister LOUISA D. PIPER, wife of R. A. PIPER, to sister MRS. E. A. CHAMBERS, mentions her decd. husband, JAMES N. HAMILTON Aug. 5, 1920, LAVENIA HAMILTON HESSEY makes a CODICIL No. 2 to her will, she is the wife of W. N. HESSEY, according to family members W. N. HESSEY was the brother of SUZANNE HESSEY who m. JOHN W. HAMILTON bro. of J. N. HAMILTON, and former bro. in law of LAVENIA, he came from Tenn. to spend the winter and they married.

SOME HAND WRITTEN NOTES: "DESCENDANTS OF ALEXANDER HAMILTON"...

"F. S. BOWMAN (1857 - 1906) m. 1881, LEULLA TIBAUT (1862 - 1939) JOHN M. TIBAUT (1820 - 80) m. 1854 ELIZABETH A. HAMILTON (b. 1835) WILLIAM ALEX. HAMILTON (1810-1894) m. 1831 JANE H. HUGLEY, (1815 - 1898) WM. HAMILTONm. 1795 MARGARET (1781-1867)
"ALEXANDER HAMILTON m. Mary .. d. 1844, parents of WILLIAM.
ALEXANDER HAMILTON (1759-1843) was placed on the pension roll 1833 of Augusta Co. Va., for service 1788 in Capt. John McEibrich's Co., and in 1781 served in Capt. Patrick Buchanan's Co. Col. Thom or (Thorn) Hugert's Regiment.
"NOTE: You see this date is somewhat of a puzzle but as I say I copied it just as I found it. In the second line you notice grandma's birth is given, but not her death as is my grantfather's but this is because at the time we joined the DAR grandma was still living. Now in the fourth line, it gives where WILLIAM HAMILTON m. and does not give either his b. or d. but we couldnt get it. We did get Margaret's though (hiswife) and Mama said MARGARET was buried in Austin and they found this information on her tombstone.
"in the last line of wife's name isnt given just her death and ALEXANDER'S. I suppose is given in this war record just below (1759-1843) where it speaks of his service in these companies that enabled him to draw a pension of his services, but it seems it should have been mentioned in the above line too."

Another handwritten couple of sheets of paper, very very old:
'Great Grand father WILLIAM HAMILTON born in Virginia March 4, 1777 died Sept. 29, 1840, MARGARET HUGLEY HAMILTON born March 21, 1781, died Feb. 28, 1867, Married 1795. Jacob HUGLEY Nov. 1808, MARGAR___ HUGLEY d. Jan. or June 26, 1807.
CHILDREN:
ALEXANDER HAMILTON b. Sept. 10, 1807 d. Feb. 5, 1811.
PEGGIE HAMILTON b. Nov. 16, 1809 d. Oct. 16, 1813;

WILLIAM HAMILTON b. April 10, 1810 d. April 27, 1894;
(underneath this: JANE HEUGLEY died May 14..)
RACHEL HAMILTON June 12, 1812;
JAMES HAMILTON, Aug. 30, 1814 (descendants now in Tenn. Legislature of Tenn)
SAMUEL HAMILTON April 18, 1817 ? (PEARSON):
ELIZABETH HAMILTON Aug 19, 1819,..1888
FRANCES HAMILTON Oct. 25, 1825... "
A line is drawn across the sheet.
"Cousin Luella's grandfather) married JANE HUGLEY
WILLIAM ALEX HAMILTON of Lebonon, Tenn. born in London Co. Va. April 10, 1810. His father WM. HAMILTON was a Va. of Scotch-Irish descent. His mother's maiden name was MARGARET HUGLEY of English descent born 1781..died Austin Feb. 28, 1867.., his father and mother were united in Holy wedlock by Bishop ASBURY, first Methodist Bishop in America in 1795..(ALEXANDER HAMILTON was of Scotch-Irish descent. His grandfather (our ancestor) (Wm.-Alex) His great-grand father (Wm. Alexander Hamilton)moved to America from Nevis with three sons and when the war of the revolution broke out his gr. father ALEXANDER HAM...one of these three sons, joined an artillery Co. Commanded by ALEXANDER HAMILTON (of histories fame) whom he claimed was his first cousin.
"His grand father (ALEXANDER HAMILTON) remained in the army as a private until the close of the war.
"He was at Battle of Brandyvine (wine) of Germantown and Mammoth. Also the siege of Yorktown.
"His two brothers were not heard of after the close of the war. Do not know what became of them but the records say one was severely wounded in the Battle of Hot water.
"(Ancestor born Sept. 1759 died 1843)
his wife b. Ba. died 1844)"

Another handwritten sheet:
"EARNEST, EUCLID MADISON, b....d....m. FRANCES MATHILDA HAMILTON b.d.
1. Amanda M. b..d...m. McFARLAND: had ADDIE m. M. C. BURNETT; Fannie m. Peters,; DAVID, BENNIE and WADE, all died young unm.
ADDIE b. d. M. C. BURNETT: Eugene, had one boy m. Mrs. Helena Burnett Maresh, DAR Houston, Texas; they adopted 2 girls; ELMER d. young unm
JESSE m. COLLINS: ERMIE m. DORFLINGER, Conn, 2 ch: Marjorie and Evealyn or Erialyn.
FANNIE b. d. m. ..PETERS: WILLIS, Had one child; FRANK & MARK died.
2. JAMES WILLIAM EARNEST, b. d. m. JENNIE CAIN (martha J. on Mamie Earnest Campbell's death cert. d. 10/6/1965); BEULAH EARNEST m. JARMON (Alice J. Lewellen; Earnest Jarman and Eliz. Jarman)
EDNA m. FISHER (burned to death), WILLIE EARNEST, BELLA EARNEST m. WHIPPLE; EUCLID, EDWIN, b. 1212/1885 d. 10/6/1965 (Note: this must be MAMIE EARNEST CAMPELL's statistical data) MARY ELIZABETH EARNEST m.
..CAMPBELL of San Antonio; CLYDE EARNEST.
3. BENJAMIN E. EARNEST b. d. m. MARY JANE FELLS SARGENT: Bennie Wooten, d. y. and unm. and NELL M. b. Feb. 22, 1885, d. July 5, 1972
4. MATTIE EARNEST DIETRICH, b. d. m. TOM DIETRICH: MELCHORA m. D. LANDRUM (John McCrae; David McCrae, Frank Landrum and Claud Landrum) ALBERT b. d. m. Addie (girl, Ansel D. Austin and Roy D. died); Tom.. Calif. children; GEORGE, Calif. children; ANNA D. m. Hammond, Calif. Children; Frank died young.
5. ANNA EARNEST b. d. m. JAMES MURDOCK: ENOCH, ED MURDOCK, BIRDIE JAMES m. WARNER (best W.; Thelma W. Earl and George); Grace Chiles.
6. JOSEPH SAMUEL EARNEST, never married.
7. ROBERT EARNEST m. Lee Ivey, Baxter, Frances and Mary".

ANOTHER HAND WRITTEN NOTE: " LOUISA J. WRIGHT m. GEO. W. WALLING, SR. Dec. 23, 1855. He was b. Feb. 29, 1816."

NOTE: Much of the foregoing four (4) sheets came from family BIBLES brought to Texas, ca 1850, 1860.

645/416 affidavit of heirship: JOSEPH WRIGHT, d. Dec. 4, 1898, his wife RACHEL, d. Nov. 8, 1893. Theirchildren: ROBERT p. b. Jan. 12, 1848 d. Oct. 8, 1872, m. FANNIE ELIZABETH EARNEST, had two children; FANNIE

M. died Jan. 18, 1908, m. WILLIAM F. GIBSON, had: A. J., EUGENE, JAMES W., LILLIE D. never married, ELLISSA R. never married, WILLIAM B. and MINNIE, who died in infancy; LOUISA m. GEO. W. WALLING.

377/28 affidavit of heirship: by T. B. WALLING and R. W. WALLING:

GEORGE W. WALLING, SR. d. Feb. 29, 1916, m. Dec. 23, 1855, LOUISA J.
CHILDREN:
CATHERINE m. P. C. WELLS:
CORA m. JAMES A. WALLING, d. 4/25/1912;
ROBERT W. WALLING,
GEO. W. WALLING, JR.
THOMAS B. WALLING:
MARY ELLEN m. CHAS. C. WILKINS:
RICHARD B. WALLING;
LOUISE d. 11/24/1910, childless; m. LUKE C. ROBERTSON, Williamson Co.
CLARIBEL, d. 9/25/1919 m. A. B. CLARKSON d. 9/14/1919, both in storm in Corpus Christi, Texas; Helen, only child.

ADDENDA, not indexed.
-A-
ABBOTT, Miss R. 123;
ABELL, Alice Louise 69, Catherine J. 69, CHAS. LEE 69, Eunice E. 69,Harriet M. 69, Helen M. 69, Louisa R. 69, Margaret 69, Mary Edna 69, Thos. 153, Thos. G. 69, Wm. A. 69, Wm. H. 69;
ABNEY, W. D. 136, 142;
ABRAMS, Elizabeth A.74, M. C. 74;
ACKERMAN, Jesse 18, Mary A. 18;
ADAMS, Alberta 77, Chas. W. 2, Cornelius 68, C. R. 115, D. 39, David 24,87, 95, David G. 9, 88, 95, Mrs. E. E. 136, F. E. 77 95, 129, Francis E. 9,95 Frank E. 77, 87, 95, Geo. 68, Geo. William 127, Hannah 68, Henry 9, 12, 67, 84, 98, 140,Hugh 76, J. A. 77, J.Alberta 77, John 68, John A. 78, Katherine Louise 62, Lewis Harris 62, Margaret J. 95, Mary H. 133, Mary L. 78, Perseany 95, Robert 68, Ruth 95, Sarah 140, Thos. 24, 35, 87, 88, 95, 97, Wm. 68, 127, Wm. J. 62;
ADDISON, Wm. 141;
ADKINSON Wm. 16;
ADKISSON, Eliza 17, John G. 17, Mary J. 17, Wm.17;
ADRIANCE (ANDIANCE) John 138, 23;
AINSWORTH (AYNSWORTH) Wm. C. 7, ...76;
AKE (AE, ABE) John J. 141, Joseph 148, Wm. 57, 148;
AKEN, Hudson S. 81;
ALBERS, Alford 38,Catherine 88, Susan R. 88;
ALBRIGHT (OLDBRIGHT) Julia I. 82; ALDRIDGE,J.
ALDEN, C. H. 13; 115;
ALEXANDER, Edward H. 80, Mrs. Dorothy D. 31, Jerome B. 15, John T. 5, 11, 80; John Thos. 80, Joseph 114, Louis 54, Mathilda 114, Millenium K. 80, 111, Newton J.80, Saml. 140, 144, Virginia E. 80, Wm. A. 80;
ALFORD, B. S. 25, 92, Chas. 25, Chas. F. 92, Elizabeth M. 80, Geo. F. 143, Harriet Emily 92, Isaac 68, Jannice 25, James 80, J. L. 92, Jennie C. 92, Julia H. 92, Julia 25, Mary C.25, 92, Mollie D. 92, Polly 68, Mollie 25, Thos. F. 92; Wm. T. 25, 92;
ALGONER, John 94, T. W. 12;
ALLAN, John T, 7, 8, 9, 17, 21, 30, 34, 64, 71 101, 102, 110;
ALLEN, Annie B. Glasscock 24, 145, Benj. 57, Elisha 143, 144, G. W. 71, Major R. D. 115, Maria 78, R. N. 81, 100, W. C. 24, 145, W. T. 78;

ALLMON, A. A. 98;
ALMQUIST, Emil 139, Sallie 139;
ALTERS, Henry 58, Wilhelmine F. 58;
ALVIS, J. A. 74, James A. 48;
ALYSTYNE, MRS. Van 124, Wm. A. 59;
AMERICAN POWER MILLS 21;
AMORY, Nathan 124, Nathaniel 57;
ANDERS, W. C. 125;
ANDERSON, A. A. 2, 79,98 107, A. G. 87, Allie A. Cluck 143, Anders J. 58, A. P. 134, 142, A. W. 11 Carl J. 58, Chas. E.24 37, 41, Charlotte G. 58, Clode 98, Cordie C. 91, E. A. 48, 58, Ed 11, Edith 73, Eldridge 48, Eva 48, Eva Hope 73, Frank 73, G. G. 138, John Alford 58, John G. 114, John W. 143, J. Hadley 98, Julia Dean 46, Julia 48, K. L. 14, Mabel 73, Mary Ann 139, 143, Oscar W. 58, Rex 116, R. H. 91 Rosetta 120, Shade 98, T. S. 43, 100, Thos. 51, 52, 139, Tommie 116, Wallace 48, Washington 8, 138, 139, W. B. 120 Wm. I. 140, 144, 145 Wm. J. 140; U. H. 152;
ANDIANCE (ADRIANCE) John 23;
APPLEGATE (APPLEGAIT) John 21;
ARCHER, Amanda 143, J. M 143, Mary L. 11, Osceola 69, W. W. 11;
ARCINIEGA (ARCEMEGA) Miguel 114, 129;
ARLITT, Fred R. 35,Sallie 35;
ARMSTRONG, Mrs. Arnette P. 87, James 51, Jane 51 Louis J. 69, Mary V. 82, Wm. 51;
"ARNEY'S PLACE, 66;
ARNOLD, JOSEPH 146;
ARRINGTON, John L. 110;
ASH, George W. 58;
ASTOLL, F. G. 45, Maude Wheless 45;
ASHER, D. C. 150, G. W. 143, Levi 150, Mollie F. 143, T. B. 145;
ASHLAND,M. 60;
ATCHISON, D. D. 23, E. 137, J. W. 147;
ATEN, Imogene 80, Ira 80;
ATKINSON, Chas. B. 137, 138, Lillie A. 137,138;
ATTWOOD, J. W. 140, Wm. 57, Wm. W. 100, 112, 148;
AUSTIN AMERICAN (paper) 79;
AUSTIN CITY GAZETTE, 103;
AUSTIN COUNTY, 114
AUSTIN, Edward T. 36, John 127, Moses 153, Norman 110, Saml. W. 60, St. F. 27, Wm. T. 60;
AUSTIN N. W. RY CO. 41, 71, 119;
AUSTIN REAL ESTATE & INV. Co. 97, (STACY family);
AUSTIN RUNNELS CO. LAND & STOCK CO. 97;

AVERY, Elizabeth 80, J.H L. C. 80, Nettie Tweedle 79, 80, Willie 24;
AWALT, Eliza S. 116, John M. 116;
AYRES, J. H. 135, Julina 109, Mattie 135, Sallie 55, Wiley 55, 62;
AYNSWORTH (AINSWORTH) Aansenath 89, A. F.140 Wm. C. 7.

-B-
BABCOCK, Chas. 141, 147, 150, Nancy 141;
BACKUS, Alcemeda 121, James 136, John K. 120, Mattie 136, Sallie G.120 Sanford 120;
BACON, Adalaide Vann 87 E. L. 40, E. M. 56, J.B. 19, 87, John B. 87,Julia Ann 19, 87, Martha E. 19 Thos. 139, Thos. H. 19, 36, 64, 110,139, Thos. S. 150, T. W. 61;
BACOT, Pensuella H. 71, P. H. 71, T. W. 72;
BAGBY, Mary Ann 124, T.H. 148;
BAGDAD CEMETERY 149, 150;
BAGGERLY, Susan I. 2;
BAILEY, Addie 120, G. W. 19, J. R. 62, Julia 19, Lou 19, Rosine 62, T. B. 19;
BAIN, N. M. 83, Noel M.59;
BAKER, Alice Ann 65, 89, Andrew 89, DeWitt Clinton 89, Davis 41, D. W. 89, D. W. C. 22, 45, 66, 89, Elizabeth 89, Ethel 89, Mrs. Frances 45, Graham 89, Hanna 124, Henry F. 57, Horace 108, Isiah 108, James 8, 45, 107, James A. 125, Jane 65, 89, 111 Jennie Waldo 89, J. N. 88, John 65, John L. 4, 61, John R. W. 45, J. P. 140 Julia 89, Kate 35, 53, Leona 120, Lola 119,Lucy 124, Lyman M. 69, Mary 89 Mathilda 65, 111, Nellie 89, Norma Burleson 41, Octavia B. 89, Richard R 65, 111, Sheppard 148, S.W. 62, 89, Wm. 65, 111 Wm. R. 74, 99, 100, 124, 127, 128; 45;
BALDINGER, A. 14, Andrew 14;
BALDWIN, Kinchin 112; 91;
BALES, Anthony 104, Timothy 105;
BALLARD, A. J. 27, 44,76 Catherine Elizabeth 27, 44, Cato 21, J. W. 125, Kate 21, 76;
BALLEW, Robert S. 9, 76;
BALL, HUTCHINGS & Co. 6, 23;
BALLINGER, R. C. 141, Harriett 152;
BALSER, J. C. 115;
BANKS, Charley 130, John B. 62, N. R. 130, W. H. 130;
BAPTIST CHURCHES 50;
BARDIN, A. J. 136, D. C. 136, J. T. 136;

BARGSLEY, Amanda Bratton 65; BARBER, Wm. 84;
BARINGER, Elizabeth 12, J. C. 12;
BARKER, Calvin 20, 144, Leman 80, Nancy 20;
BARKSDALE, Lewis 110, Mary 110;
BARNARD, Levi M. 57, 58, Mary 58;
BARNES, A. H. 88, Alex H 26, Charles 56, Jay W.48, Jefferson 51, J. H. 78, John 44, 58, 88, Julia Vada 48,Maggie Dillingham 73, Mary Jane 52,;
BARNET, Andrew J. 115, Anna 115, T. L. 115;
BARNHART, H. B. 47, 70;
BARNWELL, JAMES H. 75;
BARR, ROBT. 99;
BARRETT, D. C 20, L. M. Alonzo 22, Macajah 51, Sydney 51, Thos. C. 14, 36, 93, Wm. W. 57;
BARON de Bastrop 127;
BARROW, M. G. 78, T. H. 37;
BARRY, Nick D. 137;
BARTHOLOMEW, Annie 133, E. C. 96;
BARTLETT, Alamanta 51, J. C. 51, Jesse 20;
BARTLING, Louise 122, Wilhelm 122;
BARTON, Anna B. 84; Cora B. 31, Elisha W. 114, Mary Jane 43, Robt. 31, Spings 28, Wayne 43,54, 79, 84, 103, W. E. 84, Wm. 43, 103;
BASFORD, D. B. 15, 98,112;
BASTROP CITY CEMETERY,116;
BASTROP COUNTY .1,
BASTROP MILITARY INSTITUTE 115;
BATES, Sarah 120,Timothy 105;
BATTS, see BOTTS
BAUCHMAN, Wm. R. 110;
BAUGHN (VAUGHN) & WALKER 97;
BAYLOR UNIVERSITY 22;
BAYS, J. S. 28, Sallie 28 B. B. & C. RY. 20;
BEACHAMP, A. J. 132, Sarah J. 132;
BEALL, Duval 88, Heberden 88, Josiah 104, 105; Margaret N. 30, 88, P.R. 137 Thos. J. 30, 88·
BEAN (DEAN) I. V. 51 Tilford 51;
BEARD, J. R. 11, Mollie83;
BEARDSLEY, Lewis 110;
BEASLEY, John F. 136;
BEATON, Jane 115, M. 115, Marmaduke 115;
BEATY, M. H. (H. M.) 2, 26, 51, 53, 76, 86, 98; Wm. S. 104, 105, W. T.107;
BEAUKISS CEMETERY 117;
BECK, Carl 58, Catherine E. 58, J. B. 22, Joseph 4 Lydia 4, Mathilda 4, T.B. 7, 69;
BECKER, Herman 48;
BECKETT, Cornelia James (Jones) 9, 83, D. H. 9, 83, G. H. 9, G. K. 83, Mary D. 9, 83, Minnie 9, 83, Ola 9, 83, Thos. A. 9 83, Wm. K. 9, 76, 95, Wm.

Karr 9, 83, Wm. L. 9, 83;
BEDFORD, J. 136, Jose Ramon 129;
BEE, Bernard E. 97;
BEHNKE, Mrs. Henrietta 13;
BEIMER (WEIMER) H. 99;
BELL COUNTY, 118;
BELL, Buck 42, Calon 111, Dumps 42, Florence 34, D. H. 115, H. N.115, Irene 123, J. H. 142, James H. 85, 142, L. E. 123,Maggie C. 46, Mary 107, Ouida 138; Peter 42, P. H. 102, Sam 115, Thad C. 34, Wm. 107, Wm. Elias 42, Wm. N. 115;
BELLAMY, A. 13;
BELLS, John H. 121;
BELCHER, Allie C. 68, Eugene Horace 68, Jerald Gay 68, W. C. 68;
BELT, W. D. 137;
BENDY, Clara 125, Henry W 125, H. W. 125, 126, James H. 125, 126, Margaret 125 Napolean G. 125, N. B. 126, W. H. 125;
BENNETT, Benjamin C. 66, Cora Cook Rice 18, 60, Cora K. 18, E. T. 56, Ethel L. 75, Eugene 111, George H. 42, Hiram 63, 64, 66, James T. 6, James 35, 66, Joshua 66,108, L. P. 18, Milton 102, Richard P. 18, 60, Sarah T. 42, Virginia 18, W. H. 75.
BENSON, James,B. 110,T.6;
BENTON, Lena K. 44;
BERGEN, DANIEL & GRACY 3;
BERGMAN, Swen M. 130;
BERGREN, Chas. B. 88, Mathilda 88;
BERGSTROM, A. F. Base 36, 83, Amanda 42, G. A.41,42;
BERKMAN, Albert 13, Claud T. 13, Hulda 13, Lillie 33 Louisa B. 13, Robert 33;
BERNHAM (BERNHEIM) Lelia 42, Max 42;
BERNDT, Babette 93, Carl (Karl) 93, Chas. 93;
BERNHARDT, Helen 141, Jos. 141; M. E.153
BERRY, A. J. 124, S. E.120;
BERRYMAN, C. W. 94, Emma McCall 64, Mary 94, S. M. 92;
BERRYMENDI, Marcos A. 129;
BERTRAM, Julia O. 15;
BEST, Jacob 122, Karolina 122;
BETTS, Saml. R. 20;
BETZ, JOSEPH 109;
BEVENS, Wm. C. 53;
BEVERLY, Mrs. Mary E. 47, 48, W. D. 48;
BICKLEY, Chas. 8, Roberta 8;
BIGGS, Daisey 150;
BIGLOW, Levi 69;
BILLINGSLY, W. B. 105;
BINFORD, Josephine 92, R. Alexander 92;
BINJACK, Mrs. L. D. 74;
Wilend Roberts 74;
BINNZ, John 58;
BIRD, I. B. 55, 63, J.B. 55, 63, Joe 55, 63, John 63, John W.55, J.W. 55,63 99, Lizzie Elliott 63, Maggie 55, 63, Mary E. 55,

64, OLIVER 55, 63, POLLY 63, 123, Polly Ann 55, 63 Rhoda 63, S. E. 55, 63, Thos. 55, 62, 63, Tom 55 63, Trimble (Trumble) 55 63, Wm. 55, 63, Wm. B.63 Wm. H. 55, Wm. R. 55, Willie 55, 63;
BISHOP, Nancy C. 112;
BISSELL, Edward 32, Theodore 8, 9, 32, 75;
BITTING, J. W. 74;
BITTNER, James E. 136;
BLACK, Adam K. 27, Amy 27, Betty 28, Beulah 27, Caroline 27, Chas. 27, Claude 27, David 27, Deams or Geanie 27, Doctor 145 Easter 27, Emma J. 5, 83 Ethel 27, Geo. 27,Harriet 27, Jack 27, Jane 27, Henry 27, J. C. 147, J.M 139, Joe Z. 117, Maria 27, Mary 27, Mary Jane 27, Millie 27, M. Ora 117 R. C. 80, Richard 28. Richard A. 28, Sam 27, Selestine 27, Thos. 5, 83, Tom 27, Wm. 27, 139;
BLACKBURN, Alexander L. 33, Anna L. 33, 80, Helen Elizabeth 33, Henry P.33 Mary B. 33, Nathaniel L. 33, T. M. 33, W. A. 20, 33, 73, Wm. 33, Wm. D.33;
BLACKLOCK, Pat 135, S. Doyle 135;BLACKMORE,T.M.33
BLACKWELL, D. N. 39, J.J 133, J. M. 10, 39, 78, Lydia A. 133, Mary F.133;
BLAIN, Sam A. 98;
BLAIR, A. E. 115, Geo.D 145, Geo. W. 94, J. W. 115, Martha 145, Wm. H. 82;
BLAKE, W. W. 51;
BLAKY, H. G. 100;
BLANCO County, 118;
BLANKS, Dr. John C. 122;
BLANTON, Joseph 89, 90, Lela 89, 90;
BLEDSOE, Joseph 81;
BLENDERMAN B. 19;
BLESSING, Henry 53, Monroe 53, Moore 153;
BLOCKER, Abner P. 111, Annie 13, Ann Lane 35, 96, A. P. 31, J. R. 13, 35,96;
BLOMEKE, A. 15, Emeline 15;
BLOUNT, G. W. 14, Stephen W. 153,54, CLEMENTS 89;
BLUE CEMETERY 115;
BLUM, DANIEL 20, H. 152 Leon 152, Leon & H. Blum Land Co. 152;
BOAK, Harriet R. 47, 48;
BOCK, Sophie 14;
BOARDMAN, Fannie E. 77, Geo. P. 45, Geo. T. 9, 95, T. 77;
BOATMAN, Columbus 71, Mary 71;
BOATNER, Margaret C. 24, 145, S. W. 24;
BOATRIGHT, Ella 83, Mabel 83;
BOESEL, Oscar 6;
BOGGS, W. M. 58;
BOGGUS, Henry J. 58;
BOGLE, John C. 17;
BOHLS, Adlia A. 152, Anna H. D. 15, H. D. 15, Dieterich 15, Emeline 15,

Gustav 15, Henry B. 15, Jack B. 15, Jack Ed 15, Laura E. A. 150, Ola L. S. 152, Olena 15, Thedora 15, Theodor O. 58, Wm.15;
BOHN, Herman 58;
BOLES, Wm. (wiliem) 99, 111, Dieterich 111;
BOND, MRS. E. D. 54;
BONDS. J. E. 47, 95,R.E. 47, 95;
BONDIES, Geo. 57;
BONNELL, Geo.105;
BONNER, Betty J. 47, E.E. 47, John C. 33, J. W.111 M. H. 143, Seymour R. 10 Wash. 45, Wm. 109;
BOOKER, Carrie 53;
BOOTH, Mrs. A. C. 24, J. S. 24, Lemma Agnes 117, Mollie 24, R. C. 24, Wm. Russell E. 24, Wm. A.118 W. R. E. 24;
BOOTY, J. H. 23, Mary 23;
BORDEN, John P. 98, 102 147, J. P. 98, Thos. H. 36, 114; John P.155;
BORGUGH, J. M. 23;
BOSCHE, Phillip 48;
BOSTICK, John 84, 98, Martha F. 5, Pamelia 84, 98, Thos. 5, Wm. Barber 84;
BOSWELL, W. A. 42;
BOTT, Joseph J. 68;
BOTTS (BATTS) B. A. 125, Benj. a. 124;
BOULDIN, Bell 54, Belle B. 10, David W. 9, 10, D. W. 10, 54, James B.10 James E. (Jr. & Sr.)9, 10 28, 33, 77, 128, J. E.10 Minnie E. 9, 10, Mintor T. 9, M. T. 10, Powhattan W. 10, R. E. 10, Robert E. 9, 10, W. D. 10, W.P. 10, Wm. 9, 10;
BOUNDIES & DONATIONS 152;
BOURKE, Patrick 149;
BOURLAND, C. D. 136;
BOWDEN (ROWDEN), 102;
BOWEN, Wm. N. 51;
BOWERS, M. H. 24, 62;
BOWMAN, Burket B. 148, Mrs. Peter 145, Peter 148;
BOX, Reuben T. 94;
BOYCE, Aaron F. 62, 79, 101, Amanda Melvena 79, Ann 29, Anne E. 74, 109, A. P. 3, Benj. C. 80, Boeurgard 79, B. R. 79, David A. 80, Elizabeth Ann 74, Emma 74, H. 99, Geny 74, Isaac 79, Jas. 79, 108,145, Jenny 74, John E. 80, John P. 80, Lee 74, Marcella Elizabeth 79, Mary M. 79, N. 79, Nicholas 79, R.A. 29, Richard 79, Stephen A. 79, 145;
BOYD, Alice 16, Amy Ewing 16, Bryce H. 99, J.Earnst 16, J. N. 16, John S. 29 V. V. 131;
BOYED "Wiley" Thos. 120, Addie Bailey 120;
BOYLE, Andrew 43, Catherine 43;
BRACKEEN, Lemuel 18, 94;
BRACKENBOROUGH, M. C. 24 61, Sallie F. 24, 61;
BRACKENRIDGE, Geo. W.
23, 88, J. T. 11, R. J. 13;
BROCKER (BRAECHER, BRAKER) August 21, 27, Augusta 21, Frederick 21, 27, H. 136, Johan 21, John 20, 27, 110;
BRADFORD, Wm. 11, 94;
BRADLEY, Betty A. 77, Leonard 77, Lucinda (Lurinda) 39;
BRAGA, JOHN 111;
BRANCH, James 146, Nicholas 146, 150;
BRAND, J. D. 123, LOUISE 123;
BRANDON, John 84;Elex 134;
BRANNON, D. E. E. 96;
BRASS, Amelia 42, 89, Amelia , Jr. 42, Clara 42, 89, Emma 42, Euna 89, G. M. Sr. 42, 89, Gustav Moritz Jr. 89, Ida 42, J. Mathilda 42,Mathilda Pauline 42, 89;
BRATTON, Amanda 65, 143, F. C. 140, Geo. W. 65, Geo. 108, John 97, 107,154 153, Robert 103, 104, 153 Wm. 7, 65, 107, 143, W.R. 140, Williametta 143;
BREASHEAR, H. 124, J. 99, John 69;
BREED, Thos. H. 67;
BREEDING, John 66;
BREEDLOVE, I. M. (J. M.) 129;
BREMOND, Eugene 11, 23, 37, 43, John 62, 109, Paul 125;
BRENMAN, Mary Allen 26;
BREWSTER, E. Jefferson 56, Henry P. 12, Sue Turner 56;
BREWTON (BRENTON) J. A. 91, Sarah E. 83;
BRICHTA, Amelia 51, 63, Augustus 63, Cecelia 63, Francis (Jr. & Sr.) 51, 63, Frank V. 63, Robert H 63;
BRICHTAG, Frank F. 28;
BRIDGES, Fannie D. 149, Gilford 149, G. W. 149;
BRIEGER, Mrs. Mary 115;
BRIGHAM, Asa 82, 106;
BRINKMAN, G. L. 38;
BRISCO, DORCASNA 111;
BRITTON, Lucian G. 87, Mrs. Rebecca 87;
BRODIE, J. C. 9, M. C. 83 Minnie 9, 83;
BROECKER, H. 136;
BROOKE, J. A. 14, J. A. G. 86, John C. 14, Margaret 14;
BRONDON, Elex 134;
BROOKS, John C. 63, John P. 31, Samuel B. 104, 105, W. E. 97;
BROSIG, Henry 126;
BROTHERS, John 15;
BROWER, BROWER & STUMPF 20 P. 20;
BROWN,Adella More 24, A. J. 123, Albert 5, 113, Albert P. 24 Allen E. 100 108, Ann 44, A. R. 123, Beatrice 40, Buddy 11, C. C. 110, Caroline A. 64, 75, Carrie 45, Chas. 17 Corelia G. 5, 46, 51, D. 55, Daniel 53, David F.
4, 34, Dennie 40, Eva 44 Frank 8, 10, 16, 33, 39, 61, 71, 78, 97, 100, Frank W. 62, HENRIETTA 39, 40, Henry 39, 40, H. H. 123, Irene 123, Isaac M. 19, 87, J. 17, 67,J.A. 34, J. Frazier 24, 60, J Gordon 56,63, Jane 114, James 44, James F. 24 49, 61, James L. 5, 40, 46, 51, Jasper 11, Jim 114, J. J. 114, J. N. 137 John 25, 123, John W.60, 69, Joseph Potter 24, 61 J. porter 34, 86, 24, Leander 63, 86, 96, 99, 108, Lillie 40, L. C. 130, Louisa Z. 34,Lurinda 39, Maloney 40, Margaretta 39, Martha A. 93, Matthew 109, Mary A. 24, Mary C 24, Mary McLaughlin 43, M. I. 123, Millissa 112, Mrs. M. J. 86, Mattie B 40, Mossie M. 44, Nelson 39, O. J. 123, Ola 83, Owen 123, Peter R. 93, Rachel 114, R. D. 123, Reuben R. 10, R. L. 10, 23, 56, Robert 40, Saml. P. 16, S. P. 109 Sarah C. 24, Sarah O. 86, S.C 130, Sidney P. 64, 75, Stephen 43, Susan 137, S. W. 137, Thos. H. 2, W. D. 123, W. K. 31, 110 W. M. 136,137,
BROWN COUNTY, 118,
BROWNING, C. C. 8, 62, Christopher C. 21, 84, Christopher Columbus 98 Daniel 9, 67, 84,98, 103 David 67, 103, Frances 98 G. W. 105, John 84, 98, Martha 98, Many 98, Nancy 84, 98, Pamelia 98,Penina 8;BROWNRIGG, R. T. 77;
BRUCE, J. J. 147;
BRUGGERHOFF, Wm. 38;
BRUNK, M. S. 126;
BRUNSON, Martha S. 74, N. J. 74;
BRUSH, Elhanah (Elkanah) 91, Lizzie 91, Sarah 91 S. B. 39, 112;
BRUSHY SCHOOL, 143;
BRYAN, Guy M. 127;
BRYANT, Arminta (Mattie) 28, H. R. 28, James C. 114, Lula M. 114, M. B. 28, Mattie Hollar 28, Pearl 28, Ruth 28, H. W. 28, W. M. 28;
BRYCE, H. 99;
BRYDSON, Warren 140;
BRYSON, Grace 138;
BUCHANNAN, B. H. 149, F. M. 66, James Richmond 151, John 17, J. R. 66 Maggie 151, Margaret B. 66, Mary E. 66, 151, N. A. 66, R. 151 Rebecca V. 118, S. H. 135, W. T. 66;
BUCKNER, Bill 117, J W 117, Mrs. 117;
BUCHARD, N. 13;
BUCKS, John B. 137, J. M 125;
BUCKMAN, Oliver 107;
BUDA, Village of 127;
BUDD, Isabella F. 123;

BUDDINGTON, A. G. 53, Alb.
F. 53, Albert G. 90, Carrie 53, Fannie M. 53, Ida
53, Maud 53, Ralph W. 53
Rebecca V. 53;
BUFORD, Mary 27;
BUGG, G. P. 128;
BULLARD, Chas. K. 2;
BULLOCK, B. W. 140, 146,
J. E. 146, Martha 140,
146, Mary R 153, Uriah
104;
BUNDIC (BUNDICK) Delila
119, J. E. 123, M. H.
127, R. 123, Thos. D. 63,
T. W. 127;
BUNDY, J. H. 126;
BUNKER, Hanna 148, Henry
148, Isaac (Jr.&Sr.) 148
Joseph 148, Justin H.148
Lizzie 148, Mathilda B.
148, Pileg 148, Slocum
H. 148, Sylvia S. 148,
Thos. S. 148;
BUNTON, Desha 29, 31, Jas.
M. 111, John 29, J. W.
20, 75, Parks 114, Sarah
A. 29, 85;
BUQUAR, P. L. 97;
BURCH, Calloway 3,Houston
3, Martin 3, Reuben 3,
Sarah Jane 3;
BURDITT,(Burdett) A. M.
92, MRS. A. M. 31,Catherine 92, Giles 32,Giles H.
32 55, 63, 68, 74, 92,
109, Giles W. 5, 32, 63
Henry N. 92, H. M. 32,
H. N. 63, 68, Houston 3
James A. 94, Jesse 2. 6
25, 32, 40, 45, 74, 80,
90, 92, 100, 112, Jesse
F. Jr. 40, 55, 68, 92,
J. F. 63, J. H. 100,Joel
A. 92, John W. 2,32,40
Josephine Rowe 92, Julia
B. 98, Lavina 92, Laura
K. 94, Martha 92,108,
Martin 3, Mary J. 74, M
C. 62, 63, Missouri C.92,
Mildred 40, 74, 92,Minus
C. 92, Minus G. 6, 55,
57, 65, 92, Minus D. 63
Mrs. M. 92, Newell 108,92
Newell F. 40, 55 Newell
W. 55,63, 68, 92, 94, N
W. 32, Sarah B. 55, 57
Sarah E. 63 Sarah J. 63
Thos. Minus 92, W. B.32
68, 92, 101, Wm. B.108;

BURGESS, W. H. 52;
BURKE, Andrew G. 23,Andrew
J. 6, Franklin A. 99, J
M. 125, W. L. 142,Jas.
114;
BURLAGE, John 112;
BURLESON, Aaron 5, 22,
34, 42, 44, 55, 65, 75,
83, 105, A. B. 76, 99, 100
Bettie 124, Cecil 59D.D.
124, Ed 30, 34, 44, 65,72
76, Edward 34, 44, 65,105
129,Elizabeth 105, Genl.
75 Geo. W. 124,Icabud
Erpe 44, Ida 124, Jacob
5, 105, James 44, 64, 83
139, James G. 68, Jane C
34, 42, 66, John 5,Johnny
116, J. W. 55,Lafayette
44, Levi 42, Libbie 34,
Madge 41, Maggie 116,
Martha 45, 116, Mary Jane
50, 116, N. 115, Norma 41,

Naurine 83, Rugus 34,40,
41 Sarah Ann 105;
BURLESON COUNTY, 118;
BURLEY, Arthur G. 141, 148
Mollie Neans 27, Wethyan
L. 141, 148;
BURMINGHAM, D. W. 27,
Mollie Neans 27;
BURNAM, B. H. 149, M. A.
149, Sallie 94, W. T. 94
Zura 149;
BURNE,.Mamie 54, R. H.54;
BURNET CO. 119;
BURNETT, David G. 2, 40,
45, 123, Hannah E. 40,
Henry 28, Lacy 118, M. E.
153;
BURNEY, J. G. 4, 102;
BURNS, Alice 135, Callie
135, Christine 40, Frank
40, J. H. 99, Georgia 132
James M. 100, J. H. 99,
J. W. 135, Lucy M. D. 23,
Mattie 135, Maude 135,
Myrtle 135, M. L. 135,
Robt. 23, Susan 135;
BUROUGHS, James Merrell189
Margaret 89, Mary E. 89,
Mary Ellen 89;
BURR, Jasson 13;
Burris, James 57;
BURROWS, Amy K. 19, Bessie
Emily 19, Elizabeth 19,
John 19, John C. 18, 19,
Lenna M. 18, Mary E. 19;
BURSCHWALE, H. 90;
BURT, Ervie 55, James M.
100, Laura 55;
BURTNELL, Emma B. 60, Henry B. 60;
BURTON, Isaac W. 2, 5;
BUSH, Annie 52, Catherine
52, Mary A. 52, M. A. 52
M. C. 52, Mc T. 52,M. T.
52, W. T. 52;
BUSSEY, B. 71 Mrs. F. J.
71;
BUSTER, Michael 82;
BUTTE, GEO. C. 37;
BUTTS, B. H. H. 103,106,
113, Maria 108;
BUTLER, James 60, Mary Ann
147, Simon 89;
BUTTERY, John 136,/Wm. 90
BUTZ, Augusta 130, Carl L
130, Emily 130, Herman H.
130;
BYARS, Georgia M. 131,
Joseph J. 131;
BYBEE, John E. 46;
BYRD, Geo. J. 60,Hannah
60, Ida L. 60, Wm. 24;
BYRNE, Bridgett 54, James
37, 54, John 54, Mamie 54
Miles F. 24, Mary C. 54,
Patrick 54, Roger 54,
Timothy 54;
BYRON, James W. 153.

-C-

CABANISS, J. C. 24;
CABEEN, Catherine C. 91,
E. A. 91;
CADY (CODY) D.. C. 8, 29,
30, 50, C. C. 2, 83;
CAGE, Mary W. 143, Rane
127;
CAHILL, Camby 47, 72, D.T
121, J. D. 47, 72;
CAIN, C. 80; Christopher
150, Emma 80, J. V. 79,
J. Y. 79, 80, Joel Y. 112

M. J. 79, Nettie 80, S.M.
79, 80, Sugar M. 79, Susanna 79;
CALDER,Affa 85, Alexander
85;
CALVERT, Mrs. Mary 73;
CALDWELL County 121
CALDWELL REGISTER (paper)
121;
CALDWELL, A. C. 57, Asabel
C. 57, J. A. 5, 41, 83,
84, 85, 91, 106, James L.
87, J. L. 41, 86, 87,John
3, 45, 114, K. K. 147,
Lora L. 41, 87, Loretta
86, 87, Lucy M. 57, O.B.
92, R. T. 136;
CALHOUN CEMETERY 132;
CALHOUN, Eliza P. 132,
James H. 132, L. C. 114;
CALLAHAN, Verlin 110,116;
CALVERT, Mrs. Mary 73;
CALVEN (CALVIN) John 110,
W. H. 119;
CAMBY, A. D. 107;
CAMERON, D. M. 135,Eleanor
Amanda 135, L. R. 95;
CAMERON DAILY HEROLD 136;
CAMFIELD, F. L. 13, Irene
13;
CAMP, John B. 144, Susan
144;
CAMPBELL (CAMBELL),David
9, 76, Dover Walter
148, Felix Morris 18,
Forest G. 143, Gilbert 4,
Hugh 9, 76, Henrietta
Park 9, 76, Isaac 98,
James Lawrence 18, J.E.
31, 42, Joe E. 42, 45,67,
91, J. K. 139, Josephine
F. 25, Lenora 4, Mary E.
80, Mary Smith 18, Matthew M. 18, Mildred L.143
N. F. 25, Phebe J. 25,
Ruth Helen 18, R. F.25,
44, T. G. 80, Thos. J. 63
Thos. L.110, Walter 150
Wm. H. 18;
CAMPFULL, Thos. W. 51;
CAMPOS, Juan Vicenti 129
Guadalupe 129, Dona
Guadalupe 129;
CANADA, 1;
CANE, Wm. E. 28;
CANNON, Agnes K. 17,Chas.
C. 17, Mariah 78, Mary 17
Sylvenas T. 55, Wm. 17,
31, 32, 65, 68, Wm. R.
17, 18, 19, 78;
CAPITAL BLDG. 82;
CAPITAL FREEHOLD LAND &
INVESTMENT CO., LTD. 134;
CAPITAL RESERVATION 134;
CAPITAL STATE FAIR ASSN.
77;
CAPE (COPE) Walnette 55,
W. O. 55;
CAPPS, F. W. 87;
CAPT, LOUIS 2, 13, 108;
CARBON, Frank 24, 37;
CARDEN, Rev. H. S. 123;
CARDWELL, J. M. 121,
Mattie 121;
CARLSON (CARLETON), A. A.
4, Fred 62, 81 Polly S.
59, R. A. H. 7, Robt. A.
71;
CARLISS, Albert H. 39;
CARLOS, John 107;
CARLSON, Albert C. 33,
Carl Ed 33, Esther 33,
Henry G. 33, Herbert 33,

Hilda D. 33, Irene 33, Lawrence 33, Lillie 33,Lottie 33, Madora 126, Margaret M. 125, Pete 33, Peter C. 33, S. E. 125;
CAROTHERS, F. W. 137, 138 142, Margaret 149, Saml 145, 148, W. N. 149;
CARPENTER, C. M. 127,Mary 121, W. E. 7, W. S. 121;
CARR, John A. P. 84,R.D. 78, ...121;
CARRIESE, Joseph 124;
CARROLL, Caroline 74, John 79, Jane 16, John 7,9,43, 52, 70, 95, 106, John Wesley 16, J. R. 16 Kitie Jane 16, Lewis Vincent 16, Lula 74, Mary Ellen 16, Percney E.95, MRS. P. E. 95; Rachel Amanda 16, W. C. 74, Wm. 74;
CARRINGTON, Edith 128, Ed H. 73, Mrs. E. H.128 Fannie E. 128, H. E. 133 Katherine L. 125, L. D. 128, 133, Louisa 128, Mary C. 128, Mrs. M. E. 128, R. E. 92, 128, Mrs. S. A. J. 128, W. A. 124 125, W. D. 128, 133, W. H. D. 51 64, 81, 133, W. L. 128;
CARRUTH, Emma Tweedle 79 T. P. 79, 80, W. L. 80;
CARSON, Joseph 118, Myrtle M. 19, Saml. L. 153;
CARTER, Benj. F. 70, Elizabeth 114, G. Dewey 117 Joel 114, Joseph E. 9, M. F. 16;
CARTMELL, Theo. P. Jr. 30, 34, 94, 101, 111;
CARTWRIGHT, Amanda 23, Anna W. 23, A. P.23, Columbus C. 23, Mary C. 23, Matthew 3, 12, 22,23 32, 90, 91, Matthew C.Jr 23, M. 52;
CARUTHERS, DR. A. E. 129 John D. 129;
CASE, Frank 132, Quncy 109, Sherman 109, Wm. 11 110;
CASEY, W. F. 137, W. T. 142;
CASHION, Ann Elizabeth 122, 144, 145, 146,Lidia 145, 146, Thos. J. 144, 145;
CASNER, J. W. 137, Martin 109;
CASTANEA, I. 17;
CASTLEMAN, Alfred 44, Amelia E. 46, Anna 44, 46, E. A. 89, E. H. 44, 89, Lena 46, Maggie 44, 46, Richard Walton 44, 46, R. M. 44, 46, Sylvenus 127;
CASTRO, Marguita, 79;
CASWELL, Hattie 71, Julia 74, Timothy 74, T. 48, W. R. 71, W. T. 48;
CATCHINGS, Maggie 116;
CATER, America P. 64, Eliza Maria 64, Emma 64 Hamby M. 64, Lula V. 64, Maggie 64, Margaret 64, Marguaritta 48, M. Mc Dougal McCall 64, Marie 64, Susie 64, Thos. 64,

Thos. E. 48, 64, Wallace 64;
CATES, W. 115;
CATHOLIC CHURCH of Tex,43
CATIN, T. C. 39;
CATO, Julia E. 25, 92, Osceola C. 25, 92;
CAVE, Wm. E. 28;
CAVETT, Fannie 94, S. R. 131, R. W. 131, Thos. 94 Virginia 94, 131;
CAWFIELD, James 132, John Stephen 132, Walter 132;
CEARLEY, Mary B. 48, 57;
CERELL (CARROLL) John 106;
CEZNEAU, Wm. L. 18, 106, 107, 153;
CHADWICK, R. A. 39;
CHAFFEE, Annie R. 88;
CHAFFIN, J. A. 14;
CHALMERS, A. B. 92, Alex 47, Alex H. 50, A. H.43, 150, David G.8, 95, D. C. 37, 95, Eliza (Lizzie) 47 Fanny 47, Hugh 8, John 47, Julia 37, Julia V. 8, Julia Vaughan 8,Leigh 8, Marcia P. 50, Mary 47 Mary Jane 8, 36, 37,Sarah 47, Thos. G. 8, 22, 37, Wm. Hugh 8, 37, Wm.Leigh 36;
CHAMBERLAIN, A. W. 126, J. E. 69, J. H. 69, Nevi 69;
CHAMBERS, A. H. 150, M.A 137, Margaret 115, Talbot 98, 150 Talbot C. 10, 147 Thos. Jefferson 1, 12, 13 18, 25, 28, 36, 41, 43, 54, 64, 66, 81, 82, 85, 89, 96, 97;
CHAMBLER (CHAMBLEE) John 98;
CHAMPION, John 5, 46, 51 Mary E. 5, 46, 51;
CHANDLER,Anne 133, Carrie W. 133, Chandler & Mc Farland, attys. 24, Chas. H. 133, E. H. 128, Elizabeth H. 133, Frederick W 43, F. W. 9, 11, 34, 39, 40, 41, 43, 59 65, 100, 146, 150, Geo. W. 133, Jacob T. 133, James A. 60, 61, 128, 133, J. A. 133;
CHANEY, J. F. 24;
CHAPMAN,Celenda 136, E.T 140, James 136, M. A.130 Mason 146, Ola 146, Thos F. 93, 111, W. T. 130 Wm. 144, 36;
CHAPPEL, Alice K. 31, Wm. C. 31;
CHARLES, L. W. 128;
CHASE, E. 119;
CHEIRS, H. R. 115, Sam 115;
CHENAULT, F. 75, 125, John 103, 105;
CHEVAILLIER, CHAS. 57, Sarah C. 57;
CHIPPERO (CHIAPPIRO) Catherine Boutall 38, Norman A. 38;
CHILDERS,Elizabeth120;
CHILDRESS, Amanda 118, Beatrice 83, Beulah 83, C. A. 83, Caroline 118, Catherine 118, C. W. 83, Ella 83, Elmo 83,Eunice 83, Geo. W. 127, Goldsby

118, Graham 83, H. F. 135 James Franklin 118, John 83, John C. 83, J. T. 83 Lilon 83, Mrs. M. A. 83, Mabel 83, Mary Davis 83, Mary G. 135, Michel 83, Ola 83, Maye 83, Mollie 83, Prior 118, R. 118 Robert 118, Thos. 118, W. W. 83;
CHOTE (CHOATE) B. 31,32 33, Benj. 32, 33, 109, 111, Frances F. 32, 33, Frank F. 33, Lula H. 33 Mary 33;
CHRIETZBERG, Anna Marie 138, B. E. 138, Mrs. Bell P. (F) 138, Bond B. 138, Chas. P. 138, C. Perkins 138, Edgar M.138 Edwinia 138, Fannie 138 Grace 138, Hilliard Timbroke 138, Lillie 138 Robt. Henry 138;
CHRISMAN, Horatio, 2, 5, 36;
CHRISTIAN, Ed Loomis 78 Edward 26, 60, 77, 78, E 112, Maggie H. 78, Mathilda 77, 78, Nannie P.78
CLAIBORN (CLABURN) Phil 23, 25, 70, 148;
CLAMP, C. A. D. 148;
CLARE (CLORE) Martha 120
CLARK, A. R. 33, Mrs. Delia 22, 70, Francis A. 71, Jane 105, J. E. 141, 152, J. O. 102, John O. 107, Joseph A. 105, Julia W. 124, Kate R. 88, Madge Burleson 41, Mollie D.92 Robt. B. 92, Thos. D.105 Thos. M. 74, Virginia 74 W. J. 143, Wm. 57, Wm.R 88, Wm. Yates 71;
CLARKSON, A. B. 8, Claribel 8, Helen 8, Wm. H.32;
CLAYTON, Brittie C. 69 Harriett 27, James 62, J. E. 69, John 27;
CLAY, Muriel 48;
CLEMENTS, A.L. 2, Blount 89, Geo. 114, J. C. 113 Lizzie 114, Robt. H. 100 101 Wm. 89, 93, 94;
CLEVELAND, C. C. 7,Chas Dexter 7, John T. 7, J. T. 7, Louisiana 7, Wm. D. 125;
CLIBURN, Henry 149;
CLICK, E. S. 73, J. E.73
CLIFTON, Josiah 80, Mrs. R. E. 86;
CLOPTON, Benj. M. 75,109 Justina A. 75, Mary K. 56 R. M. 96, W. A. 56;
CLOUD, Elizabeth G. 150, Lillie 21, R. L. 21, W. A. 148, 150, W. T.60;
CLUCK, allie A. 143, Alvin G. 143, C. A. 143, Clarence A. 143, David A 143, Emmett 143, Ewell S 143, Geo. E. 143, Geo. W 143, G. W. 143, Harriet M. 143, H. L. 143, John O. 143, Julia M. 143, Mildred L. 143, Myrtle H. 143, Thos. E. 143, COAHUILA & TEXAS, 1,129;
COATS, Damon 34;
COBB, David R. 147;
COCHERAN (CROCHERON)

Henry 6, 21, 45, 48, 49, 56, 57, 84;
COCHRAN, Chas. 144, Henry 23, Henry K. 130, James 146, Nathaniel H. 144, T. B. 53, 56, W. P. 37, 49;
COCKBURN, Mary J. 30, 94 Wm. 15, 18, 29, 30, 40, 50, 62, 94, 113;
COCKRILL, Annie J. 118, John 118, John Eddie 118 John Sr. 118, Mary J.131;
COCKS, H. D. 110, Sarah H. 110;
CODY (CADY) C. C. 83, D. C. 2, 28, 29, 30,50;
COLE, James 32, 37, 67;
COLEMAN Co. 122;
COLEMAN, A. 15, 107, Geo B. 93, J. H. 76, James 17, 67, Robt. Morris 115 116;
COLLEGE HILL, 1;
COLLETT, GUY A. 12, J. H 58;
COLLIER, T. A. 129;
COLLINGSWORTH, Lucinda Ophelia 98, Mary C. 98;
COLLINS, Austin 55, Bertie C. 55, Chas. W. 69, Hugh 39, L. B. 76, L. W. 28, 38, 47, 69, 76, 85,Oscar 55, T. C. 2, 29 36, 62, 97, 102, 113, T. M. 137 Thos. 97, 98, W. V. 100;
COLORADO Co. 123;
COLORADO RIVER, 1;
COLVILLE, S. C. 5, Silas C. 83, 84, 85, Silas Cheek 84;
COLWELL, James A. 54;
COLVIN, Saml. 102;
COMPTON, Chas. F. 35, 110 Robt. 4, 61;
COMSTOCK, Ann M. 53, Arthur 53, Blanche Huggins 52, 53 Edward 53, Ella 53 Geo. 53, Jessie R. 53, Raymond 53, Thos. B. 52 Theo. Bryant 52, 53;
CONDIT, Chas. L. 52;
CONE, Joseph 136;
CONES, Charley 16;
CONEY, (CONNEY) Chas. 7, 21, 29;
CONLEY (CONLEE) Preston 31, 32, 44, 65, 138, Solomon B. 8, 75;
CONGRESS AVE. 1, 153;
CONFEDERATE SCRIPT, 152;
CONNELY, Wm. 119;
CONNOR, Henry D. 35, John H. 7, Mollie 35;
CONRAD, Frank 8;
COOK, Abner H. 9, 10, 18 35, 45, 80, A. H. Jr.9 Alexander Terrell 10, Bessie S. 26, Chas. 19, C. S. 12, 128, Constance 9, 10, Constance T. 9, 10 35, Earnest 9, 10, Hugh 10, Hugh Bouldin 10,John 127, J. G. 119, Linda May 10, Mrs. Lottie 73, Louis P. 18, 60, 72, 76, Mary 60, Mary A. 18, 60,Nellie 26, Peter 26, Terrell 10 Wm. G. 102, W. P. 26;
COOKE, Cora K. 18, 60,66 Lottie 73, Louis P. 18, 60, 66, 76, Mary A. 18, 60, Mary L. 66, Virginia

B. 18, 60, 66, Wilds K. 66,W. Katzebun(?) 98;
COONER, J. H. 97;
COOPER, A. J. 137,Armond 22, Dillard 22, James 103, J. E. 137, 142, R.T 137, 142, Sarah Wilbarger 142;
COPE (CAPE) L.Walniette 55, 139, W. O. 55,139;
COPES, J. S. 13;
CORBELL, Alton W. 117, Daisy Lois 117, Katie117;
CORBIN, WM. P. 60;
CORCASAN, W. W. 93;
CORNWALL, ESTATE 127;
CORNELISON, John 148;
CORTARI, Vicenti 129;
CORWIN, D. 16, Dennis 21 42, 52 91, J. W. 103;
CROSBY (CROSSBY) James H. 105;
COSTA, John B. 4, 9, 16, 34, 38, 41, 43, 45, 53, 54, 70, 98, 101, 102, 110 L. B. LaCosta 129;
COTTON, C. W. 126, John B. 85, Joseph 39, Mary 85 86, Noah R. 85, 86;
COULSON, B. V. 137;
COURSEY, Miss Stella 136;
COVERT, F. M. 52;
COVINGTON, W. B. 134;
COWAN, David B. 150, D.C. 150, Giles H. Josephus 84 J. W. 103, 105, Saml. 84 Saml. K. 84, Jennie Patterson 84;
COWIN, D. C. 150, 145, J. W. 105;
COX, Andrew M.110, B. M. 20, Cora 149, E. U. 20, Francis 84, 98, Perry B 126, V. E. 20, W. H. 149 Wm. 84, 98, Willie A. 20 Mollie 126;
CRADDOCK, Amanda 118, H.F 29, John 118, Mary E. Johnson 29;
CRAFT, John S. 45, R. B. 58, 96, Robt. B. 116, Russell B. 96, Saml.43;
CRAIG, James C. 3;
CRANDISH, Lyman 102;
CRAVEN, George 149, Jane 149;
CRAWFORD,Carrie 22, Danl 94, F. A. 39, Fannie 27, J. M. 22, Wm. Carroll 153;
CRAYTON, John 62;
CRARY, (CREARY) J. A. 102 107;
CREUZBAUR, Edward 111, Robt. 83, 111;
CRIDDLE, Tom 125;
CRIM, G. N. 145;
CRISER, (CRESER), C. W. 45, D. J. (Della J.) 45 Geo. S. 56, Nannie A. 14;
CRISMAN, Farrior 72, W. P. Jr. 72;
CRISWELL, H. H. 69;
CROCKERON, Henry B. 6, 45, 48, 49, 56, 76, 84;
CROCKETT, E. I. 129;
CRONKRITE, Henry 59, 94, Lyman 59, 94;
CROOKER, Alanson 97;
CROOKS, Henry 63, Martha 63;
CROSBY, Chas. A. 7, 21, John A. 106, James H. 65 105;

CROSLIN, Edna 33, Norman 33;
CROSS, David L. 94, 111, M. 118;
CROSSLEY, Edward 55, John 55;
CROSSLEY & SONS, LTD.55;
CROSTWAITE, MRS. E. M. 93 112;
CROZIER, Arthur R. 6;
CRUMLEY, Albert 55, Ben 55, Elmer 55, Euell 55, Joe 55, Mary 55;
CRUMP, N. J. 140;
CRUZE, Wm. 108;
CRYER, Hempstead Morgan 23, Mildred Duty 23;
CUDE, John M. 128, 129, John W. 128, Nancy N. 128 129;
CULBERTSON,Pauline S. 33 Pauline T. 80, Wm. J. 33 80;
CUELLER, France 129, Francisco 129;
CULLANE, Smith 17;
CULLEN, O. H. 10, 16, 31 32, 35, 41, 45, 47, 76, 78, W. H. 33, 35;
CULLING, Aaron 115, Eliza 115, Jane 115, John 115, Nancy 115, Rachel 115;
CULP, Davis D. 99;
CUMMINGS, Eliza 123, Dr. Josephus 151, Nancy G. 14 151, Stephen 2, 14, 93, 109, 113, 101, 139, 151, Texas 151;
CUNNINGHAM, Ann 31, David A. 3, 91, Freida 13,James 4, 35, 70, 90, 109, J. C 20, Levi C. 57, Leander C. 6, 23, 30, 31, 32, 57 L. C. 3, 5, 6, 10, 23,28 57, 96, Leander C. CUNNINGHAM & CO. 6, 23, Susannah 70,T. J. 13;
CURRY, David 146, David A. 147, M. H. 41;
CURTIS, Elijah 6, James 6 CUSHMAN, Chas. C. 62, C. C. 113, 153, F. E.85 CUSHING, Wm. H. 69;
CUSHNEY, Lydia Jane 50, Mary J. 50, W. B. 60, 69 Wm. H. 12, 50, 60, 69, 76 100, 109, 112;
CUSTARN, Wm. 20, 35, Mary Ann 108;
CUTHBERT, Anne 68;
CYPHER, David A. 26, L.A 26.

-D-
DOBBS, Wm. 144;
DAFFLEMEYER, W. C. 55;
DALLAMITE, Gilley 121, James 121;
DALLAS MORNING NEWS 83;
DALLMAN, Annie W. 87, James Wm. 87;
DALRIMPLE, W. C. 140,141 142, 144, W. T. 142;
DALY, JAMES 63;
DANCER, Jonas 12, 136;
DANCEY, Lucy A. 44, 49;
DANIEL, Aaron C. 125, Addie121,Barbour Jane 125, B. F. 121, C. W. 3, 47,60 C. Waverly 3,Eliza 121, Ellen 121, Geo. 125, Georgia S.(A) 121,J. T. 121, Mary 121, Mary L. 121,

Oliver B. 121, Walter 121 Wiley 31;
DAMON, H. G. 126, Saml. Sr. 142;
DARLINGTON, JOHN W. 108, 111;
DAUGHERTY, Mrs. D. 48, N 136, Robert 54;
DAVENPORT, Cora L. 87, Wharton 87;
DAVY, (DAVEY) Nancy A. 139, Thos. P. 3, 139;
DAW, Elsie 114;
DAVIDSON, A. M. 2, 47, 48 55, 63, Andrew M. 2, 101 A. W. 55, James M. 99, Genl. James 99, J. Justin 22, Justin 7, Mary E.47 48, Nancy 27, Plas 42;
DAVIS, A. L. Sr. 131,A. M. 14, Alexander M. 14, Alex J. 57,Allie A. 118, Ann 92, Anne E. 85, 93, Ann Eliza 59, Mrs. Annie 32, Ann Elizabeth 85, Bell 92, B. H. 4, 36, 71, 72, Mrs. Blooming 91, B. R. 143, Britton S. 85, Catharine 4, Cordelia Cordie 81, Cordie 32, C. L. 118 Daniel 17,67, Doctor Robt 2, 59, 83, Daisy 32,91, Easter 27, Edmund J. 85, E. J. 87, Elvira 4, 74, Emiline P. 4, 71, 96, Emily 2, 50, 59, 82, 83, E. T. 4, Finas 32, Finas Ewing 91, Frion (Fryon) 59, 92, G. W. 4, Geo.66 Geo. W. 4, 18, 19, 24,34 35, 58, 61 66, 70 71, 86 87, 92, 96, 113, Glenn Owen 4, G. W. C. 8, 86 H. A. 4, H. T. 44, H.W. 101 Henry T. 128, Isaac 59, I. M. 92, Isabella 59, 83, I. V. 4, 12, 77 83, 92, James P. 8, 19, 64, 70, 87, 102, 112 Jennie 32, 91, J. J. Sr. 31, 91, Joe 32, John 148 John T. 122, John W.128 J. M. 4, 41, 56, J. R.38 Joseph J. Jr 91, Josiah B. 148, Julia H. 92, J. W. 128 129, L. B. 129, L. H. 52, Lindsay 81,152 Lucy L. 12, 77, M. 23, M. B. 75, Martha A. 58, Martha Ann 4, Mary 32, 83 91, 127, Mary Elizabeth 91, Mathilda May 81, May W. 77, Mollie D. 92,Nannie 32, Nathan 98, N. I. 131 R. M. 4, Robert 36, 50, 59, 83 92, Robert I. 77, R. I. 92, Robert W.(Dr.) 2, 36, 59, 83, R. T. 92, Sallie 4, 96, 130, Sarah 81, 152, Stephen 43 79,Susan A. 75, Thos.Hearne 59, 83, Walter 85, W. 137 W. A. 146, W. C. 31, Wm. J. 4, W. L. 4, W. R. 31, 78, W. T. 92, W. W. 131, Y. 148;
DAWSON, Fielding 150, James 146, Jennie 32, 91 Nicholas 110, N. A. 32,91; DEAN, A. B. 41, B. W. 16 E. W. 10, W. W. 41, Nellie Stewart 46, I. V. 51, H. Edwing 46, Agnes L. 46,

Lee Ellen46,Marion 46, Bobbie May 46, Jane 46, Lee 46;
DEATS, Elizabeth H. 7, 40, 41, Eliza A. 7, 41 Jane 34, 40, Martha F. 7 41, Mary E. 7, 41, Paul 7, 41 Paul M. 7, 41, Robt A. 7, 34, 40, 41, T. A. 7, 41, Tennie 34;
DECKER, Isaac 1, 3, 28, 67, 98; 154;
DECHERD, Benj. 45;
DECLARATION of independence 1;
DEEN, A. B. 41, 48, Agnes S. 46, Boggie Mae 46,Daisy 3, I. J. 94, I. V. 51, Nellie Stewart 46, W. W. 48;
DELANCY, C. H. 142, 144;
DELGARDO, Juan 15;
DELLENCY, James 4, 14, 61 142;
de CORDOVA, H. M. 29, J. 62, Jacob 128, 129, P. 10 12, 36, 44, 66, 76, 83, 85, 94, 95, 97, Rebecca 128;
de LASHMUTT, E. B. 44, Frank 44, John H. 44;
del VALLE, S. 2, 5, 36;
de MASS (MOSS) James L. 47, James 97, Nancy 97;
de MASEE, Mrs. 145;
DEMENT, (DIMMITT) Fannie Francis 117, Wm. Berry 117 De Merse, Chas. 53, 75, 153;
DENHAM, W. E. 125;
DENMAN, Golden 53, W. E. 125;
DENNEY, C. A. 59, W. C. 58;
DENNIS, James 64;
DENTON, J. M. 31, 52, M. J. 31;
de NORMANDIE, Catherine S. 29, Peter 31, W. P. 8 29, 43, 63, 100, 101, de NORMANDIE & TEN EYCK 112; de PRAS, John A. 17, de PRE, Village of 127, 133;
de VERAMENDI, see VERAMENDI de WAR, Hal P. P. 26, Henry Hamilton 26, Hamilton Marguerite Alleene 26 Mary K. 26;
de WHIRST, Wm. Thos. 55;
de WITT, C. C. 8, Green 129;
de ZAVALA, see "Z"
DIAF, Saml. Z. 122;
DIAL, Garlington C. 20;
DIBRELL, A. W. 129;
DICKERMAN, Cyrus 51;
DICKINSON & McFARLAN, 54;
DIESON, Ann Elizabeth 11 C. H. 11, Elijah C. J. 36, Harold H. 11, W. G11;
DIETERICH, (DEDRICH, DITTRICH, DEDRICK), Albert 62 Annie 63, Dorothea 62, Caroline123, C. E. 62, F 94, 101, Francis 62,90, 96, 97, 101, 102, 107, James 62, Mable 46, 51, Mary 73, Mrs. M. D. 73, Melchora 62, Richard 73 Thos. 62, Wilhelm 123, Sarah 62, Will F. 46, Wilhelmine 123, Wm. D. 73

Wm. F. 51, Thos. R.135;
DIGNAN, D. T. W. 12, Mrs. Harriett F. 70, J. F. 70;
DILLAHUNTY, Edward 100;
DILLENAY, James 142;
DILLARD,Absolon 143, Gabriel 143, Isaac 118, John 143, John H. 143, Mahala D. 143, 132,Nancy 143, Paleman 143, Susan 143, Thos. 142, 143, Wm. 143;
DILLINGHAM, Elen G. 73, G. N. 73, Margaret 14, Maggie 23, S. R. 73;
DIMMITT, Amanda 137,Mrs. Amanda Shell 138, Mrs. Beulah H. 138, Birdie 138, C. A. 138, James H 138, J. J. 137, 138, John J. 138, Josia 138,Lillia A. 138, Lilburn Angetine Eubank 138,LILLIAn C. 137 Lillie A. 137, 138, Mrs Mamie Hinley 137, 138, Mrs. M. L. 138, P. H. 137, 138, Rosa L. 138, W. W. 138;
DINKINS, Mary O. 44, 49 90;
DINSMORE, Silas 75, 96;
DIRMLAN, Dee 127;
DISMUKES, Frederick D. 13;
"DISPATCH" (Austin) 85;
DITTMAR, Adolph 3, Alma 3, Annie 3, Anton A. 4, Augustas 3, A. E. 91, Casper 4, 90, 91, C. B. 91, Catherine 4, C. A. 91,Clara J. 3, Clara L. 91, Dorrace 3, Edna 3, Emilia J. 3, 91, Emilie R. 3, 91, Frank J. 3,91 Franz J. 91, Geo. 3, 90 91, Geo. B. 3, 91, Geo. D. 4, Geo. F. 3, 90, 91 J. A. 91, John A. 3, 4, Lydia 4, L. M. 91, M.90 Martha 3, Martin 4,Mary 3, Mary A. 3, 91,Mathilda 3, 4, Rosa J. 3,91 Tillie 3, Wally 3, W. Martin 3;
DIXON, Shadrack 130
DOBBS, Wm. 144;
DODD, C. M. 60, Louise 60;
DODSWORTH, Elizabeth 132 Thos. 132;
DOHME, F. 13, 111;
DOLAN, Patrick 43;
DOLLAMITE, Gilley 121, James 121;
DOLSON (DOTSON) Geo. M. 107, 129;
DONATHAN, E. J. 123, W. H 123;
DONNAN, Folts & Donnan 126....126, John K. 37 126;
DONNELL,Alice 149, Anna 149, Bell 149, C. E.149 Cora 149, Dora 149, Ed 149, Emma 149, Eunice 149, Fannie 149, M. A. (Minerva Ann) 148, 149, W. J. 148, 149, Wm. 149 W. H. 149, Zura 149;
DOOLEY (DOLLY), S. V.139;
DOOM, D. W. 38, John R 23, Lillie H. 23, Randolph C. 95, R. C. 62, 69, 95

101, 108, 113;
DOR, John M. 5;
DORBANDT, Fannie 71,Thos. 71;
DORRENBERGER, Austin D. 55, A. L. 55, Ellen 55, Laura 55, Robt. 55;
DORRAH, Lonnie (Mason) 143;
DORSEY, Chas. H. 152, Joshua 8;
DOUGHERTY, Eugene 13, H J. 13, John 20, James 82, Nancy A. 13, Robt. 54, W. J. 59, Zuella 59;
DOUGLASS, Cullen 30, 88 Elizabeth 88, Jacob 142 Jesse 143, Nancy 143;
DOURON, M. W. 52;
DOVER, J. 37....league 140;
DOWELL, John 71, 91,John W. 92, Miller & Dowell 92;
"DOWNTOWN" AUSTIN 153;
DOXEY, Harriett 41, Hattie 41, J. D. 95, James 41, 42, Margaret J. 41, 95, M. J. 95,Spencer 41; Thos. A. 42;
DOYLE, James 101 122;
DRAPER, Joseph G. 55;
DRAKE, Simeon J. 88;
DRISCOLL (DRISKILL) Chauncy t. 66, Wm 128;
DRISYMEGER, Conrad 107;
DUBLE, H. N. 36, 84
DUDLEY, B. W. 138, 140 Maria B. 138, 140;
DUFFAU, Francis T. 22 32, 36, 43, 93, 101, J. T. 7, Mary 63;
DUFFIELD, W. C. 14;
DUGAN (DUGEN) Thos. 144;
DUNBAR, Wm. 127;
DUNCAN, "DUNCAN'S PLACE" 120, John Bruce 120, Penelope 120, Wm. 85, John 108;
DUNKER, Addie 67, Adeline 68, Anna 67, 68, Carl H. 68, C. H. 68, Clara 67, 68, Clark D. 67, Lena 67 68, Marie 68, Norine 67 68, Patricia Ann 68 Thelma 68, Walter 67, Walter H. 68, Wm. 68, Wm. Walter 67, Wm. C. 68;
DUNLAP, Alex 6, E. Alex 6, James T. 6, John H.6 J. T. 6, 7, Richard G.6 Ripley E. 6,Wm. C. 6;
DUNLAVY, H. F. 123;
DUNN, M. J. 119, M. S. 89, Mrs. S. A. 119, W. B. 27, W. C. 119;
Du PRE....133;
DURAN, Amanda Soirells 117, Bonnie L. 117, Lillie E. 116, Ola Pearl 117;
DURAND, Annie Julia 82 Chas. 82, Emilia 82, Jessie 82, Mary 82, Nellie 82;
DURHAM, Geo. J. 41, 101 108, Geo. John 28, 30,50;
DURST, Barbara 14, Anna Catharine 14, Catharine 14, John W. 14, John Ulrich 14, Matodi (Mathlodi) 14, Peter 14, Sophie 14, Veronica 14;

DUTY,Geo. 23, Henry 109, Lucy Margaret 23, Margaret 23, Margaret M. 23, Matthew 23, 75, Mary 109, Mildred 23, Richard 23, 106, Solomon M. 23, 115; DuVal, John C. 83, Marcellus 111, Thos. (M) H 8, 36, 47, 65, 75, 78;
DWYER, C. C. 16;
DYBALL, Chas. Fritzwilliams 134;
DYCHES, Josiah 57;
DYE, A. T. 131;
DYER, James T. 16;
DYSON, C. W. 81.

-E-

EANES, Alex. 13, 25, 31 H. Clay 99, Dr. R. H. 95;
EARNEST, Benj. E. 73, Bennie Wooten 73, Edwin B. 80, Clyde D. 80, Euclid M. 73, Fannie 81, Frances M. 73, James M. 81, Jane 90, Joseph S. 73, J. W. 79, 80, Mary Fells 73, M. J. 79, 80, Nathaniel 90, Sarah Ann 90;
EARY, Birdie 126;
EASTLAND, N. W. 15, 39, Wm. M. 21, 66, 75;
EAVES, James I. 120, Rhoda S. 120;
EBELING, Otto, 37, 38,49;
EBORN, Thos. 78, Wm. 78;
ECK, (EYCK, TEN EYCK) Leonard 69;
ECKHARDT,F. G. 65, Lilla T. 38, Mary 39, Mary Ann 65, O. G. 38;
EDBERG, (EDBORG) Anton 33, Esther 33;
EDMINISTON, David G. 108;
EDMONDSON, T. R. 127;
EDRINGTON, A. J. 80, Harriett 90, James F. 54 60 Mollie 79, V. S. 79, 92;
EDWARDS, Chas. 45, Cuthbert 103, Eric S. 133, Hattie H. 130, Hayden H. 57, Henry D. 110, John 127, 109, Joseph R. 133 Lewelon D. 18, Sallie 72 S. D. 79, Saml. G. 109, Susan 79, Susan Cain 79 Susanna 79, Wm. H. 12 Will 72, W. J.130...57;
EDWING, WM. H. 12;
EGERTON, T. H. 131, W. P. 131;
EGGAN, Shad R. 146;
EGGELING, Louis Carl 38
EGGLESTON, E. T. 28, Everett T. 68, Irving 26, 93, John M. 127, Julia 127, Julia Ann 127, Mina 127, Maria 127, Louis Carl 38, Mary 127.Sarah R. 127, Steven V. R. 127 S. V. R. 127, Zelphy 127, Zina P. 127.;
EGGER, B. F. 55, Cynthia 133, Ellis B. 133, H. N 55, James L. 133, John L. 133, Liddy Harris 133, Lula 139, Moses Bond 133, R. L. 55, Robt. 139, S,A 55, 139, W. C. 55, 133, W. E. 139, W. T. 139;
EQUA, (Yawall, river) 141;
EH, Clara 12, Frieda 13 Friedricka 13, Herman F

12, Hermine 12, Hilda 13, Karl 12, 13, Pauline 12, 13, William or Wilhelm 13;
EHLINGER, John P. 39;
EHRHARDT, FREIDERICKA 151, Karl 151;
EHRLICH, Mary A. 3,Max 3;
EICHBAUM, Ada 47, Louis 47;
EIDSON, J. A. 126;
ELAM, Joel 28, 84, John 127, Mary L. 28, 84;
ELDER,Arthur Clyde 83, Chas. Augustus 83, E. J. 8, Emma J. 83, J. A. 83, James Wm. 83, Lennie L. 48, Minnie Alton 83, T H. 48;
ELGIN, Robt. M. 19, 74, R. M. 97, Thos. C. 145;
ELKINS, Clyde 61, Ella Hill 61, S. A. 137;
ELLER, Margaret E. 147, Robt. 147, Robt. W. 147;
ELLIOTT,Geo. 44, G. W. 45, J. D. 137, Lizzie 55, 63, W. W. 38;
ELLIS,Amanda Mitchell 56, Amanda M. 55, 56, C. C. 56, Caswell G. 56, Emmett A. 56, Francis T. 56, Geo W. 121, India Myrtle (Dorothy) 56, L. A. 56, Littleberry Ambros 56, Lazarus 59, Leigh 56, Littleberry A. 55, 56, Louis Geo. 116, Mary G. 152, Martha Mildred 121 Mary 59, Nolan V. 152 Pink Owen 56, Olive Graves 56, Richard15 3, Sallie 59;
ELLISON, Rebecca 121, Wm. 121;
ENGELBOCK, P. 53;
ENGLAND, 1;
ENGLAND,Geo. 4, Geo. D. 4, 96, James E. 4, 96 James W. 4, 96, Martha Ann 4, Sarah (Sallie) 4. 96;
ENGLISH, Aaron 133, Bailey (Cemetery) 83, Sarah Ann 133;
ENNIS, Cornelius 125, Mattie 83;
EPPRIGHT, Alice L. 59, Anna Riggle 59, Mary Jane 65,David 24, 59, 65 108, G. F. 65, Isaac 109 Mary Ann 58, 65;
ERATH, Geo. 138;
ERHARDT, A. A. 115, Adolph Anton 115, C.128,Cayton 115, 129;
ERWIN, W. E. 99, W. S. 71;
ESPY, Elizabeth M. 149, Thos. H. 149;
ESTRANGE, Frank L. 92;
EUBANKS, Caroline K. 140 144, Curus 140, 144, Geo 104, 105, Lilburn Anzetine 138, R. G. 140;
EVANS, Alfred C. 39, Mrs. C. 31, Emmeritta McCall 60, L. D. 63, R. B. 31, Thos. P. 141, Nannie E. 39;
EWART, Wm. Quarters 134;
EWELL, Alexander 148;
EWING, Amy 16, Margaret E. 119, Presley K. 124;

EYCK, A. 31, Alfred 31, Edward (Edmund) 31, 101, TEN EYCK & CO. 128,, Mrs J. A. 112. (TEN EYCK, ECK, EYCKE).

-F-
FAIRIE, W. A. 24 ;
FAIRLY, (FRILY) Danl. P. 130, James 111;
FAISON, N. W. 15, 24, 39 75;;FALEY,Thos.136;
FALCON, Jose Miguel 36;
FALK (FOLKS, FULKS,TALK) John 69, 73, R. A. 73;
FALL CREEK CEMETERY 132;
FANNIN, Colonel 103;152
FARISH, A. H. 36, Oscar 2, 36, 92;
FARLEY, H. N. 85, M. 6 29, 104, 147, Mossilon 29, 62, 106, 153, W. A. 12, W. N. 85;
FARMERS NATL. BANK, Manor, Tex. 69;
FARR, David Henry 43,110 James K. 94;
FARRELL, Carrie 52, James K. 35, 88, Marshal 52, Sallie 35, 52, Sarah 88;
FARRIS, L. 73, Wm. A.15;
FARWELL, Chas. Benj. 134 John Villeirs 134;
FAUBION, Ann Elizabeth 145, Elizabeth Stephens 149, J. H. 151, J. M. 144, 145, John 144, 149 150, Margaret C. 151;
FAULK, Henry 69, J. D. 112;
FAULKNER, A. 18, 58, Caroline 74, Emretta E. 18, James Alexander A. 18, Julia C 18, Mary A. A. 18, Mary J. 18,Nellie 18, Wm. H. 74;
FAUNTLEROY, Thos. T. 15, 34, 64, T. F. 95, T. T. 109;
FAYETTE Co. 123;
FAYETTEVILLE Cemetery 123;
FEARN, Chas. E. 134;
FEIMSTER, Mary 3,Russell 3;
FELLMAN,Emma 78, E. 112 Leopold 152;
FELPS, (PHELPS) Benj.F. 132, Britton 132,Catherine R. 132, David 132, Ida C. 132, Jacob 132, Julia A. 132, R. W. 132;
FELTEN, Frank James 26, John Isadore 26, Julia Betty (Elizabeth) 26, Louis 26, Louisa B. 26, Mary Theresa 26, Nicholas Lewis (Louis) 26, Peter Joseph 26, Theresa 26;
FELTER, Edward W. 82, Clarence Durand 82, Geo. 82, Mrs. Jessie 82, Roscoe H. 82;
FENNER, V. A.70, 97;
FENNEY, J. M. 44;
FENTRESS, F. 102, Lamuel 45;
FERGUSON, Austin H. 126 Christi Ann 52, Clara E 126, E. A. 126, Elizabeth A. 126, Elizabeth H.125 126, Elizabeth J. 126,
Fannie 99, Fanny 99, Geo. R. 126, Laurence 52,Lewis T. 126, Pleasant L. 126, Robt. L. 109, Wm. 17,Wm. A. 125, 126, Wm. F. 126;
FERRELL, Carrie 52, Marshall 52;
FERRENASH, Chas. 115;
FESSENDEN, Joseph 106;
FEUERBACKER, Clara J. 3, Willie 3;
FIELDS, Henry 140, H. H. 121, Mary 71, Mary Ann 71, Mary R. 121, Mollie 71, S. H. 71, T. A. 70, 71;
FINCH, Anna T. 37, 49, H. H. 37, 49, Dr. J. J. 117;
FINDLAY, Geo. 134;
FINKS, W. J. 137;
FINNEY, John M. 89;
FISCHER,Augustus 113;
FISHER, Anna 25, Annette P. 87, Cass M. 123, C. J. 16, F. K. 87, Frederick Kenner 87, Fannie P. 92, Geo. A. 21, Harper D. 123 James 25, 102, James V. 92John 92, King 148,Lewis 87, Lillie H. B. 87,Malinia 141, Martha E. B. 123,Mary M. 87, Rhods 16, Sam R.87 Thos. B.123, Thos. D. 123, Walter P. 87, Wm. C. 87;
FISK, Ann Elizabeth 118, 144, 145, 146, G. 145, Greenleaf (Greenleif) 3, 20, 72, 96, 118, 122, 138, 141, 144, 145, 146, 147, 150, Isaah 35, JAMES 145, 148, 150, James B. 118, 122, 144, 145, John 17, Joseph 30, Josiah 4, 14, 16, 21, 28, 30, 48, 49, 56, 61, 67, 76, 93, 94, 97, 118, 122, 145, 146, 147, 148, 150, Lidia 146, Mary 146, Mary A. 144, 145 Mary Ann Lindsey 118, 122, Mary E. Wood 118, 122, Mary Ann Manlove 146, Margaret Jane 122, 145, 150, Wm. A. 118, 122,145 150, Wm. F. 145 ;
FISKVILLE CEMETERY 40,74;
FISKVILLE & LITTLE WALNUT CREEK SCHOOL 94;
FITZGERALD, John 17,
FITZHUGH CEMETERY 73, 74;
FITZPATRICK, Catherine 99 Fanny 99, Joseph 99;
FITZSIMMONS, F. E. 4, T. T. 4;
FITZWILLIAMS, Capt. James W. 115, Nell 115;
FLANIGAN (FLANNIGAN), Elizabeth 133, E. F..133 Mary D. 4, P.4, R. E. 4, Robert E. 4;
FLANIKEN, Mary 53, Robt. E. 53, 108, Robt. D. 70;
FLATT, J. E. 126;
FLESHER, Palser 109;
FLINT, Ed. 103, 104, 106, Saml. 103;
FLOREZ, Antonio 141;
FLUCKINGER, Ed. 90;
FLUITT, D. Frank 120,Isaac N. 120, Sarah F. 120, S. J. Julia 120;
FLUSER, O. 14, 94;
FLOURNOY, G. M. 50;
FOLKS, John D. 64;
FOLSOM (FOLSUM) E. 104;
FOLTS, ...126, & DONNAN 126, Thos. W. 126, T. W. 126, 143;
FONTAINE, Edward 22;
FOOT, Mary Novella 106;
FORA, James 128;
FORBES (FORBIS) A. A. 34 Collin 90, 108, 153,Lillie 34, Robert M. 57
FORBUS, C. 94, Catherine J. 69;
FOREE, E. K. 41;
FORCE, A. E. 51, H. B. 51 Wm. A. 106;
FORD, Annie McBrearty 54 Emily 50, Emily Rowe 92, H. C. 31, H. E. 56, John S. 113, Marcus 92, R.Todd 94, W. H. 125, Zoe 94;
FORE, Augustus 63, 110, Austin 60, Diana 60, Mike 60;
FOREHAND, Docha 97, Nancy 97, Richard 97;
FORREST, G. B. 41, 86, 87, Rebecca L. 41, 86, 87, W. H. 57;
FORSBERG, August 13, C. J. H. 139, Herman 13, John (Johan) 13; Leontina (Tina) 13, 139, Rosalie 13, 139;
FORSTER, C. L. 7, Mahala 7, W. J. 7;
FORSYTHE, Anton 14;
FOSTER, Albert 60, Fannie 138, Lewis T. 125, Louisa J. 45, 96, Nannie 140,144, Thos. G. 29, 102, Thos.W 109, Wm. 109, 140, W. D. 140;
FOWLER, H. C. 42, 140 W. D. 140;
FOX, Francis St. Joseph 9, 10, J. M. 10, Joseph M. 10, Lawrence H. 38, Lillie 9, 10, Lackey 9,10 Mary W. 9, 10, Nellie 9, 10, Sidney 9, 10;.
FRANKHAUSER, Lucia 13, Saml. 13;
FRANKLAND, Chas. Colville 44, 78, 88, Mrs. Eleanor P. 78, Mrs. Ellen P. 88;
FRANKLIN, Jos. 61, Martha 140, Mary 132, Mary D. 47-Robert E. 47, W. C. 132, Nancy Williams 140;
FRANCIS,....102;
FRANCE, 1;
FRAZER, Ellen J. 44, John 95, Wm. B..57;
FREDDERSON, Johannes 57;
FREEMAN (FREEMEAN),C. L. 99, D. C. Jr. 10, G. R.22 27, Mary F. 22, N. B. 135 136, Thos. 7, 17, 65, 81 97, Thos. F. 125;
FREES, Mrs. Rosa 42,Wm.42;
FRENCH, DANIEL 16, 80 Horace 115;
FRENCH EMBASSY, 153;
FREYTAY, Anna F. 57,Catherine Elsa 58, Clara 58, F. 58, Fred 58, Henry F. 58, Henrietta 57, Elsa 58, J. Frederick58, Wilhelum F. 57;
FRISK, Gustav 151;
FRIEDSAM, Julia M. 143;
FRIEND, Henry M. 137, Leonard S. 109, L. S. 11, S. G. 45 (S. S.)
FRIERSON, Elias C. 99;

FRILEY, D. 145;
FRIETHIOF, Bernhide 89,
Simon 89, S. S. 44;
FROST, Harriett H. Head
123, Hezikial 104, 105,
Saml. M. 123;
FRUD, (FREID, FRUIT,FRUTH)
Bessie (Elizabeth) 26,E.
29, Erhardt 26, 29,95,
110, Henry M. 137, Jane
29, John 112, Mary 26,
Theresa 26, L. A. 26,
Mathilda 26, Christiana
M. 26;
FUCHS, Alfred E. W. 152,
Edgar 152, Emmett L. W.
152, James 152, Maria
152, Walter O. W. 152;
FUHRMANN, (PURRMAN)
August Sr. & Jr. 19, Carl
49, Chas. 19, Dennis
Sheehan 19, Effie 19,
Emilie 19, Hanna 19,
Helen 19, Robt. 19,
Wallie 19;
FULHAM, Elen 16, Leo 16;
FULKS, Albert A. 14, 63,
Bessie 63, Chas. 63,
Elizabeth 63, John 63,
John D. 64, Kate 52, W.D
63, Will 63;
FULLER, Amelia 15, E. M.
121;
FULMORE, Z. T. 5, 24, 37
40, 41, 79;
FULWINDER, David R. 17,
M. A. 17.

-G-
GADDY, J. J. 120, Mattie
Maud 120, M. E. 120, M.
M. 120;
GAINER, Ridin 124;
GAINES, WM. P. 93;
GALLANT, Percy E. 26;
GALLIGER (GALLIGHER)
Nicholas A. 43;
GAMBLE, George A. 57,
Wm. P. 57;
GAMMEL, H. P. N. 24, 37,
Josephine M. 37;
GANSS, G. L. 93;
GANZERT, Fritz 151;
GARCIA, A. 28, 75,Josefa
V. 129, Luciano 129,
Francisco 44, 59;
GARZA, Felipe 127,
Rafael 129, V. 129;
GARDNER, Isabelle M. 93,
Wm. 93;
GARIETY, Joseph W. 107,
Mays 102;
GARMES, Henry 145;
GARNER, Isaac 57;
GARR,.....121;
GARRETT, Caleb 5, H. W.
32, Ira 130, Irene 5,
Jacob 3, 91, Lillie 61,
S. H. 31, Thos. B. 3, 9,
Wm. H. 31;
GARRISON, J. W. 143,
Laura L. 143
GARZA, A. J. Rafael 129,
Felipe 127, Rafael 129,
Josefa Veramindi 129,
Vicenti 129;
GASKINS, J. P. E. 28;
GASSER,J. B. 38, J. J.
11, 38, Joseph M. 33,38,
Josephine 33, Katherine
F. 33, 38, Lucy 38;
GASTON, Margaret Hemphill
67, Wm. R. 103, 105;

GATE, Alex T. 153;
GATLIN, A. 127, A. J. 48,
Elisha 127, Holland 42;
GATTIS, Damon H. 107,
D. H. 83;
GAUCHMAN, Eugene 126,
Madora 126;
GAULT, Ben T. 48, 55, 57
63, 74, 112; Ed. 48, 56,
57, 63, Ed. H. 56, James
(Jim) R. 48, 57, 56, Jim
G. 57, Joe E. 48, 56, 57
63, John M. 48, 57, Jos.
F. 48, Julia 56, Mary B.
48, 57, Muriel 48, 56,
Nancy 48, 55, 57, 73,
Rachel 48, 57, 63, Rena
56, Ruth 48, Sarah Ellen
48, 57, Vada 48, 57, 56;
GAYE, Geo. T. 21;
GAYLE, Alxander T. 47;
GAZLEY, Thos. J. 20, 64;
GENERAL LAND OFFICE, 152;
GENTRY, E. R. 112, Ferdinand 108, G. N. 121;
GEORGE,Elizabeth 114,
Henry 114, James 109, 114,
Margaret 114, Mary Jane
114, Mathilda 114, Rachel
114;
GEORGIA, 1;
GERLEY, John H. 102;
GERMAN EMIGRATION CO.136;
GIBBS, J. L. 98;
GIBSON, Andrew 81, B. M.
131, 120, Elissa R. 81,
Geo. 121, Geo. W. 121,
Lillie 81, Martha 131,
John H. 152, Sarah Jane
120, Wm. 81, 103;
GIEBER, Preston 147;
GILBERT, Danl. J. 28, 58
81, Francis 8, Jasper 68;
GILCHRIST, Anthony J. 125
GILDART, Frank 78, J. B.
52;
GILES, Edward S. 74, 111
Sallie A. 25, 92, W. L.
25, 92;
GILFILLAN, W. L. 22;
GILL, Henry Lawrence 55,
Mary Jane 53, Nathaniel
32, Wm. H. 76;
GILLASPY, Reb. J. H. 116
Margaret C. 116;
GILLESPIE,Ben M. 119,
Berry 34, James H. 2, 6,
23, 24, 31, 44, 45, 64,
68, 89, 141, 116, J. H.
72, 116, John H. 8, 11,
J. R. 84, Louisa A. 119;
GILLETT, Alice Kate 67,
Chas. 67, 88, Emily
Margaretta 67, 68, Kate
88, Mary 67, Mary Ellen
67, 88, Wm. Wharton 67,88;
GILLILAND, Geo. M. 127,
James 5;
GILLIAM (GILLUM) Bell 152
J. P. 152;
GILLUM, John D. 66, Plly
Ann 66;
GILMORE, Aquilla 133,
D. C. 69. 96;
GILPIN, E. J. 131, S. D.
131;
GIRARD, R. A. 124;
GIRARDY, Camille E. 85,
86, Eva G. 85, 86, Helena
85, 86, Marie Leopaldine
Emma 86;
GIVENS, C. C. 2, 36, 114
147, Cezar 99,Chas.C.92;

GLASS, John 90, Lena 90
Roy 90, T. H. 90;
GLASSCOCK,Albert H. 24,
49, 141, 145, Andrew J.
24, 49 141, 145, Anna B.
24, Anna E. 89, 145,
CynthiaC. 89, Elizabeth
24, 145, Geo. 16, 128,
Geo. W. (Jr. & Sr.) 24,
33, 49, 77, 89, 114, 141
145, 144, G. W. 142, Margaret C. 24, 145, Mrs.
Mary P. 8, Mathilda J. 74
Sarah J. 24, 145, Thos.
113, W. E. 95, W. L. 39,
101;
GLEEN, Florence 5, Florence
R. 5, John W. 5;
GLENN, D. 8, Hiner 126,
John P. 144, Robert A.
99;
GLENNON, Sarah Ann 46,
Stephen 46;
GLOSSON, James 130,
Susan 130;
GODWIN, John 135, Sarah
Elizabeth 135;
GOETH, A. C. 50;
GOLDEN, Geo. W. 108, P.
113;
GOLDTHWAIT, Ella 141,
Joseph G. 141;
GOLDSBY, Mrs. Agnes W.
17, Joel W. 19, John A.
19;
GOLLMAN, Mrs. F. W. 73;
GOLSON, O. F. 136;
GOMEZ, Jesus 94;
GONZALES Co. 125;
GOOCH, Alex 97, B. 20,
138, 139, 140, 144, G.
140;
GOOD, Eliza Jane 3, H.
125, Margaret Parsons 149
Mary J. 21 76, Mary R. 44
W. B. 149, W. R. 149,
Wm. J. 44, Wm. 21, 76;
GOOCHER, Saml. 66;
GOODLETT, J. R. E. 72,
148, 150, John 148, Nicholas 148, R. E. J. 148;
GOODENOUGH, Amanda L.111
GOODMAN, W. H. 3, Laura
A. 3;
GOODRICH, Betty 77, Beverly G. 24, B. G. 21, 24,
77, 97, Fannie E. 77,
F. E. 77, G. W. 89,Henry
97, Lucy L. 77, Mrs.M.A.
77, 95;Mrs. M. G. 77,
Mandy 97, Mary 83, 89,
Mary A. 12, S. E. 77, 95
S. Ed 77, Sterling W. 12
21, 24, 77, 97, Tennessee
97, Texannia C. 3, 77,
Texelen 77, Texas E. 22,
Walton 97, W. A. 83, W.
E. 77;
GORDON, John 46, John
Campbell Hamilton 134,
Louisa R. 46, Thos. G. 54
83, 103, 104, 100, 105,
106, W. A. 96;
GOREE, Brooks 131;
GOSET, Lucretia Abbott
63; GOULD,John M.154;
GOTCHER, Eva Lee 119;
GOWER, Henry 145;
GOWAN, Martha M. 141,
Sidney M. 141;
GOYE (GAYE) Geo. T. 21;
GRACY, Building 153,3,D.
B.79, 85, 96;154;

GRAHAM, A. H. 151, B. 11, 99, Geo. T. 11, 21, John 132, Louisa 151, M. A. 132, Mary L. 151, R.Niles 87, R. N. 137;
GRANBERRY, M. C. 41, 77, R. N. 137;
GRANGER, James W. 45;
GRANT, D. V. 142;
GRAVIS, John A. F. 105 106;
GRAVES, Fannie E. 128, Ireland 62, John T. 100, T. A. 143, W. L. 23;
GRAY,A. A. 134, Geo. H. 29, 32, 35, 43, 52, 100 G. J. 136, Geo. W. 43, Fanny 38, J. M. 134,Louis N. 26, Marguerite Turner Lane Winn 26, Peter W. 2 Thos. 72, 76, 95, 78, Wm Fairfax 2,67, 89, 127, 153, Wm. 144;
GRAYSON, Benj. 22, Benj. S. 153;
GREEN,C. T. 39, Ed. J. L 128, Eliza C. 22, General 22,47, Geo. E. 60, Jesse A. 118, Jesse B. 118,John A. 16, 21, 22, 63, 75, 76 78, 80, 98, 100, John Jr 17, John W. 98, John Hamphill 22, Mary W. 22,Nancy 60, Sarah B. 118, Thos. 8, 22, 43, 47, 92, 100;
GREENHAW, E. L. 132;
GREENWOOD, Wm.36;
GREER, Ellis 66, J. A.14 Wilson 66;
GREISON, (GREESON)Wm.65;
GREGG, Abner 138, Alex 16, J. J. 19;
GREGORY, D. G. 123,David 35, Davis 94, Mary 123, Texania 123, Umbleton123;
GRESHAM, J. G. 115, M. L 115;
GRIFFIN, D. E. 55, 63, Mrs. D. E. Bird 55, 63, Ed. 30, Geo. L. 37, Maggie 55, 63;
GRIMES, Bersheba 82, Emmanuel 135, Frances Jane 135, Henry 145,Jesse 82, Jesse R. 116, 118, Jas. F. 135, John B. 135 John W. 135, M. A. 135, Martha 82, Mary G. 135, Mary Campbell 135, Rufus H. 116, 117, Rosanna 82, Sampson 82, Sarah Elizabeth 135, Wm. H. 102,107 111;
GRINNELL, W. F. 55;
GROESBECK A. 74, 124, Abraham 124, 125, Anna E 125; GROCE,Ann C.Jared 154
GROOMS,Alfred 18, 22, 65, 72, 76, 96, 110, Betsy 22, 76, Horatio 65, 72, 96, 108, Sarah 72;
GROPP, Wm. 73;
GRUMBLES,Anderson 13, Benj. 108, 113, 153, Caroline 13, Dora 55, Ellen 55, Jane 13,John D. 13, John F. 43, John 107, John G. 102, John J 9, 13, 43, 67, Mary 13, Medora 13, Lula 55,Jos. W. 13, Nat 99, Peter B. 13, Saml. G. 13, W. E. McCall 55, Wm. 109, Norman 55;

GRUNDY, Susan 60;
GRUPE, Hannah F. 132, Henry 132;
GUARDIAN SAVINGS & TRUST Co. 33;
GUARDO, Bonita 60, Fuliaso 60;
GUINEATY, Patrick 110;
GUISEWELLE, Elizabeth 21 Fred A. 21;
GULLETTE, F. G. 41;
GUNN, E. C. 120, F. L.120;
GUSTAFSON, Annie 88, F. W 45, J. 88, Nell 45;
GWIN, Doviol T. 111, J.J. 109;
GWYNN, Frank 26, Ivan S. 26.

-H-
HAAS, Annie F. 58, G. 102 106;
HABAN (HABIN) J. R. 137;
HABER, Frank 86, Frank L. 86, James E. 111, Mrs Jane 86, Jeanie 86,Rosine 86;
HACKBERRY CEMETERY 135;
HACKENBERG, Caroline 50, 3eo. PETER 50, James 50, Mae Dannie 50, Newton50;
HADEN, J. W. 75, Wm. T. 75;
HADLEY, Wm. A. 11;
HAENEL, Chas. 59, Eliese 59;
HAFTER (HAFFLER) John 103 104, 106;
HAGGARD, James P. 3, 65;
HAGUE, Martha A. F. 111;
HAINES, MRS. D. M.Thornton 67, Emily 67, James 67, Melissa W. 67;
HAIR, J. F. 27;
HAIRSTONE E. 15, Ezekiel 15;
HALBERT, Alethia E. 39, O. I. 39;
HALDEMAN, Allen S. 43,145 David 25, Jesse 115;
HALE (HAILE) John 149, Thos. 149;
HALEY, Chas. Q. 98;
HALL, Alex 55, Anne E. 89, Ann Ethel 144, Anne 49, Anna Lenora 26, A.W. 146, C. E. 26, C. J. 144 C. K. 78,Delinda 131, Edward 2, E. E. 8, F. M. 49, 89, 145, Frank 146, H. 74, Jennie L. 26; James C. 131, J. D. 144 J. M. W. 52, 81, 94, 109 John A. 55, Julia Chalmers 8, 37, Lenora 26, R. B. 146, Nelia 55, Phebe 146 P. M. W. 30, P. W. 49, Sarah J. 49, W. K. 8, W. M. 37, W. L. 26;J.W154;
HALLFORD, E. M. 120, James P. 131, John 120, J. N. 120;
HALLMAN, John G. 94;
HALLETTE, Thompson 18;
HALSEY, Julius N. 133;
HAMBLIN, W. K. 52;
HAMBY, Harvey 121, Mary F. 63, Thos. K. 76, Wm. K. 63;
HAMILTON, Co. 125;
HAMILTON, A. L. 40, 65, Andrew J. 26, 34, 43, 65 69, 77, 141 Andy 149, Betty H. 26, B. J. 40,

Hamilton Bros. 40, Carrie 23, Chas. 66,Everitt 23, Ella 31, Frank 23, 41, 79 94, Frank H. 26, G. H.40, H. R. 71, Jack 23, Jane H. 7, J. N. 7 , John C. 31, Johanna L. 149, Jos. 31, Kate 23, Lilly 26, Mary 26, 31, Mary J. 26, 69, Mary Jane 26, May 23 Margaret 73, M. C. 9, 26, 29, 70, 77, 88, 95 Morgan C. 8, 13, 26, 29, 69, 70, 77, 94, 144, 43, Robt. 31 153, Sarah 149, Susan R. 116, Tommy 23, Wm. A. 7 W. E. 40, Wm. 116;
HAMMER, H. W. 53, James Park 9, J. P. 9, John W. Jr. 9, May 9;
HAMMAN, Wm. H. 134;
HAMMOCK, E. E. 84, Nancy 84;
HAMMETT, America T. 86, Isaac 31, 32, 35, 51,68 Isaac M. 32, 68, 86, Jackson 32, 51, 68, J. M. 68 J. W. 11, Jos. B. 32, 68, L. 32, Martha J. 32, 68, Martha G. 32, 35, 51, 68 Washington 32, 68, Wm. B. 32, 68
HAMMOND, Chas. Hayer 27 Mattie Neans 27, Robt. J. 37;
HAMNER, Alma 3, Paul 3, H. C. 125;
HAMPTON, Chas. 81, Charlotte 112, Cynthia R. 81 Jos. W. 81, J. W. 81 82, Laura 81, Margaret 81, Mary 81, Robt. 81;
HANCOCK, Aaron 42, Allen E. 49, HANCOCK & WEST 63 E. B. 15, 16, 33, 36, 41, 62, 82, 96, E. 84, Eliza Louise 23, Geo. 5, 11 23, 32, 34, 35, 36, 40, 45 46, 59, 62, 63, 66, 77, 82 85, 98, 100, 101, Geo. F. 82, 83 G. D. 66, Hattie May 49, James W. 46, 82, J. 70, John 15, 16, 23, 24 33, 34, 38, 39, 40, 41, 45 46, 49, 59, 62, 77, 82, 97 101, Joseph 83, Josiah F. 74, Lewis 11, 23, 45, 46, 82, Louisa 11, 23, 46, L. S. 45, 53, Mary Ann Elizabeth O'Quinn 74, Mary E. 83, Marie 62, Melissa 83, Mollie 71, Nancy 17, 84, Polly 112, Reuben K. 83, Richard L. 83, Salem 71, Susan E. 15, 23, 33, 82, 83, 96, 98,Thos. 123, Wayne 83, W. L. 45;
HANDLEY, A. B. 114, Mathilda 114;
HANKE, HUGO 116;
HANKS, Nancy 42;
HANLEY, A. L. 114, Mathilda 114;
HANNA, ADELAIDE E. 151, A. J. 151,LIllie 151, Robt. H. 47;
HANNER, Dr. J. F.'s wife 76, James P. 76, James Park 76, John W. 76, Mary 76;Frances76,John76,Wm.76;
HARKEY, W. H. 52;
HARNES, J. B. 144;
HANNIFORD, (HARRIFORD,

HEREFORD, HERIFORD) Jas. 54, Josephine 54, Millie 53, Peter 53, 54;
HANNIG, JOS. W. 21, J. W. 21;
HANSBOROUGH, Elijah 57;
HANSEN, Catherine 46, Henry Fred. 26, John H. 46;
HARBERT, Crockett 122, Daniel G. 123, Nancy W. 123;
HARDEWAY, Annie M. Wilbarger 142, Geo. W. 142;
HARDIMAN (HARDEMAN), Elizabeth 55, J. N. 34, Mary E. 54, 57, 63, Wm. M. 55, 57, 63,
HARDIN, Alan 55, Martha 55, Martin 55;
HARDY, Emily M. 67, 88, Henry C. 67, 88, Henry C. Jr. 67, 88, John F. 18, 60, Mary A. 60, Mary Ellen 67, 88, Mary L. 18, 60;
HARGRAVES, C. E. 12, Mrs. C. Isabel 12, J. L. 150;
HARGROVE (HARGRASS) Nannie M. 148;
HARMAN (HARMON), Edwin C. 139, 148, E. D. 20, 138, Elijah 148, Elisha D. 138, 139, 147, 148, 150 141, Ella G. 139, 148, Henry 13, H. Louisa 139, 148, Isaac D. 139, 141, 148, Lillian 139, 148;
HARNES, J. B. 143;
HARNEY, Genl. Wm. S. 65, 66;
HARPER, Elijah H. 62, J. C. 42, S. E. 42;
HARRELL, A. J. 7, 145, Anderson J. 15, 44, 97, 145, David 56, Dorthula 145, Emma B. 145, Euer? 145, India Myrtle 56, Jacob B. 144, Joab M. 76, 106, 138, J. 58, James G. 138, 139, 145, J. M. 100, 103, John 51, 145 James H. 146, Joseph 48, 52, Mary 145;
HARRELLSON, Hugh A. 36, Jas. 56, J. C. 86, J. E. 69, K. L. 50;
HARRINGTON, Edward 57, 74;
HARRIS, Co. 127;
HARRIS, A. D. 117, A. J. 118, Annette 117, Anne P 87, Augustus Storey 62, Bessie B. 116, Charlotte 144, Cora L. 87, E. S. 144, F. 124, F. M. 76, Gladys 62, Isaac 20, 108 James Byron 57, James M. 69, Jeannette Marletta 62, Jefferson Storey 62, Jesse 20, 110, John W. 54, 87, 94, J. W. 32, 54, Kent Clay 62, Katherine 117, L. B. 116, Leasal 34, Leondas Sidon 62, Lillie B. 87, Louise 62, Margaret W. 57, Millie Ann Ruth 55, Dr. N. B. 117, Patrick Sidney 62, Rebecca P. 87, Robt. A. 116, S. B. 116, Saml. 16 45, Sarah 20, 32, Sidon 62, Wiley 139, Wm. H. 57;

HARRISON, Daniel Murchison 106, Elezabeth 135, 137, Greenberry H. 106, John T. 114, Lesea 114 N. C. 123, R. P. 132, W 8, W. D. 91; Col. Chas. 135;
HERROD, J. Q. A. 126;
HARRY, C. E. 25, 95, Edwin 25, Martha G. Morrow 25, 95;
HART: Fred P. 34, James H 34, James P. 34, 41, John R. 121, Mary E. 34, Mary P. 34, Simon 66, W. D. 34;
HARTENSTEIN & SON, 112;
HARTSON (HORTSON), Bartie 75, Bartie Leonard 96, Eliza J. 87, J. M. 66, John M. 75, L. 87, Susan A. 66, 75, Wm. 75;
HARVEL, J. M. 103;
HARVEY, John 96, 110, John H. 103, W. C.(T. C) 137;
HARWELL, D. M. 100, J. M 103;
HASKINS, Elizabeth 114, John 114, J. T. 116, Mary 116, Sarah 114, Thos. 114;
HASMER, Chas. B. (G) 139 141, Lucretia 139, 141;
HAWKINS, David L. 35, L. 146, Mary Annette 81 82, Mary A. 82, Thos. 66;
HAWKE, Eliza 69, Wm. 69;
HAY, John W. 23;
HAYAN, D. 14, Hazel 76, Thos. K. 76;
HAYDEN, Elizabeth B. 75, John W. 105, 106;
HAYNES, Chas. 121, John T. 74, 111;
HAYNIE, H. H. H. 16, 45, 92, 112, James A. 79, L. G. 104, Saml. G. 40, 51, 59, 112, S. G. 16;
HAYS, Co. 129, 130, 131, 132, 133;
HAYS, Geo. Lewis 106, Jane 132, Nicholas 51;
HAZLETT, Saml. 147;
HEAD, Albert 135, Albert A. Harrison 119, E. J. 140, Barbour Jane 125, Elizabeth 135, Elizabeth A. 125, Harrison 119, 125 Frances Jane 135, James 125, James Madison 125, Susan 151, Thos. S. 123;
HEADRIGHT CERTIFICATES 152;
HEADSPETH, Carrie V. 70 J. B. 70, John B. 70, Saml P. 70, 93;
HEARD, J. F. 126;
HEBITS, Ann Bush 52, J. C. 52;
HEBGER, Geo. 136;
HEDGECOCK, Oliver H. 11;
HEFFINGTON, David 50, Elizabeth 114, F. P. 91 Frank P. 68, James G. 114 123, L. J. 68, Tom 12;
HEGERTY (HAGARTY) John 54;
HEISE, Christian 136;
HEINATZ, John F. 146;
HEISSNER, Geo. 90, 93, Geo. D. 32, Martha 32, Myra 32;
HELM, Betty Grooms 22, 76 Thos. 22, 76, Wilson 104 105;

HEMPHILL, Cornelius M. 32 David 67, James 67, Jane W. 67, John 40, 64, 96, 110, 153, John N. 67, John W. 67, Jos. 114, Morgan 67, Robt. 67, Robt. N. 67, Sarah 114, Sarah J. 116, Theodora 66, W. 3, W. L. 117, Wm. R. 67, Wm. 91, 2,;
HEMSTOCK, J. D. 116, Minnie S. 116;
HENDERSON, E. H. 47, James 106, J. H. 52, J. W 17, Mary 47, Wm. F. 47;
HENDLEY, Jerimah 141;
HENDRICKS (HENDRICK) Abram 92;
HENRICKS, Thos. D. 14;
HENDRIX, C. 117, C. L. 117, Cordelia 117, F. J 117, James H. 117, John D. 117 Josephine Sorrels 117;;
HENKLEY, Sally 59;
HENNINGER, Mrs. Elizabeth 93, Herman 19, Jacob 93 John 112;
"HERMIT", The 47;
HENRIE, Arthur 124;
HENRY, Amanda M. 6, 16, Davis N. 6, Eliza T. 6, Elizabeth B. 6, Franklin D. 6, Hugh G. 6, James M. 6, John D. 6, 12, John D. 109, John R. 6, J.R. 143, Mary J. 6, Meredith W. 6, Texanna C. 6, Thos J. 6, Wade 64;
HENSON, ANN 94, Walton 94;
Hentz, Conrad 106;
HEPPENHEIMER, Ernest J. 26, 95, Ruth Norris 26;
HERBERT, Mary B. 2, Peter Walter 2, P. W. 6;
HERMANN, Alma E. 118, J. W. 118;
HERNDON, Algey 136, Edward W. 141, Herod Thos. 136 John 34, J. W. 128, 130 Zachariah K. 147, Z.K.147;
HEROD, Alay, 136;
HERRING, F.T. 15;
HERRON, A. 153;
HERSHALL, B. 6, Levi 6;
HERWIG, Elizabeth 132 Roscoe H. 132, Warren 132;
HEYE, Kathryn Alice 40, Otto Joseph 40;
HICKS, Amanda 148, Catherine 148, James 148, James W 148, 150, Jos. 148, Mary 148, 150, Milton 147, 148 150, Presley 148, R. H. 37, Saml. 148, Sarah 148 Wm. 148;
HICKMAN, Bartlett 148 Chas. C. 120, Effie M. 120
HIGGINS, Eli C. 81, Col. J. C. 115;
HIGHSMITH, J. 113, M. B 6, 23, Saml. 6, 45, 72, 76, 108, Theresa 72;
HIGHTOWER, Richard D. 139;
HIGSBY, E. 26;
HILL, A. C. 61, Addie 61 Anne G. 61, Asa 82, C.F. 97, Chas. W. 34, Eli 129 Elvira A. 48, 49, 64, Emilie 93, E. P. 124, Hattie M. 48, 49, H.B. 93, Henry 51, Henry P.13,

43, 47, 65, 97, Ira B. 48
49, 64, J.Pinckney 9,
Jessie May 61, Kate E. 70
Lou H. 61, Mary P. 34,
Pinckney 127, R. D. 51,
R. J. 141, Robt. Jerome
70, Stephen D. 48, 49, 64
Tennie 34, Washington 54;
W. H. 32, 74, 111, W. L.
86, W. Pinckney 67, 96,
Wm. H. 32, 74, T.T.52;
HILLEBRAND (HILDEBRAND)
Emma L. 77, Louis R. 77,
94;
HILLYER, J. L. D. 33;
HILTON, Beulah 25,Lee 25;
HINCKELS (HINKELS, HINKLES
HENKLES) Anna C. 11,Jacob
Lebrecht Max 11,
Leonard 11, Mary Mathilda
11;
HINCKLEY, James 86, Mrs.
Mary Cotton86;
HINDLEY, Jeremiah 141;
HINDS, B. J. 130, Catherine 118, E. C. 118,
E. P. 85, Matthias 136;
HINES, WM. 30;
HINGES, Ruth 94;
HIRSCHFIELD, Henry 8, 42,
93, Jennie 42, John 42
Laura 42, Lelia 42,
Morris 42, Rosa 42,Sam 42;
HITCHCOCK, M. M. 143;
HITT, Geo. C. 56;
HOBBS, Mrs. G. A. 132,
J. D. 132;
HOBBY, Wm. 130;
HODGES, Mrs. Eddie 83,
H. A. R. 121;
HODGSON, Mary 149, Thos.
149;
HOFFAT, Elizabeth 141,
Joseph 141, Louis 141,
Willie 141;
HOFFMAN, Caroline 122,
Ernest Gustav 122, P. H.
32;
HOGG, A. 125, Arc'D 126,
James C. K. 125, 126,
Philip 109, Quinton 134;
HOLDER, Martha Jane 138,
Prior A. 138, Wm. 138;
HOLLAND,Elijah D. 114,
Elizabeth 114, Eugene 13
John M. 99, M. J. 51,
Phillip 138, Mrs. Sallie
13, Samuel E. 109;
HOLLAR (HOLLOR) A. H. 28,
Arminta 28, A. P. 28,
Carrie 28, Dorsia 28, E.
W. 93, Hwnry 28, Lucretia
28, Mary 28, Mittie 28,
Nannie 28, R. W. 28, S. W
28, Sallie 28, W. W. 28,
Theodorsia (Theodosia
Dorsia) 28;
HOLLINGSWORTH, G. W. 137,
James 115, B. 137, J.
S. 132, Mrs. J. W. 132,
K. G. K. 21, 26, O. N.
21, 26, Rachel 115;
HOLMAN, H. C. 100, I. P
66, I. W. 66, James S.66
Jasper 66, Martha W.
66, Mrs. O. N. 55, 63,
Sallie 55, 63, W. F. 66;
HOLMS, Algy 136, Flusie M
Phillips 36, S. 57, Walton
36, Walter H. 38;
HONEY, Geo. W. 99;
HOLT, J. W. 143, Lucretia
143;

HOOD,Bettie 124, E. J.124
Ella 124, Mrs. Fannie 124
H. I. 124, Ida 124, Joe
124, Lula 124, Margaret
Elizabeth 124, T. H. 124
W. F. 124;
HOOPER, Richard 80;
HOPEWELL CEMETERY 151;
HOPKINS, Andrew H. 30,153
Andrew S. 94, A. N. 30,94
97, 100, 102, 108, 112,
127, 153, A. V. 62,
Francis M. 70, 86, Jane
30, 94, Jurlan M. 112,
Matthew 16, 95, Rachel A.
70, Rachel E. 70, Richard
86, Sarah E. 70, 86;
HORAN, John 10, 15, 81,
100, 101;
HORMAN, L. Kinnard 131
Tabatha 131;
HORNBURGER, F. 100;
HORNE,A. A. 86, A. C. 62,
Alex 44, Amanda A. 86,
Andrew Jr. 86, Andrew O.
67, 86, 97, 108, A. O.Jr
86, A. O. 86, A. Archibald
86, A. Archibald G. 86,
A. G. 86, Elizabeth 86,
Mrs. Elizabeth 86, James
M. 86, John C. 86, Malcom
G. 86, Mariam 86, Mary C.
86, Mattie L. 86, Mattie
Lou 86, M. G. 86, Nellie
G. 86, Sarah M. 86, Sarah
O. 86, Saml. D. 86,Susan
C. 86, Wm. 86, W. T. 86,
109;
HORNSBY, Bessie Emily 18
19, Duke 150, Felix 150
Jesse 18, 19, John W. 41
138, 150, John 150, July
Ann 138,, M. D. 150,
Moses S. 147, 150, Reuben
3, 12, 16, 20, 66, 100,
105, 138, 150, R. 150,
Sarah A.150, Susanna 138,
150, Thos. M. 138, 150
Wm. W. 3, 58, 59, 66, 105
138;
"HORSES PRAIRIE" (Indian
Massacre 1870) 135;
HORST (HOIST) August 78,
Chas. 78, Edward M. 96,
Emma 78, James 78, Louis
29, 63, 78, 106, 107,
Louisa 78, Margaretha 78,
Mathilda 78;
HORTON, A. 3, 14, Albert
C. 2, 30,39, 63, 64, A.C.
2, Charlotte A. 61;
HOTSCHKISS, (HOTCHKISS)
A. 124, Corelia T. 5,46
51, DeWitt 46, DeWitt H.
46, 51, Daniel W. 5, 46,
Elizabeth 75, Hanna 5, 46
Hannah B. Puckett 5, 46
51, Kate Westfall 46, 51,
Martha 5, 25, 46, 51,
Mary E. 5, 46, 51, Mary
S. 5, Milton S. 46, 51,
Oscar T. 46, 51, Ralph 46
51, Wm. H. 46, Wm. Henry
51, Wm. J. 74, Wm. S. 5,
46, 51, 93, Wm. 51;
HOUCHINS, Betty W. 130,
Geo. W. 130;
HOUGHTON, Annie E. 144
Horace 106, Joel A. 146,
T. M. 143, 144;
HOUSE, J. H. B. 125, T.
W. 125;
HOUSTON, A. D. 108, 109,

A.S. 60, E. T. 69, J.S.
66, Laura 94, L. S. 94,
Marion A. 64, Sam 40, 100
153, T. J. 40, 70, Victorine 40, 70;
HOWARD,J. L. 129, Julia
A. 38, Lula 124, M. 124
Mary 41, N. C. 125, W.
Frank 38, 96;
HOWELL, A. B. 75, D. A.
J. 22;
HOWLETT (ROWLETT) James
147, 150;HOXEY,Asa 154;
HOYLE, Stephen 106;
HOYT, Saml. C. 111;
HUBBARD, Elizabeth 17,
Zadock 17;
HUDDLESTON, Thos. 20;
HUDGINS, Annie E. 80,
T. E. 80;
HUDSON, Edward 55, L. M
118, Rev. Wm. A. 118;
HUDSPETH, Narcissa R. 121
Nathan 121;
HUELLEMAN, Erma 35, Paul
R. 35;
HUGG, Fred J. 23;
HUGGINS (HUDGINS) Anna
I. 80, Blanche 53, Eli
C. 110, J. T. 149, T.
E. 80;
HUGELY, Chas. 81;
HUGHES, A. A. 31, Chas.
97, Henry W. 115, J. D.
137, John D. 137, 138,
M. Eliza 115, Nancy 115
Rosa 137, 138, S. 115,
Thos. P. 138, 147, 150
HUGHES & VENTREES, atts
145;
HULING,Alamanta 51,
Elizabeth 51, 142,Henry
51, John A. 51, John,
Hamilton 142, Marcus 109
Marcus C. 57, M. B. 51
R. D. 51, Sadie R. 51,
Thos. B. HULING & CO. 51
151, Thos. B. 50, 51,139,
140, 142, 144, 151, Wm.
N. 51;
HUMPHREYS, D. 60, P. W.
54, T. W. 102;
HUNNICUTT, James B. 132
Shanny M. 132;
HUNT,A. J. 140, Francis
K. 138, 140, J. D. 52,
John D. 52, Jonathan S
(1) 99, Julia G. 138,
140, Marie E. 52, M. E.
52, Nathaniel 14, Serepts
140, Wm. H. 60;
HUNTINGTON, John F. 127;
HUNTER, Mrs. C. 13;
HUPPERTZ, Chas. 41;Emmie
15;
HURLEY, C. W. 143;
HURLOCK, H. V. 124;
HURST, Charlotte 68, 86,
109, Edward M. 68, 86,
HUTCHINS, James H. 81,
109, J. V. 130, W. J. 124'
HUTCHINGS, BALL-HUTCHINGS
& CO. 23, J. H. 23;
HUTCHINSON, J. C. 125,
Eugene 137;
HUTCHISON, Annie Cuthbert
68, Beverly 68, James H
81, 109, J. V. 130, Lenore
S. 68, Louis 68, Mary Louise
68, Oscar C. 68, W. J.
124, W. O. 68, 129;
HUTSON, David 98;

HYDE, A. C. 107, 147,John C. 16, 17, 67, Nancy 17;
HYLAND, Molly 146, R. R 134, Will 146;
HYATT, Alice Kate 67, 88, Geo. E. 67, 88.

-I-
ING, Chas. 26, Christina 26;
INGRAM, Austin C. 117, C.B. 117, James H. 23, Mary C. 23;
I. & G. N. Ry Co. 25, 58, 61;
IRELAND, 1;
IRELAND, John 77;
IRIAN, R. A. 57;
IRVINE, James C. 149, Jas O. 149, Sarah J. 149;
ISAACS, Harry G. W. 12;
ISBELL, Alexander 118,154 Amanda 118, Amanda I. 125 Anna 118, James 118, Jas. H. 125, James R.118, 140, J. M. 118, John H. 118, Kate 118, L. A. 125,Lenora J. 132, Lola 118, Rebecca J. 118, Rebecca T. 118, Vista I. 118, W. H. 118;
ISLAND CITY SAVINGS BANK 152;
IVEY, J. J. 119.

-J-
JACK (JACKS) Laura H. 114 Patrick C. 10, 12,Wm. H. 114;
JACKSON, Alex M. Jr. 71, Chas. 84, Curtis M. 57, Elizabeth 114, John M. 57 Milton 13, N. R. 48, R.M 58, Susie 125, T. C. 45, T. M. 3, Thos. C. 85, Wm. R. 125;
JACOBS, Euel 94, Joseph 60, L. J. 94, R. P. 94, Well 128, Zoe 94;
JAGER (YAGER) Andrew 110;
JAMES, Ashby S. 37, 38, C. A. 16, Chas. A. 16, John G. 16, Margaret E.16 Phoebe Peck 34, Thos.H.34;
JAMESON (JAMISON) R. S.5;
JAQUA, A. E. 86, Sarah 84, Sarah M. 86;
JAQUES, GEO. B. 60;
JARMON, Alma B. 80, R. E. 80;
JARRELL, Stephen 141;
JAYNE, J. 153, Juliet 30 Joe J. 72, Joseph 71;
JAYS, Jacob 127;
JEFFERSON, Lillie 60, May 60, Silas W. 60,W.W. 60;
JEFFREY, John K. 147;
JEFFRIES, Rebecca J. 118;
JEMISON, W. J. 45;
JENKINS, home 115, Thos. H. 130, Virginia E. 130;
JENNINGS, Aarene 132,Anna 133, Delila Elizabeth 120 Gordon C. 24, James J. 132, J. T. 133, L. S. 132, Saml. K. 31, 90, 109;
JESSNEY, Anna Catherine 14, Jacob 14, Mathlodi (Malodi) 14, Sabel 14;
JESTER, S. B. 79;
JEWETT, H. J. 127;
JOBE, P. W. 44, 76, Phillip 50;

JOHNS, B. F. 107, C. K. 128, 136, Clement R. 8, 76, Emily H. 67, J. P. 135, P. R. 99;
JOHNSON, A. G. 106, Alex C. 24, Alice Ruth 59, Annie 88, Augusta 20, 88 Benj. 145, Benj. F. 24, 68, 78, 100, B. F. 8, 32 36, 38, 104, Ben H. 102, 105, Ben J. 24, Betty J. 46, Chas. 36, 112, Chas. A. 32 88, Chas. J. 88, Chas. P. 59, C. C. J. 88 Cornelia J. White 18, Cornelia Jane 3, 35, 39, D. 102, D. A. 59, Dallas 29, Dallas Kyle 29, David A. 59, D. A. 59, Emily 88 Emma Virginia 108, Enoch 2, 35, 39, 58, 66, 70, 110 E. S. 18, 35, Fannie A. 29, Frank C. 59, Frances Lyons 59, Franklin 147, Fred 88, Gus,88, Helen Elizabeth Morse 59, Jas. F. 16, 26, 58, 66, 69, Jas. R. 23, 24, 37, 41 97 John 99, John C. 32, John O. 7 46, 58, 93, John R. 29, Henry 88, Ira B. 59,Josephine G. 29, Julius 88, L. B. 65, 145, Lucius B. 145, Marcia 38, M. 102, Martha A. 93, Mary 59, 88 Mary C. 24, 37, 38, Mary E. 29, Mary Jane 59,Mary Olivia 88, Maud 53,Moses 98, 106, M. M.37, Raymond 24, Richard M. 29, 47, R. D. 36, R. M. 5, 47, Robt. D. 2, Sarah 32, Solomon L. 106, Mrs.T.M. 135, T. J. D. 53, Walter 88, 97, Wm. H. 22, W. H. H. 26, W. H. W. 6, W. J. 20, 56, W. Wm. 76, 108 145, Wm. R. 97, Wilbur J. 61, Zuella 59; Frank 155;
JOHNSTON, Alex 111, Ella 141, Franklin 52, 145, Helena 141, James 141, John C. 141, Johnston & O'Banion 141, Mary Ann 141, Robert 141;
JOINER, H. H. 136;
JONES, A. E. 46, 92, A.F. 10, 54, A. S. 119, Albert C. 45, Alick 21, Annie E. 93, Anson 22, 34, 69, Bennett J. 151, Calvin 96 106, Chas. 116, Chas. G. 48, 56, Crawford 45,Delia J. 45, E. C. 45,Edward 61 E. 60, Edmund C. 45, 60, 61, Eleanor P.78, Elizabeth C. 45, 61, Emma Lee 3, Emily E. 111, F. H.48, Geo. 25, Henry 105, 107, Ira B. 59, I. M. 92, Isaac V. 3, 92, 111, Jas. R. 19, James W. 93, Jane Ferry 83, Jay Jarvis 60, Joel W. 17, Jos. 116, 117 J. J. 8, J. W. 46, 92, John R. 130, John Rice 20 J. R. 20, 29, John S. 92 John L. 84, Klebar 3, Linton 3, Louisa 59, Louise 61, Louisa J. 96, Maria L 3 Marsha 151, Mattie A. 45, 96, Mathilda 88,Mary 151, Oliver 127, Olivia 3,

Peter 24,Randall 82, Richard Payne 44, 78, 88, R. R. 92, Rufus R. 3, 111, R. F. 45, 96, Robt. 45 96, R. A. 45, R. P. 44, Sam Houston 108, Saml.6, Scharlotte 88, S. M. 147 Theo. H. 2, 3, 8, 12, 36 54, 59, 62, 92, 101, 102 108, Thos. L. 107, T. M. 46, W. B. 85, W. C. 45 Wiley 114, Willie R. 28, W. W. 132, Zilphy 127;
JOLLY, J. G. 93, J. H. 121 Mary Tennessee 52, M. E. 121;
JORDAN, Albert A. 23, Frank W. 130, Mary 130, W. M. 130;
JOSEPH, Thos. M. 36, Wright D. 112;
JOURDAN, Amanda B. 25, 52, 74, 92, Anne 25, Arch P. 25, C. W. 92, Fannie P. 25, 92, Frederick 25, 92, Geo. W. 25, 92,Harriet Bell 92, Harriet E. 92, James 25, 92, Jennie L. 25, John B. 25, 92, J.L. 92, Julia E. 25, Mary C. 25, 92, Sallie 25, Wm. Waldermore 92, Zacharest P. 25, 92;
"JOURNAL" The, 123;
JOYNER, Joe J. 72,Joseph 71;
JUNG, Adolph 116.

-K-
KAPPLER, J. G. 73;
KARNEGAY, D. S. 15;
KARNES, Francis 24;
KASCH,Amanda 73, Betty Ann 73, Ed 73, James Warren 73, Milton 73, Milton Edward 73;
KAUFMAN, Joseph 25,Theresa J. 25; Thos. 25
KAVANAUGH, Clem 44, Eva K. 44, Geo. 44, Leila 44 Lena K. 44, Jacob (Jake) 44, Margaret 78, Matthew 44, Robt. 44;
KAZINE, Ann 71 72, Caroline 72, Chas. 71, 72, Delphia 72, Fannie 72, Glen 72;
KEEL, Marion 86, Mary E. 86, Robt. M. 86;
KEEN, Mrs. Ella Hamilton 32;
KEES, August 111;
KELLAM, A. B. 29, Sarah A. 29;KELLOGG,V.L.106;
KELLER, O. 148;
KELLEY,Florence 77,Francis 44, 79, 80, 81, Susan 77;
KELLY, A. K. O. 122, Francis 11, 35, 44, 79, 80, 81, 108, John W. 11 79, 122; Lennie 122, Mary A. 11, 79, 80, 81, Mary Ann 11, Mary Jane 11,79 M. Calhoun 55, Wm. T. 11 79;KELLUM,A.R.85,S.A.85;
KENDALL, Haywood H. 77, Hutchison 77, Nathan 77;
KENABLOCK, C. A. 118;
KENNEDY, E. J. 132, J.B. 132, John J. 5, M. 132 M. J. 132;
KENNEY (KINNEY), KINNIE)

Mary 138, Thos. 138;
KENRICK, C. 81, Harvey 54;
KEY, W. M. 141;
KENSINGTON, Edward 134;
KENTUCKY, 1;
KEPLER, Wm. 104;
KIDD, Cincinnatus 136, Harry Walton 131, H. P. 131, T. B. 131;
KILGORE, Agnes 61,J.M. 61;
KILLINGSWORTH, E. P. 88;
KILLOUGH, I. G. 21,J.G.21 S 42, Mamie L. 42, Phillis 115, W. T. 151
KIMBALL, Wm. H. 76;
KIMBLE, Albert G. 108;
KIMBRO, Daniel 117;
KINCHEON, Julia 48;
KING,Amanda 144, Ben. L. 119, Benj. Lewis 120, Clarabel 119, 120, Chas. F. 57, 107, Coy 116, Delila Elizabeth 120, E. A. 148, Eva Lee 119, Mrs E. M. 52; Frank A. 148, Grace Ann 120, H. F. 121, Henry G. 148, H. C. A. 148, James C. 119, John E. 148, John M. 51,Julia D. 121, Lillie Rosa 120 Mary Sue 119, Martha 80, N. J. 31, Nick 120, Richard 31, Sylvia 148, Sue Miles 119, Susan M. 119, Tecumceh 120, Thos. J. 80, Wm. A. 51, 52, W. C. 144, W. F. 121, W. H. 96, Mrs. W. M. 52, Watkins 120;
KINGSBERRY (KINGSBURY) S. G. 7;
KINGSTONE, Wm. 45;
KINNARD, L. 121;
KINNEAR, Francis 148, Mathilda Bell 148;
KINNEY, Beulah E. 89, Chas. D. 89, David R.13, 89, Ed P. 26, F. G. 12, Frances Grace 12,Francis J.89, Geo. P. 89, Gladys A. King 89, Harry B. 26, Harvey Lee 89, Hattie B. 26, H. B. 13, John D. 89, L. B. 12, Lillian B. 12, Myron D. 89, Martha A. 26, Martin M. 124,Olivia T. Cleveland 89, Olivia S. 89, Ophelia L. 89, O. T. 13, R. H. 12, Roland D. 89, Roswell H. 12, S. E. 12, Smith Evans 12 Warren 6;
KIRBY, Isaach 51, J. C. 85, Jacob C. 84, Joseph C. 96, Marie M. Spence 84; 96;
KIRK, Nancy 123, Nancy W. 123;
KIRSCHER, Wm. 103;
KIRSCHNER, Christian 110;
KIRKLAND, Geo. W. 125;
KIRKPATRICK, E. S. 42, Mattie L. 42;
KIRCHBURG, Gustavus 111, Wm. 107;
KIRVEN, O. C. 124;
KLEIN, Albertine 37, Arnold 37, Barbara 37, Caroline 37, Chas. 12, 37 108, Elizabeth 21,John P. 21, Mary J. 21, Mary N. 21, Peter 21, 110,

Peter J. 21; Chas.155;
KLOCKE, H. 129;
KLOPPENBERG, H. 107;
KLOTZ, Carrie Isabell 12 30;
KNIGHT, Caroline 140,144 Eliza 140, 144, Isabel M. 85 James 57, 140, 144, J. B. 140, 141, Joseph B. 144, J. R. 124, Martha 140 144, 80, 146, Martha Ann 80, 140, 144, Mary A. 140 146, Nancy 144, Nannie 140 144, Thos. J. King 80, Wm. 140, 144, 146, Wm. H. 95;
KNOX, Isaac J. 118;
KOEGH, M. H. 60;
KOENEGER, L. 93;
KOFAHL, Chris. 19;
KOPPERL, B. J. 71, M. A. 52, Montz 12, Waldine Zimpelman 12;
KRAFT, Sabastine 43;
KRAMER (see von KRAMER)
KRAUSE, Bertram 65, Eleanor 65, Helena 65, R. 90, Rudolph K. 65, 72;
KRAUSS, A. B. 78;
KREMPKOW, Otto 145;
KUEHNE, F. 37;
KREUENCKE, Edna 3;
KUNZE, Frank52, Mabel Julia 52;
KUPFER, Rosiana Barbara 15, T. S. 15;
KYLE, C. 100, Claiborne 153, Dorothula 56; Emma Jane 57, Fergus 29,Margaret W. Harris 57, Martha T 57, R. B. 56.

-L-
LABENSKI, Victor L. 108;
LACY, H. 50, Martha 50, M. A. 50;
LACKEY, N. M. A. 47, U. G. 47;
LaCosta L. B. 129;
LADD, Caroline 141, Henry Hoxie 26, (See Winn) Wm. F. 141;
LaFour, F. R. 85;
LAMAIR, Chas. 19, Mary E. 18, 19;
LAMAR, Gazaway B. 65, Mirabeau B. 41, 54, 65, 66, 83, 100;
LAMB, CO. 134;
LAMB, James 107;
LAMPASAS Co. 134;
LAMPKINS, D. 137;
LANDERS, John 120, Mary Elizabeth 121;
LAND OFFICE, 82;
LANE, Addison 109, A. E. 65, 69, Annie 13, 35,Burleson 65, D. A. 59, 65, Fannie 53, Frances E. (Betty) 65, Gertrude 59, Hanson, 55, H. S. 53,Jas. M. 110, Jas. S. 13, 35, John Lafayette 121, John 31, John W. 59, 65, Jos. L. 84, L. B. D. 5, Lelia (Lena) Clay 26, Laura E. 31, Martha Jane 120,Mary 59, 65, Mary Ann 65, Mary Jane 59, 65, 69, Mattie 65, M. H. 94; Manervia Anne 121, Maud 53, Newton Givens 13, 35, R. N. 13, 22, 35, Sarah 32, S. G. 94

Watts E. 59, 65, Wm. A. 72, 76, W. H. 62, 65;
LANCASTER, J. N. 121,Mary A. 121;
LANFEAR, Ambrose 44;
LANGERMANN, A. B. 59, 60, 94, Marie Althalie 59,60;
LANGSTON, Jesse E. 74, Roxina F. 74;
LaRUE, Amanda 4, 14, 47, 72, Edward 14, Emily 72, Geo. F. 47, 72, L. M. 14 Mary 72;
LANTERMAN, A. 131,Catherine M. 131;
LARABIE, Chas. .102;
LARKINS, Warren 57;
LASTLEY, Robt. 134;
LATHAM, M. M. 121, W. J. 121;
LATIMER, W. W. 61;
LaTROBE, Chas. Albert 134;
LAUBSCHEO, Gustav A. 38;
LAUCK, Mrs.E. B. 151,Geo B. 55, T. H. 151;
LAUGHLIN, D. 7, 106, David 102, 104, 106, 107;
LAVACA CO. 135;
LAWHORN CEMETERY 135;
LAWHORN, Hugh M. 110, 111 W. C. 25;
LAWRENCE John R. 12, J.R 10, J. W. 9, Mills Whitley 131;
LAWSON, Vera 94;
LAY, Sylvester 62;
LEA, Joseph C. 58;
LEACH, John 55;
LEBERMANN, H. F. 126, N. V. 126;
LEBOLD, C. H. 38, Lillian 38, W. F. 38;
LEDBETTER, J. W. 145;
LEE COUNTY 135;
LEE, A. 43, Abner 7, Chas. H. 3, 92, Emma 3, 92, Green 103, 105, H. G. 8, 96, Horatio Grooms 72, H. Grooms 72, 77, J. C. 138, John C. 18, Joseph 9 11, 18, 26, 58, 65, 66, 69, 72, 76, 77, 86, 100, 101 113 106, 107, 147, Lydia 7, Mary 55, 63, Nancy 119 Rhoda 55, Rhoda Bird 63, Robt. E. 131,Sarah 11, 72 77, Sarah J. 72, 77;
LEFTWICH, Robt. 145, 147 Wm. 53;
LEGETT, Mary A. 112;
LEME, John H. 13;
LEMONS, G. W. 140, 144;
LENSING, Elizabeth 66, James 66, Lemuel 94;
LENTZ, Eliza 117, Gabe 117 LaRue 52, Martha 117;
LEONARD, Chas. 44, Jas. 54, Lanier 54, Mary C.54 Marguerite 54, Mary Margaret 54, Miles Jr. 54;
LEON & H. BLUM LAND Co.152;
LESER (LESSER) Jacob 89, John 97;
LESTER, Fountain 62, 63, 68, James S. 21, 66, 75, J. G. 121, J. S. 121(Mrs);
LeSUERER (LaSuer), Anna E. 44, 49, 90, C. M. 44 90, Lelah N. 3, Noel Winston 3, Saml. J. 3, Maria Leopoldine Emma 86, W. N 3;

LEVI, John 127, 128;
LEVITT, Benj. 149,
Lucinda 149;
LEVY, Wm. 153;
LEWIS, Allen Lewis Place
30, Andrew J. 134, D. K.
3, Elizabeth 50, Ira A.
18, Ira R. 46, James 50
John L. 10, John P. 50
L. L. 119, Louisa 46,
Lucy Ann 3, M. Henrietta
94, Wilson F. 94, Wm.
50, 51;
LEWRIGHT, Estelle 70, J.
B. 70, J. C. 70, Mary V.
70, Maud L. 70;
"LIDEL" The 37;
LIESSE, John 110;
LIGHTFOOT, W. F. 2, W. H
F. 92, W. T. 16, 36;
LIMERICK, Eliza 43,
Joseph 43, 111;
LINCOLN, Abe 42;
LINDHOLM, Augusta 88,
S. L. 88;
LINK, J. A. 137;
LINN, Geo. 58, John E.6;
LINDSAY, A. M. 128, C. H
28, C. M. 28, Luetta
Kinney 12, Nannie 28,
W. G. 12, Wm. 129;
LINDSEY, Mary Ann 118;
LIPSCOMB, Abner S. 103;
LISMAN, Thos. P. 137;
LITTON (LYTTON_) John
114, J. M. 35, 81,
Sarah 114;
LITTLE, James M. 51,
Simon 137;
LITTLEPAGE, H. 101,
James B. 111;
LIVINGSTON, J., E. 131,
J. S. 126;
LLOYD, Richard 103;
LOCKE, Richard 83;
LOCKETT, Al 39;
LOCKHART CITY CEMTERY,
121;
LOCKHART POST REGISTER,
121;
LOCKHART, C. L. 8;
LOCKWOOD, S. 99;
LOESCHMANN, Ottellie
Charlotte 72;
LOFLIN, Sarah 91, W. T.91
LOGAN, A. T. 24, 49,Eliza
J. 24, 49, 145;
LOGREN, Amanda Christiana
13, 139, Sallie Alma 13,
Sarah 13, 139;
LOHMAN, Antonette 12, H.
12, Henry 109, John
Henry 12, Mary 12, Rosine
12, Theodora 12;
LONG, Catherine Emily J.
50, Harford 14, James M.
15, 36, 48, 67, 79, 83,
100, John 50, Josephine
50, Lucinda E. 50, M. A.
50, Minus M. 77, Penelope
120, Virginia 50, W. E.
50, Wm. 50, Wm. G. 14;
LONGBOTHAM, J. O. 124,
Louisa 124, Lucy 124, 123
R. B. 124, Thos. 124;
LONGLEY, Alfred H. 36;
LONGSCOPE, Chas. S. 41;
LONGSTREET, Gilbert 118;
LOOMIS, Celeste 26, Chris-
tian 26, Lydia May 26,
Simon 26, Simon Christian
26;
LOPEZ, Theodore 136;

LORD, Chas. 32, Chas. W.
32, Laura G. 32;
LOUGHRAN, Maggie Mc
Brearty 54;
LOVE, Lelia 26, Robt.
45, W. H. 26;
LOVETT, R. S. 127;
LOVING, H. H. 30, James
M. 61, R. J. 61, Virginia
F. 61;
LOVELACE, DeWitt 84;
LOWE, Peter B. 49, 90,112;
LOWREY, W. G. 93;
LOYD, F. 106, Simpson 52;
LUCIANO, Cabasos 119;
LUEDECKE, Wm. 75;
LUCKETT,Alfred 8, 27,
Alfred Thornton 8, Alfred
T. 8, 36, 37, Alfred W.
8, Ann C. 8, A. W. 7, 36
95, 102, 105, Basil H. 27
Ed H. 27, Henry H. 27,
H. Powell 27, John H. 27,
Levin H. 8, 36, L. H. 8,
17, 25, 27, 33, 36, 39,
53, 58, 64, 66, 67, 81,
101, L. Horace 8, 27,
Louise 27, Mary Jane 8, 36
N. M. 36, 69, 100, 108,8,
Nowland W. 8, P. P. 24,
Susan E. 27, T. Dade 27,
Wm. 8;
LUCKSINGER, Mary 37, Saml
37, 40, 97;
LUMPKIN, G. F. 90, P. V.
105;
LUNATIC ASYLUM 77;
LURRY, Anne P. 31, Roy
31, W. C. 31;
LUTHERAN Church Cemetery
122;
LYNCH, Catherine 46, John
L. 64, 75, 98, Sarah Ann
46, Thos. 46;
LYON, Francis 59, 65,
Pincus 136, W. W. 28,30,50
LYTLE, James T. 57.

-Mc-
McALISTER, G. A. 130, M.
L. 125;
McANNELLY, R. D. 43, 136,
145;
McANULTY, Sarah 124;
McARTHUR,Isam 99, J. P.31
James P. 31, 108; N. 103,
Nicholas 41, 54, 82, 103
106, Wm. 134;
McBREARY, Catherine Mc
Laughlin 43, ...John
54, Mary 54;
McBRIDE, John 125, Mattie
71, Wm. 94, W. W. 71;H.63;
McCALL America P. 64,
Jennie C. 92, J. S. W. C.
64, John R. 29, 64, John
125, Sarah S. S. 46, W. C
64;
McCALLA, Jannet 67, John
67;
McCARTHY, E. F. 69, 71;
McCARTY, A. B. 71, A. J.
71, Annie 71 E. F. 69,52;
McCASHIN, Neill 78;
McCAULEY, Daniel 7;
McCLAIN, Dorsea (Theodus)
28, J. M. 28;
McCLANAHAN, J. M.2, W. A.
23;
McCLENDEN E. H. Herndon
131, Jane 131, J. 131,
Leila Miles 119, Wm.S.131;
McCLINTOCK, Geo. W. 68,

Phebe 68;
McCLURE, Fredonia 140,
Geo. 140, H. 90, Susan
C. 143;
McCLUSKY, Geo. B. 105;
McCONNELL, A. J. 90,
Bessie 90;
McCONOUGHY, David W.85;
McCORD, A. F. 18, James
E. 128, Julia C. 18;
McCORMICK, J. R. 13, H.
129;
McCOY, John C. 85,
John M. 85;
McCREA, G. P. 143;
McCREARY, John 139;
McCUISTION,Annie P.
Slaughter 31, Ellenor
133, Elisha 133, John J
31, 108, Noah 141;
McCULLOCK, H. E. 15;
McCULLOUGH, James H. 77
Margaret 77;
McCUTCHEON (McCUTCHIN)
Jesse A. 21, 55, Joseph
T. 21;
McDADE CEMETERY 115,116
McDANIEL, J. W. 125;
McDONALD, Alexander 106,
Burt 26, Ellen C. 5,
John 5, 88, 96, Thos 119;
McDONNELL, Sam J. P. 34;
McDOUGLE, Etta May 149,
John 149;
McELLENNY, Bernard 43,
Mary Ann 43;
McELROY, Ada 133, Chas.
S. 17, Elizabeth 16, 17
Francella 17, Gault 57,
Henry 16, 17, Howard C.
133, Phillip 16, 17,
Sarah Ellen 48, 57, Thos
E. 133, Wm. A. 133;
McEWER, John B. 76;
McFALL, D. A. 71, J. K.
84, Mary 84;
McFARLAND (McFARLANE),
Abel 5, 84, Alexander
C. 98, A. C. 84, Mrs.
A. M. 73, Bernice E. 73
Chandler & McFarland,atty.
24, David 73, DICKERSON
(DICKINSON) 54, DICKERSON
& McFARLAND 54, Jane 5,
84, Joseph 54, J. B. 15
M. J. 5, 84, R. J. 5, 84
Saml. N. 84, Sarah Jaques
84, Wm. 84, W. H. 73;J.84;
McFADDIN, A. C. 105, -
D. W. 20;
McGAFFY, Neal 140, 144;
McGARY, James D. 94,
J. D. 36;
McGEE, Anna 33, 35, Eliza-
beth 7, James M. 99,John
T. 33, 35, James L. 33,
M. H. 7, Robt. Bruce 7,
Saml. 7;
McGEHEE, Chas. L. 82,112;
McGILL, Ashford B. 7, 10
12, 15, 21, 28, 30, 53
54, 65, 75, 83, 98, 102,
108, 112, Bridget 43,
Isabella 43, John 43,
Patrick 43;
McGINNIS, Anna M. 115,
John 142, O. H. P. 115;
McGONIGAL, Jos. C. 44,
45, James 45, James M.45
McGOWAN, Georgia 25;
McGOWEN, Alexander R.
99, Edward 99, Geo. 99
Geo. R. 99, James 99,103

John 103, 104, Thos. M. 99;
McGREAL, H. 107, Peter 10, 12, 44, 58, 78;
McGUIRE, John 94, Marguerite 54;
McGUNDY, Lucinda H. 121, Wm. 121;
McGUYER, A. J. 134;
McHUGH, Bond B. 138, Edwinia 138, Isabella McLaughlin 43, John 43 Patrick 43;
McINTIRE, Richard 85;
McKEAN,Mrs. A. C. 56, A. T. 56, E. T. 56, T. 153, Timothy 15, 16, 29, 72, 102;
McKEE, F. V. 14;
McKELVEY, Alice 16, J. J 16;
McKENSIE (McKINZE) David 35, John 35, Rowland 35;
McKINNEY (McKINNIE), Anna G . 66, Clement P. 130, Collin 153, James F. 10, James P. 2, 10, 92, 108, Marcellus 130, Nancy 114, Thos. F. 2, 32, 36, 64, 75, 82, 92, 114, Thos. J. 55;
McKINSEY, Donald 74, Mary E. Saunders 74;
MacKENZIE, Amanda 70, Amanda J. 70, Ann 70, 86 Asa 70, 86, Francis 70 Frances M. Hopkins 70 Geo. W. 70, Harriette E. 70, 71, J. A. 146, James 70, Kenneth 103, 105,, Lacy 70, 71, 94, Lasa 70, 86, Martha M. 70, Mary Ann 70, Mrs. Maud Sparks 146, Rachel A. 70, Richard 70,Sarah E. 70, 86, Wm. 106;
McKNIGHT, James 2;
McLAREN, Angus 109;
McLAUGHLIN, Catherine 43 Chas. 43, Elijah 100, Ellen 43, Ellen Ann 43, Isabella 43, Mary 43, Mary Ann 43, Rose Ann 43;
McLAURIN, Angus 150, Farrior 72, Irene E. 70, J. T. 24, 32, 33, 35,55 59, 62, 68, 98, 101,114 J. J. 109, James 100, M. H. 56, W. W. 70;
McLEAN, A. A. 97, E. 10, Ephram 10;
MC LENDON, Isaac 128, 131 Jane Seal 128, 131;
McLEMORE, Jim 11, June W. B. Norris 143;
McLENDON, Lila Miles 119;
McLENNAN Co. Texas
McLENNAN (McLILLIAN) Rufus 13;
McLESTER, H. 23;
McLEOD, Hugh 64, 102, 105
McLILLAN, Rufus 14;
McMAHON, Perry F. 123;
McMARTIN, D. C. 26;
McNEESE, Amanda 143, Ben 143, C. W. 143, Edd 143, Ellen 143, Franklin 143, Lena B. 143, B. F. 143 L. M. 143, L. M. 143, Mollie F. 143, T. R. 143 W. E. 143, Williametta 143;
McNICHOLAS, F. 77;

McNULTY, Sarah 124;
McQUEEN, Axis 122, J. A. M. 122, M. D. 122;
McRAE, A. L. 5, Maranda 5, Wm. 51;
McSWEENY, James 144;
McWILLIAMS, Agnes C. 44 John H. 44.

-M-

MARKS & BRANDS, 108-112;
MAAG, Adam 58, Roxine 153;
MAAS, Clara 84, M. 84;
MABEN C. E. 134, 135, L. E. 134, 135, Mary Ann 34, Mary E. 135, M. O. 135, W. B. 33, Wm. P. 34 101;
MABRY, W. P. 59;
MABSON, W. P. Sr. 48;
MACHAEL, Ziller 53;
MACKENZIE, J. A.146,Maud Sparks 146;
MACKEY, James H. 78, Jas. Willis 78, John 128;
MADDEN, J. E. 135, J. N. 136, S. M. 136;
MADDING, J. M. 130,Mary Elizabeth 130;
MADDOX, Andrew 132, C. H. M. 132, Danl. H. 132; Elizabeth C. 132, Frank M. 24, 37, 41, F. M. 79, John 79, John W. 24, 37, 41, 79, L. A. 132,MADDOX BROS. 24, 37, 41, MARY D. 79, Mollie D. 79, Robt. BOWlen 132, Selety 132;
MADISON, Jennie 90, Jesse 90, Mary Jane 27;
MAGEE (MAIGE, McGEE) Annie 35, Herny 97, James 141, John T. 35, Joseah 65;
MAGGINSON, Joe 44;
MAGILL (Magreil) Cora 146 J. D. 146;
MAJOR, Eliza 47, Col. Jas. P. 47;
MAKEMSON, W. K. 140;
MALLERRY, E. 114;
MALONE, James 80, James L. 11, 128, 153, Mrs. Lilly 27;
MANEY, Wm. F. 92;
MANLOVE, Abrella 138, B. 21, 138, 140, 146, 152, Mary Ann Bartholomew 146;
MANN, Mrs. Anne L. 139, C L. 80, J. W. 37;
MANNING, Ben 27;
MANOR, Ann E. 74, Catherine G. 74, Elizabeth A. 74, Elvira T. 74, James 64, 69, 74, 75, 84, Joseph 98, Joseph J. 108, Lizzie N. 74, Lucy 74, Lavenia 74, Mary 37, Mathilda J. 74, Phebe S. 75, Mrs. U. S. 47;
MANSBENDEL, Peter 50;
MANSON, Edward Randall 152, Mary Randall 152, Mary Grant (Gautt) 152, W. F. 152, Wm. F. 152;
MARCHITTE, G. 55;
MARCONNIER, A. C. 77, Gertrude 77;
MAROHN, Gottfried 112;
MARSH, B. J. 131;
MARSHALL, John 66, 111, L. A. 123, Vesta I. 118, M. & Oldham, atty. 75;

MARTINUS, Raphael 111;
MARSON, Elizabeth 114;
MARTIN, Archibald 11, Beulah 83, Emily 130, Eva 48, Geo. W. 143, Henry 6 Henry B. 36, John H. 37, 49, Linee M. 115, Lucy H 37, 49, Matha W.143, Thos. Wm. 134, W. H. 144 Wm. O. 111, W. P. 120;
MASON, Addie 151, A. J. 151, Alpheous 151, A. S. 151, Augusta A. 151, Betty 151, C. C. 141, 149, 151 Chas. 151, 8, 101, 113, Chas. C. 150, Elizabeth Bell 151, Harriett M. Cluck 143, James A. 60, James N. 151, J. M. 151 J. N. 151, John 143,151 John D. 151, Julie 143, Louisa 151, Mary J. 149, 151, Mary Jane 151, Mary L. 151, Maggie 151, Nancy 151;
MASSEY, Andrew 53, Greenberry 118, Ida 53, Martha A. 132, W. 7;
MASSIE, John M. 101;
MASTERSON, Annie W. 87, Alpheous (Appolus) 87, Branch T. 87, 125, Birdsall 127, Evelyn 87, Harris 127, Harrison 127, J Harris 87, Leigh 127, May M. 87, N. T. 127, Ralph 127, Rane 127, Rebecca B 87, Sallie 127, T. R. 127, T. W. 87, Thos. G.10 Thos. W. Jr. 87, Wilman D. 87;
MATHEY, C. F. 125;
MATHER, Anna 90, Saml.90;
MATTHEWS,A. B. 140,Abner 47, 53, 77, Agnes H. 53, Anne 22, 138, Ascenetha 47, 53, Dan B. 34, 87, E. J. 53, Eric 22, E. S.47 53, 65, E. S. M. 53, Elizabeth 47, 53, Esther H. 47, 53, Ezekel S. 47, Frank 22, 87, G. S. 41, Ike 138, Jake 138, J. A. 33, James S. 87, J. H. 112 John A. 47, 53, John C. 109, John J. 113, Joseph 98, J. Steele 76, Libbie 34, Louisa D. 47, 87, Mary D. 47, 53, Mary E. 22, 87, Martha M. 47, 53 Ouida Belle 138, Paul 22 Robt. F. 47, 53, Robt. H. 87, Rosa 22, Rufus P. 87 Thos. A. 110, Wm. S. 87, Nancy H. 53; J.H.39 64,75
MATTICE, A. W. 130;
MATTINGLY, Delfah 117;
MAULDING, Elisha C. 146;
MAUTHE, Carrie Isabel 12 30, Henry 12, 30;
MAXWELL, A. Carson 61, Agnes 61, Alex. Carson 61 Annie L. 61, Cynthia A. 61, E. 61 Ella J. 61, F.A 61, Forrest O. 61, F. P. 61, Frank H. 61, Florence 61, Harriett V. 61, Henry J. 61 J. C. 25, J. A. Carson 61, James C. 55, 92, James H. 61, J. C. 92, Jennie L. 25, Jesse W. 61 Garrett 61, Louise 61, Louisa Jane 92, Maggie L

61, Matthew W. 61, Owen
Hickman 61, R. Henry 61
Sadie 61, Thos. O. 61,
Thos. Q. 61, Virginia F.
61, Wm. W. 61, W. W. 61;
MAXEY, T. S. 16;
MAY, Gibson 84, Morris
14, Pearl95;
MAYER, S. B. 137;
MAYHEME, Alice 19;
MAYNE, W. W. 3,;
MAYTUM, Martha Ann 4,
W. H. 4;
MAYS, Danl. 128, G. H.
Sr. 52, J. E. 90, John
59, Nancy Elizabeth 52,
Parolic E. 56, Sina 90,
Thos. H. 11, 6, 28, 30,
35, 44, 58, 59 64, 65,
66, 76, 138;
MEARS, C. M. 140;
MECKLING, W. J. 66;
MEDLIN, Hall 11, 35, 81,
109, S. C. 94;
MEEK, John W. 46, Louise
S. 46;
MEEKS, John 109, S. Ann
134, W. J.134;
MEGG, Adam 153;
MEGRATH, C. R. 38;
MEINERS, Augusta 130
Chas. 130, Emilie 130,
Wm. O. 130, Willie O.
130;
MELTON, Strand 134;
MELVILLE, Wm. B. 106;
MENARD, Michael B. 2, 36
92;
MENCKE, Joseph 136;
MENEFEE, B. 150;
MENGER, A. F. 135;
MERCER, Elizabeth 139,
Fannie B. Nelson 11, Geo
H. 139, Geo. R. 139,
Matthew 139;
MEREDITH, Francis 59,
Sallie 59;
MERIWETHER, Wm. H. 121,
130;
MERONEY, O. H. 14;
MERRELL (MERRILL,MERIL)
Nelson 39, 64, 65, 70, 98
108, 138; 155
MERRIMAN (MERRYMAN) Alice
F. 39, E. T. 2, 64, 96;
METCALF, Delphana 123,
Julie O. 40, Thos. D. 40;
METHODIST EPISCOPAL CH.
93;
METHVARN, Joseph T. 57;
METZ, M. H. 8, 11, 12,
41, 47;
MEURER, Mrs. Elizabeth
117, Mrs. John 117;
MEYER, Alma 95, Antonio
60, August 95, C. 51,
Elsie 95, Lilie 95,
Sophie 95, Theo. P. 60;
MEYERHEFER, Joseph 136;
MICHAEL, Ziller 99;
MIDDLEBROOK, M. A. 131,
Mrs. N. L. 131, S. G.
131;
MIDDLETON, M. S. Dunn 89;
MIERS, ANN Castner 117,
H. T. 117;
MILAM Co. 136;
MILAM Bartley B. 91, Benj
R. 10, 28, 36, 68, B. M
91, Brice 91, John J.T.
148; Ben 155;
MILES, A. H. 127, Benj.
119, C. S. 119, F. B.119

J. T. 138, Lelia 119, Ora
138, Susan 119, Wm. P.10
Walter 138;
MILLARD, Frederick S. 51,
151, Henry B. 51, 151,
Col. Henry 51, 151, Henry
K. 106, 144;
MILLER CREEK CEMETERY 132;
MILLER, C. A. 140 Cain 114
Catherine 93, Chas. F.148
Chas. W. 51, Doris 15,
Mrs. E. A. 93, Evelyn 55,
Frances 114, Hanna 148,J.
A. 51, Jane Dean 46, J.K.
114, John 98, John G. 69,
93, John T. 6, 36, 77, 93
J. R. 53, Joseph A. 51,
L. R. 104, Lizzie 114,
Mattie 114, M. C. 41,
Martha 114, M. D. 21,
Mildred 33, 35, N. J. 119
N. S. 55, Owen 114,Saml.
R. 20, 44, 54, 64, 96,
105, 127, Sophie W. 21,
Thos. R. 129, Washington
D. 36, 110, W. A. H. 100
136, W. D. 2, 18, 33, 35,
36, 93, W. J. 15, MILLER
& DOWELL attys. 92, W. H.
92; James B. 155;
MILLETT, C. F. 70, C. S.
40;
MILLICAN, E. B. 34, Fannie
Peck 34, O. H. 24, 34, 35
69, 77, P. 4, 61, Peter
94;

MILLS, Dean Clough 55,
Maggie 15, Mary Hamilton
26, 27, Saml. A. 104, 105
W. W. 26, 27;
MILUM Burris 91, J. H. 91
Sarah Ann 91, Tennessee
91;
MINER, J. 49, Joel 153,
M. 101, Phillip 148;
MINGER, G. S. 143;
MINOR, Cynthia B. 42, J.
4, 62, 65, 100, 101, Joel
35, 68, 108, 153, Phillip
57;
MISSISSIPPI, 1;
MISTRAT, Felix E. 137;
MITHVARN, Joseph T. 57;
MITCHELL, B. J. J. 133,
David 140, Elizabeth H.
30, 88, Mrs. E. H. 88,
Geraldine 133, Dr. James
30, 88, Martha 6,133, Martha D. 132, Martha H. 31
Martin 31,,Nathan 86,
Nathaniel 65, Randolph
132,Robt. 6, Robt. G. 132
133, Sarah G. 132, 133,
Washington 132, 133;
M. K. & T. Land Co. 77;
MOBLEY, Cora A. 116, Thos
R. 116, Waldena 116;
MOCK, Wm. N. 67;
MODEN, Joseph 13;
MODGLING, Margaret 84;
MOELLER, Agnes 15, H. W.
15, J. C. 93;
MOFFATT (MOFFITT) L. H.
5, Margaret 67, Martha J.
67, Wm. S. 67;
MOHLE, Flavius Down 40,
Nellie Lenora Margaret
Pauls 40;
MOLE, (MALE) John 13;
MONOGUE,Alberta 77,
Brigett 77, Margaret 77,
Mary 77, Thos. M.77,W.77;

MONROE, Martha M. 47, 53
P. A. 53, Rachel Amanda
16, Wm. N. 16;
MONTANDON...54;
MONTGOMERY Almira 128,
Edmund D. 88, Eliza 140,
Elizabet Ney 88, F. L.
77, James 128, 140, John
122, Lorne N. 88, L. L.
18, Musidors 18, R. H.
148, Robt. W. 108, W. C
57, W. J. 49;
MONTOPOLIS BRIDGE, 82;
MOODY, F. A. 143;
MOONING, G. M. 51;
MOORE, Adella 24, A. E.
56, Mrs. Belle 12, 95,
Betty (Elizabeth) 20, C.
A. 56, Darthula K. 56,
E. A. 15, 35, Eliza 123
E. E. 38, 88, E. L.136,
Elizabeth Ann 3, 15, 35,
39, 49, 90, Enoch 94
E. T. 21, 47, 49, Elizabeth O. 56, Eucilia 5,
Frank 25, Fred W. 29,
F. W. 99, Geo. F. 12, J.
24, James G. 35, 88,
James W. 3, Joe D. 26,
John H. Jr. 123, J. T.
137, Kate L. 35, 83, 88,
96, L. 15, L. B. 56, 92,
110, Lamar 16, 53, 65,
Larken B. 56, Louisa 35
88, Louise Luckett 27,
Luke 127, Martin 3, 15,
35, 39, 49, 53, 108, Mary
J. 17, Mary K. 57, Mollie
35, Maurice B. 12, N.148
Nat. 99, Nathaniel 5,
R. A. 56, Paralic E. 56,
Sallie 35, Sallie A. 136,
Sampson C. 17, Sarah E.
15, 35, Sarah 88, 136,
Susie Lou 56, Thos. 105,
Thos. Jr. 108, 137, T. K
114, W. W. 27;
MOORMAN, Carrie 90, Wickley 90;
MORELAND, A. T. 41, 87,
A. Turner 86, J. J. 41,
86, 87, J. N. 99, J. T.
41, Joseph 41, 54, 75, 86
87, Lee L. 86, L. L. 41,
87, M. A. 41, 87, Mary
Ann 86, 87, Rebecca L. 41
W. F. 54;
MORGAN, Gabriel M. 43
Henry 14, Hiram S. 2, 23
64, Mattie J. 132, Richard
S. 43, Saml. 12, Thos.
132;
MOREY, Nelson 134;
MORLEY, S. K. 96; Wm.153-4
NORMAN MILLS 36;
"MORNING STAR" 127;
MORRALL (MORRILL) Amos
98, Benj. 52, Thos. 52;
MORRIS,A. R. 20, 37, 41
65, 73, 101, J. B. 28,
71, J. M. 21, 73, John
21, John E. 141, John W.
73, Lucy M. 120, Mary
46, M. E. 21, Mila 28,
Milton 61, M. M. 73,
Myrtle Mae 135, Nella T.
59, R. M. 120, S. W. 135
Timothy B. 19, 46, V.
Vallie S. 73, W. A. 101;
MORRISON, A. 17, 67,
Archie 55, Geo. 3;
MORROW, A. J. 135, Arm=
strong 82, A. W. 25,Chas.

52, Elizabeth 135, I. D.
(. J. D.) 135, James 82,
James F. 135, Louise 135
Martha G. 25, Mary V. 82
Nancy Ann 135, Prudence
82Richard 82, Wm. 82;
MORSE, Chas. S. 61;
MORTON, Geo. W. 71, Jane
71, John H. 137, Wm. I.
92;
MOSELEY, T. D. 39, 77;
MOSES, M. 137;
MOSSON (MASSON) ...80,
MORRISON & SAMUELS 112;
MOSSONS, E. 2, Elias,
58, 66, 81, Herman 58,
66, 81;
MOTLEY, Wm. 153;
MOTE (MOTT) Joseph 144,
M. A. 140;
MOUNT ZION CEMETERY,119;
MOWINKEL (MOWEINCKLE)
John E. 15, John Ernst
110;
MUDD, B. H. 141, Delphana
123, Thos. Nathaniel123;
MUELLER, Laura 60, Rudolpy Q. 60;
MULKEY, Allen 94, B. J.
94, Callie 94, Eugenia
94, Inez 94, J. A. 94,
J. H. 94, John H. 93, 94
Laura 94, Mark M. 94,
M. M. 94, Mary May 94,
O. A. 94, S. C. 94,Ruth94
Susan E. 94;
MULL, Peter 105;
MULLINS Chas. 112, John
H. 47, Thos. O. 52;
MULLOWNAY, John F. 8,
S. D. 108, 109;
MULRYNE, T. H. 127;
MULLUSK, Geo. 137;
MUNGER, Ligilious S.123,
Sarah E. 123, W. E. 123;
MUNSON, Ira 53, 102, Jos
55, Lucy Margaret Duty
23, Millie Ruth Ann 55;
MUNOS, Lucas 91;
MURCHISON, Cameron 116,
John P. 116;
MURPHY, Linda May 10;
MURRAH, Tom 58;
MURRAY, A. L. 146, Bell
64, C. A. 148, G. W. 64
J. A. N. 76, J. E. 123,
James 113, Jessie 64,
R. V. 64, Wm. F. 2, Wm.
H. 143;
MUSE, H. K. 105, Hymena
80, Mrs. Ruth 74;
MUSGROVE, A.. P. 99;
MUSQUIO, Ramon 129;
MYER, C. 51,
MYERS, Lou 55, Wm. 144;
MYRICK, J. S. 24, 37,
41, 97, Wm. 138.

-N-
NABORS, Wm. 15;
NAGLE, J. A. 97, James
C. 52, Louise T. 7;
NALLE, Joseph 78;
NANCE, Ezekiel 85, John
W. 111;
NAPIER, Emma B. 145,
J. B. 145;
NARUNA CEMETERY 120;
NASH, Edwin 17, 101;
NAVARRO, Lucian 129, Jose
Antonio 36, 45, 153, Josefa
Maria 129;
NAYLOR, Calvin H. 110;

NEAL, Andrew 153, James
P. 14, Mabel Julia 52,
Walter 52;
NEANS (NEENS) Charley 21
Fannie E. 27, Henry Jr.
27, Mary Jane 21, 27,
Wm. 21, 27, 110;
NEBGEN,Antonio A. 4, 90,
91, 111, Catherine 4,
Catherine M. 90, 111
NEEDHAM, John 109;
NEELY, Chas. 27, C. N. 27
Henry 21, 27, H. Park 9
76;
NEESCE, Lola 118;
NEIGHBORS, Robert S. 65,
R. S. 136, Sarah H. 148;
NEILL, Geo. J. 32, 68, .
James 43, James C. 31;
NELSON, A. 57, A. J. 139
Andrew J. 151, Adla
Christine 151, Carl August
151, Fannie B. 11, 94,
Geo. Waltner 151 Hedwig
151, J. A. 139, J. C. N.
31, Lizzie Page 11,Mary
D. 79, Mary Bell 151,
Mary Jane 143, Oscar
Andrew 157, Thos. Edward
151, Wm. 79, 94, W. H.38;
NESEN, Capt. 91;
NESS, C. VAN 129;
NETTLESHIPE, Thos. 120;
NETTLETON, Chas. 32;
NEVILL, Hardin 120;
NEW, John C. 56;
NEW RED ROCK CEMETERY 116;
NEWALT (AWALT) John D.105;
NEWCOMB, Dr. Wm. B. 118;
"NEW ERA" 46, 47;
NEW HOPE CEMETERY 81;
NEW JERSEY, 1;
NEWLAND, John A. 127, Wm
125, 126;
NEWMAN, Caroline 37, H.
H. 56;
NEWNING, Chas. C. 88;
NEWSHAM, Joseph 12;
NEWTON, Geo. 93, Mary J.
65; Ida 85, H. H. 109;
NEWYORK , 1;
NEY, Elizabet, 88·
NICHOLAS, John 148, W. B
100, 109;
NICHOLS, Amanda Milvena
79, B. F. 84, Callie 94,
John B. 28, Lorenzo D.
142, Quella J. 100,Maggie
A. 84, O. J. 82, O. W.
52, Susan 54, Wm. 57,
Wm. B. 127, Wm. M. 54;
NICHOLSON, Clementine
139, Harriett E. 15,
James 139, John W. 99,
M. H. 15, 106, Wm. 115,
Wm. H. 102;
NIERHOFF, E. M. 143;
NITCHKE, Edna 72;
NITE, Bertha 116, Erasmus
W. 116, Rhoda A. 116,
Thos. C. 116;
NITSCHKE, H. F. 64, Winnie
64;
NIXON, Elizabeth 75,Ethel
L. 75, Ed J. Geo. Ant.123,
Greg J. 75, Jimmie 75,
John 112, Jorge Anton 123,
Marian Dean 46, Mary E.D
75, Robt. F. 128, Robt.
J. 75, Robt. W. 75;
NOBLE, Benj. D. 102;
NOBLES, D. B. 105,Watkins
104, 105;

NOEL, Nicholas 148;
NOLEN (NOWLAN) Anne 32,
B. E. 32, Elizabeth 91
H. C. 32, Homer 32, Mary
32, Mitchell 32, M. S. 42
Lizzie 32, Martha 32
Myra 32, Sarah J. 32,
46, S. F. 32, Thos. S. 32
T. W. 31, 32, Thos. W. 32
46, W. A. 32;
NORTH, Wm. F. 41;
NORTON, N. L. 93, W. T.
98;
NORTH CAROLINA 1;
"NORTHERN STANDARD" 82;
NORTHROPE, Amyas Stafford
134;
NORVELL,N. J. 31, S. G.
31;
NORVILLE, Wm. L. 118;
NOWLIN, Drury 49,Martha
W. 44, 49, Martha J. 90,
Payton D. 49, Payton W.
44, 49, 68, 76, 90, 109,
P. W. 21, 68, 77, T. W.
63;
NORWOOD, Mrs. M. E. 130,
W. J.130;
NUMBERS, Artie B. 77,
Emily L. 77, Melita 77;
NUNEZ, Manuel 129.

-O-
OAKWOOD CEMETERY, 73, 81
82;
OATS, Thos. 145;
O'BANION, Hamilton 141;
O'BRIEN, Owen 101;
OCCUPATION TAX 136,137;
O'CONNEL, Wm 8, 10, 43,
81, 100, 102;
O'CONNER, Joseph 6, 23,
Mollie 16;
ODIN, J. M. 97;
ODIORNE, Dr. James 132,
Sarah E. 132;
O. HENRY, 82;
ODOM, H. S. 76, Hugh 44
L. M. 24, 37, M. J. 76;
OLDHAM, Agnes H. H. 59,
D. 8, David 8, David B.9;
Elvira 9, Jane 9, John O
9, Oldham & MARSHALL 75
P. B. 27, Sallie 9,
Williamson S. 8, 32, 59,
75, W. L. 100;
ODUM, Hugh 21, 44, Minerva
J. 21, 44,;
OGDEN, James M. 107;
OIENS, Sarah 118;
OLD ANDERSON MILL 30;
OLD FORT PROVIDENCE CEM.
118;
OLDBRIGHT, Julia I. 82;
(Albright)
OLIPHANT, Elizabeth 139,
Margaret F. 16, Sanford
139;
OLIVER, E. R.108, J. B.
J. 128, J. W. 99;
OLLE, Emma 48, Theodore
48;
OPPENHEIMER, A. 85, August
85, Ida 85;
O'QUINN, James 74, Mary
Ann Elizabeth 74;
O'RICE, James 89;
ORLENDORF, Chas. 11;
ORR, Mrs. W. S. 53;
OSBORN, B. M. 69;
OSBURNE, Claiborne 108,
Thos. 83, 108;

ORTEGA, Guadalupe Campos 129, P. P. 129, Pablo P 129;
OSTENS, Henry 58, John F. 91;
OTIS, Wm. O. 11, 26;
OTTINGER, Ethel May 119;
OTTO, August F. 42, 68, 94;
OTTONS, Henry 58;
OTTOWAY, H. F. 31;
OVERBEY, H. C. 28;
OVERTON, David 62;
OWEN (OWENS) Amelia 75, Benj. F. 2, 7, 119, B. L 149, C. C. 98, E. A.140 Ellen 16, F. C. 149,R.B 19, Webb 141.

-P-

PACE, Gideon S. 8, Hardy 51, James R. 4, 17, 58, 63, 66, 67, 113, Robert A. 104, 105;
PADDOCK, James 146;
PADILLO, Vedaurine Juan Antonio K. 18;
PAGE, J. M. 140, 142, J. W. 26, Margaret 16, Moses 58, Nannie 140, R. H. 17, Saml. 16;
PAIGE, Annie E. 124, David S. 124, E. H. 124 H. C. 124, Henry C. 124, Wm. A. 124;
PAINE, Mary A. 52, Mary J. 5, 83, W. S. 5, 83;
PAKRANT, Hermine 12, Irene 12, Paul12- Ray 12;
PALLEY, Melinda E. 121, Robt. E. 121;
PALM, J. G. 37, Johannas 139, Swante 139;
PALMER, Chas. O. 25, 52, Dora 25, 52, E. A. 63, Ed Allen 55, 63, Freda 63 Geo. W. 32, Martha Elizabeth 115, Martin 17 May E. 42, Mecca 63,153-4 Myrtle Freda 63, Oswald J. 55, Wm. 6, Thos. J.42;
PANGLE, J. B. 19;
PENNELL, Anne P. 89, Fuller M. 89;
PAPE, Henry 111;
PARIS, W. D. 15;
PARISH, A. H. 29, 36, J. D. 13;
PARK, Francis 9, Francis A. 76, James 8, 9, 32,76 James W. 9, John Park Jr 9, John A. Sr. 9, John S. 76 Joseph L. 76, M.H. 39, Saml. 24, Wm. 9, 76 Wm. A. 9, 76;
PARKER, A. G. 51, E. H. 128, Emretta E. 18, Elizabeth H. 128, Horatio S. 75, J. H. 128, Peter 109 R. F. 63, Richard T. 72;
PARKS, Cermiller 69, J. D. 54, Saml. 20, Tom 69;
PARMER, Martin 113;; 152;
PARRIS,Richd. 94, Wm. D. 94;
PARRISH, Dillwyn 56, N. S. 93;
PARSONS, Cragg 149, Edmund 149, E. J. 125, 149 E. S. 149, Geo. W. 39, Jacin 149, Margaret 149, W. A. 149, Zenus 149;

PASCHAL (PASCHELL , PAS= KELL) Betty 18, Emmett 26, Geo. W. 18, 57, 148,62 Harriet 26, 18, Maria 18;
PATE, Elijah 17, 67;
PATRICK, A. T. 70;
PATTERSON, Edmund D. 84, Edward W. 84, Isabelle Spence 84, James 57, Jennie 84, J. B. 84, 98, J. M. 37, 41, John C. 130 Joshia 20, 44, MRS. Leney L. Thompson 31, Martha 84 98, M. E. 31;
PATTON, J. L. (S) 30, Moses L. 43, S. D. 58;
PAUL, Sophia 78;
PAULIN, Albert T. 126 Edith G. 126, Leila I. 126, Lewis 126, Mamie G. 126;
PAULS, Cornelia 40, Edward Conrad 40, J. E. 40, Kathryn Alice 40;
PAXTON, Bonita 60;
PAYNE, B. 4, Banyan 47, 53, 109, Elizabeth 47, 53, Elvia 114, Hanley 114, Sallie E. 144, W. T. 144;
PAYTON (PEYTON) , Mrs. A. B. 25, A. J. 63, Amanda B. (Jordan) 25, 52, 74, 92, Andrew J. 25, 52, 92 Bell R. 25, B. N. 52, Bradford N. 52, 92, (Buck) C. W. 92, Daniel R. 25, 74, 92, Daniel Rufus 52 Dora 25, 52, E. F. 25 73, Ephram F. 52, 92, Era PEARL 52, Eula Lee 52 Eula P. 25, Fannie P. 92 Geo. W. 92, Gerald Lee 52, Homer Leon 52, James 92, James W. 74, Joel Bradford 52, John B. 92, John W. 25, 92, John Wesley 52, Joy Truman 52, Julia E. 92,,Kate 52, 63, Louisa Jane 92, Lura 25 Mabel Julia 52, Maggie 52 Mary C. 92, Myrtle Freda 63, Maggie Margaret 63, Norman 52, Pauline 25, P. Dora 92, Zack P. 92;S.A.92
PEACE, Lillie 94, Walter P. 94;
PEAK, Howard W. 137;
PEAL, Mrs. Dorothy C. 112
PEARCE Mattie A. 45, 96 Thos. P. 45, Thos. J. 96;
PEAR, Chas. 136;
PEA..SON James 117, Robt. 117;
PEASE, E. M. 20, 39, 64, 81, 100, L. C. 94;
PECAN SPRINGS SCHOOL HOUSE, 65;
PECAR, Dr. Joseph 122;
PECHT, Bernard58, Theodore 111;
PECK,Chas. 119, 151, Chas R. 119, Earnest W. 140, Edward F. 8, Edward R.100 Elsie 140, Emma 151;Ethel May 119, Fred 34, Mary 34, Odis 120, O. J. 94 R. H. 34, 94, 100, 111, Thornton 15, Wm. Earnest 151;
PEEL, Thos. 111, Wm. A. 111;
PELHAM, Chas. T. 110, Wm.

90;
PENDLETON, Miller F. 38;
PENDLEY, P. F. 31;
PENN, Lucinda 60;
PENNAL R. W. 144;
PENNINGTON, Levi 4;
PENNSYLVANIA 1;
PENTELL, T. M. 31;
PEREZ, Manuel 129;
PERKINS, E. S. 107;
PERKLE,S. H. 121;
PERRY, Mrs. Ben 78, Burrel P. 141, C. R. 78, Mrs. Ethel 78, Isabella 84,A.G84 James F. 127, J. T. 84, Martha J. 136, Mary Ann 141, Milton 21, 84,Nathaniel 141, Orville 141, Richardson 141, Sadie 78, Sally 78, Wm. M. 44, 76, 89
PERSON, John 119, Ralph James 119, Sarah Jane 119 Ursula Ann 119;
PETERS, Mrs. C. A. 27, Chas. 27, Caroline 74 Josephine M. Wolf 27;
PETERSON, C. A. 41, 96, Louisa 41, 96;
PETRI, Fredericka 43, Henry 43;
PETTEE , James C. 33, 38 Josephine G. 33, 38;
PETTUS, Edward W. 17, S. O. 127;
PETTY, Elsie A. 116, Hanford 116, Inez M. 116, T. Earl 116, W. A. 117;
PEVETO, Michael 51;
PFAEFFLIN, Fanny 38, 70, H. 38;
PFENNIG, Wm. 38;
PFLUGER (PFEGER, PFLUEGER) Christian 38, Geo. 23, Helena 38, Henry 111;
PHARRASS, Saml. 144;
PHELPS,J. W. 140, Mollie 126, Neil S. 140, Mrs. N. V. 126, R. R. 140, S. A. 28 Sophronie E.126 W. P. 126,...119;
PHILECK, Eunice 83;
PHILLIPS, Cleve 55, Don 48, 56, Florida 35, J. Hall 35, John 35, 110, Mary E. 35, Muriel Gault (Clay) 48, 56, N. B. 98, Oleta Crumley 55, Penelope 35, 38, Walter D. 36, Wm. C. 9, 32, 33, 35, 38, 81, 94, Wm. P. 35;
PHILQUIST, S. A. 38;
PHOENIX SALOON, 43;
PICKETT, Joe 31, Lee 72, Lizzie 72;
PICKLE, D. J. 38;
PICKNEY (PINCKNEY) T. F.96
PIERCE, Mary Ann 3;
PIERSON, Jesse 153, Michael 128;
PILAND, S. J. 129;
PILLOW, Geo. Lee 135;
PIPER, Benj. 119,
PITT, Thos. J. 79;
PITTMAN, S. C. 104, 105;
PITTS, Ann S. 5, John D. 128;
PITZAH, Ed 11;
PLATT, Colon M. 4, Fanny Gray 38, Joe H. 4, Lenora 4, Mollie L. 4, Ona 4, Radcliff 4, 14, 23,38 63 Sam. M. 4, W. M. 132;
PLATTNER, Anne (Adeline)D.

68, Addie 67, Irv.in 68;
PLUMLEY, J. T. 13, Mary 13;
POLK, C. I. 14;
POPE, J. B. 96, John B. 114, John H. 114;
PORTER, E. 5, Fannie C. 93, Florence 61, J. B. 115, John M. 115, John Thornton 115, John W. 115, Milton H. 115, Newell F. 115, Nicholas 141, Robt. V. 115, Saml. 57, Susan Catherine 115, Thos. A. 115;
POTTER, James Brown 56, James O. 99, J. L. 67 84, 98, Mary 84, 98, Robt. 54, 105, 153, William H. 152;
POTTS, C. S. 37;
POUNCEY (POWNCEY) A. W. 62, 113;
POUND D. Joseph M. 131, Louisana 131, Sarah D. 131;
POWELL, Geo. W. 17, James 82, 114, 139, John 82, Joseph 82, Mark 82, Mariah 114, Saml. G. 45, 46, 54, Sarah M. 116, W. C. 116, W. G. 116, Wiley 107, Thos. B. 46;
POWER, James 153, John M 103, 105, Thos. B. 45;
PRAL, Inez 129;
PRATHER, Mrs. Elizabeth 74, F. H. 74, Geo. 128;
PRE EMPTION CERTIFICATES 153;
PRENTISS, Francis 107;
PRESBYTERIAN COLLEGE for GIRLS 142;
PRESBYTERIAN THEOLOGICAL SCHOOL 142;
PRESCOTT, WM. Chase 134;
PRESLEY, Joseph H. 148;
PRESSLER, Herman 79;
PRICE, Clara Bendy 125, 126, Earl 135, James R 117, Joe B. 53, John A. 14, John T. 78, 98, J. T 117, Kate 53, Mary H. 31 32, 78, N. E. 117, Verdie 135, W. C. 125, 126, Wm. D. 18;
PRIEM, A. H. 13, Hilda 13
PRIEST, Bell 25, James Armstrong 144, Wm. 94;
PRIESTLEY, Perl 7;
PRINCE, Wm. L. 98;
PROBST, Clara Bell 117, J. 117, L. P. 117;
PROPER, Daniel H. 8;
PROPHETT, Chas. Woodson 58, Emma C. 58, Oglesby S. 58, Woodson Z 58;
PROSKE, John 73;
PRUITT, John T. 32, 51, 68, Martha J. 32, 68;
PUCKETT, Chauncey P. 5, Chancey R. 5, Cyrus Jr. 5, Edward R. 99, Eucelia 5, Hannah B. 5, 46, 51, Irene 5, Leon 5, Lorenzo D. 5, M. C. 5, Miranda 5, Mollie W. 33, Nancy 5 Thos. 5, T. W. 5, W.W. 33, 133; A.W.113,M.W.35;
PUGH, R. N. 118, S. A. 94;
PULSIFER, S. M. 141;
PUMPHREY, R. B. 145;
PURSER, J. A. 115;

PURSLEY, August 7, Bathsheba 131, Elizabeth 7, Hiram 7, Jennie 7, J W 7 M. 131, Myrtle 7, Sam 7 Wm. 7, 131, Cemetery 131.

-Q-
QUATTLEBAUM, W. A. 149;
QUEEN, John N. 150, L.A 119, W. W. 119;
QUICK, J. E. 131, Mary Ann 131.

-R-
RAATZ, Eugenia 94, Herbert 94;
RABB, John 11, Texas 11, Thos. J. 75, Virgil S. 11, V. S. 11;
RADKEY, Ben 21, 58, Bernard 16, Martin A. 21, Mary A. 21, Mary L. 21, Olean H. 21, Stephen D. 21
RAGLAND, Adelia 17, James P. 17, 37, J. R. 24;
RAGLIN, H. W. 76;
RAGSDALE, James 57, Jas. R. 88, James W. 30, Margaret N. 30, 88, Nancy H. 30, Walter G. 30, 88
RAIGER (REAGER) Ann Baker 64, Wm. C. 65, 138;
RAILEY, James 25
RAINARD, Ellenor 109,133;
RALPH, S. W. 4, 61;
RAMBO (RHAMBO) R. I. 110
RAMEY, Robt. R. 102, Maria 27;
RAMSDELL, Addie 61, Robt. L. 61;
RAMSEY, Bell 64, Euphie 64, F. M. 136, F. T. 64, 76, 96, J. M. 64, Jessie 64, Mercy P. 64, R. D. 3, RAMSEY MINING CO. 135, 136, Winnie 64, W. R.136;
RANDALL, Albert G. 84, Edward 152, Dr. Edward 152, Harriett Ballinger 152, Mary 152;
RANDOLPH, C. B. 49, C. H 44, 47, 90, C. P. 44 76 H. C. 57, James M. 84, Susan B. 44, 49, 90,T.J. 43, Wm. Colville 84;
RANSOM, Elizabeth O. 56, J. M. 56, 102;
RAPP, John F. 109;
RAPPALLO, Chas. A. 19;
RATHKE, Henry 111;
RAWLES, Caroline M. 111;
RAWORTH, Eghart A. 97;
RAY, Cal 11, E. A. 20, 47, 73, Ed 73, F. S. 25 James M. 95, J. R. 20, 47, 73,Lucretia 20, 47, 73, Thos. J. 7;
RAGLAND, J. R. 24;
RAYMOND,Alice 62, James H. RAYMOND & Co. 24,37,41 128; H. C. 65; James H. 7, 9, 12, 15, 16, 21,23, 24, 36, 37, 41 53, 62, 66 79, 89, 95, 97, 99, 102, 108, Margaret J. 15, 24, 37, 79, N. C. 110;;
RAYNOR, Moses 19, 43;
REAGEN, Wm. C. 46; 154;
RECTOR, Arthur 10, Harriet C. 77, James E. 10, 31,

32, J. Bouldin 10, John b. 49, 72, 93, 97, J.R 94, Lilla B. 10, Lillie 9, Lizzie 10, N. A. 76 NelsonS. 36, 43, 74, N L. 92, N. S. 27, 77, Pattie Townes 59, Richard T. 10, Thompson N. 74;
RED ROCK CEMETERY (new) 116, (old) 117;
REDDING (REDING) Catherine Elizabeth 27, 44, 89 Hugh S. 27, Isabella M. 49, Jane Elizabeth 27, 44, 49, 89, Joseph 76, Kate 21, 76, Laura 21, Laura Josephine 21, 76 Margaret Laura 27, 44, 89, Mary Indiana 27, 44 89, Mary J. 21, 76, Minerva Jane 21, 27, 44 76, 89, Nancy Josephine 27, 44, 89, R. L. 11, 27, 32, 44, 48, 49, 68, 89, Robt. 76, Robt. S. 21, 49, Robt. L. 27, 44 48, 49, 96, Wm. Mac 21, 27, 44, 76, 89, Wm. R 49, 76, 96;
REDFORD, Jose Ramon 129;
REED, Ann Elizabeth 11, A. S. 122, Barton 11, David C. 122, Mrs. E. A. (E. H.) 122, Eleanor 11, Eleanor Rogers 11, G. B. 144, G. D. C. 122 J. L. 29, J. M. 11,John James 11, J. W. 122, John B. 111, Madison 11 Marymum Lavinia 11,, Nannie 111, S. B. 33, Seth B. 11, S. H. 98, Theodore 122, T. S.122;
REESE, Chas. K. 148, Terry (Perry) 105;
REEVES, Cynthia T. 22, Wm. T. 22;
REID, A. E. 95, Ellen 36, J. M. 13, Miranda 132, S. B. 94;
REILEY, Edward F. 55, Jas W. 19, Wm. 19;
REINER, Wm. A. 69;
REISHAW, Frederick 112;
RENICK (RENCKER) Barton 9, Burton L. 95, J. L. 135, Sam H. 21;
REPUBLIC of MEXICO 1, 152;
REPUBLIC of TEXAS, 1, 152, 153;
REYNOLDS,DAvid 96,Lafayet 63, Rhodie 63;
RHODES, Dora M. 117,Gadfrey 55, John H. 117, Wm. H. 28, 30, 50;
RIBBICK, Henry 65;
RICE, Albert G. 134, Aluheous P. 150, Cora K 18, 60, F. A. 74, 124 Horatio H. 60, James O. 20, 148, July Ann 138, Mary E. 60, Margaret 114 Thos. 114, Wm. B. 124 Wm. M. 125;
RICH, Isaac 123;
RICHARDS, Ada 60, C. W. 121, John 60, Madeline 60, Mary Ann 60, Robt. David 60, Saml. 60, Sarah B. 121;

RICHARDSON, F. D. 134, J
F. 31, J. P. 71, 100,128
Susan 82;
RICHLER, Fr. 136;
RICHTER, G. F. W. 75;
RICHARD, Robt Theo. 116;
RICKS, Geo. W. 110,John
T. 146;
RIDDLES, Emma 116, Jim
Abner 116, John 116,
Julia 116;
RIDGE, Ilse 114, Sol 114
RIGGLE, Alice L. 59,
Anna 59, Madison 111;
"RIGS" 91;
RIGHT, (WRIGHT) Saml. M.
89;
RIGSBY, A. J. 126;
RILEY, Clementine B. 46
Cyrus 128, David 48, H.
B. 4,35, 36, J. D. 119,
James W. 46, Mary J. 48,
R. W. 48, 70, 84, Sarah
46, 48, S. M. 48,Walley
4, Wm. 46,;
RINARD, Elleanor 109;
(RAINARD) 133;
RISHER,Ada 39, Alethea E
39, Benj. A. 36, 39,
Harry 39, Henry C. 39,
Laura B. 39, Nannie E.
36, 39, N. Kate 39;
RITCHIE, C. B. 14;
RIVERS, Mary 91, M. L.91;
ROBARDS, A. L. 50, Willis
99, W. L. 28;
ROBBINS, Aaron 148, Geo.
B. 85, Irabel M. 85, John
S. 85, Lillian E. 85,
Marie S. 85, Mary J. 131
Rowland A. 32, Russell
32, Wm. H. 131;
ROAKE, M. O. 141;
ROBB, G. T. 13;
ROBERTS, Albert Saml. 47
Anna W. 23, A. P. 73, 131;
B. B. 130, Benj. T. 23,
B. M. 122, Chas. E. 120,
C. E. 45, C. C. 136, Edward 102, Eleanor A. 131
Elizabeth A. 120, Ella L
124, 130, 131, Fanny 47,
H. V. 130, Henrietta 58,
Henry 47, Henry W. 131,
Isaac D. 130, 131, J.
121, Jesse E. 121, John
136, J. F. 130, 131S.110,
John Gordon 47, Joseph 58
K. P. 124, Lizzie 122,
O. B. 73, O. M. 73, Oran
73, P. L. 136, Robt F.
127, ROBERTS SCHOOL HOUSE
9, 76, Cemetery 122; Saml
110, Stephen R. 12, 34,
T. A. 121, Wm. H. 100;
ROBERTSON, Benj. C. 107,
C. C. 144, Charlotte 144
C. J. (Cynthia) 144,
Elijah S. C. 145, 147,
E. S. C. 39, 65, Eugene
144, Geo. L. 19, Green F
(L) 144, H. A. F. 144,
James 54, James H. 37,49
64, J. B. 33, 102,Jessie
144, J. M. 107, John B.
106, John W. 144, Joseph
106, 144, Joseph W. 7, 13
19, 35, 58, 59, 66, 100,
106, L. L. 19, L. S. 145
Lucke C. 8, Louise 8,
Lydia A. 146, Mary 144,
M. E. 144, M. V. 144,
Nancy 106, N. J. 144,

Nathaniel H. 110, Perry
N. 144, Peter 146, P.N.
144, Sallie E.144,Sarah
E. 86, Sarah E.McKenzie
70, Sterling C. 96, 153,
Susan M. 54, 64, 80,
Wm. 86, Wm. 70;
ROBEY, Francis A. 109,
John C. 109;
ROBISON, Neill 24;
ROBINSON, A. 148, Addie
44, 49, Adeline 90, A.
H. 16, 31, Al 16,Alfred
H. 16, 31, Alonzo 16,
Andrew 153,4Annie 94,
Bessie 16. Chas. 94,
David M. 90, D. N. 49,
E. B. 73, Eda 72, Edna
72, Ethel 73, Elizabeth
16, Eva 73, Eva Hope Anderson 73, Fannie 71, 94,
Florence 72, Hattie 71,
Geo. E. 78, 100, J. B.
20, 71, 72, Jack 72,
Jane 35, John 16, 72
John B. 20, John H. 11,
16, 31, 35, 50, 62, 100,
112, Joseph B. 71, 72,
Joseph C. 71, 72,Josephine
16, 27, Kate 16, Kelsie
72, Lorella 72, Lillie
94, Louis 78, Louisa 78,
Lula 47, Mary 16, Mary A.
48, Maggie 78, Mollie 71
Nancy 20, Norvella 90,
Olive 72, Ottelie 72,
Pauline 16, Pauline
Bremond 16, Salem 90,Sam
71 72, Sam H. 71, S. H.
71, Sarah E. 71, S. E. 70
T. P. 48, Wm. F. 70, 71,
72, Wm. M. 54;
ROBLE, D. 121;
ROBUCK, ...Survey 148;
ROCKWELL, Annie R. 88,
Barnard 88, Geo. 88,Geo.
A. 88, Kate R. 88, Susan
R. 88, Thos. Hawley 88;
RODGERS, Ella Comstock 53
ROESSELL, Christopher M.
108;
ROESSLER, Octava B. 89;
ROGAN, Leo. 122, Leonard
122, Mary Smith 122,
ROGERS,B. W. 152, Dora 55
Edward H. 48, 54, 62, 63,
Eleanor 11, Ethel 55,AW23;
Ellen 55, Evelyn 55,Frank
55, Mrs. H. 93, James 24,
44, 45, 48, 54, 55, 56,
57, 58, 59, 62, 63, 64, 70
76, 92, 152, Jonathan 21,
27, 44, 76, John I. 28,
29, J. I. 28, J. P. 92,
Joseph B. 48, 54, 62, 63,
Josephine 21, 27, 44, 76,
L. A. 54, 63, Lula 55,
Lavenia H. 59, 92, Mark
M. 44, 89, Mary A. 62,
Mary E. 48, 63, Mary May
94, M. M. 44, 89,Minus C
48, Nancy Josephine27,
44, Nancy 48, 63, Norman
55, Olive 55, Rachel 44,
48, 54, 57, 63, S. A. 55,
Sarah B. 48, Sarah E. 63,
Sally 54, Wm. 55, Wm. E
31, 55, 58, Wm. H. 48;
ROLLY, Henderson 114,
Mattie 114;
ROONEY, Catherine (Kate)
46, Eddie 46, John 46,
John Francis 46, Kate 46

Tom Morton 46;
ROOT, Irving 18, Sarah
E. 77;
ROSBOROUGH, A. M. 99;
ROSENHERMER, John 129;
ROSE, Geo. W. 112, L. 51
Leon C. 116;
ROSS, David K. 14, 106,
D. S. 137, Manda 135,
O. R. 135, Robt. 131;
ROTHE, John C. 14;
ROUND ROCK SEMINARY JOINT
STOCK Co. 145;
ROUNDTREE, Bettie A. 18,
Goran 18, Hal L. 18,
Herbert 18, L C. 143,
Musidora 18, 108, Robt.
F. 18, R. F. 17, 18,
Smythe 18, Thos P. 110;
ROW, J. R. 115, S. E.
115, W. E. 115;
ROWDEN, James 102;
ROWE, Arthur 50, 92,
Catherine C. 80, Elizabeth
114, Emily 50, 59, 82,
92, 93, Horace 50, 92,
James 82, Jesse J. Fletcher
2, 92, Joseph 2, 6, 50
59, 80, 93, 101, Dr.
Joseph 50, 92, Josephine
50, 92, Lavinia 92, Thos
E. 57, 74, 80, Thos. H.
57; Thos. 79;
ROWLETT,Danl. 83, James
150;
ROWLAND, Fannie 130,
James O. 130, Mattie E.
130;
ROWLEY, Joseph F. 133;
RUCKER, Geo. G. 58;
RUGGLES, Dixie L. 63,
Gardner 63;
RUIZ, Francisco 153;
RUMPFF, Martin 100;
RUMSEY, James A. 148;
RUNNELS, H. R. 100;
RUSK, Thos. J. 153;
RUSSELL, Alexander 153
Daniel A. 39, Helen
Clarabel 8, James A. 8,
J. H. 11, Lillie 39;
RUST, Carrie 22, Ed 22
Phebe 22;
RUTH, Lemus C. 85;
RUTHERFORD, C. N.27, 61
Elizabeth 27, 45, Eleanor
45, Erin 45, 61, P. A.44
89, Robt. A. 27, 45, 61;
RUTLEDGE, Alice 144, -
Franklin 144, H. M. 44
John T. 144, J. T. 66,
151, Martha A. 144,
Margaret F. 16, Mary E.
66, 151, Sam A. 144
Susan 144, W. P. 144;
RYAN, Nancy A. 119,
Wm. 119;
RYSINGER, A. 39.

-S-
SABIN, D. C. 33;
ST. DAVID'S EPISCOPAL
CHURCH 47;
St. MARY'S CATHOLIC
CHURCH 43;
SALEM, Chas. P. 38;
SAMPSON, Geo. W. 92, 101
102;
SAMUELS, Hart 58, 66, 81
SAMUELS & MOSSON 112;
SAMUELSON, John D. 37;
SAN ANTONIO de BEXAR, 1;
SANCEDO, Don Jose Antonio

127;
SANCHES (SAUNCHES) A.13;
SANDERS, D. M. 80, Elizabeth M. 80, Geo. 55, Martha 80, Mary Elizabeth 80 Richard H. 80, Wm. 80 Wm. H. 80, Wm. J. 80;
SANDERSON, Mary Elizabeth 80;
SANDIFER, Willie 114;
SANDOZ, Evelyn 87, Dr. X 87;
SANDUSKY, John C. 103, Wm. H. 1;
SANFORD, A. J. 17, 42, 67 Andrew J. 67, Earl Palm 16, 67, Earl May 67, Eliza 17, 67, Lillie Bessie 67, Lewis Thiele 17, 95, Pearl May 17, S. L. 67;
SANSOM, Cooper 142, 151, Gussie 151, P. M. 130 Richard 142, 145, 146, T. L. 130;
SARGENT, Mary Fells 73;
SASSMAN, Annie 19, Archie Clifford 19, Geo. 94, Isabel 19, James 18, 19, Joe. W. 18, Josie Ida 19 Lela May 19, Lenora M. 18, Myrtle M. 19, Wm. F. 19;
SATTLER, Wm. 11;
SATTERLIE, Wm. A. 38;
SATTERTHWAITE, C. A. 48;
SAUER, Wm. 11, 99;
SAULS, (SAWLES) Dicy 149 Elenor 133, Francis 72 Geo. 72, John 149, N. 104, Nieland 75;
SAUNDERS, Edwin L. 74, Geo. 74, 94, J. C 9 John H. 129, Mary E. 74, Sara E. 74, Wm. M. 99;
SAVERY, C. S. 98, Caroline 49, John Preston 49;
SAWYERS, Washington 24;
SAYERS, David 115, Gov. Joseph D. 115;
SAYLOR (TAYLOR) John 23;
SCAGGS, J. H. 10;
SCALLORN, Elizabeth R. 41 Geo. W. 41, John W. 15, 39, Mariam 15, 24, 41, Stephen 24, Thos. J. 24 41, Wm. 15, 24, 33;
SCARBROUGH, E. M. 37;
SCATTS, James Walter 123 J. C. 123, J. R. 123, M. J. 123;
SCHAACK, Caroline von 50;
SCHAEFER, P. A. 23;
SCHERMERHORN, Anne 8, James 8;
SCHIEFFER, H. 71;
SCHILLER, Wm. 29;;
SCHMIDT, Chas. 69, H. 22 Peter 31;
SCHNEIDER, Catherine 93, Mrs. Frithoaf 89, John 73
SCHNEIDERWIND, Friederika 13, Pauline 12, 13, Wm. or Wilhelm 13;
SCHOOLFIELD, Chas. 105;
SCHRIVNER, Joseph 32;
SCHROMAN, Gustav 23;
SCHROPHSHIRE, Ben H. 60;
SCHUBER, F. 37;
SCHUFFER, Herman 69;
SCHULLE, Christian 122, Dorothea 122;

SCHULZ, Henry 34, Otto 73
SCHULTZ, Michael 136;
SCHUPBACK, Saml. 121;
SCHUTZE, Emil 3, Emilie R. 3;
SCHUWIRTH, Anna 42, Dora C. 42, Geo. 42;
SCHWAB, Richard 6;
SCHWARTZ, August (Augustus) 14, 80, 112;
SCHWARZKOFF, GOTTLIEB 112;
SCOTT, Clara 18, Elizabeth J. 147, E. S. 147, Ezra S. 147, G. W. 9, 43, G. M. 113, 134, Geo. R. 11, J. W. 127, Jonathan 109, Josephus 108, Paul R. 18 Rachael B. 108, Sam T. 36 39;
SCOTLAND, 1;
SCOTTISH AMERICAN MTG. CO Ltd. 23;
SCOTTISH RITE TEMPLE, 153;
SCRIBNER, Harvey A. 150, Wm. A. 150;
SCROGGINS, Wm. J. J. 57;
SCRUGGS, W. C. 6;
SCUDDER, F. V. 7, Frank V. 7;
SCURRY, Wm. 81;
SEALE, Chas. 128, 131, Della Mae 131, Elizabeth 120, Exe A. 120, Isaac D 128, Jane 128, M. A. 120 Thos. Arnold 120, Thos. J. 120;
SEALY, Geo. 6, 23, 141, Magnolia 141;
SEATON, C. 109;
SEAY, Caspain 146, Nancy 146;
SEDWICK, J. B. 39;
SEEGAR, Augustus 76;
SEICKE, C. L. 73;
SEELY, Horace 26, Wm. M. 124;
SEGUIN (SEQUIN) Erasmos 129; 155
SEIDERS, Alice 83, Edward 3, 35, 39, 53, 90, 95, Edward 3, H. B. 83, E 83, Henry B. 3, 53, Letitia 3, 95, Louisa Maria 3, 39 53, Pinckney W. 3, 53;
SELLSTROM, Carl 69;
SENECHAL, Augustus 127;
SENOUR, Joseph T. 130;
SENTERFITT, Kate 135, R. B. 135;
"SENTINAL" 103;
SESSIONS, Geo. 35;
SETTLE, Chas. 111, Susan 112;
SEWARD, B. V. 131, F. L. 131;
SEXTON, J. R. 69;
SEYMOUR, Andrew 38;
SHAFFER, John Henry 132;
SHAKER, J. W. 137;
SHANDS, E. W. 11, 34, Mrs Eugene 140;
SHANKS, Amy 27, Wm. 27;
SHARPE, J. M. 90, Lena 90, Louisa Jane 127, W. C. 136; Wm.99;
SHARPLESS, Joshua 85;
SHAVER, Bell D. 149, James 149;
SHAW, A. A. 3, Bess A. 3, Daisy B. 3, Frank D. 77, James B. 34, 36, 41, 54, 64, 65, 83, 85, 91, 92; 94

John A. 3, J. W. 3,,Kate E 3, Laura A. 3, Texanna C. 3;
SHEA, C. J. 115, John 127;
SHED, Alice 135, A. E.&V. 135, G. H.135, James 135, John W. 135, J. T. 135, Mollie 135, Myrtle Mae 135, Nancy 135, Pat 135 Pauline 135, R. E. 135;
SHEEHAM, Dennis 19, Edward 137;
SHEEKS, David 63;
SHEEL (SHELL) John 57,141;
SHELBY, H. I. 144,Lemuel Evant 81, Mabel C.Wright 81;
SHELLEY, Henry E. 133, James J. 95, Lula A. 95 Mollie G. 95, N. G. 13, 62, 95, Percy L. 95, Robt. M. 95, R. C. 30, Wm. D. 95;
SHELTON, J. R. 14, John 110;
SHEPERD, Chas. 103, 128 Hugh 124;
SHEPHERD, B. A. 6, Benj A. 6, 23, Joseph D. 11;
SHERMAN, Amanda E. 74, A. M. 94, Louise Mason 143, M. C. 93, Morgan D. 74;
SHERRILL, A. W. 135;
SHERWOOD, Palmon 51;
SHILBURN, Silas 135, Witt 135;
SHIPE, M., M. 77, 97;
SHIVERS, GOV. 87;
SHOEMAKER, Sandy 23;
SHORT, Irene 134, Squire W. 134, S. W. 134;
SHRAVEN, Jacob 112;
SHREVE, John M. 53, 103
SHROPSHIRE, Ben H. 60;
SHUBEY Rose Z. 121;
SHUBERT, Alma 35, Erna 35, Frieda 35, Hildegard 35, Ottoman R. 35;
SHUFF, Washington 103;
SHULTZ...119;
SILLIMAN, Catherine 8, W. B. 8;
SILLURE, J. W. 145
SILSBEE, Albert 44, 59, Archelous 44, 59, Howard 59, Joseph 59, Mary 59;
SIMMONS, Daniel P. 53, Carrie 53, C. L. 140 Elizabeth 137, John T.137, O. A. 94, Solomon 128, T. F. 77;
SIMMLER, A. J. 36, E. 74 S. 124;
SIMMS, Bartlett 2, 5, 6 28, 36, 44, 64, 65, 92, 98 W. B. 8, Wm. 112;
SIMON, Geo. 131, Sophie131;
SIMONDS, Geo. 134;
SIMPSON, A. J. 136, Bob 11, Cora B. 11, H. H. 137 J. S. 34, J. T. 136, L.W 34, Mary E. 34, Wm. 106 107;
SIMS, F. W. 87, J. C. 5 Wm. C. W. 6;
SINCLAIR, Mrs. Claire J 12, L. B. 12;
SINNETT, H. C. 9;
SIRMON, G. W. 131, Mrs. M. 131;
SISLER, Andrew 23;

SISSON, P. C. 78, 85, Phillip C. 85, P. G. 85; PHILLIP G. 85, Phillis S 85;
SKINNER, S. M. 147, 150;
SLAUGHTER, A. B. 31, 111 Alice V. 31, Anna P. 31 Ann 31, Augustus B. 31, Cora B. 31, F. 31, F. A 31, Francis A. 31, H.31 H. B. 9, Lucy 31, Lucy A. 31, Stephen F. 30,31 127, S. S.136;;
SLEEPER, Laura B. 39, W. M. 39;
SLINGER, Mrs. R. 13;
SLOCUM, Caroline 49, John R. 49, 103, 153;
SLOAN, R. E. 53;
SLOSS, M. M. 33, 35; Sallie B. 33, 35;
SMALLEY, Franklin 146; Freeman 138, James K.146, 147, Sintha A. 147, Wm A. M. 147;
SMELSER, Harmon 138, 150;
SMILEY A. M. 22, E. K.22;
SMITH, A. E. 111, Ada C. 117, Agnes S. 46, Alfred J. & Sr. 15, 22, 44, 46, 75, 133, Amelia 15,Amelia Owens 75, America N.139, Angelina D. 12, 69, 95, 106, 153, Annie 44, 46, 117, Anthony 144, A. S. 75, Augustus V. 57,Benj. 140,Bettie A. 18, Caroline 75,Caroline A. 22, 75, Chas. T. 139; DeWitt C. 141, Donald 32, Duncan 138, E. 74, Earl 48, 56, Elizabeth 74, 143, Elizabeth B. 22, 75, Elizabeth B. Hayden 75, Ella Lee 131, Ellen 143, Elmore L. Anderson 18, Emma 117, Emma Walker 38, F. E. 31, Felix E. 17, 18, 31,F.H. 37, 38, 70, 96, Feilding G. 46, Fenwick 50,Gilbert Stovall 18, Geo. 18, Gertrude Lane 59, H. A. 72, Harvey 50, 106, H. Clay 65, H. C. 65, H. E. 131, Holly 25, Isaac 11, Jas. 22, 44, 64, 75, 89, Jas. B. 56, Jas. M. 18, Jas. S. 54, Jas. W. 43, 46,54, 58, 64, 69, 75, 76, 106,66 141, James W. Jr. 12,14 18, James Woods 8, Jeannette 15, Jennie Gertrude 65, J. H. 143, J. M. 74 J. R. 57, 137, J. W.49, 86, 100, 102, John 3, John F. 22, 75, 110,John L. 135, John M. 118., JOhn T. 18, John Willard 117, John W. 129, Joseph F.23 Juan C. 129, Juan O. 129 Julia Ann 121, Julia H. 69, Jourdan 115, Lina B 143, Mrs. M. A. 140, Mamie 18, Margaret 14, Martha 82, Mary 11,Mary A. 82, Mary E. 15, 22,75 110, May E. 14, 75,Mary S. 18, Matthew M. 18, Miles F. 145, 147, Maud E. 74, Mumford 99, Myra 14, Myrtle B. 47,Nannie 18, Norvella Wade 18, O. B. 138, Obadiah B. 139;

R. A. 39, 70, 100, Rebecca 50, 106, Rena G. 48, 56 R. H. 65, Robt. A. 24, 37 69, 79, 94, Robt. S. 139, R. J. 137, Ross 19, Roy Albert 117, Ruth Helen 18 R. T. 57, Saml. 109, Sam S. 129, S. H. 141,Speedy 140, Smith Springs Cemetery 135, S. R. 82, Stephen Girard 18, Susan A. 22, 66, 75, 110, Sylvester T 112, Taylor 140, 144,148 Taylor Jr. 57, 140, Thos. 75, Thos. A. 69, Thos. F 84, Thos. J. 139, Thos. S. 75, Thos. W. 12, 50, 106, Van M. 48, Wade M. 18, Wallie 19, Ward T.137, Wiley 140, Will 18, Will C. 47 (The "hermit") Will E. 117, Will S. 18, Wm. A. 105, Wm. 50, 121, Wm. M. 135, Wm. J. 117, Wm. Rogers 18, Dr. W. P. 123 W. R. 143, W. S. 8, 18;
SMITHERSON, Edward 62;
SMITHWICKE, Noah 106;
SMYTHE, Geo. W. 15, Peyton 128;
SNAVES, D. W. 22;
SNEED, Alex. W. 6, G. L. 150, Sebron G. 32, 75, 81 90, 89, 102, 147, T. E. 64, Thos. E. 89;
SNIVELY, David 66, Jacob 66, 153, James 66;
SNODDY, Wm. M. 32;
SNAUTS, (SCHNAUTZ) WM.110;
SNYDER, C. J. 147, Dudley H. 147, John W. 146,147;
SOMMERVILLE, H. S. 17;
SORRELS, MRS. A. M. 130, F. P. 130, James S. 122, Mary A. 122, P. B. (T. B) 24, R. (?) G. 130, Sallie 130, W. L. 122;
SOUR, Wm. 108;
SOUTH AUSTIN, 153;
SOUTH CAROLINA, 1;
"SOUTHERN INTELLIGENCE" 43;
SOUTHMAYD. I. A. 17;
SOUTHWESTERN AMERICAN,43;
SOUTHWESTERN UNIVERSITY 143;
SPAN, Mrs. Maggie 73;
SPANISH LAND GRANTS, 152;
SPARKS, Benton H. 146, Chas. M. 146, Elsberry 84, Henry 125, John 53, 146, Lee Elan 46, Leland 146, Maude Rachel Knight 146, Nancy Elnora 146, Rachel 146, Wilkinson 10, 12,90;
SPAULDING, C. 96;
SPEAR (SPIER, SPEER)Abner B. 57, A. B. 65, Geo. W. 3, 15, 33, 39, 41, 54,91, John 141 Miriam 15, RebecaJ. 15, 33, 35, 39, 41, Sarah 121, Thos. S. 118;
SPECKELS, A. W. 48;
SPENCE, Isabell 84, John B. 84, John S. 16, 33, 84, 97, Joseph 7, 39, 40, Mrs. Maria M. 84, 96, Theodore P. 14;
SPENCER, Joseph 7, Lillie Bessie Stanford 67, Wm. 106;
SPILLAR, Bliss Robison 40 Ruby Cornelia Pauls 40;

SPILLMAN, Chas. H. 38, Edward 3, 91, H. 15, Lydia 4, Otto 4, Olena 15, Rosa J. 3, 91;
SPIVEY, Cullen 103;
SPRINKLE, Mary C. 25, 92; E. F. 92;
STACHE(STOCKE) W. H. 137;
STACY, STACY=ROBBINS CO. 38, James 57;
STAFFORD, S. 99;
STALNAKER, Beulah Beatrix 12, Guy C. 12;
STAMPER, Wm. D. 2, 36, 113;
STANDIFER, James W. 109 Maria 127;
STANDLEY, Thos. E. 109;
STANFIELD, Lesia 114;
STANFORD, Andrew J. 96, A. J. 67, Earl May 67, Eliza 67, S. L. 67,Lillie Bessie 67;
STANGIER, Mathilda 66;
STANLEY, Becker F. 32, Becker T. 32, Elias S. 32, Geo. T. 32, HOLLAND Gatlin 42, 46, Martha 13 Mary E. 32, Thos. Ed 31, 32, 42, 46, Wm. H. 13;
STAPLES, Louisa 132, Thos. J.132;
STARK,Amanda Christiana 13, 139, Carl Oscar 13, 139, Hendrick Theofel 139 Herman 13, 139, Hulda 13 Johann August 13, 139 Leontina (Tina) Rosalie 13, 139;
STAR STATE SAVINGS 40,96;
STARR, Emeline 128, Jas. H. 15, 57, 98, Solomon 110;
STATE of COAHUILA & TEXAS 1, 10, 17, 36, 68, 114 127;
STATE GAZETTE, 81, 66;
STATE NATIONAL BANK 41;
STAVELY, Bryant O. 111;
STEIL, Henry J. 53;
STEELE, Guillermo H. 145 147, Wm. H. 147;
STELFOX, John 81, Wm. 66;
STEEN, Isaac 126, Rev.58;
STEINER, Henry H. 93, Joseph M. 80, Josephus M 36, 59, J. M. 66, 93, J. Ulrich 122, Sophie 122;
STEPHENS, Chas. 71, Delila 136, Elizabeth 149, M. C. A. 136;
STEPHENSON, B. T. 131, Mrs. G. A. H 131, Jane C 84, James C. 84, Mary Jane 84, Nannie 131;
STERN, G. M. 36, Hattie May Kavanaugh 44, Jacob 13, Robt. Allen 44;
STERZING, Fred 70;
STEUSSEY, Albertine 37;
STEVENS, R. M. 137;
STEWART,(STEWARD) Anna 67, 96, A. J. 143,Benj. K. 68, B. K. 86, Bud 68 D. T. 141, Earl Palm 95 F. C. 136, H. 97, H. B. 87, Jasper 17, 67, 96, James P. 68, Jesse G. 68 86, J. N. 143, Lelon 143 May A. 95, O. E. 86, Pearl May 95, P. L. 143,Robt. 80, Rutha Ann 97, Saml.N 68, 91, Sarah 68, Sarah

Frances 68, S. M. 91, T. J. 143, Wm. A. 13, Wm. F. 143, Wm. H. 13;
STICKNEY, Catherine M. 118, E. L. 118, E.Lawrence 92;
STILLWELL, Webster 59;
STOCHE (STACKE) W. H. 137
STOKES, Chas. 13, Wm. P. 13,
STOLLEY, Gertrude E. 152 Otto 152;
STONE, Clark M. 99, Mary A. 101, 109, Mary Ann 78 Saml. 78, 101, 113,Saml. T. 78, Sarah N. 78, S.T. 78, Thos. J. 99, 100,112
STOREY, James G. 128, Mary 62;
STORM, WM. H. 142, Wm. J. 56;
STOVALL, Mary T. 18, V. A. 18;
STRAHORN, N. P. 65, N. T. 89;
STRALEY, A. J. 134,Fannie E. 134, J. L. 134, Mary E. 134, S. H. 134;
STRANGIER, Mathilda 66;
STRAWN, Nancy 20, W. B. 20; STREMME,CC, 155;
STREET, J._ M 55, Park 99
STRICKLAND, E. A. 90,140;
STRICKLIN, Mrs. Alice 74;
STRICKLE, D. F. 124;
STROTHER, C. J. 79, 114 Christopher J. 79;
STUBBS, Chas. J. 38, J.J. 124;
STUBBLEFIELD Clement 38, 139, 144, John J. 142, W. O. 140, Woodruff 142;
STUDOR, Elizabeth 15, Henry 15, John J. 15;
STULER, J. 4, 91, Anne 4 91;
STUMPF, BROWER & STUMPF 20, Joseph 20, 26, 61, Mathilda 26,
STURDIVANT, C. W. 45, Elizabeth 45;
SUBLETT,Catherine H. 148 Henry W. 14, 45, H. W.14 100, Saml. 148;
SUDERLAND, W. M. 55;
SUDDUTH, H. W. 144;
SUECHES (SEUSE) M. E.73;
SULLIVAN, L. P. 72;
SUMMERROW, Ed 68, Electra 34, Michael 33, 34, M. Edward 33, W. P. 34;
SUMNER, Benj. Franklin 120, 126, Frances 19, James Henry 126, Mary Frances 126, Sarah Jane Powell Sargent 120, W.E. 73;
SURBER, H._ M 130;
SUSMAN, Geo. 111;
SUTON, John G. 8;
SUTOR, Fried 81, F. W.40;
SUTTLE, Chas. 150, Chas. G. 109;
SUTTON, Wm. 21;
SWANCOAT, Lizzie 13, 16, R. J. 13;
SWANK, Wm. 31;
SWANN, R. M.58;
SWARTZ, August 80, Bell 92, Oscar 92;
SWENSON, Eric P. 23, Mary E. 23, S. M. 51, 139, S. M. SWENSON & SONS 23,
S. M. 23, Susan M. 23, Swante M. 34, 90,Swan (Swen) Alben 23;
SWEENEY, Elizabeth M. 105, Wm. B. 105, 107;
SWIFT, Alice 19, Caroline 19, Frank S. 19, Frederic 19, Henry 19, Henry Sumner 19;
SWISHER, Annie 35, 96, Elizabeth 13, 35, 96, F 13, James G. 9, 10, 21, 22, 28, 34, 35, 36, 39, 62, 90, 96, 101, 102, 108; James M. 14, 16, 21, 41 64, 68, 98, 101, 102,112, James Monroe 35, J. M. 99 John M. 3, 9, 12, 21, 22 36, 89, 102, John Milton 35, Swisher Hotel 62, Swisher's Tavern 98,
SWISHER, RAYMOND & CO. 128;
SZANO, A. A. 124, Harriet M. 124.

-T-

TABER, J. S. 143, Mary A. 143;
TAFT, J. S. 153;
TALBOT, Chas. P. 25, Mrs. E. J. 89, Elias W. 25, Elizabeth J. 49, James W 25, Jos. W. 25, S. G. 49 Thos. 25, Virginia B. 18, 60;
TALIFERRO (TALLAFERRO TOLIAFERRO,TOLIVER) Betty V. 139, C. 120 Chloe 139 Chloe H. 139, Fennie M. 139, Mrs. R. H. 120, W. A. 139;
TALK (FALK) John 22, 69, 108, Thos. 22;
TALLEY (TALEY) E. D. 46, G. I. 120, J. C. 46, Lola M. 120, Thos. 136, W. P. 120;
TANNEY (TANEY) John 110, 127;
TANNEHILL (TANNEHILL) Frank R. 34, 42, 64, Geo C. 8, Jesse C. 20, 21, 42 64, 66, 75, 96, 91, 102, Jane 66, John J. 42 64, Mary Ann 42, Will 42, Wm. J. 42, 75, Wm. P. 42;
TANNER, Jonathan 108;
TARBOX, Lyman 63, 64;
TARLETON, James 83;
TARRANT, Jacob 17,67, 95;
TARVER, B. F. 12;
TATE, Mrs. Margaret M.120;
TATUM, Amanda 27, James 27, Willis 48;
TAYLOR, Abner 134, A. C. 146, 147, Bell 12, B. G. 147, Bessie 12, Beulah 42 Campbell 115, C. H. 42, Chat 57, Clara Louise 134, Chas. P. 57, Darcus S. 147, Emzy 140, Eliza 22, Emily 124, E. F. 133, Euphie 64, Fannie M. 139 Horace D. 124,Green I.67 Isaac M. 147, James 80 J. B. 147, John 23, 90, John W. 83, 147, Jos. C. 22, Mathilda 147, M. A. 101, Melita 147, Mary Ann 12, Naurene 83, Paul= ine 80, P. C. 12, 90,Robt Jr. 114, Samuel C. 100,
Sarah C. 147, Stewart 38 Thos. F. 24;
TEABAUT (TEABE, TIBAUT) E. E. M. 7, Eliza 7, John M. 111, 112;
TEAGLE, Joshua 79;
TEAGUE, Wm. 13;
TEGNER, (TIGNER) Fritz 71 Wm. 100;
TEMPLE, Lee Dean 46;
TEN EYCK, A. 31, Alfred 31, Edward (Edmund) 31, 101, de NORMANDIE & TEN EYCKE, 112, Mrs. J. A. 112, TEN EYCKE & CO. 128
TEMPLETON, Mrs. Lula C. 96;
TENNESSEE, 1;
TERRELL, Alexander W. 33 Ann Elizabeth 33, Arthur J. 10, 33, A. W. 30, 32, 33, 66, 77, 88 Elizabeth 9, 10, C. J. 124, Con= stance 10, 33, E. B. 33 Earnest Bouldin 33, Genl. Geo. W. 81, Henry 107, Howard D. 88, John O.12, Lilla 33, Mary Lee 33, Pearl 12;
TERRY, B. F. 115,Clinton 44, Nathaniel 19, W. S. 136, TERRY'S TEXAS RANGERS 40;
TEXAS DEMOCRAT, 47;
TEXAS LAND, 152;
TEXAS MILITARY INSTITUTE 16;
TEXAS STATE CAPITOL BLDG 82;
Texas University 143;1;
THACHARD, Christiana 12, J. H. 12;
THAXTON, Clara 18, Felix S. 18, Henry J. 18, Mary T. 18, Mamie Smith 18, Nannie S. 17, 18, Robt. C. 143, 150, W. H. 17. 18, 38, Wm. 31;
THAYER, Elizabeth 73, EVA HOPE 73, Jera Payne 73;
THIELE, Alice H. 40, Anna 40, Chas. 11, Christine 40, Edward A. 40, Jaye 40 Josephine S. 40, Julia O 40, Mattie A. 40, Otto F. 40, Richard A. 40 Robt. E. 40, Wm. 40;
THOMAS, A. J. 128,David 25, 110, 113, D. 12, Clyde E. 152,Henry 2, 30, 58, J. W. 55, 143, Marcus 90 Mark 90, Warren L. 7, 52 Wm. D. 17, 108;
THOMPSON, Abby C. 36, 41 97, Alex C. 46, Agnes H. 47, 53, Benj. 35, 53 96, B. H. 59, Benj. J. 35 88, 92, Betty J. 46, C.W Cornelia Rebecca 39, Cyrus 36, 97, 41,Danl. E. 46, Dorothy D. 31,D.W. 54, Ellis 66, Frances 114, Geo. W. 92, 93, Jackson 31, James 39,Jas A. 92, Jasper M. 46, J. H. 41, 87, 98, 102,112 J. R. 41, Joseph R. 86, John DeKalb, 47, 53,Kate F. 53, Kate L. 35, 53, Knox 46, Lucinda M. 93, Laura E. 31, Lenora L.46 Luck 48, Louisa R. 46,

L. H. 92, Lavenia H. 59, 74, Mary A. 41, 87, M. Amelia 86, 87, Mary Jane 53, Norman F. 126,Nancy H. 47, 53 Permelia A.R. 46, R. M. 49, Rebecca Caroline 3, 83, Thad A. 49, Singleton F. 51, S. G. 51, W. D. 31, 46, 54, 138, 139, Wm. 28, W. R. 31, W. L. 66, W. W. 106, 107;
THOMSON,Wm. D. 139, W. L 66;
THORNE, Francis 114, Frank 114, John L. 103, 105, Laura Wright 81, T. W. 129, W. R. 114;
THORNTON, D. M. 151, Elsie 140, Geo. H. 50, G. W 151, J. M. 50, James J. 50, Mae Dannie 50, Margaret 151, Mrs. M. S. 77, M. Coatney 77;
THORPE,B. C. 83, Carrie 52, Chas. Jefferson 52, Christi Ann 52, Era Pearle 52, John Wm. 52 J. J. 28, Mabel Julia 52 Mary Jane 52, Mary Tennessee 52, Milam 52, Melissa 83, Milton A. 52 Nancy Elizabeth 52, W.P. 15, 110; 154;
THRASHER, Chester 91, Daisy 32, 91, Elizabeth A. 41;
THURMAN, A. 91, Henry 109, J. A. H. 91, Mary E.83, Sarah Ann 91;
TIEMANN, Katie 48, Otto 48;
TILLETON COLLEGATE & NORMAL INSTITUTE 97;
TIMMERMANN, Edward 94;
TINNIN, Ed 101, 102, Hellen Mary 85, Hugh 22 51, 85 90, 102, 153, Mary H. 51;
TIPS, Eugene 50, Walter 50;
TIPTON, W. A. 13;
TOBIN, R. H. 147;
TODD, R. S. 60;
TOLER, Dan I. 129;
TOLMAN, John 3;
TOMPKINS, Griffin 55;
TONGAT (TOUNGATE) M. 17 39, 111, Nancy 17, 39,67;
TONSEY, Isaac 150;
TOOLE, Margaret E. 16;
TOUNGATE, C. A. 55, Ephraim 55, John 42;
TOWERS, Harriette E. 69;
TOWNES, Alfred E. 88, Alfred 28 Allen 81,Allen R. 59, Bettie 28, Edgar E. 37, 49, Edward T. 59 Eggleston D. 57, 58,E.T. 68, 81, Everard 28, John C. 37, 49, N. Cobb 68, 81, Pattie 28, 59, Polly 28, 59, R. A. 28, Ric hard A. 28, Robt. J. 28, 59, 68, 81, R. J. 28, 68, 81 Saml. 65;
TOWNSEND, A. B. 74, Angelina L. 20, 39, 54, 73 80, Anna L. 33, Benj. R. 20,33, 39,73, 80,Caroline 74, Cecelia 28, 63,Halsey 20, 73, 80, James W. 33

Kate 135, Lela 74, Lou Ella 74, Lavenia H. 74, Maria 20, 73, 80, Marie 54, 73, Martin W. 28, 32 63, M. W. 30, McDonald 6, Nathaniel 20, 33, 39, 42 51, 53, 54, 64, 73, 80 Nathaniel Jr. 20, 32, 73 Palmer S. 33, Pauline 33 80, Randolph W. 53, 80 Sallie M. 74, Serena M. 6, Susie M. 33, 64, 80, Wm. 74;
TRAMMELL, Burke 84, Dennie 84, J. 84, James 75, 84, Margaret 84, Sampson 84 Wm. 103;
TRAUTWEIN, Adolph A. 93;
TRAVIS COUNTY, 1;
TRAYLOR, John 90, M. A. 101, (Taylor);
TRIGG, B. 99, Cam 114;
TRIMBLE, C. A. 127, Mrs. Cornelia A. 127, 133, David 133, D. A. 127(see TRUMBLE)
TRIPLETT, Joseph 3, Marcella Elizabeth 79;
TRIPPETT, W. W. 137;
TRUBE, Henry J. 14,John C. 14, Sophie 14,Veronic Durst 14;
"TRUE ISSUE", 82;
TRUEHART, H. M. 92, James S. 129;
TRUETT, A. F. 10;
TRUSSELL, J. W. 134;
TUBBERVILLE, W. S. 125;
TULK (TALK) John H. 32;
TULL, Geo. 3, 91, J. H. 31;
TULON Geo. K. 107, Geo. R. 49
TUMLINSON,..Survey 147;
TUMMEY, T. H._ 33, Thos. 31; TURLEY, James M. 110;
TURNER, A. 128, Addie E. 117, Amasa 128, Anna Lenora 26, Ariena C. 117, Bell 26, Bessie S. 26, Bonnie S. 117, Cassie 56 C. J. 124,David A. 56, E. B. 11, 25, 34, Elias Ambrose 56, Ella 117, Ethel 73, Garland 117, Geo. M. 26, J. M.59, Jennie L. 26, L. A. 117, Lucy Baker 124, Mary P. 38, Mina 127, Nellie 26, Pink Owen 56, P. R. 6, 23, Rita Leora 56,Roger C. 117, R. R. 26, Sallie 127, Sarah J. 26, Sue 56 Wallace A. 117, W. G. 137 Wm. Baker 124;
TUTTLE, Mrs. E. H. 117;
TWEEDLE, Emma 79, Fielder 74, L. C. 79, Mollie 80 Sarah 79, Mrs. Sarah 74;
TWINNING, Scharlotte 88, W. 88,
TYNES, B. R. 31;
TYSON, E. Jane 44, 76, Jane Elizabeth 27, 44, Wm. Mac 27, W. S. 44.

-U-
UNIVERSITY of TEXAS, 1;
UPCHURCH, Bertha 146,Cora 146, Green 146, Henderson 146, John 147, Lizzie 146 Martha 146, Mary 146,Mary Elizabeth 146, Millie 146

Mattie L. 146, Ola 146, Phebe 146, Ruby 146, Sarah G. 146, W. G. 146 Zora 146;
UPHAM, C. B.69
UPSHAW (UPSHURE) H. L. 9, 67, Horace L. 98;
U. S. GOVERNMENT HOSPITAL 83,
UTLEY CEMETERY, 114.

-V-
VALDEZ, Manuel M. A. 18;
VALENTINE, Mrs. Jane P. 20;
VALLANORA,...League 5;
VALLE, SANTIAGO del 2, 5, 36;
VALLMERING, Katie 118;
VAN ALYSTINE, Wm. A. 59 Marie A. 125, Mrs..124;
VAN CLEAVE, Berry L. 106 J. 17, Lorenzo 50;
VANDEVER, Logan 66,103;
VANGRANDT, Emily 50;
VANLANDER, Z. A. 106;
VANN, Adalaide 87,Lorarus T. 87, Thos. 35, T.J.36;
VANPELT, Wm F. 57;
VANZANDT, Emily 92;
VARNELL, W. M. 57;
VARY, D. W. C. 53;
VAUGHN, I. D. 119;)BAUGHN)
VAUGHN & WALKER 97;
VEAL, W. G. 124, 143;
VEHLEIN, Joseph 127;
VENTREES, ED 139, E. H. 146, 147. 150, VENTREES & HUGHES 145;
VERAMENDI, Juan Martin 129, Josefa 129, Rafael 129, Maria Josefa 129, M. A. 129, Marcus A. 129
VINCE, John 127, Robt.127;
VINSON, John B. 39, W. H. 34;
VIRGINIA, 1;
VOIGHT, Georgie E. 116, Geo. F. 116;
von BOECKMANN, Antonio 60, Eugene 60, Franzeska 60, Laura 60;
von KRAMER, F. A. 50 Mamie E. 50;
von QUINTUS, Anne 3;
von ROSENBERG, _Arthur 81 Arthur W. 81,Devereaux 81, Edna 81, Edgar 81, J. Leslie 81, Mary K. 26 Mary Holland 81, Nannie 81, Harriet S. 26, Paul 31, Rosa 81, Wm. Jr. 21, 96, 136!
von SCHAAK, Caroline 50;
VOWTER, Sallie (Hallor) 28.
VEATCH, John A. 154;

-W-
WACKSMAN, Adolph W. 73, Agnes 72, Clara 73, Emmet W. 73, Geo. 73, Herbert 73, Rosa Bernhaum 73;
WADDELL, D. F. 82;
WADE, David 123, E. B. 72, Geo. W. 125, Mary Jane 131;
WADSWORTH, Wm. A. O. 103 105;
WAFFORD, Doctor 92,Emily 50, Henry 50, 92, J. H. 50, 92, J. W. 82, Robt.

Davis 50;
WAGGONER, A. P. 146, John 146, Mattie L. 146, Mollie 146, W. G. 146;
WAHRENBERGER, Caroline Kline Newman 37, John 15, 108; F.155;
WAIT, J. S. 95;
WALDEMORE, Geo. W. 25, Mrs. H. E. 25, Wm. 25;92;
WALDEN, Alice L. 17,L.R. 17, R. E. 24, 37;
WALK, J. A. 119;
WALKER, A. G. 134, Alex S Jr. 142, Anna J. 142,A.S 69, 86, 142, BAUGH & WALKER 97, Chas. 65, 92, 104, David 6, D. C. 89, E. A. 145, Elizabeth 82, Emma 149, E. Y. 120, F.I. 149, Rev. F. M. 131,Geo. 93, H. S. 55, 139, Henry 55, 139, John 17, John E 142, Jim Tom 116, J. S. 114, Julia 127, LORENZO 2 98, Louisa 142, Lula 55, 139, Martin 114, M. H. 131, Mrs. O. J. 116, Prudence 82, Richard 57, Sarah Margaret 142, Shelby 55, 139 VAUGHN & WALKER 97, Wm. 82, WALL-netta 55, 139;
WALL, James 35;
WALLA, James 148;
WALLACE, Geo. C. 28, Jas. P. 24, 48, 49, 62, 70, 95 96, J. L. 19, John E. 94, Wm. S. 112, Wm. G. 98,108;
WALLER, Edwin 147, Joseph 132, Rody 132; S. O. 132
WALLERS, D. F. 62, Edwin 147, Saml. Oliver 132;
WALLING, amy 8, Annie Tibaut 81, Catherine 8, Clarabel 8, Cora 8, Geo. W. Jr. 8, 42, Geo. W.Sr. 8, 72, 81, Jas. A. 8, Louisa J. 8, 81, Mary Ella 8, Richard B. 8,Robt.W. 8, 41, Roberta 8, Thos. B. 8;
WALLS, John O. 13, Wm.106
WALSH, D. 108, Sarah D. 153;
WALTERS, L. B. 144;
WALTON, E.Payton 29, Geo L. 7; Meredith 6, P.A. 63, Sarah A. 29, Wm. 8, 100, Wm. M. 37,63, 139,;
WANSLEY, J. Y. 132;
WAPPLES (WAPPELS) Jos.57;
WARD, Adda 55, H. 103, John 117, J. W. 106, Lucy 117, Rosanna 82, Sarah C. Taylor 147, Susan L. 62, Susan M. 119, Sylvester 147, Thos. 15, 55, 58, 66 100, 101; Thos. Wood 55, 98, 108, Thos. Wm. 62 64, 65, 68, 83, 101, W. J. 102, W. K. 37; T.W.155;
WARE (WEAR) John D. 85 Fines E. 108, Wm. R.144;
WAREFIELD, Dr. Elisha 140
WARNELL, Henry 64;
WARNER, Clara 68;
WARREN, Burleson 44, 152 Campbell 93, Eugene 136, Frances 116, Geo. 93, Geo P. 90, John P. 108, Jos. 58, 80, Lyman 74, Margaret 44, Minnie 74, Nancy 116,

Robert J. 116, Thos. 12;
WARRICK, E. E. 132, Mary 132, W. 132;
WARWICK, V. V. 48, Minnie E. 48;
WASHBURN, Howard 45,Sadie 45;
WASHINGTON, ELLA J. 61 Lewis M. H. 62, Thos. P. 45, 83;
WATERLOO, 76;
WATERS, Geo. W. 65;
WATERSTON, Jas. 94, Sarah 94;
WATROUS, John C. 2, 36, 39, Lydia Ann 2, 36, 39, Nathaniel H. 2, 36, 39,64, 92;
WATSON, Alex 146, E. A. 114, Mrs. E. A. 114,Hiram 114, J. M. 68, WATSON & COCHRAN 146;
WATTS, (WATES) Haden 138 150, John 138, 150;
WAY, H. W. 23;
WEAKLEY, Jane90;
WEAR (WARE) Fannie 71, Scott 71;
WEATHERBEE, James H. 79;
WEAVER, Alman 106, 107, Gilmore 106, Phillip I. 2, Tilmon 107;
WEBB, A. M. J. 38, David K. 97, 106, 107, D. K.Sr 54, 97, 105, J. 2, Jas. 2, 6, 26, 34, 40, 43, 62 65, 68, 69, 76, 72, Jas. W. 6, L. P. 15, 24,Rachel E. 6, Wm. G. 24, 33;
"WEBBERS PRAIRIE", 102;
WEBBER, Agnes C. McWill-iams 44, Athalania Caro-line 3, Caroline 3, John F. 137, Louis 3, Mary Frances 131, P. Leinna 13;
WECHSTER, Andrew 153;
WEEKS, David 119;
WEEMS, B. F. 124, 125, Emily Rowe Ford, 50,59, 92, 93, John B. 59, 92, 93; Katherine L. 125;
WEICKIND, T. F. W. 110, Katherine L. 125;
WEIMER (BEIMER) H. 99;
WEIR, A. G. 81, 112, Col. 112, A. C. 3, Edward M. 41, Mrs. E. 60;
WELLMER, Lena 41, Wm.41;
WELLS, A. C. 3,B. C. 29, Caroline S. 3, Catherine 8, Emily 72, Geo. H. 14, 72, J. M. 4, 14, 47, Jas 3, Jas. Morgan 47, 72, Lucille J. 14; Martin J. 146, Mary 47, 72, Mary Eva 14, Mary MARGARET 54 Margaret 14, Maye E. 14 M. I. 13, P. C. 4, 8,Peter C. 14, 72, Peter K. 47, R. D. 3, Richard 127, Richard B. 3, Thos. W. 72, W. F. 4, Wayman F. 13, 14 24, 47, 72, Wayman Thos. 47;
WENDE, Emelia 3, Emily J 4, John B. 91, Wm. 3,Wil-helm 111, W. T. 4, 14,;
WENDLAND, August 117, Cla-ra 12, Fritz 12, Mary 117;
WENDLANDT, C. 38;
WERNLANDER, G. A. 106;
WESLEY, John 21,
WEST, C. S. 28, 39, 40,

62, 68, 72, Caroline F. 74, Clarence E. 22, C. W 38, Dorcia 121, Emma S. 22, HANCOCK & WEST 63, Harry S. 22, J. C. 32,68 North K. 22, W. H. 74
WESTCOTT, N. D. 51 R. D. 51;
WESTEN, L. L. 26, Sarah J. 26, Thos. G. 147;
WESTFALL, Kate 46;
WESTLING, Hilda D. 33, Lottie 33;
WESTMORLAND John W. 99;
WESTRICH, U. 153;
WHATLEY, Seaborn James 24, 57, 65;
WHEAT, Agnes 15, Davis 15, Emmie 15, Julia O. 15 Moses H. 15, Wm. 67;
WHEELER, Mrs. Catherine G. 74, Henry H. 136, T. B. 21, 26, 74, Thos. J. 25, 26;
WHELESS, Carrie 45, Elizabeth 45, Gladys 45, Jas. 45, J. J. 90, Lena 45, Lillie M. 45, Maud 45, Mildred 45, Norma 45 Nell 45, Robt. 45, R. L. 45, Ruth 45, Sadie 45, Thos. H. 21, W. J. 90;
WHERRITT, T. 29;
WHETSTONE, A. H. 58;
WHIPPLE, B. G. R. 65,Jas E. 141, Jas. W. 147,John M. 141, 151, J. W. 8, 62 80, L. B. 62, Nancy 141, Ruth I. 80, Sarah E. 8, 62;
WHITE, Ada 83, A. H. 11, Cornelia Jane 3, Eleazer H. 28, 84, Elizabeth 3, Elizabeth Ann 3, Gideon 3, 39, Ike D. 37, Jas. A. 128, Jas. M. 99, John B. 28, John G. 84, John M. 28, Joseph 127, Louisa Maria 3, Mary 84, Mary L. 28, Mary Monroe 48, Monroe 48, Narcissus Lucinda 3, 39, Rebecca Caroline 3, R. E. 38, Saml. E. 28, 84, Thos. 28 Thos. W. 84;
WHITEMAN, Mary 61, Wm. B 61;
WHITEHEAD, Carrie Isabel 30, E. L. 12, Hattie C. 12, L. K. 12, R. L. 12;
WHITING, T. P. 75, Sam 49;
WHITIS, Chas. P. 34, 64, C. W. 34, 36, 64, 66, 77 97, Ellen P. 34, 64, Florence 34, 64,Gertrude 34, 64, John 34, 64, Jno H. 24, 34, Mary 34, 64, Mollie 34, Rufus 34, 64 Thos. P. 34, 65;
WHITT, Henry 25, John 25 J. W. 25, Jesse 25, Nancy Kirk 25, Patrick 25, R.H 25, R. W. 25, Thos. 25, T. J. 25, Wm. 25;
WHITLEY, Addie 93, Hen=rietta 93, Jane 93,Jennie 93, Mary 140, Rainie 93, Sam 104;
WHITNEY, John S. 94, Saml. 107;
WHITTEN, Bostick 46, Martha E. 46;
WHITTIKER, Anna 67,68,

L. G. 68; WHORTON,Wm.155
WICKES, H. G. 12;
WIDEN, Carl A. 42, Elin Augusta 42;
WIEHL, Joseph 153;
WIELAND, Anna 15;
WIERSIOH, F. G. 111;
WILCOX (WILLCOX) Alice 29, Bobbie M. 29, Chas. G. 29, Dallas 29, Henry 15, Mary K. 29, Ozwin 100 112, 113, Robt. M. 29, S. C. 1;
WILDE, (WILD) Frederick 82, Herman 82, P. A. 38;
WILDBAHN, F. M. 74,Isaac 20, 57, 74, J. E. 37,Jos. 58, Wildbahn Land Co. 37 49;
WILBARGER (WILDBARGER) Anna Jane 142, Anna M.142 Elizabeth 114, Geo. C. 142, H. C. 142, Henry Clay 142, James 142, Jas. Harvey 115, John 79, John W. 80, 140, 145, Josiah 64, 80, Josiah 58,115, Louisa 142, Lucy 80, Mathias 80, 141, 142, 148, 150, Sarah 142, Sarah M. 141, 142, Virginia 142;
WILEMAN, Alice Donnell 149, Ed 149, J. E. 149;
WILEY, Amanda H. 148, A. B. 120, Elizabeth 118, H 148, Isaac 120, Inez 94, Lutie 120, Nancy Ann 120, T. B. 120, Thos. 118;
WILHELM, Christian 34, Fred 96, Wm. 110;
WILKE, Gustav 59, Mary 59 Wm. 92;
WILKES, Jane 151, Joe 55 Loncescia 55, Wm. 65, 94 104;
WILKINS, A. H. 11, Chas. C. 8, John H. 105, Lavender S. 98, 105, Mary Ella 8, L. S. 2, Richard R.127;
WILLENBURG, Corelia T. 51 Robt. J. 51;
WILLIAMS, Abe 17, Alex 32, 121, Amanda M. 121, Amy 8, Anne 140, B. Frank 27, Carrie C. 72, Chas. C. 25, Charlie 27, Cleve 55, David 13, 40, Dora T. 55, Elizabeth 140, Emeline 46 55, Eugene 56, Ferdinan 145, Fridonia 140, Geo. W. 140, G. T. 141, 144, Henry 55, Henry H. 61, James 8, J. Henry 55, James H. 6, John H. 61, 140, J. L. 71, Joseph 55, Kate 40, L. J. 72, L.W.14 Mary 140, Martha 140, Nancy E. 140, O. A. 135, Mollie Pauline 135, Rebecca Ann 61, Saml. M. 2, 16, 36, 92, 127, 129,S.L.5 Serapts 140, Sophronie 140, Susan 140, Thos. 140 Wm. 140, W. T. 55;
WILLIAMSON, Elizabeth 137 James 137, James W. S.144 150, John W. 137, J. H. 121, Lewis 137, Mary Frances 121, R. M. 10, 28 127, Susan 137, Wm. 137;
WILLIAMSON County, 137;
WILLIE, A. H. 61 Asa H. 70 Maud L. 71;

WILLIS, Peter J. 141, P. J. WILLIS BROS. 137, 141, Richard S. 141,R.S 134, W. E. 134, Wm. H. 141;
WILSON, Albert S. 33, 35 Anna 33, 35, B. H. 33, 35 Don Wilson 32, 86, David M. 32, 33, D. M. 33, 35 Dan 8, 33, Edna 33, 35 Elizabeth P. 33, 67, J. C. 31, 33, J. M. 33, 35 115, J. P. 137, Jennie L. 33, John 128, John C. 31, 32, 33, 35, 68, J. B 33, 35, Joseph W. 120 Julius E. 141,Martha J. 67, 115, Mary E. 31, Mattie J. 120, Mary 33, 41, Mildred E. R. 32, 33, 35, 68, Mollie 33, 35 Pete 94, R. F. 129,Rhoda 31, 33, R. L. 33, 35, Scott 31, Sallie B. 33 35, Sarah 33, Walker 30, 127, Washington 116, Wm. M. 5, 7, 8, 41, 43, 64, W. Scott 21, 33, Wm. W. 7, W. S. 33, 35;
WIMBERLY, Amanda 129, Andrew J. 129, Calvin H. 129, C. H. 129, C. W. 30 Fannie B. 129, Mary W. 129, Pleasant 30, 129, Rachel 129, Rosa Mable 129, Rufus 30, Zack T. 129;
WIMBISH, J., A. H. 38, James H. 38, Virginia F. 38;
WINDER, Barsheba 82;
WING, C. L. 22, W. C.153
WINN, James 105, Marguerite Turner Lane 26;
WINSTON, J. A. 19, John A.17, John Anthony 17, 19, W. O. 17, 19;
WINTERS, Nancy N. 128, Wm. 128, Wm. C. 128, Willie 128
WISDOM, Benj. H. 94, B.H 28, Henry 28;
WISE, E. R. 78;
WITHERS, W. P. 111;
WITHROS, Carl M. 52, Dora 52;
WITT, Mary J. 132;
WOFFORD, James 105, Wm. 12;
WOLF CROSSING CEMETERY 120;
WOLF, Chas. 27, 53, Josephine M. 27, T. H. 135;
WOLFINBARGER, Saml. 114;
WOLFSON, Joseph N. 85,86;
WOMACK, Ida 80, R. M. 80
WOOD, Campbell 30, Douglas 13, G. W. 15, Hallum 16 Hiram 148, James A. 97 James H. 126, James S. 13 John 7, 26, 104, Joseph 31, Kitie Jane 16, Moses 7, 107, Mary E. 122, Nannie 30, 88, Nathan 13 Norman 41, 54, P. C. 128 Saml. A. 97. James 7;
WOODALL, John C. 8 32;
WOODY, Sarah A. 42 , Wilson 42, W. 42;
WOOLDRIDGE, A. P. 21, 41 70, Jasper 76;
WORD, David A. 114;

WORTHAM, Wm. B. 24;
WRIGHT, ada81, Amy K. 18 19, Betty Paschel 18, Bessie 90, Carrie 90,Caroline 90, Chas. 94, 97, Elizabeth A. 73, 76, E. P. 18, Etta May 90,Eugene 90, Fannie E. 81, Francis W. 18, 19, H. 52, Henry 90, Henry Jr. 90, H. W. 90, James E. 73, James 90, James A. 27, 71, James H. 90, Jennie 90, John R.125, Joseph 7,8, 30, 50, 73, 81,89, Jos. 81, Julia 81, L. A. 125 Laura 81, Lila 90,Lennie 90, Mabel C. 81,Milton 90, M. & C. 90,Norvella 90, Rachel 7, 8, 73, R. P. 7, 81, Saml. M. 44, 73, 76, 89, 111, S. E. 73, Tennie 81, Tom 90 Wm. M. 90;
WROE, H. A. 7;
WRONKOW, Herman 55, Serena 55;
WUFLGIN, J. D. 147;
WUTHRICH, Anna E. 13, Christian Michael 13, Johann 13, John 111, Johann Ulrich 13, Lucia 13, Mates 13, Peter 13, Ulrich 13;
WYATT, Wm. 17;
WYCHE, John 30, Wm. P. 6, 30;
WYNNE, James 105, Robt. H. 26, 102, 153.

-Y-

YAGER, (JAGER) Andrew 110;
YANCEY, A. B. 114,Lizzie 114, Robt. J. 145;
YARBROUGH, C. C. 144, John Y. 144;
YARRINGTON, A. H. 38, J. E. 125;
YATES, A. P. 151, H. W. 151; Anna Liza 121, Jas. 121, Fannie 121, Grover Cleveland 121, Bruce C. 121;
YAWALL, 141;
YBARRBO, Candelanus 25, 26, J. A. 25, Jose Antonio 25, 26;
YEAGER, T. A. 126;
YERBEY, John H. 107;
YOAST, Elizabeth 114, F. 120, Francis 114, Frank 120, M. 120;
YOE, Robt. 119;
YOUNG, Emma J. 83, Frank P. 5, 83, Harrison 103, 105, 108, J. W. 90, Jas. 17, Jane L. J. 83, 84, John S. 5, 83, 84, John M. 65, Louisa 84, J. W. 90, Mary J. 83, Michael 137, Richard S. 93, W.A. 128, Walter Scott 84; YOUNGER, Louis H. 41; YOUREE, Mary Frances 126.

-Z-

ZAVALA, Lorenzo de 153;
ZEPADA, Jesus Valdez 129 Victoriana 129;
ZILLER (ZELLER) Michael 111, 112; 153;

ZIMPELMANN (ZIMPLEMANN)
Geo. B. 31, 77, 82, 91,
Geo. W. 91, James Lee 91
Lee 12, Sarah C. 91, Thos
91, Tom 12, Waldine 12,
91;
ZINCK, John N. 103,
ZIMMERMANN, Edward 110;
ZIVELY, John 84;
ZUCHLAG, Conrad, 111.

www.ingramcontent.com/pod-product-compliance
Lightning Source LLC
Chambersburg PA
CBHW020650300426
44112CB00007B/318